Exploring
JEWISH
ETHICS

Books by Eugene B. Borowitz

A Layman's Introduction to Religious Existentialism
A New Jewish Theology in the Making
How Can a Jew Speak of Faith Today?
Choosing a Sex Ethic
The Mask Jews Wear
Reform Judaism Today
Understanding Judaism
Contemporary Christologies, a Jewish Response
Choices in Modern Jewish Thought
Liberal Judaism
Explaining Reform Judaism (with Naomi Patz)

This book published with the assistance
of a grant from the family of
Leonard N. Simons

Exploring

JEWISH
ETHICS

Papers on
Covenant Responsibility

Eugene B. Borowitz

 Wayne State University Press   Detroit   1990

94 93 92 91 90   5 4 3 2 1

Library of Congress Cataloging-in-Publication Data

Borowitz, Eugene B.
    Exploring Jewish ethics : papers on covenant responsibility /
Eugene B. Borowitz.
        p.   cm.
    ISBN 0–8143–2199–2. — ISBN 0–8143–2200–X (pbk.)
    1. Judaism—20th century.   2. Ethics, Jewish.   3. Judaism and
social problems.   4. Judaism—United States.   I. Title.
BM565.B68   1990
296.3′85—dc20   89–29202
                                                    CIP

For Nan, Andy, Noah Isaac, and Emily Rose

Contents

Contents

10

Preface

What is a theologian doing appearing here in the guise of an ethician? Somewhat to my own surprise, I gradually realized that my interest in the structure and content of Jewish belief required me to work out some of its ethical entailments. Often my need arose in reaction to a pressing contemporary problem, practical or academic. Sometimes it came about because I was invited to present a Jewish view to a meeting considering a given topic. The result has been two decades or so of continual writing about ethics. This has led me not only to reflect more deeply on these matters but, with my students—whom I here fondly recall with thanks for bearing with my struggles—to seek a new path in liberal Jewish ethics. This process has now reached, as I hope this collection demonstrates, a measure of closure, one that arises from arriving at a new stage in the effort. It seemed, therefore, a good time to set my present contribution before those interested in the ongoing development of Jewish ethics, and I am grateful to the Wayne State University Press for making this possible.

The attentive reader will quickly see that these papers have been addressed to different audiences, lay, clerical, and academic, and have appeared in formats as diverse as services, popular magazines, conferences, academic journals, encyclopedias, and learned books. While I have tried to keep the materials within a reasonably limited span of styles, the reader's indulgence for the considerable variety that remains will be gratefully appreciated. Aside from a rare deletion, I have not made any changes in the papers (or their transliterations) as they originally appeared—with two exceptions. First, I became aware of the problem of sexist language in 1973 through a review of my book *The Mask Jews Wear*. Convinced then that it was ethically wrong to continue to write and speak as I had for nearly four decades, I began learning how to make my references to God *(sic)* and humankind gender-free. In a book of ethical thought I simply could not allow an old unethical usage to stand. I believe the changes I have introduced into those papers do not disrupt the ideas developed there. Second, the published form of my 1986 B. G. Rudolph lecture at Syracuse University developed my theme, "The Ideal Jew," at considerable academic, even pedantic length. Because its concern is central to this work, I have abridged it and its notes to a form more congenial to the other papers presented here.

The fifth part of this collection, "Relating to Groups, Mine and Others," is unusual enough to call for special comment. Too often one finds that the high ethical ideals one manifests toward people differ from those expressed when one considers the problems of one's own religious community or the appeals of competing groups. The alien remains a continual ethical provocation. It therefore seems to me that intra- and inter-religious affairs pose a special challenge for religious ethics. In my case, I hope this section will indicate my resolute effort to apply a common ethical approach to groups as well as persons. Regardless, the reader will find here the most extensive analysis I know of the entailments of Jewish ethics and faith for the proper conduct of theological dialogue between faiths.

I follow certain linguistic usages. By "liberal" Jews, I mean all those who are not Orthodox, whether Reform, Conservative, Reconstructionist, vaguely traditional, or otherwise devoted to a modernized form of Jewish faith. When I mean one specific group, I refer to it by name and with a capital first letter; Orthodoxy refers to Orthodox Judaism, while orthodoxy refers to the general human pattern of loyal adherence to a given teaching. I similarly distinguish by capitalization between God's covenant with all humankind, the covenant with Noah, and the Covenant with Israel, the Covenant of Sinai. Following a suggestion made by Professor Yehuda Bauer, I write anti-semitism without a capital "S," hoping thereby to indicate that it has nothing to do with Semites but only with Jew-hatred. Finally, the words *ethics* and *morality* overlap so that I do not try to make a rigid distinction between them, though I mostly use the former term in these papers because of its overtones of abstract reflection.

I should like, also, to acknowledge formally and gratefully the permission granted me by the various copyright holders of my work before 1979 who have allowed me to include here works that they published. Their names and the specific publications involved are given at the beginning of each paper included in this volume. Seven papers have not heretofore appeared in print.

My thanks are once again extended to the staff of the Library of the New York School of the Hebrew Union College-Jewish Institute of Religion for their gracious help over the years. My good friend Carolyn Toll Oppenheim was gracious enough to read through the large mass of my writing that could conceivably have been included here. I have not always followed her thoughtful recommendations about exclusion or arrangement, but her guidance was invaluable in getting me to the present plan and contents of this volume. May everyone be blessed by such friends. The graciousness that has accompanied each of my contacts with the staff of the Wayne State University Press and, most especially, its Managing Editor, Anne M. G. Adamus, and its former director, Dr. Robert A. Mandel, has made working on this volume a particular joy. I wish also to give public thanks to Jana Currie Scott for the great care she exercised in preparing my ungainly manuscript for publication. I should like also to record one small apology. By one reckoning, my second grandchild, Zachary Aaron Glick, should be entitled to have this book dedicated to him. But his entry into our family was preceded by his uncle Andrew Langowitz, whose mention for honor must be given priority, particularly as he is now to be linked with his son Noah Isaac Langowitz and daughter Emily Rose. May Zack soon have more than this small public recognition of his precious worth.

As the years add up, I am increasingly grateful for the gift of time and strength to continue my work, and in heartfelt appreciation I say, בָּרוּךְ אַתָּה יְיָ. אֱלֹהֵינוּ מֶלֶךְ הָעוֹלָם. הַמֵּכִין מִצְעֲדֵי־גֶבֶר: We bless You, *Adonai* our God, ruler of the universe, who makes firm our human steps.

An Introduction to Old Certainties
and New Problems

1

Jewish Ethics, a Historical Overview

Numerous issues divide scholars seeking to characterize the ethics of Judaism. Two general difficulties prevent easy delimitation of the field: lack of agreement as to what constitutes "ethics" and the philosophic contention that theocentric moralities, such as that of Judaism, may not properly be termed "ethics." More troublingly, the authoritative Jewish sacred texts, the Bible and the Talmud, do not use the term "ethics" or reflect so Hellenic an intellectual category. The holy, rather than the good, seems to be their most inclusive value. Efforts to describe the ethics of Torah, God's "instruction," began only in the 9th century C.E. when Jews encountered Greek philosophy via Muslim culture. These treatments struggled to discover generalizations that would be true to the multiple, discrete behests of the Written and Oral Torahs (one dynamic whole), God's instructions.

When the fifteen-century European segregation and persecution of Jews ended (beginning about the time of the French Revolution), Jewish thinkers responded to the grant of equality by creating new theories of the ethics of Judaism. The most notable of these, that of Hermann Cohen (1842–1918), radically identified the ethics of Judaism with neo-Kantian ethics. In some watered-down sense, that notion lies behind the use of the term "Jewish ethics" in most discussions. But despite the continuing efforts of a few to rehabilitate this position, most Jewish thinkers, for historical and philosophical reasons, have abandoned it. Consensus now exists only on the problems involved in working on the ethics of Judaism and on

From *The Westminster Dictionary of Christian Ethics* (Philadelphia: Westminster, 1986).

certain themes it encompasses. But how to respond to the former and structure the latter remain highly contentious. This article seeks to communicate a representative historical overview plus an account of divergent contemporary approaches to this field, all necessarily filtered through one perspective.

For the biblical authors, human responsibility derives from God's reality. One God and no other created the universe, set its rules, oversees its affairs, and participates in its activities in both ordinary and extraordinary ways. This sovereign yet involved God created humankind different from other creatures, making people uniquely capable of knowing and doing God's will. Remarkably, the undisputed Ruler of the universe gave human beings the freedom to do or not to do the divine commands. The ethics of Judaism begins at this juncture: a God who might but does not coerce persons and a person created for special intimacy with God who may freely will to obey or transgress God's stated will.

The distinctive urgency connected with the Bible's injunctions to action stems not only from their being God's stated behests but from the knowledge that God "cares" supremely about human action. Diverse human metaphors are employed to make the divine priorities plain. God weeps, pants, suffers, roars, regrets, rages, threatens, punishes, and much else, in response to humankind's freely chosen sinfulness. God's concerns embrace much more than what the Greeks considered ethics, e.g., the interdiction of idolatry. Nonetheless, moral considerations occupy a major place in the biblical legislation, are a constant theme in the historical books, run strongly through wisdom literature, and dominate the prophetic condemnations of their people. Classic Judaism summons humankind and the Jewish people to action for God's sake. One can only hope to understand its character and the ethics it encompasses if one appreciates the manifold religious levels on which its teaching is communicated and experienced.

This centrality of ethics in the service of God applies to all human beings equally. Neither the Bible nor the Talmud contains serious denial that God is the God of all humankind and established and maintains a covenant with them all. The early chapters of Genesis specify God's ethical expectations of humankind. As the fate of Sodom and Gomorrah indicates, God cares about Gentile behavior even after there are Jews. More tellingly, God's acceptance of the repentance of the utterly sinful Ninevites, for all that Jonah found it a personal affront, indicates how firmly the relationship between God and the Gentiles remains in force.

In rabbinic Judaism, this universal doctrine was reflected in Jewish law. On the basis of the covenant God made with Noah and his children, the rabbis held Gentiles to be bound by seven fundamental commandments: not to blaspheme, or to practice idolatry, or to steal, or murder, or commit sexual offenses, or to cut limbs off living animals and, positively, to establish courts to administer justice. Obviously, authoritative Jewish teaching has an embracing sense of the (religious) ethical competence of all human beings, one which rabbinic tradition amplified in its customary extension of these basic laws.

The rabbis' teaching about human nature similarly applies equally to Gentiles and Jews. Two inner urges, the will-to-do-good and the will-to-do-evil, battle within each human soul. No one ever fully staves off the will-to-do-evil, but like Moses, God's most intimate servant, all eventually sin. With sin understood as a choice, its rectification also takes place by a free human act: repentance, the turning back to God. If, however, one has sinned against another human being, one must first make such restitution as one can before asking for God's forgiveness (which, the rabbis stress, is always forthcoming to the sincere soul). All this transpires without benefit of special rite, personnel, or occasion, as the case of the Ninevites demonstrates.

One other aspect of the ethical theory of human nature deserves attention. For the biblical authors and the rabbis, human nature remains critically social. One is indissoluble not only with one's family but with one's folk or nation. Thus the classic ethics of Judaism address the community or society as much as the individuals who constitute them. So seamlessly do these notions blend that often in the book of Psalms we cannot tell whether an individual or the nation speaks or is being addressed—and occasionally the poet moves between the two with no apparent unease. So too the traditional ethics of Judaism manifests an utter interpenetration of what might elsewhere be distinct domains of individual and social ethics.

The biblical authors and the rabbis believe God brought the Jewish people into being and established a special covenant with it because the Gentile nations consistently sin. God's election involves the gift of God's Torah, the divine "instruction." The Torah proper, i.e., the first five books of the Bible, indicates the acts God's people ought to do, expressing this more in the form of law than of the stories and teaching which extend its application and give it its meaning. The rest of the Bible—the rabbis spoke of the whole as the Written Torah—includes considerable exhortation but little commandment. In the latter books of the Bible, Torah-instruction occurs as intimate poetry and practical apothegm, touching short story and detailed history, social criticism and bizarre vision of a distant future.

The ethical thrust of the covenant with the Jews hardly comes as a surprise given the biblical view of God and humankind. It urges Jews to be just with others and yet more than just. A repetitive theme in the commandments demands special concern for the powerless: the widow, the stranger, the orphan. So, too, the community must take care of the poor; not to the point of perverting justice for them (one may also not pervert justice for the rich), but in acknowledging the right of the indigent to community support. Such laws, so to speak, command compassion, seeking to make personal response as urgent a responsibility as obedience to specified duties. For God's justice and mercy can never be completely spelled out, and the fullest service of God must come through living up to one's personal likeness to God.

19

The Oral Torah, i.e., the dynamic, still continuing, rabbinic elaboration of the Written Torah and the received traditions, only amplifies these tendencies (for Jews read the Bible through the rabbinic tradition). Ethics remains a subcategory of holiness, and the rabbis impart ethical instruction in many different ways.

Their vast literature has customarily been read in terms of two levels of authority. The one, *halakhah*, "the way," had the power of law and was enforceable in Jewish courts (though some of it remained more ideal than practical). The other, *agadah* (or *haggadah*), perhaps "the lore," included all that was not *halakhah*; while an integral part of God's Oral Torah, it allowed for greater individual freedom of response and action. Ethical prescriptions abound in the *halakhah* with its detailed concern, for example, about fair business practices. Since much of the agadic literature is homiletic or exegetic, it contains many general comments on how one ought to live—but also a puzzling diversity of opinion. Students of ethics have found agadic teachings of particular interest because they appeal to one's self-determination. Thus, while the *halakhah* enjoins some obligations of parents to their children, the bulk of the famous Jewish family ethos is taught in the *agadah* and in the community traditions which are its complement.

While neither the teachers of the Bible nor those of the Talmud define duty primarily in terms of virtue (or vice), it may convey something of the flavor of Jewish ethics to indicate some characterological concerns of the rabbis. They abominate lying, stealing, sexual immorality, violence, and bloodshed. They decry gossip, slander, faithlessness, injustice, hardheartedness, arrogance, and pride. They glorify the industrious, honest, compassionate, charitable, trustworthy, humble, forgiving, pious, God-fearing soul. Their sense of the social emerges in homey fashion in their continuing emphasis on "acquiring a good name" and such customs as requiring even the poor supported by community funds to contribute to the communal philanthropic funds.

The rabbinic understanding of duty focuses on this world and prizes life as an ultimate if not absolute good. The rabbis believe devoutly in the resurrection of the dead. (They made it central to postbiblical Judaism). And they often invoke its promise of eternal life and its threat of judgment-punishment as motives for righteous living. But these themes, like the love and fear of God, which medieval thinkers were to write about, remain in the background of their thought. Being intensely conscious—overawed would not be too strong a word—at possessing God's own instruction/instructions, they devote themselves to studying, explicating, applying, and living them. They disparage speculation on what happened before creation, have some greater tolerance of theories of what will happen in the days of the Messiah, but remain resolutely agnostic about what will follow it in the future-to-come.

One result is a passion for life and whatever will make it possible. Should someone's life be at stake, every law of the Torah which stands in the way of saving it *must*, as a divine command, be broken, save three: the prohibitions against idolatry, murder, and sexual sins. Thus, Jewish medical ethics has been relatively open to experimentation and advance whenever they could be shown to save threatened lives. This "bias toward life" cannot be reduced to an easy formula. Thus, rabbinic law on the dying patient is strongly weighted against hastening the end. But though the rabbis have great respect for a fetus as a potential person, if its mother's life is threatened by it, it must be aborted. In the latter case, note that the "is," as determined by competent medical personnel, becomes fundamental to the legal-ethical decision of the rabbi.

From the completion of the Talmud to the beginnings of Jewish modernity (roughly from 500 c.e. to the French Revolution), several intellectual movements affected the further development of Jewish ethics. Each based itself on the Bible and the Talmud and accepted the ongoing developments in Jewish law as the context of its teaching. They all learned from one another, making the distinctions between them somewhat artificial. Nonetheless, for clarity's sake scholars speak of the separate genres of *musar*, or pietistic literature, of philosophy, and of mysticism.

The nature of *musar* literature is epitomized in the title of its first major work, Bahya ibn Pakuda's *Hovot Halevavot*, the Duties of the Heart, a Spanish-Jewish book of the late 11th century. Bahya sought to clarify the inner responsibilities that devolve upon the Jew and complement the external obligations specified by the rabbis. Primarily, he urged individuals to cultivate an intimate sense of God's greatness. That would lead them to act so as to gain God's favor and avoid God's judgment. This inner sensitivity would also bring them to deep concern for others, seeking to do more than merely fulfill their obligations toward them. The cultivation of piety and with it compassionate living so characterizes this work and the literature which followed it that some scholars have characterized the *musar* books as primarily ethical.

The pietists introduced other themes of ethical import into medieval Jewish thought. They counseled heightening one's sense of the evil of sin and of the terror of God's punishment so as to strengthen one's will-to-do-good. They also thought of the body as the antagonist of the soul in the fight to remain pure in heart and deed. Though rabbinic Judaism recognizes some dichotomy between body and soul, the rabbis had a far more integrated and less dualistic notion of the self than that of the musarists. However, whatever temptation they had to move on to full-scale asceticism was reined by the law which commanded marriage, procreation, festive celebrations, and other worldly activities.

The *musar* literature was intended for the masses and became widely read. Its influence may be judged from the growth of the custom, in late medieval times, of writing an "ethical will" for one's family. Few significant pietistic works appeared after the 18th century, largely because they seemed out of place in the humanistic, self-confident 19th century. An attempt to recast the insights of the pietists was made by Israel Lipkin

(1810–1883). He founded the Musar movement, which introduced pietistic-ethical devotion and practices into the traditional East European *yeshivot*, the academies devoted almost entirely to the study of *halakhah*.

Medieval Jewish pietism arose amid Muslim civilization, and scholars have sought to explicate its roots in Muslim piety, particularly in Sufi mysticism, as well as in the Neo-platonism that figures so strongly in them. This Hellenic-Muslim mixture also formed the background of medieval Jewish philosophy and was responsible for the ethical treatises which form a minor part of it. In these, however, the Aristotelian heritage, with its emphasis upon intellect and its understanding of human nature, became dominant.

Medieval Jewish mysticism was, like Jewish philosophy, an essentially elitist enterprise until its last period, that of Hasidism (beginning in the 18th century). Through its long history it retained a strong ethical content. While teaching its adepts the proper way to intimate communion with God, it affirmed the immutability of God's Torah and hence of the content it commanded. Thus, Jewish mystic experience did not become antinomian. Rather, it reinforced and extended the content of classic Jewish teaching, particularly the *musar* stress on ethical sensitivity as a means to holiness.

After fifteen centuries of segregation and persecution, the grant of equality which came fitfully to various European Jewries shattered the old patterns of Jewish life and thought. Modernity meant secularization, certainly for Jews, whose only hope of social equality lay in the creation of civic domains where religion, i.e., Christianity, did not rule. It also changed the scope of Jewish responsibility. Where Jews had once been excluded from civic affairs they were now expected to be good citizens and think in terms of the general welfare. The classic Jewish sources had not considered such an eventuality. Much talmudic and later Jewish law assumes (with good reason) existence in a hostile social environment. It therefore divides Jewish duty into the spheres of those who share one's laws and values, other Jews, and those who do not, Gentiles. One's kin receive more generous treatment than do the oppressive outsiders, though God's covenant with Gentiles mandated significant ethical duties toward them. When, however, social equality came, it required a new Jewish social ethic. Elaborating it became a major intellectual task for 19th-century Jewish thinkers.

Producing a more explicitly universal Jewish ethics required facing another challenge: secularization made human experience the substitute for divine revelation, the foundation of classic Jewish thought and ethics. The successful resolution of this intellectual problem gave rise to what has become the accepted ideology of contemporary Jewry—and also to the criticisms which have brought into being three alternative theories of modern Jewish ethics.

In Immanuel Kant's ethics, 19th-century Jewish thinkers found a philosophical framework by which to specify what they now took to be the

22

essence of Judaism. In the work of Hermann Cohen, the founder of Marburg neo-Kantianism, this effort achieved academic fulfillment. Cohen argued that the ethical dimension of human rationality must be said to undergird its other Kantian modes, scientific and aesthetic thought. To integrate these three activities of the mind, every rational world view requires a unique, transcendent idea, what religions call God. Philosophy therefore mandates religion of reason, ethical monotheism.

In actual history, Cohen argued, this idea first appeared in the prophets of Israel and it remains the rational unity integrating all the subsequent development of Judaism. Thus, Jewish law is at heart a training for ethics, and that ethics, for all its limitation to one community, ideally aims at universal inclusiveness. In the modern period, with Jews freed from the ghetto, this universal core could now freely express itself. Jews should give up anything in their tradition that contradicts ethics and preserve everything that either teaches or abets it. Contemporary Jewish duty must now be as directed toward humankind as to the Jewish people. Indeed, Cohen argued that Jews had a historic mission to teach this concept of ethical monotheism to all of humanity since their religion possessed it more purely than did any other.

Ideas such as these had an almost incalculable influence upon the lives of all modernized Jews, though they were for long particularly cherished in Reform Judaism. Even those Jews who have given up Jewish belief have often still maintained a commitment to ethics as the criterion of true humanity. The statistically disproportionate involvement of Jews in every activity for human betterment derives from this reinterpretation of Jewish responsibility. The same is true of the standard apologies for Jewish practice—that they are, essentially, training for ethics; and for Jewish continuity—that no other religion produces such devotion to ethical living.

Critics have challenged the Jewish and ethical adequacy of this theory. Its identification of Judaism with a universalistic ethics has been rejected as untrue to Jewish history and destructive of particular Jewish duty. Over the centuries, Jews have thought of themselves as rabbinic rather than "prophetic" Jews, and rabbinic law may have some universal, ethical themes but cannot, without distortion, be equated with a humanistic morality. Rather, this theory says more about 19th-century German philosophy than it does about the Jewish tradition. If proof of this charge is required, it can be found in the "commandments" generated by this system. It commits Jews primarily to universal ethics, relegating Jewish ritual and communal responsibility to a secondary, optional role. That may create good people but might also lead to the disappearance of the unique Jewish service of God.

In reaction to Judaism-as-ethics, some thinkers advocated a historicist approach to Jewish duty, and though it has found institutional expression in Conservative Judaism it has not yet been given academic theoretical explication. These thinkers contended that history indicated that there could be no Judaism without its legal system, *halakhah*. Any modern Judaism, to be worthy of the name, must therefore operate within the classic legal framework. That, however, should now be understood in terms of the modern notion of historic development. As scholarly research indicates, Jewish law has changed over the centuries, not infrequently as the result of growing ethical sensitivity. Were a modern scholar class to respond dynamically out of Jewish law to questions of the day, contemporary Jews might hope to have a properly ethical and Jewish determination of their responsibility.

This view, too, has had its critics. Orthodox Jewish thinkers have charged that while it properly identifies Judaism with *halakhah*, it perverts the classic Jewish understanding of how the law develops. Changes in Jewish law in the past arose primarily out of concern for Jewish teaching and only secondarily to adapt to the Gentile world. The inauthenticity of the historicist treatment of the law has been made manifest by its validating changes in practice that traditionalist scholars and the bulk of the observant community have found contrary to *halakhah*. Considering the moral and spiritual emptiness of much of Western civilization—a civilization which could give rise to the Holocaust—its values should not become a guide to the Jewish service of God. Rather, the determination of Jewish law and ethics should be left to those who have come to merit the respect of the observant, learned Jewish community. Reverent continuity, not presumptuous change, should be the hallmark of Jewish obligation.

Feminists have radically challenged the ethical sufficiency of the historicist and Orthodox interpretations of Jewish duty. By universal standards, Jewish law is sexist and unethical. This is not to deny that the *halakhah* may have extended women's rights over the ages and given Jewish women a higher communal status than that of other women of their time. Nonetheless, it denies women equality with men, most troublingly by insisting that men make all the decisions about women's Jewish religious status. Despite these charges, the sages of Orthodoxy have ruled that *halakhah* prohibits any major changes in Jewish law and practice with regard to women. The historicists have split over this issue. The more traditional among them agree with the Orthodox that loyalty to the procedures and precedents of Jewish law makes it impossible to grant many of the changes feminists desire. Others argue that Jewish law does not explicitly prohibit greater equality for women, such as their right to be ordained, but, dynamically read, can authorize changes in women's status.

A personalistic, Buberian approach to these issues has also been advocated. It accepts the liberal notion that a universal ethical sensitivity must be basic to a modern Judaism. But it denies the continuing adequacy of the Kantian understanding of the ethics, which derives from a conception of the self as fundamentally a construction of one's reason. Instead it proposes to integrate rationality into a more comprehensive, existentialist sense of the self, producing thereby an ethics of relationship rather than of rational rule. Likewise, it reinterprets Jewish authenticity in relational terms, suggesting that Jewish responsibility derives from personally sharing the Jewish people's covenant with God. The *halakhah* and *agadah* may then be the Jew's best guides to authentic obligation—but they must now be read in terms of a given individual's present response to God as one of God's dedicated ethnic community. The proponents of this view find its pluralism amid traditionalism appealing, but its critics charge that its individualism will destroy the community cohesiveness necessary for the Jewish people to continue to serve God in history.

Two centuries of growing freedom have so ingrained the expanded ethical commitment of Jews that it has become fundamental to their Jewish existence. But the community and its thinkers remain deeply divided as to just how to define the character and content of Jewish ethics.

2

"Jewish?" "Ethics?" "Jewish Ethics?"—The New Problems

Since Jews began leaving the ghetto, no facet of their new self-image has carried more symbolic weight than the complex of ideas associated with "Jewish ethics." It justified their participation in general society, validated their emancipated Jewish identity, explained and shaped their secularity, refuted Christian claims to superiority—and much more. Yet today the entire notion of "Jewish ethics," as we have commonly understood the term, has become questionable, engendering the search for new meanings. Though the papers gathered in this book treat only aspects of this development (as was appropriate to the occasion of their writing), bringing them together here should provide a fairly comprehensive view of the problems and my suggested solutions.

I

To begin with the history, the early nineteenth-century Emancipation of "ghetto" Jewry—a gradual process rather than an event—revolutionized Jewish life to an extent free Jews can hardly comprehend. After roughly 1500 years of segregation, oppression, and then persecution, European Jews became social equals. (Jews under Arab rule were not similarly benefited as were, in even happier ways, those coming to North America.) This drastic social relocation made a revised understanding of Jewish identity indispensable for the masses who eagerly embraced the new freedom. Thinkers reflecting on the heady experience of equality worked out a Jewish response to it in terms of ideas we have come to know as "Jewish ethics," a theme that became central to modernized Jewry's self-image.

26

Traditional Judaism had not addressed the abstract concern with conduct called "ethics." No book of the Bible or the Talmud has ethics as its topic or major theme; however, once one thinks in terms of ethics one becomes aware of the strong ethical thrust found in the Written and Oral Torah. Ethics is, of course, a Greek way of looking at duty, a duty derived from reason. Judaism had a more reliable source of obligation, God's revelation, and thus it spoke of commandments, ones that dealt with very much more of life than how one should treat other people. Not until Jews learned about Greek philosophy in the ninth century did they occasionally reflect specifically on ethics. Thus, the modern Jewish understanding of Jewish ethics and its exaltation as the primary means of being a good Jew were very much more a creative innovation than a simple evolution.

The concept primarily derived from the startling experience of having rights as a citizen. This only became possible when the modern state enfranchised individuals, not classes like the nobility, or institutions like the church or the Jewish community. The new status of the single self was confirmed as democracy increasingly expanded. Now each citizen had a share in determining who would rule and, more important for our theme, who would legislate. Though people had to share their political power with numerous others, the act of voting taught them about their newly enriched personal worth. Since then, participation in determining the laws ruling one has been a critical indication of individual dignity, a reality the worldwide passion for self-determination continues to demonstrate.

Democracy came, and still comes, as a wonder to the previously disenfranchised. To European Jewry, it seemed nearly miraculous, for political equality was given to *everyone*, including, despite controversy, those millennial outsiders, the Jews. The intellectual-ethical roots of the emancipation of Jewry were rationalistic. Citizenship was to be universal; ideally no one was excluded from the democratic process and no one within it was to have more power than anyone else. Moreover, the new opportunities available to Jews seemed, compared to the ghetto's limited arena of activity, to encompass little less than the whole world. Not the least of these were economic opportunities, offering the hope of advancing from penury to security.

The overwhelming majority of Jews found the lure of modernization irresistible; neither force nor special incentive was ever required to get them to leave the ghetto. Subsequently, whenever equality has been honestly offered to Jews, they have avidly taken advantage of it. One cannot hope to fathom the character of modern Jewish life today without acknowledging its foundation in the Jewish passion to be an integral part of democratic society.

Living largely among gentiles created a conflict with what the rabbinate taught was the necessary form and tone of Jewish life. To some extent the Torah directly mandated a good measure of Jewish separatism; more critically, the recent centuries of segregation and persecution had heightened the desire for self-isolation. They brought about a defensiveness that opposed modernization, including such adaptations as recent generations of the observant have found compatible with Jewish law.

In response, many Jews simply did what modernity had taught them: they made up their own minds about what they ought to do. Mostly on their own, but learning from one another and occasionally in concert, they created their own versions of how to be Jewish *and* modern. In the West, the religious model proved most efficacious, so Jews modernized their worship and other religious duties through the movements we know as Reform and Conservative Judaism. In the East, nationality offered a better way of modernizing, so Jews there turned to secular patterns such as cultural enlightenment, Zionism, and Jewish socialism for a new self-image. In all these new modes of Jewish existence, the modern concept of ethics was essential, providing Jews with their essential view of being human and staying Jewish.

Many reasons came together to commend the notion of Jewish ethics. Negatively, by its reliance on individual conscience and reason, Jewish ethics persuasively superseded the now embarrassing doctrine of God's revelation, as well as the restrictive power of the traditional rabbinate. Positively, the concept affirmed the dignity of the individual, not the least by exalting the Jewish virtue of simply doing good. Jewish ethics also provided an easily understandable criterion for what was lasting in the Jewish heritage—its ethics—and what might be changed—its other observances. At the same time, it clarified why responsible Jews should devote much of their energy to a world dominated by gentiles, making such social involvement an essential Jewish duty. In this way, it mandated a Jewish way of life that, because of its universality, transcended the encumbrances of particularity, yet simultaneously justified why Jews should stay Jews. Judaism, with its classic emphasis on "works," was, particularly when modernized, simply more ethical than Christianity, which prided itself on its concern with faith. Modern Jews had no difficulty reading historic Jewish law as essentially moral law, but they denied that one could create a realistic social ethics from the Christian doctrine of love. And since ethics derived from human reason and made believing in God Jewishly irrelevant, this notion appealed equally to Jewish secularists.

Because of this multiple appeal, the various understandings connected with Jewish ethics were at the ideological heart of every movement to modernize Judaism. Despite much criticism, Jewish ethics remains the single most important way Jews validate their traditions to themselves and justify their community against its detractors. This continuing commitment lies behind the tensions American Jews feel whenever they perceive the United States or the State of Israel transgressing decent ethical limits.

Acknowledging the social functions of the concept of Jewish ethics does not lead to the cynical conclusion that the concept merely rationalized Jewish group interest. It did serve Jewish social needs and almost certainly gained its power from its social origins, but most Jews affirmed the concept because they believed it was true; they knew instinctively that

28

the essence of Judaism was being a good person. They saw their heritage uncommonly devoted to creating good people and caring communities, though its modes of doing so in other times and cultures now occasionally clashed with an unsegregated existence.

No thinker more effectively demonstrated the academic legitimacy of ethics and thus the primary principle of a rational interpretation of Judaism than Hermann Cohen (1842–1918). Based on his internationally recognized philosophic revival of Kant, this great turn-of-the-century German philosopher gave the concept of Jewish ethics its enduring distinctive form. Cohen's thought was brought to American Jewry by the many students who went to Germany to pursue doctorates in Jewish studies. Since Cohen's ideas permeated German Jewish intellectual life, everyone who studied in Germany absorbed them. Then often, as professors at American seminaries, these former students taught Cohen's ideas to their rabbinical students, who in turn transmitted them to their congregations.

On a less academic level, the centrality of ethics to Judaism was made an intellectual staple by the widely read Hebrew essayist writing under the name Ahad Haam (Asher Ginzberg, 1856–1927). His Zionism envisioned the Jewish homeland serving as a "spiritual center" for worldwide Jewry. By "spiritual" he meant nothing religious since he was a committed secularist. An uncompromising elitist, Ahad Haam believed the human spirit could only be fulfilled in high cultural creativity. He therefore wanted the Jewish people to return to their land to revive an authentic Jewish culture. In this, Jewish ethics would have to play a vital role since he insisted that the Jews had a special national gift for ethics, one their reestablished cultural independence would clearly make manifest. In equating Jewish nationalism with high ethical attainment, Ahad Haam was exceptional among the early theoreticians of Zionism—the reason, observers suggest, that he is no longer considered relevant by most Israeli intellectuals. Since Ahad Haam never fully explicated his view of Jewish ethics or its distinctiveness, and his brief references sound much like Hermann Cohen's neo-Kantianism, let us sketch in some of this thinker's relevant ideas.

Like Kant, Cohen argued that ethics was as fully significant a dimension of the rational mind as was science (with esthetics the third such mode). In the Kantian understanding, reason presses toward comprehensive explanations so that a rational ethics can be recognized, in part by its universality; that is, it has respect for all moral agents (human beings), granting them intrinsic dignity and including them in all truly ethical rules. Moreover, Kant argued, just as in science a rational mind seeks to establish the laws of nature, so a rational person will seek an ethics structured in law, the so-called "moral law."

Cohen developed his neo-Kantianism in heavy academic tomes, quite independent of any Jewish overtones. Yet as a proud Jew, he would occasionally write an essay showing how his philosophy illuminated, indeed, lay at the core of the Jewish tradition. Applied in virtuoso fashion by his

29

many followers, this neo-Kantianism seemed so true an understanding of what it meant to be a modern, rational person and yet so clear an evocation of the soul of traditional Judaism that it became the grounding premise of modern Jewry's intellectual self-understanding.

One further theme of particular American significance remains to be mentioned: the identification of Jewish ethics with liberal politics and social-action activities. European Jewish socialists had stressed the moral power of politics—particularly as contrasted to piety—and they brought their ethical activism with them to the United States. By the mid-twentieth century, with the massive East European Jewish migration acculturating, the United States, itself catalyzed by the reforms of the New Deal, seemed ready for a fuller democracy. After the World War II victory over the Nazi totalitarians and with an expanding economy providing more for everyone, America began making good on its promise of equality to the minorities it had previously scorned. Jews delighted in this process not only as a response to their social agenda but as a powerful means of ensuring their new gains. If even those lower on the ladder of social acceptability had guaranteed rights, then Jews would surely be more secure in their status as equals. Moreover, since anti-semitism seemed largely to arise from social discontent, it was prudent for Jews to support governmental action to alleviate problems such as unemployment, inadequate housing, job discrimination, and so on. (Speculatively, this belief in the government as moral leader has its roots in the experience of Jewish emancipation and in the classic Jewish belief in the power of law.) Consequently, as the 1950s moved along and then as the 1960s gave birth to a newly demonstrative, confrontational politics, Jews were to be found in every liberal cause in highly disproportionate numbers.

In sum, by the late 1960s most American Jews took it for granted that the most important thing about Judaism was its ethics and that Jewish ethics meant liberal politics.

II

This remarkable amalgam of social experience, self-interest, and moral intuition then began to fall apart as each of its components came under increasing challenge. As a result, the meanings popularly associated with the terms *Jewish, ethics,* and *Jewish ethics* were thrown into doubt. How one might properly speak of such a concept and, certainly, what its content was became matters of considerable argument. One period's certainty had become another's perplexity.

To begin with the social context again, American democracy, with surprising quickness, lost much of its moral stature. A strong civil-rights law did not lead to full equality for blacks, and as numerous other minority groups learned the politics of confrontation and protest, the limits of American tolerance became clear. The Vietnam War made suspicion rather than respect the common attitude toward government, and the continuing scandals, typified by Watergate, completed the desacralization of democratic politics. At the same time, the university, the family, the arts, religion, all the institutions we counted on to nurture character now showed themselves equally capable of corrupting it. Then, too, our economy could no longer promise most people expanding economic horizons, and our society began tolerating actions that once would have been condemned as vice. Above everyone's head hovered the plagues of violence and drugs. A shift in ethos from idealistic hope to cynical resignation could hardly be avoided. Modernity had become a deep disappointment; individual freedom was more than conscience could handle so that the old stabilities suddenly became preferable to the new openness.

In the Jewish community, the general misery had pointed focus in the special pain of the Holocaust. Modern culture, even democracy, did not prevent such ineffable evil. It took American Jews nearly twenty years to face this horror—one intimately connected, I am convinced, not with the death of a biblical God that a largely agnostic community no longer affirmed, but with the loss of its operative faith in Western culture and human competence. Then came the further revelations that the democracies, including the United States, had not done all they could have to mitigate the slaughter. The depth of anti-semitism in Western culture seemed immeasurable, and the continual incidents that indicated its unabated virulence made modernity's potential for malevolence painfully unavoidable.

Intellectually, too, the vision of humankind as rational and rationality itself implying a Kant-like ethics lost its old compelling power, perhaps mostly as a result of the incredible carnage of World War I. What remained of Kantian ethics faded as psychoanalysis from within and anthropology and Marxism from without demonstrated that, realistically, "conscience" mostly meant the introjected parent or group interest. Moreover, if one tightly identifies the rational with "clear and distinct ideas," then only science and logic qualify as rational, rendering ethics more personal preference than reasoned truth. With the increasing acceptance of this technical sense of rationality, one could credibly claim to be quite rational yet a-ethical, a dichotomy unthinkable to Kantians. Today many philosophic varieties of "rationality" compete for our intellectual allegiance, none able to demonstrate why it rather than its competitors should structure our thinking. Even worse, with philosophy itself largely conceived as a "construction of reality," none can establish why, to begin with, we ought to strive to be ethical and, as a consequence, why its ethics command imperatives rather than merely offer counsel.

In this radically changed intellectual environment, few can retain the old Kantian liberal certainty that ethics is more certain than belief, and therefore religion must first begin with a rational ethics and then include only what is compatible with it. The postmodern situation begins with the recognition that ethics has lost its old certainty and priority. The deconstructionists unabashedly construe ethics as only another form of word-play. But most religious believers, unwilling to let the new midrashic anti-rationalism overrule their sense of truth and right, have turned the modernist premise around: they now ponder the role of belief in establish-ing the ground and content of ethics—and thus, too, of Jewish duty as a whole.

It should come as no surprise then, that the familiar identification of Jewish ethics with liberal politics also has been rejected. Neo-conservative criticism has devastatingly demonstrated how much evil has been created by the government's efforts to increase our society's welfare. Why must every burden be thrown upon government when so often its major virtues, power and reach, degenerate into inflexible rules and unresponsive bu-reaucracies, defeating its humane aspirations? Surely there is nothing un-ethical about exploiting what private initiative might do—and perhaps do better—to foster social benefit. As to the Jewish content of ethics, our tra-dition has long commended industry, sobriety, moderation, modesty, the family, and public decorum as against the liberal temper that so delights in self-fulfillment, experimentation, sexual liberation and the toleration of aberrance, and government spending as social therapy.

The needs of the State of Israel have also militated against identifying Jewish ethics with liberal politics. Most Jews give higher priority to its immediate survival than to assuring long-range local security by improv-ing America. Or, in the classic terms, Israeli guns, it is argued, should con-cern American Jews more than butter for the American deprived. Such political clout as American Jews have should, therefore, be targeted to lob-bying for the State of Israel's needs. Moreover, with the Soviet Union and Red China sponsoring terrorists and otherwise impeding a Middle-Eastern settlement, Jews should scorn any semblance of support for the left and fight the moralistic rush to detente.

Such thinking requires a rethinking of what should be meant in call-ing an ethic "Jewish." Liberal Jews once understood this term so univer-sally that they fought for every people but their own. But only an odd sense of the good would require sacrificing one's family—or one's uncom-monly admirable people—for the sake of humankind. Are we not ethically entitled to ask "What's good for the Jews?" and to reject categorically a supine Jewish acceptance of whatever modern ethics allegedly mandates? In simple self-respect, we must insist that just as modernity may criticize and enrich Judaism, so our problem-riddled culture can often benefit from Jewish reproof and recommendation.

Believing Jews can now readily see that Western democracy, by its drastic secularization, has cut itself off from its biblical foundations. Los-ing its certainty in the moral standards laid upon us by our Creator—the One who gave us our "unalienable rights"—our civilization has let free-dom have its head with traumatic social consequences. Its highly problem-atic ethical sense can no longer, as it did in the heyday of liberalism, dictate what remains valid in Judaism. Rather, our society needs to reappropriate its Jewish—some say its Judeo-Christian—roots to restore its moral well-being. Judaism as a whole and Jewish ethics in particular now ought to be seen as independent sources of guidance for a society desperately requiring ethical and metaethical help.

If the Jewishness of Jewish ethics no longer means uncovering the rationalistic, liberal imperatives embedded in Jewish sources, what does it mean? The early protagonists of modern Jewish ethics generally utilized the biblical prophets and rabbinic *agadah* (lore) to make their case since these materials often stressed the priority of moral duty. But Jewish teachers have long insisted that one finds the authoritative delineation of Jewish duty in the *halakhah* (rabbinic law). If so, any ethics that claims to be authentically "Jewish" ought to validate itself by *Jewish* standards, that is, by serious attention to the dialectical working out of the *halakhah* over the centuries.

This critique of the liberal version of Jewish ethics has convinced some Jews, as have similar arguments in their communities persuaded some Moslems and Christians, to turn to orthodoxy. The choices before us are painted starkly: either a failed modernity or a return to old religious ways, which, despite an occasional problem, have proven themselves over the centuries to be truly humane precisely because they are God's own ways for us. If retaining proper values entails the sacrifice of certain cherished modern freedoms, like sexual openness, then it is well worth the price. Every generation requires absolutes—ours more than most, the blandishments of relativism being so seductive.

As a result, the movement in other communities to fundamentalism is paralleled among Jews in a strong, if minority, return to Orthodoxy. For believing Orthodox Jews, the *halakhah*, the God-given system for determining Jewish duty, is the only authentic Jewish form of what has been called "Jewish ethics," a term it does not customarily use even as it denies the secularists' universal human ethics an independent role in fixing Jewish obligation.

In response, most Jews, despite their disillusionment with modernity, have refused to give up its teaching about ethics. Three issues clarify this demurral, all deriving from moral lessons taught by the experience of democracy. The first arises from a revulsion at the extremism and fanaticism that an unmodernized religious traditionalism can readily engender. Judaism has the same potential for zealotry as does every faith that claims possession of the only God's own truth. This empowers religious leaders, as the situation requires, to punish the wicked drastically, for this will restore them to a right relationship with God. The result has been the sorry human experience of religion as persecutor. Today, allowing their perception of rampant anti-semitism to unshackle their tongues, Jewish religious bigots on the right have publicly demonstrated Judaism's halakhic resources for intolerance.

One can give this line of argument positive form. For all the faults of democracy, no political system does more to enhance the dignity of individuals and promote tranquillity between antagonistic groups. Religious orthodoxies commend themselves for their moral absolutes, which also means they are, in principle, not committed to pluralism. Jewish Orthodoxy, despite its meritocracy of the learned and its appreciation of individuality, has not yet made plain whether its relationship to democratic pluralism is pragmatic or principled. Until it does so, the basis of its effective control of its potential for fanaticism will be in doubt. As long as that is so, most American Jews will seek spiritual guidance in a liberal reinterpretation of their religion.

Modernists also reject Orthodoxy as a therapy for our society's moral ailments, because they find its social vision more inner-directed than they believe right in our democratic situation. They do not deny that Jewish survival ought to be a major Jewish priority and that anti-semitism remains a dangerous threat in Western cultures. But they believe we require greater emphasis on our God-given duties to humankind entire than our traditionalists commonly give them. The classic texts of the *halakhah* contain legal conclusions derived by applying the behests of Torah to life carried on under conditions of political subservience, social segregation, and comparative economic scarcity. They therefore naturally instruct Jews to direct almost all their energies to their duties toward other Jews and the Jewish community. But closely following these precedents today does not create a major Jewish religious imperative to work for the common welfare of humanity. In our unparalleled social equality and economic well-being, that seems a less than ethical response to our society and its ideals. And when emotion turns "What's good for the Jews?" into the overriding criterion of Jewish duty, one has the obverse Orthodox equivalent of the liberals' old sin of only asking, "What's good for humankind?"

This issue becomes particularly upsetting when some Jews insist that the Holocaust proves people cannot be expected to act ethically toward Jews so we have good reason to concentrate on taking care of ourselves. Though there is some truth in such realism, there is much more to be said. Were there not a universal sense of ethics, one every human being ought to acknowledge and obey, why should we expect every decent human being to be outraged by what the Nazis did? If ethics are merely local standards or group values, the Nazis acted properly according to the (perverted) "moral" values of their (demented) culture. Only if we affirm that there is a universal ethical order, one whose commands everyone can know, can we rightly demand, as we regularly do, that people resist "unjust orders" despite fearsome pressure. Because there are universally accessible ethics, we are right to be scandalized by the Holocaust, by the guilt of the "good Germans," and by the collusion of the leaders of the democracies. And we ought not to forget that the equality of Jews in democratic societies is premised on universal, not local, ethics. By some such line of reasoning, most modern Jews know that an explicit, effective universalism must be a necessary and significant element in Jewish duty, a truth they do not see unequivocally mandated by our Orthodoxy.

Third, feminism has provided a dramatic, specific focus for the limit to the modernist's embrace of the Jewish tradition. If all moral agents ought to be treated with ethical equality, as Kant taught and democracy exemplifies, why should Jewish women not have equal obligations and thus a religious status equal to that of Jewish men? It will not do to say that women are inherently spiritual and, hence, require fewer duties than men, or that feminist goals refute themselves by seeking to obliterate all the differences created by biology. The debate can be easily limited to a few practical but deeply felt questions: Why should Jewish law, as most traditionalists understand it, debar women from being counted in the quorum for formal Jewish worship; and is that, indeed, a good enough reason to prohibit their leading such services? Why should the overwhelming majority of sages prohibit women from studying the advanced texts of rabbinic law? Why may they not generally serve as legal witnesses, or divorce a husband, or be a rabbi? And, most tellingly of all, why do women have no effective role in answering these questions, no significant share in the decision making that affects their lives as Jews?

American Jewesses are the most highly educated group of women in human history. Their accomplishments have been awesome. Most American Jews, aside from their residual sexist conditioning, know that women and men should rightly live by the same standards of piety. But just in the face of the changes called for by this intense moral conviction, the potential immobility of an institutionalized religious absolute becomes a chilling reality. That does not always happen. It can change some of its old ways or rules. But other changes cannot or do not take place regardless of what appears to be their spiritual value—and that, so far, has been the response of most of the leaders of Orthodoxy to Jewish feminism. This reaction has taught most American Jews that for all their deepened respect for their tradition as an independent source of moral guidance, they know they cannot rely on it exclusively—and this has brought us back to the emancipated Jew's project of creating a proper Jewish ethics.

III

I wrote the papers gathered in this volume to gain insight into this religious situation and, as I did so, to learn how to respond to it. I see them as clearing the ground for a postmodern Jewish ethic. It must be postmodern not in the sense of being deconstructionist, for taken rigorously that position relativizes all values into verbal play. By using the term *postmodern*, I mean to point to our rejection of the old rationalist assumption that universal ethics defines our essential Jewish duty and that neo-Kantianism provides the necessary form and political liberalism the proper content of Jewish ethics. There are many places one can learn about Jewish duty today, the most important of which is rabbinic literature. Certainly when it comes to the critical metaethical determinations

35

from which we elaborate our ethical reasoning, the classic wisdom of the Jewish tradition instructs me more reliably than any single body of modern knowledge I know. And this primal Jewish commitment is the standard by which I gauge where I may find the good in the welter of opportunities our society sets before me.

Though Judaism is my most significant guide, I cannot accept its classic absolutism, its consequent structure of authority, and its delineation of Jewish obligation. Accepting neither modernity nor Jewish tradition as providing my life's determining rule, not even understanding how they combine in sacred alliance rightfully to indicate what I must do, I seek to redefine "Jewish ethics." For me this term now involves less a content than a process, one of mediating between the values I find in each. But I have not found nor think I will find a rule by which rightly to do that. I do not possess that much confidence in the power of human reason (though it is the major instrument utilized in these papers).

What mediates between these two sources of guidance is, I suggest, my self, specifically the Jewish self I have tried to describe here (most notably in Chapter 14). It must carry the work of self-exposure, criticism, and learning I see as basic to this new kind of engaged Jewish ethics. I am therefore deeply committed to pluralism in defining Jewish obligation.

In developing my understanding, I have devoted my attention mainly to specific issues rather than abstract philosophic themes. By focusing on applied ethics I have hoped—with good Jewish precedent—that inductively I might gain insight into the most responsible way of carrying on this process. These papers, then, for all that I believe them to have some substantive worth, constitute a record of work still in progress.

PART
ONE

In Search of the Ground
of Our Values

ONE

In Search of the Ground
of Our Values

The radical change in the Jew's social situation as a result of the Emancipation motivated Jewish thinkers to create a new conception of Jewish life and belief. As a consequence, any shift in that social context will have a major effect on the modern Jew's self-understanding. Where once Western culture was perceived as humanly benign, even liberating, its increasing pathology, so evident in the latter part of the twentieth century, has forced everyone whose ethics derive from the Bible to reflect on what has gone wrong.

Religious thinkers have been particularly troubled by the radicalization of modern secularity. What once was an attractive feature of the modern state—that it relegated religion to the private realm—is now increasingly seen as also the spiritual root of our social malaise. While secularity continues to benefit all citizens by the relative harmony it creates among oftentimes conflicting religious communities, it has also eroded the stability and significance of our old values. The humanism that once seemed so noble, though unbelieving, now defiles itself by additionally leading to the grossness of hedonism, narcissism, and license.

In exploring this theme over the years, I have been particularly concerned with what religion can still learn from secularism. I have also argued that without a Judeo-Christian base, the one secularity long declared dispensable, one cannot assume that the classic ethical concerns of our society and our social liberals will have any staying power. This refusal to spurn the continuing virtues of secularism remains a major reason I continue to be a religious liberal, even as my nagging effort to direct our attention to the general loss of a ground for our values firmly situates my liberalism on a religious foundation.

In one situation after another, I have found it important to say that what we believe is critical for what we shall think is the good. The God of the Jewish tradition, envisioned in appropriately modern guise yet classicly still recognizable, is the ground of my personal and social ethics. Those who share similar values but have, in many ways, been accustomed to ignoring the question of what gives them their validity, I seek to challenge with my assertion that they believe more than they know. And in the retrieval of their latent faith, I see the beginnings of hope for our civilization.

3

Psychotherapy and Religion

Appropriate Expectations

Psychotherapy and religion have so much in common, in form if not in substance, that specifying their differences is far more difficult than describing their similarities. To begin with, neither term can be satisfactorily defined and thus one can never be quite certain just what is or is not properly included under it. At its best, this indeterminacy arises from our mutual vitality, a dynamism which bring us both endless new claimants to greater truth and, therefore, similar problems of sectarianism, heresy and orthodoxy. When, then, someone writes comprehensively about our disciplines, as I am doing, thoughtful readers reasonably speculate about what may be called the author's political location among colleagues. I, for example, write as a believing Jew—note the modifier—and as a Reform, not an Orthodox or Conservative Jew, to omit a number of other small if important Jewish religious groups and cultural orientations.

Furthermore, in both fields, providing a movement label is hardly satisfactory identification since every group has its liberals and conservatives, its orthodoxy and radicalism. In my liberal religious community, I am comparatively traditional in belief and practice but also far more liberal than are those of my traditionalist colleagues who keep calling for us to institute group disciplines. Thus, I speak mainly for myself, which, to my surprise, I hear some otherwise good Catholics today saying even about the Pope. The situation seems no different in "psychotherapy," a

Reprinted from the journal *Religious Education*, Volume 69, Number 6, by permission from the publisher, The Religious Education Association, 409 Prospect Street, New Haven, CT 06511–2177.

catch-all designation created to encompass a similarly bewilderingly comprehensive enterprise.

Clergy and psychotherapists are most intimately linked by a mutual concern: deep devotion to human beings and their welfare. Idealistically, we aspire to assuage suffering and foster wholeness. We regularly attend to people so anguished that others everywhere have tended to withdraw from them. We hope our ministrations and presence will help lessen their pain, particularly when it is self-caused, and strengthen them so that they may live with greater well-being.

Sometimes our help comes with dramatic suddenness, but in the usual case the benefit depends on being able to maintain a certain discipline. One must come with constancy, apply oneself to the process conscientiously and, through the ofttimes tedious, demanding work, seek out a newer, richer truth. We learn humility, to surrender the false righteousness that blinds us from seeing how we have defeated our highest ideals. More humbling still, we come to acknowledge how our ideals themselves were distorted by the accidents that shaped or the perversities that stunted our emerging selves. Painfully, healingly, we discern what was not ours to change and what we still can do. Embracing the past more fully, we gain a newly enlarged future and thus an immeasurably richer present.

This curious enlightenment arrives largely by attending to symbols, the words or acts or images which testify to a reality that critically impinges upon us but of which we commonly remain unaware. Learning to accept this initially alien otherness—which then turns out to be so intimately a part of us—becomes central to our reeducation. For most of us, language is the chief medium of our contact with this deeper reality. What was or is now said can carry immense significance and therefore invites intense examination. We practice ever new, subtle forms of interpretaton—exegesis—and thereby learn how deeply our sense of reality depends on our way of reading our data—hermeneutics. For others of us, acts are the primary means of asserting our humanness. In this mode, learning how to do what once we were incapable of doing becomes, in the very doing, an opening to oneself. This pattern, it should be noted, places strong emphasis upon justice, the faith that right action will be consistently rewarded.

We often come to religion or psychotherapy because of a momentary crisis in our lives yet both disciplines aim at having a more than temporary effect upon us. They propose to change our lives lastingly because they hope to reach to the very core of our being. Thus, the art of self-perception they expect to impart to us needs to be a steady part of our lives lest we forget who we are and lose our clearer vision of what, in fact, we are doing. Should we let the new powers we have acquired atrophy, our perverse and self-destructive self will surely return and overpower us. Besides, life has its surprises, the blessings and traumas which so quickly arouse in us heretofore dormant dangerous impulses. Our psychic gain is thus, necessarily, less a possession one always has available than an excellence which, for all that it has been acquired, must forever be worked at or lost.

This must be a lifelong process because the truth we seek is infinite. The more we learn, the more we sense what yet needs to be learned. We operate, then, with a curious mix of knowledge and ignorance, of faith and agnosticism. Our insights can arrive with such immediacy that they are self-confirming, perhaps overwhelmingly so. We cannot believe that but a little while ago, for all that others said there were such things, for all our intimations of it, what we now know so certainly was nonexistent. Now, we shall never know how much more such knowledge awaits us. It is entirely possible that the greater part of what most deeply affects our lives is still hidden from us. We cannot know and we may never find out. We shall have to live by such truth as we have, building upon it whenever we can and testing every new insight by its integrity with our knowledge and life.

For all the demands these disciplines make upon their participants, neither of them can scientifically demonstrate its effectiveness. Of course, we personally may have seen people under our care change their lives radically for the better, and there are surely many others who would gladly testify that our help was uniquely valuable to them. Some of us have even seen shattered selves miraculously transformed. Nonetheless, thus far, there is no disinterested, quantitative proof that our ministrations lead to our goals with reasonable consistency. Worse, there is equally little proof that any one of our processes is better than any other or even that, if left alone, people might not equally have benefited.

So, for all our scholarship and erudition, we operate as much by faith as by knowledge, serving an ideal we know to be worthy of our finest efforts even though unprovable, in devotion to a human accomplishment so valuable that, despite its rarity and unpredictability, we know it rightly claims our dedication. To put it now in religious terms, we celebrate the incomparable glory of the exodus experience, the joy of bringing human beings from slavery to freedom, of liberating them from the taskmasters of sin and tangled emotions so they may walk the hard but rewarding way through the wilderness of realism to the promised land of fulfilled maturity. We are then, jointly, priests of the little redemptions, the ones which despite their ordinariness and day to day character, reflect the ultimacy we have known and lure us toward the consummation we envision.

In all these respects, then, one may expect something similar from psychotherapy and religion. Yet each regimen also brings to bear upon our human condition its own special strengths. In exploring these, I am conscious that what I see as distinctive of each field is not exclusive to it but is, in considerable measure, found in the other as well.

Psychotherapy is based on a detailed knowledge of human behavior that religion rarely attains, despite its centuries of intimate experience with people. In part that arises from psychology's concentration of attention, its detailed, meticulous study of human behavior and its causes. In greater part, I believe, its special expertise arises from its insight that our emotional lives are far more determinative of who we are and how we act than people had once thought.

Consider, for example, how much religion has benefited from the study of the psychodynamics of dying and bereavement. Religion has, of course, been incomparably significant over the ages in helping people meet these inevitable traumas. Yet, now, through a better understanding of the emotional stages through which the dying and bereaved usually pass, we are far better equipped to help others and, let us hope, ourselves to face the psychic tasks involved. In this instance, obviously, religion and psychotherapy each has something to contribute to the other. Nonetheless, we rightly expect those psychologically trained to be especially knowledgeable about how people may be expected to act *in extremis* and what help is likely therefore to be of the greatest psychic benefit to them. It is no wonder then that secure religionists have been so eager to learn about and, to considerable extent employ, psychotherapeutic insights in their ministry to the dying and the bereaved as in so many other areas.

Psychology has also created an impressive variety of techniques by which we can effectively help people be more themselves. My example is as simple as its effect has been revolutionary: psychotherapists have created a special way of listening—and listening in depth has helped us know better how we might appropriately respond to others. Religion's classic figures generally have been speakers, not listeners. Their successors, it must be acknowledged, tended to employ admonition and exhortation rather than consolation and sharing to move their flocks to greater goodness. Preaching still has a central place in the religious life but hardly as the monologue it once was. Congregants who know what it is to be heard do not long listen to preachers whose speaking does not proceed from a great depth of hearing. They regularly are more deeply moved by the clergy's attentive presence than by their words. This psychological emphasis on interaction as the best means of helping people now affects almost every aspect of clerical-lay relationships.

With the growth of psychotherapeutic proficiency, many problems that once would have come to a minister of religion now clearly are better directed to a psychotherapist. Depression is a common and compelling case. Sometimes a profoundly unhappy soul can be transformed by love or commandment or community or will or devout acceptance. In the usual case, attendance to the pharmacological and emotional sources of the depression, as difficult as they sometimes are to unravel and treat, will be of greater benefit. Such diagnosis and treatment should appropriately come only from someone with extensive psychological training and clinical experience. In such cases, wisdom consists, as so often in life, in knowing when and to whom to turn for proper help.

Moreover, psychotherapy generally shows its effectiveness more quickly than does religion. True, sudden, transformative conversion experiences do occur to radically alter personalities for life. Something like that can also happen to people as a result of otherwise ordinary events in their lives. Most people, however, do not know such grace and they must eke out their wholeness day by day. When they face an immediate inner problem, they are more likely to make progess overcoming it by consulting a psychotherapist rather than by relying on their faith and their minister. Thus, guided by a psychologically trained counselor, a reasonably healthy family can often quickly see what engenders their bickering and then learn how they might change their relationships. The cases could quickly be multiplied, all yielding the conclusion: therapy often works—and works quickly enough that one soon feels its positive results. By contrast, religion operates by a rather elongated time scale, not infrequently deferring full gratification to life in a world yet to come. In a narcissistic time, with self increasingly the measure of all things, it is not surprising that psychology easily becomes a substitute for religion or is itself repackaged as a pseudo-religion.

Once more we hear the lesson repeated again and again since the time of Copernicus: religion does not know everything; it has much to learn from those who study nature in general and human nature in particular. But in its hard-won humility religion will still assert that what it does know—in the somewhat uncommon way that it knows it—are simply the most important things: the grace of existence, the values we ought to live by, the human context in which we ought to live them and the unalienable reason why we must strive to live this way.

To begin with, religion is not essentially a therapy, a remedy for a problematic condition. It is rather an elemental, joyous response to the surprise of existence. It arises from our astonishment that riches we could not claim as a right have graciously been lavished on us. Cosmically, it celebrates the wonder that a world exists; existentially, it glories in God's gift of life and partnership. And it directs us, in thankful response, to live in accord with our Creator's will, giving love and creating goodness. Before there is sin or suffering, there is the amazement of covenant and the gratitude that obligates. In some such primal sense, religion is essentially pre-therapeutic and value-filled.

Assume, then, with the late Freud that aggression and love are our fundamental human drives. Therapists will surely know much more about their etiology, development and psychic manifestations than will the clergy. They will also know very much more about how problems arising from either drive might best be treated and the psychic energy involved in them might be redirected. But to what end ought this treatment lead? That is, to take the one case, what should patients be doing about their aggression after they have been helped to be in touch with it? The question is a troublesome one indeed, particularly since we have known cultures which valued war and antagonism most highly. To say that values are not our concern opens the door as much to every stupidity as to every decency. But to say that full humanhood involves proper values impales us on the dilemma of asking a descriptive understanding of psycho-dynamics to become the prescriptive source of the values we call health. For all its failure to exemplify its own great message, Biblical religion has known that justice is better than violence, peace than war, love than hatred, though violence, war and hatred are as much a part of our humanity as are justice, peace and love. And it is to this vision of what human beings ought to be that religion directs us.

Our sexuality also makes the problem of values unavoidable. To learn just how intimately our personalities are bound up with our genitality does not thereby enlighten us as to what we ought to do with our driving, random urge to pleasure. That can only come from a realm that generates value, and it is precisely our arguments over what value to place on sexuality that spark our fiery debates concerning it. To most of us who cherish the Bible and the moral values of democracy, it seems clear that sexuality finds its fulfillment in faithful love. We need to do everything we can then to make it possible for people to love and to love faithfully—and that surely includes helping people attain psychic readiness for it. It is such understandings of the "oughts" of human existence that Biblical religion, for all that we argue about its true teaching, is uniquely competent to provide.

But enabling us to love maturely today immediately points us to another distinctive concern of religion, humankind as a whole. Where psychotherapy focuses essentially on individuals, religion is concerned finally with the world. It may begin with helping free people from inner constriction, but it cannot rest until it has redeemed humankind as a whole. A simple logic grounds this grandiose concern: psychic health will not long survive in a society which, while doing great good, tears apart the soul. Thus, with regard to sexuality, therapists can largely fulfill their professional responsibility by helping individual patients come to terms with their genitality. Believers must go beyond that and seek to create institutions and a social order which is less sexually exploitative than ours is and one more fully conducive to faithful loving.

Or let us turn outward to the problem of urban homeless souls. They usually are unable to present themselves to therapists for treatment. Social agencies aside, homelessness is thus not a usual psychotherapeutic problem. Were it, therapists would likely define their duty as helping the clients gain enough psychic strength to set about changing their way of life. Religion obligates believers in a more embracing and activist way. It knows human beings to be as social as they are individual, and it therefore defines selfhood largely in terms of neighbors and society—specifying, accordingly, our duties to the powerless among us, "the widow, the stranger, the orphan." So, through their own institutions or those of the society generally, believers must help the homeless and improve a social order that breeds homelessness.

How troublesome and obscure is that little word *must*. In the secular world it is no longer clear that anything is authoritative for people other than what they will. Surely that is important as a safeguard against coer-

46

cion in all its tyrannical forms; autonomy, then, comprises a large part of what we mean by the dignity of the individual. But when naked will is all that commands us, we logically ask critical metapsychological questions about why "we must" or why "we ought" and why to these ends and not to others.

This issue runs deep through our society and is the metaethical fault-line along which our social order has been trembling. Consider its effect in the psychotherapeutic situation. Suppose the patient does not wish to enter therapy or does not think its possible results are worth the effort it involves. Many therapists would consider that statement verification of an underlying personality disorder and thus in itself a justification for treatment. But why? If the issue is whether psychotherapy itself is to be valued, entering treatment to find the correct answer cannot logically be suggested as an answer. In other words, to give the psychological equivalent of Godel's mathematical theorem, psychotherapy is not ultimately self-justifying. A grounding value or ideal vision is at stake here, one which only something as metaphysical as religion can supply.

The same issue appears in many other guises. Some years ago R. D. Laing suggested that schizophrenia ought to be considered a realistic response to our disordered civilization. Why, then, should we insist people try to become more fully integrated personalities? Or, to take the limit case, why, once all the neurotic reasons have been worked through, should we assert that people whose lives are utterly empty or filled with suffering ought not commit suicide?

For all such questions of ultimate meaning and motivation, we appropriately turn to religion. Its compelling if elusive genius deals with such utterly deep and lastingly significant questions. And it brings to us not merely the ideas of one great spiritual personality and a number of memorable disciples but the wisdom of communities which have refined their truths over centuries and millennia. They set before us their models of the sanctified life and the holy community, the people who, in all their ordinariness and humanity, nonetheless brought God once again into time.

For the final word is God, the One whose unity stands over against us as a goal, we who are created in God's image, the One whose transcendent goodness calls us, lifelong, to become better. In our self-centeredness, we are reminded that God made the world for God's own purposes, not necessarily for ours though, thankfully, our goals are often congruent, particularly as we mature. And in our despair and misery, so often the result of expecting the creation to center about us, we are told that God, no matter what our willfulness, still holds us in loving, demanding covenant. Where faith abides, hope lives; God will not fail. We humans are frail, obdurate, perverse and even malevolent, yet God elects us as covenant partners to transform the world. This exquisite blend of realism and idealism can keep us from the cynicism or folly that so quickly destroy our humanity.

But honesty demands a return to a final commonality. We believers and therapists are, after all, only people, human beings whose high calling has not made them perfect. Proposing to guide others to more abundant life, we rightly stand under special judgment when we fail our cause, as we often do. Yet we are also often the means by which small redemptions come into human lives. Sinners though we be, we also do God's work and as we help others, we help save ourselves.

4

Religion and America's
Moral Crisis

There is a crisis in public morality. Apparently the decline in our standard of behavior is so obvious that, despite our political and class and religious differences, we can agree upon the disorder if not the therapy. I therefore propose not to document our ills any further, but I do wish first to diagnose them and only then to suggest a line of significant treatment.

I see our problem less as one of ethics than of metaethics. Our difficulty is not rules or values. There are so many of them around that our difficulty is in choosing among them. Worse, it is in caring at all about being moral. I suggest that our ethics have become so anemic because they have lost their support system. More, I shall argue that our characterological breakdown is the result of misplaced faith.

Let me begin my analysis of our condition by applying to it Paul Tillich's understanding of what it means to be religious. For him, and for me in this stage of the investigation, one's religion is best thought of in existentialist terms: What is, in fact, one's ultimate concern? This is an untraditional and uninstitutional way of thinking about having faith. For all its novelty, it is highly appropriate to our task, for we are concerned with the moral crisis of our civilization and thus require a tool which enables us to understand how believers and unbelievers alike have caught the plague.

I will begin by applying the Tillichian concept of religion to morality. I suppose my Jewish sense of the centrality of duty, of action, of good

Reprinted with permission of the Carnegie Council on Ethics and International Affairs, from Eugene B. Borowitz, "Religion and America's Moral Crisis," *Worldview*, vol. 17, no. 8 (November 1974): 52:56.

deeds manifests itself here. Yet in this enterprise I know I do not betray Tillich's sense of Christianity nor that of many other Christian thinkers, like the great nineteenth-century thinker Albrecht Ritschl, who taught that religion is primarily the realm of human value judgments. I shall, however, turn Ritschl on his head and argue with Tillich that, rather than our values being our religion, we have lost our values because we have lost what was, existentially, our religion; and that we have lost our religion, not because we never had any, but rather because we have now discovered that we have had an inappropriate one.

What has been the operative faith of most Americans for the past generation or so? Note that the question is not, What would people say to a pollster?, nor even, In what religious buildings might they, with some frequency, be found? When we inquire about ultimate concern we reach far beneath the level of conventional behavior or locations. We ask, rather: When people were faced by significant, demanding choices, to what did they give the major free energies of their lives? What did they really care about more than anything else? In phrasing the question in this existentialist fashion we are debarred from the precision of an empirical answer. Hence my response is admittedly subjective and impressionistic—but not therefore eccentric or unsupportable.

What most Americans have believed in, I submit, was not God or Church or Torah but the burgeoning American society. In simple terms, we put our trust in ever greater affluence: once deprived, we gained sufficiency; once degraded by unceasing want, we came to the self-respect of a steady, decent income. For us Exodus or Resurrection was the liberation from a slum flat to clean rooms, thence to a decent neighborhood, a garden apartment perhaps, or on to a home in the suburbs, even a second home. This process, repeated on many levels, promised not only satisfaction but, in its own way, salvation.

I do not mean to describe us as merely economic animals. We were, amidst our upward social striving, also concerned about the quality of our existence. In our aspirations for our families we can most easily see the close relationship between greater good and greater goods. And a similar broad sense of the promise of growth was felt in other areas of our civilization. We looked to schooling not only as preparation for a good job but also for a richer life. So as adults we turn to books and records and magazines and concerts and hobbies to deepen our minds and increase our sensitivity. The arts would give us character; recreation would restore our soul. Psychiatry would solve our personal problems, science our technical ones, politics and community work our social ones.

By calling this a misplaced faith I do not mean to denigrate these activities. They were, and are, legitimate concerns, productive of much that is morally worthwhile. The question is: Is this complex of interests and values worthy of our ultimate trust? Does it create and sustain the morals it contains, or must they be drawn from another, deeper source? Can the

American way of life bear the full weight of our ethical existence, or must it derive its sense of quality and direction from something that lies beyond it, a "more ultimate" concern?

The key issue here is the power of secularity. We had put our trust in man and his capacities. That is, our ultimate hope was in ourselves, singly and jointly. Either we abandoned the God of the Bible or made God marginal to more significant concerns. In either case we based our lives and our values on our secularity, and it is this, our old, fundamental, existential faith, that has now been thrown into question. For it is no longer clear that secularity mandates morality. To the contrary, it seems abundantly clear that secularity is compatible with amorality and can even accommodate and encourage immorality, by the standards of the Bible. I do not think this feeling was created in the hearts of most Americans by any of our contemporary scandals. I think they only made the issue of the past decade or so all but inescapable.

For most of us the new realism about secularity began with a changing sense of perspective. Instead of taking certain rules or institutions for granted as exemplars of ethical practice, we began asking what, in truth, they did to people. Segregation was the classic case. It had claimed the sanction of law, tradition, established practice, and the apparent will of the majority of voters in a wide region. But when we got down to thinking about what it was doing to people, we knew it to be wrong. We knew that when one cannot think of a certain group of people as persons, entitled to the rights of all persons, then one is immoral. And that from the perspective of being a person, the great good is freedom, the great goal is being true to oneself. We also came to see the great problem in human relations as power and its abuse: If you use your power over me to constrain my freedom you render me less a person. There was recognition that when our society or members of a group coerce another group they effectively reduce their own humanity. Of course, it might be necessary for the common good for each of us to sacrifice something of our individual freedom. But too often we were not asked to participate in the process of determining what limits shall be set upon us.

With persons as the criterion of the good, with power seen as a common force for the bad, a new moral realism began to dawn on us. The institutions whose goodness we had taken for granted now showed themselves to be run by relatively insensitive power, and thus to be injurious to persons. We became aware of tyrannies we had never before noted, at home, at school, in business, in sports, in our social relationships and our politics. Noble terms were being used to cover power drives and ego trips. And it also seemed clear that we should be able to find better ways to structure our lives with others.

So we set to work. A hundred causes claimed our allegiance: civil rights, better housing, decent education, care for the aged and the sick, peace abroad and peace at home. We had some successes. They only made clear how much yet remained to be done. Increasingly we learned the hard lessons: Most of us are not very willing to change. We are comfortable with our evil and at ease with our sin. We do not propose to live up to the values supposedly inherent in our culture.

More disturbing, it began to dawn on us that the morality we thought was demanded by our secular culture was only another option to it. What was there in a secular view of things that could mandate concern for all other persons as well as self-interest? Why should we indeed care for the weak and the powerless, the ungainly and unattractive, the failures and the bores, as long as we get what we want? Our science is value-free, our economics interested in profit, our politics concerned with power, our arts dominated by questions of technique, our lifestyle devoted to strategies of escape and indulgence.

Perhaps we might have come to terms with that, for people have often lived poorly in the name of great ideals. But secularity also took away our sense of guilt. Ethics became reduced to conditioning, to convention, to education, to psychic mechanism—anything but a commandment, a duty, a summons.

A great part of our crisis, then, is that many people today are effectively amoral. In Freud's day neurosis was most commonly traceable to an oppressive sense of duty and guilt. Today it is more commonly associated with having no firm set of values and by having no sense of limits or direction, thus having no true sense of self at all.

Another part of our crisis is that those of us who still retain a strong sense of biblical morality suddenly feel alien and ill at ease. The moral America we took for granted is not the America we see around us. We are depressed and sickened by its strange hospitality to evil acts and evil people. Our civilization has become our problem—how then can it continue to deserve our existential faith? We now stand in judgment over the secularity which once comprised our ultimate concern. How can we any longer put our most basic trust in it? We are deeply disturbed because we have lost our faith. We believed in a god who was no god. The idol of secularity has fallen, and we are shaken to our core.

A number of Americans do not participate in the sense of moral crisis I am describing. For one group the old secular style still remains the only true way.Their problem is largely that they do not understand why everyone else has lost their moral nerve. They are disturbed only because they are increasingly isolated and marginal in our society. Where once they seemed to be moving with what was the major mood of the times, now they seem somehow old-fashioned and out of touch.

Unsecularized religionists are similarly untainted by our society's ethical malaise. If anything, they are somewhat elated by it. They always knew secularization was wrong. Now that the pseudo-faith created by it has come to grief, they have been justified by history. Relying now as before on revelation, they remain unperturbed. They still know what they must do. But because they have never been through the refiner's fire of secularization, I find their ethical horizons narrow and their sense of responsibility limited essentially to themselves and their kind.

One need not agree on secularity as revelation. But that does not mean there was nothing to learn from it. The notion of humanity, of one global humankind, was surely implicit in biblical faith. It took the rationalist rigor of secularity to make it clear and unavoidable. That is a precious gain I am not willing to sacrifice. I repeat: Many of the concerns of secularity are legitimate and remain morally compelling. My major quarrel with it derives from its being made a god.

No, America is not all bad, but at the very least it has lost heart. It still does many good things, but it isn't sure they still count. It no longer knows what to care about. It isn't even certain that caring itself still makes much sense.

Yet, paradoxically enough, this moment of doubt creates a new openness to a more adequate religious faith. Insofar as we are deeply disturbed we evidence deep moral concern. We show that somehow we know our ethical values are right, for it is in the name of those values that we deny the old idolatry. We have here the dawning recognition that our ethical commitments transcend us and our society, though we had, for a while, lost sight of that. We are now willing to search for a faith adequate to this new sense of personal depth.

Apparently a good many people in our country share this feeling, for we live in a time of unprecedented American religious search. Six or seven years ago no self-respecting magazine or lecture platform was complete without some comment on the death-of-God movement. It was explicitly stated then that henceforth it would be necessary to do theology and practice religion out of the knowledge that God was dead. This year two of the leaders of that movement, William Hamilton and David Miller, having already passed through the stages of religion as celebration and as play, are announcing a new stage in our religious life: the rebirth of polytheism. From a time when they identified the chief religious reality of our lives as the experience of the absence of God they now apparently feel that there is so great a sense of the holy among us that one god is not sufficient to describe that reality.

In any case, the identification of our new polytheism by those who said God was dead is fitting, if ironic, proof that America is experiencing a resurgence of spirituality. One might almost call it a rebirth of enthusiasm, in the technical sense of that term, were it not that much of this movement is highly personal, determinedly quiet, and deeply suspicious of religious institutions. Indeed, many people touched by it are afraid to share their quest with others, despite their longing for community, lest public exposure kill the tender shoots of their spirituality. The dramatic manifestations of this surge are regularly brought to us by the media: the more established Asian cults like Vedanta and Zen, as well as the currently fashionable sects like those of the Maharishi or the Maharaj Ji. And in our own communities we see extraordinary signs: Catholics who are charis-

53

matics; Protestants who as Jesus people turn legalistic, while others from sophisticated churches talk in tongues and heal by faith; and Jews who take a fresh interest in Hasidic devotion and Orthodox discipline.

I submit that these phenomena arise from a sense of the new emptiness at the heart of our culture. They are a desperate, sometimes unthinking, effort to fill it. And something similar may be seen as far away as the Soviet Union.

What Judaism and Christianity can uniquely bring to the American culture at this juncture (in other areas of the world we should, of course, have to add Islam) is their root religious intuition that a transcendent God stands over against us and our society, summoning us to moral conduct. These biblical religions proclaim, against almost all of Asian religious teaching, that God's ultimate character, insofar as humans may speak of such exalted matters, is not neutral. The Lord we serve is not finally beyond the categories of good and evil. Our God is not to be approached through a realm that ultimately lies beyond morality. God's holiness is intimately linked with God's ethical command. There is a direct movement from "You shall be holy for I the Lord, your God, am holy" to "You shall not hate your brother in your heart but you shall love your neighbor as yourself." True, the God of the Bible stands in covenant with us, but this intimacy never negates the distance between creature and creator, never destroys God's right to command. Our God in personal presence comes to us as compelling love and purposing forgiveness. We are summoned and sent and judged and held accountable—and in just such moral suasion we also see the signs of God's close caring.

We Jews and Christians will argue between us and among ourselves whether the new or old law is in effect and in what mode it is to be followed. We shall differ as to the form and nature of the commandments. But I think we will both insist that those who know God should devote themselves to doing good and those who love God ought to love people and dedicate their lives to creating a humane and holy social order.

Not so long ago this Judeo-Christian sense of reality linked to responsibility was taken to be the basis of the American ethos. It gave the American way of life a strong, metaphysical impetus to sustained moral striving. It was, of course, not the only and perhaps not the most important factor in creating that unparalleled mixture of idealism and opportunism we recognize as American. Yet despite the frontier and our lavish natural resources, despite immigrant vigor and extraordinary industrialization, it was the accepted sense of a transcendent ethical demand laid upon us which gave us Americans our special brand of national idealism. The hand of the Puritans still rests upon us.

In secularizing our culture in the past generation or so we have carried out an experiment, so to speak, to see what might happen to our way of life if we abandoned the Judeo-Christian view of human obligation. We did not do too badly for a while. Our commitments to our biblical past run so deep that despite our putative secularity we remain quite faithful to biblical values; much of the remaining moral content of our culture is there, I would argue, not because it is intrinsic to secularity, but as an inheritance from an earlier, more religious age. Only now is it clear what cutting ourselves off from our transcendent source of values does to us and our society.

I am not saying that if all Americans were instantly to take up Jewish and Christian religious duties or, better, were to share Jewish or Christian faith and the ethical responsibilities they entail, all the moral problems of America would be solved. The question of the ground of our values is only one of the many difficulties facing this nation. But it is our root problem. I do not see how, until we reestablish our ultimate sense of why we ought to do the good and in what direction that good lies, the rest of our moral efforts can hope to succeed.

The temptation is for religion to seek to reestablish itself in our society by denouncing secularity as it criticizes every moral evil that has been created in its name. Surely there is ample biblical precedent for us to assert our roles as the critics of society. The prophets were continually involved in political and social judgments, for they could evaluate human affairs from a transcendent perspective. Since we claim something of their vantage, ought we not be the people most sensitive to every wrong and the most courageous in pointing it out? And since our civilization is relatively understanding of the evil men do, knowing "they are only human" and "that's the way things have always been," is it not our special responsibility to remind our fellows that to be human is to bear the divine image, that the way things are must give way to how things ought to be?

I do not see how, without the greatest peril to our soul, we can shirk the prophetic role of denunciation and witness and proclamation and dissent. Better to run the risk of looking foolish by being overly sensitive to sin than to retain our respectability at the price of learning to live in peace with it.

But in a time when so much has gone wrong it is too easy to fatten one's sense of righteousness by concentrating on the sins of others. I do not think prophetic criticism is what people most need from us today. Indeed, I am far from certain that they will take our prophetic role seriously until we establish our credibility on a more substantial basis.

The truth is that institutional religion shares in the crisis of our time. The skepticism that runs so deep through our society is no less directed toward religion. Consider, for a moment, the frequent distinction made between religiosity and institutional religion. We may find some grounds for optimism in the fact that presently the sense of religious concern is widespread in our society. Yet at the same time we must acknowledge that interest in churches and synagogues seems to have passed its peak. Like it or not, Judaism and Christianity, in all their variety, are closely connected with the American style of the past generation. What has been our great accomplishment these past twenty-five years? Our institutions—building them and staffing them, yes, and democratizing them. That was what dominated our activity in the expansionist 1950's and 1960's. Only now we live in a time when all institutions are suspect. We despair of government and are disturbed by schools. We aren't even terribly certain about the family. No wonder church and synagogue are suspect.

If anything, sensitive people will set higher standards for religious bodies than for any other institution in our society. I think they are right. If we are the unique agencies of a transcendent morality, then we should exemplify it. But can we say we have done this? Have we transcended our society in moral stature? There is, at the very least, serious doubt about our moral performance. I suggest, therefore, that as people now turn to religion to help them in their search for a firm moral ground, they will want to know what religious organizations have done and are doing to merit their ethical confidence. They will care little for what we say. But they will care much about how we conduct ourselves. They will apply to us the same searching test they have used on all our social institutions: How do we use our power? They will ask: What do we do to persons in their freedom as we operate our hierarchies, our agencies, our commissions, our seminaries, our churches and synagogues, our ministries? So if we are to be able to carry out our mission as transmitters and celebrators of transcendence in a decadent age, we shall have to pass at least three key tests.

First, how do we, as we go about preserving what is good in our heritage, encourage the creation of the new and the better? Surely there is something timeless about God and what we ought to do for God. Yet people are not timeless. We do not, cannot, should not be expected to live as our grandparents did, perhaps not even as our parents lived. And we know that our religious traditions have changed in previous ages, sometimes radically. If we now change too much, we run the risk of losing what was good in the past, those truths and practices which carried the generations forward and linked them to each other in a history-transforming continuity. Yet if we do not change, we run the risk of losing the present generation and thus our ncessary link with the future. The question then is: How will we place the burden of the past on the shoulders of the present?

The *second* challenge puts the same question in more individual terms: How do we propose to maintain the purity of our faith while fostering individual expression? We cannot be all things to all people; the recent decades have surely established that. We do see clearly that God is the source of our individuality and personal dignity. But if God can make no claim upon us and must be satisfied with whatever we choose to be, then God has no dignity; we who are created in God's image, for all our vaunted freedom, will have only the hollow worth of our freedom to choose it matters not what. Yes, we have a right to be persons and to be true to ourselves, but God has a right to be God and thus to make demands upon us. The proper question is: How will we lay God's command to humanity upon the individual?

But mainly, I think, people will judge us by seeing to what extent we serve ourselves and to what extent we serve others. To be sure, if Judaism and Christianity are to be strong enough to influence America, they must be organized and institutionalized. That means a structured constituency which shares a common dream and supports its members as they seek to achieve it in a hostile environment. And it means a social apparatus that transcends any group of persons and thus can survive to keep the old hope alive from generation to generation.

Yet, in this process, what happens to people? How do we now relate to other human beings who are not of our group, whether of another faith or of no faith at all? What happens to our need for human community with other believers in our faith as church and synagogue rightfully seek to maintain their institutions? This *third* issue, I am convinced, is the most sensitive we face. For surely religion ought to bring us together as people, to show us how to share our true humanity with one another in the presence of the one God who is the source of our unity. Yet so often, in religion's name, we feel we are attending the clergy or the lay leadership rather than God; or we are too busy carrying out the heavy formalities of religious etiquette to be able to feel for one another. If we are to be God's people, then surely we should be encouraged to feel like people, sensitive, individual, concerned, open to one another, as we gather in God's name. We should be more a community of human sharing as we gather in God's assembly than anywhere else. And at the moment that is rarely true.

What makes these demands on us so difficult is that they cannot be met by following a rule. They are true dilemmas, mutually contradictory demands, and we must learn to live with these dilemmas. For even as we affirm the continuity and tradition and institution, so we affirm the precious significance of each individual soul. In the face of such demands we have no security and can only act out of our most basic faith and intuition. That is what many people know, and that is why they will examine this focus of our power and their need to make their judgment as to who and what we truly are. And we shall restore our credibility with them only insofar as we have met this searching test.

I do not see that we can approach this challenge with any special confidence. We have been tried in the past and found wanting. We must acknowledge that it is quite possible that this beloved country of ours, and we with it, have passed by the moment of our highest moral potential and entered into a period of moral stagnation, if not decline. The crisis is real, our loss may be quite serious indeed. But for all their realism, Judaism and Christianity are religions of hope. We not only believe in the coming of God's kingdom, we believe that, with God's help, we can live in it here and now. It is our difficult task in this difficult hour to live in the reality of God's rule despite all pessimism, and by our words and deeds to summon people from their sinfulness to God's steady service.

5

Beyond the Secular City

Gone is the lilting optimism of earlier generations. As the evidence of human perversity grows, and with it our sense of inadequacy, so we sink deeper into disappointment and despair. Our leaders seem incompetent and, not infrequently, mean and venal. The institutions in which we once trusted—the university, politics, the professions, even the last bastion, the family itself—have failed us. Our economy is unreliable, our cities violent and their citizens often irrational, our inner life unstable and troubled. We feel threatened by ills we cannot anticipate, much less fend off. Nor have we plausible hope that there is anything that can be done to repair the human condition, or anyone to do it; anxiety and apathy and cynicism spread. Against the pessimism, grim realism is the most positive alternative we can manage.

To our present distemper, the most that religion appears to offer is superficial solace. Yet a closer analysis shows, I believe, that a serious effort to restore religious values and understandings to this most secular age can offer more, far more, than a lift to our spirits; it can, indeed, lead us to happier and healthier circumstances.

Religious values and understandings? But is it not the failures of religion that have helped bring us to our unhappy state? So the secularists have argued—and there is much to what they have said. However painful it may be to review their critique, no person of faith can seriously propose a restoration of religious values without first confronting its components. (But the secularist, witnessing the pain, ought not gloat; we are all in this

From *Moment*, vol. 10, no. 8 (September 1985).

together—and secularism's failures, in any case, do not permit its champions to be smug, as I will soon show.)

First: We were obscurantist. Having God's word, we felt we had all significant knowledge. We therefore objected when people proposed to investigate matters we thought already settled or produced data that disagreed with our received truth. Galileo heads the long list of intellectual martyrs, a list that we cannot yet say is finally closed.

Second: We had only a limited respect for the rights of individual conscience; our assurance in spiritual matters was even greater than our certainty about nature. Since ours, we believed, was the sole truth, the One truth, we were only being helpful when we coerced others into believing as we did. It was natural that we deny believers and gentiles alike the possibility of following their spiritual search in directions that might lead outside our tradition. Baruch Spinoza's case, though uncommon in Jewish history, testifies to a religious propensity that Jews shared with adherents to other great religions.

Third: Marx and his followers were not wholly wrong. In the perspective of Marxian sociology, religious institutions are revealed to be far more concerned with maintaining good relations with the rich and the powerful than with championing the cause of the poor and downtrodden. Perhaps unwittingly, but nonetheless damningly, religion has encouraged the oppressed to remain satisifed with their lot, to eschew radical change.

That indictment can be directed inward as well. Like all institutions, religion seems to operate primarily for self-aggrandizement. As the Marxists noted, the biblical priests ate meat every day, while the rest of the people were lucky to eat meat at festival time. Of course, one can rationalize that the clergy must be attentive to the wealthy and powerful if only to garner the support they need in order to help the unfortunate. But somehow, that pact, born of necessity, often led to high-living clergy and sumptuous sanctuaries. Historically, religion's self-concern has set a poor example for those to whom it preaches altruism.

Fourth: Religion has made people—all people, not merely the poor—more passive than they ought to be in dealing with their problems. Religion, after all, taught that the almighty power of God is working for our good in whatever comes to pass; we need only be perfect in our faith. The biblical religions did not teach fatalism, but they did leave in God's hands the critical initiative in human affairs. We need only compare the traditional religious teachings to the activism of modern secularity to understand the association between religion and passivity. No, religion cannot be accused of being against the building of dams, the careful management of water resources, or the detailed study of weather. Yet it required a radical change for us to stop relying on prayers and fasting in the face of drought, for us to turn our energies instead to science and engineering. Secularity liberated human energy for the incredible burst of accomplishment of the past two centuries. Those of us who take for granted the availability of pure water and the practice of hygiene on which our health and longevity depend should not airily dismiss the attainments that the secularization of Western civilization has made possible.

Positively, too, secularity created new ways of living that now commend themselves even to believers. In the secular world, for example, one is encouraged to think critically; that is, one subjects every claim to authority to the most searching questions possible. True, very many people remain gullible, many continue to prefer belief—belief in almost anything—to the anxiety of personal responsibility and decision. But secularism's endorsement of skepticism has encouraged countless other people to think carefully and critically, to see life as choice, hence to be more responsible.

Out of such a temper, the temper of secularism, has come the disciplined investigation of virtually every aspect of our world and of our selves; it is skepticism, rejection of received authority, that accounts for the knowledge explosion of our times. And not only the explosion of knowledge, but also the explosion of opinion, and even of taste. The consequence is a highly variegated culture, a culture of so many disparate choices that without an ethic of tolerance it would be neither conceivable nor viable. But secularism provides just such an ethic. Secularism begets diversity—and insists on respect for the choices that diversity implies, as also for the conscience that has dictated those choices. Secularism creates and extols the notion of living harmoniously with others, particularly of learning to work together on projects of mutual concern with those with whom one otherwise may radically disagree. Indeed, secularism teaches that it is good for us—in our separate groups or as individuals—to be exposed to other groups, to other individuals. It teaches that pluralism enriches and extends our finitude.

Nor is secularism just a doctrine of skepticism and diversity. It recognizes, as well, the common humanity that underlies differences of race, nation, culture and religion. Hence secularists enunciate without equivocation the unity of the world's people. Where ethnocentrism or religious creed had always divided the world into the civilized and the barbarians, the believers and the infidels, secularism's blunt attention to basic human needs and aspirations shows our fundamental similarity to others to be greater than our difference. Biblical religion had, of course, always known the theory of one human family, but it took rationalistic secularism's universalism to make the theory part of the functioning world view of every ethical person.

Most daringly, secularity projected the notion of group tolerance and individual responsibility into the realm of politics. Previously, power had almost always required centralization to be effective. The new view of humankind diffused power into a plurality of centers and gave everyone an ultimate share in it. The democratization of government lets every citizen participate in the determination of public policy and, perhaps more effectively, in rectifying its errors. At its best, democracy is an awe-inspiring social accomplishment. We owe this achievement primarily to the secularization of our Western civilization, not to the simple maturation or creativity of biblical religion.

I do not believe this appreciation of secular democracy is excessive. Indeed, I have here understated my true feelings. If I be thought over-enthusiastic, bear in mind that my human sensibilities and biblical faith are reinforced by centuries of persecution of my people. One hundred years ago, members of my own family lived the precarious, even dangerous, life of the *shtetl*-dweller; today, my children enjoy the extravagant benefits of America. For Jews such as I, secular democracy is a passionate personal commitment.

And for all adherents of religion, I hope, accepting the accomplishments of secular democracy is the necessary first step in our search for an appropriate relationship between religion and secular society. It would be neither honest nor useful to press the case for religious values by condemning secular insights and achievements. Our problem is not how to defeat secularism, but how to tame it; the solution is not to revert to a pre-secular mode but how to revive values that can bring vitality where morbidity is setting in.

Secularization, which once appeared capable of perfecting humankind, turns out, for all its very real gifts, to have demeaned us. In the free world, life seems tawdry and vulgar; elsewhere, oppression has risen to new heights of inhumanity. It is the very genius of secularity—its openness to new truth—that has proved its undoing. Openness, which was highly therapeutic as tolerance, soon degenerated into relativism and now threatens to become nihilism. The rationalism and humanism we had counted on to channel our skills toward worthy goals have lost authority in the face of secularity's built-in skepticism. We have lost our ground of value, and, with the steady dissipation of the inherited capital of our Western faith in biblical values, we begin to contemplate the decline and fall of our civilization.

The most obvious evidence of this threat is our steady turn to irrationalism. No theory seems too bizarre to attract adherents, and the imposition of absolute demands that previously would have been rejected as absurd now seems to be the very thing that makes cults attractive to so many. The political implication of our liberated notion of rationality is totalitarianism. The state usurps religion's place, arrogating to itself the fullest possible passion and commitment. Having no peer in secular power, it claims to be the Absolute. Therefore, it goes on to announce, it is justified in doing whatever it deems necessary to accomplish its ends. Individual conscience has no countervailing rights, and no transcendent realm exists outside the state to legitimate critical prophecy. The human spirit, uprooted from its biblical ground, may now be directed to the service of what not so long ago would have been perceived as monstrous evil.

But if this be the case, do we not learn therefrom what is needed? For if the problem is that in this secular world we have lost our biblical sense of value, is not the task of religion precisely to restore that sense?

Five specific aspects of that restoration seem to me especially important, all of them amplifications of the Bible's view that human dignity is ineradicably intertwined with human responsibility.

First: We begin with the assertion that every human being has inestimable worth. The Bible story of creation describes human beings as the only creatures specifically made in God's image. This unique human status is fulfilled in the biblical notion of covenant. Despite humanity's sinfulness, God calls people into partnership. Jewish tradition took the covenant with the Children of Noah so seriously that its teachers later could assert that "the righteous among the gentiles have a share in the life of the world to come." (It is this high estimate of humanity's enduring tie to God that explains why the Jewish tradition is only marginally interested in proselytization.)

Secular society hardly sees such intrinsic worth in human beings. Ideologically, it values them for their productive capacity—one reason the Soviet Union opposes free emigration. Most of us are not that crass, but we nonetheless equate our value with performing, with what we do rather than in the simple and fundamental fact of our humanity. The Bible knows our faults and our failures; it regularly condemns us for being sinners. It calls on us to turn back to God. But even should we ignore that plea, it insists we retain such cosmic status that God will not let us go. What we do not do, God will do. God "seeks" and saves us. The Bible knows that our worth is in our very being, not merely in our doing. By virtue of having been born human, each of us has an ultimate and infinite value that no one can ever take away.

From a naturalistic point of view, to single out the human animal and endow it with such unparalleled worth makes no sense. After seeing what "good" people were capable of during the Holocaust, to speak of the infinite worth of all human beings seems ludicrously optimistic. Even considering what we have intimately had to face in ourselves or in others we have come to know closely, calling us "but little lower than the angels" (Psalms 8:5) seems deluded. Secularity need mount no theoretical argument against our delusion; it need only cite the empirical data.

Against those data, religion comes, with its affirmations drawn from the transcendent realm. Knowing God's abiding covenant with us, biblical teaching unhesitatingly proclaims each person's cosmic value. Extrapolating from the empirical, we are bound to despair; insisting on the transcendent, on personal dignity, we secure the basis upon which any hope of rebuilding the morale of our civilization must rest.

Second: Though being has primacy in the Bible, its authors depict the relationship between God and people as anything but static. Human beings share God's capacity to do works of love and justice. No other creatures can create goodness as they can, discerning and doing the will of God.

Covenant requires the application of that capacity for goodness. It generates and motivates commandment. The biblical authors are appalled by sin, for by it we have willfully rejected our unique human capacity and denied our partnership with the Divine. In fulfilling God's behests we are truest to ourselves and the God who made us unique. Human dignity is therefore fulfilled in doing acts of righteousness.

Ever fewer people today connect self-realization with doing one's duty. Creativity, not responsibility, is heralded as the sign of authentic personhood. We do not feel dignified by the many demands made upon us, for we do not attach very great value to the authority behind them. Fashion is capricious, convention arbitrary, and role inconsiderate of our individuality. Our personal interests change rapidly, and what we will want tomorrow we cannot quite know today.

Paradoxically, being free to do almost anything, we feel chronically unfulfilled. We know we have depths of ability we cannot bring ourselves to summon. We dream, then, of some situation or person who can evoke the slumbering hero in us. Even war can seem rewarding, for it legitimately makes ultimate secular demands upon us. How good, too, were the days when some overriding political cause could similarly summon up the hidden best in us. With war inhuman and the political process no longer morally commanding, we are left dissatisfied by a secular existence in which our capacities are only partially utilized or are applied to what we know to be ephemeral or limited purposes.

How appealing, then, to accept a guru and an encompassing doctrine. In answering the absolute demand for faith and observance one finds the long-sought dignity—but only at the price of sacrificing one's autonomy. We reach inner peace, but only by denying a most precious part of ourselves. Most of us, therefore, take another road. We retreat to the new epicureanism. We seek to replace the self-esteem derived from exercising significant responsibility by "being good to ourselves." When hedonism becomes an ideology, a civilization testifies to its spiritual emptiness.

If religion could help our society regain a sense of self that equates being human with doing good, we might be able to overcome our moral debility and ennoble the awesome energies released by secularity.

Third: The Bible also insists that the self is not only necessarily, but desirably, social. Preceding the creation of the first spouse, Genesis says simply, "It is not good for a person to be alone" (2:18). From that moment on, the personages of the sacred story are seen as part of marriages, families, clans, communities, nations and humankind as a whole. For the Bible, individuals realize themselves through interpersonal relationships, not in isolation.

How different is the current notion of the self! We so identify selfhood with individuality that we are extraordinarily wary of involvement. We judge institutions and activities largely by how they benefit us. We even evaluate personal relationships in terms of what they do for us. The difficulty with our attitude is not our lack of sainthood, that we are unwilling

63

to live in complete giving to others. Self-denial is not the only alternative to self-centeredness. What is at stake is whether selfhood essentially matures in individuality or in relationships.

No doubt, the excesses of others against the self have properly prompted our revolt against heteronomy and for increasing self-assertion. The impositions of tradition, class, custom, role, and the old conception of propriety often did violence to the self. When we think of human beings at their best as free, responsible and creative, changing in their needs and desires as they grow, autonomy becomes infinitely precious. In that context, only one's self is worthy of being the ultimate arbiter of our judgments.

As in so many other cases of innovation, autonomy—which came on the cultural scene as a worthwhile corrective—is now trumpeted as an end in itself. In its imperial cause, every social responsibility is seriously challenged, not excluding marriage, procreation and family.

The deification of the self resulted from all our previous secular substitutes for religion having failed us. We were left with nothing but ourselves to believe in. The results have been disastrous. The isolated, individual self cannot carry the weight of the authority we have placed upon it. When we can muster the strength to avoid rationalization, we know we are not finally worth that much trust. We are not the answer but the problem. Illusionless, we wander in a void, stripped of worth and dignity—the experience of nothingness that produces the depression so characteristic of our culture.

Strictly speaking, our problem is not identity but the utter insignificance of our individual existence according to secular standards. Ironically, the attention to self that was to have fulfilled us shows us to be unworthy of ultimate concern. In the midst of the greatest opportunity individuals have ever known, despair reigns. We cannot say who we truly are, for we do not know what we ought to be. The consequences for our society are severe. With persons concentrating on self, we forget that it is largely through meeting responsibilities to others that we might become the selves we dimly know we ought to be. Many of the human gains of our time—support for the poor, help for the handicapped, education for all, an income for the aged—have come from our banding together, beyond our individual needs, to care for everyone. No invisible hand of nature may be relied upon to create a just and compassionate society while we determinedly pursue our private good. Sin is too strong for that, and it has fertile ground when self-interest is espoused as the highest value. The rebuilding of our social morality depends upon our again linking our self in an unbreakable bond with all the other selves with whom we inhabit this planet.

The Bible teaches that individuals are not separable from relationships. The most basic of these is our relationship with God. That may well be too pious a stance for a secular society to utilize as its basic source of self-understanding. Still, even our society retains enough biblical roots to be comfortable with the implications of the relationship between the individual and God. A self arises in a family and, regardless of its autonomy, has responsibility to its kin. A covenant links the generations, those that preceded us and who are entitled to appropriate honor, and those that should proceed from us. We and they exist in large measure to fulfill the hopes and striving of those who prepared the way for us. The path to God's reign runs through biology.

More intimately, in the covenant experience of marriage, in the unconditional responsibility of raising children, our selfhood is commonly given its most searching test and greatest opportunity. Through them we momentarily mirror the covenant between God and humankind. Our families exist in communities, and they in turn in nations and in humankind as a whole. With one God over all, we are part of a global human family. Our actions may have less effect as the circle enlarges, but, wherever we are, what we do with such power as we have determines, through an infinitely complex calculus, what happens to us all.

By situating the individual in this intricate web of relationships, religion gives us a personhood that is as much a gift as an accomplishment. We need not bear alone the burden of validating our worth; we can share it with others who will help us bear its limits and appreciate its virtues. By knowing that all people share the same situation and that the everlasting, good God maintains covenant with us, we may accept our condition in its limits and in its glory.

If religion could restore a social sense of self to secular society it would heal the narcissistic wound that today enfeebles our corporate identity.

Fourth: The Bible's teaching about responsibility is balanced by its message of forgiveness. Covenant may imply duty, but freedom and willfulness, to say nothing of sheer human limitation, lead us to failure and sin. Still, because our human dignity is in our being and not in our productivity, our failings do not break our covenant with God. Our limitations come as no surprise to God; rather, as part of God's relationship with us, God forgives the repentant and makes possible an ever-renewed opportunity for us to create the good.

Secularity's great strength came from the success we achieved when it freed our power by teaching us to rely only on the best human judgment. So much good was accomplished—so much capacity we did not know we had came to the surface—that we thought we now might accomplish anything. We prepared to create God's own realm on earth. We did not anticipate the possibility of deep or lasting failure. We could not believe that our best ideas might be too small, our plans inadequate, our character mean, our will perverse, our human situation too restricted for us to accomplish perfection. And we certainly did not expect that in doing righteousness we might also create evils, that the unintended consequences of our ambitions might add to pain and to misery, might outweigh the good we had done or sought.

65

There is little in secularity to help us with our finitude and waywardness. It has little to say about our limitations, expecting as it does that greater effort and more research will solve everything. The human situation has turned out to be more complicated than that. We might seize upon the common explanation that we are, after all, only human. Such forgiveness evenhandedly excuses any errant behavior; it makes no demands on contrition or repentance. To accept people's sins as natural creates license to transgress.

The result is not only moral malaise but a time in which, amid the greatest freedom and affluence people have ever known, our common psychiatric problem has shifted from guilt to depression. Knowing our failings, we cannot truly believe in ourselves. We cannot even do the good that lies within our power, because failure has convinced us that nothing we might do is worth anything. Ironically—and tragically—the very secularism that demonstrated humankind's enormous creative potential has been trapped by the contradictions of its own success. It has left us to stare at our moral impotence.

The Bible teaches that what we cannot do for ourselves God does for us. We are not called to be perfect but to be holy, to do what we can as faithful covenant partners. The biblical understanding of our relationship is astonishingly dynamic. Insofar as we succeed, we bask in the joy of having lived up to our responsibility. More important, insofar as we have failed, have even done evil, we know God will forgive us if we turn to God in deep contrition and new resolve. God, so to speak, is more faithful to the covenant than we are. God does not let us go but holds us in a constantly renewed relationship. And that brings us to the next act and command, the next opportunity, as if it were the first of our lives.

If religion could teach secular society to accept significant failure without becoming paralyzed through self-abnegation, and to reach for forgiveness without mitigating our sense of ongoing responsibility, we might end the dejection and moral lassitude that now suffuse our civilization.

Fifth: This insight needs to be extended to the farthest range of human vision. Something radical must be done about our massive loss of human hope. The quiet despair we feel personally has its social counterpart in our pervasive cynicism about the possibility of substantially improving our world. We have lost our secular faith that one or another program might end our troubles. In the current shift from Marxism and liberal politics to conservatism and libertarianism our disenchantment with social reconstruction via government is politically manifested. Such political excitement as is now available derives not from the old hope of creating God's realm by our efforts, but from anticipating relief from the oppressive power of the state. No one has any compelling plans to transform our social order morally. The pundits are so divided on every question from astrophysics through economics to psychiatry that we can no longer believe that any of them is right. The intense pluralism of our time, instead of promoting intelligent choice, overwhelms us with the feeling that our problems are insoluble.

Worse, we have seen evil pervasively at work in human affairs. When we refuse to cover up reality in the name of love or custom, we see what damage we have done in the family, the school and every other human institution. We have been most tragically disappointed by politics, where our power to harm is wildly amplified. We had counted on the democratic process to limit our sinfulness and perhaps even to summon forth our moral power. Instead, venality, corruption, malfeasance and even malevolence have nightly appeared before us in television newscasts. Internationally, the behavior of people and nations has been utterly disheartening. Human nature seems deeply flawed, no social structure being peopleproof. We face the future with futility and a desperate wish that we may be spared the worst of what will, as likely as not, soon transpire.

This near fatalism—and the moral withdrawal associated with it—is the dark underside of our rush to saving cults, secular or religious. Few if any of them ask us to use our moral powers for the good of improving the common human lot. The cults give us inner peace by relieving us of our personal responsibility for working out our social problems here and now. They succeed because they appeal to our despair. Given the exaggerated hopes we placed in ourselves and in our projects in recent years, our present hopelessness seems almost logical. Today it would be laughable to try to rally people under the banner of human perfectibility, to assert that we are called on to achieve the Messianic Age through a combination of education, culture, psychotherapy, political action, recreation, nutrition, or such.

For all the proximate value of such activities we religionists have a different source of faith in the possibilities of humankind. We believe, despite all the difficulties we have in understanding it, that God rules supreme. The world is not dominated by chance, and history is not abandoned to randomness or neutrality. The universe is not inimical or indifferent but hospitable to goodness. In what we experience minute by minute, day by day, we see, mainly, a goodness and beneficence that we do not deserve and cannot claim as a matter of right. We call God good and see God's goodness as fundamental to the universe—to such an extent that as long as our faith is strong we are able to accept the evils that befall us, even though we cannot comprehend their purpose or significance.

Out of that daily affirmation we join the great biblical affirmation that God's rule will one day be realized among humankind. No matter how obdurate human beings remain, no matter what transpires in a given era, God will not ultimately be defeated. Sin will not always be the norm among people. God's power is the power of God's goodness. The good God will not violate humankind's freedom of decision—yet, paradoxically, God's goal of a fully righteous creation will not be denied. We fail, our plans are frustrated, our cultures become empty, and our civilizations decline—the condition the Bible calls exile—but God's goodness will one day bring us to the coming of the Messiah.

Through some such eschatological faith biblical religion has taught its adherents the power to endure. There have been many dark days in human history, and we may well fear that there will yet be others, though we pray not. They wound the human heart and make us sick of soul. In the tumultuous and unsteady times in which we live, who can avoid the doubts that bring one down to the darkness of the pit? But how much more, then, are we grateful for those saving moments when we have been drawn up from the depths by a strength greater and more enduring than our own. And the righteous live by that faith.

If religion could impart something of that eschatological strength to our secular society, it would help us surmount the hard times we witness, enbolden us to persist in our efforts to change things for the better.

There are five ways, then, in which religion might challenge and complement secularity's work in meeting the needs of the human situation. Once upon a time, the secular mind brought religion under prophetic judgment and proposed to fulfill its frustrated promise. Now it has come time for a reversal of roles. Religion must now assert in full force that secularity has lost much of its power for good, that it urgently requires the restoration of a freshly compelling sense of values if it is to resume its positive role in human affairs.

We can hope to carry out this role effectively because we do not approach secular society as outsiders or antagonists. We, too, have been, in part, secularized. The many failures of secularity give us no excuse for denying that we were ever guilty of the obscurantism and moral insensitivity of which we were once accused. Rather, it is as beneficiaries of the secular revolution that we call upon it to remember the truth in which it was born and that it has come to forget.

Secularity appealed to humankind because of its high moral vision. It chided religion for not believing enough in people and for not exemplifying in person and practice the ethics we proclaimed in God's name. Without that high commitment to human dignity and social cooperation, secularity loses its exalted claim on our allegiance. And that is what has been happening in recent decades. The biblical foundation from which the secular prophets emerged to criticize us has largely been abandoned. The humanism and rationalism that we once thought might take religion's place have failed us in the face of history and our growing skepticism. We therefore call for the forging of a new covenant between a chastened, undefensive, yet strongly faithful religion and a newly weak and dispirited, yet still humanly powerful, secularity. We share enough that we can find many areas in which to work together for the common welfare. We differ enough in our perspective—the one focusing primarily on the transcendent as it intersects with the human, the other steadfastly concerned with what people can yet do with their power—that we can enrich and enlighten one another.

I do not mean to suggest that we shall thereby find answers to all the troubling problems of our time. For all that religion seeks to mediate God's word and apply it to the realities of life, there is much we do not know and cannot do. Belief does not end the gap between goals and capacity. It does not stop history or render it free of surprises, tragic or triumphant. From decision to decision, we must still ponder and choose and propose and determine and try to act. Faith does not make us infallible. Besides, we do not always agree with one another, within our faiths or in the discussions between them. We may commune with the Absolute, but away from the sanctuary or pulpit or dais we are only people.

So we cannot claim to offer solutions to our society. Besides, who but the gullible could believe such a claim today? But there is one infinitely important thing we can do: We can help restore our civilization to its classic biblical ground of value. That ground was once the source of our standards and goals; thereby, it sanctified our human striving. In detaching itself from that foundation, our society has undercut the very basis of its call to freedom and creativity. We come to all people of goodwill with the ancient religious call to turn and renew their covenant with God. And we pledge ourselves to utilize such power as the Lord has given us, to work together with all who share something of our vision of what people on earth may yet accomplish.

6

Individualistic Ethics

A Dispute with Robert Nozick

I remember the old woman from the years when I would visit in the neighborhood. Somehow, among the many other acculturated East European grandmothers who lived there, she stood out. She had a touch of natural grace about her, a sense of her own dignity that led her to withdraw from vulgarity and said that in her presence people should act with sensitivity.

I admit that because of her present condition I may be retrospectively exaggerating her charm. I see her now only when I am visiting at the Home. She is hardly recognizable for she is senile and despite the good medical attention and personal care she receives, her debility grows each month. Some time back she could still recognize me and engage in one of the ritual conversations that were the framework of our relationship. Today she can no longer speak, not even the gibberish that temporarily became her substitute for language; her head is bent most of the time as she endlessly attends to some detail of dress, or chair, or floor, and she does not respond to my greeting. She is incontinent and feeds herself only with much spilling. So she wears a continuing series of shapeless institutional dresses which are clean but often have a button missing or a ribbon hanging. Like most people, I am sure she would have hated to think of herself as ever coming to this: Not the least of her sadness would be that she is essentially supported by the state; were she not another of New York City's famed welfare cases and a beneficiary of special government programs for

Originally published as "The Old Woman as Meta-Question: A Religionist's Reflections on Nozick's View of the State," *Journal of the American Academy of Religion*, vol. 44, no. 3 (September 1976): 504–15.

the aged and the infirm, her social security pension and Medicare insurance would not be sufficient to pay for even modest institutional care.

I first came to associate her with the Nozick-Rawls controversy, I think, when, after the meeting of the National Book Award judges at which we selected the nominees for the field of philosophy and religion, I visited at the Home and saw her. Since then, her image hovers at the margins of my consciousness when I think about the problem of an appropriate theory of the state, particularly as it concerns the obligations of citizens to one another. Apparently the old woman confronts me with some deeply challenging meta-questions. These go beyond the realm of politics and reach out to the general relationship of much contemporary philosophy to much religious affirmation—certainly to mine as a liberal Jew. In this series of reflections, then, I propose to identify, analyze and thereby clarify the perplexities I find the old woman raises for me.

Robert Nozick's book, *Anarchy, State and Utopia* (New York: Basic Books, 1974), is an effort to sketch a reasonably comprehensive, logically tight theory of what, from the presupposition of private rights, a state might justifiably be. I esteem Nozick's work highly enough to have joined in voting it a major award and to be troubled by it for many months. To my mind its argument is usefully pictured as a two-pronged, dialectical polemic. Nozick begins his case with an argument against anarchy. There is something quite directly appealing about the contention that states are inevitably coercive and hence their existence is a violation of personal dignity. In this view all states are illegitimate and hence only the irrationalities of history or the perversity of human nature "justifies" our having governments. Nozick refutes this position with a precisely worked out argument for a minimal state. But this effort to overcome anarchy sets the context for all that follows, that is, how the rights of the single self can be made to yield a social entity with its own "rights." Hence the other prong of his polemic is directed against those who would argue for more than a minimal state, most notably John Rawls and his view as given in *A Theory of Justice* (Cambridge: Harvard University Press, 1971). Rawls' major opponents are not the anarchists but the utilitarians. Rawls refutes any validation of government on the basis of corporate benefit the famous "greatest good for the greatest number." Yet in arguing for the return of political theory to an individualist foundation, Rawls cannot forget some of the moral benefits of utilitarianism. These derived from the fact that this theory (and the liberal politics connected with it) considered the state obligated to promote the well-being of its citizens. Rawls cannot go that far. But the moral advance of the utilitarians over the individualists would seem to have been the former's mitigation through social initiative of the exploitation and oppression which, in practice, become the consequences of political individualism. Rawls' sense of justice, his feel for fairness, thus leads him to find a way to validate, from his individualist premise, the state's duty to ameliorate the worst social effects of its individualistic ordering. This move to corporate responsibility draws

Nozick's criticism. Though against the anarchists he justifies the existence of a minimal state, he does not see how Rawls, or anyone else, can show that an association of individuals may do more than is strictly necessary to enable citizens to exercise their private rights. For the government to coerce them in any way to compensate those disadvantaged by the operation of the system is a violation of the premise of its existence and therefore illegitimate.

The old woman does not fare well in Nozick's proposal. True, he insists that all persons, senile or not, have rights and that no one, least of all the state, whose powers derive from individuals, may deprive persons of their rights. Hence the old lady need not fear that a Nozickian state in some Nazi-like, biological perversion of the greatest-number-good rule will subject her to euthanasia. Nor is she, because she is reduced in status, not entitled to her natural rights of liberty, the pursuit of economic gain and the free exercise of the property derived therefrom. Considering what some cultures have done to the old and the incompetent among them and recognizing how many constraints various governments place upon individuals, Nozick's defense of the liberty of the single-self, regardless of rank, race, belief or biological condition has much human appeal.

Yet the old woman faces two special problems in Nozick's minimal state. While no one will take away her rights, she is not in a position to exercise them. And she is not unique in this respect. To be sure, her civic incompetence is physiological; we cannot think of a large-scale social arrangement in which a person with such a damaged nervous system could function reasonably well. Most other incompetents are merely functionally so. Because of poor training, bad experience, inhibiting emotions, social trauma, the complexity of the system, or the rapacity of the powerful, they have—and know they have—little or no chance of effectively exercising their rights. Industrial democracy has, of course, given them a much greater chance of doing so than did feudal or monarchic forms of organizing society, and the efforts in recent years to provide enabling institutions to the disenfranchised have somewhat expanded their possibility of being able to act effectively on their own behalf. Nonetheless, the old woman in her dramatic incompetence is a proper case with which to raise questions about the nature of Nozick's state. If some exaggeration may be permitted (Nozick's own range of permissible philosophic moves is admirably broad), one has the impression that the Nozickian citizen is a superb young athlete, who has the strength and stamina to gain reasonable rewards in the competition of each with all. In fact, a good deal of Nozick's reference is to individual producers and their rights to the products of their labor. I do not consider that problem an unworthy or insignificant one. The old woman, however, keeps reminding me that many people in a society are not producers or are inefficient or deficit producers. Since in a Nozickian social order rights exist in practice insofar as citizens can exercise them, she and her kind may have the negative liberty of noninfringement but not the positive liberty which, practically, is available only for the vigorous and determined.

On this level then the old woman raises the question of the philosophical anthropology on which this political theory is based. Nozick (and Locke, whom he follows here) appear to posit a homogenous citizenry, alike in its capabilities. This is not true of humankind as we know it and not merely for the sort of historical reasons that Nozick, to create a proper theoretical model, rules out of order. Rather humanity is most diversely unequal in intellect, psychic predisposition and the like, to the tasks of social living. One can logically couple this fact of humanity's natural diversity with an insistence upon equal political rights with little more difficulty than associating it with the paternalism or elitist notions of government with which it is commonly linked. In any case, individualists should give some attention to the diverse nature of the human beings whose individuality is central to their constructions. Nozick does not do this at least because of the need to delimit an already far-ranging study but more likely because here the old woman has raised the sort of meta-question with which he does not wish to deal.

The other problem the old woman raises for me is that the government takes my money to pay for her keep. We are, in contemporary America, constrained to surrender the product of our free labor to enhance the welfare of all sorts of other people. This is precisely the sort of liberalistic, utilitarian coercion of individuals that Nozick considers rationally untenable. He is not inhumane and favors philanthropy for there people give freely to causes they choose. (He argues that his sort of social arrangement would not discourage philanthropy. Apparently he favors it, and I see in this advocacy a useful mitigation to the harsh effects of his individualism, but he does not indicate why people would or should cherish this virtue, another example of a problem caused by inattention to the anthropological meta-question.) Nozick is opposed to the state forcing me to do what, on the basis of my rights, I need not do and the state's not giving me the decision as to which if any social "philanthropies" I will support with my goods. For Nozick's citizens have no obligation to each other. They are true individuals whose duties are only to self. They should, if Nozick's anti-anarchy argument is correct, be willing to join with other individuals to form a state for mutual protection, contiguous living, joint functioning and the equally minimal like. But they have no responsibility to one another beyond granting each other social space. Hence it is a primary violation of a national social order, in Nozick's view, for the state, in effect, to seize the property of its citizens, even if an equitable measure for such seizure is employed, and distribute it to various of the citizens, even if an equitable measure of distribution is employed. If such as the old woman cannot take care of themselves, then let their children, or relatives, or friends, or good-hearted people in the community take care of them. She—and all like her—have no political claim on others. The minimal state defines welfare in terms of the freedom to exercise rights; senile old ladies are not its proper concern.

I have grown up with a sense of the state and society which has a radically different criterion for measuring the adequacy of a political arrangement. Being a Jew who, against the odds, has rather regularly been in synagogues for most of his post-bar-mitzvah life, I have had it drummed into me by repetitive Torah and prophetic readings that a social order is judged by the test cases of the stranger, the orphan, and the widow. (The old woman's husband has been dead about ten years.) Or the poor. The Bible believes that we are positively obligated to one another. Hence when some people have special needs it is our duty to help them. Much of what Nozick advocates is consonant with the Biblical view of social justice. We must not pervert justice for the poor or prevent it functioning for the stranger, the orphan or the widow. The weak and the powerless must not be disenfranchised. But the Bible goes far beyond structural entailments. It prescribes our substantive obligations to others less well-situated or competent. We must plead the case of the widow and the orphan. We must give food and money to the poor. (The nearby poor are our first but not our only responsibility.) We must leave the corner of our fields and what fell in the harvesting for the poor and the stranger who dwells in our gates. We must separate a tithe for the poor. These are not options, warmly recommended to the good-hearted. They are commandments, religious laws of the state in that odd theo-political situation (to borrow and re-direct Buber's term) which the Bible describes. All such positive action, enjoined for another's benefit is anathema to Nozick.

The Bible's different sense of duty derives, so to speak, from its different fundamental premise. Y', God, the creator and ruler of the universe, brought humanity into being and is concerned about its individual and corporate behavior. Though people incline to sinfulness, God has made them capable of building just social orders. God commands them to fulfill this capacity and, on occasion, dramatically punishes them when they, in their freedom, refuse to do so. (So Sodom and Gomorrah; and the Kingdoms of Israel and Judah.) People are intimately involved in each other's welfare because God says so—but also because that is the way God made them, needing others for completion. The single self, in its separate identity, is created in the image of God. But, on the other hand, individuality is not an exclusive good. For the Bible, people are essentially social—("It is not good for a person to be alone," Gen. 2:18). Human singleness finds its proper context in family, community and folk. So too the People of Israel, for all that it "dwells alone" (Num. 23:9), is part of humanity as a whole, and its function in history involves not merely reestablishing the Davidic monarchy but bringing the Kingdom of God for all humankind.

The old woman now lives in a Jewish Home though I think its benefactors would prefer to think of it in the euphemism made famous by Brandeis University, "Jewish sponsored, non-denominational." She receives the fine care she does here because, ultimately, Jews over the centuries lived

74

the Biblical sense of common responsibility. Thus even though most Jews today no longer believe God commands them, they still tend, in secularized fashion, to live by many of the values of a prior, pious time. So this Home would almost certainly not exist nor be operated at its present high standards were these old Jewish commitments not still operative.

Near the Home is a large discount department store, always very busy. When I look into the faces of the good people going in or out of it, I sense their frustration that they cannot buy all they want or, perhaps, need. Even when our anomalous inflation mixed with depression passes, they will be a difficult group to raise funds from to erect or maintain a home. Yet, when, through the process called democracy they are forced to be contributors to this home and other welfare activities, they are largely willing to do so, in no small part, I think, because they know all other citizens share in this interhuman burden and they too retain something of the Bible's view that we are responsible for one another. Most Jews, I would guess, still have so high a sense of social obligation that they see in governmental programs promoting social welfare an extension of their own community values. This is what is meant, I think, by the suggestion that Jews tend to be liberals. And this explains the special sadness in much of the Jewish community that the people indicted in the New York nursing home scandals were Jewish, in one case, an apparently pious leader of a world-wide, traditional Jewish religious organization. Fraud is not only an American crime but a Jewish sin. Committed on a grand scale so as to attract public attention, it is doubly heinous for it brings shame on the Jewish community as a whole. But if the objects of one's dishonesty are the poor, the widowed, the aged and the infirm, then one is especially vile and no public display of a head always covered by a skull-cap can make up for what will seem to most Jews a perverted hierarchy of Jewish values.

To Rawls' credit, he is disturbed lest the shift from a utilitarian to an individualist foundation for political theory deprive the old woman and others like her of the substantial dignity which, by virtue of governmental coercion, her treatment in the Home confers upon her. He therefore argues for what he calls a "reasonable" addendum to individualist politics. He begins from a hypothetical position in which rational people, not knowing what would be their lot in a society now about to be formed, are asked to establish basic principles for it. He suggests that it would make good sense for them first to have "equality in the assignment of basic rights and duties while the second (principle) holds that social and economic inequalities . . . are just only if they result in compensating benefits for everyone, and in particular for the least advantaged members of society" (pp. 14–15). If we take the stranger, the orphan, the widow and the poor as Biblical equivalents for "the least advantaged" then Rawls' sense of justice is akin to that of the Bible. Nozick, however, while agreeing with Rawls' first principle, points out that Rawls has no good basis for the adoption of his supplemental rule. It is clear why the disadvantaged—or those who think that they might turn out to be disadvantaged—would want this compensatory regulation. They would receive a maximum return from the increase of benefits in the society. Then why shouldn't the advantaged similarly be entitled to a maximum return for their efforts and thus not have to give to others? Why is it "reasonable" to suggest, as Rawls terms it, that the advantaged—or those who think they might be—should agree to work for others as well as their own gain? Surely, Nozick argues, it is not enough merely to say as Rawls does (p. 103) that we need some rule for society and this is a "reasonable" one. Rather one should say the supplemental principle is unreasonable, for how can one logically move from an individual's right to his labor, to depriving him of it to benefit someone else? In terms of the joint Nozick–Rawls individualist structure of political theorizing (the first principle), I must admit that Nozick's critique is quite successful. For all Rawls' Biblical appeal he has not made a case for nonutilitarian social responsibility. But now the vision of the old woman and her fellows rises before me. Shall I, moved beyond my old values by the precision of Nozick's argument, join the fight against welfare programs and let the old woman and her ilk live on such charity as I and others choose to provide?

The question disturbs me profoundly, and I sense that it touches me at a level far deeper than mere sentiment or the natural reluctance to give up old political commitments. Something far more basic to my self is at stake.

I am not alone in my distress. Nozick knows that his rigor has brought him to a surprising set of conclusions. He remarks that readers will want to reject "anything so apparently callous toward the needs and suffering of others." He continues, "I know that reaction; it was mine when I first began to consider such views. With reluctance, I found myself becoming convinced of . . . libertarian views, due to various considerations and arguments . . . my earlier reluctance is not present in this volume, because it has disappeared. Over time, I have grown accustomed to the views and their consequences, and I now see the political realm through them" (p. ix–x). Nozick acknowledges that his conclusions are, by customary ethical standards, reprehensible. He suggests by the use of the word "apparently" that his conclusions are not so morally base as they might seem to the unenlightened reader. We may infer then that he believes that the common ethical criteria need to be revised most likely in terms of the political premise of the book. That is, these conclusions are apparently callous when one's morality still contains a social thrust. Here we are operating with an individualistic base for political theory that is morally decisive as well. Ethics is essentially only the duties the self has to other selves which makes it possible for them to function in full consonance with their individuality. Perhaps, then, in Nozick's case the beauty of the argument not only commended the conclusions but drove the thinker back to see that he had not drawn the full implication of his premise. It was morally as well as politically significant.

There is another road he could have taken were his old ethical concerns deeply rooted. Thus a person with any sort of Biblical values would reverse Nozick's procedure. Instead of revising one's ethics one would re-examine the premises which sent one on a rational way to "apparently" sinful conclusions. The meta-question cannot be repressed. If individualism leads to callousness is it worthy of being the stringent basis of all one's argument? Why did Nozick accept and maintain this meta-stance?

Nozick's "justification" for adopting a "state-of-nature" theory as the foundation of all that follows (Locke's term; what I have in this paper preferred to call by the more substantive identification "individualism") runs about 6 pages at the beginning of the book.

Despite the brevity of this early treatment and the results this premise generates, Nozick never returns to reexamine the idea. Hence we must examine his meta-political position in terms of a highly limited statement, a fact of some significance for this sort of philosophizing. Nozick begins by commenting that while one can give "reasons why it is important to pursue state-of-nature theory . . . (and) fruitful . . . the best reason is the developed theory itself" (p. 3). But surely a heuristic justification will not do here. If the developed theory leads us to apparent callousness then despite the interest and fun of the ensuing argument the results of adopting the premise can hardly be said to be self-evidently desirable. And if this is "the best reason" for beginning with a rigorous individualism then the entire enterprise collapses on its unhappy foundation.

Nozick then goes on to give two specific reasons for adopting Locke's state-of-nature premise. The first is devised in due course from the need to overcome the appeal of anarchism. The latter position, "if tenable, undercuts the whole subject of *political* philosophy" (p. 4). So Nozick proposes to rule out the anarchist option by showing that a state would be more desirable than the best possible situation of anarchy, which he describes (after excluding some other possibilities) as "a nonstate situation in which people generally satisfy moral constraints and generally act as they ought" (p. 5). For the debate to be joined with someone advocating such a society requires finding a common ground within a highly restricted set of conditions. If Nozick now posited that people are inherently political animals or by nature are meant to live in society and thus, necessarily, have government (e.g., 1 Sam. 8), he would rule out a discussion of anarchy *ab initio*. Yet note that morality is included in the anarchist-Nozick presupposition. Nozick says flatly, "moral philosophy sets the background for, and boundaries of, political philosophy" (p. 6). However, the conditions of the debate assign special semantic limits to the term, and "moral" is now used here without its common sense of social obligation but in the strictly individualistic understanding which alone would be acceptable to anarchists. Thus the moral shift Nozick traces in himself relative to the "apparent" callousness of his conclusions derives, in this first validation of his individualist premise, from the need to be able to engage the anarchists in mutually meaningful discourse.

Nozick's second reason for adopting a state-of-nature basis for his argument is more technically grounded than the first. He begins with a brief discussion of what constitutes a good explanation. Then he asserts that state-of-nature explanations of the origins of government are a logically good kind of explanation and they "pack explanatory punch and illumination, even if incorrect. We learn much by seeing how the state could have arisen, even if it didn't arise that way . . . we also would learn much . . . by trying to explain why the particular bit of the real world that diverges from the state-of-nature model is as it is" (p. 9). Thus the explanatory power which comes from adopting this premise is so great that Nozick holds on to it despite its leading to conclusions he once saw as callous; he can now call them only "apparently callous"; and "over time . . . grow(s) accustomed to them."

A major source of my distress at this sort of philosophizing is that I am not clear whether it is meant as a hypothetic-deductive academic language game (with perhaps some limited use for better understanding reality) or whether it is model-making with practical overtones. The distinction is quite important to me, for the old lady is no literary device of mine invented to make a theoretical article come alive. She is a real person; so are her kind. In the fiscal-crisis of New York City and State, where welfare programs are a prime target of budget cutters, am I to read Nozick for intellectual pleasure or as a guide to political action (since I believe I have a moral responsibility to effectuate the best form of government I can think of)? If it is only the former, then I have little but admiration for Nozick's accomplishment. To take a promising thesis and explore its implications, indeed to show a certain daring but no lack of discipline in applying it in ways not previously done, is a triumph of man's rational capacity and thus a humanistic achievement I highly value. But much of contemporary philosophy that overlaps religious concerns seems to slip over from mental possibility to practical suggestion. Analytic philosophy, which regularly takes the form of exploring "If . . . then . . . " often ends up preaching "Since . . . then . . . . " The argument over verifiability is, perhaps, the classic example. If statements may be said to have meaning only insofar as they are empirically testable, then even non-literalistic God-talk turns out to be meaningless—a not-so-surprising discovery since Biblical religion taught that God is not subject to empirical test. Now one could not object if analytic philosophers were content to leave matters at that, namely to say that "IF you want to participate in the analytic philosophy game THEN it does not appear that you can make any statements about God here that may be said to have meaning"; such gamesmanship is unexceptionable. But what begins as good methodology covertly acquires metaphysical status. Judgments about reality emerge: what religion knows is not "knowledge"; what religion says is only emotive; perhaps it has moral power, but surely not coherent meaning; philosophical theology is a contradiction in terms; philosophy, properly done, in fact, shows the nonsense of almost every major proposition derived from Biblical faith. Obviously some people will insist on remaining religious despite these demonstrations but no intelligent person should do so. I am not alone in

78

detecting something of an evangelical fervor in the work of Flew and Nielsen, to mention two outstanding practitioners of the analysts' art though not the most egregious practitioners of analytic meta-claims. What is somewhat restrained by the proper canons of literary presentation has often been liberated on campus by the rights professors feel they have to extend their expertise from the narrow realm of "if ... then ... " to the real world which stretches so far beyond it.

In Nozick's case it is clear that the state-of-nature "If ... " is utilized primarily for the good politics-explaining-game it sets up. In this game as it is now played one takes anarchism seriously enough to make one's first moves by refuting it, and thus justifying the game. To do this Nozick adopts a minimalist thesis about social responsibility and when he then discovers that applied with verve it explains political problems interestingly, he claims, retroactively, to have justified its employment. For playing a demanding mental game that would be fine. But Nozick goes further. He does not say at the end of his effort what many recent Jewish legal documents do *"halachah v'en morin kan,"* which may loosely be rendered, "I have here deduced a proper legal ruling but you may not use this correct theoretical decision for instruction as to authorized practice." Rather Nozick speaks of using the model he has produced as a basis of explaining "why the particular bit of the real world that diverges from (it) ... is as it is"; he has changed his moral perceptions in terms of it for what was once callous is now, with time, only "apparently" so: and, in fact, he now "see(s) the political realm through" the conclusions reached here. What began as a useful way of playing an interesting game yielded such stimulating results that it commended itself to its practitioner as the way the real world ought to be organized.

To exaggerate slightly, the root of Nozick's libertarian politics is his need to refute the anarchists. (I take it other political meta-principles than state-of-nature could yield explanations that are proper and have "punch.") This is one useful way of approaching a meta-question conflict. One accepts the opponent's meta-ground, in this case the anarchist's affirmation of (moral) individualism, in my perspective, radical individualism. And then one hopes, on the opponent's ground, to build a case for one's own, contrary position. This is the sort of thing Braithwaite did in accepting the empiricist definition of meaning and then justifying religion as a special sort of moral activity. The dangers of this strategy are clear from these two instances: by accepting a foundation to the argument which, to accommodate the opponent, is reductionist in terms of one's prior (pre-argument) understanding, one almost always arrives at conclusions which are far less embracing than one held before. Thus Nozick, by adopting a meta-stance acceptable to anarchists, must almost inevitably give up his prior belief that governments should tax the rich to help the widow and the orphan, while Braithwaite, to speak to the empiricists, must reduce Christianity to an ethical motivator and guide. On the game level this can be valuable. "If" we were to play with anarchists / empiricists / etc.,

79

"then," though their stance is reductive of our prior sense of reality, we could see what a newly formulated politics / religion / etc. would be. Exploring how our premises effect our conclusions is useful in itself. It may, in the real world, help us see how our values and goals derive from our meta-ground. And it may send us back to reexamine that ground when we now see that another premise would lead us in different directions. But if it is reality which is, in fact, at stake, then the validation of a meta-stance surely cannot be whether it is the accepted or desirable way to play a given intellectual game. We need to consider whether, as best we can figure it out, this meta-stance reasonably corresponds to reality. I take it that there is no logical connection between the "is" that an idea game evokes in a certain group of thoughtful Western professors and the assertion that it does reasonably correspond to reality, or "ought" to be used as if it did. Hence when philosophers suggest that I change my politics/religion/etc. (and perhaps work to get others to do so) on the basis of what I agree has been uncommonly engaging mind-play, I must as a rational and moral being inquire, "What has your game to do with reality?" or more specifically when conclusions are odd and arguments are tight, "What has your game-premise to do with reality?"

I now require a far more substantial justification of the other theorists' meta-ground than I would if we were only to engage in another "If . . . then . . ." game. On this level a statement of a premise's utility cannot be substituted for a truth-claim on its behalf. Yet I must confess that my agenda has become polemical. Seeing that what I call their reductionism would necessarily strip away much of what I know to be true (with all the qualification and self-doubt that I, as a modern, necessarily attach to such a claim) I am not prepared to accept their premises as a basis for our discussion. The price is simply too high. Surely, I should not surrender an informed, tested meta-ground because they are authorities and I am not (a frequent undertone of philosopher-religionist controversies); nor because among academics they esteem this is the best way of doing things (no wonder many philosophers, anxious to avoid facing their "gentleman's agreement" on passing over meta-questions, do not find the sociology of philosophic knowledge valuable to their enterprise). Shifts in meta-grounds with consequences for life and action (something like Lonergan's "conversion") should take place only when one is convinced another's meta-ground is, in fact, a better approximation of the truth than one's own. Alas, our current intellectual situation has no good way of handling inter-meta-stance disputes. Without a reasonably common metaphysics or epistemology, living in a cultural pluriverse, we find we cannot reasonably talk to one another—Nozick to the anarchists (without accepting their individualism) and now, perhaps, I to Nozick. Mostly we are limited to the exchange of phenomenological data which conveys insight into a given position without allowing us a basis for debating it.

How can one directly conduct a meta-conflict? I shall make little headway reminding Nozick that, factually, people as we know them in an original "state-of-nature" are not radical individualists but members of groups. Indeed in the earliest human writings identity for most people seems more a matter of being a member of a group than the sort of self-conscious, autonomous self-hood we hear so much about today. Nozick knows all that, but it is, essentially, irrelevant to his enterprise for he is "doing philosophy," not anthropology or history.

I shall be even less effective if I seek to argue my feeling that the emphasis Nozick places on individualism is carried beyond reasonable proportion. There is surely some intellectual value in pointing out that the sort of individualism we are talking about is a relatively recent human phenomenon. (While we may find some early post-Cromwellian British roots for the theory of anarchy, it is largely a product of 19th century, post-Enlightenment conceptions of the nature of being a person.) Moreover, while social and political control of the individual has proceeded to frightening lengths in our time, thus commending a vigorous individualism, we have gotten to the not uncommon historic stage of pushing a new, good idea too hard. Thus someone with my sort of Biblical perspective sees the concentration on self leading to disturbing life-options. Let me give two examples of what I see as excesses of contemporary individualism: one may responsibly spend one's life on a-social fun and pleasure; and one has a perfect right to commit suicide when one wishes to do so. In the former case, the individual accepts no significant positive responsibility toward society (what the rabbis called our duty "to upbuild the world"); in the latter case, there is not even a positive response to what secularists call nature or the world (to which one has ecological and other such responsibilities) and surely not to what religionists call God. In both cases people feel fully free to dispose of themselves, a sign to me that the modern notion of individualism has proceeded to the point of blindness to one's bio-physical and social ties and certainly to one's meta-physical roots and responsibilities.

Not only could Nozick argue that such arguments are essentially subjective—history can be read many ways and one man's "extreme" is another man's progress—but that attacks upon individualism are self-refuting in the mouth of a liberal Jew. When society was organized on an essentially corporate basis only Christians had full rights. Not until the emergence of the modern state and its notion that rights were individual, not corporate, could Jews attain full citizenship. Hence for someone whose personal liberty is directly the result of the modern sense of the individual, to object to its further development seems ungrateful as well as inconsistent.

This brief exploration of my meta-conflict with Nozick has only made my problem more complex for while I cannot accept his individualism, I do not totally disagree with it either. Liberal Judaism, that is, the non-traditionalist interpretation of Jewish faith and belief that arose in the early 19th century and is so widespread today under various labels, is essentially an effort to link the notion of autonomous personhood with Jewish tradition. It has sought to give the individual a greater role than prior Judaism did in the relationship with God and what it is understood God wants of the Jewish people. Hence the commitment of the non-Orthodox Jew to the significance of the individual now has theological as well as a political base. But that will not normally lead on to an acceptance of the meta-politics Nozick is commending. In this regard the difference between the individualisms of Jean Paul Sartre and Martin Buber is illuminating. Sartre's early sense of the individual was radically a-social. He would not marry, beget children, or even accept awards. He could write "Hell is other people." Buber is the most radically individualistic interpreter of what it means to be a Jew. His anti-nomianism has won him the antipathy of almost all institutionally significant leaders in the Jewish community. Yet Buber's individualism is simultaneously thoroughly social. By contrast to Sartrean existentialism, Buber had said (years earlier) that one does not truly become an "I" until one addresses another as "thou." Yet in the I-thou relationship, the one, true human situation, one retains one's individuality even as one gains full selfhood in the being-with-the-other; the hyphen separates as it joins. Buber speaks for my sense of individualism as necessary yet insufficient, as adequate only when it has a social context and hence obligation.

It would be tempting to say against Nozick that religion is concerned with the old lady while he and philosophers of his sort play language games, often with damaging social overtones. But it is not true. Much of what relilgionists write is unrelated to life, some of my own work being no exception. (The time spent puzzling out the intellectual problems explored here was obviously not spent on the orphan, the widow and the stranger.) Nor can religionists claim that we alone see and care about the old woman as, apparently, I do. Many a believing Jew and Christian would vote to abolish the government's involvement in welfare activity and do so on what would be argued were religious grounds. Thus I cannot claim then that my response to Nozick is fundamentally the result of the clash of two disciplines for whatever such a technical argument is worth when reality is at issue. However, it is fair to point out that religion is uncommonly concerned with meta-questions. It centers around some disclosure of ultimate reality and its implications for human existence. On the common sense level, one is largely unaware (or totally so) of the true (religious) nature of reality and of the overwhelming significance of the fact that humanity, through religious insight, now knows what is truly the case. Religions will indeed spend much of their effort on the rites and institutions through which this glorious knowledge will be lived. Yet though doctrine and faith retreat far into the background, they remain essential to religion. Everything depends on the meta-vision. Hence I think philosophers must expect religionists to be more than commonly concerned with meta-questions and to insist in these conflict situations that religion is most appropriately understood as a meta-stance and its consequenes. (I take it this is what Hare was trying to convey with his concept of religion as "blik" and Ramsey kept trying to clarify when he spoke of the "penny drop-ping.") This will not ease the difficulty of our discussion with the philos-ophers but the consciousness of our concern and its importance to us should make the meta-discussions somewhat less dissonant.

What then can we hope to accomplish with one another in such con-frontations? We can try to understand something of the other person's meta-ground, most particularly by seeing its distance from our own. In such a process of negating another's position we are necessarily affirming something as well. Hence, with a little self-scrutiny, we should simulta-neously gain greater insight into our own ultimate commitments. We can also try to help others see the entailments of their position, particularly where, as in this discussion, a difference in meta-ground makes a substan-tial difference in consequences. And again, the same is true as they help us see where our own views lead. If, by chance, we affirm the same values and hence judge consequences by a similar standard, we may be able to call into question one another's premises and not just their arguments. We thus need to be open to searching criticism of our faith if, as part of honest interchange, we expect to make judgments of others.

I think all that is valuable yet it will, with the rarest exceptions, not bring us to a resolution of our conflict. None has been reached here. I leave my confrontation with Nozick intellectually stimulated but not, to my way of thinking, very much enlightened about what I take to be the real world and what my duties are in it. Nozick's great game is not worth a change in my faith. I suppose that renders me a "fideist," a term that in the mouths of many is a formula for assignment to philosophic perdition. In my present state of belief I should like to think I would gladly bear the opprobrium rather than give up my sense that my responsibility to the old woman is part of the very nature of the cosmos. If being a rationalist or any other kind of "ist" requires that I surrender my existential sense, that I, my individual destiny, and my welfare are inextricably tied up with all those among whom I live and thus all humanity, then I must surrender a claim to all such labels and the honors associated with them. Yet, this position seems to me not so much a dogmatic assertion or a truth be-stowed by special revelation, as a divine command which is at the same time a reasonable idea. There are thus some basic things about my faith which I think some sort of philosophy could reasonably well ground and clarify. I am disappointed that much of the philosophy l read does not come close to doing this and that I do not seem to have the means to create a non-fideistic validation of my faith. I suppose it is another of the odd characteristics of believing but, despite all these intellectual difficulties, I do not propose to give up my faith, or the duties it entails, or the search for a philosophy adequate to what seems explicable in it. And this is not just my religionist's language-game. It is my life.

7

Toward a More Moral
Social Order

Conscious of the dignity of this occasion and of the honor bestowed upon me to speak to this convocation, I prepared an address which, I hoped, responded to a major religious concern we Americans share. This weekend, when the Rosh Hashanah celebration ended, I learned of the massacre at Shatila and Sabra. The event and the response to it by Jewish leaders have filled me with such moral anguish that I find the text I have ready inadequate to this time of pain. But I have not found the wisdom, or the power, perhaps because I have not had the courage, to discard what I wrote and adddress myself to this spiritual calamity. I hope that you will understand and that God will forgive my yielding to prudence rather than heeding my conscience. For I have decided to continue now with the address I wrote for the occasion.

> We bless you Adonai, our God, ruler of the universe, who has kept us alive, sustained us and brought us to this moment.

For the Jewish community these are the *yomim noraim*, "the days of awe." This past weekend, on *Rosh Hashanah*, as the new year 5,743 began, we celebrated God's annual reenthronement and once again formally accepted God as our sovereign. Now, during these first ordinary seven days of the year, the observant few submit themselves in fresh consciousness to the Divine judgment. On all other days, we end our daily petition for good leaders and worthy politicians by blessing God as *ohev tzedakah umish-*

1982 Harvard Convocation sermon. Entitled "Lessons for our Society from the Days of Awe," in the *Harvard Theological Review*, vol. 75, no. 3 (October 1982).

pat, "the one who loves righteousness and justice." During these solemn days, we conclude instead, *hamelekh hamishpat,* "We bless you, Adonai, our God, the sovereign who is justice."

We could not bear confronting God's awesome holiness if we had not been promised, on the tenth day of each year, the sure mercies of *Yom Hakippurim,* "the Day of Atonement." For this period of dwelling on our guilt was ordained to spur us to repentance. Ezekiel taught our people, " 'Cast away from you all of the transgressions with which you have affronted Me. Create within you a new heart and a new spirit. Why should you die, O household of Israel. I do not desire the death of the one that dies,' declares *Adonai,* God. 'Repent, therefore, and live!' " (18:31–32). If we can find the courage to accept God's judgment upon us and turn from our evil ways, God will this year, as every year, make atonement for us. And that will indeed make 5,743 a *new* year.

But it would smack of cheap grace to vault over judgment and speak now of the comforts of God's atoning love. These are still the days of awe. Let us, then, muster our spiritual strength and aproach the throne of justice. Much in our world, or in the Middle East, or in western civilization cries out for moral scrutiny. But it will be burden enough to apply the teaching of this observance, the least particularistic of the Jewish calendar, to the condition of our society.

The special moral pain of this hour has been accumulating for years. A decade or so ago, in the Watergate era, we idealists gave up, we thought, whatever naive notions we had about the ease with which we might improve social order. We became realists. But any hope that we had that giving up our illusions might itself improve things has been shattered by subsequent events. They have regularly out-stripped our imagination of the human capacity for folly, ignorance, prejudice, selfishness, callousness, ruthlessness, and malevolence. We "realists" simply had not learned Jeremiah's lesson, "The heart is the most devious of all things—and desperately sick. Who can understand it?" (17:9).

Much of our society has now moved on from ethical realism to simple dejection, and, where energy remains, to cynicism. The moral despair which suffuses our civilization implicitly denies God's rule. It may therefore be termed the root sin of our time.

Its evidence is all about us. I do not mean those cheap shots of despair we often discharge to prove how hardened we have become. What troubles me is the growing number of people who live by the crass credo that everyone cheats, that justice is a joke, that ideals are for suckers, and that the only sensible ethics is looking out for number one. Such jungle mores seem reasonable when we look at the perverseness of human nature. They make a virtue out of the heartlessness that even the decent must employ to survive the infinity of each day's moral burden. But many people know in some intimate way that that exploitation denies a cosmic reality. It must be resisted: only the prodigious challenge we then face can easily turn realism into despair. What chance has the spirit in a carnivorous world? If, flaunting Eugene O'Neill's teaching, we refuse to take refuge in illusion, how can we have hope? Our mood is very much like that of a certain small-town poker player. When asked why he regularly played with people who cheated, he remarked: "I know it's a crooked game. But it's the only game in town."

I have little doubt that Reinhold Niebuhr's thesis of another time applies equally to ours: the depth of our present disillusionment is directly proportional to the height of our previous self-confidence.

For more than a century, we idealistic Americans have believed that our science, our politics, our psychotherapy or the like, would cure the perennial ills of humankind. Research, or revolution, or the right candidate, or insight, or affluence, or station, or getting in touch with our bodies, or running, or natural foods, or meditation, or some holistic combination of them, would bring us to the equivalent of the Kingdom of God. Technique has been our messiah—and in subtle transformation, still is for many people. No matter that again and again our most recent saving know-how has disappointed us. That has not shaken our basic trust in human competence. We still pick up our ears when people start telling of a new regimen which has worked wonders for them.

Increasingly, however, Americans sense that they must abandon the optimistic humanism inscribed in McGuffey, exemplified by Horatio Alger and evangelized by *Reader's Digest*. With each traumatizing year the conclusion becomes ever more inescapable: we cannot give the final answers to our human problems, because it is we human beings who are the problem. We can corrupt our noblest visions, vitiate the best products of our decency and undermine the good we do create. If all we have to rely on is people, then acknowledging what we realistically know about them and us, we are right to be pessimistic about the human condition.

The futility of exclusively relying on humankind now powers our American flight to cults, sects and saving doctrines of every sort—and, more wholesomely, back to traditional religion. Immanence, that is, trust in our ourselves, has lost its salvific power. Instead, we have begun humbly to confess that our strength finds its fulfillment and proper application in the Transcendent, by whatever name we identify it. We are ready to acknowledge that our universe testifies to a power, a standard, a reality, a personal presence greater than us, one that properly commands our allegiance and directs our conduct.

Knowing its transcendent reality obligates us not to despair, regardless of what we see about us or within us. Despite our realism, we then recognize that our finite goodness will be urged on and completed by its encompassing worth. And our failure and sinfulness will be forgiven and compensated for by its victory in "the end of days." Some such healing vision, I suggest, lies at the heart of our generation's growing concern with spirituality.

I even find unwilling confirmation of this thesis in the elaborate efforts people make to avoid speaking about God or participating in a religion. Note how much we enjoy our fantasies about life on other planets.

Twenty years ago, when we still prided ourselves on our growing domination of the universe, we feared lest some blob or slime descend upon our planet and frustrate our steady march to mastery. Today, chastened by what we have made of this earth, we long for close encounters with creatures from a civilization radically more benign than ours. Were an extra-terrestrial to visit us, his tormentors would be people seeking, they say, to protect humankind. Carrying the keys of this kingdom, they lock some people in and other people out. Those who seek to save a life by injecting, pummeling, cutting and shocking, end up taking it. If only the pure love of the undefiled, pre-pubescent child could stay unsullied. It would recognize a savior even though "He had no form or comeliness, that we should look upon him, nor beauty that we should delight in him" (Isa. 53:2). For he might raise us above our persecutors, heal our wounds and revive our dead blooms.

Those who cannot believe God would directly save us can now comfort themselves with the image of a visitor from another planet who suffers at the hands of people, dies unreasonably and is put into a cold tomb—only to be resurrected by love and then, after assuring his disciples he will be with them always, ascends into the heavens whence he came. We are too sophisticated for Michelangelo's brawny, anthropomorphic God. We now symbolize creativity with E.T.'s bony finger stretched toward ours.

In these inter-planetary day-dreams we express our longing for a more than terrestrial but less than traditional revelation. We yearn for a place somewhere in the cosmos where biology has outwitted the serpent, for there we might find a species which has fulfilled the potential we have so befouled. These fervent imaginings are perhaps the only hope left to our old, faltering naturalism.

Our compulsive avoidance of God—and of church and synagogue—stems from our great fears of returning to traditional religion. Feminists dread the revival of a transcendent God who might be used to revalidate male dominance. Minority groups fear that the old-time religion will bring back the old-time intolerance. Worse, our drive toward religious traditionalism or commanding orthodoxies often arises from a profound mistrust of human reason, thereby opening a door to creative superstition and sincere fanaticism.

Unfortunately, I do not see how contemporary rationalism can be of much help to us in meeting our moral crisis. For over a century now, the subjectivization of reason on the one hand, and its dialectical technicalization on the other, have been the intellectual source of our ethical malaise. Kant's rationality commanded—and did so categorically. Since then, reason investigates, or explains; it constructs possible world-views, analyzes reasonable choices for rational people or is an art form for the cognitively inclined. It does everything but give us imperatives, the compelling sense of duty by which we might once again put muscle into our flabby ethics. And where this or that system rises to the level of rational command, its cultural impact is impaired by thinkers of another bent who emphatically deny that such substantive thought can properly be called "rational."

I esteem philosophy and devote much of my life to trying to think more precisely. But I side with those who feel we need a rebirth of faith if intellect is once again to produce true humanism. I also know the perils of unreflective commitment. I therefore feel a special obligation to guard against the possible unethical consequences of our turn to transcendence.

Feminism is so likely a victim of traditionalizing belief that it often identifies itself with immanentist doctrines of religion. But its own call for equality makes sense only when based on a transcendent source of value. Wherever we look, nature displays dominance and subjugation. To collect with care ethological evidences of sharing and deference, of mutuality and beneficence, only raises the issue of why one chooses this rather than that data on which to ground one's life. If there are only immanent standards of judgment, and there is nothing else to go by, why should reasonable people devote themselves to reform what is?

The hope for a transforming redemption arises from a twofold intuition. Initially, we have sufficient insight into a transcendent criterion of values that we know people and nature have fallen from the condition of Eden. Thereafter, we come to recognize that God's transcendent sovereignty requires that a transfiguring goodness eventually effectuate itself among us.

I have stressed the monarchic metaphor of God's qualitative distance from us to the point where I may have misled you. God's rulership ought not be mentioned long undialectically. Doing so obscures the astonishing counter-thesis of Biblical faith. The unutterably sovereign God is also the one who makes covenants, binding infinite Godhood as well as humankind in mutually responsible relationships. One glimpses a bit of the Biblical authors' appreciation of God's unfathomable graciousness in the *hen* and *hesed* of Jewish tradition and the *kenosis* of Christian teaching. Loving-kindness and covenant-loyalty in the one faith, and the self-emptying of God in the other, are the breathtaking manifestations of God's transcendence. God does not use the exalted Divine status to oppress but rather as a place from which to reach for partnership. God's rule need not, then, set a model for one sex dominating the other.

Martin Buber guided us well when he suggested reinterpreting God's covenants as I-Thou relationsips. Nothing could command persons more compellingly than the ties of love. Yet they also affirm the partners in their distinctive humanness, to which gender is secondary, as manifest in the encompassing terms "I" and "Thou."

The more difficult, political aspect of equality for women is closely bound up, as I see it, with the fate of other partially enfranchised American groups. They fear that under the guise of ending ethical anarchy, America will grow more repressive.

The theological root of this strategy lies near the surface. Regaining the Transcendent quickly becomes owning the Absolute. First one reclaims enough truth to ground one's life and that of one's society. Then one insists one has all the truth anyone needs. For many people this becomes the prime attraction of a religious group: its leader possesses the consummate revelation, so complete surrender to the leader's will is perfect freedom. And I shall not deny that traditional religions, my own included, once claimed such universal competence that no significant truth lay outside them and no opinion which strongly differed from theirs could be tolerated.

Must the reappropriation of the Transcendent lead on to faiths that may promote fanaticism and zealotry? Is there no way to hold an ultimate strong enough to ground and guide us without simultaneously saying that those who vigorously disagree with us should do only what we know to be right?

Traditional religion's over-bearing self-confidence once made secular democracy a necessity for all who had some independent sense of the worth of humankind. We cannot now be asked to renew our faith in ourselves at the cost of diminishing our tolerance of others. We cannot be asked to accept the principle that, afffirming the one God, we must deny the virtues of pluralism. For myself, I would rather run the risks of the occasional abuse of freedom than face the profanation of God and degradation of people that religious persecution and intolerance create.

Our generation now needs to learn how to proclaim the truth of faith and liberty simultaneously. Such commitment without absolutism can come from maintaining a profound theological modesty. Though I know enough about transcendent truth to base my life on it, I also realize that it expresses and manifests itself in ways far more complex than I can fully understand. If so, other people may rightly have apprehensions of transcendent reality which differ with mine. Besides, I cannot insist that my conscience alone deserves the right of free decision. For all my personal conviction, I must bow to your right to make up your own mind. My spirit and my intellect tell me that my understanding of the ultimate is the best that anyone has—but that does not imply that those who disagree with me are necessarily in error and have no spiritual right to what I perceive as their religious folly. Against the old logic and the old theologies, we now assert the religious virtue of approaching the truth pluralistically.

Transcendence without fanaticism, pluralism without permissiveness, the moral courage of the old faiths with modern democracy's respect for differences—America should have taught us that. We, who seek to bind up her spiritual wounds, need to be true to what this blessed nation has given her successive generations of immigrants, the many who have come here, since the days of the Pilgrims, as refugees from intolerance.

Twenty-five hundred years or so ago, an unknown prophet, whom we call the Second Isaiah, came to his people in exile and brought them a message of hope. His charge in that time of despair was as simple as it was profound. " 'Comfort, O bring comfort to My people,' says your God." He could not do that by relieving them of their political sufferings or restoring them to well-being in their homeland. He could only help them try to see beyond the idolatry which surrounded them and he could spur them to fresh belief in their transcendent yet immanent God. Confident of God's reality, he could say to them as I now say to you,

> "Why do you say, O Jacob,
>   Why declare, O Israel,
> 'My way is hid from *Adonai*,
>   My cause is ignored by my God?'
> Do you not know?
>   Have you not heard?
> *Adonai* is God everlasting,
>   The creator of the earth and its limits.
> God never faints or grows weary,
>   God's wisdom has no end.
> God gives power to those that faint
>   And to those lacking might, God
>   adds strength.
> Though youths faint and grow weary,
>   Though athletes fall by the way,
> Those who trust in *Adonai*
>   shall renew their strength
> They shall mount up with wings
>   as eagles,
> They shall run
>   and not grow weary,
> They shall march
>   and not grow faint."

And, now, in memory of the dead of Shatila and Sabra, and in remembrance of all people who have died as victims of prejudice, hatred and hard-heartedness, let us rise for a moment of silent prayer.

> May their souls be bound up in the bundle of eternal life
> and may they rest in peace
> and let us say, "Amen."

PART
TWO

America as Challenge
and Opportunity

PART
TWO

America as Challenge
and Opportunity

The United States (and Canada to a lesser extent) has had a special impact on the Jewish experience of modernity. This country was founded with an eye to avoiding religious intolerance and providing a relatively neutral public ground in which previously antagonistic religious groups might live peaceably, if not happily, with one another. Thus, by its founding, ideal America was the most open gentile society Jews have ever encountered. Moreover, while the various immigrant groups brought their heritage of prejudice and intolerance with them, the newness of much of the American social order freed it of any long history of persecution or entrenched discrimination. As Americans built their new cities and societies, creating the new American style that went with it, they provided an unusual opportunity for those perennial outsiders of Western civilization, the Jews.

In recent years, Jews reflecting on their fortunate situation have been loath to say, "America is different" from other countries where, in due course, bitter persecution erupted. That was the boast of German Jewry until Hitler. Even in this extraordinarily humane America, there remain low rumblings that anti-semitism is alive and virulent. But America's Jews have largely found in this country not only a hospitableness they hold precious but a moral reality that they have sought to incorporate into their lives.

In many ways American Jewry is the test case of the Jewish experience of modernity generally. It has most fully realized the hopes of the Emancipation. It has made a once quite poor group quite rich; a group relatively ignorant of Western culture among its major savants and contributors; and a group of aliens very much a part, for all its minority status, of those who move and shake things.

It has also given its Jewish community two special problems. America, because of its wealth, dynamism, and long tradition of neutrality to religion exacerbates all the problems Western civilization faces about re-establishing a ground of values. In confronting this issue, American Jewry pioneers a response to the problem facing all modernized Jewries. Then, too, by its very openness, America challenges its Jews as to how best to share the goals of all Americans while preserving and enriching their distinctive Jewish identity. How can we avoid a universalism that negates the ethnic basis of our ethical passion, yet also guard against an ethnocentrism that denies the human reality that has given us such unaccustomed security?

I have sought to be faithful to both great ethical passions, discovering to my great joy that in practicing this political-religious bigamy one can be true to each of them in ways in which they both approve.

8

Our Jewish Duties
to Humanity

Contemporary Jews take citizenship so much for granted that we can hardly imagine a time when it seemed an unattainable dream. In some American Jewish families European grandparents still tell tales of growing up amid pre-Nazi persecution. Sephardim from the rural areas of North Africa or the Near East may recount more recent experience with political discrimination. The record is a long one. In 313 C.E. Christianity became the official religion of the Roman Empire, and Jews, while tolerated, were relegated to the fringes of society. Islam began in the seventh century and, shortly thereafter, Moslems instituted the first formal pattern of segregating and degrading Jews. After the First Crusade (1096 C.E.), Christian countries intensified the maltreatment of Jews, including various forms of spiritual coercion and physical violence. Not until the eighteenth century did some people argue that Jews (and other exotic social aliens) might become full participants in the life of the nation. A revolutionary change in political theory made this possible. Since it still provides the context for modern Jewish life, it deserves careful consideration.

The religious character of the premodern state made Jewish participation impossible. Thus, in Saudi Arabia today, as in all unsecularized nations (Christian and Moslem), religion and the state are thoroughly intertwined. (Islam, being organized as a "nation," not as a church, engenders an even closer relationship than does Christianity.) In such countries,

Entitled "What are our Duties to Humanity?" in *Liberal Judaism* (New York: Union of American Hebrew Congregations, 1984).

sharing an odd faith prevents one from swearing the religious oaths by which all important agreements are made. An infidel then exists outside the law, technically, an "out-law." In some European areas special legal arrangements were created to legitimize Jewish residence, and educing them from medieval legal records is a major interest of contemporary Jewish historians.

Jews could be citizens only when religion and nationality were separated, that is, when the state became secular. Once faith had nothing to do with citizenship, Jews could be equals. After 1,500 years of segregation and oppression, secularization provided Jews with the opportunity to reach their present unparalleled level of security and well-being. As a result, liberal Jews have been passionately devoted to the separation of "church and state."

The Intellectual Challenge of Citizenship

Fifteen centuries of growing anti-semitism had prepared neither Jews nor Christians for western Europe's enfranchisement of the Jews. The experience in France illustrates the difficulties Jews later faced everywhere in being emancipated.

After a revolution fought for "liberty, equality, fraternity," the French should have had no questions about Jewish rights. The revolutionaries had broken the church's tie to the state because of its identification with the old order. Instead, they looked to reason as their social guide. They therefore should have quickly given French Jews full citizenship. Such logic overlooks the power of old usage and prejudice. In fact the new French Assembly debated for three years before deciding to enfranchise the Jews.

This initial determination did not end the matter. A decade later, when Napoleon came to power, Jewish rights still troubled French officials. In 1806 Napoleon issued an imperial decree calling for an Assembly of Jewish Notables (and later a "Sanhedrin") to provide a formal answer on behalf of French Jewry to a number of questions. A certain Count Mole submitted twelve inquiries to the assembly of which three are relevant to our inquiry: "(4) In the eyes of the Jews, are the French their brethren or their enemies? (5) In either case, what duties does Jewish law prescribe toward the French who are not of their faith? (6) Do those Jews who are born in France and who are treated as French citizens regard France as their native country? Do they feel themselves obligated to defend it, to obey its laws, and to submit to all regulations of its civil code?"

Hearing these questions, American Jews often respond with outrage. How dare they suggest that Jews consider their neighbors their enemies and are not loyal to their country! Our emotion in such matters betrays our anxieties over the Gentile's perceptions of us. No matter what extraordinary contributions we make to our society—further evidence of our insecurity—nothing washes away the prejudices of our fellow citizens, or, at least, some portion of them.

Perhaps this feeling can help us imagine, two centuries later, the attitudes Jews faced when they took their first exploratory steps outside the newly destroyed ghetto wall. They encountered a populace accustomed to think of Jews as misanthropists, haters of humankind, and lovers only of their co-religionists. Not the least difficulty Jews had in responding to this charge was its unconscious origin. The civilization which had despised Jews for fifteen centuries now projected its hatred on to its victim. Getting Gentiles to acknowledge their own prejudices before presuming to make judgments about Judaism has been a major Jewish battle ever since the Emancipation.

Fashioning a Jewish Philosophy of Non-Jews

On one level, the notables of the Jewish community had little difficulty giving an answer to Napoleon. They could base themselves on the long history of Jewish loyalty to regimes that had treated them fairly. They could also see that, if the ideals of the Revolution were carried out, undreamed of opportunities would open up for the French Jewry.

In their formal statement they outlined a position later adopted by the leadership of all Jewish communities who received freedom. Here are some critical sentences taken from their protocols: (To question 4) "When the Israelites formed a settled and independent nation, their law made it a rule for them to consider strangers as their brethren. . . . A religion whose fundamental maxims are such, a religion which makes a duty of loving the stranger, a religion which enforces the practice of social virtues, must surely require that its followers should consider their fellow citizens as brethren." (To question 5) "At the present time, when the Jews no longer form a separate people [in the literal sense] but enjoy the advantage of being incorporated within the great nation France—which privilege they consider a kind of political redemption—it is impossible that a Jew should treat a Frenchman not of his religion in any other manner than he would treat one of his Israelite brethren." (To question 6) "Jeremiah [chapter 29] exhorts the Jews to consider Babylon as their country even though they were to remain there only for seventy years. He tells them to till the ground, to build houses, to sow, and to plant." Most Jews took his injunction so to heart that only a few returned with Ezra to rebuild the Temple. "In the heart of Jews the love of country is a sentiment so natural, so powerful, and so consonant with their religious opinions that, visiting in England, a French Jew considers himself as among strangers, although he may be among Jews; and the case is the same with English Jews." The answer closes by reminding the emperor of the many Jews who have fought in his campaigns against Jews of other nations and the many scars they now proudly bear as a sign of their bravery.

Beyond Politics to Doctrine

Jewish scholars and thinkers later sought to clarify the Jewish religious bases on which these positions might authentically be taken. They could not simply cite the texts exhorting Jews to be good citizens for no prophet or rabbi had ever written on Jewish duty in a democracy. How could they have? There was no democratic, secular state in their time. For all the Jewish participation in the cultural life of Hellenistic Alexandria or Moslem Spain, the Jews there had not been political equals.

Not only were Jews outsiders until modern times but for much of that time they chose isolation. In the days of the Bible, only the Jews worshiped the one God. "The nations" practiced idolatry and lived by standards the Jews found spiritually repulsive. Participation in gentile affairs then would have meant the end of ethical monotheism. The Talmud largely reflects the same attitude. In later years the antipathy of Christianity and Islam to Judaism excluded the possibility of developing a guide to Jewish citizenship.

The Emancipation required Jewish thinkers to clarify a Jew's duties to the non-Jewish society. They did this by explicating traditional Judaism's positive attitude toward humankind and by gathering the sages' few comments on the topic. They fashioned these sources into so persuasive an outlook that most modern Jews accepted it. Let us sketch in some of their central ideas.

The Ethical Implications of the Creation Story

God did not begin the world with Jews. Instead, God created humankind undifferentiated (except for having two genders) and established a covenant with it. The God of the Jews is first the God of all humanity and retains that status in all subsequent Jewish teaching. The Bible takes the ultimate worth of all people for granted; the prophets would not rail so against the nations if they did not believe that all human beings were God's covenant partners.

In the Talmud the rabbis carry forward the concept of one human family. Here is the Mishnah's statement of the exhortation given to witnesses before they testify in a capital case, "Therefore but a single man was created in the world to teach that, if anyone has caused a single soul to perish from Israel [some texts omit 'from Israel'], Scripture imputes it to him as if he had caused a whole world to perish. And he who saves a single Israelite [some texts omit 'Israelite'] soul, Scripture imputes it to him as if he had saved a whole world. Again, [but a single man was created] for the sake of peace among mankind. Now none can say to his fellow, 'My ancestor was greater than your ancestor'; and also that heretics should not say 'There are many ruling powers in heaven.' Again, [but a single man was created] to proclaim the greatness of the Holy One, blessed is He. For a man stamps

98

out many coins with one seal and they are all identical but the king of kings of kings, the Holy One, blessed is He, has stamped every man with the seal of the first man, yet none of them is like his fellow. Therefore, every one must say, 'For my sake the world was created' " (San. 4:5).

Modern Jewish thinkers added their own interpretation to this theme. Few took the Torah's creation story literally for they accepted the evolutionary view of the origins of humankind. They nonetheless steadfastly affirmed the moral values of the creation myth. They saw in its having God begin humankind with but one pair of people an early intuition of the truth that ethics is necessarily universal. Put symbolically, one Divine Parent meant that all human beings have familial obligations to one another. To limit one's ethical duties only to those of one's neighborhood or nation or religion was unethical. Human relations had to transcend all the old barriers or else no one could be truly human. By including Jews in the family of humankind, the European nations had shown the power of universal ethics to overcome prejudice. In what had happened to them, Jews could recognize the fulfillment of one of their oldest, most central ideals.

What Does the Law Enjoin Jews to Do?

This theory was bolstered by pointing to the provisions of Jewish law regarding duties to non-Jews. The Mishnah says, "For the sake of peace, impoverished idolaters are not prevented from gathering gleanings or forgotten sheaves or from the corner of the field though the Torah provides only that these be left for poor Jews" (Git. 5:8). In the Talmud, this is extended in terms of an anonymous teaching, "We support the poor among the idolaters along with the poor of Israel, and visit the sick among the idolaters along with the sick of Israel, and bury the poor among the idolaters along with the dead of Israel, for the sake of peace" (Git. 61a). While there are some other halachic passages which deal with duties to Gentiles, the notion of *mipne darche shalom*, for the sake of peace, constitutes the central theme of the subsequent discussions of this issue in Jewish law.

Several features of the later legal material are noteworthy. Some halachic authorities are troubled by the prospect of allowing non-Jews to take Jewish agricultural produce (in the Land of Israel) or benefit from Jewish charity funds. Both the produce and the money as good as belong to the poor Jews for whom they were set aside. *Tsedakah* funds in particular are a community trust whose terms may not be violated. To use such money for heathens is tantamount to stealing from the Jewish poor. Though such arguments are raised, the authorities agree that needy Gentiles are not to be denied succor because of scruples about improper disbursement.

A similar indication of the weight attached to these laws may be found in the unexpected development they underwent. They specify that, when needy Gentiles come for help along with needy Jews, we assist them. But what if the gentile poor alone solicit our aid? The medieval authorities rule that they are still to be helped "for the sake of peace" (and once again they insist that such exclusive disbursement to Gentiles is not *de facto* robbery of the Jewish poor). Considering the treatment of Jews then, this ruling, for all its likely defensive motivation, shows exceptional commitment to the interdependence of humankind.

The Jew as God's Representative

A broader theological consideration reinforced the legal tradition. Quite commonly, the rabbis call the attention of Jews to the religious impression created by their acts. They want Jews to consider what non-Jews will think of the Jewish religion when they observe Jewish behavior. It will indicate to them the sort of God the Jews have. This conception of the public consequence of Jewish deeds is termed the doctrine of *kiddush hashem*. The rabbis demand that a Jew's acts should always "sanctify God's name" (in effect, God's reputation) among people.

At its extreme, *kiddush hashem* leads to martyrdom (and is the common Hebrew term for it). Then a Jew, who normally can do anything under extreme duress except commit murder, idolatry, or sexual offenses, refuses to do what is demanded and instead accepts death. Under the extraordinary circumstances of the Middle Ages, we even hear of Jewish communities where parents killed their families and then committed suicide for *kiddush hashem*, to sanctify God's name.

Jews have discouraged martyrdom as a means of gaining God's special favor; people punish themselves enough and history has been sufficiently cruel to Jews that our sages considered it a virtue to avoid unnecessary suffering. But, in its broader connotation, *kiddush hashem* was part of everyday Jewish life. There was little more one could say to condemn an act than to call it a *chilul hashem*, a profanation of God's name, thus the opposite of *kiddush hashem*. A well known use of *chilul hashem* applies directly to our topic. "Robbery from a Gentile is more heinous than robbery from a Jew because it also involves *chilul hashem*" (Tos. San. 10:15). In Jewish conduct toward non-Jews no less than God's honor was at stake.

The positive ideal is portrayed in a legendary story about Simeon b. Shetah. He once bought an ass from an Arab. When his servants brought it home they found a costly jewel in its harness. Simeon at once ordered it returned on the grounds that he had intended to buy only the animal. This caused the Arab to proclaim, "Blessed be the God of the Jews who renders His people so scrupulous in their dealings with others" (Y., B.M. 2:5, 8c). This constitutes *kiddush hashem* at its highest.

These biblical and rabbinic traditions informed the Jewish ethos. No matter how oppressed Jews were they did not deny the basic unity of humankind. Two comments from recent centuries illustrate this even if we cannot say that their authors had Gentiles primarily in mind. Yaakov

Yitzhak was the chasidic *rebbe* of Pzhysha. His identification with the Jewish people was so intense that he was known simply as the Yehudi, the Jew. He once inquired, "Why is the stork not *kosher*? After all, the Talmud says that its name, *chasidah*, the loving one, stems from its tender concern for mate and young. Why should such a bird be ritually unclean?" He then answered himself, "The stork is not *kosher* because it gives love only to its own." Something of the same universalism is found in the Yiddish maxim created by common folk, "You must love your neighbor—even when he plays a trombone."

The Liberals' New Sense of Jewish Priorities

The liberal Jews who had developed these sources into a full-scale doctrine of democratic responsibility added a startling emphasis to it. They argued that Judaism's general ethics—its "universalism," as they termed it—was its most important and hence unchanging element. Jewish rituals and customs had altered over the centuries, as historical study demonstrated. But, they insisted, the ethical essence of Judaism had remained constant. It had not always been expressed, as, for example, in the biblical laws of slavery. But, even then, it gradually made itself felt in the abolition or the modification of the inequitable pattern, as in the case of Jewish slaves. Modern thinkers, they asserted, have merely clarified an old Jewish trust. We must reject any Jewish tradition which clashes with it, such as segregating women at services. But we ought steadfastly maintain all our Jewish ethical teachings as well as those ritual practices which enlarge our moral sensitivity.

Their program went even further. They contended that universal ethics, our duty to humankind, was the ultimate test of our Jewishness. Until then, most Jews had connected being a good Jew with punctilious observance of the commandments, particularly the rituals. The liberals now proclaimed that, in an emancipated community, how one acted toward one's fellow human beings (now largely gentile) must be the standard of our Jewish virtue.

In this reordering of Jewish priorities, these thinkers considered themselves the heirs of the prophets. They enthusiastically cited those biblical texts criticizing trust in ritual as a compensation for moral failings. In the opening chapter of his book, Isaiah says God is weary of all the Jewish rites at the Temple and desires rather that the people change their ways.

Put away your evil doings
from before Me.
Cease doing evil;
learn to do good.
Devote yourselves to justice;
aid the wronged.

101

Uphold the rights of the orphan;
and defend the cause of the widow. (1:16–17)

Jeremiah (in chapter 7) denounces his countrymen for thinking that they can be unethical with impunity as long as the Temple is in their midst. They so misunderstand God's priorities, he announces, that God will now allow His Temple to be destroyed. And Amos's denunciation of the Jews of his day uncannily sounds as if he knew modern America.

The Political Implications of Prophetic Judaism

This identification of Jewish duty with universal ethics came to be known as "Prophetic Judaism." For more than a century and a half it spoke powerfully to Jews who modernized. Remembering the discrimination which pressed down on their parents, Jews leaving the ghetto and shtetl were euphoric that ostracism was giving way to equal rights. In their physical well-being, their personal security, their educational, cultural, and economic attainments, they saw the messianic power of inclusive ethics. They had no difficulty imagining a day of universal peace, justice, and compassion if all people would only live rationally. It seemed self-evident that the ancient Jewish hope for humankind would best be fulfilled by pursuing universal goals, not parochial ones.

Despite their rhetoric, hindsight discloses that these liberals were almost certainly also motivated by an unconscious Jewish self-interest. They knew Jews were the scapegoat of Western society. If social frustrations rose, Jews would suffer. To remain secure Jews should do what they could to defuse social discontent before it became explosive. Social ethics was a preventive strategy as well as an ethical ideal. With belief and self-interest as motivations, Prophetic Judaism became a dynamic theme in modern Jewish life. Only the mutual reinforcement of these basic drives explains the record of extraordinarily disproportionate Jewish involvement in universal social causes over the past century or so.

Occasionally an additional unconscious impulse also added its special impetus, one strongly tainted by self-hate. When Jewish duty is essentially universal, one need not do acts which distinguish Jews from other people. Judaism as pure universalism can achieve assimilation without the stigma of rejecting one's heritage.

These motives all surfaced in the Jewish fascination with Marxism. Many Jews in Europe found various kinds of socialism the only realistic way of reaching the Messianic Age. They were convinced that only a complete reconstruction of the social order could eliminate the exploitation and oppression built into Western civilization. Unless ethics became politics suffering would continue.

With their acculturation, most American Jews spurned Marxist substitutes or supplements to Judaism. Instead they happily espoused a democ-

102

ratizing capitalism which gave them a steady accretion of social gains and personal freedom. What little was left of Jewish Marxism suffered irreparable damage from the actual behavior of Soviet communism and the more recently organized Marxist states. Instead of ethical paragons, they regularly showed themselves to be cynically political, humanly reprehensible, and continuingly anti-semitic.

Social Action, the Application of Prophetic Idealism

By the 1930s American Jewry felt sufficiently at home that modern Jewish ethics found a new outlet, liberal political activism. The federal government was now seen as an agent for social change. Remedying the Depression provided the initial impetus for government leadership. The ethical agenda soon expanded to include legislation outlawing discrimination and providing the underprivileged with effective opportunity. The fight against dictatorship overseas in World War II made it subsequently possible to insist on fully functioning democracy at home. The civil rights struggles of the 1960s and the bitter difference of American opinion over the Vietnam War brought these decades of ethical activism to a climax.

In these American struggles Jews were involved in numbers far beyond their proportion of the population. And the same was true of most local causes like good education, better mental health facilities, and more adequate care for the needy, handicapped, and aged. Institutionally, synagogue social action committees involved their congregations in general ethical causes while national Jewish organizations regularly passed resolutions taking a liberal stand on issues of social concern. In overwhelming numbers, American Jews had accepted civic responsibility as a major element in Jewish duty. Even disaffected Jews regularly chose the secularized path of Jewish duty, activist politics, as their surrogate for Judaism—often to find that a high proportion of their universalistic comrades were other marginal Jews.

When the Holocaust came to the forefront of Jewish consciousness in the early 1960s, it added a special Jewish incentive for participating in liberal politics. The demented Nazi program was carried out not by deranged savages but by ethically passive ordinary people. The silent German now became the model of what good people can do to create monstrous evil. If everyone had a duty to protest when inhumanities occurred, Jews surely had a special obligation to cry out. They had long been commanded. "Do not stand idly by your brother's blood" (Lev. 19:16). And they had just undergone the most awesome suffering in their history while humanity and not just the Germans stood by in silence. Joachim Prinz summed up the ethical Jewish devotion of this period when he said at the great 1963 civil rights march in Washington, "When I was the rabbi of the Jewish community in Berlin under the Hitler regime, I learned many things. The most important thing that I learned under those tragic circum-

103

stances was that bigotry and hatred are not the most urgent problem. The most urgent, most disgraceful, the most shameful, and the most tragic problem is silence."

How Shall We Live Out Our Jewish Ethics Today?

By the 1980s the almost total identification of Jewish ethics with the agenda of liberal politics had ended. Two major shifts in attitude had produced differing views about Jewish social responsibility.

The first of these arose out of disenchantment with government as a moral leader. In the sixties the automatic solution for major problems was the passage of a new law or the establishment of a new agency. Experience with this approach in employment, education, welfare, mental health, and other fields was mixed. We and our experts do not seem as competent as we once thought. The ills perpetrated by government programs, from creating dependency in the needy to building immobile bureaucracies, have not infrequently offset or overbalanced their successes.

The second change in Jewish attitudes came with the rise of an urgent sense of self-interest: If the Jewish community did not give primary attention to its own problems, its survival might be in doubt. One major reason for this new particularism was the perilous situation of the State of Israel. Without sustained, heavy American Jewish support, the Israelis would find it most difficult to maintain a viable country. Practically speaking, energies summoned in this commanding ethnic cause would not be available for universal social programs. More troublingly, universal and particular concerns could now directly clash. American Zionist leaders argued that the Israeli army depends upon American military supplies in an emergency and that a powerful United States is the only deterrent to further Soviet provocation in the Middle East. Hence they insisted that American Jews ought to support a strong United States military posture even if this meant cuts in the funding of human welfare programs.

The internal aspect of this new self-concern was the community's anxiety about its own future. The symptoms of its failing health were immediately evident: a high rate of intermarriage, a low rate of reproduction, static or declining institutional involvement, and widespread ignorance, apathy, and indifference. Externally, American culture no longer offered anything like salvation, and the increase in anti-semitic incidents and intergroup distance impelled Jews to search for their roots. A sizable minority of Jews began giving Judaism increased priority in their lives. Some particularists now demanded—in private, to be sure—that Jewish energies be exclusively devoted to Jewish causes. Others counseled a pragmatic strategy: participating in universal causes only as required to maintain our political alliances and keep us from bad repute. On the whole no new community consensus has appeared. The majority of Jews seems to accept neither a new particularism verging on self-isolation nor a universalism so devoted to humankind it ignores Jewish needs.

This ambivalent situation is unlikely soon to disappear. Contemporary liberal Judaism affirms both the universal God and the particular people Covenanted to God. We remain devotedly liberal because we personally are living testimony to the human benefits that come from actualizing universal ethics. As supreme beneficiaries of democracy, we have a special responsibility to be involved in the solution of its problems. We are also devoted Jews. The survival of our people must be one of our highest priorities. Whatever we can do for humankind must begin with our efforts to see that our own people flourishes. Yet our people's vision has always transcended its own well-being. Most Jewish generations could do little directly to contribute to this greater goal. Jews in democratic lands have an unparalleled Jewish opportunity to make our idealism felt in our nations and among humankind as a whole. We cannot say simply how Jews ought to face those social choices which seem to pit their loyalty to their people against that to humankind. Yet we know that we will not be true to the special situation in which God has placed us if we do not make the human issues of our age a major part of our Jewish duty.

9

This Land Is Our Land

What It Begat

In a place and at a time when society offers so many possibilities for cultural enrichment and apparent fulfillment, far more possibilities than anyone can "use," why should a Jew engage with Jewish life and with the Jewish community? Now that Judaism has become—for all the ties that bind us and the ideals that inspire us—a voluntary enterprise, why should the Jew "volunteer"? Where is the motive?

For a while, immigrant solidarity and fear of the stranger provided the answer. Later, helping the State of Israel or savoring the ethnic joy of our emerging American Jewish style offered adequate reward. More recently, our reaction to our passivity during the Holocaust has prompted a new Jewish vigilance. And, in addition, the turn of many Americans during this socially turbulent period from public concern to their particular roots has its Jewish parallel; we, too, have sought to reclaim our ethnic heritage.

For some Jews, these and similar motives impel great devotion to Judaism. But neither fearfulness nor nostalgia nor clannishness nor emergencies can fully answer the question of motive. These will not produce the rich culture and spirituality that have marked other great Jewish communities and that must be available if we are to attract Jews voluntaristically. Neither, by itself, will Jewish education: knowledge is one thing, caring about what one knows quite another. Stocking the cranium with Jewish data and concepts does not necessarily engender the will to be Jewish—as demonstrated by the excellent gentile students in my university courses on Judaism.

From *Moment*, vol. 9, no. 5 (May 1984).

I see only two sources of Jewish idealism that are sufficiently compelling to counteract diaspora lassitude: Zionism and religious belief. In my view, the two are inseparably united, but my argument here will be clearer if I treat them as if they were distinct.

We all know of the positive effects the State of Israel has had on our community, not the least because of its effect on the world. No other Jewish concern regularly moves American Jews to their very depths as does the fate of our Israeli kin. But ours is an unusual Zionism, for it functions most powerfully when it is negative—that is, when it moves us to repel the enemies of the State of Israel. Its positive effects appear most movingly when we visit Israel and are touched in ways we have not previously experienced or imagined possible. Returning to the United States, we may find that we have been moved to new levels of Jewish commitment, particularly to involvement in community affairs—but our Zionism does not move us to a new way of life as American Jews.

It is no small thing for people who were just a few decades back ambivalent about their Jewishness, often eager to hide from it, to find themselves willingly, eagerly taking up the public struggle for Israel's safety and welfare. But that struggle cannot be said to be a way of life, for it is about doing for others, not for ourselves. A self-respecting life cannot, in the end, be built on so servile a premise.

If, for example, we turn to the positive Zionist *"mitzvot"*—learning Hebrew and moving to Israel—we can see how far involvement with Israel remains from informing the ways we live. Introductory courses in Hebrew are regularly the most popular offering in adult Jewish education programs. But the number of American Jews who attain anything remotely resembling bilingualism remains pitifully small. Even among the *literati*, Hebrew is hardly ever a primary form of Judaic expression. And, so far as immigration to Israel, *aliyah*, is concerned, the facts are equally dismal. The overwhelming majority of American Jews simply have no interest in *aliyah*, not even in their retirement. They are therefore very far from perceiving America as a way-station in Jewish life, from building American Judaism into a preparation for life in Israel.

Plainly, the prime motive for this latter-day territorialism, this attachment to where-we-are, is materialistic. Never have so many Jews had it so good, economically and socially. And the sizable migration of Israeli Jews to the United States attests that we are not the only Jews so motivated. Yet our general rejection of *aliyah* cannot be explained exclusively in terms of avarice, nor even, more simply, in terms of inertia. Account must be also taken of the very deep-seated Jewish appreciation of the American democratic ideal.

For something unique in human history is happening in this country. What the French first prophetically enunciated and then bungled, what the English gloriously proclaimed and then stifled, has here become manifest. In political terms, it is the simple notion of equal rights for every

107

citizen, including the right to participate in deciding who shall govern and for how long. In social terms, which are not less important, it is the idea that people of the most diverse backgrounds, interests and commitments can live together in harmony, work together for the common good— and not need to obliterate their differences. Here, tolerance is a uniquely compelling civic virtue, fanaticism and dogmatism are social blights.

Considering human history, considering the conditions that even today prevail in most of the world, democracy is hardly an ideal that can be taken for granted. And considering what Jews remember, the American commitment to democracy and its expression, both political and social, in this country, are powerful magnets. The sacred myth of this country begins with the Pilgrims, come here as religious refugees, the Hebrew Scriptures their text. From that experience and that text, America has derived its sense of moral obligation; hence Jews have here found a unique compatibility and felt a unique devotion.

In recent years, some Jews have become so intent on asserting the primacy of Jewish interests that they have come to deny that we ought to be significantly involved in general American concerns. The task of Jews, they have insisted, is to defend the ever-threatened Jewish interest; it is a snare and a delusion for Jews to invest in the general welfare.

Such vulgar ethnocentrism deserves public attention and requires public rebuke. It is unbecoming to encounter such ingratitude among people who profess so to rejoice in freedom. Unbecoming, and immoral—and we would denounce such a perspective were we to encounter it in others.

Are we by now not sufficiently secure in our American Jewish distinctiveness so that no one will accuse me of "assimilationism" if I assert that it is time for us to rekindle the old American Jewish passion for democracy? No other diaspora land has ever thought of itself as a new nation, composed of people of diverse national and racial origins. No other country has taken such great pains to live up to its doctrine that religious bigotry is unpatriotic and that minorities should have full equality. For more than 200 years now, and despite recurrent spasms of prejudice and xenophobia, America has extended ever-greater equality to ever-greater numbers. With all its failings, this country remains the greatest exemplar of democracy the world has ever known. More, it remains humanity's best hope that political freedom can not only work but can be ever more fully realized.

American Jews love this country because they love its ideals. They see in the realization of the American vision the fulfillment of many of their Jewish hopes and the remedy of much of their historic Jewish pain. They even find in America's obsessive moral masochism something of their own idealistic *krechtzing*, a shared recognition that no matter how much we have done that is good and right and wise, we remain woefully short of the Messianic Age.

Should America's ethical lapses one day overcome her ability to resuscitate her idealism, God forbid, then *aliyah* and the preparation for it

108

might become a reality for us. Under such circumstances, we might even learn Hebrew. Until then, for all our devotion to the State of Israel and its/our dreams, we overwhelmingly propose to work out our Jewish destiny here. For America, too, offers an inspiring challenge to Jewish idealism. Surely one major cause of our occasional racking disagreements with certain policies of one or another Israeli administration stems from this Americanized moral sense of the proper Jewish use of power. We are a generation committed centrally to folk-faithfulness—but we also believe that being a Jew must always mean exemplifying Jewish ideals. We have already come a long way in learning to live up to both these imperatives; may our wisdom ever be adequate to prevent a clash between them.

Still, if the American Jewish community is to reach for Jewish quality and excellence, it requires a driving source of Jewish responsibility. In our time, that source can only be some form of Jewish faith and practice.

I say that "only" Jewish faith and practice will do for us not merely because religion rather than nationality is the accepted form of American distinctiveness, but because of what has been happening to authority and value in western culture generally. We have been going through a seismic intellectual shift in these regards. Secularism, which was once our surrogate for traditional religion, indeed so great an improvement on it—so we believed—that we invested it with messianic power, no longer holds much promise. A century or more of secularization has left the west disappointed, perhaps even depressed.

Yet our devotion to human betterment persists even as the vehicle of secularism grinds to a halt. Increasingly, modern men and women turn back to religion, hoping there to find the energizing values that can fuel our highest hopes. Some, of course, come to religion because unlimited freedom has cast them into panic; they seek refuge in constricting orthodoxies, authoritarian leaders and enveloping communities. But far more broadly, the renewed interest in religion reflects our effort to regain confidence in the validity of our old, deep-rooted intuition about the ultimacy of high human value and social concern. We will not, we do not accept that such concern is merely another "alternative life style."

There are those who would dismiss this turn because it can lead to alien places. Dissatisfied with over-achieving Jewish secularism, some of our young desert us not to change the world (via revolution, the university or liberal politics) but for the certainties of sects and cults. They assert that their spiritual quest cannot be satisfied within our secular midst.

Already, at the turn of this century, in the wake of the Kishinev massacre, we abandoned our belief in the hands-on operator of history described in the books of Deuteronomy and Judges. And then, within a few decades, like a powerful exclamation point should anyone have missed the earlier horror, came the Holocaust. By mid-century, most of us were, as many of us still say we are, agnostics. The only "God" in whom we allowed ourselves to believe was humanity itself. And why not? What need had we of any other god? Did not all educated, cultured people know their human duty?

Plainly they did not and do not. Our utter faith in the goodness of human nature and the competence of human rationality has sustained intolerable battering; our optimistic trust in humanity has collapsed. The Holocaust has become the enduring symbol of our human as well as our unutterable Jewish loss.

Shall we, then, believe nothing? Are the nihilists right? Is one value as good as another, does nothing make sense, is all striving equally meaningless, empty?

Surprisingly, we resist such grim conclusions, and we resist them by invoking God; in the face of the challenge to our hopes, something elementally Jewish reasserts itself. Reaching deep into some ultimate recess of our soul, we know that our dreams for ourselves and all humankind are not deluded. We know that our lives are touched by a cosmic standard of goodness and decency that properly commands our response. When we can muster the courage to respond to this hint of the transcendent—the ineffable reality our tradition calls God—we also recognize that we in our day are only doing what our Jewish forebears did in theirs. Jewish duty, at its depths, is our way of acknowledging the utter ultimate supremacy of quality in the universe and of expressing it in our lives.

It is for such sometimes dim and often unconscious metaphysical reasons that Jews—like others—have been turning to their religion. We seek to regain the grounding for an idealism that will not be quashed. One unanticipated consequence of this centripetal turn among American Jews has been the rise of a vigorous Orthodoxy, impressive less for its numbers than for its devoutness. While it is true that sentimentality rather than discipline characterizes the majority of those affiliated with Orthodox Jewish institutions, the emergence of a learned, observant, believing American Orthodoxy has added new strength to our community. Much of this new strength derives from the survivors who came here after World War II from the old heartland of Ashkenazi Jewish life. Many of these had long been observant Jews. (Indeed, that was one reason they had not previously joined the general migration to these religiously defiling shores.) Secularization did not tempt them; sure of their faith, they did not come here in search of a new faith to replace the old.

Today, after some decades of economic progress and social accommodation, their attitude towards the gentile world still ranges from wariness through fearfulness to hostility. They often do not identify with the American ideal. For them, the United States is another barely distinguishable stop on the long, sad trek of our Exile.

I do not know whether time and contiguity will bring them, as it has generations of immigrants before them, to a more positive accommodation to America. In the meantime, we must now count as a significant part of our core community a deeply devoted group that does not substantially share the general social ideals of most American Jews.

110

And, as in the State of Israel, the Orthodox far right has much more influence than its numbers would appear to warrant. In our case, that is largely due to its stiffening effect on the greater Orthodox community, those who often describe themselves as "Modern Orthodox." Left to itself, this group, numerically preponderant, believes in the acceptance of whatever is worthwhile in modern society, with Torah—that is, the law and its sensibilities—as the arbiter of that integration. The piety and observance of the caring Modern Orthodox are impressive in their own terms; beyond that, Modern Orthodoxy has particularly happy implications for the future of the American Jewish community, because most of its members are native born, the products of our homes and our day schools, people who accept the American ideal and have become an important source of our Jewishly concerned community leadership, lay and professional.

But the "stiffening effect" I have mentioned points to potential problems, as the Modern Orthodox seek to reconcile the competing claims on their commitment. Indeed, the emergence of the several Orthodoxies into community prominence may prove especially problematic if and as religion becomes the major motivating force for our community. American Jews, including many affiliated with Orthodoxy, have not only modernized but Americanized. That means that they accept the American ideal that individuals have unchallengeable rights, that all groups ought to work together in equality, and that compromise is usually our best road to the good.

Such notions have little standing in any orthodoxy, secular or religious. As a result, we now face increasing polarization in our religious community. At one time, the polarization was largely confined to a small group who denied that Orthodox rabbis could legitimately work together with non-Orthodox rabbis in so-called "umbrella groups." Today, the clashes are broader and more serious—as witness the debate over the legitimacy of non-Orthodox conversions to Judaism. It requires no gift of prophecy to see how serious the intensification of such disputes might be for our future, not the least because the major source of our hope may equally bring tragedy instead.

I do not see that this rift between a spiritually experimental community and an absolutist leadership can ever be easily resolved. In our community, the critical issue is women's rights in Jewish practice—most dramatically, the right of women to be ordained. With the decision of the Conservative movement to join the Reform and Reconstructionist groups in permitting women to be rabbis, the will of the community has, in effect, superseded the formal judgment of the most widely accepted *halachic* sages. If that principle continues to dominate American Jewish self-consciousness and behavior, polarization will intensify. At the very least, it will put a very heavy strain on the gingerly worked out American mechanisms of intracommunal religious cooperation.

The liberal willingness to risk such an admittedly lamentable confrontation is not simple willfulness. It is, instead, the necessary consequence

111

of our acceptance of much of the American ideal as instructive for our Jewish faith. The people, we now affirm, not only its scholars, is properly a major participant in determining what constitutes Jewish duty and responsibility. Our institutions and their leaders, to be sure, must provide us religious guidance—but at the same time they must be as responsive to the popular intuition of what God demands of us as they are to Jewish precedent. In the nature of things, and especially of American things, we will not all have the same response to the Holy nor an identical notion of how best to express its mandates in our lives. We are quite likely to disagree as to what personal and corporate actions are "good for the Jews." The different paths of our piety will generate much more debate than our religious community has traditionally been able to tolerate. For some of us, the diversity will be painful. But if I am correct about our developing sense of the spiritual implications of democracy, most of us will see in the new Jewish pluralism happy signs of both Jewish vitality and Jewish faithfulness.

Granting power to the people can have baleful consequences. Democracies are plagued by people who do not vote, who remain uninformed, who spurn their political responsibilities. A religious community that permits such sloth is likely to be flabby and weak, hardly worthy of bearing the name of that tradition whose adherents, by their utter dedication, carried it through the wilderness we call history.

The power of Orthodoxy derives from a different source, from Orthodoxy's sure knowledge of what God wants from God's people, here and now. Each Jew knows, then, that nothing less is at stake in Jewish duty than obeying or defying the one single sovereign of creation. Because Jews knew that God wanted them to be Jews, they were indomitable. So they outlasted enemies and overcame crises, brought us to this day. Such is the awesome power of orthodox belief.

But we cannot hide from the fact that the same absolutism that produces so much good can also lead to extremism, dogmatism, fanaticism. For most American Jews, such behavior is so repugnant that they shun any system that might permit it—even if that system promises at the same time to arouse unbounded Jewish devotion.

These dialectically related problems, arising directly from the strengths of each religious sector, set the critical agenda for our community. From my liberal perspective, Orthodoxy needs to tell our community what it believes Torah-true Jews can learn from democracy, not merely how they can use it. Until now, the Modern Orthodox have been content to proceed out of a mixture of pragmatism and a lack of power. They had little to lose and much to gain by limiting their responsibility for the community's spiritual welfare to their own adherents. But now that they have come of age, it is time for them to think through, for everyone's benefit, just what place democracy may authentically have in their vision of the American Jewish community.

At the same time, the non-Orthodox need to clarify and demonstrate just how they propose to motivate significant Jewish dedication and discipline in a democratized Jewish faith. Thus far, they have been living off the Jewish capital of the immigrant generations and the democratic enthusiasm of their optimistic offspring. They could (and did) experiment boldly in the rough confidence that American Jewish life was basically healthy. But now the signs of our environmentally induced pathology are too great to ignore and the challenges of Jewish authenticity and continuity cannot easily be evaded. What, then, do the non-Orthodox affirm with sufficient conviction so that, despite the emphasis on personal rights and community tolerance, we may feel ourselves required to dedicate our lives to Jewish pursuits?

To answer these questions, and to fulfill the Jewish promise of this extraordinary community in this extraordinary place, both groups will need a special measure of creative sagacity, will need to find ways to bind us to one another in love and communal devotion. That is the only way we shall be able to make of this house a true home, worthy of what America has taught us, worthy of what our tradition instructs us.

10

Between Anarchy
and Fanaticism

Two concerns prompted Thomas Jefferson and other founders of our democracy to distance religion from government. In the spirit of the Enlightenment, they esteemed human nature most highly, trusting that as knowledge replaced ignorance and superstition, the goodness latent in each soul would emerge. They coupled this idealistic view of humankind with a profound revulsion at the long, ugly history of religious warfare and persecution. Ideologically, they believed that the classic religions had probably done more human harm than good, so people free to think for themselves would likely be far more decent than the pious of recent centuries. Practically, many of America's earliest settlers had come to the New World to escape religious persecution. They could not dissociate religious liberty from political freedom. Of course, they initially wanted it only for themselves and their kind. But the push of prudence confronting pluralism and the pull of the Golden Rule led Americans to universalize religious liberty, though not unreluctantly so.

Were intuition and experience so mutually reinforcing today, we would not be as perplexed as we are about just where the proper exercise of religion becomes the practice of politics. History has forced many of us to surrender the Enlightenment's optimisim about human nature. As we now see it, the founders' deism evolved into secularism. That term may be academically indefinable and its cultural triumph was surely not all-pervasive. Nonetheless, by mid-twentieth century the Judeo-Christian commitments which once morally powered American life had lost their

Published in abridged form in *The Christian Century*, July 15–22, 1987.

dominance in our social ethos. Civic religion—if it may properly be called "religion"—was about all that inspired our political leaders while our culture heroes regularly disdained the traditional faiths as obsolete or analgesic. Most Americans had become practical realists believing that applied reason and creative politics would do more to bring the Messianic Age than would prayer and piety.

But detaching Enlightenment secularity from its biblical roots and putting humankind essentially on its own, has been disillusioning. Instead of increasing justice, educated Germans, dialectically enlightened Russians, and the best and brightest of American leaders have taught us how much evil human beings can do, even when acting with the best intent. Amazingly attractive and competent people regularly display shocking moral insensitivity, amorality or malevolence. No day's news seems without fresh moral trauma and our character as a society seems in significant decline. Even the self offers little comfort, for we have turned out to be more the problem than its solution.

With education for character a far more complex and frustrating task than the Jeffersonians imagined, the optimisim of the Enlightenment seems untenable.

Existentially, the reining in of human self-confidence has led our generation to a passionate search for a new sense of self and ultimate reality. And it has allowed religious leaders to turn against their secular critics the very charge with which they once chastised the classic faiths: that those who promised to lead us to messianic fulfillment have, in fact, been our betrayers. Many Americans now agree that an ethos unrooted in biblical faith or the equivalent does not produce the moral striving demanded by the prophets and sages of the Bible. Thus, unless we reappropriate America's old Judeo-Christian spiritual base we cannot hope to rebuild our country's ethical morale and regain our pride in it. This mood has brought conservative religious groups to the forefront of our American political life, the North American manifestation of a spiritual-cultural phenomenon widely observed in countries from Iran westward to Asia.

It is important for this discussion to emphasize that liberal religion as well as secularity has been denounced by the traditionalists. They have condemned liberal religionists for attending more to the lessons of the times than to their timeless knowledge of God. Worse, suborning the very faith which might have shielded us from social iniquity, liberalism has given religious sanction to acts prior generations plainly called sin. Therefore, the religious right calls on the liberal faiths for repentance, not instruction on how to succeed in modernity.

In the religious right's proclamations of prophetic righteousness, a note of triumphalism may often be heard. It arises from memories of the scornful way in which our leading educational and cultural institutions treated traditional religion in recent decades. A neutral secularity would merely have relegated all religion, liberal and traditional, to the private realm. As secularity attained preeminence in our culture, it dismissed

liberal religion as irrelevant while scornfully deriding religious conservatism as benighted and obscurantist, if not dangerous. Not long ago, professors and *literati* felt commissioned to save the naive public from the
myths of its scripture and the superstition of its ritual. This rankling treatment engendered a searing resentment now being expressed. For today
the facts appear to vindicate the traditionalists. The supposedly old-
fashioned and outmoded faiths grow and flourish while the modernist
liberal ones decline, apparently having little distinctive to say to a deeply troubled generation. In this unexpected reversal of fortune the religious right sees God's just reward to those who maintained their inherited
religious standards while others went hankering after society's new-old
allurements.

Ironically, the challenge of the religious conservatives has now begun
to revivify the liberals. The conservatives have been most effective attack-
ing the moral vacuum underlying our present social ills. But as they have
turned from critique to legislation, they have resurrected the concerns
which created liberalism. Should some people's orthodoxy be forced upon
those who conscientiously hold different standards of personal and social
virtue? Suddenly, the mortal sins of classic religion become newly relevant: Gallileo and Spinoza, heresy hunting and inquisition, the suppres-
sion of free inquiry and intolerance of dissent, all for God's sake. Liberal
religion was born to dissociate God's name and God's people from such
practices. Its strength arises from celebrating human freedom as God's
great gift to us, our finest spiritual resource living, as we do, across the
chasm separating God's own truth from humankind's religions.

The American religious community is itself, therefore, beset with tension. On the left, religious liberals see the various spiritual orthodoxies
inevitably productive of extremism. And every act of spiritual zealotry—
like bombing abortion clinics—awakens in them the spector of religious
fanatics controlling America. In that mood, the slightest hint of an in-
fringement upon the separation of church and state must be fought to save
our country from impending obscurantist theocracy.

That paranoid fantasy has an equally corrosive counterpart on the
right. If Americans are not educated, industrious and sober, if our streets
are violent and our sexuality pagan, if our family life is unstable and our
personalities unsound, in short, if America has lost its moral stature and
thus its national self-respect, it is due to those who prate of freedom and
thereby sow anarchy, most treacherously, the liberal religionists. So every
lover of God and America must rally to defeat those who condone everything because they seem to believe nothing.

These ghostly figures, religious fanatics and spiritual and ethical nihilists, haunt our theological discussions of what religious freedom means
in America today. I have no illusion that, by this exercise in raising them
from the pit of our unconscious, I shall thereby exorcise them. I only hope
that by encouraging us to face our wild imaginings I may make it some-

what easier for us to distinguish them from reality, as difficult as that is to discern.

My theological approach to this conflict begins from a common assertion of religious self-respect, namely, that religion ought not look to secular disciplines to assign it its role in helping determine our social policy and ought vigorously to resist the frequent efforts to tell it to stand at the distant sidelines. Rather, like many religionists of the left and the right, I believe we must play a far more significant role in the life of our culture than we recently have if our democracy is to restore the ground of value which long gave it its strong moral tone.

But beyond this initial statement of unity, the two religious perspectives radically and disturbingly divide. Though both proceed theologically, they do so in utterly incompatible universes of discourse.

To begin with the camp in which I may be found, religious liberals appreciate pluralism and tolerate divergent life styles because they know that theirs is a limited truth. Indeed, they see all religion deriving as much from human spiritual striving and creativity as from God's instructive presence. They know enough of God's truth to devote their lives to it, perhaps even to seek to share its benefits with others who could benefit from its truth. But that truth being refracted through human finitude, they cannot consistently insist that their version of it must now become the one way for everyone—and be enforced by government. For just as they are Divinely commanded and spiritually committed in their way, self and soul and conscience may lead others to different forms of God's service. This openness to the human diversity of religious insight, this willingness to appreciate and even learn from others, is the glory of religious liberalism, keeping it forever fresh.

Traditional religion speaks in more certain terms. Its holy books are God's own words, not merely inspired literature. In them God has given humankind specific, clear instruction for individual and social conduct. The exemplars of the faith have taught God's own truth in their lives and the classic exegetes have faithfully explicated its meaning in succeeding generations. True, every religion has had discord and its forms have changed with time. But legitimate pluralism and diversity have accepted the discipline of God's word or been recognized as heretical. True, there are limits on the demands that can be made of sinners and every person's conscience deserves some respect. But to cultivate a social neutrality toward God's fundamental teachings adds to the sinfulness of our time and denies a proper concern for all humankind. This certainty in knowing God's one, true way generates the courage to stand against the majority and endure any suffering. It is the glory of traditional religion.

Religious liberals and traditionalists have utterly divergent intuitions of ultimate truth. There is no theological way of reconciling these different understandings of God's and people's role in creating our religions and hence of their appropriate social assertiveness. So, too, no tactical procedures, like getting to know one another or dialoguing in good will, for all their intrinsic worth and moral significance, will overcome so fundamental a disagreement.

Realistically, then, we must expect to continue living with considerable religious tension. As long as present conditions prevail, our clashing views of religious truth and their diverse social entailments will keep bringing us into conflict. Expecting this may keep us from being shocked that our views on social betterment are strongly opposed by others. Perhaps a benign providence will enable us to learn from our experiences how to mitigate the acrimony such confrontations commonly arouse and how, also, each in integrity to our own faith, to create new patterns of living that reasonably accommodate the views of others.

I do not consider this continuing lack of religious serenity a major threat to our democratic future. It should rather give us greater insight into the moral daring our founders displayed by separating religion and government. They did not erect their symbolic "wall" because they disparaged religion. Rather, they considered it self-evident that a reality transcending nature validated democracy by mandating concern for the common welfare and respect for every individual. Because belief empowered and thus shaped political life, they granted all religions the right of free exercise. Knowing the human desire to dominate, they also courageously required the state to refrain from coopting religion's power and insisted that our government refrain from infringing upon its operation. They even made it possible for some uncommon believers to be exceptions to the nation's laws, a breathtaking acknowledgment of the power of religious belief. And the price of such benign disinterest by the state was that the faiths refrain from intruding credal matters into our political affairs.

Let us face up to the inherent instability of this odd arrangement. It seeks to unite two contraries, a positive regard for religion in theory and a complete indifference to it in government practice. True, for a long time this instability manifested itself only in the exceptional situation. A vague culture-Protestantism effectively provided an officially unestablished but conventionally expected basis for our society. More recently, as disbelief and secularity began to dominate our universities and cultural life, as minorities became more insistent upon their rights and American religiosity became more radically variegated, the old pragmatic center has not held. And now, the resurgence of religious orthodoxies has brought to the fore the issue of the religious ground of democracy and its effect upon our social planning.

As I see it, Jefferson and his co-workers displayed further creative genius by not seeking to resolve this problem. Clearly, they gave us no rule by which to mediate the conflicts arising from the state's positive need for religion despite its legal distance from it. Perhaps, they did so out of political shrewdness, knowing the futility of seeking to forestall the problems future centuries would bring. They surely had no model for the place of religion in their ideal republic since they were convinced that the previous arrangements had been disastrous for the common weal. They simply left it to the democratic process to resolve future conflicts between our religions and our government. I assume they could accept so indeterminate a structure because of their confidence in democracy. What the Constitution or the Bill of Rights could not specify or only ambiguously indicate, the ongoing give and take of an engaged citizenry would slowly clarify, altering its judgments as time and experience demanded. Politically, they were pragmatists, though morally they remained idealists. It is an unphilosophic combination of standards, but one which, I am convinced, can hardly be improved on for those who would govern democratically but humanely.

Our generation is less sanguine about the practice of democracy than were the Jeffersonians, and the high emotions of our politics of confrontation testify to our insecurity. How, then, shall we idealists who are also determined to be realists find the courage to walk the open, uncertain way they marked out for us? Seeking to serve God, where can we find compelling reason to treat with civility the arguments and the people we know to be profoundly wrong?

To begin with, though we have had to give up Jefferson's moral confidence in a rationally enlightened humankind, we have good reason to share his other motive for separating government from religion, namely, humankind's tragic experience with melding the state's unlimited power and religion's absolute truth. Though we no longer see classic wars of religion, most Americans are repelled that religion is used to exacerbate the conflicts between Irish Protestants and Catholics, Lebanese Christians and Moslems, the Israeli right-wing Orthodox and Palestinian Christians and Moslems, as well as Indian Hindus and Sikhs and Pakistani Moslems. Surely the pseudo-religions of our time, communism and Naziism, have acted with equal if not greater inhumanity. But they, at least, made no claim of fealty to a God whose supreme concern is peace. So, too, when religious leaders like the Ayatollah Khomeini and Meir Kahane, for all their differences, similarly propose to run a country strictly by what they understand to be God's revealed word, and hence to do so undemocratically, most American believers become deeply troubled. Conscience, for all its intimations of the Transcendent, is outraged by the inhumanity regularly resulting from mixing government and religion. It thus bids us maintain a critical distance between them.

Moreover, we can draw on an experience unavailable to the authors of our religious liberty, namely, two hundred years of American history. Their bold experiment in separation has, on the whole, succeeded remarkably well. It has kept America free of religious wars, persecution and established intolerance. It has enabled us, with spasms of regression, to steadily overcome prejudices entrenched for centuries and to be increasingly humane to those whose faiths seem to us odd or even offensive. It has fostered an ethos in which most Americans see religion as a beneficent contributor to our nation's social welfare. And it has largely benefitted the

119

life of the faiths themselves. Forced to rely on persuasion and example, rather than on government support, American religions exhibit a vitality and personal significance unmatched in most other societies.

I see no contradiction between this eulogistic description of our religious situation and my prior lament about the decline of American belief and its deleterious social consequences. American religion, in my estimation, has weathered western civilization's turn to secularity comparatively well and that, I think, is largely due to its need to stand on its own.

But I am also speaking out of my personal experience of the swing of the religious-secular pendulum from one side to the other. Growing up as a child in the 1930s in Columbus, Ohio—no home then of aggressive religious orthodoxy—I regularly felt the coercion of the dominant Protestant mentality. I attended the Heyl Avenue Elementary School. I realized one day that the song we were expected to sing as we marched into assembly was "Onward Christian Soldiers." In high school, years later, our principal did not hesitate, when chiding me for my immaturity, to call me to fulfill the injunction of Scripture, that is, of Paul, to give up childish things and act like an adult. Were America a Christian country, as the administrators I encountered took for granted, then we non-Christian patriots might well have to find a way to participate in a religion we did not share. But we were also being taught that all citizens, regardless of religion, had equal rights in this country. To all of us who did not share the dominant though unevangelical Protestantism, the secularization of public education and thus of all civic life was a liberating ideal.

After World War II, the pendulum shifted. Secularity seized the cultural sway from Protestantism, to some extent carrying its revolution so far it destroyed its own moral foundations. We are now seeking through our present democratic disputes to determine just where the line between civic secularity and religious practice should be drawn. In trying to do so, the evils of the present ought not erase from memory—it certainly cannot erase them from mine—the evils of the prior stage. American secularity came to power because of religion's failure to respect the simple human rights Americans have long felt everyone had. If secularity itself now requires reining in, it ought not come about by losing the human gains an expansion of freedom brought our citizenry. Indeed, with American religion and secularity becoming increasingly diverse, no single religious position can hope to speak for us all. Any practice so bland as to be unobjectionable will surely be too empty to rectify our lack of spirituality.

Religious liberals, who claim to find God in human experience, should find the two centuries of this American experiment with religious openness normative. For them democracy has been revelatory, teaching how religious institutions themselves can best serve God and indicating how each person's God-given individuality can be combined with that of quite diverse others to build a moral social life.

The same cannot easily be said of the classic faiths. For them, history dare not usurp the supreme authority of God's given word. Yet human ex-

120

perience does have an important though subsidiary role in religious ortho-doxies. On the simplest level, they have achieved much of their recent success by learning the current fashions for successful communication. Their content, too, has not been unaffected by socio-cultural develop-ments, as their present celebration of the joy of marital sexuality indicates. More important, they know that Americans will largely judge the value of their faith by its fruits in human relations. When, to give a recent example, his superiors removed the Roman Catholic archbishop of Seattle from ar-eas of leadership where his soul had led him to gentle yet prophetic dis-sent from them, many pious Americans were appalled.

Thomas Jefferson may well have been America's greatest political thinker and draftsman, but Abraham Lincoln, I suggest, remains our model believer. By the conservative standards of his day, he seemed almost an infidel, refusing to attend a church or even to avow Christian faith. But no one then or now, in a far less religious age, doubts the utter depth of his devotion to humankind and the awesome responsibilities that can lay upon us. Something like Lincoln's faith runs strongly through the Ameri-can psyche. Its persistence goes far to explain why, though institutional affiliation remains low, public opinion surveys consistently show Ameri-cans overwhelmingly affirming religious beliefs. Most traditional religious groups in this country can, I think, find ways of learning from this elemen-tal American commitment to humaneness.

In the years ahead, as we walk the uncertain road of religious free-dom, it would be of great help to all Americans if each of the contending wings of American religiosity would clarify its social doctrine.

Liberals have already valuably explored for us the spiritual virtues of human freedom and creativity. They now need to make plain why their demythologization of sin and commandment does not eventually lead on to a destructive anarchy. In a time when freedom is regularly abused, what limits do they place on the exercise of the individual will? What do they consider an irresponsible, irreligious exercise of personal autonomy and how do they propose to teach and exemplify their doctrine of religious constraint?

Conservatives have tellingly demonstrated the spiritual fruits of faith-fulness to God's expressed will. They now need to explain why a doctrine of inerrancy is not likely to lead on to the sinfulness and profanation of fanaticism. What value does their understanding of God's revelation place upon democracy? What sort of freedom is appropriate in their midst and how much difference in other people can they grant full dignity?

Few theological tasks could be as critical for our time as these: teach-ing us how, while loving freedom, to mandate high human standards; or how, while maintaining God's truth, to accommodate variety and dissent.

Social freedom of religion is not a condition achieved once and for all by a statute in Virginia or by statements in the Constitution. It is today what it has always been, an incomparable American adventure, a coura-geous effort to solve in life what cannot be reconciled in theory. And it has ennobled the existence of this great, diverse American people for two shining centuries. In great measure, we owe this to the creative genius of Jefferson and his compatriots, and it is the basis of our enduring gratitude to them.

11

Judaism and the
Secular State

The logic of religious utterance is admittedly odd, but the range of constructs which can simultaneously be contained within the legal mind is equally unexpected. First the United States Supreme Court prohibited the practice or teaching of religion in American public schools. That decision, climaxing years of litigation, carried such an air of finality about it that the proponents of school prayer abandoned further court action and sought legislative redress instead. With the failure of the Becker amendment, it seemed, an era ended. Yet at the same time as it uttered its definitive "No," the Court, or rather several of its justices, took the occasion to indicate that they did not by their prohibition intend to oppose teaching "about" religion in state schools. To the contrary, the justices specifically commended such instruction and suggested that competent school personnel look into certain specified subject areas for newly authorized offerings.[1] Thus, while locking and barring one door more firmly than many a separationist had dared expect, the justices simultaneously provided another entry for religion into the public school system which opens farther than the eye can see at present. So indeed a new era begins.

What should be done with this new-found public pedagogic freedom? This question comes with particular poignancy to believing American Jews. Their tradition has long emphasized the great virtue of education and they have had a magnificent experience pursuing it in the American public school. What they found there was not merely economic access to the social order from which they had so long been barred. Because of the unique American separation of church and state, religion had no place in the public school and, thus, the school was the place where American Jews first found effective social and human equality. That is why they viewed, generally with great satisfaction, the progress made in recent years to eliminate the remnants of religious practice and indoctrination which still persisted in the public school.[2] Now they must face up to the possibility of schools that will consciously seek to teach about religion. If there is anxiety in the Jewish heart at this development, it is because such instruction will have all the power and prestige of the state behind it.

The Power of the State

The might of the state is critical to this discussion. The issue is obviously not whether private schools may teach about religion. The right to private education has long been established as consistent with American democracy. The issue is precisely centered on the public school, and it is hardly a volitional institution. Once a parent does not choose to make private provision for the education of his child, the law in all its majestic power—no less great for not being blatantly brandished—takes over. Public educators do not like to think of themselves as agents of the state in the full coercive potential of a role more commonly associated with the police or tax collectors. Yet the full executive power of the government stands behind them. Without it they would be compelled radically to revise their programs.[3] Indeed, what has largely concerned the Supreme Court, as the essays in this volume by Ball and La Noue *inter alia* make abundantly clear, is what the government through its educational officials may impose on the child. Let us not dodge the reality: legal compulsion is the foundation of American public education.

Now that governmental power and prestige may be placed behind programs of instruction about religion, what guidance might the believing Jew offer to officials who are considering implementing this new understanding of American democratic procedure? More specifically, what light can Jewish theology (with all the methodological difficulties involved in this formulation) throw upon the proper relation of the state to educating about religion?[4] Three questions seem logically to require answers: (1) Since the authority of the state is the critical factor in this program, what attitude did traditional Judaism take to human governments, Jewish and non-Jewish? (2) How did it view their responsibility for education? (3) How might these views guide believing Jews today to seek a responsible answer to the problem of teaching about religion in the public school?

Judaism's View of Government

The traditional Jewish attitude toward states is inevitably dialectical. It cannot be categorically propositional, for biblical Judaism affirms fundamentally both that God is the undisputed Sovereign of all creation and fulfills this sovereignty in human history through individuals and social institutions (without thereby infringing on human freedom). The first belief sets limits to the authority of human governments; the second authorizes them.

The Sovereignty of God

The universality of God's sovereignty in early Israelite belief is still a matter of debate among students of the Bible. Minimalist estimates concede only that God was already in the days of the Judges the exclusive God of the Hebrew people; others now argue that Hebrew monotheism originates with the Patriarchs.[5] More important is the dimensional question. This God, apparently from the earliest days, transcends nature and may not be identified with anything in it. That is in many ways God's most characteristic attribute. It gives rise to the unrelenting fight against idolatry which some consider central to the biblical experience.[6] It is equally the source of that other unprecedented biblical passion, that human kings are themselves fully subject to God's law. They may not, as in other nations, seek to identify themselves with God, nor insist that what they do is necessarily God's will. The seer-prophet who authenticates Hebrew monarchy and in increasing glory, until its disastrous end, stands over against it in judgment and rebuke is the incarnation of God's claim to undivided ultimate loyalty.[7]

No wonder then that when the Hebrews request a king, God is heard to say, "They have rejected Me from being King over them" (1 Sam. 8:7). God alone should be the Hebrews' immediate ruler as in the wilderness or in the period of early settlement when God raised up occasional leaders to serve the Divine purposes in times of crisis. To impose a lasting human government between the ruling, transcendent God and the chosen people seemed blasphemy. That sense of limit to human self-government is surely at the heart of this classic chapter. It is so much a continuing reality in Jewish religious thought that centuries later, after the Exile, it reappears in Ezra's validation of Jewish existence without political autonomy as already evidenced in the changes made in Zechariah's proclamation to Zerubbabel.[8] There, too, the ideal Israelite king, the Messiah, is not an autonomous *Übermensch*, but one who rules in God's name to effect God's law. God alone is truly Ruler, Sovereign, Governor.

Yet the other side of the covenantal understanding of religion is also affirmed. Though God is transcendent, God is not normally withdrawn from creation. God cares for it and participates in it. God guides it in revelation, redirects it in justice, and preserves it in love, awaiting with infinite patience and understanding its ultimate free acceptance of the Divine rule and, thus, the full establishment of God's Kingdom. God is, therefore, intimately involved with marriages and inheritance, with slavery and the stranger, with priests and seers, and thus ultimately with kings. They are the very stuff of history in which God's sovereignty must be made manifest. The author of 1 Samuel attributes the Israelite call for a human king to the people's baseness, in itself a human historical reality not to be ignored. The modern mind cannot help noting that a crisis had arisen which made the inherited social structure unworkable. In the face of Philistine military organization and technology, a divided Israel could not long survive. If Israel now insisted on maintaining forms of social cooperation suited to a previous period, when foes were few and temporary, it would die at the hand of a persistent, powerful Philistine people. But—for God's sake—Israel must survive! It exists not for itself or for the moment, but as God's instrument for the transformation of all human history! It must wait and work in history until the Messiah comes. To withdraw from history by suicide or social paralysis would be to deny its Covenant root and branch. Thus Samuel learned what later Jewish sages institutionalized, that in the face of social change God will teach Israel how it may find the new forms which will enable it to continue to serve God amidst the realities of history. In this case God unexpectedly permits a king, providing, to be sure, that this new social structure not be construed as any diminishment of God's real if ultimate sovereignty over this people. In succeeding centuries God's Torah tradition, progressively developed by the rabbis, will be the continuing medium of reconciling the simultaneous demands of Divine rule and Israel's need to serve God in history.[9] Thus, in a word, governments are authorized, but only conditionally.

Establishment of a Jewish Monarchy

The Jewish tradition views the account of 1 Samuel as the adumbration of the Mosaic commandment to appoint a king (Deut. 17:14–15). The interpretation accorded these authoritative verses by the classic rabbinic texts illustrates well the fundamental dialectic being described here. Because the Deuteronomic wording exhibits the ambiguity typical of much biblical formulation, the Tannaitic commentators (pre-200 of the Common Era) are divided as to whether the appointment of a king over Israel was obligatory or optional. Their positions, theologically, are but another form of the biblical dialectic.[10] These differences were already reflected in the Hellenistic Jewish thinkers of the first century. Philo, reflecting the Greek philosophic concern for proper political organization, apparently believed monarchy a Mosaic mandate.[11] Josephus, whose background was aristocratic and Boethusian/Sadducean, follows the latter's predilection for a priestly, theocratic rule and therefore considers the text only permission, not a religious requirement.[12] To all these Jewish thinkers, the question posed live, political options. When two Judean revolutions failed and time passed, it became increasingly hypothetical. When no normal historical ruler seemed imminent for the Jewish people, Jewish politics became almost completely eschatological. That, it seems to me, explains why the monarchists gained the ascendancy, since all discussions of a Jewish king were now conducted in the context of waiting for the promised Son of David.

Thus almost all medieval Jewish comment on this question is to the effect that the establishment of a Jewish monarchy is obligatory. Maimonides lists it as one of the 248 positive commandments[13] and the *Sefer Hachinuch* specifies it as one of the duties incumbent upon the Jewish people.[14] Such major intellectual and legal figures of the thirteenth and fourteenth centuries as Nachmanides, Moses of Coucy, Gersonides, and Bachya ben Asher may be mentioned as sharing this position.[15] By contrast, only two dissenting authorities can be cited.

Abraham Ibn Ezra, commenting on the Deuteronomic provision, regards it as an option, but we are unable to tell whether his comment has more than grammatical significance. Only Isaac Abravanel presents a major argument against having a Jewish king.[16] His position almost certainly derives from his experience as a statesman and practicing politician and is focused upon immediate historic reality. Having served under several monarchs (always with tragic result) and having been influenced by the Christian and humanist political thought of his day (unlike his Jewish philosophical predecessors), Abravanel revives the anti-monarchic arguments of the Book of Samuel. He is too much a realist to believe that men in sinful history can actually be ruled by God directly. Rather, he considers monarchy an inferior form of government to what might be called a democracy of the elite.[17] That is the best hope of doing God's will until the Messiah comes, for he alone can be a king pleasing in God's sight.

Attitudes Toward Non-Jewish Governments

Abravanel, commenting on the law of the Torah for Jewish states, is undoubtedly thinking of what it may teach non-Jewish governments. Yet Deuteronomic law is not addressed to the nations of the world, but only to Israel. Does the inner tension it knows between the Divine and Jewish kings extend to non-Jewish kings ruling over a non-Jewish state? Though there is little generalized opinion available on this topic, the answer may be ventured with some confidence that the same basic dialectic holds true.[18] It may most conveniently be exposed by a consideration of the attitudes clustering around the concepts *dina d'malchuta dina*[19] and *galut*.

The Amoraic master Samuel enunciated the principle *dina d'malchuta dina*, "the law of the (non-Jewish ruler of the) land is the law (for Jews)," early in the third century in Parthia (Babylonia), and it became an accepted legal norm for succeeding Jewish law and thought.[20] Samuel was referring only to non-Jewish legal procedures, such as witnesses and documents, but the sense of his pronouncement must be seen as far more inclusive. By the third century Jewish life in the Land of Israel was in serious decline both as to numbers and in communal vitality. The spiritual strength of Judaism was to be found in communities widely scattered through the Roman and—more influentially—the Parthian empires. If Israel was to survive amidst the realities of human affairs as God's witness, it had to find a social pattern other than independent national existence on its own land to make that service of endurance possible. And it had to be as authentic to Israel's messianic purpose in history as it was useful to its survival.

All this was implied in Samuel's dictum. Jews could bind themselves to the civil law of the land in which they found themselves, as part of their Covenant with God. They therefore could be loyal to their non-Jewish king even as they remained loyal to God in their special Covenant relationship. Though no Talmudic references are made to it, the modern mind sees here the recapitulation of the message Jeremiah sent centuries earlier to that same Babylonian Jewry: "Seek the welfare of the city where I have sent you into exile, and pray to the Lord on its behalf, for in its welfare you will find your welfare" (Jer. 29:7). This passage may be called the charter of authenticity for Diaspora forms of Covenantal existence.

"The King's Law" and "The Law of the Kingdom." Samuel's principle, affirming the religious legitimacy of non-Jewish governments and their rights, is not without limits in its development in later Jewish law. Two qualifications are relevant to the question of the general Jewish attitude toward non-Jewish states. If the king acts in an arbitrary and capricious fashion, such as taxing one group of citizens or one province in a way incommensurate with what he has demanded of others, then his decrees are not considered binding by Jewish law; they are *dina d'malka*, "the king's law," rather than *dina d'malchuta*, "the law of the kingdom." The other case is more obvious. The authority of the non-Jewish king does not extend to more strictly "religious" matters such as what is ritually clean or unclean, permitted or forbidden. What Judaism seeks in non-Jewish governments is obviously God's righteousness fulfilled. According to Jewish law the sons of Noah (that is, all people) are commanded by God to be just to one another. Thus the non-Jewish king is obligated to establish justice and authorized when he does so. Therefore Jews have a religious basis for civil responsibility to such a non-Jewish king. The fuller obedience to God would, of course, be for Israel to live as a community whose life was structured by God's Torah. The non-Jewish world is not commanded by and does not observe that fuller law. Hence life for the Jew in the midst of a non-observant people can never have the same quality of sanctity that independent life on its own land might have. That is the source of the negative religious attitudes toward non-Jewish states and they may best be analyzed in terms of the concept *galut*.

Galut. Galut may be translated "exile," but the political and geographic connotations of that English term are misleading.

Since the biblical God is the God of history, politics and geography can be religious matters to Judaism. God grants a land to the chosen people as part of their Covenant and makes their continued happy existence on

128

that land contingent upon their observance of the revealed command-ments. God authorizes a king for them as noted, but he and they are ex-pected to be no less observant of God's behests because of it; when they are, God's prophets warn both king and people that God will exile them in punishment for their sins. Thus *galut* is fundamentally a theological category.[21] It testifies to Israel's past infidelity and her present punish-ment, for that is what life under a non-Jewish government is when com-pared to full Covenantal existence on one's promised land under the divine law. And as centuries went by and the experience of cruel and op-pressive monarchs multiplied, the sense of *galut* deepened and messianic expectation grew more fervent. How soon this concept was applied to God too, saying that God has become an alien in creation, is difficult to say, but early in the Common Era Israel's political-geographic-religious situation was seen as a symbol of God's own alienation, and the hope of Israel's restoration to its land under its messianic king became inextricably iden-tified with the return of God's presence to the world and the full establish-ment of the Kingdom. (That is why the religious Jew will still be able to say, much to the consternation of the Israeli nationalist, that the State of Israel itself is *galut*. Zionist theoreticians in their thoroughgoing political secularization of traditional Jewish religious concepts transvalued *galut* into simple geographic exile. For them, therefore, to return to the Land of Israel and live as part of the State of Israel is the end of exile.[22] What a warning this should sound in the ears of those who are eager to give sec-ular, particularly political, interpretations of traditional religious concepts! For the present State of Israel in this Zionist system becomes the answer to centuries of Jewish prayer for the end of exile and the resolution of the mysteries of the people of Israel's millennial service. Believing Jews, how-ever, know that the real *galut* is metaphysical and so cannot end until God manifests God's Kingdom. For them the State of Israel is at best, as the mystics put it, *atchalta d'g'ula*, "the beginning of redemption," and, as we shall see below, they are therefore preserved from jingoism and uncritical nationalism. Rather they must judge that state as they judge other states, by the prophetic criterion of its fulfillment of God's law.[23])

Judaism and the Modern Democratic State

The dialectical "Yes"/"No" of Judaism toward non-Jewish kings took a radical shift in the direction of an almost unqualified "Yes" with the rise of modern democracy and the secular state. Where there had been for cen-turies only Zoroastrian, Moslem, or Christian governments, now there was to be a government which was not directly concerned with religion. Polit-ical loyalty was one thing, religious commitment another. The state cared only about good citizenship; religion was in effect a private decision re-moved from the public domain. Because the non-Jewish state no longer held a religion antagonistic to Judaism, because it had no religion at all but was secular, Jews could be a part of it, and equal in its midst.[24] Indeed, for the first time it became their state as much as anyone else's.

No wonder the Jews hailed Napoleon with messianic fervor and gladly rushed from their enforced segregation to share a new life.[25] Much of the history of nineteenth- and twentieth-century European and American Jewry may be read as one continuing fight to find ways to win in practice the opportunities promised in this emancipation. In some countries democracy was largely fraudulent, and Jewish rights never became widely meaningful. In others it provided a measure of opportunity rarely equaled in the history of the Jewish dispersion. The newness of the gift of freedom and the continuing effort to expand and safeguard it still set the dominant tone of Jewish life and thought in the United States. This may be somewhat more sophisticated today than in the days of mass immigration and frenzied acculturation, but with the overwhelming number of American Jews only three generations away from the degradation of the *shtetl*, equality is still too fresh to be taken for granted by most American Jews.

That mood of euphoric acceptance and wholehearted commitment lies behind the virtual absence of *galut* concepts from the religious thought of Jews in democratic countries in the past century or so.[26] By comparison to the oppression of religious governments, the tolerance created by secular governments seemed in effect an end to *galut*. Nothing made Zionist theoreticians (largely East Europeans) of the late nineteenth and early twentieth centuries more unpopular with their Western brothers than their assertion that Jews would never fully be accepted in modern democracies and needed a country of their own. Nor did the Jewish masses of Europe accept the argument, for they directed their migration in overwhelming numbers to the United States, and only the later immigration laws and Hitlerian conquests made the Land of Israel their personal goal. Metaphysical conception of *galut* similarly had little meaning for them when contrasted with a country whose streets, rumor said, were paved with gold and whose social and economic opportunities proved realistically far greater than any Jewish immigrant to these shores could have anticipated. Compared to the grim poverty and human misery of life in Eastern Europe, America seemed too much like the answer to a prayer to be considered exile. The Jew has had a rapturous love affair with America, and it has made him almost unable to say "No" to her.

The Threat of State Power

Yet the time has clearly come to reassert the negative side of the dialectical Jewish view of states. In part this is motivated by the profound general sense of personal alienation which marks so much of the criticism of contemporary society. For believing Jews it is the duty deriving from their affirmation of the Covenant. To take God and God's demands seriously provides a perspective in which even the best of secular, democratic, welfare states is not nearly good enough. To wait and work for the Kingdom of God requires a renewed commitment to the concept of *galut* in all its theopolitical depth.

This is a matter of particular urgency because the contemporary nation-state is the closest thing to an effective absolute we know. The totalitarian states are only a dramatic example of what seems to be happening wherever governments organize and, in the name of efficiency, centralize. Let the needs of the state become paramount, as in a war, and the almost unqualified nature of its power and the absence of any significant right greater than its self-preservation are made abundantly clear. No wonder Orwell could predict that the normal political situation in 1984 would be continual war. So, too, where states agree to join in international parliament, their sovereignty in internal affairs must be guaranteed them, with some countries even being granted a veto over the will of the entire body.

As the democratic state has effectively made its rights increasingly paramount, so it has moved to neutralize or control all potential rivals for social power. It does this not as in the days of tyranny by proscription or persecution, but more dangerously by paternalism and patronage. Who then can stand up to so beneficent a federal government? States' rights mean little in the face of necessary federal aid; independent capitalism is a fantasy exploded by non-legislated economic guidelines and luscious defense contracts; academic autonomy walks a cliff-edge, lured below by research grants and building loans; now artists of every variety are to benefit from government largesse. The next step, one may be certain, will be fellowships to stimulate protests and dissent. Economic determinism aside, when one's mouth is full of gravy, it is difficult to cry out.

The threat of government without significant opposition will hardly be affected by American politics or secular morality. Since World War II Americans have shown themselves substantially unwilling to commit themselves to any large-scale political ideology that might make radical criticism of government a necessity. Perhaps no more than a minority of Americans ever was active politically, but there was always hope that the creative few might change social policy. Hot politics, except for some few specific face-to-face issues, is out of place in a world seeking to play it cool. Passionate conviction is even less evident as an effective offset to governmental self-aggrandizement. Affluence has had its dulling effect on individuals as on institutions. Most Americans could define the immediate good as being left alone by the government to enjoy what they have, or perhaps as being given a little more. The morality of private-ism may make for better families and friendships, but its foundation is withdrawal from responsibility for politics and history.

The issue becomes more painfully difficult as the state takes on what must be termed a new and broader ethical responsibility. Today it seeks to fulfill many of the injunctions the Bible taught that God demanded of people. Moreover, it does its work of righteousness in a technically competent, full-scale outreach whereas the religions operated, at best, with great spirit but also in a piecemeal, frequently ineffectual fashion. By finding work for the poor, teaching the illiterate, housing the dispossessed,

131

healing the sick, dignifying the elderly (throughout the world!), the American government may claim a certain religious merit. How easy then for the state to excuse its other failings by the goodness it does. How soon a little righteousness becomes a general justification, and like the bad Pharisees and impious Christians of every generation, even what little was good now becomes an instrument of self-delusion and thus moral perversion. Niebuhr's burden concerning immoral societies joined to Acton's confession of the teleology of power should at this late date free us sufficiently from our illusions to see that the very good the state does demands more than the religious "Yes"; it demands religion's watchful and chastening "No."

Temptations and Duties Faced by Religious Groups

Join to these harsh realities the special temptations confronting American religious groups. Protestantism is not only a minority faith; it no longer dominates the American ethos. Could it not somehow use governmental control of children to complement its lagging evangelical outreach? Catholicism is no longer an outsider to the American consensus. Can it not somehow utilize the lessened hostility to parochial education to garner aid for its non-religious aspects while seeing that the government schools provide some useful information to that increasing number of children who cannot or do not wish to attend church-sponsored schools? And the Jews are no longer an oppressed minority. They have arrived, but only so recently that they worry about the permanence of their situation. Would it not be possible, therefore, to utilize the government's new openness to religion by teaching everyone about Judaism, thereby not only checking such prejudice as arises from ignorance but, more significantly, placing the prestige of the state behind the acceptance of Judaism as one of America's three great religious groups?

These decades-old temptations have not been ended by the firmness of the Supreme Court decisions against teaching religion or conducting religious observances. Like all self-seeking they reappear as soon as a new pretext is available. In this case, the eager ego need not create an imagined opportunity. The several justices immediately and objectively provided it in authorizing teaching "about" religion. The old hopes may have been thwarted. They merely reassert themselves in a different guise, this time with full legal sanction. Why should not the religious groups take the fullest possible advantage of the new openings, delimited though they be, that the government has now provided?

The answer from my Jewish religious perspective (intertwined with a social-political analysis as is always required of a religion of history) is that religion is the major remaining social body that has hope, as long as it maintains its loyalty to a transcendent God, of standing over against the government and its idolatrous self-seeking, and that every alliance with or dependence upon the government weakens the possibility of its fulfilling that role. To put it less socially and more theologically, as it serves God religion must criticize government, particularly where the state seeks to

132

supplant or ignore God, and the more a religion relies on government, the less it will be able to remain faithful to its primary tasks, to serve God before all else.

Israel's prophets may serve as the classic example of this truth.[27] As long as they were hirelings—royal seers and diviners—the men of God could in only rare instances, as Samuel, Nathan, and Elijah did, rise to the heights of later prophecy. Perhaps of that latter group Isaiah was part of the Establishment. If so, he is an even greater genius than men have thought. For it is only when the herdsman is taken from the sheep, almost against his will, and the unknown Amos confronts the professional visionary Amaziah in the royal sanctuary, that prophecy reaches classic proportions. The vicissitudes of Israel's prophets, loners almost entirely, are proof of the stand one must be ready to take and the cost one must be ready to pay to bring God's judgment to bear on society even when one stands in the midst of a people covenanted to God. How much more is this the case in the secular state. This is not to argue that the sole function of religion in modern America is prophetic criticism. There is ample room for the appreciation of what the state has and can continue to do, for the religious "Yes." Yet that is the easy word in a day of politics by consensus and social manipulation by human-relations techniques. Religion will be most true to itself today as the home of all those alienated ultimately from any government but the Kingdom of God, and therefore uniquely valuable to American democracy as the institutionalization of the principle and practice of social judgment and dissent.

Judaism's View of State Responsibility for Education

In view of the attitude toward the state and its powers, set forth above, which I derive from my Jewish religious tradition, what may be said about the Jewish conception of the state as educator? The biblical tradition, though its instruction concerning educational responsibility is quite specific, does not consider education a matter for the state. Every father is commanded to teach God's word to his child. This duty is of such importance that it follows shortly after the *Shema Yisrael* ("Hear, O Israel") and is the first explicit obligation given the man who loves God with all his heart, soul, and might. Such community obligation for education as exists in the Bible is directed essentially to adults.[28] In Ezra's reading of the Torah on New Year's Day to the whole Judean community, Jewish tradition saw the beginning of the custom to read scripture to the people each Monday, Thursday, and Sabbath, a practice, it should be noted, which precedes the establishment of a formal, communal liturgy for worship outside the Temple. Since God's law is not primarily intended for children, Jewish education as a religious duty has always aimed at the adult. By the time of the rabbis the public reading and explication of Torah and Prophets to adults had become a significant religious practice. It was not until 64 C.E.

133

that the community as such became involved in the education of children. Joshua ben Gamala (Gamaliel), the High Priest, is reported to have established elementary schools for children in every sector of Judea. These schools did not usurp the responsibility of parents with regard to education, for the well-to-do still had their children privately tutored. They did, however, make it possible for the children of the poor also to receive an education and so made the education of Jewish children in effect universal. This pattern of public assistance to those who could not fulfill a private obligation continued unbroken down to the modern period. Of special note is the fact that while rabbinic law also required the parent to teach his child an occupation, there is no record of a Jewish community's considering it so important a communal obligation that it established vocational schools, though the many and advanced religious academies with quasi-communal support are among the proudest accomplishments of Jewish history.

From these religious positions it should be clear that the non-Jewish state, even the democratic one, has no competence from the Jewish religious point of view to teach Jewish children Judaism and should not teach Jewish children Christianity. That is why Jewish religious and organizational authorities have with almost complete unanimity welcomed the Supreme Court decisions barring the practice or teaching of religion in the public school system. Indeed, for a notoriously quarrelsome folk, American Jewry has had an unprecedented singleness of mind over the years in support of a strict interpretation of the separation of church and state as applied to the schools. Now "separation," in the constitutional sense, is no longer the issue. Our concern is teaching "about" religion, and that has been legally authorized, or nearly so. The response must be given in religious, not legal, terms; that is why I have spent the major part of this analysis clarifying my Jewish understanding of religion's—that is, Judaism's—role vis-à-vis the state in general and its educational competence in particular.

Since I believe that in contemporary America the most authentic and useful thing Judaism can do is to reassert its distance from the state so that it may remain an effective prophetic critic, my attitude toward teaching "about" religion is essentially negative. Intrinsically, I consider it of limited value where it is not reductive and therefore damaging to religion. Symbolically and socially, since it creates a tentative alliance between religion and government, it is a most undesirable breach of what should be the theological wall of separation between church and state.

Issues Involved in Teaching About Religion

Negative Perspective

Let me begin my practical analysis and recommendations with several negative theses.

1. The public school will merit greater confidence if it first acknowledges that it has limited aims in the education of our children. As is typical of government activities, there is a strong temptation, considering how many children one has under one's expert control, to utilize the school to correct every major social problem.

It was hardly a surprise, therefore, when a psychiatrist recently suggested that schools should educate to prevent alcoholism, and since this was best done by practicing beneficial drinking patterns early, he suggested mild drinking as part of elementary school training.[29] Somewhat similarly, teaching "about" religion has meant for some the possibility of educating for those ultimate commitments about being which are the foundation of a healthy and integrated personality. Yet even before one reaches this existential level, it seems reasonably clear that the single factor which effectively prevents most Americans from making mature commitments is their emotional maladjustments. Before teaching "about" religion in this way, the schools might better spend their time doing psychotherapy (which is obviously not "guidance") so that the child might be free enough to make responsible religious decisions! It should be obvious that the school is not set up to deal with every social problem, and the more intimate and personal the problems are, the better they are left to others, such as home or church or social agency, to handle, and that specifically applies to religion as the ultimate ground of personality structure.

Some enthusiastic supporters of teaching about religion have argued for it on the ground that its omission from the school program is one effective way of indicating to children that religion is not really important. Religion, objectively taught, needs to be part of the school program so that the child will know that it is a significant part of life as far as the majority of our society is concerned. Such truth as is contained in this argument seems to me to be satisfied by far less radical curricular revision than is generally suggested by its proponents. Ending the silence about religion in the public school to allow for a proper appreciation of its social significance is one thing; full-scale teaching about religion is another. The school is not the mirror of life. Every child knows (though graduate students must keep reminding themselves) that the school is always an artificial creation and not reality itself. Children know that the most important things of life are not found in school. Why must administrators seek to bring everything, like love, faith, psychic wholeness, and other ultimate realities, under their programmatic sway?

The public school cannot long continue to take on every teaching function that parents once held, and then wonder why parents do not take an active interest in their child's education. Castration rarely begets gratitude. The home and synagogue may be educationally delinquent, but the school will not strengthen them in their proper tasks, or win them as the allies it requires in its legitimate tasks, by taking *in loco parentis* as a justification of its own omnicompetence.

2. The objectivity which lies at the heart of teaching "about" religion

is badly in need of demythologization. The customary argument about objectivity is the unavailability of adequately trained or properly oriented personnel. That is a real and valid argument against the practicality of the new proposals. It needs no reiteration here. But the matter must be seen in its full theoretical difficulty as well. Philosophically, I must insist, there is no such thing as objectivity; there are only varieties of subjectivity held in check by certain contrivances whose subjective foundations are masked by the academic mystique called methodology. Perhaps an exaggeration will help: In most undergraduate instruction in the humanities, as students quickly discover, "objectivity" means learning the instructor's lingo for structuring phenomena and repeating it on examinations as if it were one's own. A liberal approach includes studying opposing views and learning the instructor's refutation of them. Objectivity is generally a species of brainwashing, at least to what constitutes proper objectivity!

The matter is of special importance here because in the field of religion objectivity can never hope to mean the same sort of impersonal public testing and agreement that it attains in the natural sciences, or even in the social sciences, some of whose aspects are quantifiable. The best it can hope to be is a delimited subjectivity which gives heavy weight to documents, chronology, and the community of scholars. As anyone knows who has participated in the field, that still allows for an extraordinary range of subjectivity. The use of the magic term "objectivity" should not be allowed to conjure away the serious problems involved in defining the material to be included in teaching "about" religion.

These complications become insupportable on the instructional level. Nothing, for example, could be more deadly than to try to teach social studies or great literature as objective data. Knowing Salinger's biography or the plot outline of The Catcher in the Rye is no substitute for arguing, even deciding, whether people are as phony as he describes them. If you wish to change behavior you must drive your argument to the existential level. Merely giving pupils the facts about smoking or reckless driving is useless. To the contrary, the first rule of decent pedagogy is to show the relevance of the material under study to the student's own life, to involve the student personally and not just verbally in the issue. Thus if the teaching "about" religion is to be meaningful, it must involve opening up the student to the truth of the religion under discussion and confronting its relevance. That is hardly what proponents of teaching "objectively" would seem to be advocating; yet it is the logical parallel to what is being done to teach the social studies and literature effectively.

3. Nor can religion be satisfied to have the aesthetic experience once again substituted for the holy. Genesis was not written so people could worry about the appropriate form of the short story. Had its authors been aware that people would be more concerned with their style than their God, they would have considered it blasphemous. Though we are far more distant from the Holy One than they, we should not seek to increase the distance by reading the good book for the wrong reasons. By abetting such

typical secularization of the religious we foster that substitution of the pretty for the sacred which impedes every effort at genuine liturgical revival. The bridal party needs marching time to be ogled properly; that is why the rabbi should "keep it short."

Reading the Bible as literature rather than as revelation is worse than not reading it at all. In the latter case, at least, the word waits for us without a superimposed secular construction. Yet to read it as literature but really hope it is heard as revelation, which is probably the hidden agenda of most religionists advocating this practice, is as immoral in its deception as it is illegal in its substance.

4. And I do not see how with the best of good will I can approve of having Jewish children study the New Testament under non-Jewish, almost certainly Christian, auspices.[30] The matter is sensitive, but it is not to be avoided. From my Jewish religious perspective the New Testament is inevitably a polemical document. Its very name, the "New" Testament, implies that the people of Israel's Covenant (Testament) with God is archaic, if not obsolete. The Gospels are replete with references to Jesus as the fulfillment of Jewish prophecy; thus they always make a claim upon the Jewish reader, and this situation in a government-sponsored, Christian-dominated classroom is quite uncomfortable. To accept the Gospel claim is to reject Judaism, from the Jewish point of view. To reject it is, from the Christian side, at best odd, perhaps willful, at worst sinful. The Epistles deepen the predicament. Though they affirm God's continuing love for Israel, they seem to a Jew radically to reject the saving power of the "old" dispensation. For a believing Jew to study these books must therefore inevitably mean involvement in apologetics and polemics. They need not today arouse fanaticism or lead to violence as they have in the past. Yet if the fundamental challenge of the New Testament is not openly met with counterchallenge and argument, they are not being read fairly, from a Jewish point of view. Such controversy is inappropriate to the public school as it is outside the competence of even most well-trained non-Jews to handle satisfactorily from the Jewish standpoint. (These strictures apply with lesser effect to study about Islam and are largely inapplicable to Far Eastern religions.)

Positive Perspective

My positive recommendations should be seen within the foregoing perspective. They must, however, be prefaced with a plea for full-scale attention to the still barely met challenge of teaching ethical values in the public schools. Concern for the new possibilities the Supreme Court has opened up should not blind us to the fact that we have not yet done much to create imaginative means of arousing ethical concern and genuine human understanding in our youngsters. The effective teaching of moral and spiritual values in schools would be of far greater significance to Judaism and to America than the new efforts to teach "about" religion.

1. The most useful thing the Supreme Court has done for us is to re-

137

move the sense of anxiety that gripped so many conscientious teachers when it became impossible for them to avoid mentioning religion, religious institutions, or religious concepts. The negativism involved in that sense of absolute separation communicated itself to students. Surely teachers ought to feel free to mention religion and religious institutions where these legitimately come up in the course of their teaching. Lifting that barrier of silence has conferred upon religion the dignity of equal mention, if not time and value, with James Bond and the National Football League. Recognizing the existence of religion and religious institutions as an integral element of American life and the history of man is long overdue and would end the curious hiatus in the study of humankind which has made religion seem somehow unimportant today.

2. There are some places in the current curriculum, such as in the study of history or literature, where an understanding of religious backgrounds would provide greater insight into events or ideas. It would seem reasonable in these circumstances to spend some time clarifying the underlying religious context. Here the discussion about religion might hope to retain substantial objectivity since it would be a tangential issue, not the central matter under discussion. Nor should one minimize the effect of introducing such learning along the way rather than by units of their own. The indirect and unexpected materials are often the ones which make the process of education most interesting and are therefore the best retained.

3. Rather than try to teach religious data it would be far more helpful to encourage those universal human experiences which, though germane to general education, in our present understanding seem to be the basis of a religious outlook. In this way the school could make the possibility of religion real to children while leaving its development and interpretation to the home and religious institutions. Two such experiences seem widely significant: One is the sense of awe, the other the sense of unity which underlies all multiplicity. Too much of our education these days seems designed to empty children of wonder and transfer them into another efficient switching point in the giant communications-production complex we call society. Instruction in the arts is supposedly oriented in this direction, but even the arts are often technique rather than experience oriented, and everyone knows most art is elective where math and science are required! Without lapsing into "see how the miracles of nature prove the existence of God," one could make the study of nature less technical and more personal. Together with indoctrination in methodology, quantification, and classification, the child should learn a basic surprise that there is anything present at all and continuing astonishment that the human mind can find ways to cope with these multiple experiences.

The sense of unity offers a similar opportunity and one which is missed because it is simply taken for granted. Yet though the world about us is incredibly diverse and multifaceted, the most astonishing interrelationships appear when one insists on seeing it in its unity. That sense alone makes possible the concept of development basic to the social sciences and the concept of the integrity of universes which is the foundation of all mathematics. To foster these experiences in the public school curriculum would allow students to have personal sense about religion that no amount of dispassionate data could ever provide.

4. If Martin Buber is right, an even more important form of teaching about religion would be that sort of instruction—better, that sort of student-teacher relationship—which would help students know what it means truly to be a person.[31] Buber insists that the heart of all religion is the experience of genuine encounter between persons. In an age so obviously bereft of opportunity for being and meeting a real person, that is something our schools might well dedicate themselves to. By helping students find themselves as selves, the school would not only develop them in the deepest personal sense and teach them critical communal values but simultaneously help them know that basic human sense of reality which Buber says lies at the heart of all religion.

5. The discussions of possible curricular changes based on the Supreme Court suggestions have thus far paid little attention to the appropriate age for such instruction. If, as I believe, the questions of objectivity and polemical materials are not to be underestimated, a partial solution to dealing with them would be to reserve the instruction for an appropriate level of maturity. Older students have grown up insofar as they have learned to think in an ever more autonomous fashion. So, too, the instruction they receive becomes more nearly "objective" as they become older. One simply cannot compare the style of instruction in even a good twelfth-grade class with that of most universities but one year and probably two years later. Although perhaps it is more social change than psychological maturation, still most children do not arrive at reasonable intellectual independence until they have spent some time at a university—and too many not even then. College age would seem the most reasonable age level on which to experiment with direct teaching "about" religion. Such courses would normally be elective and thus have the advantage of not coming with the compulsion of the state behind them while yet being made available to large and increasing numbers of students. Since state universities have experimented in this direction, now may be the time to move forward with new and different offerings in the field of religion.

Nevertheless, my essential negative orientation returns. If religion is to maintain a prophetic stance on the American scene, the final word must be one of caution. Anything that would encourage or seem to involve religious alliance with or reliance upon the state should be steadfastly avoided. The religious groups should therefore exercise the greatest possible self-discipline in their expectations of such new school programs as are begun and should be as tentative as is responsible in advancing or cooperating with any suggestions for teaching "about" religion under government auspices.

139

Notes

1. The critical cases are *McCollum v. Board of Education and Abington v. Schempp*, with the remarks of Jackson to the former and of Clark, Brennan, and Goldberg (concurred in by Harlan) to the latter the basis of the understanding. Fuller documentation is provided in the legal discussions in this volume.

2. Though several groups in the Jewish community dissented for the first time from the strict separationist position on the issue of federal aid to private schools in nonreligious areas of instruction, the only one to have deplored the ruling barring prayers in the public school was the leader of the Lubavitcher group of Hasidic Jews. On the former topic see Milton Himmelfarb, "Church and State—How High a Wall?" *Commentary*, July, 1966.

3. In the several years I served as national Director of Education for Reform Judaism I often noted the difficult problem of adjustment many competent public school administrators had when they sought to lead synagogue schools, because the latter were fully voluntary institutions.

4. The problem of whether there is, or can be, Jewish theology is rather less heated today than it was some years ago, probably because American Jewry today largely considers itself a religious community. As it asks with increasing seriousness, "What do Jews believe?" the answers are Jewish theology. Today the discussion seems more to turn on proper method than on the feasibility or virtue of the enterprise. For the earlier level of discussion see my "The Jewish Need for Theology," *Commentary*, August, 1962, and the resulting correspondence, February, 1963. A good picture of the methodological argument may be seen in the *Yearbooks of the Central Conference of American Rabbis* for 1962, 1963, and 1964 in the papers on theology.

5. So Theodore Robinson can write, ". . . such doctrines as those of Amos and Isaiah must lead *in the long run* to a pure monotheism . . ." (*A History of Israel* [Oxford University Press, 1932], vol. I, p. 407, emphasis added). The discussion by Gerhard von Rad is far more tempered but essentially skeptical of early monotheism (*Old Testament Theology* [Harper, 1962], pp. 210 ff.). E. A. Speiser's revisionism gives vigor to the more traditional position (*The Anchor Bible*, Genesis [Doubleday, 1964], pp. xlv ff.).

6. "The dominant tenet of Hebrew thought is the absolute transcendence of God. Yahweh is not in nature." This, by contrast to Mesopotamian and Egyptian thought, is the summary of H. and H. A. Frankfort (*Before Philosophy* [Pelican, 1946], p. 241). Walther Eichrodt links this emphasis on transcendence with the sense of His immanence, though that is a different thing from being "in nature" (*Theology of the Old Testament* [Westminster, 1961], p. 205). The centrality of anti-idolatry to biblical Judaism is itself the dominant motif of Ezekiel Kaufmann's *Toldot Haemunah Hay-israelit*. See the very first sentence of vol. I, Part 1, p. 1, Dvir, 1937.

7. The inner experience is clarified by R. B. Y. Scott, *The Relevance of the Prophets* (Macmillan, 1944), pp. 52 f. and 106 ff. On the king's role and Israelite law see Roland de Vaux, *Ancient Israel* (McGraw-Hill, 1961), pp. 144 ff., especially section 5 on the king's legislative and judicial powers.

8. Robert H. Pfeiffer, *Introduction to the Old Testament* (Harper, 1941), pp. 605 f., is more graphic but less detailed than Otto Eissefeldt, *The Old Testament* (Harper & Row, 1965), pp. 430–432.

9. The early statement of R. Travers Herford in *The Pharisees* (Macmillan, 1924), pp. 69 ff., on tradition supplementing the written Torah remains basically

correct. Succeeding scholarship has only extended this insight that law is an adaptive instrument which allows change to enter Judaism without the loss of Judaism's essential character.

10. The same material is given in three places with some variation, none of special conceptual note: *Sifre* Dt. par. 156, p. 105a; *Midrash Tannaim* to Dt. 17:14, pp. 103–104; *Sanhedrin* 20b. In the former text, R. Judah, who considers the Deuteronomic injunction mandatory, gives this explanation for what then seems the surprising rebuke of 1 Sam. 8, viz., they asked for the king at too early a date. The dichotomy of views continues into later rabbinic literature. Positively, one should recite a blessing upon seeing a Jewish king (Ber. 58a); impudence to him is like impudence to God (Gen. Rab. 94); when the people obey their rulers God does what they decide (Dt. Rab. 1); for even the smallest of appointees has great status, some say he acts with God's authority (R. H. 25b and B. B. 91b); and even the Roman government might be called "good" for it established justice (Gen. Rab. 9.13). Negatively, many a remark approaching the cynical is recorded with respect to the action of Jewish community officials, much less non-Jewish governors. (See P. A. 1.10, Pes. 87b, Tan. Mish. 2, *Midrash Hagadol*, ed. Schechter, p. 412, and Yoma 22b, which notes that Saul's kingdom ended because it was not dishonest!)

11. *De Specialibus Legibus*, IV, 30, 157, read with Harry Austryn Wolfson, *Philo* (Harvard University Press, 1947), vol. II, p. 329.

12. *Contra Apion*, 2.16; *Antiquities*, IV, 8, 17, 223. The interpretation of his Boethusian background is taken from *The Rise and Fall of the Judaean State*, vol. II, by Solomon Zeitlin, which will shortly be published by the Jewish Publication Society of America. Simon Federbush contends, however (*Mishpat Hameluchah Beyisrael* [Mosad Harav Kuk, 1952], pp. 26f.), that Josephus' position on theocracy has been misunderstood and that only later generations ever thought it meant hierocracy, the rule of priests. Jewish faith demands equality for all religions and peoples. Hence religious and political powers were always separated in Israel. The exceptions, the Hasmonean rulers, were derogated by rabbinic Judaism. His proof, aside from a rather general statement in the Jerusalem Talmud, is a citation from the thirteenth-century Nachmanides. The ideological intent behind this reconstruction is discussed in note 17 below.

13. *Sefer Hamitzvot*, positive commandment 173, and note the implicit assumption that the king is expected to follow the Torah to be worthy of preeminence. Monarchy is given a generally Aristotelian justification in *The Guide of the Perplexed*, II, 40. The legal prescriptions are given in M. T. *Hilchot Melachim*, and note that the messianic laws are part of this discussion of Jewish kings (chs. 11 and 12). See the discussion in Leo Strauss, "Abravanel's Political Theory," in *Isaac Abravanel*, ed. Trend and Loewe (Cambridge University Press, 1937), pp. 106 ff.

14. *Sefer Hachinuch*, par. 497.

15. So Strauss, *op. cit.*, p. 119, referring to the biblical commentaries to Dt. 17:14 f. of the former two. An instructive parallel to the Moslem position is drawn by S. D. Gotein in his "Attitudes Toward Government in Islam and Judaism," in *Studies in Islamic History and Institutions* (Brill, 1966). Since the Koran contains no references to political regimes, some authorities could argue that the Caliphate was not religiously required and no form of political organization is preferable to another. While such arguments were heard when the Caliphate made its appearance, they gradually disappeared in the face of the reality. The matter apparently caused no intellectual concern to later generations for the topic of monarchy is not dealt with in the later Moslem codes or later philosophies.

16. Strauss, *op. cit.*, is particularly helpful for his study of the context of contemporary political theory in which Abravanel's departure from past theory is best to be understood. A somewhat more detailed discussion of Abravanel's ideas in their development is found in Ben Zion Netanyahu, *Don Isaac Abravanel* (Jewish Publication Society, 1953), pp. 183 ff. His rejection of the influence of contemporary political thought on Abravanel is not convincing to me after Strauss's demonstration.

17. Simon Federbush seizes upon this position as a means of arguing that traditional Jewish law does not require a monarchy and hence the establishment of a democracy in the contemporary State of Israel is fully halachic! His treatment of the prevailing, opposing view may be seen in his comment, "But from the simple meaning of the Torah text it is clear that it is not commanded; and the phrase 'like all the nations' is a clear implication of derogation, which is also clear from the simple meaning of Samuel's reply to those seeking a king" (*op. cit.*, p. 39). He further points out that since there is no prophet or Sanhedrin today to induct and ratify the king, a monarchy is a practical impossibility. The conclusion is, however, made *"lefi ruach hatorah,"* "according to the spirit of the Torah," a phrase and concept he would roundly condemn when utilized by non-Orthodox interpreters for similar treatments of traditional law to allow for more modern social arrangements (*op. cit.*, p. 40).

18. The dialectic developed by Joseph Baer Soloveitchik regarding the two kinds of peoplehood, the one biological and compulsory, the other an especially human response because free, is of a different order. Soloveitchik operates here, characteristically, with a typology which he uses to understand history but which is not fully reflected in any historical phenomenon. His contrast is not so much the rule of God versus the rule of men in actual institutions, but the two modes of Jewish existence as a people, biological and theological, not separate but intertwined. This makes possible the positive acceptance of the current secular State of Israel but demands an effort to help it live up to its full Jewish character (*"Kol Dodi Dofek," Torah Umeluchah*, ed. Simon Federbush [Mosad Harav Kuk, 1961], pp. 11–44).

19. An alternate possibility for these positive attitudes may be found in the prohibition against rebellion, the laws of *mored bemalchut*. These are, however, less central to Jewish law, and the attitudes around them seem to have developed most clearly at a much later period. See the somewhat abstract discussion by Simon Federbush, *op. cit.*, pp. 84 ff. For a brief description of the legal tradition see J. D. Eisenstein's *Otzar Dinim Uminhagim*, art. *"Mored Bemalchut"* (Hebrew Publishing Co., 1917), p. 211. I know of no English discussion of this theme. A brief list of *aggadic* passages calling for reverence to kings is given in *The Jewish Encyclopedia*, art. "King," section "In rabbinical literature," vol VII, p. 502. A more realistic picture of what the average person expects of a king is given in the imaginative contrasts between the immorality of earthly kings as contrasted with the righteousness of the King of Kings. See the index entry "Earthly Kings" in *A Rabbinic Anthology*, ed. Montefiore and Loewe (Macmillan, 1938), p. 791.

20. See the full discussion of this principle, noteworthy for its full citation of later and occasionally diverging authorities, in the *Talmudic Encyclopedia* (Hebrew), Jerusalem, 1956, art. *"Dina Demalchuta Dina,"* vol. VII, columns 295–308. However, Salo Baron cautions that this principle was never given definitive limits or fully clarified. (*The Jewish Community* [Jewish Publication Society, 1942], vol. II, pp. 216 ff.; *A Social and Religious History of the Jews* [Jewish Publication Society, 2nd. ed., 1957], vol. V, pp. 75 ff.).

21. The major study of this concept to date is Yitzchak B. Baer, *Galut* (Schocken, 1947), the English translation of a German text published in the early thirties. Baer's nationalistic and rationalistic concerns seem to me to constrict his treatment of what he recognizes as the essentially religious origins and connotations, of the concept. Thus there is no discussion of the biblical concept of *galut*, only a short discussion of the *aggadic* notion of the Exile of God's Indwelling Presence, and but brief mention of medieval mysticism. Hence Baer's study cannot be relied upon for a rounded understanding of this doctrine, particularly from the standpoint of its meaning and place within the structure of Jewish faith.

22. For an excellent introduction to Zionist ideology see Arthur Hertzberg, *The Zionist Idea* (Doubleday, 1959). Of particular interest are the Introduction, which carefully distinguishes between Jewish religious tradition and modern secular thought, and the selections in Parts 4, 5, and 6. Note that a separate section, and only one at that, is given to religious Zionism (including, quite properly, Martin Buber). David Ben-Gurion's secular messianism is a particularly interesting effort to blend the two streams from the secular side.

23. A sensitive discussion of this problem is to be found in Ernst Simon, "Are We Israelis Still Jews?" *Commentary*, April, 1953. See also my brief, popular statement, "Who Is Israel?" *Jewish Heritage*, Fall, 1961.

24. See the convincing analysis of Arthur Hertzberg, "Church, State and the Jews," *Commentary*, April, 1963.

25. The story of the period is engagingly narrated by Howard M. Sachar, *The Course of Modern Jewish History* (World Publishing Co., 1958), particularly chap. III but *passim*. Napoleon was quite harsh to French Jewry, yet they bore his rigors patiently and then exalted him as the founder of their freedom. The latter was what they found surprising. See the perceptive remarks of Zosa Szajkowski, "Judaica-Napoleonica," *Studies in Jewish Bibliography and Folklore*, June, 1956, p. 108.

26. It is typical of the mood of the times that *The Jewish Encyclopedia* of 1904 treats "Exile" with a brief linguistic note and then refers its readers to articles which deal essentially with the biblical experience of "Banishment" or "Captivity" (in Babylon) but treats Jews off the land of Israel by the neutral term "Diaspora."

27. Note the comment by Harry Orlinsky on the possibilities of Israel's prophets' taking pay ("The Seer in Ancient Israel," *Oriens Antiquus*, vol IV, fasc. II, 1965, p. 154). Bear in mind too that the entire burden of this study is the uniqueness of Israel's prophets (as contrasted with her seers) from so-called prophets seen elsewhere in Near Eastern literature. From a quite different perspective there is the still relevant preachment of Martin Buber in "False Prophets," *Israel and the World* (Schocken, 1948), pp. 113 ff.

28. A good brief description of the history of Jewish education and its institutional forms is given by Julius Maller, "The Role of Education in Jewish History," and Simon Greenberg, "Jewish Educational Institutions," chaps. 21 and 22 of *The Jews*, ed. Louis Finkelstein (Jewish Publication Society, 1949).

29. As reported in the *New York Times*, January 12, 1966, and *Time*, January 21, 1966.

30. Steven S. Schwarzschild argues that for a Jew to read even the "Old" Testament means to utilize the rabbinic understanding of what the biblical text says, thus effectively preventing reading even that text jointly ("Judaism, Scriptures and Ecumenism," in *Scripture and Ecumenism*, ed. Leonard J. Swidler [Duquesne University Press, 1965]).

143

31. The working out of the educational implications of *I and Thou* is most clearly given in the essays "Education" and "The Education of Character," reproduced in *Between Man and Man* (Macmillan, 1948). Cf. the interpretation given by Maurice Friedman, *Martin Buber: The Life of Dialogue* (Harper Torchbook, 1960), chap. XX.

12

Hope Jewish and Hope Secular, a Response to Jürgen Moltmann

The work of Jewish theology today must be carried out from a post-secular stance. Because that position determines the view of hope offered here, some preliminary remarks concerning it are required.

With the Emancipation of the Jews from ghetto existence beginning about the end of the 18th century, Judaism underwent a steady process of secularization, in the contemporary, limited sense of that term. On one level this was associated with the radical change in the political status of the Jews. Only with the emergence of a secular as contrasted to a Christian state was it possible for Jews to have full rights as citizens. The Jews, therefore, welcomed the secular state in Western Europe and avidly took advantage of its new opportunities for civic participation. This basic political secularization was amplified by the urban concentration of Jews and their speedy movement into the universities wherever this was permitted. As the 19th century proceeded, this process moved toward self-consciousness. Traditional Judaism saw the need to explain itself to the surrounding world, or, what is the same, having adopted the style of the general society, it now had to explain itself to itself in society's terms. This meant using the language of secular philosophy to talk about Judaism, and, while German idealism was more hospitable to religious interpretation than today's secular philosophy is, the very process of employing a philosophic hermeneutic made demands for the transformation of Judaism. These social and intellectual pressures were so great that when Orthodox

Originally published as "Hope Jewish and Hope Secular," in *Judaism*, vol. 17, no. 2 (Spring 1968) and revised for this volume.

Judaism emerges in the person of Samson Raphael Hirsch, it, as well as Reform Judaism, appears as a self-consciously "religious" movement and thus, as contrasted to the older synthesis of folk and faith, one touched by the modern secular spirit. The effects were internal as well. Among Reform Jews the service was translated into the vernacular, the legal disciplines were reduced to subjective desirables, and the clergy lost its aura of infallibility. Yet even among the traditionalists the observance of Jewish civil law speedily gave way to the use of the governments' courts, and general as well as Jewish education became acceptable—both unthinkable courses of action a century before. The decades since have only increased this involvement with secularity.

The process took a more radical turn at the hands of those Jews who felt that modernity meant some sort of scientific or materialistic positivism. By the last quarter of the 19th century many Jewish intellectuals knew God was dead and religion hopelessly outmoded. They wrote about it, preached it, and organized in terms of it. Their substitutes for Jewish faith, which were very effective in the Jewish world, took the form of Socialism, if they were determined to transcend their Jewishness; or Zionist nationalism, if they were proud of it; or Socialist Zionism, if they wanted the best of both worlds. They demythologized Jewish religious concepts into politics. The prophets were early agitators for social justice. *Galut*, exile, was a matter of political geography rather than equally the metaphysical alienation of God and humankind in this world. *G'ulah*, redemption, they took back to its early sense of reacquiring one's national land in Palestine instead of equally meaning the establishing of the Messianic Kingdom. The State of Israel is the fulfillment of that secularization of Judaism.

I

In the United States these European activities came much later, mass migration being a late-19th-early-20th-century phenomenon, and were transformed by the special social situation of an open and expanding society. Its early and perhaps characteristic American example was the establishment of the Ethical Culture movement by a Jew and the large number of Jews who once flocked to it as a perfect synthesis of the non-sacred in Judaism with the moral in democracy. Today it would seem that the high point of American Jewish secularization was reached just before World War II. There were by then enough native-born Jews and aspiring young immigrants in the universities or involved in the general, secular culture to provide a positive intellectual inducement for giving up one's ancestral religion. What gave this movement tremendous force in the Jewish community was its linkage to the psychosocial pressures generated by the cultural distance between the immigrant Yiddish-speaking elder generation and their American children. As a result, for Jewish youth Americaniza-

146

tion meant non-observance of Jewish law; sophistication meant atheism. Statistically this may have not been the majority style, yet it was widespread, well known, and much worried over. No wonder that Jewish thinkers in that period sought secular syntheses by elaborating naturalist, that is, functional, non-metaphysical explanations of Jewish faith (like Mordecai Kaplan), or that they experimented with other, even less God-oriented, forms of humanism.

Anyone who lived through these past few decades of American Jewish history or who has vicariously made his own the difficulties of the Jewish community since the Emancipation began a century and a half ago, cannot help but marvel at the revolution which the discovery of the secular realm has apparently initiated in both Protestant and Catholic circles. We thought that the church was in the world and part of culture while we were still emerging into them. Now we wonder what kind of spiritual ghetto Christianity seeks emancipation from. Usually Jews borrow theological patterns from their neighbors. For a change, a theological movement seems to have passed through Judaism before reaching Christianity, almost certainly because we are structured as a folk or a people and not as a church. We could not therefore, even in pre-Emancipation days, be as separate from the "secular" as Christians have felt themselves to be.

From the perspective of our many decades of experience with secularity, it is both sad and astonishing to hear it being welcomed by Christians as a religious aid of messianic proportions. Of course, we must understand and in part accommodate ourselves to contemporary secularity. Of course, we must speak to moderns in a modern way. But our experience is that translating the service not only makes it understandable but also unbelievable to many; turning law into a matter of individual decision leads not only to willing compliance but to gross non-observance, almost to anarchy; and humanizing the authorities makes them not only more approachable but less influential in most people's lives. A religious concern with the secular style of our time may solve some of our older pressing problems and so may be necessary, but it will also lose us many of the old values we have treasured and create new problems which will then demand newer solutions. This is what brings us to the post-secular stance.

Since World War II the Jewish community seems to have rounded a theological corner, at least in some small minority of its members. I do not refer now to the unexpectedly high proportion of Jews who affiliate with synagogues, who have built an incredibly large number of beautiful religious structures, and who in some measure participate in their activities. While no observer of American Jewish life in the late '30s could have expected it, such a return seems today more often a new way of secularizing Judaism than a genuine religious movement. What is even more unexpected and important is that small group who, having come through atheism or Socialism or ideological Zionism or pure secularist indifference, are now seriously seeking the meaning of Jewish faith. On the intellectual level it is an inter-denominational group of theologians and rabbis who are

147

trying to go beyond Buber and Rosenzweig in the search for a new sense of Covenant, law and community. They cluster around JUDAISM and dominated the under-50 group in the *Commentary* symposium, "On the Condition of Jewish Belief." They are met in every Jewish community they visit by a small but thoughtful group who are anxious to hear about Jewish belief, and the more existentially challenging the presentation the better. They are not many, but that they exist at all, that they care as they do, is what provides the social reality to this post-secular stance of Jewish theology. In concern if not yet in theological substance they know why they are Jewish. By contrast, why should one who takes secularity seriously care about his Jewishness? Ethics are universal; psychic needs are for doctors to treat or experiences to fill; belonging is supplied by Americanism; ethnic enrichment by folk music or crafts, imported from the whole world; culture is forced on one by a booming culture industry. Thus a large number of Jews are too secular to take Judaism or even Jewishness seriously, yet have too much self-respect to surrender them entirely. This is what the alliance with secularity has brought us to, and that is why, living with it for years now, I approach the analysis of modern man's sense of hope in the future not uncritically.[1]

II

There can be little doubt that all of us today are very much concerned with what is new, with what is coming to be. On a vulgar level much of our economy is based on it. The annual change in automobile models sets a tone which appliance, clothes, and other manufacturers emulate. We engineer for obsolescence. We are equally concerned with the novel in our social styles, looking for the new restaurant, resort, or thing-to-do. And our omnipresent communications media put their great energy into what they know will sell, the sensational and the different.

That is the superficial side of what technology and history have taught us. Invention has demonstrated again and again that things need not be what they were. Looking back over the ages, the men we most admire are the innovators who have improved the human condition or broadened the horizons of our spirit. Those movements have not stopped. That good future we would like is even now coming into being. Today is always becoming "the old days."

There is much in this modern mood about which religion and the contemporary secular spirit can agree. Both are discontent with the present situation of the individual and society. They know things are not what they ought to be and that it is critical for us to devote ourselves to making them better. Secularists propose to do so by what we may call horizontal transcendence. By projecting human creativity forward through time they hope to overcome the present problems. There is in all logical rigor no present evidence that such a positive outcome is possible. All we can see are difficulties, false solutions, and creative discontent. We do have some experience of such problems having been met in the past. Still, this says nothing about the principle. Thus, even in secular hope there is also a certain measure of faith, a commitment that goes beyond the present evidence and is strong enough to build one's life upon.

Here those who are religious and those of a secular temper can meet, for this horizontal conception of hope is clearly to be seen in the Bible. The major Hebrew term for hope, *k-v-h*, means in the Bible not just a state of soul but an expectation in time. The dictionaries often give its meaning as "to wait for." Hope in God is the trust one has in one's present distress that God will soon act to bring one relief. This temporal sense of hoping is reinforced by the frequent parallelism of terms from the root *k-v-h* with those from *y-ḥ-l*, which far more specifically means "to await" or "look for." Another root similarly but less frequently used in these contexts, *ḥ-k-h*, even more concretely denotes temporal expectation. Much has been written about the historical orientation of Biblical faith, and this is surely a striking corroboration of it. Our most natural inclination today would be to think of hope as something inner, emotional, essentially subjective; yet for the Bible it is quite objectively connected with events to take place in time.

Moreover, where we would assume that hope was primarily for the individual or perhaps our loved ones, it is in the Bible as much a concern for the community, the people of Israel. When the Hebrews express their folk distress and hope in God they say they wait for God, which is to say: to make the Divine power felt in history on their behalf. This sense of communal hope is one of the most common prophetic and psalmic themes. And the individual and corporate levels do not conflict with each other; rather, they seem complements. Thus it is very often difficult to tell in the *Psalms* whether the usage, though expressed individually, is not meant communally. On occasion a clear-cut community usage suddenly slips into the first person or vice versa. In Biblical times individual and people were not nearly as separate as they are today, when subjective autonomy and individualism are methodological necessities.

This may help us understand why even individually there was such a strong sense of temporal hope in Biblical Judaism. The major historic event it knew and celebrated was the Exodus from Egypt. God had brought the people forth from slavery and given them a law and a land. *Adonai* became the Hebrews' God by overcoming a tragic historic situation and turning it into one of fulfillment. No matter to how many tribes this actually happened, the Exodus became the major religious memory of all the people of Israel. Now they hoped that God would be their saving power in history. Individual Hebrews, one may surmise, by participating in their people's sense of having a saving God, came to understand the experience of their own lives in similar bondage-transcending, Exodus-granting terms. They, too, could hope that God would act on their behalf in their situations of peril. Both levels of expectation, that people and individual alike

149

would find God working on their behalf to bring them out of their trouble, were confirmed by their experience. God often did help them. This does not mean that God always gave them prosperity and success. They had the capacity to see God working for their benefit even in what otherwise would have appeared as defeat or disaster. Their trust that God would yet act was often strained, and they expressed their feelings to their God in terms of desperation. Yet it held fast through centuries of trial, and after every new Exodus-experience the old Egypt events seemed ever more reliably the faithful paradigm of God's living, active relationship with this chosen people and each of its members.

III

This sense of God's present power in history is a major ingredient in the Hebrew conviction that the relationship with God is best symbolized by the concept of Covenant. God's responsibility in this relationship is, among other things, to save the Jewish people. One might then say that because Israel has a Covenant with God it can hope that God will act for them in history. This describes it in fairly clear Biblical terms, though I think the religious reality is better put this way: Because the people of Israel knew its God to work on their behalf in history it could use the juridic concept of Covenant to symbolize their relationship with God.

What is critical from the point of view of our modern theological problematic is the dialectic sense of action under the Covenant. That God is expected to act does not mean that people may do nothing but simply wait. The Hebrews must walk themselves out of Egypt though they know they were borne on eagles' wings. The Hebrew Judges and Kings must lead their armies into battle even though they have been told that the Lord will fight for them. To be sure, God occasionally takes quite independent action in the form of a miracle. That is God's free right as sovereign Lord. Yet the law forbids testing God in this regard, and waiting for God's help therefore does not mean giving up the responsibility for what we must yet do. Only when everything has been done does one wait for a miracle.

The human side of the Covenant dialectic of action is, as befits our stature in contrast to God's, far more limited. For people to act simply on their own, that is to say, without regard for their Covenant partner, is always wrong. It may seem to lead to success, but it is nonetheless sin and will be met with punishment. Human action is truly significant only when it takes place in accordance with God's will. Since God is sovereign in history, only such acts can endure and bring blessing. Moreover, when one does them one knows one does them with God's help, for that is the direction in which God is moving history. The act is now quite precisely a Covenant act, in which people and God join together to do a deed, yet the partners retain their own integrity. This sense of Covenant partnership in the deeds of the every-day is in principle the same as its more dramatic

150

manifestation, that in moments of danger, personal or communal, we trust that God will act on our behalf. Here, too, it is normally we who must petition, appeal, fight or go into exile. Yet we know our acts mean nothing without God's help. The pious, however, have realized that this is equally true of every act we do in calmer days.

This Covenant dialectic of people and God eventually and inevitably, so it would seem, leads to a third level of hope, that God will use the Divine saving power in such a way that there will be, so to speak, no more need for God to act again. One day there will be an ultimate Exodus from the human slaveries that we call history and an entrance into the Promised Land of God's rule and humankind's full-hearted obedience. If God is truly sovereign over the creation and concerned that the Divine will be done among us, if God repeatedly acts to make this happen and covenants with Israel to bring it about, then it seems reasonable that in due course God should see to it that this effort reaches a proper conclusion. This alone is commensurate with the sole rule of God. It also reinforces and is in turn strengthened by the individual and folk levels of Biblical faith. When the individual or the people of Israel verged on despair, they were buoyed by the knowledge that any defeat they might now suffer could not impede God's and therefore Israel's ultimate triumph in history.

Jews have always been incredulous when they have been told that Israel's Covenant and its eschatological hope are contradictory, that only by its Covenant being broken or superseded could its messianic visions be fulfilled. Jews today remain no less incredulous. If anything, they are somewhat astonished that so archaic an attitude, so pre-Conciliar a point of view can still be heard in serious scholarly circles. Were the Exilic and post-Exilic prophets of the Bible not truly God's prophets when they called for the re-establishment of the Temple, the observance of Jewish law, and affirmed the eternity of Israel's relationship to God? Was the Jewish people which heard the prophets, preserved their writings, and transmitted their message in unbroken tradition over the centuries completely misled and deluded? Even more important, has the community of Israel throughout the ages, indeed is the Household of Israel today, not God's people, not truly bound to God in a Covenant as real and as effective today as when it was made at Sinai? Any such imputation that there can be no living religious reality to Israel's presence in the world today or that there cannot be any integrity to its structure of hope must be rejected as blind to the reality of Biblical faith and its living manifestation in Jewish lives both today and through the ages.

By the early centuries of the Common Era Jewish eschatology was as fundamental to Jewish hope as was God's trustworthiness toward individuals and the people as a whole. It is true that some Rabbis speak of the messianic era in quite naturalistic terms, while others give a miraculous interpretation. Often that spectrum of opinion exists because of a distinction between a naturalistic messianic time which is only the prelude to the trans-naturalistic Kingdom of God's own rule, though this usage is not consistent. The Rabbis did not encourage such post-historical speculations, yet allowed great individual freedom when they occurred. They could do so because they firmly fixed eschatological as well as personal and communal hope into the pattern of Jewish observance. Thus, in the daily prayers it is a leading motif of the *kaddish* doxology, is found in four of the last five of the regular petitions of the daily service and is the major theme of the New Year's and Day of Atonement liturgy. Indeed, the place where the word "hope" figures most prominently in Jewish liturgy is the original New Year's prayer for the establishment of God's Kingdom which for about six centuries now closes every Jewish service. Its second paragraph begins: "We therefore hope in Thee, O Lord our God, that we may speedily behold the glory of Thy might, when Thou wilt remove idols from the earth and the non-gods shall be utterly destroyed, when Thou shalt establish the world as the Kingdom of God...." And one can see the eschatological dimension of Jewish hope intertwined with the individual and folk concerns in the opening paragraph of the petitions recited three times each day: the mighty God who helped one man, Abraham, is now addressed as the One who will bring a redeemer to save all the Household of Israel.

IV

This brief survey should be sufficient to indicate why the old Jewish hope is unacceptable to secular moderns. Though Biblical Judaism, too, knows dissatisfaction with the present and has faith that it will be transcended in time to come, it affirms this horizontal trust because it knows a vertical reality. It believes the present can be transcended because it believes in a transcendent God. Here the paths diverge. Secularists by popular definition, know no transcendent reality. Their hope for the future is in the enhancement of human capabilities. With the improved techniques and knowledge time will bring, humanity will be able to overcome problems which are not now soluble. This represents only faith in humankind and its capacities, perhaps, too, a trust in nature's accommodation to the human, or a sense that to change things may change the quality of existence. All these must still be called horizontal factors.

This is what makes Marxism such an interesting case in the contemporary secular world. At one time a Marxist view of society and history might well seem to have qualified as the height of secularity. Today our secularity is too radical for such a judgment. Marxism still bears the genetic signs of its idealistic parentage, for it retains a sense of transcendence even though it has sought to stand the Hegelian dialectic on somewhat materialistic feet. The classic Marxist believes that there is at work in and through human history a process which will inevitably bring about the Socialist state or some other such messianic surrogate. It would be wisest for people to identify and cooperate with this inevitable development, but even if they do not it will surely come to be. What powers this hope is its recognition of a process beyond our ultimate control that moves history to a pre-determined end. It may be located in nature and closely identified with economic structures and dynamics, but, insofar as it is beyond deflection or control, it is in the category of transcendent realities. Moreover, though it cannot be tested or empirically verified, it explains everything. It therefore seems, in Marx's own sense, an ideology—and a religious one at that. There may be great virtue in creating dialogues with Marxists today, particularly in Europe, yet that has little to do with the problem of interpreting religion to those of a secular mind. Because they reject all transcendence and ideological formulation for their tentative commitments and pragmatic understandings, they are essentially post-Marxist with regard to history even where they use Marx's sociology—and that seems increasingly true in Europe as in the United States. Indeed, one cannot help but wonder whether it is not a recognition of its failing intellectual appeal that makes Marxism open to discussion with religion.

The fundamental question then between secularists and Biblical religion is: To what extent is hope possible without faith in a transcendent reality? Are the problems of human existence ones which are in principle within human competence to resolve, or must the future inevitably involve human beings in the same fundamental human difficulties? Let us assume that by the elaboration of medical techniques people could have great stretches of time, perhaps even endlessly extended, and the vigor to use it. Would this answer the problem of self-fulfillment? If being a person implies a sense of intellectual, aesthetic, and more particularly, moral excellence, if it implies dissatisfaction with anything less than a fully integrated self in spirit and in action, the human problem is not time or technique but the distance between finite self and infinite aspiration. Our problem lies in the quality of existence, and while we may modify it we cannot change it. Even endless time could bring us only to despair, for with many years and undreamed of help we still could not yet live in the fullness we know we ought to reach. Even without death to dramatize our limits, endless time itself could only bring us an endless sense of ultimate frustration.

If this is our existential reality, it would be absurd for us to face the future with an attitude so fundamentally positive as to be worthy of the term "hope." It is even more difficult to believe, except by some quixotic self-assertion against the universe, that we could in some secular fashion make hope the fundamental principle of our existence. As I see it, a modern trust in the future must necessarily be self-contradictory. If we know nothing which can radically change the present, then the future can only mollify or alleviate our existential discontent. As important and as useful as that may be, such a sentiment hardly qualifies as hope. If we know that the years to come will be essentially as disquieting as now, though with some improvements and conveniences, then we should speak of our attitude toward them as expectation, anticipation, desire or longing, but something quite distinct from the old religious virtue of hope. And I believe a fresh look at our continual concern with what is yet to be will show this, in fact, to be the case.

V

We have, however, come to a fundamental methodological problem, one which is insoluble, yet unavoidable. Out of the plethora of evidence available, how do we know exactly what the secular mentality is? How can we be certain that we are talking about real people in modern times rather than our fantasies concerning them? Since they are considered scientifically oriented, one would think that empirical factors would be critical. Yet, as in the death-of-God dispute, we ignore such statistical data as exist because we assume that most people are really behind the times. In talking of the secular mind, then, theologians are playing at spiritual sociology. I suppose the only way we shall know who is right is by applying one Biblical standard for prophecy and waiting to see whether things turn out as predicted. In the meantime, the best any such speculation can do is to provide a useful hermeneutic for understanding some of the movements in our society, though just which ones and how many one cannot say. I would suggest as one handy rule for understanding such analysis that we tend to find the significantly new in reaction to what we are tired of seeing. Again Hegel refuses to die. In the interpretation which follows I admit my amateur standing as a social diagnostician and confess that if there is anything I am overly acquainted with it is Jewish secularity usurping Jewish religiosity.

I see our modern concern for the future as quite spurious, a rationalization or an escape, but not a genuine hope. On one level I believe this is true because in substantial part we have had the experience of reaching a hoped for future and found it wanting. American society has made a tremendous leap forward in the past two decades. Many people today—unfortunately not all—have had an entirely unexpected number of their fondest dreams fulfilled. The cars, the clothes, the homes, the vacations, the appliances, the recreation are often far better than they ever could have imagined twenty years ago. Then they believed that if only they had this or that they would be happy. Now they have been given much of what they asked for—and it has not solved anything. They do not want to go back to life at it was, but they have learned, decisively, I think, that having is not being. They may still want more and better things. That is only because the present might be better, not because they can any longer have genuine hope in the future. And the disappointment that has come to Communists with the achievement of Communist states is a commonplace of the post-modern world.

This, it seems to me, explains why we are less oriented to the future than to the present. The most obvious economic fact of our times is not that people invest but that they live on credit, that they mortgage their futures to pay for pleasures now. They do so because they do not trust in the future as much as did their parents. They cannot be certain they will ever get there, so everyone is on a pleasure spree seeking to fill the now with the justification of existence. The "squares" experiment with restaurants and travel, the liberals with sex, and the radicals with drugs. Even the multi-media discotheques are no voyage into the future, only a non-pharmaceutical way of blotting out time by over-loading the senses. I cannot see how we can ignore this massive redirection from the future to the present, nor do I see what else can explain it but our lack of faith in the future.

On a far more intellectual level, Albert Camus had seen this in the 1940s. In his novel *The Plague* and elsewhere he characterized us moderns as those who must learn to live without hope. If modernity to man is, by definition, to sacrifice all illusion, then the most dangerous illusion of all, the one we must therefore most thoroughly surrender, is hope. Camus knew that without some transcendent standard or reality the future could be no better than the past, and he also knew that transcendence was no longer accessible. Being as humane as he was honest, he asked how we could now keep from despair, most radically suicide, and how we might come to exercise common decency toward others. He failed to validate ethics without transcendence, yet his quest remains the productive model for courageous secularity.

VI

I have presented these three aspects of the modern experience not only to argue that it is not essentially future-oriented but equally to remind us of its radical rejection of transcendence. If our apologetic strategy leads us to try explaining religious hope in secular terms, we must inevitably compromise the fundamental nature of Biblical trust. The secular concern for the future and, indeed, its current escape into the present do afford us an opportunity to speak of similar dissatisfactions which must similarly be met by faith. Still, at some point our apologetics must give way to a certain polemical thrust, no matter in how friendly or open a way it is put forward. Surely no dialogue is worth entering into if one cannot stand one's own ground in full and equal dignity.

The strange fate of hope in modern Jewish history is worthy of special consideration in this regard. The old tri-partite structure of Biblical hope, personal, communal, eschatological, held with some variety in the configuration throughout the Middle Ages. Then, with some individual exceptions, such as Spinoza, it was the concept of autonomy created by the Enlightenment, systematically elaborated by Kant and given special power by the secular state and modern science, which required it to undergo major reconsideration. Validation now meant personal experience, rational, moral, or religious. Eschatology was the prime victim, for what could the

155

individual personally know of what waited beyond historic time? The folk-hope somehow managed to survive, though how personal evidence could mandate group existence was a problem which disturbs Jewish theology down to the present more rigorously individualistic time. Hope for the individual still remained, since that was the dogmatic foundation of the concept of autonomy. If, then, the Jewish people helped individuals and even humankind, then one might trust it would survive in history.

The Holocaust under Hitler destroyed that liberal reconstruction and yet prevented a return to the traditional modes of belief. It was no longer possible to make the goodness of humankind the cornerstone of Jewish faith. Yet, who could see God acting in this horror-filled history? That is not because it was traumatic. The Jewish people had been able to see God in disaster before. The prophetic interpretation of the Biblical catastrophes had long since set the standard which Jews utilized to explain disasters as substantial as the destruction of the Second Temple, the defeat of Bar Kochba, the Expulsion from Spain, the rampage of Chmelnicki. None had caused a break with the Jewish tradition of hope, though often it has been reinterpreted. Now, however, the social suffering was too great to be seen as any sort of divine punishment or instruction. And the pain of endless individuals was too great to find explanation in the survival of the people or in such eschatological promises as might still be extended. If God did not act for individuals and Israel, then how could one hope God would ever act again? How could one even trust God was there?

It is characteristic of Judaism that if any new statement of atheism was to move the Jewish community since World War II it had to come on the basis of what happened in history rather than because philosophers worry whether statements about God can have significant intellectual content. Jews, for all their intellectuality, do not seem so rationalistic as to consider linguistic problems a compelling reason for saying God is dead. And, in turn, they have been amazed that the major death-of-God thinkers have not discussed the unparalleled destruction of Jews under Hitler as a reason for disbelief in God. That alone has agitated the Jewish community whenever it sought to speak of Jewish faith.

This social interpretation is, of course, subjective but, I think, quite widespread. Here we come to the problem of how to read the social evidence on an even more significant level. How does one know that this and not that event is revelatory? Why did the Hebrews say it was the Exodus and Sinai and not the 400-year slavery or the Golden Calf that taught them what was finally true and ultimately real? I do not know the answer to these questions. I only know that for me and, I believe, for the Jewish people as a whole the Holocaust was shattering but not determinative. It was not the Sinai of our time. It burned us, tortured us, scarred us, and does so yet today. Nonetheless, its obscene brutality did not become our paradigm for future history. I have never been able to cease wondering, in the technical, Biblical sense, that after the Holocaust there was no mass desertion of Judaism. If anything, there arose in the community as a whole a conscious desire to reclaim and re-establish Jewish existence. It was no more than that. Yet, considering what Jewishness had just entailed, that spontaneous, inner reassertion was uncanny. It testified to that which is more than human wisdom and courage, which yet sustains and carries humankind through the terrors of personal and social history.

I also find it significant that despite the substantial secularity of our community, the very few Jewish death-of-God advocates have found very little acceptance. I attribute this to the social fact that, while to others to hear of religious atheists sounds new and radical, to us it is somehow very old-fashioned. Atheism is where we all were in the '30s and the '40s, in the days when we still thought university rationalism would redeem the world. That is what those of us who care about Judaism seriously turned away from; to revive it now for a new Judaism seems strangely behind the times. What is more important, the very phenomenon it should explain to us it rather destroys. To say there is no God means that everything is permitted. Now, the Holocaust explained is the Holocaust neutralized. It does not even have a negative power. By what right are we disgusted, nauseated, overwhelmed, outraged, at what happened to the innocent if it was only an honest reflection of reality and not an intolerable violation of a standard of right inherent in the universe itself? The new atheism would rob us of our moral indignation, and it is just that which the Jewish community knows better than to surrender. Some decades back it could be tolerant of an atheism which left ethics standing. Today secular ethics is a vanishing myth, and atheism means nihilism. That is to lose the very moral ground from which the protest against God was launched.

Post-Holocaust Jewish theology found itself in a period when only a negative methodology might be intellectually bearable, though hardly emotionally effective. Any effort to explain the Holocaust would betray the event and our reactions to it. So, nothing could be said. Yet unbelief was equally impossible, because of the moral affirmation inherent in the very protest. We could not speak, but we could not not believe. We could only have a theology of non-non-belief. That was not much, but it was more than nothing. Considering what we had been through, considering that some of us had been through it and refused not to believe, that would until recent days have been the realistic content of Jewish hope.

VII

Now, once again, historic events have shaken us to our foundations. One cannot speak of Jewish hope today without discussing the June 1967 Arab-Israeli war—and this within a Biblical frame of reference. Hope for individual Jews was until recent times intimately linked with the fate of their people. The individual Jew shares God's Covenant as one of the people of Israel, and this means that each Jew is by divine act tied to all Jews, everywhere in the world, especially those who live in the Land of Israel.

This ethnic closeness in a religious faith may be more than what one normally expects in a church, but then God called the Children of Israel as a folk and not as a church. This social structure has over the ages been found fully appropriate to its purpose of endurance through history.

Jewish hope, moreover, is linked to what God does in historic time. If the Jews find themselves in a house of bondage, they await God's saving action in the here and now. That was the trauma of the Holocaust. Therefore, if we are to speak of Jewish hope we must speak of the fate of the Jews, and in our times that means, among other communities, quite specifically the State of Israel. That sounds like politics to many Christians and hence strangely unreligious. But Christian categories will not do here. The destiny of the Household of Israel is a theo-political matter now as it was in Biblical times. Neither our human institutions for channeling governmental power nor God's concern with what this people must yet do in history can be eliminated when discussing the Jews and their Judaism.

That Monday afternoon when the Six Day War began and no news of what was taking place came through, there was black anxiety throughout the Jewish world. The question was not military: Who would win? It was theological: Would God abandon the people of Israel again and allow the citizens of the State of Israel to be slaughtered by Arab armies? For weeks we had heard Radio Cairo's threats to exterminate the Jews of the State of Israel, and we had watched as the mobs there and in other Arab capitals were whipped into a frenzied hatred of the Israelis. We knew the danger was real and not exaggerated, that if the Arab armies drove back the Israelis there would be an incredible massacre which the Western governments would not intercede in time to stop. And God had shown us already once this century a Divine withdrawal from history sufficient to allow the Chosen People to be slaughtered. Could we survive another Holocaust? It was not only the Israeli armies that were on trial that day but, in very earnest, God.

Then came the victory, clean, sharp and decisive; gained by intelligence and skill backed by moral will and determination; unsullied by brutality, vengefulness, atrocity or vindictiveness. We sophisticates thought we knew historical reality and, therefore, had discounted much of the Bible. Now, before our very eyes, history turned Biblical once again. Of course it was relief, elation, a victory at last, and a great one. This only begins the explanation, for the truth is that to our own surprise we sensed the presence of a transcendent reality operating in history that we had almost come to believe could no longer make itself felt there. We knew all the technical reasons for the Israeli success, but we also knew they did not explain what had happened. Without soldiers and generals, without equipment and training, nothing could have happened; but what happened was more than what they alone could do, and so we naturally and necessarily gave thanks to the One who works wonders and delivers God's people from Egypt. We saw Divinity once again as the God who remembers the Covenant. I am not saying that the Israeli victory proves to Jews there is a

158

God. I am saying that what happened in June spoke to us in a way that, for example, the Sinai campaign of 1956 did not. For a moment the tight, naturalistic structure through which we secularized souls see everything cracked open, and we saw God's hand. As a result, we cannot speak of Jewish hope today as we would have done after the Holocaust but before the Six Day War.

You will have noticed that I have not spoken of what happened to *them*, there in the State of Israel, but of what happened to *us*. This was, of course, their politics, their war, and their immediate suffering. But, while we are not bound to them politically, we were, by virtue of being one people under God, intimately involved in their crisis. How could we who have been through this Holocaust and post-Holocaust era together now stand divided in trial or in triumph? Perhaps neither of us knew how closely we felt tied to them until the moment of crisis arrived. And it is certain that neither of us realized how deeply we were still rooted in Jewish tradition until we all stood once again, so unexpectedly, before the Western Wall of the Temple in Old Jerusalem. Irony of ironies, it is that archaic religious symbol which more than anything else explains to agnostics and to religious liberals, to secularists and the non-observant, who the people of Israel is.

Thus in one incredible week we reclaimed two strands of our old Jewish hope: we saw God save our people Israel; and we recognized personally how our individual being was tied to our Covenant folk. And now we could feel free to speak of what had sounded so hollow in the post-Holocaust days, that we, personally and individually, have from time to time felt God's helping presence in our lives. In the face of our people's disaster, schooled in secular disbelief, how could we say God still works in human lives and we hope in God. Now what we have seen broadcast before the entire world makes it possible for us to say in all humility: God has helped us, too. Our experience as a community is once again linked with our individual experience, and the old pattern of Covenant hope on these two levels reasserts itself.

What we have now regained is not a soothing, easy hope. It encompasses of necessity the reality of pain, even of incredible, inexplicable suffering. It does not relish such experiences nor find them a virtue to be cherished. The suffering of the servant has been foisted on us. Crucifixion is not one of our models. Gladly would we await the Messiah with the normal tests of endurance. Yet in the midst of whatever bondage history may now bring, we can once again hope in God's action on our behalf. God did so for our fathers. God did so in our time. We trust God will do so again for our children and our children's children. God's Covenant with us remains unbroken.

We do not understand how to explain in technically coherent terms our strange history of service, of suffering, and of continued hope. We know what we have seen gives us no intellectual clarity about the continuing suffering of individual Jews and Jewish communities, of persons

159

and peoples of every faith and none. We still can say nothing about the Holocaust. History is grimmer than we ever imagined and human existence far more difficult than we believed. Still, amidst that very realism, we have a sense of hope. We know that God may try us, but God does not entirely abandon us. We know our individual existence and social destiny do not escape God's saving power. In such a world as ours that is a lot to know. It is the only kind of hope which has a chance to transcend despair.

And knowing that much, must not even we secularized Jews follow the organic development of Biblical Judaism and move on from personal and social hope to a full-throated eschatological belief? That surely is incompatible with secularity, but now that we have seen the secular transcended in our own lives we may find the way to reassert in our own accents the coming of God's Kingdom which will transform and redeem history. That is more than can be said at present. Indeed, already the cynics and the sophisticated are eager to analyze away the religious reality of what we have so freshly gained. I trust that despite their numbers and their stature they will not succeed but rather that the promise of the unknown prophet of the Exile will be fulfilled:

> They that wait for the LORD shall renew their strength;
> They shall mount up with wings as eagles;
> They shall run, and not be weary;
> They shall walk, and not faint.

(Isa. 40:27–31)

Note

1. The argument which follows is in response to the presentation by Jürgen Moltmann, elaborating a theology of hope based on the secular philosopher Ernst Bloch's theory that the key to modern secularity is its commitment to the future.

The Jew as Individual:
Personal Ethics

THREE

The Jew as Individual:
Personal Ethics

For all the concern with social context exhibited in the prior sections of this book, I see the self as the rightful locus of moral decision and thus the necessary center of a contemporary Jewish ethic. Happily for my theorizing, that is how most loyal Jews today approach questions of responsibility. They wish to know what guidance their tradition offers and they are respectful of the opinions of rabbis and scholars—but as the incomparably well-educated, self-respecting persons they know themselves to be, they then insist on "making up their own minds." Except for the devout Orthodox, American Jews who stress the importance of Jewish law regularly take its rulings as guidance, not as discipline—and so, too, do the large number of merely nominal Orthodox Jews.

Classically, the Jewish tradition does not bestow such power upon the single self, for all that it esteems and honors it. And many moderns have done prodigies to demean the self's dignity by warping its freedom into willfulness and self-indulgence. No self-respecting Jew can accept that perversion of autonomy. Hence the major theoretical problem of contemporary Jewish ethics, as I construe it, is how to give the self the ethical rights modernity has shown it to deserve—particularly against the institutions that have so often betrayed it—while channeling its energy in ways that befit Covenant responsibility.

I begin this enterprise with a rejection of rationalism's construction of the self, which I find inadequate to its immediate reality. To that extent, I have been influenced by existentialism. But knowing my Jewishness to be utterly basic to my being, that is, in these terms, to my selfhood, I have sought to describe what might constitute a proper "Jewish self." And it is the autonomy of the *Jewish* self, not the rationalistic moral agent of Kant or the secular, isolated self of philosophic existentialism that I have sought to characterize and guide to moral action.

Perhaps I should not be surprised that sexuality has been the ethical area to which I have most applied this dawning understanding—indeed, the area in which I first wrote at length about ethical matters, though I did so more out of a need to respond to a human problem than because I knew clearly how Jewish ethics ought to be done today. Surely no modern transformation of human values has been at once more persuasive and problematic than that in the sexual realm. I am somewhat comforted that the stands I have taken on these matters over the years appear to me, except in some subsidiary judgments, still to reflect my understanding of Jewish responsibility.

13

Autonomy Versus Tradition

The reform of Judaism to meet the situation of an emancipated Jewry became possible only when, even unconsciously, human autonomy could be asserted and given precedence over the authority of Jewish tradition. Because Moses Mendelssohn could do so only in the realm of theology and not in that of practice he remains "orthodox." When Israel Jacobson believed the individual's duty to follow mind and conscience was more important than following inherited forms of liturgical observances, reform could begin. Jacobson and other innovators consciously directed their autonomous will to the continuation of historic Judaism and so considered their modification itself Judaism. Indeed, if change was once central to Judaism, liberalism is now the most authentic form of Judaism.

Theoretically, the autonomy is prior to the tradition and has hierarchical superiority in matters of decision. Practically, the German liberals were men who used it to renew their Judaism. They are Liberal, Progressive or Reform Jews, with the autonomous adjectives modifying the tradition, which remains the continuing substantive term. When Moses Mendelssohn's children and grandchildren could not autonomously affirm Judaism they followed their enlightened will into the church. Today they would become some variety of secularist. Only now they are so often joined by other refugees from Judaism that they form a Jewish class and it is difficult therefore to tell on which side of the margin of continuing Jewishness they still stand.

From *CCAR Journal*, vol. 15, no. 2 (April 1968).

This paradox of a logically prior autonomy used to affirm the value of Jewish tradition has, in fact, been basic to all non-orthodox Jewish theology since the early 19th century and the source of its inevitable intellectual tensions. Already in Zechariah Frankel and Samuel Holdheim of that time, progressive Judaism had to face the demand for a reactionary or a revolutionary turn. Voices at either extreme are again heard today. By their very opposition to one another they drive the divergent positions yet further apart and tend to polarize all liberal Jewish thinking. It should be helpful therefore as well as intellectually interesting to explore the problematic of affirming in the present situation the simultaneous value of the autonomous will and Judaism's demands on the Jews.

Liberal Jews should not underestimate their great stake in the concept of autonomy for it is the source of their special contribution to Judaism. They came into being because they were not content simply to accept what the Jewish past brought to a radically transformed Jewish present. Their 19th century forefathers had the courage to insist against what their Jewish teachers had taught them, that Judaism's creative adaptiveness through the ages is one of its chief characteristics and, against what the authorities of their community insisted, that it can change. They defended themselves ultimately on the basis of what Kant had already defined as the key principle of enlightenment: the autonomy of the individual. The early liberals did not apply the concept as individualistically as did the philosophers of their day or this. The German rabbis wrote and thought more of the autonomy of each generation or epoch, thus validating in a rather corporate way their right to differ from their ghetto forebears. Thus they preserved a community aspect to their sense of rightful change and hoped to avoid the anarchy or defection which would be the fruit of radical individualism. In their reform of Judaism they hoped to fuse the best of the tradition with their modern sense of truth and value. They tried to shape a Judaism that they felt would stand the scrutiny and fulfill the standards of autonomous individuals. So they selected and adapted as well as transmitted the Jewish heritage. They stressed prayer in the vernacular, sermons that spoke to mind and heart, instruction for girls as well as boys. They wanted understanding to bring commitment, insight to transform faith by continuity into one of willed acceptance.

It was a grand and noble enterprise. Not so long ago, in the multiple forms of modernized Judaism it had engendered, it seemed to have succeeded nicely. A contemporary style of Judaism had come to seem the most natural thing in the world. Not only do most Jews no longer live in the ghetto manner and yet consider themselves to be loyal Jews, but even the traditionally observant have changed the tone and emphasis of their practice in a way that seemed unthinkable in the early, acrimonious debates.

Alas, that happy balance between modernity and tradition is breaking down. On the one side people under the influence of a secular civilization, have become more radical in their demands for autonomy. Everything is valued in terms of the self, its needs, its fulfillment. On the other side, the rising rate of inter-marriage, poor attendance at prayer and the general apathy of practice seem to force the admission that if Judaism is to continue in any significant way, it must create a deeper piety and express it in richer observance.

Consider the problem as it arises with teenagers or college youth, those apostles of individuality. They rebel for more freedom, more independence, the right to be only what they choose to be. Their Jewish teachers know they and their parents are not good enough Jews. The young want greater autonomy. The synagogue wants more Judaism and it defensively tends to see in the cry for more freedom not an appropriate affirmation of human responsibility but a threat to everything it holds dear. For insofar as choice is fully free it may settle on anything as well as Judaism and there is enough historic as well as contemporary experience to show that this fear is realistic. Moreover it would be fantasy to assume that some new philosophic or social scientific answer will quickly solve the problem. Religion is as social and psychological a phenomenon as an intellectual one. Hence the response it gives must be as institutional as it is philosophic, if not more so. For anyone who wants continuing commitment to Judaism how can the pursuit of autonomy and not Jewish discipline be the ultimate good?

That is the reactionary wing of liberal Judaism speaking and one hears in its words the instinctive adult response to youthful demands for autonomy: lay down the law and require its observance. Often this keeps the children in line—for a while. Is that then what progressive Judaism should do? Stem the rising tide of indifference and unconcern by defining necessary beliefs and setting forth required standards of practice?

Were this position only negatively motivated it would have little appeal. Its power stems from the reality of the failure to help liberal Jews understand Jewish belief or instruct them in the value of Jewish observance. How can one expect to win their autonomous assent to Judaism in a world which fights religion and considers Jewish faith odd if they are not given sophisticated, thoughtful guidance as to their living Jewish alternatives in thought and practice? Where are the books on belief and observance serious enough to be considered worthy of reviews by others than colleagues who owe the authors attention?

There is, however, a critical distance between guidance and authority, between education and legislation. Liberal Judaism was created over precisely this issue and despite the risks it is difficult to see how it could remain true to itself if it took a dogmatic tack. Where is the theory of revelation which today could authorize by God's own will statements of belief or practice? Is there any human authority to which people should surrender their autonomy? Practically, who would listen to this new insistence on discipline? Surely not the youth, the group about whom most of the worrying is done. They know they are or will be as free as they wish in religious matters. They show it today in their attitudes, tomorrow in their indifference to campus religious activities of every sort. The appeal to tradition for its own sake, the insistence upon authority lest the whole thing fall apart will only strike them as a typical effort of the old to deprive them of their rights so the aged may stay in power. And their parents are far too much part of the secular world to be any more willing to accept authority. The emancipation of the Jews was based on the secular notion of personal freedom of religion. Having joyously accepted its benefits Judaism cannot now avoid its risks though they grow increasingly great.

So the call comes from the radical pole to admit that Jews are fully part of the modern world and follow wherever that leads. The appeal here is to the unimpeded pursuit of truth, even should it lead far away from the past. One might argue, somewhat homiletically, that this was always the fundamental concern of Judaism. Was not Abraham the first Jew by virtue of smashing his father's idols and thereby boldly breaking from his religion? This is an age of scientific advance, of intellectual acceleration, of technological conquest. How can Jews remain content to speak in terms of old semitic or rabbinic mythologies?

The arguments are so familiar they run the risk of being rejected because they have become boring. Yet at this extreme too there is much truth. Surely Judaism has known since the days of the prophets that Jewish survival depends not on old institutions meticulously preserved but on the God of truth served, if need be, by the destruction of God's own house. The old intellectual structures of 19th century German idealism which still serve as the staples of modern Jewish liberalism are hardly fit for a world where the great work of Freud and Einstein is half a century old and Auschwitz and Hiroshima are nearly a quarter of a century gone. There surely needs to be a statement of Jewish faith as adequate to this age as the neo-Kantian was to pre-World War I German liberal Jewry. The problem, of course, is where to find a proper conceptual matrix for such an explication of Judaism.

The older liberalism could believe that the modern secular mind knows a truth worthy of such trust that it should be allowed to determine what is permissible in modern Jewish belief. To reassert such a relatively uncritical dependency on contemporary philosophy or culture after the lessons of the past century and a half of parasitic liberalism seems unfathomably optimistic amidst a secularity whose chief characteristic is realism pressed almost to the point of pessimism. Yet that is what the radicals propose. They keep hoping they can do for this age what the German Reformers did a century ago. They reached out into the culture, into general philosophy and found a means of explaining Judaism in terms of universal truth. That kept Judaism alive then and only a similar effort can do so today. (How odd to hear such a decidedly Hegelian assertion in the mouths of supposedly post-Hegelians.)

There are two reasons why this will not work again, one intellectual and one social.

When the German Reformers sought survival by fusing their Judaism with the spirit of the age, they were in an intellectual climate suffused by a Kantian emphasis on the ethical and a Hegelian concern with history. Both were religiously oriented and thus there was available to the early Jewish liberals a secular, rational spirit relatively accommodating to their Judaism. That is what the radicals would like to find today. But how accommodating are the major philosophic structures of today? None of them, naturalism, existentialism, phenomenology, linguistic analysis, offers hospitality to anything like traditional ethics much less religion or God. Judaism even in its progressive form would have to change itself radically to adjust to any one of them. The German Reformers sounded modern to their contemporaries because everyone except the materialists was some kind of idealist then. There was a *Zeitgeist* and they could use it. Today the sacrifices of such reintegration would produce little return. There is no detectable, pervasive, single Zeitgeist. None of the philosophic styles is or shows sign of becoming dominant. Worse, they partially contradict one another. To select one as the new Jewish language means alienating the adherents of the other positions. One cannot hope to convince most moderns in an age of such philosophic pluralism. One can only choose which minority of intellectuals one wishes to address.

That being so, it will not do to see the purpose of progressive Jewish theology as essentially the elucidation of a proper modern concept of God. That might be the goal set by a neo-Kantian theology in which ideas are all important and the idea of God plays a central role. In a contemporary world of contrary conceptual systems it is fantasy to hope to create one idea so compelling that it will unify most Jews in Jewish belief. It is even more incredible, after the German experience, to believe that knowing such an idea will bring people to live by it, much less bring them to Jewish observance or the love of the people of Israel. The hope that adopting one philosophic style or another will save Judaism is so reductive of the complexities of the situation that it must be considered some sort of rationalist wishful thinking, a delightful contradiction in terms indeed.

These methodological considerations might be extended by asking by what criteria one selects the philosophy which will become the judge of what remains true in Jewish faith. Having dealt with that topic before (*C.C.A.R. Yearbook, 1963*, p. 215 ff.) let me pass on to the social realities which stand against the radical position.

We moderns, like people in every age, do not live by philosophy or hold back on life's major decisions until they have achieved full intellectual clarity. Most people want a rational component in their life style and we moderns seek to amplify it. Our time is often termed post-modern because we have come to realize how little intellect can rule persons, how much we are the creatures of our will and our times. On the surface the German Jewish effort to move with the Zeitgeist seemed a straightforward intellectual decision in the Hegelian spirit. Yet it had a significant social foundation. The early Reformers must have sensed that they could depend on their society to encourage ethical religion while setting limits for Jewish assimilation. Accommodation to the culture in their world implied a morally oriented concern with spirit, while negatively its anti-semitism would keep most Jews within their ancestral community. Besides their Jews came from an observant community and were surrounded by the historic evidences of their folk past. Many were learned. All had Jewish memories. Their community being deeply Jewish the thinkers could concentrate on the lesson of autonomy. Their primary thrust is rightly called a Jewish universalism.

That is far from the contemporary Jewish situation. As the secularity of the American society grows it fortunately has less and less place for overt anti-semitism and more and more appreciation for Jewish productiveness and creativity. Yet it also has little place for real religion or substantial ethnicity. The rise of democracy and technology means greater freedom for Jews as individuals but less use for them or anyone as a religious community. Indeed what Judaism must recognize is that contemporary culture is moving toward an a-moral, pleasure seeking, present oriented human style. One cannot count on educated people to be religious, or spiritual, or even moral when a real crisis occurs. Modern secular society has no institution, no philosophy or even cultural thrust with which to divert or control its inherent drive toward use and payoff. That, not philosophic inadequacy, is the real challenge confronting Judaism. Moreover, one can no longer count on anti-semitism or sentiment to keep Jews Jewish. Increasingly American Jews have few rich memories of Jewishness to fall back on as a last, lowest level of Jewish identity. So it is folly for contemporary Jewish thinkers to elaborate a new Jewish universalism in the unconscious hope that social forces may be counted on to keep people ethical, religious or Jewish and thereby counteract their centrifugal thrust. Today such a major outward thrust implies what one could hope it did not in 19th century Germany, committing most of the Jewish community to the new American paganism.

For most liberal Jews, I believe, that is too radical a stance. On the minimal level that is because they believe in the lasting significance of what may for the moment be too simply described as ethics. They may consider freedom a great value but if it leads to moral nihilism it has vitiated its own virtue. Freedom is not an end in itself, no matter where it leads, as Sartre and other atheist existentialists argue. For most Jews, even those of little faith, autonomy is precious as the pre-condition of a mature morality. It is itself an ethical commandment, hence when it is used to destroy ethics it negates itself.

To hold such a high view of ethical standards in contemporary society is already to share a minority faith. It is no longer widespread in the contemporary civilization and surely not self-evident or rationally demonstrable. Where one is to find the foundation for it in the future becomes increasingly problematic. So when the children of a community which made law precious and the doing of commandment supreme speak, against the crowd, for freedom confirmed in ethical responsibility, that may properly be understood as the old Jewish faith expressing itself in modern though truncated form.

Others are more positively Jewish. Having given themselves whole-heartedly to contemporary civilization, particularly its high culture and its politics, and having done so to the point of forgetting or forsaking their Judaism, they find themselves betrayed. With all its greatness, with all its promise, there is a stinking rot near the core of Western, industrial, democratic society. The moral revulsion Jews felt at the Hitlerian destruction of European Jewry could by the nasty be ascribed to Jewish ghetto sensitivity on the one side and German totalitarian madness on the other. Yet the appalling record of the succeeding decades has made it seem more prophetic than exceptional. Wherever one turns—black men, yellow men; the aged, the poor; the military, the industrialists; the educated, the respected—there is violence and exploitation, madness pretending to respectability, infirmity masquerading as competence.

If that is what a good part of today's world is like then many people will healthfully want to dissociate from it. The Jewish activism remains too strong for adults to drop out with the flower children or by way of drugs. But to identify completely is likely to mean surrendering values that now suddenly are as dear as they are nonconforming. The cultivation of a proper alienation has become a human necessity. So Jewish roots become a needed source of strength and Jewish forms of expression a helpful way of reaffirming self by taking one's distance from the majority. Having a Jewishness to assert against freedom gone wild has suddenly become a precious privilege as even the novelists have now discovered.

These realities reestablish the classic paradox of liberal Jewish theology. Only now, so to speak, there must be a change in its social orientation. Jewish universalism has had its day. It has shown, and indispensably so, that Jews can be modern. Now it is time to move to the next task. What is required is a stress on Judaism strong enough to serve as an antidote for paganism and an appreciation of the individual powerful enough to make us recognize how much of our fulfillment depends on our own acts. That sense of partnership between people and God was basic to the traditional Jewish belief in the Covenant. Yet it strikes a progressive, liberal note in giving human beings a greater share in its working out—and if God's absence in the Hitler days taught Judaism nothing it should have taught Jews they must do just that. What is needed today in liberal Judaism then is what I propose to call an open traditionalism.

It cannot be a simple reiteration of classic Jewish faith for what has been learned from a century and a half of progressive Judaism cannot be denied. Traditional Jews had once become so dependent upon God and God's saving power they seemed to have forgotten how to help themselves. They were abjectly passive before social injustice and historical abuse. They could only go to Palestine to die, not to rebuild themselves or the

171

Jewish people. The Reform Movement came into being in reaction to that denigration of human moral agency. Its history has legitimated in a way that cannot be gainsaid the modern Jew's fundamental concern for autonomy. So our reasserted traditionalism must be open, recognizing the basic importance of the free choice of human action, including, therefore, the right to conscientious dissent from what Jewish tradition once required or strongly urged.

Such openness led the early reformers to place all their trust in humankind and its creativity. They were self-confident and optimistic about society. It was enough for God to be an integrating moral idea. History was our province. In the light of later events their faith seems childish and naive, an over compensation against traditional belief as understandable for them as it is unacceptable today. Jewish humanism with religious trimmings and certainly more radical forms of openness will not do at this moment of crisis in civilization. So the openness affirmed here is first directed inward toward Jewish belief and practice. Historic Judaism is claimed as the ground of one's personal existence, yet in that act the right to dissent is carried along. If the differences with the tradition which arise become fundamental they might shatter the essential paradoxicality of the stand and a radical individualism would have to be reasserted. Or one might discover there was a principle of dissent and that represented the highest truth to which one's autonomy was pledged. Liberals would have great respect for either of those outcomes though they might lead the searching soul out of Judaism. For the reasons given above it can be hoped that this will not become the common case for those reestablishing their Jewish faith. It should also be noted that there is another possibility which might occur. It might turn out that one discovers one has no reason to dissent from the tradition whatsoever and is, in fact, orthodox. Liberals should see in such an autonomously reclaimed orthodoxy a surprising but a happy Jewish result indeed.

This emphasis on tradition, though open, makes it possible to believe that for the first time in liberal Jewish history a reverse relation to the culture may become possible, that Jewish faith may now be legitimated as its possible critic. Ever since the emancipation the judgment has come steadily from the outside. It was enough to make one wonder whether there was anything in Jewish faith which could stand up against a widely held modern belief. Now Judaism becomes precious for just that which once made it undesirable, its quality of alienation and transcendence of the society.

This has direct application to the problem of relating Judaism and philosophy. In this new approach to Jewish thought it is the tradition, openly held, which is the most important criterion of the philosophy used to interpret it. Which of the modern options is most congenial to its content, not which is most widely held or persuasively represented on campus this decade, determines the mode of doing theology in an open traditionalism.

172

In terms of my Jewish affirmations, religious existentialism is the most complementary philosophic style available. It supplies the hermeneutic instrument for interpreting Judaism in modern terms but may not usurp that role as a means to replace the primacy of traditional Jewish faith for me. That is what this self-conscious commitment to open traditionalism clarifies. Now when the religious existentialist insights contradict what study shows is classic Jewish faith, as is true in the areas of society, history and law, I do not automatically judge Judaism to be wrong. Rather I investigate to see what it is that I truly affirm. Perhaps I believe as the existentialists do and thereby discover a principle to my dissent and thus a higher faith which I affirm. Perhaps here I do autonomously uphold traditional belief and am thus led to criticize and correct religious existentialism. In the case of society and history it seems to me the existentialists are wrong and need the inter-personal, time-oriented vision which Jewish faith provides. In the case of law I dissent from both positions. That leads me to a Jewish sense that all authentic existence must be structured, an understanding foreign to existentialism. Yet I am also moved to an existentialist reworking of Jewish law in personalist terms it could not traditionally tolerate.

It is also important to keep in mind that this approach is not normally static. Openness implies new ideas, new insight, new consideration, the ongoing process of again and again winning one's traditionalism by personal affirmation. There is no guarantee that what is cherished today will not be discarded tomorrow. That is the risk of freedom without which mature humanity is unobtainable.

An open traditionalism would necessarily shake itself into incompatible pieces if it tried to come into being primarily as either a body of coherent doctrine, as the radicals generally prescribe, or as a body of required practice, as the reactionaries insist. The former is too abstract to tolerate paradox, the latter too specific to tolerate freedom. What is needed rather is something far more existential, what may be termed style. Without sophistication one has behavior but not style. Without structure one is only erratic. In recognizable style mind and action interpenetrate, integrating in life what if left to mind alone would be paradox. The present stage of Jewish theology should work toward the creation and definition of this modern style of Jewish being. One way of doing so is to show through analysis that the fundamental dialectic of such a style is not a matter of arbitrary decision but a necessary relatedness in the two basic faiths.

The key to such a demonstration comes from the recognition that any life lived in devotion to autonomy must, despite a cool exterior or a therapeutic humor, at some point reach a sense of high seriousness. Playing super-autonomy demands dedication to survive. A casual concern with it in this culture means its speedy demise, a self-contradiction not to be resolved. Modern Judaism, however, can be hospitable to the autonomous approach because it knows that when we face ourselves in ultimate seriousness we stand ready to transcend ourselves. We cannot serve as the ground of our own dignity. We are not self-explanatory or self-justifying. The question "who are we?" leads on, if it is radically affirmative, to "who is God?" Anthropology in depth is the contemporary way to theology.

Seriousness means that at some point in seeking to be true to oneself one turns back upon one's assumptions with enough power to ask radical questions about them. What is the faith implicit in the passion for autonomy? What commitments ground the right of people to take themselves and to be taken by others with such seriousness? Those become the critical questions on the way to reconciling the paradox.

The individual may claim that one's concern for one's autonomy was simply one's own idea, that it is a self-validating, willed value. Yet if it is important to make a similar assertion for everyone, if such a universal sense of autonomy should be one of the most fundamental considerations in organizing society, then it will not do to rest such comprehensive weight on so arbitrary a basis. For one may well ask in all seriousness today as one would have hesitated to do in more liberalistic times, why should people affirm themselves? Most people know themselves to be in many respects deeply unworthy of high regard. That is not a neurotic symptom. After all one's childish fantasies have been brought to consciousness and made to face reality one may still wonder at one's worth. Even the mature continually fail to meet their own standards or the reasonable demands of those they love. Self-acceptance is one of the great moral and psychic commandments of this era precisely because it is so difficult if we are expected to be realistic about ourselves and what we ought to be.

The imperative to be autonomous cannot be grounded in oneself and surely not in a culture which regularly tramples on it. Nor does the faith of every religion lead to it. Confucius would have us bend the self to the old social values. Lao Tsu asks that the self empty itself so the way of nature may become its way. Hinduism would lose the soul in the World Soul. Buddhism does not consider the self a reality to be enhanced and strengthened. Only in Judaism and its daughter religions does autonomy become possible, indeed necessary.

The Hebrews know human beings as the single creatures formed in God's image and bound to God as covenant partner. Not even our sins break that relationship as our punishment by God under the covenant shows. That is how radically the worth of our existence is asserted. Yet the covenant relationship does not require us to surrender ourselves or to escape from the self. Rather we must affirm our selfhood to participate in it for it is made with us quite specifically as human beings. We are not asked to be an angel to fulfill our part in it. Its commandments call us to be only what a person can be. In the rabbinic understanding people are not only the focus of the commandments but the master of their elaboration against all miracles or other supposed divine intervention. Under such a covenant people can, in rare instances, stand on their rights as partners and question God directly. Our more normal role is to accept God's sovereignty and live by God's law. That we always remain free to accept or reject. Even against God we have a certain autonomy.

That traditional understanding is not the same as our modern sense of autonomy since there the superior status of the Divine and the specificity to God's revealed will tend to keep human freedom to respond at a minimum. Still it is the root whence, by way of Greek abstraction and modern rationalist universalization, it grew to the affirmation of each person's moral dignity. Jewish faith still knows such a God and such a relationship of acceptance and obligation with humankind. That is the theological root of its contemporary moral disgust. Moreover Judaism has had extraordinary experience in translating this faith into a daily way of life. It has had such success that Jewish patterns still substantially survive in the general human concerns of Jewish lives despite widespread disbelief and non-observance. So the Jewish child receives that special welcome and concern which befits a new manifestation of the Divine image. Every Jew is pressured to study or to learn because great value is attached to our working out our unique capacities. The family and the community form the social matrix which keeps this attitude toward persons alive and functioning. Intense folk bonds keep the people an identifiable community linked to its ancient traditions though history has been cruel and perfidious. With all its fostering of commonalities, this is a people of fierce individualists, a folk which glories in argument and abhors hierarchy. If autonomy is precious in an anti-personal society then being Jewish gives one the kind of faith, the sort of life, the community support, the historic experience which makes it possible even today. It is not clear where else in the modern world, except in Christianity, one might otherwise find adequate substantiation for a vigorous affirmation of human autonomy.

So the paradox of living by autonomy and tradition simultaneously may now be resolved. That does not take the form of subordinating one of the affirmations to the other as both the radicals and reactionaries desire but rather by showing that neither can claim priority over the other. Each depends on its polar opposite. Jewish faith increasingly cannot be the passive continuation of a social heritage which is what it essentially was in previous Jewish generations. The more modern one is the more one insists it to be a matter of responsible willing. One should choose to be Jewish and resist as non-determinative the claims of family, history or personal sentiment. That choice, particularly since it is a fundamental commitment of one's life, must be made autonomously to be authentic. Yet the high value attached to autonomy is no longer self-explanatory. One can explain one's seriousness about it and one's determined pursuit of it only in terms of a prior faith, for the Jew, Judaism. The tradition grounds the autonomy—but it must be the basis of affirming the tradition—and so endlessly. The circle of faith is complete and in its harmonious closing the integrity of liberal Jewish existence despite its paradoxical foundation is established.

175

14

The Autonomous Jewish Self

Questioners commonly challenge me with a Jewish version of the fallacy of misplaced confidence. For generations now, liberal Jews have made western culture their surrogate for Torah—with disastrous results. While one might have accepted some Jewish sacrifice as the necessary accompaniment of a seismic shift to living in a new and better world, thinking in such other-directed terms in our situation seems ridiculous. Western civilization itself ails desperately. It not only does not merit being our religion, it seems likely to escape paganization only by the rebirth of the sort of moral devotion which faith in a commanding God can alone provide. Why then do liberal Jews not stop asking first what our society demands from them and attend instead to the claims that Judaism makes of all who wish to be authentic Jews?

Socially put, why are liberal Jews so half-hearted about their well-advertised return to traditional practices? Do we not know, no matter to what depth conscious pride or embarrassment have caused us to repress it, that genuine Jewish piety means living by traditional Jewish law? If we are not ready to accept the whole law, then for the sake of the unity of all Israel, can we not now immediately move in one limited but critical area: to follow orthodox Jewish law, in all its diversity, as our basis for Jewish marriages and divorces?

On rare occasions these challenges sound a metaphysical tone. Questioners cannot understand why Jews who acknowledge that religious du-

From *Modern Judaism*, vol. 4, no. 1 (February 1984).

ties are largely of human origin cannot simply accommodate those who know their standards are not their own but God's. How can liberal Jews utter an occasional absolute "no" when they proudly boast that all authority is substantially human and therefore open to revision?

My sort of liberal Jews will want to begin a response, I think, by carefully distinguishing between the failures of Western civilization and its lacking any value whatsoever. Many of the vital and creative aspects of contemporary Jewish life arose as a result of our emancipation. Jewish esthetics has moved beyond ritual silver, manuscript illumination and synagogue music to embrace arts and styles that greatly enrich our Jewish lives. Jewish scholarship is not only fecund beyond our fondest expectations of but twenty years ago, it excites us intellectually through its use of a western hermeneutic applied chronologically to texts examined critically. American Jewry exhibits an activism unique in the Diaspora Jewish experience. Zionism was the first great fruit of the fusion of the western notion of social responsibility and the Jewish commitment to life. By now we consider it a premise of Jewish duty that we should help determine the course of our society and take political action for the state of Israel or Jews in peril. And—limiting this list to four examples—by adapting ourselves to America we have created a Jewish style which shows signs of being a worthy successor to other great amalgams of Jewish life and a host culture, such as Spanish and Polish Jewish life.

These and many other smaller triumphs exist because many Jews, against the advice of their leaders, believed that the spiritual survival of the Jewish community would never be assured by seeking to preserve Jewish life as isolated as possible from the newly opened up western world. Rather, they knew that Jewish well-being depended on accepting the risks of entering the general society and actively seeking to benefit Jewish life from it. In the mid-19th century—and even now in some quarters—this commitment to energetic involvement with western civilization was seen as the death knell of Judaism. Today, a century or so later, the overwhelming majority of Jews, including a very substantial number of Orthodox Jews, is determined that they and their children shall have the best of both heritages. Liberal Jews like myself see in this historic transformation of Jewish community values a validation of our general sense of commitment to modern civilization and some of its central values.

The very most significant idea the Emancipation taught us, I venture to say, is the notion of the autonomous self. As we emerged from the ghetto, *shtetl* and *mellah*, we encountered a view of human nature that radically extended ideas which we had occasionally seen mentioned in our traditional texts. The western world gave these old Jewish notions an emphasis and power the admittedly high Jewish sense of self had not come to. For the Enlightenment thinkers taught that human beings ought to make their own minds and consciences the *ultimate* basis of their decisions and actions. When they ceded to some external reality—tradition, convention, custom, class, society or even the church—the final right to tell them what they ought to do, they gave away the greatest human capacity: the ability to think for oneself. Instead of utterly depending on others, people need to educate themselves and develop their moral and esthetic faculties, so that they might then responsibly join with other people to freely determine the course of their common existence. Human dignity became identified with rational self-actualization rather than with faithful obedience. Liberals today have lost the optimism connected with that 18th century notion but we are far from ready to give up its high estimate of the human value of self-determination. If anything, our experience with the moral failure of every kind of institution and collective has forced us back on the self as the proper, ultimate touchstone of righteous existence.

The importation of the notion of the self into Jewish thought has proceeded under many guises and still remains incomplete. But, in practice, the masses of American Jews have made it the foundation of their relationship to Judaism. Our "non-observant Orthodox" affiliate with institutions pledged to the *halakhah* but, after listening respectfully to what the law requires, do "what is right in their own eyes." The new young traditionalists of whom we are so proud, pick and choose their Jewish law from a three-volume catalog. Only the liberal Jews proclaim the autonomy of the self (in their transformed sense of that term, as we shall see) to be a fundamental principle for living Judaism today. When they perceive how much of the Jewish community, regardless of ideology, lives by the autonomous self, they feel confirmed in explicitly championing this western notion.

Emancipated Jewry also enthusiastically adopted the Enlightenment assertion that ethical responsibility has a primary place in the functioning of the autonomous self. In matters concerning inter-human obligation an unparalleled imperative quality enters the life of the liberal Jew. Liberal Jewish duty extends far beyond ethics (in its several explications) but nothing else one must do manifests its supremely commanding power. It confronts us as a transcendent demand and lays an ultimate claim upon us. Not to grasp the compelling power of the ethical upon devout liberal Jews dooms one to misunderstand them. To be sure, Enlightenment thinkers spoke largely in terms of secular ethics (as in Kantian autonomy) and liberal Jews, in adopting their ideas, turned them into religious ones (thus substantially changing the Kantian autonomy). This, rather than mitigating the power of the ethical, only made it stronger.

Liberal Judaism proclaimed that a properly autonomous self exists essentially in response to the commanding power of ethics. The point needs emphasis. I wish to provide it by recalling the unanimous agreement of the great exemplars of modern Jewish thought in this matter. Our one great philosophic mind, Hermann Cohen, continued Kant's view that we hear the ethical command as a categorical imperative. The other path-breaking rationalist, Mordecai Kaplan, provides even stronger testimony to the sovereign power of the ethical claim. In Kaplan's naturalistic understanding of reason, the social group creates all significant human value—with one exception (not explained by the common canons of naturalism): moral law. A folk has the right to do anything with its culture that it deems proper (Kaplan's liberalism) except to contravene ethical standards. They remain so powerful that they constrain the otherwise omnipotent Kaplanian group. In both thinkers the self finds the ground and guarantee of ethics in its idea of God.

The non-rationalists also uphold this view of ethics, though one must understand them in their personalistic sense and not insist that because they are not Kantians they have no ethics at all. Martin Buber rejects the concept of a binding rational ethical law (and Kant's notion of autonomy) but he has a Buberian equivalent for it, the command which arises from genuine encounter. Whenever two persons truly meet, God is present as the third, enabling partner of their relationship. And every direct I-thou with God itself provides a mission on which we are sent. Because dialogue brings persons most fully into contact, it also most directly issues forth in a sense of duty to other human beings. The ethical imperative we carry with us as we leave our meeting is, then, our response to God. It comes with such imperative quality that even a received law should not be allowed to stand in its way if they differ. This may be anti-nomian but it clearly manifests a sense of ultimate religio-ethical claim.

Abraham Heschel's treatment of this theme—and certainly the fashion in which he lived—similarly relates the personal experience of the reality of God to the need for an ethical life. In Heschel's treatment of revelation, the ethical occupies a powerful place and in what little he wrote about the Holocaust, most of his remarks are addressed to our perverse use of our powers to do good.

On no other single theme I can think of, not God, or the people of Israel, or revelation, or messianism, or law, or how we should think about these issues, do these thinkers so completely agree. For the liberal Jew then, ethics binds the self, regardless of the intellectual form in which one describes it. And, I hasten to add, it has a priority in Jewish duty over all other categories of Jewish responsibility, as necessary to a rounded Jewish life as they are. Despite the current disparagement of the old notion of Prophetic Judaism, the hierarchy of Jewish values proclaimed by many of the prophets still speaks to the religious perceptions of many liberal Jews.

Please note that for all these thinkers the old Enlightenment terms have significantly changed their meaning by being organically fixed in a religious context. For them, as for thoughtful liberal Jews of less intellectual distinction, the self is no longer fully understandable independent of God, and the autonomy of the self, primarily seen in ethical responsiveness, makes sense only in terms of the self's actualization of God's will since God is the source and standard of its own being.

I have not placed such stress upon the virtual identification of selfhood with religiously autonomous ethics so as to defend the old liberalism and its equation of Jewish duty with universal human ethics. That doctrine now appears to be less a timeless truth about Judaism than a re-

179

sponse to the historic situation of liberal Jews in another day. If Judaism was to survive the Emancipation, acculturation was a spiritual duty. In that time one could well take the Jewishness of most Jews for granted. Hence the immediate task of liberal theologians was to clarify the ways in which Jews were not only permitted to be active participants in general culture but should see this as a new Jewish duty.

Living in a vastly different time, we have almost the diametrically opposite liberal Jewish theological agenda. Our universalism is largely secure, as our continuity at the university, in large cities and our subsequent secularization attests. Our new Jewish excitement comes from our turn to our particular roots. Liberal theologians now hear themselves summoned to recapture a compelling particularism without sacrificing the gains of the universalization of Judaism. Or, to translate that into my personalist language, we need to transform the older, liberal, general human self with its accretion of Jewish coloration into what I call the undivided Jewish self. Specifically, I wish to clarify some aspects of the Jewish self's "autonomy."

In putting the question this way, I have departed from Mordecai Kaplan's ingenious effort to make a Jewish rationalism commandingly particular. While I admire Kaplan's rounded sense of Jewish ethnicity, I believe that his sort of religious humanism cannot satisfactorily resolve the critical contemporary human problem, the need of a ground of value. I agree with those many thinkers who deny that any immanentism, even those called a "transnaturalism," can legitimately call us to prefer one aspect of nature over another and devote ourselves to it to the point of substantial self-sacrifice. Kaplan illogically attempts to use sociology prescriptively and contradicts much of our recent experience when he insists that collectives can properly command autonomous selves. Custom does have power but not to the point of empowering long range imperatives. For several decades now we have continually been disillusioned by groups and institutions to the point where we greet their calls to sacrifice with considerable suspicion. The over-arching symbol of this development is the American involvement in the Viet Nam War. I must therefore leave it to others to clarify how the Kaplanian option can meet our ethical and spiritual needs and what limits it sets for community cooperation in the process.

For me, Buber took the important first step toward a new theology when he characterized the self as fundamentally relational. To put it starkly, Buber contends that one cannot be a proper self without a relationship to God, whether reached by a direct or indirect I-thou encounter. The daring of this assertion may most easily be grasped by the contrast to Jean Paul Sartre for whom individuality remains utterly unrelievable. Buber's self is not only essentially social but involved with God. Thus, while retaining the experiential base of all liberalism, Buber radically breaks with humanism by pointing to God's role in every I-thou meeting.

The Buberian shift from liberal religion as *ideas* to religion as *relationship* further transforms the notion of autonomy. Because every relationship manifests distance as well as communion, the self retains its full identity even in its most intimate involvement with the other. Specifically, I-thou involvement creates command without heteronomy. Despite all that you and I now mean to one another, neither of us must now surrender to the other our power of self-determination. Yet because you are here with me, my self, formerly so potentially anarchic, now has a sense of what it must choose and do—and it knows God stands behind this "mission." For Buber, then, the "autonomy" of the self is fulfilled in relation to the other and God. This interpretation of religious experience is too individualistic for any orthodoxy and too other-involved for anarchy. Because Buber preserves autonomy while guiding it in terms of a social-Divine involvement, his thought has been highly prized by many contemporary liberal religious thinkers.

Buber was an enthusiastic particularist, in fact a cultural Zionist, for almost two decades before writing *I and Thou*. He believed all nations were addressed by God, though the Hebrews had uniquely responded to their summons. He served the Jewish people devotedly, not the least by recalling it to its responsibilities to God, particularly that of bringing reconciliation into Israeli-Arab relations. Yet Buber never clarified how he made his intellectual way from individual "command" to national duty. When pressed on this issue, he insisted on an uncompromising individualism with all its universalistic overtones.

To meet our particularist needs we must find a way to reshape Buber's relationally autonomous self so that it has a direct, primary, ethnic form. I suggest, prompted by some hints in Rosenzweig, that my sort of liberal Jew is constituted by existence in the Covenant. (The capital "C" usage distinguishes between the universal Noachide covenant and the particular Israelitic one.) A Jewish self is characterized not only by a grounding personal relationship with God but relates to God as part of the people of Israel's historic Covenant with God. Being a Jew then, may begin with the individual but Jewish personhood is structured by an utterly elemental participation in the Jewish historical experience of God. Jewish existence is not merely personal but communal and even public. In the healthy Jewish self one detects no place, no matter how deeply one searches, where one can find the old liberal schizoid split between the self and the Jew. One *is* a Jew, existentially.

In responding to God out of the Covenant situation, the relationally autonomous Jewish self acknowledges its essential historicity and sociality. One did not begin the Covenant and one is its conduit only as part of the people of Israel. In the Hebrew Covenant, tradition and community round out what the self of the Noachide covenant already recognizes as God's behest and the universal solidarity of humankind. With heritage and folk compelling values, with the Jewish service of God directed to historic continuity lasting until messianic days, the Covenanted self acknowledges the need for structure to Jewish existence. Yet this does not rise to the point of validating law in the traditional sense, for personal autonomy remains the cornerstone of this piety.

This matter is so important and generally so poorly understood that I would like to devote some space here to analyzing in some detail the dialectic of freedom and constraint in the liberal Jewish self.

The relational interpretation of the structure of Jewish selfhood I am suggesting here radically departs from the usual Jewish understandings. Traditionally, the Jewish self is firmly held within the *halakhah*, Jewish law. With modernity, liberals began to think of the Jewish legal process in terms of its social context. The folk, through its institutions, customs and folkways, could be seen as providing the forms for Jewish self-actualization, including a developing law. These two ways of interpreting the structure of Jewish existence have the advantage of furnishing us with common, public, objective standards of what it is to be a Jew. They do not "command" my sort of liberal Jew precisely because of their external, heteronomous nature. That is, I and many Jews like me can accept Jewish tradition as guiding us, indeed as an incomparably valuable resource, but not as overriding "conscience." Identifying our dignity as human beings with our autonomy, we are determined to think for ourselves. However, we are not general selves but Jewish selves. Thinking personalistically about our Jewishness, we identify our Jewish variety of self-structure in relational terms, a rather new way of envisioning authentic Jewish existence. Specifically, the Jewish self gives patterned continuity to its existence by a continual orientation to God as part of the people of Israel's historic Covenant. Four aspects of this situation deserve comment.

First, as noted above, the Jewish self is personally and primarily involved with God. Jewishness is lived out of a relationship with God which precedes, undergirds, and interfuses all the other relationships of the Jewish self. Where the Biblical-rabbinic Jew had essentially a theocentric existence, the modern Jewish self may better be described as theorelated in ultimate depth. That being the case, the highest priority must today be given to the fight to overcome the pervasive agnosticism which resulted from the modernization of Jewry. Without a personal sense of involvement with God, this relational, Covenantal Jewish existence cannot be properly attained.

Second, and inextricably bound with the first, though subsidiary to it, is the Jewish self's participation in the Jewish people as part of its ongoing relation to God. All forms of radical individualism on the human level are negated by this stance. The Jewish self lives out the Covenant not only as a self in relation to God but as part of a living ethnic community. This people then seeks to transform its social relations as well as its individual lives in terms of its continuing close involvement with God. Jewish "autonomy" need not be sacrificed to what other Jews are now doing or think right, but the Jewish self will be seriously concerned with the community which is so great a part of its selfhood. Naturally, this individual autonomy will often be channeled and fulfilled through what the Jewish people has always done or now values. For the sake of community unity, the Jewish self will often undoubtedly sacrifice the exercise of personal standards. That most easily takes place when the demands are obviously necessary for community action—e.g., a folk not a personal Jewish calendar—or when the demands are not seen as onerous—e.g., *Kiddush* over wine and not the whisky or marijuana one might prefer. We shall deal with more significant clashes later.

Third, the Jewish self, through the Covenant, is historically rooted as well as Divinely and communally oriented. Modern Jews not only did not initiate the Covenant, they are not the first to live it. While social conditions and self-perceptions have greatly changed over the centuries, the basic relationship and the partners involved in it have remained the same. Human nature, personally and socially, has not appreciably altered since Bible times (as we so often note reading ancient Jewish texts). Hence much of what Jews once did is likely to commend itself to us as what we ought to do. More, since their sense of the Covenant was comparatively fresh, strong and steadfast, where ours is often uncertain, weak and faltering, we will substantially rely on their guidance in determining our Jewish duty. But not to the point of dependency or passivity of will. Not only is our situation in many respects radically different from theirs but our identification of maturity with the proper exercise of agency (in Covenantal context for a Jew) requires us on occasion to dissent from what our tradition has taught or enjoined.

Fourth, the Jewish self, because of its intimate connections with God, folk and tradition, is sensitized to more than the present and its call to decision. All persons, as I see it, but certainly Jews, should put the immediate exercise of autonomy into the framework of attaining personal integrity. For a person lives in time and the self persists as well as chooses. The soul which lives only in the present with little connection to previous experience and minimal thought to the future denies not only the chronological character of creatureliness but the most creative of human acts, to give wholeness to an entire life. Form, habit, institution and structure have a necessary role to play in such fulfillment of the self—as long as they continue to express what the individual, at some level of choice, still wills to do. And almost all of us, out of frailty or indecision, will often depend on previously chosen patterns to carry us through life, particularly its trials. But in the clash between a pressing, immediate insight and an old, once-valuable but now empty practice, we will know ourselves authorized to break with the past and do acts which more appropriately express our deepest commitments.

With these theoretical matters clarified, let me now turn to the Jewish self's attitude to Jewish law. Since the Covenant must be lived, not just believed in or thought about, Jewish law has been the primary means of being an authentic Jewish self until modern times. As the effects of the Emancipation were increasingly internalized, the overwhelming majority of Jews insisted upon an autonomous relation to Jewish law, thereby utterly changing its character for them. But I am arguing that if they could relate to Jewish tradition as liberal Jewish selves and not merely as autonomous persons-in-general, they would find in Jewish law the single best source of guidance as to how they ought to live. That is, wanting to be true to themselves as persons—understood now immediately and not secondarily as *Jewish* persons and thus intimately involved in faithfulness to God, people and historic devotion—they would want their lives substantially to be structured by a continuing involvement with the prescriptions of Jewish law. But as *autonomous* Jewish persons, the provisions of the law would ultimately be tested by appeal to their conscientious individual Jewish understanding.

Over a decade ago, in *Choosing a Sex Ethic*[1] I gave an extended example of the way in which a Jew might candidly engage the choices confronting a mature, autonomous self in dialectical involvement with society and the variegated guidance provided by historic Jewish law. While some details of the judgments I made then seem to me now in need of revision, the fundamental delineation of the modern Jewish liberal decision-making process I provided there still seems to me fundamentally correct. Autonomy should not be subservient to the *halakhah* in sexual matters but at the same time, the law, in all its details, does not hesitate to make its claim on the committed autonomous Jewish self.

I suggest that, from a relational perspective, the Jewishness of the Jewish self should now be seen less in its obedient observance than in its authentically living in Covenant. Its Jewish acts result from their expressing that relationship. And, I would add, again following Rosenzweig, that everything one then did and not merely some delimited activities would be Jewish. Against Rosenzweig, I do not see how, even in principle, Jewish law can be imposed on such a Jewish self. Rather, with autonomy essential to selfhood, I avidly espouse a pluralism of thought and action stemming from Jewish commitment. I also look forward to the day when enough Jewish selves autonomously choose to live in ways sufficiently similar that they can create common patterns among us. A richly personal yet Jewishly grounded and communally created Jewish style or way would be the autonomous Jewish self's equivalent of "*halakhah*." It would give us universalism without assimilation and a commanding particularism which has full respect for the dignity of the individual.

This multiplication of simultaneous responsibilities—to self, to God, to the Jewish past, present and future, and to humankind as a whole (through the Noachide covenant of which Jews remain a part)—obviously creates special problems for decision makers. Facing any choice, one must take account of many commitments. And not infrequently there will be conflict among them. This constitutes a further reason for acknowledging the legitimacy, indeed the desirability of pluralistic Jewish practice and thought. More, we must remain continually open to the possibility that new and unanticipated forms may arise to express genuinely the imperatives which flow from existence in Covenant.

Does not this reassertion of liberalism's call for community openness make the character of the Covenant folk so shapeless that it hardly has distinct identity? Has not autonomy again manifested its anarchic and therefore ultimately un-Jewish character?

I cannot deny the risks involved in the path I am suggesting. Before saying they are too great to bear I want to direct our attention to one highly esteemed western value I omitted from my previous list, namely, democracy. Liberal Jews passionately embrace what the western world has taught us about the way in which people ought to conduct their societal life. The universalization of power by the enfranchisement of every citizen remains for all its faults and abuses, the least humanly destructive form of government. Democracy calls for pluralism and tolerance of others' radically differing views, a concept which has produced social harmony unprecedented in human history. By contrast, wherever absolutisms have attained political power, human degradation has shortly followed, not infrequently in the name of the highest moral ends.

Liberalism's insistence on individualism will surely yield only a flabby sort of structure. But it will have no difficulty directly and organically authorizing and commending democracy. I do not see that the same is true of the orthodoxies I know or have read about. When one possesses the one absolute truth, how can one be expected to turn any significant power over to those who deny or oppose it?

The problem of an orthodox doctrine of democracy can only temporarily be settled pragmatically, that is, by arguing that because of the large number of unbelievers or the need to reach out to as many people as possible, one may expect that the true believers will practice democracy. Once the usefulness of the democracy ends, the absolutism will then naturally express itself. It will also not do to discuss how this or that tradition contains resources by means of which one might validate democracy. The hypothetical revisionism must yet make its way against the tradition's absolutistic beliefs, its history, established tradition, practice and ethos. Consider the situation in the Jewish community were the religious parties to come to full power in the State of Israel. Once their rule was consolidated, what would be the status of Noachides who refused to accept the Noachian laws as revealed by the Torah? What rights would Christians have? Or, a less questionable case of *ovde avodah zarah*, idolatrous Bakhti Hindus and imagistic Buddhists? Though I have tried to be aware of contemporary Orthodox Jewish theoretical authentifications of democracy as desirable for a Jewish polity, particularly a Jewish state, only one is known to me, Michael Wyschogrod's paper on "Judaism and Conscience" which appeared in the Msr. John M. Oesterreicher *Festschrift, Standing before God.*[2] Let me summarize its argument.

Wyschogrod contends, convincingly to me, that despite some hints of a similar notion, a fully self-conscious concept of conscience does not appear in classic Jewish tradition. This follows consistently from the Jewish emphasis upon the affirmation of God's highly contentful revelation to the people of Israel. Judaism must certainly reject the autonomous conscience in its common, humanistic form for, as Heidegger is used to show, it radically destroys obedience to anything other than ourselves. And I would add, precisely this separation of conscience from its transcendent source has been the intellectual cause of our gradual loss of a social consensus about the standards and nature of moral value.

Wyschogrod then carefully delineates a notion of conscience which might be acceptable to Judaism. Here the individual's sense of right is understood to be a faculty given humans by God so that they might discern and respond to God's will. Wyschogrod thus follows the philosophical path by which personal autonomy is fulfilled in theonomy, thereby avoiding the problem of a religious ethic being heteronomous.

He then sets about assimilating this notion to contemporary traditional Judaism. This he accomplishes by calling attention to the way in which the determination to remain Orthodox today must necessarily be made against the crowd. One can say, he suggests, that a significant measure of autonomy is involved in the continuing will to be a believing, practicing Jew. To be sure, in any possible conflict between the *halakhah* and the will, one sacrifices one's self-determination, our personal version of the binding of Issac. And in the very sense that this can occasionally take place, one phenomenologically detects the role of autonomy within Orthodoxy.

Of particular interest, certainly in connection with the theme of this paper, are the motives Wyschogrod manifests for undertaking this unique intellectual enterprise. He acknowledges that the concept of autonomy has correctly pointed our attention to a critical locus of human dignity. Without some such self-actualization, we would be less the creatures that God formed us to be. Hence Orthodox Judaism needs to make room for the idea and function of conscience.

A practical consideration is also at work, one not explicitly stated but one suggested by the context in which this paper appears and by the consequences which follow from the argument. Consider the following breathtaking issue Wyschogrod carefully develops. If conscience may legitimately command one, may it still do so when we judge the person utilizing it to be acting in error? That is, if we adhere to an orthodoxy we have an objective notion of God's true will. Shall we still grant conscience its rights when someone uses it *against* what we know is true and good? One cannot help but hear in such thinking the overtones of the old Catholic teaching that error has no rights.

But Wyschogrod strongly argues the opposite, that the individual conscience must be granted rights even when to us it appears to be acting in error. Not to do so would negate the very concept of conscience for a heteronomous revelation would have effectively usurped our God-given right to think and judge for ourselves.

Wyschogrod's purpose in all this, I believe, is to try to make a theological place in Orthodox Judaism for Christians to be allowed to be Christians. He does not sacrifice the absoluteness of God's revelation but carefully provides room for individual conscience within it. Then those who cannot read its message plainly may still claim the right to go their deviant way. If I remember correctly, John Courtney Murray mounted an argument of this sort for many years within the Roman Catholic church to help it attain a positive attitude toward democracy and pluralism. His position was substantially adopted by Vatican Council II and now constitutes the church's official teaching. Perhaps the thought occurred to me because the central citation of Wyschogrod's argument about the right of the erring conscience is taken from Thomas Aquinas.

Wyschogrod makes only one stipulation about the employment of conscience other than genuineness. He requires serious, reverential study of God's revelation, the sacred texts of Judaism.

I shall be most interested to see what sort of reception Wyschogrod's argument receives in the Orthodox Jewish community. If accepted, it could provide a theoretical basis not only for inter-faith but intra-faith understanding. Specifically, I believe the autonomous Jewish self I have described more than meets Wyschogrod's conditions for a conscience which Orthodoxy should respect even when it errs. The ethical sense of such liberal Jews is founded on theonomy, not humanism, and, because the Covenant sets the field of its perceptions, they are spiritually guided by classic Jewish texts. By Wyschogrod's standards, Orthodoxy should acknowledge the legitimacy of authentic Jewish liberalism despite its sinfulness. More, my Jewish Covenantalists can lay claim to even greater Jewish legitimacy. The Covenant clearly links them to the Jewish people and they are mandated to realize their Jewish selves in community. That goes far beyond Wyschogrod's demands—a further indication that his paper speaks to the question of Christian legitimacy. Of Jews who follow their conscience, it would seem reasonable to demand, certainly in a post-Holocaust time, not only reverence for God and study of texts but passionate loyalty to the Covenant people.

One further point about Wyschogrod's paper—this rare effort to validate tolerance and democracy within Orthodoxy does so by arguing, against precedent, for a broad acceptance of the autonomy of the individual. If the well-known liberal move to the right could be met by this kind of Orthodox theoretical opening to the left, we might have another instance of the mutual redefinition of positions which often in the past has made possible greater human unity. In any event, we liberals will, at the least, see Wyschogrod's noble effort as further proof of our old contention that a vital contemporary Judaism must make greater place for the concept of personal autonomy than did our tradition in the past (though it requires reworking from its rigorous Enlightenment individualism to become the new autonomy of a Jewish self).

Experience further indicates that we are less likely to run into difficulty seeking communal agreement in practice rather than in theology. Different beliefs often lead to similar acts, as our joint work for the State of

Israel, Soviet Jewry and *tzedakah* demonstrates. Liberal Jews enthusiastically participate in such communal activities for they happily unite autonomy and Covenant responsibility. They become quite troubled, however, when their autonomous sense of their Covenant obligations conflicts with other views of Jewish duty. With regard to marriage and divorce practices, that means the *halakhah* as interpreted by the sages of contemporary Orthodoxy.

I think it will best serve my purpose of getting others to understand liberal Judaism better if, before turning to the contentious area of marriage law, I deal with one likely to arouse less emotion. This case should give us greater insight into the way a liberal as against a traditional *posek* might balance the conflicting claims of Jewish commitment.

J. David Bleich, in one of his summaries of recent *halakhic* literature[3] discussed the issue of dwarfism and the problems its treatment raises. The condition, troublesome to those who have it and often a heavy burden for their relatives, does not constitute a genuine threat to life which would then merit the exceptional activities of *pikuah nefesh*. Jewish law, it should also be noted, imposes no special disabilities upon dwarfs. Some urgency for the treatment of dwarfism arises from the greater than usual difficulty dwarfs have in conceiving children. They therefore not only merit help for general humanitarian and Jewish medical reasons but so as to enable the males more likely to fulfill their Jewish duty of procreation. However, the accepted therapy, growth hormone, must be collected from human corpses. *Poskim* (rabbinic decisors) must then seek to reconcile the laws of *kibud hamet* (honor for the dead) with the desirability of curing a distressing but non-life-threatening condition. Disturbed by the need to cut into the corpse, they give considerable attention as to how this must be done so as to create the least disfigurement. Ruling permissively they are able to find ways to maintain the law and its values while meeting a human need.

The autonomous Jewish self would face the situation somewhat differently. A corpse is surely entitled to respectful treatment. Indeed, in our day of lessening concern for the dead—fewer people appear to be saying *kaddish* and visiting graves—some special effort ought to be made to remind Jews that we cannot envision a self as utterly distinct from its body. While a corpse is surely far from a person, our psycho-somatic sense of personhood requires us to give dead bodies reverential treatment.

However, when one thinks primarily in terms of selfhood, there cannot be any value comparison between, much less subordination of, the needs of a living person to a dead body. While the corpse exercises claims upon us, its proper honor must yield to the vastly more significant needs of the living. One can surely be a self and a dwarf, yet the selfsame psycho-somatic view of the self which authorizes honoring corpses requires us to recognize that dwarfism imposes very severe personal handicaps on its victims. Liberal Jews would then likely argue that the human suffering of the dwarf, not respect for the corpse, ought in this case be our primary consideration in determining our personal responsibility under the Covenant.

Fortunately, where dwarfism is involved there will be little difference in practice between traditionalists and liberals. But were rigorous *poskim* to impose such stringent conditions that the collection of pituitary glands was seriously impeded, liberal Jews would demur. We would not believe God would have us act so today to fulfill the Covenant. We might be in error but we could not follow the *halakhah* then if we were to fulfill what we know to be our Jewish duty.

Jewish marriage and divorce laws raise more directly ethical issues, as the two classic conflict cases *agunah* ("abandoned wife") and *mamzerut* (the category of "bastard") indicate. Traditional Jews do not need liberals to tell them what agony these issues create. However, traditionalists are willing to sacrifice whatever stirrings of autonomous rebellion they may feel in such cases so that they may follow God's law. Liberal Jews, for whom autonomy tends to be ultimate, cannot easily take that course. They are far more likely to react in ethical indignation. In the name of proper legal procedure a woman can be debarred from remarrying and establishing a fully ramified Jewish home. Or, in compensation for a parental sin, a child is prevented from ever contracting a normal Jewish marriage. These ethical considerations already carry heavy Covenantal weight. They become overwhelming when we think of the Holocaust. Does much in Jewish life now take priority as an obligatory response to the Holocaust over contracting a Jewish marriage and creating a Jewish family? Yet also in the name of the Holocaust, liberal Jews are asked to accept traditional Jewish marriage and divorce law. While that will create more uniform practice in the Jewish community, it will necessarily also involve us in preventing some Jews from founding Jewish families!

To the autonomous Jewish self, the ethical and Covenantal damage done by the laws of *agunah* and *mamzerut* cannot be explained away by any form of mitigating defense. Our overwhelming sense of duty cannot be stilled by hearing that the decisors may be relied on to minimize drastically the numbers of *agunot* and *mamzerim*, or that we should consider the few unresolved cases a small price to pay for effecting the familial unity of the Jewish people. The fact is that, with all the compassion and legal creativity contemporary *poskim* display, there are *agunot* and *mamzerim*. And the legal disabilities are enforced on them whenever they come under Orthodox jurisdiction. For liberal Jews to adopt the comtemporary Orthodox *halakhah* with regard to marriage and divorce means retroactively to validate the decisions already made and to put themselves in principle behind the possible creation of new *agunot* and *mamzerim*. As we understand our obligation to God under the Covenant, I do not see that we can do that. As I read our community, we believe God does not want Jews to relate to other Jews by categorizing and treating them as *agunot* and *mamzerim*. We cannot fulfill our Jewish responsibilities through a system which does so.

I am not suggesting that for the sake of community unity traditional Jews give up their understanding of God's law and the manner of its correct implementation. That would be a quite inconsistent application of the pluralism I have espoused. I do know that there are other Jewish laws which remain in full force but are, in practice, inoperable—an eye for an eye being the example we regularly cite to Christians. I have sufficient confidence in the resources of the *halakhah* and the creativity of contemporary *poskim* to believe that even the thorny problems of *agunah* and *mamzerut* could be solved once there is sufficient will to do so.

We face a far more difficult and complex issue when we deal with the question of women's rights in traditional Jewish marriage and divorce law. Because most liberal Jews perceive the equality of women as one of the great ethical issues of our time, we remain unpersuaded by all efforts to demonstrate the relative humanity of the *halakhah* in this area. That Jewish law has treated women better than many other legal systems have, that it has often made special provision to protect women from potential abuses of its male-oriented statutes, should inform Jewish pride about the inherent moral thrust in our heritage. To the autonomous Jewish self, all such apologetics do not validate continuing a system which badly discriminates against women. The feminist movement in western culture has made us aware how blind we Jews have been to our own ethical failings with regard to women. Acknowledging that, we would be untrue to our fundamental commitments were we to agree to operate by a law in which women are not fully equal legal agents with men.

I cannot take this issue further. I do not know what traditional authorities might do in this area and I am in no position to say what sorts of practices liberal Jews might accept for the sake of uniform communal practice. Liberal Jewish women will speak for themselves and, considering how they have suffered at the hands of men, I do not expect them to be in a mood to compromise.

As a final contribution to this analysis of Covenantal decision-making I should like to make some generalizations concerning it. Should our various Covenant obligations appear to conflict, the duty to God—most compellingly, ethics—must take priority over our responsibilities to the Jewish people or the dictates of Jewish tradition. I acknowledge only one regular exception to that rule, cases when the survival of the Jewish people is clearly at stake. Obviously, without the Jews there can be no continuing Covenant relationship and Covenant, not universal ethics, provides the framework for my Jewish existence.

What should a Jew do when confronted by a conflict between a divinely imposed ethical responsibility and a duty upon which the survival of the Jewish people seems to rest? I cannot say. A true crisis of the soul occurs when two values we cherish ultimately can no longer be maintained simultaneously. And we call it a tragedy when, no matter what we decide, we must substantially sacrifice a value which has shaped our lives. May God spare us such choices. Or, failing that, may God then give us the wisdom and courage to face crisis with honest choice and stand by us when we have, as best we could, tried to do so.

My liberal subjectivity has now been exponentially amplified by this problem of a multiplicity of basic values. Nonetheless, I believe I can help-fully illustrate how the autonomous Jewish self might function in this sit-uation by quickly sketching in my response to three diverse cases.

Many years ago, when I was breaking out of the old liberal identifica-tion of Judaism with universal ethics, it occurred to me that the Jewish duty to procreate can be objected to ethically. To bring a child into the world bearing the name Jew inevitably subjects that human being to spe-cial potential danger. All the joys and advantages of being a Jew cannot compensate for this ineradicable disability. Yet the Covenant absolutely depends on Jewish biologic-historic continuity until the messianic days come. For all its ethical difficulty then, I have no choice but to proclaim the Jewish duty to have children.

Why then do I resist establishing one community standard for Jewish marriages and divorces? Many in our community would say that the per-sonal status of Jews will critically affect the survival of the Jewish people. But I read our situation differently. In my thought, the exceptional survival-category must be used as restrictively as *halakhah* uses *pikuah nefesh*. I am not convinced that the Jewish people will not survive at all without a uniform marriage and divorce law. Though the overwhelming majority of Jews worldwide have given up the authority of the *halakhah*, they still manifest a will to Jewish continuity. I agree that the Jewish peo-ple without one standard of practice in family matters will not continue as it did when it had such consensus—but even without it, the folk as such will survive. In this instance, I cannot therefore invoke the survival clause to overcome my sense of ethical obligation.

Then why will I not perform intermarriages? After all, in the contem-porary situation, more than half the families formed by an intermarriage apparently try to live as Jews. Accepting their will to be Jewish as a means of Jewish survival would allow me to fulfill an ethical responsibility—that is, to serve two people who might seem humanly well-suited to one another despite their having different religions. I confess that I am moved by such arguments and know that my answer to this disturbing question may appear even more subjective than usual. In positive response to such people's Jewish concerns, I reach out to intermarried couples with warmth and gladly accept their children as Jews when through education and par-ticipation they manifest Covenant loyalty. I cannot go so far as to officiate at their wedding. To do this would give a false indication to them and to the community of my understanding of Covenant obligation. The relation between God and the Jewish people is mirrored, articulated and continued largely through family Judaism. As I see it, we must therefore necessarily prefer a family which fully espouses the Covenant to one which does so with inherent ambiguity. Moreover, I understand myself as a rabbi autho-rized to function only within the Covenant and on behalf of the Covenant.

My Reform Jewish colleagues who differ with me on this issue do so because they read the balance between ethics and Jewish survival differently than I do. They believe, erroneously in my opinion, that performing intermarriages will help win and bind these families to the Jewish people. Because I may well be wrong in this matter and because I respect their reading of their Covenant responsibility, I associate myself with them in full collegiality. My sense of liberal Jewish pluralism clearly encompasses this troubling disagreement.

Having devoted so much of this paper to my liberal certainties, I wanted to close it with an instance of my more characteristic tentativeness. We will not understand liberalism, at least not the sort which surfaces in my kind of liberal Judaism, without understanding the dialectic of confidence and hesitation which informs it. Perhaps with such insight we can find a way to move beyond community fragmentation to greater unity amid diversity.

Notes

1. New York, 1969.
2. New York, 1981.
3. *Tradition*, Vol. 18, No. 4 (Winter, 1980).

15

On the Ethical Moment in
Halakhah

A Disagreement with Aharon Lichtenstein

A good deal of attention has been given to the turn to Jewish tradition among those who at one time identified the essence of Judaism with universal human ethics. With the loss of confidence in the authority of Western civilization, the possibility arose that classic Jewish teaching might be the best guide to the good life.[1] The question is then often asked, in the all-or-nothing terms beloved by those who like to use intellect coercively, "Why do you not then fully embrace rabbinic teaching as developed over millennia and as amplified in unbroken tradition today?" Much of the response to that query hinges on the place of ethics within Jewish teaching or, to be more precise, on the authority given to the ethical imperative within classic Rabbinic Judaism. (On this term, a euphemism for the unbroken tradition of interpreting the Torah in inherited fashion, see below.)

This issue has been treated most intensively from within traditionalist circles by Aharon Lichtenstein in his widely read paper, "Does Jewish Tradition Recognize an Ethic Independent of Halakha?"[2] Lichtenstein has surely clarified the issue before the community, but in my opinion, has not satisfactorily faced up to the issue troubling many Jews about their heritage.

Lichtenstein focuses on an internal problem of Rabbinic Judaism. It recognizes that its legal procedures occasionally do not directly produce ethical results. It thus includes various measures for overcoming such im-

Originally entitled "The Authority of the Ethical Impulse in *Halakhah*," in *Through the Sound of Many Voices*, ed. Jonathan Plout (Toronto: Lester & Orpen Dennys, 1982).

passes. He takes particular pains to point out that some of these special processes were actionable, that they could be enforced by a Jewish court. He can then conclude that though Jewish tradition does not recognize an ethic independent of *Halakhah*, it contains within itself all the ethical resources its notion of God and humankind would expect us to find in it.

The issue of the internal ethical adequacy of Jewish tradition is not a minor one, both for theological and practical reasons. Ethical demands come with an imperative quality. They lay an authoritative claim upon us. If Rabbinic Judaism were to recognize an ethics independent of it, that would be to recognize a second source of authority to the Torah. Or, to say the same thing differently, Jews would have to admit that God had given them only a partial, not a complete, revelation. The former notion conflicts with the common identification of the one God with the one Torah, the latter with the Jewish understanding of the completeness of the Torah revelation.

Practically, too, the notion of an external ethics would raise methodological problems for a contemporary *posek*. His expertise is in Torah. He will certainly recognize the internal ethical impulses and goals in Torah and respond to them as he deems appropriate. Should external ethical considerations be included in determining authoritative Jewish duty, he would have to transcend his received methodology and learning, and become expert in general ethics and its relation to rabbinic tradition. No established institution would easily accept such a radical challenge to its accustomed ways of proceeding.

David Weiss Halivni's statement on the halakhic status of a universal ethics seems more motivated by pragmatic than theological reasons in rejecting the concept of an external morality with authority within *Halakhah*.[3] Maimonides' famous insistence that Noachides must accept their commandments as revealed by the Torah and not as given by their own reason, while a somewhat different case, is relevant here. Why he should rule this way despite his practical identification of revelation with reason has not yet been made compellingly clear.[4] The pragmatic explanation, in his case securing the ultimate foundation of the social order, is perhaps the easiest to accept, particularly if we are influenced by the "two doctrines" interpretation of his thought. Yet that would require us to accept that, in terms of the higher doctrine, such a sociological "external," if revealed, ethics exists and is authoritative. Our only other alternative would seem to be to take a radically fresh approach to the nonrational or trans-rational aspect of all of his philosophy, a reading often spoken of but not yet done.

Lichtenstein's treatment of the issue, however, proceeds beyond these issues to analyze the way in which an ethical impulse makes itself felt and operates within Rabbinic Judaism. For our purposes, it will help to grant immediately what appears to be one of Lichtenstein's main points: Rabbinic Judaism has a fundamental ethical thrust, not only manifested in the law itself, but most notably in the methods and motives it has for overcoming internal conflicts between its ethical values and its legal procedures. The vulgar contrast made in older Christian polemics between Jewish legalism and general ethics betrays ignorance of Judaism and insensitivity to its own prejudice (in the name of ethics!). Leaving that question, I wish to focus on the problem that I see arising when one speaks about the internal ethics of Judaism as Lichtenstein has done.

Critical to understanding Lichtenstein's argument is his special use of the term *"Halakhah"* (note the capital "H"). He does so in a way different from that commonly found in North American English-language writing on such matters. Through most of his paper he means by *Halakhah* the totality of the rabbinic tradition. (To conform to his meaning but to avoid the linguistic confusion which can result from his usage, I shall use the term "Rabbinic Judaism" to refer to the same phenomenon.) Lichtenstein's choice of terms is certainly justifiable, but the question posed by many interlocutors asking about an ethics independent of *Halakhah* often has a somewhat different issue in mind. That is, one regularly sees the word *"Halakhah"* used as referring to only one part of Rabbinic Judaism, the legal part, as contrasted to *aggadah,* the non-legal part. The *aggadah* obviously contains much ethical material. To ask about an ethic independent of *Halakhah* means, then, to ask whether ethical impulses arising outside the law carry full imperative quality either in their own right or, more threateningly, against provisions of the law.

Lichtenstein knows that his usage is somewhat uncommon and on the last two pages of his article makes mention of the more common understanding of the term *"halakhah"* (note the lower-case "h").[5] He thinks we would be better off calling *din* what people usually call *halakhah.* In sum, he argues that this is only a matter of semantics and that, while one may define as one thinks best, the outcome will be the same: Rabbinic Judaism has a vital, effective, internal ethics.[6]

What may go unnoticed as a result of Lichtenstein's unusual terminology is the problem of the several levels of authority within Rabbinic Judaism. Lichtenstein is too careful a scholar not to refer to this along the way, but it does not serve as one of his major foci. The best example of an accurate statement which may perhaps be misleading is found in one of his summary sentences. Referring to various ways of speaking of Jewish tradition, he concludes that it makes little difference as long as we "issue with the thesis that traditional halakhic Judaism demands of the Jew both adherence to *Halakha* and commitment to an ethical moment that though different from *Halakha* is nevertheless of a piece with it and in its own way fully imperative."[7] The critical yet easily overlooked part of this statement is the qualifying clause, "in its own way." That is, Lichtenstein does not say: "and commitment to an ethical moment that though different from *Halakha* is nevertheless of a piece with it and fully imperative." No, the "ethical moment" that is "nevertheless of a piece with" *Halakhah* is "fully imperative" only "in its own way." Just what is that distinctive way? And what are its implications? These questions will be critical to a mind sensitized by general ethics, now seeking to understand how ethics functions within Rabbinic Judaism.

Let us now retrace Lichtenstein's argument insofar as this will help us see his answer to these questions. Much of his paper deals with the sort of imperative involved in acting *lifnim mishurat hadin*, literally, "within the line of the law," which is the equivalent of the English "go beyond the letter of the law." Lichtenstein is at pains to point out that this "is no mere option." It has "obligatory character" as shown by the verses Nahmanides uses to ground his argument about it.[8] Obviously, were this matter merely optional, it would not have any serious ethical standing. That it is "obligatory" would seem as good as guaranteed by its being part of the Oral Torah, God's revelation not being a matter of mere play. Our question, however, is just what sort of obligation is involved.

The matter is not settled, as Steven S. Schwarzschild believes, by the term itself. He writes: "*lifnim mishurat hadin* is 'within,' not as the usual rendering has it, 'beyond,' the line of the law; i.e., the very term indicates that we are here dealing with a dynamic function that operates within the system."[9] As I see it, Schwarzschild confuses the meaning of the term *din* here. The reference is to the particular legal right which one could now exercise. One is rather directed to restrict one's right in this particular case and not do that which one might otherwise properly do under the law. He correctly reads *lifnim* as "within," that is, not at the limit of what one might do. But that differs from the issue here: the status of this precept as a whole. Does it itself come to us as part of the law, the *din*, or is it in another category (though admittedly part of Rabbinic Judaism and "in its own way fully imperative")? If the reference of the term *din* was the whole legal system and not the specific *din* at issue in this instance, the phrase and its effect would be contradictory. One would be enjoined to act legally—*lifnim mishurat hadin* read as "stay [well] within legal limits"—and yet be told not to do what the law clearly entitles one to do. Lichtenstein apparently does not consider this the meaning of the phrase, and this explains why he struggles to show the imperative nature of the injunction.

To continue, Lichtenstein notes: "With respect to the *degree of obligation*, however, *rishonim* [legal authorities of the period before the classic code, the Shulḥan Arukh, of the sixteenth century C.E.] admittedly held different views" (emphasis added).[10] Apparently, only Rabbi Isaac of Corbeille considered it to have the full "degree of obligation." He alone lists the need to act *lifnim mishurat hadin* as one of the 613 commandments. We can understand the issue of degree better if we attend to Lichtenstein's succeeding sentences: "Nahmanides did not go quite this far, as he does not classify *lifnim mishurat hadin* as an independent *mitzvah*, as binding as *shofar* or *tefillin*. However, he does clearly posit it as a normative duty, incumbent upon—and expected of—every Jew as part of his basic obligation."[11]

The treatment of Maimonides' position which then follows is of interest to us, despite the difficulty in giving a consistent interpretation of his position, only because he posits a somewhat different degree of obligation. Depending upon one's interpretation, Maimonides proclaims either a higher or lower level of responsibility than does Nahmanides, but in either case not as strong as that of Rabbi Isaac.[12] Regardless of the interpretation, Lichtenstein is satisfied that a "supralegal ethic" exists within Rabbinic Judaism. What remains unclear is the precise status of the "supralegal," that is, the specific way in which it is "supra" or, alternatively, just how much authority it has and how it is brought to bear upon the full legal requirements of Judaism.

Lichtenstein approaches this issue by inquiring whether *lifnim mishurat hadin* is actionable.[13] He notes that while the Rosh, and therefore probably the whole Spanish school, did not consider it actionable, some Tosafists held such action "could indeed be compelled."[14] He then immediately sets the necessary limits to what might otherwise lead to a gross antinomianism: "Of course, such a position could not conceivably be held with reference to all supralegal behavior. *Din* has many ethical levels; and so, of necessity, must *lifnim mishurat hadin*. Surpassing laws grounded in, say, the concept that 'the Torah has but spoken vis-à-vis the evil inclination' is hardly comparable to transcending those with a powerful moral thrust." This retraction, however, does not lose his point, for he concludes: "Nevertheless, the fact that some *rishonim* held *lifnim mishurat hadin* to be, in principle, actionable, indicates the extent to which it is part of the fabric of *Halakha*."[15] For our purposes, the very division of opinion and the need to qualify such opinion as coercive indicates that there remains a considerable question about just where this "ethical moment" stands within the *Halakhah*. And we shall not know very much about its actual ethical status until we know a good deal more about the already qualified way in which it is "fully imperative."

Once again Lichtenstein enables us to clarify an interpretation of Steven S. Schwarzschild's. Citing Hermann Cohen to substantiate philosophically his interpretation of *lifnim mishurat hadin*, Schwarzschild writes, "Equity is not a factor additional to the *jus strictum*, but a judgment-procedure which makes sure that the application of the law in each individual case is proper (i.e., moral); thus all of the law, statutes as well as the procedures, operationalizes ethical values (*aggadah*)."[16] Schwarzschild wants us to consider *lifnim mishurat hadin* as part of *din* and, for Cohenian reasons, necessarily so.

The facts, as Lichtenstein makes plain, are otherwise. Most Jewish authorities do not consider the need to act in this ethical fashion a *din*. And Lichtenstein indicates why. A law, or *din*, which directs one to override the law (for significant ethical reasons) might soon destroy the fabric of the law as a whole and reduce it to morality. As commendable as that might be, Judaism has classically been a religion where morality takes the form of law, not one where moral law effectively dominates the Torah's precepts. Of course, in an ideal Kantian legal system, morality and law would be identical. Cohen has in mind just such a rational ideal. Perhaps Schwarzschild means to argue that in Jewish law an inner essence makes itself seen which corresponds to the ethical ideal and slowly works its way out into reality. In that case, in addition to validating philosophically the notion of essence or ideal, he will have to deal with all the contrary historical data, in this instance, as forthrightly detailed by Lichtenstein. Until then, the famous gap between "religion of reason" and "the sources of Judaism" will continue to loom before the eyes of many contemporary students of the Jewish tradition. . . .

Lichtenstein eventually tells us what he means by the ethical moment being "in its own way fully imperative." "It is less rigorous not only in the sense of being less exacting with respect to the degree and force of obligation—and there are times, as has been noted, when it can be equally demanding—but in the sense of being more flexible, its duty more readily definable in light of the existence of particular circumstances." To the average reader, I should think, that provides so many loopholes that it seems to indicate a far less significant sort of imperative. For that reason, I take it, Lichtenstein immediately continues: "This has nothing to do with the force of obligation," though he said the opposite in the prior sentence. And: "Once it has been determined that, in a given case, realization of 'the right and the good' mandates a particular course, its pursuit may conceivably be as imperative as the performance of a din."[17] To me that seems to indicate that though the ethical impulse is there, it has much less imperative status than the din. It is explicitly termed "less rigorous." Moreover, it only gains "the full force of obligation . . . once it has been determined" that an ethical issue is involved. This determination is not a matter left to the general conscience, but is assigned to competent decisors and permitted to function by them in only a limited number of cases.

Because of this administrative structure, we note that Lichtenstein cannot say more than that, when operational, "its pursuit *may conceivably* be as imperative as the performance of a din" (emphasis added).[18]

In a later discussion he indicates that this is the case, for he can summarize the dialectic between formalist din and contextualist lifnim mishurat hadin as follows: "Quite apart from the severity of obligation, therefore, there is a fundamental difference between din and lifnim mishurat hadin. One, as a more minimal level, imposes fixed objective standards. The demands of the other evolve from a specific situation; and, depending on the circumstances, may vary with the agent.[19]

I do not think anything further in Lichtenstein's paper impinges upon the issue at hand.

Perhaps it will help us to expand a bit the way in which the "ethical moment" in Rabbinic Judaism makes itself felt. It surely is not confined to the notion of lifnim mishurat hadin, though this theme constitutes a particularly interesting and even dramatic instance of it. There are a number of other rubrics under which the rabbis act in order to extend or amplify what the *din* requires, so that one may more clearly do that which is "good and right." Isaac Herzog, in *The Main Institutions of Jewish Law*, lists a number of these.[20]

In a recent article, J. David Bleich gives a striking instance of the different levels of rabbinic injunction to action. The case will set into bolder relief the problem of the varying levels of authority within Rabbinic Judaism. Bleich notes that Rashi considers Num. 33:53 merely God's prudent advice to the Jewish people about how they should go about conquering the land.[21] Nahmanides, on the other hand, considers the verse a positive commandment. Maimonides, however, is understood by Bleich as essentially agreeing with Rashi.[22] I do not think that Bleich is suggesting that Maimonides considers the advice to Jews about settling on the land of Israel "merely optional," to return to Lichtenstein's formulation. Rather, Bleich here resolves the issue of the "degree of obligation" by invoking the notion of merit, *zekhut*. That is, he suggests that Maimonides believes that while there is no law requiring one to immigrate to the land of Israel, he follows abundant rabbinic teaching in holding that to do so brings one great reward.

The sages often sought to get people to behave ethically not as a matter of full legal prescription, but by suggesting that certain acts, while not required, were highly meritorious. These exhortations, too, are part of God's Oral Torah and, therefore, in some sense not "merely optional." But I do not know whether Lichtenstein would consider them within his category of being fully imperative though only in their own way. Bleich does not help us further with this issue, for he notes that "this issue of merit, as distinct from compensation of fulfillment of a Divine commandment, is difficult to elucidate."[23] Again, let me suggest that we shall not properly understand the place of the ethical within Rabbinic Judaism until we clarify the weight of ethical obligations encompassed by such nonlegal rabbinic injunctions to action as that of *zekhut*, particularly because they so often are used in relation to ethical concerns.

The introduction of the notion of merit, however, has taken us away from Lichtenstein's purpose. While he would not deprecate preaching, education, model-setting, and the like as rabbinically desirable, he recognized that the key issue in this discussion was showing that its proper form was *not* the relation between a required law and an optional ethics. That would not only fly in the face of the facts as he sees them, but could not suffice as an adequate defense of the ethical impulse in Rabbinic Judaism. With commandment the dominant Jewish religious sense, an ethics that was less than required would hardly have much Jewish status. Then, too, ever since the time of Kant, an ethics which does not take the form of law has hardly seemed to most Jewish thinkers an ethics at all.[24] (I would add that though ethics does not take the form of law in Buber, by being God's own behest it is clearly "fully imperative.") Lichtenstein, therefore, took great pains to show that the ethical thrust in Rabbinic Judaism was a species of command.

The result of Lichtenstein's discussion, however, leaves me, and, I would judge, some considerable portion of the Jewish community, troubled by the balance between the law and its supralegal ethical imperative. The disparity between the different levels of authority restricts the operation of conscience in a way that seems to us unacceptable. No one questions the commanding quality of the law. The ethical normally operates on a different, secondary level, with its degree of obligation not clearly known. The law is authoritative unless occasionally supervened. The ethical must make a case for itself should there be a conflict between them. Even then its legitimacy and functioning will be defined by the legists. The law is clear, with much precedent and institutionalized patterns of procedure. The supralegal functions in a hazy area, with few guidelines as to its proper application and handicapped by needing to make its way against the well-entrenched patterns of community practice, the law.

All this is not astonishing for a legal system. Rather, an open-minded student would probably show great admiration for the Jewish community in creating a legal structure which is so highly ethical. But to one who takes seriously the obligatory character of ethics—whether understood in the Kantian sense of law or the Buberian-Rosenzweigian and perhaps Heschelian sense of personal response to God—a major problem arises. The ethical, which ought to come as a categorical or unmediated imperative, operates within Rabbinic Judaism in a quite qualified, mediated way. A substantial difference exists between a system of action in which ethics is commandingly primary and one in which, though it remains imperative, it can often be a subsidiary consideration. The matter is not merely one for academics to ponder as the continuing agitation over the classic issues of *agunah*, the abandoned wife, and *mamzerut*, the Jewish equivalent of bastardy, makes clear.

With some hesitation, permit me to suggest that in claiming a pattern of subsidiary but still "fully imperative" ethics, we seem to contradict our polemical argument against Christianity. Jews have charged that by subordinating works to faith, Christianity seriously compromises the impulse to righteous action.[25] Does not, in the argument we have considered, Judaism do something similar, if not to works of law, then to its own ethical moment?

Let us take the issue presently disturbing a good portion of the Jewish community, the status of Jewish women. Two major lines of thought on this issue seem to emerge. The one finds ethical reason within Rabbinic Judaism for recognizing a problem with the present formulation of the *din* with regard to women, as well as the expectations contained in contemporary Jewish practice. Based on much internal conflict, various authorities seek remedies within the law. On the whole, the more traditionally inclined interpreters who see the problem, though recognizing the ethical need to seek solutions, find that little remedial action can be taken. That is, though the ethical moment has here made itself felt within the system, it is of such limited power in the face of law and precedent that it has no supralegal effectiveness. Such reasoning has brought some Conservative Jewish legists to challenge this classic balance between law and ethics in Judaism. In this instance, they wish to make the ethical thrust of women's equality in Judaism "fully imperative" and not allow it to function in so qualified a fashion as to rob it of any ability to shape community action. For them, the ethical issue is so categorically felt as to require the vaunted flexibility inherent in *Halakhah* to operate and accomplish an ethical revision of existing law and practice.[26] They believe, as do many in the Jewish community, that the gap between ethics and law must now be bridged so as to make our understanding of our obligations under the Torah worthy of being called the service of God.

The other line of thought illumines our difficulty even more clearly. Some authorities deny that there is a women's ethical problem at all. That God ordained a different scope of obligation for Jewish men and women is not at all contravened by notions such as God creating humankind equally as male and female, or bestowing these creatures with dignity. The diverse yet allegedly unequal categories of commandment are so well established in Torah teaching that these authorities do not even see an issue. No possibility of an "ethical moment" arises for them. They claim that the so-called ethical impulse behind the women's issue is a Gentile importation into Judaism. Had it not been for the influence of non-Jews, they charge, we would not be concerned about this question.

Historically, I think, this judgment is correct. I cannot in this paper seek to determine whether, though the issue was raised by non-Jews, the fresh reading of the rabbinic tradition prompted by them proves that women's equality was all along present in the Torah or whether substantial Jewish basis exists for moving toward it. What we can usefully do here is to inquire about our attitude toward ethics.

The broader theoretical issue concerns the status of non-Torah ethics. Is all that Jews can call ethical fundamentally given in the Torah, or may we ever gain significant ethical insight from Gentiles? Factually, we American Jews should acknowledge that the Gentile notion of universalism and common humanity has reminded us of the Torah's teaching that there is, in fact, but one human family—though some in the Jewish community would as good as say that, although Gentiles remain God's children, they are by God's will inferior to Jews. The issue of democracy takes us a step further. This extraordinary notion, with its corollaries of pluralism and tolerance, did not arise within Rabbinic Judaism. We have yet to hear a good theological argument, as against a pragmatic case, being made within the terms of Rabbinic Judaism to endorse, much less to mandate, the practice of democracy. And this matter would immediately leave the hypothetical realm should the Orthodox parties of the State of Israel come to power.

The more restricted, communal issue concerns the present balance between *din* and the ethical moment within Rabbinic Judaism. To many Jews today, the Torah's ethical behests come with such imperative quality that they can consider them properly heard only when they are accepted categorically. To qualify their functioning as substantially as do the spokesmen of contemporary Rabbinic Judaism must be seen by them as requiring less than what God now demands of the people of Israel. They therefore cannot consider Rabbinic Judaism, as presently interpreted, God's will for the people of God's Covenant.[27]

To be sure, on a vulgar level, almost all human beings prefer personal convenience to heavy responsibility. But not being tainted by original sin, they also have a strong sense of what is good and just. Though it has been difficult to call their attention to it and more difficult to get them to live up to it, many people have acknowledged that slavery is unethical and racial discrimination is immoral. In a similar ethical way they came to realize that keeping Jews from equal rights was unjust. And most Jews who have modernized agree that any proper contemporary sense of the good ought to emphasize the equality of all human beings and, in the present case, to give women the status and opportunities hitherto available only to men. The matter is so compellingly clear to these Jews today—as other matters were in recent generations—that if this impulse cannot function supralegally, that is, to change Jewish law, they will find it necessary, for all their Jewish devotion, to function extralegally.

One reason that they will do so is that they feel they have a more satisfactory understanding of Rabbinic Judaism than it offers of itself. Watching it struggle to confront ethical issues and not be able to move very quickly to resolve them, they do not see it as God's own institution, albeit a human one, for mediating the divine will. Rather, it discloses to them the same traits they find everywhere in thoroughly human institutions. It is regularly more concerned with form than with content, with precedent than present need, with regulations than with persons, with what authorities and peers will say than with what, as best we can tell directly, God wants of us now.

In a prior generation, some such belief caused many serious-minded Jews to make general ethics, rather than Torah, the law by which they lived. Even those of us who know that the universalistic path is unreliable without the corrective guidance of Torah are not willing to forsake the way of ethics entirely for a Rabbinic Judaism which, by construing its ethical concerns as it does, appears to us to vitiate them substantially.

Notes

1. See my "Rethinking the Reform Jewish Theory of Social Action," *Journal of Reform Judaism*, Fall 1980.

2. Aharon Lichtenstein, "Does Jewish Tradition Recognize an Ethic Independent of Halakha?" in *Modern Jewish Ethics*, ed. Marvin Fox (Ohio State University Press, 1975).

3. "Can a Religious Law be Immoral?" in *Perspectives on Jews and Judaism*, ed. Arthur A. Chiel (Rabbinical Assembly, New York, 1978).

4. For two recent discussions, see Isadore Twersky, *Introduction to the Code of Maimonides* (Princeton, N.J., 1980), pp. 454ff. and Lawrence V. Berman, "Maimonides on the Fall of Man," *AJS Review* V (1980), 3, note 6.

5. Lichtenstein, "Jewish Tradition," pp. 82–83.

6. In his remarks to the December 1980 meeting of the Association of Jewish Studies, J. David Bleich argued in a somewhat similar linguistic fashion. I am grateful to him for allowing my student, Mr. Marc Gruber, to tape his remarks.

7. Lichtenstein, "Jewish Tradition," p. 83.

8. Ibid., p. 71.

9. Steven S. Schwarzschild, "The Question of Jewish Ethics Today," *Sh'ma*, 7/124, p. 31.

10. Lichtenstein, "Jewish Tradition," p. 71.

11. Ibid.

12. Ibid., pp. 71–74.

13. Ibid., p. 74.

14. Ibid.

15. Ibid., p. 75.

16. Schwarzschild, "The Question of Jewish Ethics," p. 31.

17. Lichtenstein, "Jewish Tradition," pp. 76, 77.

18. Ibid.

19. Ibid., p. 79.

20. Isaac Herzog, *The Main Institutions of Jewish Law* (Soncino Press, 1936), vol. I, pp. 379–86.

21. "Judea and Samaria: Settlement and Return," *Tradition* 18:1 (1979), 48.

22. Ibid., p. 50.

23. Ibid.

24. See, for example, the criticisms of Martin Buber by thinkers as diverse as Marvin Fox and Emil Fackenheim in *The Philosophy of Martin Buber*, ed. Schilpp and Friedman (Open Court, 1967).

25. For a recent discussion, see my *Contemporary Christologies, a Jewish response* (Paulist Press, 1980), pp. 127–29; 133–34.

26. See the bold, general statement by Seymour Siegel in "Theology for Today," *Conservative Judaism* XXVIII, no. 4 (1974), 47–48. He had previously asserted these views in "Ethics and the Halakhah," *Conservative Judaism* XXV, no. 3 (1971), and projects them as part of the ideology of Conservative Judaism in his anthology *Conservative Judaism and Jewish Law* (Rabbinical Assembly, New York, 1977), p. xxiiif. Since then this position has come under increasing attack from the Conservative right-wing as a result of which Siegel was ousted from his position as chairman of the prestigious Rabbinical Assembly Commission on Law and Standards.

27. I have dealt with the liberal Jewish affirmation of personal autonomy despite an increased regard for the guidance of Jewish tradition in chapter 11 of my *Choices in Modern Jewish Thought* (Behrman House). A fuller statement of my views concerning the proper process of liberal Jewish decision making is found in "The Autonomous Jewish Self," reprinted here as chapter 14.

16

The Autonomous Self
and the Commanding
Community

The problem of authority in our Western religious institutions arises essentially from our widespread acceptance of the notion of personal autonomy. This doctrine so fundamentally characterizes liberals like me that our religious bodies must be substantially structured in terms of it, and our relationship with God is fundamentally correlated with it. In my opinion, its influence has also been widely felt even in those religious communities that affirm that their corporate forms derive in significant detail from God's revelation. How we transform that originally secular notion so that it may find a proper place in our service of God affects not only our understanding of faith but (what directly concerns us here) our conception of the legitimate authority of our religious institutions. I therefore propose to approach the issue of social discipline by first clarifying how I think we ought to frame our concept of personal religious autonomy. I shall do so by examining certain representative thinkers who have materially influenced me with regard to this issue. Then, having established what I take to be the right contemporary challenge to traditional religious notions of corporate authority, I shall seek to mediate between religiously autonomous persons and their communities.[1]

I

Any thoughtful discussion of autonomy must focus on the philosophy of Immanuel Kant. Were there space, I would begin with more than a nod

From *Theological Studies*, vol. 45, no. 1 (March 1984).

to Peter Abelard,[2] Thomas Aquinas,[3] and Martin Luther, who in their own ways pointed us toward modern individualism. I shall, however, allow myself a few sentences on René Descartes and Jean Jacques Rousseau to serve as an introduction to the great Koenigsberg thinker.

With Descartes a decisive negative principle became basic to the nascent Enlightenment and the related enfranchisement of the individual: we ought to doubt every idea until it is a clear and distinct truth to us. As Descartes's procedure of thinking from methodical doubt became a categorical imperative for the modern mind, sovereignty in the realm of value began to shift to the individual from the community.[4] Single selves now began to sit confidently in judgment over all proposals for their assent or action and demanded warrants of their personal acceptability.

In Rousseau this assertion of the authority of the self took social, specifically political, form. The negative principle now manifested itself as the indignant criticism of institutions. This leads Rousseau to the positive idea that persons ought to rule themselves and thus that governments ought to be democratic. Our personal experience of democracy—the most humane, if flawed, system of government we know—has provided the social basis for our concern with autonomy. And so to Kant.[5]

In Kant's ethics all other considerations are subordinated to the individual's manifestation of good will. Kant clearly distinguishes between will and impulse. The latter is little more than an animalistic urge and thus hardly an appropriate basis for human action. In human will our drive to action is organized in somewhat rational form.[6] Our will becomes truly good when it fulfills its rational potential. That means one which does not operate in terms of whim or caprice but only in terms of rational necessity.[7] A truly ethical will ought not function by a merely contingent principle, for it would have slight rational status and thus infringe on the individual's dignity.[8] It will therefore also not frame exceptional privilege or apply only to a favored group but will be universal. The best term for such an ethical principle is "law," and a good will is thus one which follows this sort of moral law.[9]

Immanuel Kant, then, is the champion of literal autonomy. He teaches an ethics of *nomos*, of law, for reason operates in terms of universal, binding certainties. What constitutes such law, whether in general or in any given situation, one ought to clarify for oneself, since one has the reason to do so.[10] When we abjectly accept moral direction from another, we betray our most essential human capacity. The truly ethical person relies on the self, the *autos*, but does so in terms of ethical law, *nomos*.[11] The good will is, in this sense, self-legislating, autonomous.

The unsophisticated modern ear no longer hears the Kantian overtones of the word "autonomy." Instead, it often implies the legitimacy of a privatistic permissiveness, as in the authoritative dictum of popular culture that no one can really tell you what you ought to do. What, we must ask, kept the Kantian individual from this contemporary willfulness?

For Kant, reason ought to control the will lest it become mere impulse. Anarchy, which so often seems to threaten us, is simply unthinkable in Kantian ethics. The rational mind is characterized by lawfulness, not its absence. And what is an ethical law for me personally must, if it is rational, equally be true for all humankind. Kantian self-legislation cannot yield the moral isolation we often see about us.

But why, asks the child of twentieth-century freedom, is Kantian rationality so constraining? What gives it such domineering authority? With such troubling questions, we start our hard way to our contemporary disillusionment.

As a devoted Enlightener, Kant has no doubt that our rationality, above all else, makes us human.[12] In his letter on Enlightenment, he writes that, to come of age, to be mature, means to throw off the tutelage of others and to think for oneself.[13] Not to progress in fighting the accumulated errors of humankind and to grow more free thinking for ourselves would be "a crime against human nature."[14] He has little doubt that society can only benefit from the growth of self-determination. "Men work themselves gradually out of barbarity if only intentional artifices are not made to hold them in it."[15]

In fact, for Kant the identification of our humanity with our rationality is utterly self-evident. For that reason he does not usually bother to discuss it.[16] As the Marburg neo-Kantian Ernst Cassirer puts it,

> Critical ethics affords us no answer as to why order takes precedence over chaos, free subordination to the universality of a self-given law over arbitrariness of individual desires. In the critique of reason, theoretical as well as practical, the idea of reason, the idea of a final and supreme union of knowledge and will is taken for granted. Whoever fails to acknowledge this idea thus excludes himself from the orbit of its manner of posing problems, and from its conceptions of "true" and "false," "good" and "evil," which it alone can substantiate, empowered by its method.[17]

Written before World War I, that final sentence already testifies to the melancholy fate of a sovereign reason in the century and more since Kant. And the succeeding decades have only further diminished its imperial sway.[18] What was self-evident to Kant had become, even to a leading neo-Kantian, only another possible way of posing and answering questions. Today, the *nomos* Kant empowered with reason's authority has little binding force and a drastically altered sense of the *autos* pervades our discussions of moral duty. Kant may no longer define the term for us, but he more than anyone taught us the dignity of self-determination and did so with such truthfulness that, though we feel we must transform the concept, we cannot surrender it.

The most effective practical challenges to Kantian individualism have come from Marxism and nationalism. Particularly because of our concern with social structures, we must give some attention to their critique of making the single self the foundation of our thought.

Karl Marx often refers positively to the individual, but almost always as part of his apologetic strategy. He is resolutely determined to shift the center of authority from the individual to society or even to humankind.[19] He attacks the notion of autonomy most perceptively by demonstrating that the alleged freedom of individuals in bourgeois democracy comes only with more fundamental alienation from their true humanity. By exposing the deleterious role things play in modern life, the cruel use people make of one another, the harsh power we economically face, he awakens us from our dogmatic dream of our pure inner freedom.[20] Our ideas as individuals, and the forms in which we think, he rudely insists, will testify far more to the conditions of production under which we exist than to the purity of human reason.[21]

To be sure, Marx is speaking politically rather than philosophically. That is exactly his point, that the only truly significant philosophy will be done in terms of socioeconomic power realities, not speculatively à la Hegel. He summarizes his rejection of individualism at the conclusion of his essay "On the Jewish Question." Marx here is not concerned with the specific situation of Jews.[22] Rather he wishes to discuss the abstract issue of emancipation, specifically by denying that gaining individual rights is meaningful freedom. He argues:

> Political emancipation is a reduction of man to a member of civil society, to an *egoistic independent* individual on the one hand and to a *citizen*, a moral person, on the other. Only when the actual, individual man has taken back into himself the abstract citizen and in his everyday life, his individual work, and his individual relationships become a *species-being*, only when he has recognized and organized his own powers as *social* powers so that social force is no longer separated from him as *political* power, only then is human emancipation complete.[23]

To some extent Marx has persuaded us all. We find it difficult to deny that our individuality is substantially social. For us, therefore, self-determination must mean creating a social order which enables us all to be more fully human. Even when our agenda becomes substantially economic, I do not see this view inherently contradicting Kantianism, for Kant surely knew the importance of fulfilling ethical responsibility in social relationships. The break with Kant comes when Marx says, or is understood to say, that the person is essentially social. Then one effectively nullifies individualism by universalizing it, for now society knows better than its members what their individuality ought to be and totalitarianism replaces autonomy.

The other example of a widely accepted social understanding of human existence is nationalism, which I shall consider through the thought of one of its most noble exponents, the Zionist essayist Asher Ginzberg. He wrote under the pseudonym Ahad Haam, "one of the people," itself a fine epitome of his position. He deserves our attention because he demanded that all nationalism be ethical. The Jewish national ideal, he further argued, historically goes beyond that to a commitment to moral excellence.[24] Thus, in principle, his social theory allows for the clash of wills we are studying. In practice, his understanding of Jewish ethics as well as of nationalism prevents his being of much direct help to us.

Ahad Haam's clearest statement about Jewish ethics comes in his disdainful critique of Claude Montefiore's now, as then, unparalleled commentary entitled *The Synoptic Gospels*.[25] Montefiore concluded his 1909 work by suggesting that Judaism had to come to terms with the Gospels to remain a great teaching. Ahad Haam repudiated this notion as inconsistent with the ethics of Judaism. Not surprisingly, he presents his version of the usual modern Jewish polemic against the practicality of Christian love, as exemplified in the Sermon on the Mount. If that could create a functioning ethic on the personal and local level, it would still be utterly ineffective as a guide to national or international conduct.[26] But the bulk of his argument develops from an acceptance of the old Christian polemic distinction between the two faiths. He argues that justice is superior to love as the standard for human relations. The Jewish national ethic, he opines, is distinctively dedicated to the life of justice. This he takes to be an uncompromising abstract principle, one which gives only a highly limited place to human individuality.[27] Typically, he sounds more like a Kantian than a classic Jewish ethicist when he dreams of a day when

> Justice will become an instinct with good men, so that in any given situation they will be able to apply the standard of absolute justice without any long process of reflexion. . . . Personal and social consideration will not affect them in the slightest degree; their instinct will judge every action with absolute impartiality ignoring all human relations, and making no difference between X and Y, between the self and the other, between rich and poor.[28]

As against the injustice and partiality that regularly mar social relationships, such principled justice would be a welcome human advance. But to say that ethically we ought to ignore all "personal and social considerations," "all human relations," seems not only harsh but inflexible and possibly even cruel. One wonders what Ahad Haam thought of the Jewish notion of *rahamim*, of mercy, which in Jewish teaching traditionally accompanies the enunciation of the lofty standards of God's and humankind's justice. Unfortunately, Ahad Haam never produced his promised work on Jewish ethics and we have only the comments in his essays by which to fathom his meaning. We can, however, say that where Marx sublimated the self into society, Ahad Haam universalized it to an ethical ideal.

By turning to his theory of the nation, we can ask what he would counsel a loyal Jew whose individual conscience clashes with what Jewish leaders proclaim as each Jew's national ethical duty. Ahad Haam regularly polemicizes against the modern privatization of Jewish lives and stresses the primacy of national considerations in Jewish existence. In his essay "Flesh and Spirit" he argues that individualism denies reality and that the self should be understood properly as a "limb of the national body."[29]

Yet in the one case where he directly confronts the possibility of such a clash, he backs off from subordinating our individual ethics to those of the nation. Much in his essay "The National Ethic" denies Kantian autonomy, for he declares that one who wishes to be "a whole person in one's role as Jew" should acquire a Jewish national feeling to the point where "it directs one's life and restrains one's will in all one's acts."[30] But on the specific issue of marrying a Gentile, Ahad Haam hedges. He acknowledges that from a personal ethical standpoint, a loyal Jew might feel that intermarriage was permissible.[31] He rejects this—but with what seems a sudden loss of confidence. He makes a radical shift from principle to contingency, and reasons in terms of an emergency at that. Not even making a declaration, he only inquires whether, in the present perilous situation of the Jewish people, it is "not an ethical duty of the nationalistic Jew to defend the folk and to sacrifice one's personal happiness for this."[32]

Ahad Haam surely taught much of modern Jewry that ethnicity is the authentic social form of Jewish identity, even religiously. But for all his ethical sensitivity, he did not retain sufficient respect for the individual conscience to be able to help us with the conflicts his social view of Jewishness has engendered, now so greatly magnified by the difficulties faced by the State of Israel.

Marxism and, if not nationalism, then sociology have strongly affected our sense of the self. Most commentators point to the increased privatization of American life as the major result of the flower-child rebellion of the 1960's. For me, an equally important outcome has been the continuing effort to create person-oriented communities and institutions. Most of the early communes have died. But we continue to see the creation of small groups for sharing significant aspects of one's life or to offset the intensified loneliness which has accompanied growing individuality, in the Jewish community, *havurot*. For us, any consideration of the self must, I think, pay as much attention to its social as to its rational nature. And it is this recognition of our ineradicable sociality which makes conflicts between our institutions and ourselves so difficult to resolve.

Retrospectively, the ethical problem of the self as a social reality may be said to haunt and ultimately render unsatisfactory the life work of Jean-Paul Sartre. In its initial stage Sartre emerged as the great philosophic exponent of the utterly free and unlimited individual. The difference between his phenomenological analysis and that of Descartes is instructive.[33] For Sartre, almost all the certainties of substantive rationalism have had to be surrendered. Rather, the world is technically understood to be absurd. Now, literally, there is nothing on which the authentic self may rely and still be truly for-itself. The self has only its freedom given to it. Indeed, in seeking external support to authenticate one's use of one's freedom, one already commits the primal Sartrean sin. As Dominick La Capra phrases it, "This pure and total freedom is an empty spontaneity that approximates blind will and allows only for a 'leap' into commitment."[34] Sartre can use the term "autonomy," but with rationality providing no guidance, with the *autos* defined as pure freedom, *nomos* means that it must radically be a law unto itself. The result is a thoroughgoing relativism. As Sartre says in the concluding ethical pages of *Being and Nothingness*, "... all human values are equivalent ... all are on principle doomed to failure. Thus it amounts to the same thing whether one gets drunk alone or is a leader of nations."[35] Here Sartre has given refined philosophic expression to the unanticipated outcome of Enlightenment individualism, an agnosticism so universal and profound it has led to moral solipsism.

This Sartrean individualism does admit of one social moral consideration. Sartre acknowledges that the other who stands over against me must be granted the same sort of freedom-consciousness that I possess.[36] Sartre has no good reason for this declaration, since one could hardly know any other free self as one knows one's self. Yet this moral deviation from his accustomed rigor testifies eloquently to his ethical seriousness.

Sartre had promised a work on ethics to fulfill the ontological analysis of *Being and Nothingness*. Instead, he turned to the Marxist notion of the sociality of the self in *Critique of Dialectical Reason*. Though Sartre now situated the self in its socioeconomic situation, nothing in this new analysis resolved his ethical problem of what an utterly free self should do.[37] In the *Critique* he did try to frame a way in which groups may properly be said to have a we-subject. But his does not go very far. Though he now acknowledges the many social determinants of our individuality, he does not at all shift the locus of legitimate authority from the self to the group.[38] What has happened is aptly summarized by Steven S. Schwarzschild: "*Critique of Dialectical Reason* does not differ very much from *Being and Nothingness* except for the fact that the hole of human autonomy is no longer to be found primarily in the being of some metaphysic but rather within the interstices of Marxist history."[39] Again, Sartre promised a successor ethical volume which never appeared, though a posthumous work with the promising title *Power and Liberty* has been announced.

This ethical vacuum in Sartre's thinking has now been filled, at least temporarily, by the publication of three interviews with Sartre by his last intimate associate, Benny Levy. At the end of the third interview Sartre is reported to have said that the Jewish people, by its life, constitutes a metaphysical reality. He renders this extraordinary judgment because the Jewish people has freely dedicated itself to achieving a this-worldly messianism by continually transforming and thereby transcending social reality. Such a statement would be tantamount to a retraction of Sartre's philosophy in prior years, and Simone de Beauvoir has denied that the interviews indicate Sartre's final position. However, Schwarzschild has now massively argued[40] that Sartre had to arrive at some such conclusion in order to complete his notion of ethical commitment as absolutely freely chosen by a mind rational enough to have such a project. By the time Schwarzschild's deliciously audacious reinterpretation of the Sartrean quest is over, Sartre can be called "a Jew *honoris causa.*"[41] By that Schwarzschild means one who espouses Hermann Cohen's Marburg neo-Kantian explication of Judaism's regulative idea.[42] Thus Schwarzschild can triumphantly identify Sartre's atheism as saying only "what for two hundred years Kant and H. Cohen's neo-Kantianism had said all along. . . ."[43] And it is in terms of Cohen's unique notion of messianism as an always beckoning but never attainable ethical goal that Schwarzschild interprets Sartrean ethics. It is regrettable that this fascinating study was published in a Jewish intellectual journal where scholars are unlikely to be able to benefit from and respond to its radical thesis.

Jürgen Habermas may well be said to be presenting the most interesting contemporary secular effort to situate free individuals in a thoroughly social context.[44] Habermas has tried to face up to the dire moral consequences of our ethical agnosticism in a time of increasingly powerful social structures.[45] Once again institutional evils impel the thinker to take the self seriously, even though much can no longer be said simply from within one's private individuality. Habermas has sought a ground of ethical value in our lived human social situation. In this way we may finally resolve the perennial post-Enlightenment problem of having to validate a robust social responsibility from a rigorously individualistic source of authority.[46]

Habermas points to communication as unique to human beings and universal in humankind.[47] Applying a transcendental analytic, he then inquires as to its necessary presuppositions.[48] Among the most important are the effort to be understood and, therefore, to gain assent to the act of communication (not its content). From this arises the fundamental concern of ethics, to seek the other's agreement or, conversely, the right not to be coerced but to come to one's own understanding.[49]

Rationality quickly claims its place in this process, for Habermas acknowledges the validity of one form of coercion, what he calls the peculiar force of the better argument.[50] We can then state a new criterion of truth, one which we may not be able to exemplify but which we can always endeavor to reach: that is, what would be accepted by everyone under the conditions of perfect communication.[51] In the service of this ideal we must unmask all the present distortions of communication, largely deriving from our social arrangements, and by transcending our false consciousness begin our march toward the ideal.[52]

Autonomy has now become the individual's right to resist any societal value or structure which remains unconvincingly explained. Without postulating any of the Kantian claims for practical reason, Habermas has made the individual's rationality the hope for ethical judgments and, therefore, social arrangements. By Kantian standards this is a minimalist ethic, but compared to the usual Marxist analysis of the place of the individual in contemporary society, it remains powerfully individualistic. To that extent at least, Habermas is making a significant contribution to resolving the tension between the autonomous self and its social obligations.

Yet the compelling power of this philosophy remains limited by its pragmatic evasion of the metaethical issue of the dignity of the self. In this secularism as in others, it is not clear why one should take the self so seriously and grant it such authority. What we realistically know about most people's lives, most emphatically beginning with our own, surely will not allow us to claim that they merit ultimate worth. If we are to be accorded the dignity of autonomy, it must surely be despite what we regularly show ourselves to be. That, in fact, we Westerners continue to attach such significance to individuality may only be, as Oriental critics suggest, a sign of our faulty sense of reality. Advaita Hinduism advises people to give up this illusion, which arises from a dualism that betrays the oneness of ultimate reality. Less metaphysically, much of Buddhism directs us, as the first step to enlightenment, to acknowledge the truth of *annata*, that there is no such thing as a self. Why, then, do we take it so for granted? It is hardly persuasive to respond that even the enunciation of such doctrines presupposes communication and therefore its implicit values. Perhaps at certain gross levels of understanding interpersonal communication remains necessary, but with a growth in insight speech becomes increasingly inadequate, as the record of the odd forms of religious "communication" indicates.[53]

Moreover, my Jewish sense of contact-laden responsibility makes me impatient with learning only the proper form of an ethical imperative. People luxuriating in freedom but unable to determine what to do with it need more substantive guidance. From what source can they gain the values and even the maxims by which they should live? And what might engender in them not merely a possible ethical construction of reality but an imperative of such quality that its appropriate response was one's utmost, lifelong devotion? I do not see contemporary secular reason capable of quieting our insatiable Descartesian doubt about rationalistic assertions concerning the ultimate grounds of our ethics.[54] This critique of critical reason, set against the background of such certainties as I can affirm, provides the intellectual ground for my now turning to religious thought.[55]

For me, the diverse strands of this post-Enlightenment quest come together least inadequately in the system of Martin Buber.[56] He knows no utterly discrete Descartesian ego but only a self which is always engaged with an other. So much the phenomenologists might have told us. But Buber also asserts that the self can directly know other selves, and these I-thou meetings are qualitatively more significant than our more precise customary engagement with others as objects. Indeed, Buber contends, the full self truly emerges only in the interpersonal encounter. Through its I-thou relationships it has access to a standard by which to live and an imperative to do so. The ultimate ground of all such I-thou encounters, and not uncommonly the immediate other in them, is God, the Eternal

212

Thou. Because, directly or indirectly, God relates to us precisely as the singular, individual thou we are, we know ourselves, in our specific personhood, to be endowed with ultimate worth.

The notion of autonomy functions here but in transformed fashion. The self, Buber stresses, must retain its individuality in a genuine I-thou encounter. Obviously, if you will not let me stand my ground, then "I" am no longer present to you. In contrast, my individuality only emerges in its fullness in relation to you and because of what we mean to one another. Thereafter I can no longer base my moral judgments on purely private considerations. The *autos* which now seeks the worthy act must always do so as an encounter partner.

No Kantian *nomos* can necessarily indicate the obligation that now devolves upon me.[57] Law seeks to specify the common case. It may, perhaps, speak to my-our present situation. But as I participated in and emerged from our meeting in fresh individuality, a universal law may also not know my-our need. It therefore cannot be granted its old coercive priority. For Buber, *nomos* is our acknowledgment of the commanding power of our relationships. They do not leave us content merely to bask in their significance but send us forth to live in terms of what we have just come to know. In this old-new sense, Buber's dialogical self has autonomy.

The personal effects of the notion of the I-thou relationship are so impressive that its equally social consequences are often overlooked. When we apply the distinction between I-it and I-thou relating socially, we see that our institutions disturb us so because they regularly treat us more as objects than as persons. Instead, we now consciously aspire to a social existence in which people reach out to one another in dialogic concern. Buber terms such a group a community and he, more than anyone I can think of, is responsible for the revolutionary thesis that our highest human duty is to transmute society into community.[58]

Usually this takes place only slowly, by individuals meeting and changing their social relations. On occasion groups as such directly have an I-thou encounter.[59] Then, as we may have experienced small-scale in work, prayer, or study, we are all momentarily bound up in a unity which did not negate our individuality while fulfilling it in a relation with many others. So the community forged by that experience now becomes valued in itself—and with each renewal of the experience the group becomes more important to our personal existence.

In great historic moments this happens to a folk and establishes its national character. The Hebrews shared such an experience in the events we call Exodus and Sinai—but did so with the unparalleled recognition that they were entering a covenant with God as well as with their newly born nation.[60]

All such corporate encounters, great or small, generate specific duties, thus specifying the mission on which the group now embarks. These laws retain their legitimacy as long as they continue to express the encounter that gave rise to them.[61] Social forms have a further validity to Buber.

213

People cannot remain in the I-thou state but must spend most of their lives in the I-it mode. Until the next encounter, the individual should seek to transform the I-it by what is still remembered of the I-thou.[62]

Secondarily, law provides for the continuity of I-thou reality in our I-it existence, a thesis with major social implications. Here is Buber's explication of the Torah's condemnation of Korah for rebelling against Moses (Num 16):

> Naturally God rules through men who have been gripped and filled with His spirit, and who on occasion carry out His will not merely by means of instantaneous decisions but also through lasting justice and law ... for without law, that is, without any clear-cut and transmissible line of demarcation between that which is pleasing to God and that which is displeasing to Him, there can be no historical continuity of divine rule upon earth.[63]

Korah was wrong because he argued "that the law as such displaces the spirit and the freedom and ... that it ought to be replaced by them."[64] He forgot our I-it historicity, dissolving it in the timelessness of the I-thou experience. Yet to some extent he was correct, for "in the world of the law what has been inspired always becomes emptied of the spirit, but ... in this state it continues to maintain its claim of full inspiration ... the law must again and again immerse itself in the consuming and purifying fire of the spirit, in order to renew itself and anew refine the genuine substance out of the dross of what has become false."[65] Thus Buberian I-thou autonomy holds sway over the Buberian affirmation of law.[66]

This dialogical understanding was the basis of Buber's famous exchange of letters from 1922–25 with Franz Rosenzweig concerning the authority of Jewish law.[67] Rosenzweig had suggested that Buber accept traditional Jewish law, at least in principle, as a perennial potential course of action. Buber rejected the idea. As he wrote in various letters, "I cannot admit the law transformed by man into the realm of my will, if I am to hold myself ready as well for the unmediated word of God directed to a specific hour of my life."[68] "I must ask myself again and again: Is this particular law addressed to me and rightly so? So that at one time I may include myself in this Israel which is addressed, but at times, many times, I cannot."[69] And more abstractly, "for me, though man is a law-receiver, God is not a law-giver, and therefore the Law has no universal validity, for me, but only a personal one."[70]

For Buber, concern for the presence of God should be our unqualified primary interest. By that standard, Jewish law seemed more to be serving its own institutional ends, not its Giver. To bring God back to the center of Jewish life, Buber felt he must resolutely resist any prior claims to his devotion.[71]

In his earlier years, at the turn of the century, Buber had stressed the group rather than the individual, but from the early 1920's on he felt that nothing was more important than the struggle against the collective.[72] Today, more than a half a century later, we must still oppose our collectives for regularly seeking to nullify or neutralize our autonomy. But, in addition to this struggle, the paramount one of Buber's life, we must carry on another of at least equal significance. We must reemphasize the sociality of the self, even as we envisage the self fundamentally grounded in covenant with God; for in our time, autonomy has largely shrunk into the notion of the self as a law unto itself. What began as a movement to liberate individuals has now become, through the loss of the old guiding certainties, a means for their degradation. If only to retain the validity of autonomy so as to oppose our overbearing institutions, we need to oppose unrestrained individualism and specify the sources of authority which should limit it. Redirecting autonomy has become as important a task as opposing any collective seeking to deny it. To me, then, autonomy is more God-oriented than our secular teachers admit and more social than the older Buber was willing to concede.[73] On that understanding, I now turn to the problem of living in commanding communities.

II

The first premise can be quickly stated. The self gains its worth not from itself but from its relationship with God. Much has been written on that score. More impressive is the way Americans have outgrown the alleged death of God. Adolescents think that to come of age one must spurn one's parents. But after our Oedipal acting-out we can appreciate that intimate relationships, even with persons deserving of deference, confer rather than impede maturity. So for some years now the quest for personal spirituality has been the outstanding phenomenon of American religious life.

If we can accept God in any significant sense of the term, we cannot employ our autonomy selfishly, that is, without intimate reference to the One who is sovereign and also the source of our freedom. God, in whatever way we relate to God, both bestows and delimits our independence.

We cannot as easily indicate today how human collectives validly ought to exercise significant sway over us. Let us begin by acknowledging that our group has some legitimate authority. We are not usually shaken by simple issues of social order or group discipline. Let us also confess, with some trepidation, that conscience can make ultimate claims upon us. Hence we can understand that in extreme cases we might—may God spare us—have to dissociate ourselves radically from our community. The tangled texture of our problem is most easily seen when a community behest rankles badly and we are suddenly caught between its authority and our autonomy.

The dialectical nature of our present struggle with group authority now manifests itself. As a troubled religious liberal, I feel I must begin from the side of the autonomous self, now bestriding our culture with great self-assurance. And I want to say a strong word about its essential sociality.

The Descartesian discrete self is a methodological fiction, useful for intellectual purposes and perhaps even necessary in our present under-

215

standing of our existence, but a fiction nonetheless. But what began as a heuristic device has become a metaphysical given. In truth, we are all very much more the children of our time, place, and community than of our pure thought or free choice. The very project of thinking as a pure mind, for all that it is the work of individual genius, arises within the history of Western thought, itself an elitist enterprise carried out by an uncommonly bookish group of white, middle- or upper-class males addicted to abstraction—of which I am one. The tribal and guild aspects of philosophy and theology are readily apparent to any perceptive observer at one of their conferences. Even creativity and individuality quickly become cult activities, and one identifies with them by adopting their garb, hair styles, buzz words, diets, and approved causes. Contemporary individualists did not themselves create the notion of autonomy. They received it as a social inheritance. They now assert their independence of others on the basis of a doctrine they learned from them. Kant would be appalled at autonomy as the ideology of enlightened selfishness; he took persons as ends far too seriously for that.

If we establish our autonomy on the basis of the freedom God has given us, we can hardly escape the consequent sociality of our selfhood. However we interpret the metaphor, God's voice commands not only the most intense, direct, personal love but also the love of our neighbor. Only by converting a specific directive into a vague sentiment can we arrive at a Judeo-Christian libertarianism.

The exercise of autonomy cannot, then, begin with a Descartesian initial negation of all institutions, lest we thereby deny our very selves. And in this part of the twentieth century I do not see how it can be reinstated on the basis of a Rousseauistic trust in our natural human goodness which would reproduce Eden if uncorrupted by society. The proper use of autonomy, then, begins by repudiating the self as a monad. I am individual and unique but likewise inseparably a part of all humankind. More, by my finitude I am necessarily more intimately linked to some of its vast number than to others. I am therefore morally obligated to live my life in community with them and exercise my personal autonomy in terms of them. To that extent the social critics of individualism, like Marx and Ahad Haam, were correct.

I understand that to mean that my community may reasonably demand of me that I discipline my will so that the community can function and persevere. Moreover, because I am substantially its creation, it can also legitimately expect some sacrifice of my conscience when its promptings conflict with central affirmations of my group. However, these institutional obligations are more than the dues we pay for participation or our simple duty as a result of the sociality of our being. They also derive from our recent, hard-won humility in selfhood. People are not as rational, as selfless, as morally competent as we thought them to be. Our communities and traditions often bear a wisdom far more profound and embracing, and certainly more enduring, than anything we could create on our own. In conflict with it, we must often bow to what, against our private judgment but in due humility, we accept as its superior understanding.

I have not meant by this heavy argument for the sociality of the *autos* and thus of its *nomos* to also make a case for the Grand Inquisitor. I only seek to right a balance—better, to restore a proper tension. I remain committed to the Enlightenment notion that full human dignity requires thinking and deciding for oneself. Today, as two centuries ago, that not infrequently can mean, when pressed, opposing radically what is otherwise most dear to us. As a liberal, I am regularly exasperated by a community wallowing in freedom, whose members love autonomy because it sanctions their casual nonobservance. I have therefore often tried to clarify what God rightfully demands of us.[74] Here I have tried to do something of the same for the community.[75] But when an institution begins to suggest that, on the whole, I will be better off relying on its judgment than my own, then my unrepentant liberalism makes itself rebelliously felt. I acknowledge that in any controversy my community may legitimately ask for my social *bona fides* and inquire what sacrifices I have in fact made as a more than selfish self. But, in turn, I will unabashedly ask for its *bona fides*. What sacrifices has it made of its power, its ambition, its drive to serve itself, for me and those like me who are not merely its beneficiaries but independent centers of worth and wisdom, and not infrequently the source of its authority?

Most social structures still function without essential regard for individual autonomy and its consequences for desirable human relations. Their leaders quickly revert to paternalism, punishment, or tyranny. If autonomous individuals are rightly asked to acknowledge and live by their sociality, then the dialectical demand on institutions must be that they organize and activate themselves out of respect for the fundamental dignity of their participants. Messianically, we yearn for the day when the common course will be directly determined by the common will. Practically, all we can and must ask is that our organizations manifest a major, activist commitment to achieving true community and make regular progress toward it.

I cannot go beyond this clarification of our mutual responsibilities to provide a rule by which these two sources of valid authority can settle serious confrontations. I cannot even specify very far the critical signs by which we may know when we have gone beyond individual sacrifice or institutional patience. But I can provide an old-new term for living in this kind of open, unsettled, but mutually dignifying relationship. It is "covenant," now less a structure spelled out from on high than a more equal effort to live in common need and respect. As is the case with egalitarian marriages, we cannot yet tell what forms and processes are appropriate to most people in such arrangements. We can, however, accept covenantal relationship as a central ethical challenge of our time and pragmatically see how we can sanctify our lives by employing it. For some such reason, I take it, God has put us in an open history.

217

In my view, the foregoing analysis applies to secular as to religious institutions but it takes somewhat altered form when applied to the corporate life of biblical religions.

I begin again with the sociality of the religious self. For all our contemporary spiritual search, there are few if any people whose resulting faith is not substantially another variation of a long historical tradition of the East or the West. And if we confess that our selfhood and autonomy are grounded in God, then we are commanded to live as part of a religious community.

In classic Judaism the social takes heavy precedence over the individual. The Covenant (the capitalization indicates reference to the Sinaitic Covenant) was not made with individuals but with a folk, the people of Israel. The individual Jew participates in our intense, personalistic relationship with God—no priests, no sacraments, no hierarchy—as part of the folk's religio-ethnic intimacy with God. Our modern non-Orthodox Judaisms have extended the power of the individual in that relationship. They use the concept of individual autonomy somewhat differently but they all assert their Jewish authenticity by their continuation of the people of Israel's historic Covenant.

I believe that we modern Jews properly exercise our autonomy only when we do so in terms of our relationship with God as part of the people of Israel and as the latest expression of its long Covenant tradition. Two intensifications of our general human sociality arise from this situation. As in all religions, the most utterly fundamental human bond is at stake here, namely, that with God. Hence our religious communities and responsibilities should properly be invested with profound devotion and commitment. Moreover, because of the ethnic base of its Covenant, Judaism emphasizes the social means by which this relationship is lived. The Jewish people worldwide, its local communities, its families, its progeny are the immediate means of the sacralization of Jewish existence. Though private devotion is esteemed and even demanded, though a fierce intellectual individualism has been one great source of our folk pride, living the Covenant has always meant linking oneself intimately to other Jews and their practices.

Most Jews who modernized had such great confidence in Western culture or disdain for the ghetto that they exercised their autonomy with little regard for the Jewish people, less for Jewish tradition, and little if any for God. Despite a resurgence of Jewish ethnicity, that still remains largely true. But a significant minority among us, very much more humble about the spiritual strength of our civilization, has learned a new respect for Judaism's wisdom, and even that of its God. Where this has become an affirmation that the people of Israel's Covenant is qualitatively unique, group loyalty and discipline have been even further intensified.

For their part, our religious leaders, we must admit, bear impossible burdens. How do we suggest they turn institutions into communities? Not every change they have initiated has proved entirely beneficial. Others, which have been resisted, have shown their mixed value when imple-

mented elsewhere. Besides, tradition has often held up well against modernity in recent years. Surely the accumulated wisdom of centuries
should not easily be surrendered for what may announce itself as ethics
but may soon be seen as one decade's passion.

Moreover, our leaders must make their decisions in terms of what God
wants God's community to be doing, an agenda they must largely define
and effectuate. Even as they know they are not God, they must not shirk
the special dignity of their roles which invests their decisions with a special measure of God's own authority.

Jewish institutional leadership finds these problems exacerbated by
the persistent threats to our existence. The Holocaust ended whatever
sense of ultimate security the Enlightenment and secular democracy had
given modern Jewry. The continuing peril of the State of Israel, our people's redemptive response to the Holocaust and therefore our unique contemporary symbol of the Covenant, keeps our leaders in a state of constant
alarm. The people of Israel needs vigilant defense against its foes; how can
it then easily tolerate critics and dissenters? The Jewish religion is threatened by a community which knows and practices little, and which believes even less. The modernization of Judaism has not produced a
widespread non-Orthodox Jewish piety; then, shall what has been preserved of our tradition now be further vitiated?

All American religious institutions can surely find strong warrant for
resisting further individualization as they reap the rewards of disillusion
with our secular idols. However, it ought not lull them into expecting that
we shall long be satisfied with them if they do not actively respect our
autonomy. Believers not only expect our religious institutions to serve as
social models of the humane values God demands of us as individuals; we
expect that they do so in exemplary fashion. We know that we cannot realistically demand that our religious leaders be saints and our institutions
perfect. We also cannot allow this to be their excuse for demonstrating
little more corporate righteousness than the unconsecrated do; for we can
find individual holiness by ourselves. What we seek from our institutions
is the social elaboration of our private responsibility, and we know that
only in its corporate religious exemplification can the full dimensions of
the sacred enter our individual lives.

Most Americans do not currently find their religious institutions
meeting their spiritual expectations. Against everything sociologists keep
telling us about secularization, pollsters regularly find that the overwhelming majority of us continue to profess belief in God and a broad
range of other Judeo-Christian beliefs. But these believers are dramatically
less involved in our institutions and their practices. I admit that this dis-
crepancy says something about what one can learn by polling people
about their beliefs and much more about the depth of faith being held. It
also says to me that many Americans remain children of the Enlightenment, experts in criticizing their social institutions, particularly the religious ones, for not living up to the values they proclaim. I read their

massive Lincolnesque defection from us as being in large part God's judgment upon our institutions for failing to exemplify better what God wants of us.

Here too I can adumbrate no rule for mediating between the conscientious self and the church or synagogue seeking to be true to its God-given mandate. The inspirited soul has always expressed itself in amazingly diverse fashion. Today, with individualism a primary good, with cultural lures of the most diverse kinds held out to us, we may expect people to hear God making an even broader range of demands upon them. But if they are part of the biblical witness of faith, they will, in some central way, be called to live in a community of fellow believers. The authenticity of their personal demands upon their institutions will first be ascertained by their response to their corporate obligations. What do they know of the tradition they are judging? What sacrifices have they made to its discipline? What place have they given the community in their vision of the proper service of God, and is it one by which it can legitimately hope to continue in faithful corporate service to God until the Messiah comes?

Then individuals, practicing what I have tried to explicate as a faithful biblical autonomy, will make their counterdemands upon their institutions. How have they used their power in relation to individuals and in pursuit of their corporate aims? How much dissent and pluralism have they tolerated or encouraged? How far have they sought to lead us and our society to a more humane existence rather than merely mirror or modify its present virtues and vices?

Our problems and opportunities arise from the need to refashion the covenants which have shaped the life of religious institutions. Heretofore they have derived essentially from two major centers of authority: God and God's people as a body. The rise of the notion of religiously autonomous individuals demands that a third partner now be fully acknowledged in the alliance.

I do not mean to suggest that God ought now be any less the primary figure in this expanded partnership. If my symbolism for God is less monarchical and more dialogical than has been traditional, I do not propose by stressing God's availability and gracious grant of human freedom to demean God's transcendent authority. Whether as people or as individuals, our existence devolves from God and ought to be dedicated, beyond all else, to God.

I also hope I have made clear the continuing necessity of structured religious sociality. Even as selves, we need the church and synagogue if we are to serve God properly. We therefore accept the yoke of their discipline and the guidance of their teaching.

To these two traditional foci of religious authority we now insist on adding a third: ourselves in our autonomous individuality. We are not bereft of God's presence or ignorant of God's present, commanding word. Seeking in some individual way to fulfill what we dimly but undeniably come to know God wants of us, we ask our institutions to treat us with a new, because greater, measure of covenant loyalty. We require more help and encouragement from them in working out our personhood in their midst, even if that engenders greater dissent in ideas and divergence in practice than has been acceptable heretofore. We know that there are always many good reasons for not sharing power with others, but even our humble sense of our individual dignity will not let us now be content with demanding of them any less. It is time for us to become the persons as well as the people of God.

III

Permit me now to conclude with some paragraphs on what I think I have been doing in these pages, thus fulfilling the contemporary theologian's compulsion to discuss methodology. Most theology is done from certainty. Some colleagues are confident they know how people ought to think, or the structure of universal human nature or experience, or what ultimate questions arise from our existence. Others speak with assurance about what religion is or ought to be, of how history operates, of the details of what God has told us, or even of what God is. I am unsure about all these matters and many more having to do with my faith.

What is clear to me at some moments often becomes problematic later. And what I once knew I could not accept has, on occasion, become significant to me later. Each of my affirmations seems troubled by many questions and doubts. Often I seem to hold them so lightly that the slightest thing could make them fall away from me. I do not find myself alone in this religious hesitancy.

All things being equal, we can say that most people in other ages were reasonably secure in their faith. When spiritual problems or possibilities arose among them, or when new ways of thinking about their belief came to them, they created intellectual systems which reflected their situation. Theologies of certainty thus arose and became traditional among us. Not sharing that sort of stability, religiously or culturally, I cannot properly carry on that enterprise. For myself and the many like me who find large measures of doubt and vacillation included in their faith, I work at what I have come to call the theology of comparative uncertainty—if it may be called theology at all.

I would not essay such a problematic effort were it not for two facts. The first has to do with the limits of my uncertainty. If the theologians and philosophers of religion I read regularly show me how little I am sure of, then the nihilists and humanists who surround us in this culture regularly make plain to me how much faith I still retain. For all I do not know and cannot make clear and distinct, I do not believe nothing. And what little I can say I do believe is utterly decisive for how I understand myself and

221

what I must try to do with my life. Second, for all that I am baffled by how to do so properly, I want to think very hard about my belief. Indeed, just because I cannot be very precise about my faith, I seek to clarify intellectually whatever I can give reasonable articulation. I do not find very congenial modes of abstract discourse with which to pursue this work of reflection, but I know I cannot be true to the cognitive capacity God has given me if I do not employ it in God's service as best I can. And this dialectic of faith and uncertainty engenders my kind of theological studies.

Notes

1. Readers eager to know the central methodological considerations on which this study rests will find them briefly stated in Section III.

2. "For Abelard sin lay solely in the intention. A man could not be called a sinner because he did what was objectively wrong, nor because he felt a sinful desire; sin, purely and simply, lay in consent to sinful desire" (C. Morris, *The Discovery of the Individual 1050–1200* [New York: Harper & Row, 1972] 75).

3. "The general principle he advocated was that 'every man must act in consonance with reason' . . . a principle which persuasively demonstrates the advance in individual ethics and a principle which begins to assert the autonomy of the individual in the moral sphere" (W. Ullmann, *The Individual and Society* [Baltimore: Johns Hopkins, 1966] 127).

4. On Descartes's fundamental individualism, see B. Williams, *The Project of Pure Inquiry* (New York: Penguin, 1978) 69–71.

5. The direct link between Rousseau and Kant is concisely indicated by L. W. Beck, *Early German Philosophy* (Cambridge: Harvard University, 1969) 489–90.

6. Ibid. 490. H. J. Paton, *The Categorical Imperative* (London: Hutchinson, 1965) 80, 82–83. For a more detailed analysis, see the chapter "Kant's Two Concepts of the Will in Their Political Context," in L. W. Beck, *Studies in the Philosophy of Kant* (Indianapolis: Bobbs-Merrill, 1965), particularly the conclusions reached, 221 and 223.

7. Paton, *Categorical Imperative* 211–12; E. Cassirer, *Kant's Life and Thought* (New Haven: Yale University, 1981) 244–45.

8. Ibid. 233.

9. On the analogy to the quest for pure reason, ibid. 239; Beck, *Early German Philosophy* 491; Beck, *Studies* 224; Paton, *Categorical Imperative* 81 and 207.

10. Richard Kroner does not hesitate to call this emphasis on the self "subjectivity" (R. Kroner, *Kant's Weltanschauung* [Chicago: University of Chicago, 1956] 68).

11. Paton, *Categorical Imperative* 180 ff.

12. Kant demonstrates a certain teleological interest in this regard: ibid. 44–45; Beck, *Early German Philosophy* 491.

13. I. Kant, *Foundations of the Metaphysics of Morals* (Indianapolis: Bobbs-Merrill, 1959) 85.

14. Ibid. 89.

15. Ibid. 91.

16. Again and again for Kant our rational nature requires us to come to certain

222

conclusions: Cassirer, *Kant's Life* 225; Paton, *Categorical Imperative* 240. It also determines his understanding of a rational faith: Beck, *Early German Philosophy* 487; Cassirer, *Kant's Life* 263. Kroner, *Weltanschauung* 35–37, detects some ambiguity with regard to God.

17. Cassirer, *Kant's Life* 246.

18. A similarly doleful plaint about the fate of reason from after World War II is made by another Kantian in Paton, *Categorical Imperative* 260.

19. K. Marx, *Writings of the Young Marx on Philosophy and Society* (New York: Doubleday, 1967) 457.

20. Ibid. 267, 272–73, 458.

21. Negatively, ibid. 458; positively, 281, 467.

22. When Marx does turn to the specific question of emancipating the Jews he identifies the Jewish people with everything he despises in contemporary society; the result is scurrilously anti-semitic (ibid. 241 ff.)

23. Ibid. 241.

24. Perhaps the fullest statement is given in the essay "The Transvaluation of Values," in A. Haam *Selected Essays* (Philadelphia: Jewish Publication Society, 1936) 217 ff. Thus he can say: "It is almost universally admitted that the Jews have a genius for morality, and in this respect are superior to all other nations" (228).

25. The critical portion may be found in A. Haam, *Essays, Letters, Memoirs* (Oxford: East and West, 1946) 127 ff.

26. Ibid. 137.

27. Ibid. 132.

28. Ibid. 135.

29. Untranslated: A. Haam, *All the Writings of Ahad Haam* [Hebrew] (Tel Aviv: Dvir, 1949) 350.

30. Untranslated: ibid. 163.

31. Ibid.

32. Ibid.

33. For the continuities with Descartes, see M. Grene, *Sartre* (New York: Franklin Watts, 1973) 39, 44.

34. D. La Capra, *A Preface to Sartre* (Ithaca: Cornell University, 1978) 127.

35. J. Sartre, *Being and Nothingness* (New York: Washington Square, 1966) 767.

36. Ibid. 358 ff., 641.

37. Grene, *Sartre* 258 ff.

38. " . . . there is in Sartre a scepticism regarding the possible primacy of any kind of group life, any life that resists collapse into a constellation of individual consciousnesses in which it exists as an object. . . . " (A. Danto, *Jean-Paul Sartre* [New York: Viking, 1975] 135). See La Capra, *Preface* 136.

39. S. Schwarzschild, "J.-P. Sartre as Jew," *Modern Judaism* 3 (1983) 50.

40. Ibid. 39–73.

41. Ibid. 59.

42. For insight into the rival, Heidelberg neo-Kantianism with a more substantive approach to God and thus to classic religiosity (Protestant), see R. Kroner, *Weltanschauung* 40 ff.

43. Schwarzschild, "Sartre as Jew" 59.

44. To place Habermas' highly Germanic thought in relation to the concerns of Anglo-American philosophy, see the lucid introductory essay by Charles Taylor and Alan Montefiore in G. Kortian, *Metacritique* (Cambridge: Cambridge University, 1980) 1–21.

45. Ibid. 56; D. Held, *Introduction to Critical Theory* (Berkeley: University of California, 1980) 67–69, 134–35, 349.

46. For Habermas, humans have an interest in reason which drives them toward emancipation and autonomy; moral freedom is thus the *telos* of philosophy (ibid. 254). See Kortian, *Metacritique* 70, 109.

47. His "universal pragmatics" is analyzed ibid. 118 ff., as well as by Held, *Introduction* 332 ff.

48. ". . . sometime in the mid 1960s, he seems to have been frightened by the specter of relativism, and retreated into a kind of transcendentalism" (R. Geuss, *The Idea of a Critical Theory* [Cambridge: Cambridge University, 1981] 64). See Kortian, *Metacritique* 121.

49. Ibid. 119; Geuss, *Idea* 69; Held, *Introduction* 256, 333.

50. Ibid. 344.

51. Ibid. 343–344; Geuss, *Idea*, 65–66.

52. Ibid. 70 ff.

53. Habermas recognizes that there are more forms of communication than discourse and he hopes ultimately to consider them all; see Held, *Introduction* 332.

54. Critiques of Habermas' thought on related if more directly philosophic issues may be found ibid. 395 ff. (on making communication normative and using discourse as its model) and Geuss, *Idea* 66–67 (on the absurdity of the ideal speech situation), 81 ff. (on the theoretical problems of Frankfurt School thinking as a whole).

55. Max Horkheimer, one of the leaders of the Frankfurt School, seems to have reached somewhat similar conclusions: "By the mid 1960s he felt he could not defend any philosophy or critical stance that lacked a theological moment; that is, an awareness of the transcendent, or the infinite, or the 'Wholly other' " (Held, *Introduction* 198).

56. For my understanding of Buber's thought as a whole, see E. Borowitz, *Choices in Modern Jewish Thought* (New York: Behrman, 1983) 141 ff.

57. Buber's most direct statement on this point comes in his response to his ethical critics in R. Schlipp and M. Friedman, *The Philosophy of Martin Buber* (La Salle, Ill., Open Court, 1967) 717 ff.

58. M. Buber, *Israel and the World* (New York: Schocken, 1948) 186, 193, 210.

59. M. Buber, *I and Thou* (New York: Scribners, 1958) 54.

60. M. Buber, *Moses* (Oxford: East and West, 1947) 110 ff.

61. Buber, *I and Thou* 118.

62. Ibid. 48–49, 112–15. Politically, too, M. Buber, *Between Man and Man* (New York: Macmillan, 1948) 64.

63. Buber, *Moses* 188.

64. Ibid.

65. Ibid.

66. So already in Buber, *I and Thou* 118–19.

67. F. Rosenzweig, *On Jewish Learning* (New York: Schocken, 1955) 109–18.

68. Ibid. 111.

69. Ibid. 114.

70. Ibid. 115.

71. This, then, is a strategic decision, based upon Buber's estimate of his situation and that of Judaism; it is not a matter of eternal principle. Cf. M. Friedman, *Martin Buber's Life and Work: The Middle Years 1923–1945* (New York: Dutton, 1983) 230, and note his statement about himself as a *hasid* (323).

72. Buber, *Man and Man* 80.

73. Cf. E. Borowitz, *Choices* 243–72. For an earlier approach to the issue, see E. Borowitz, "Autonomy versus Tradition," *Central Conference of American Rabbis Journal* 15 (1968) 32–43.

74. E. Borowitz, "The Old Woman as Meta-Question," *Journal of the American Academy of Religion* 44 (1976) 503–15 (reprinted here as chapter 6); "Beyond Immanence," *Religious Education* 75 (1980) 387–408; "Liberal Judaism's Effort To Invalidate Relativism without Mandating Orthodoxy," in *Go and Study,* ed. R. Jospe and S. Fishman (Washington: B'nai Brith, 1980) 149–60; "Affirming Transcendence: Beyond the Old Liberalism and the New Orthodoxies," *Reconstructionist* 46 (1980) 7–17.

75. Though written in 1981, my paper "The Autonomous Jewish Self" may be seen as a companion piece to this study, *Modern Judaism* 4 (1984) no. 1. It is reprinted here as chapter 14.

17

The Ideal Jew

I

In a typically stimulating paper, "Three Types of Jewish Piety," Gershom Scholem wrote, "I do not think there can be any doubt as to what these types of the ideal Jew are."[1] He identified these ideals as the *talmid hakam*, the *tzaddik* and the *hasid*—terms too rich for easy translation but ones that may be rendered, the sage, the righteous and the pietist. Years later, his judgment still seems correct and I should now like to extend Scholem's analysis in two directions: first, to add some nuances to his discussion of the past, and more important, to extend his thought into the present by speculating about the contemporary Jewish human ideal.

Scholem's premise was that "the basic tension in the religious society of Judaism is that between rational and emotional factors, rational and irrational forces. The ideal types formed by this society will necessarily reflect such tension." I see in this statement a reflection of Scholem's personal agenda, one powerfully formed by his response to German Jewish life. I, being part of the next generation and a product of American Jewry, see things differently. In part due to the acceptance of his work, in part because of historic events, the rational and irrational forces in Judaism, as in all humanity, seem to me more to co-exist than to be in radical tension. And, against his view, I find that to be true of the classic sources of Judaism.

Abridged from the B. G. Rudolph lecture of the same title. Syracuse University, 1986.

In that light, let me modify somewhat what Scholem said about the three ideal Jewish figures, particularly in terms of their depiction in talmudic and midrashic literature.

The first model he discusses is the *talmid hakham,* "the rabbinic scholar, or, as the extremely modest term would have to be translated literally: 'the pupil of a sage.' " He sees in this term "above all, an intellectual value and a value of a life of contemplation [as contrasted to activity]. What is asked of the scholar? A rational effort of the mind and its concentration."[2] After filling out his portrait of the sage, he sums up, "the decisive quality expected of him is his sobriety and rationality by which he is able to expound the values that have come down and been upheld by tradition, and his clarity of mind which makes him an educator, handing down those values to the next generation."[3]

This figure, I suggest, logically emerges from a distinctive characteristic of the Jewish religion, that God has given written as well as oral—as the rabbis insist—Torah, instructions, to the people of Israel. Since these include the possibility of their further elaboration, the person who knows the traditions and who can reliably interpret and apply them acquires high religious status.

Scholem emphasizes the academic character of the *talmid hakham* so heavily in order to dramatize his contrast with the *hasid,* whom Scholem will depict as essentially an emotional type, a religious enthusiast. I think that rhetorical purpose leads Scholem to overstate the case, as three themes in talmudic literature make clear.

Scholem admits[4] that the *talmid hakham* is a community figure but then radically subordinates this role to the sage's personal intellectual activity. Talmudic texts are less one-sided for they describe him as being appointed by the community,[5] and, whether or not officially installed to do so, performing various functions: as judge, preacher, teacher of students, decisor of various ritual issues, determiner of which vows one may be released from, and the agent of other such religious functions.[6] These surely require the exercise of rationality but hardly leave us with the sense of an ivory-tower intellectual as Scholem's description might.

Not the least aspect of being a community figure was serving as a role model. His disciples wanted to see how the master lived as well as to hear his teachings. And they then told their disciples what their masters did in the most diverse human situations. Their tales speak less of the sages as essentially sober, rational types, than of quite passionate men who regularly break into tears or otherwise give vent to their joy, distress or exasperation.

Scholem says of the two remaining types, the *tzaddik* and the *hasid,* that "they are not judged by the quality of their intellectual penetration, but by the way in which they perform the discharge of their religious duties in action. They are, to put it briefly, ideals of the *active* [as against the contemplative] life." He then adds, "Of course, the types are not exclusive of each other. A scholar may well-nigh be a *tzaddik* or a *hasid* at the same

227

time and *vice versa*. Each is to be judged by his own scale of values. If the *talmid hakham* represented an intellectual value in its perfection, the *tzaddik* or the *hasid* represents what we would call ethical values, values of the heart and of the deeds of man."[7] Moreover, while of the latter two types there is "no clear-cut distinction and separation" and "very often the terms could be exchanged" in the Middle Ages, particularly in the *musar*, the pietistic literature, "the distinction between the two types becomes crystal clear."[8]

For all that, when Scholem describes the *tzaddik*, he does so in terms directly derived from the Talmud.[9] "The *tzaddik* is the Jew who tries to comply with the commandments of the Law. He would be a *tzaddik* in the eyes of God if, brought before His court, it would be found that he has fulfilled his duties at least more than fifty percent."[10] Further, "The *tzaddik*, let me put it in a sententious way, is the ideal of the *normal* Jew. . . . In the moral sphere, indeed, the ideal of the *tzaddik* contains an element in common with the ideal of the scholar. This is the sobriety of the ideal, the absence of emotionalism. The Just Man is balanced in his actions, there is something deeply composed and cool-headed about him, however intense the passion to fulfill the Divine command that drives him may be. He does not lose control of himself."[11]

I believe that the notion of the *tzaddik* as the ideal for the ordinary Jew derives easily from Judaism as a religion of Torah. God's instructions, revealed to the people of Israel at Sinai and reinterpreted by the sages of each generation, focus upon the proper conduct of life. A Jew therefore serves God by trying to carry out God's behests, whether imparted as rule, ideal, model or folk intuition. The *tzaddik*, the one who has managed more often than not to carry out the Torah, thus becomes the common model for Jewish piety.

Once again, what Scholem calls the classic epitome gives us a somewhat different picture than he has drawn. He says, "The classic manuals of Jewish morals describe such training for the state of *tzaddik*, none more stringently than the famous treatise *Mesillat Yesharim* [The Path of the Upright] . . . no doubt one of the noblest products of Hebrew literature."[12] Yet that book hardly deals with sober-sidedness in religion. Rather, after its introduction, its next four chapters teach about the virtue of "Watchfulness," its acquisition and the hindrances to practicing it. And the next four chapters focus on "Zeal" in the same way. These are less a call to harmoniousness than to religious drive.

The treatise says of the proper attitude toward the commandments, ". . . we should be as scrupulous with regard to the *mitzvot* and the worship of God as though we had to weigh gold or precious stones, for they are means to perfection and eternal worth."[13] Luzzatto is quite insistent, teaching "that all decisions which incline toward leniency call for further examination. For although such leniency may be proper, it may, nevertheless, be a trick which the Evil Urge is playing upon us. Every tendency to be lenient should, therefore, be thoroughly looked into." But, in true Jewish spirit, Luzzatto does not teach asceticism. He concludes, "If, after such scrutiny, it still appears justified, it may certainly be considered good."[14]

Thus the properly zealous soul "moves with the swiftness of fire, and gives himself no rest until his object is attained. Note, further, that as enthusiasm calls forth zeal, so zeal calls forth enthusiasm, for when a man is engaged in the performance of a *mitzvah*, he feels that as he hastens his outward movements, his emotions are aroused and his enthusiasm waxes stronger. But if his bodily movements are sluggish, the movements of his spirit also become dull and lifeless."[15]

Luzzatto's *tzaddik*—and the Talmud's too, I would argue[16]—is something of an extremist, if only for taking religion so seriously and working at it so diligently.

For Scholem, the *talmid hakham* and the *tzaddik* are rational types while the third classic figure, the *hasid*, is essentially emotional. "He is never content with the middle road, he does not count his steps. He is the enthusiast, whose radicalism and utter emotional commitment are not to be deterred by bourgeois consideration. [The latter, almost certainly, is a reference to the style of the *tzaddik* as Scholem understands him.] . . . Whatever he does, he does in a spirit of spontaneous exuberance and of supererogation. . . . The *tzaddik* follows a law valid for all. I would say that he is the Jewish disciple of Kant in ethics. The *hasid* follows a law that is valid and binding only for himself. . . . There is something nonconformist and even an element of holy anarchism in his nature."[17]

While one might become a *tzaddik* through education, Scholem says, "Whether you are a *hasid* or not is basically a matter of gift and character. It is a propensity which you have or have not. If you have it, you can develop it. But you cannot educate everybody to become a *hasid*, as in principle you could educate everybody to become a *tzaddik*."[18]

Judaism's esteem for the *hasid*, I suggest, simply confirms all religion's effort to draw humankind to what Paul Tillich nicely termed "ultimacy." Thus, in polytheism the various gods had unique powers and deserved to be served with special care and attention. In monotheism, however, the one God of all the universe shares that regard with no one; the single God thus properly demands our concentrated dedication. Since Jewish practice links the acknowledgment of God's unity with loving God with all one's heart, with all one's soul and with all one's might, some of the faithful will surely do so extravagantly.

What may be lost in Scholem's depiction is that the *hasid*, for all his extremism, remains a normative Jew, one whose life is structured by the Torah. Scholem himself often commented that Jewish mysticism, for all its interiority, is essentially law-abiding. Here his focus on the *hasid* as nonconformist enthusiast unfortunately underplays the balancing dialectic.

The matter is quite clear in the Talmud if only, as Scholem has noted, because many of the *talmidei hakhamim*, who were, of course, *tzaddikim*, are also called *hasid*.[19] The same is true of the description given in medieval Jewish literature. Moreover, Luzzatto said directly that he wrote the

Mesillat Yesharium to train people to be *hasidim.* "There are but few who study the nature of the love and the fear of God, of communion or any other phase of *hasidut,* saintliness." He believes that, "Although saintliness is latent in the character of every normal person, yet without cultivation it is sure to remain dormant . . . [it is] not so innate as to enable men to dispense with the effort needed to develop [it]."[20]

Luzzatto's precis of his understanding of the *hasid* is like that of Scholem, yet less anarchic in its spirituality. "Accordingly, the principle of saintliness is that the scope of the observance of *mitzvot* should be enlarged. This applies to every possible aspect of the *mitzvot,* and to the circumstances under which they are to be observed."[21]

The extremism and radicality which Scholem stressed are found here but the non-conformity of Luzzatto's *hasid* is remarkably structured compared to what we have come to expect from apostles of religious enthusiasm.

Scholem concluded his lecture—and perhaps this thought led him to it—that, with the emergence of the Hasidic movement in the eighteenth-century, these terms underwent a "very curious metamorphosis. Never would it have occurred to earlier generations . . . to give the title of *hasidim* to people who admired *hasidim.* But that is precisely what has happened here . . . a rather paradoxical, if not to say scandalous, usage of the word—and the true *hasidim,* those who live up to the [classic] ideal, now came to be called *tzaddikim.* . . . A *tzaddik* in the hasidic sense has nothing to do with what the term meant in the traditional usage . . . but rather connotes the 'super-*hasid.*' "[22] This insight of Scholem's comes with startling effect, offering another example of the way in which new movements tend to co-opt old terms all the while redefining them. It is a stunning example of the idiosyncratic way religious traditions can transform themselves, which should caution students of religion that the same term may mean quite different things in different periods in a given faith. If so, how much the more is it possible that the same term used in different faiths is likely to have quite diverse meanings in each of them.

II

The insightfulness of Scholem's typology becomes clear when we apply it to modern times, which he did not. Jewish modernity arises with the Emancipation, the process beginning in the 19th century by which Jews were granted political rights in Europe and North America. Wherever Jews received equality they overwhelmingly abandoned ghetto life—created in response to 1500 years of discrimination—and avidly embraced the broader cultural horizon of the welcoming society. Indeed, they often over-idealized its humanity, identifying their host nation with a commitment to universal human liberation and fulfillment.

In this radical shift of social horizon, the old ideals, *talmid hakham,* *tzaddik, hasid,* lost compelling appeal. They had been empowered by Jewish faith exercised in a Jewish setting. Modern Jews lived primarily among non-Jews and largely adopted their human standards. Thus for newly enfranchised Jews—in my family as recent as my father's and my mother's emigration from Poland and Hungary—attaining social competence took priority over Jewish achievement. Most American Jews, I am convinced, still have that hierarchy of values despite their recent revival of interest in their Jewishness.

A second significant social shift accompanied the first, namely, the loss of rabbinic authority. Modern Jews, happy in a democratic social order, increasingly, if often quietly, took on the dignity of religious self-determination. They would make up their own minds as to how they would live Jewishly and whose guidance (sic) they would accept.

A minority of Jews resisted these changes in the name of traditional Jewish faith. Their way of life was determined by God's gift of the Torah, interpreted for our age by contemporary sages, not by the gentile world and its culture heroes. The overwhelming majority of Jews, however, found unreconstructed Jewish faith no longer tenable. For them, modernization meant secularization, so even when they believed, they were surer of their questions than of their affirmations.

Scholem, studying pre-modern Jewish ideal types consulted the sacred books created by the religious elite. But to look for the contemporary equivalent of a Jewish ideal, we are better advised to turn to the people itself. I confess I do not know a methodologically defensible way of doing that yet I believe it needs[23] to be attempted. What follows, then, proceeds from no sociological expertise but arises from my experience in and study of the Jewish community, both filtered through my intuition of the continuing existential validity of the Covenant.

I suggest, to begin with, that the three classic ideals have powerfully maintained themselves, albeit in universalistic transformation. The *talmid hakham,* the talmudic sage, now became realized in the university professor—explaining the uncommon proportion of Jews in academia. The *hasid,* the religous extremist, now metamorphosed into the political radical, passionate about instituting the messianic age—another social role with statistical Jewish over-representation. The more common Jewish ideal, the *tzaddik,* the person striving for righteousness, now took the path of being a good citizen and neighbor, with particular emphasis on human welfare and culture—again providing the ethnic impetus for the uncommon involvement of Jews in these activities. Substantively, the old Jewish models no longer move us; existentially, in accommodation to our new social situation, they still powerfully shape our lives.

These impressions can be taken a significant step further. American Jews, I suggest, have by now largely adopted a Yiddish[24] word to describe their contemporary ethnic ideal. It is the term *mentsh.* Put simply, a Jew may be a *talmid hakham, tzaddik or hasid* in the classic sense, or a professor, or radical, or good citizen or any combination thereof. But most of us are unlikely to esteem that Jew highly if he or she is not also a *mentsh*, a procedure indicating our adoption of a new and more significant human ideal.

What, then, is it to be a *mentsh?* As usual with such highly charged terms, no one exactly knows. And neither Yiddishists nor anthropologists have yet begun the process of unravelling its rich fabric of meanings. We shall have to proceed rather intuitively.

The word itself represents an intriguing and instructive tension. Denotatively, *mentsh* simply means "a person, a human being." Connotatively, it seems the equivalent of the English usage, "a *real* person," a phrase of similarly imprecise meaning. In the term *mentsh* the real and the ideal intersect. More important, the term's immediate reference is purely universalistic, pointing beyond Jewish standards to what anyone, anywhere ought to be. In this it shows its post-Emancipation provenance and commitment. But, of course, this is being expressed in Yiddish, as if to ground Jewish universalism in ethnicity, possibly even expressing the hope that Jewishness will give the Jew special, perhaps unique, insight into being human.

Steven S. Schwarzschild has suggested, quite correctly, I believe, that a " 'Mentsh' is *homo humanus* in one word, in one indivisible notion. In other words, the Yiddish noun carries with it, as part of its essential definition, an ethical component."[25] Indeed, nothing so disturbs the contemporary Jew as an otherwise estimable community figure who is revealed to be morally culpable. Some recent notorious examples are: the non-observant Jew Abe Fortas, forced to resign from the Supreme Court for accepting a retainer from someone whose case might come before the court; Bernard Bergman, a leader in international Orthodoxy, convicted of improper care of the aged in his nursing homes; and presently, Rabbi Meir Kahane who espouses an anti-democratic Jewish politics.

A *mentsh* ought to have a strong sense of ethics, one which reaches out to all humankind and reflects the devotion to justice and compassion that animate every true human being. This ethical commitment has such power that often, when it clashes with a Jewish tradition it transforms it, as is now happening with feminism, though somewhat grudgingly, to be sure. But it is by no means invincible. Sometimes, as with the issues of intermarriage and Palestinian rights, Jews will divide over what ought to be done, the majority remaining convinced that their commitment to their people's Covenant with God demands that Jewish particularity be given proper scope.

But the term seems to me to have much broader connotations than "being ethical," particularly in the stringently rationalistic interpretation Schwarzschild gives to "ethics." We can gain some sense of these other meanings by looking at the associations of the word *mentsh* in Yiddish folk expressions. Let me adduce some data gathered from collections of

Yiddish folk sayings, one from early in the century, the encyclopedic Bernstein/Segel volume of 1908, the others coming from more recent decades.[26]

Roughly a third of the adages listed under *mentsh* in the Bernstein/ Segel anthology had some direct ethical content.[27] Some are simple lessons, for example: "*Iber dem hat Got dem mentshen gegeben tzve oyeren un ayn moyl, kidey er zol mer heren un veniger reden,*" "God gave a person two ears and one mouth so he should listen more and talk less";[28] and "*Der mentsh iz in zikh aleyn fernart,*" "One is often fooled about oneself."[29] A somewhat larger number encapsulate the sardonic reflections often associated with Yiddish. "*Der mentsh hot groyse oygen un zet nit zayn eygene feyler,*"[30] "A person has big eyes but doesn't see his own faults"; and "*Vos der mentsh tun zikh aleyn volten im kayn tzeyn sonim nit vintshen,*" "What a person does to himself, ten enemies wouldn't wish him."[31]

Of all the proverbs perused, only two can be said to invest the word *mentsh* with high humane or ethical content. "*A mentsh iz umetum a mentsh,*" literally, "A person is always a person," implying that one's innate worth remains regardless of events.[32] And "*A groysser oylem un nito keyn mentsh,*" "A great assembly, and no man in it!"[33]

From the Bernstein/Segel sample, then, one must conclude that *mentsh* is used overwhelmingly as a simple descriptive—human being, person—and not as an accepted ideal. The proverbs in the other sources I consulted similarly use the term *mentsh* in folk observations of human nature, about half of which may be called sardonic.[34] In fact, more maxims referred to how unethical one may expect people to be than to the ethical humanhood they ought to manifest. For example, "*A mentsh darf iber zikh kayn ergers nit hoben vi a mentshn,*" "A person can't have anything worse over him than another person";[35] "*Far Got hot men moyre—far mentshn muz men zikh hitn,*" "Fear God but beware of people";[36] and "*Got shtroft, der mentsh iz sikh noykem,*" "God punishes but people take revenge."[37] More positively, we can see *mentsh* used in its typical a-ethical sense in a maxim like, "*A mentsh mit gute maniren shlogt zikh durkh ale tiren,*" "A person with good manners can break through all doors."[38] Matisow calls our attention to the common Yiddish expression "*nit far keyn mentshn gedakht,*" "may —— be unthinkable for any person." One of the phrases most frequently invoked to ward off possible danger, it carries no connotation of high humaneness or rational morality. Thus, his example is "*Un geven iz er a kaptsn, nit far keyn mentshn gedakht,*" "And he was a pauper—may it be unthinkable for any person."[39]

To me, the common use of the term *mentsh* speaks rather more of Jewish realism than of Jewish idealism, of *metshlekhkayt* as simple humanness not literary or moral/intellectual creativity. It exhibits, on the folk level, a modern shift of concern, away from the Torah and the God who gave it, to the human beings who must try to live it. At the least, it gives priority to exhibiting one's common humanity no matter what one's position or power. It also displays the new scepticism of modernist Jewish self-consciousness, one that deflates all sweeping claims to certainty with the evidence drawn from keeping a steady eye on people. I hear these overtones and more in such adages as "*A mentsh is doch nor a bosór vedom*," "A person is only flesh and blood," which is to say something like, "People are only human."[40]

In the Yiddish that sentiment has quite a different effect than in English. In our society we regularly aver to our humanity to excuse our failings. "I'm only human," has something of a pathetic tone, calling on the listener to acknowledge that people should not be expected to live up to high standards.

The Yiddish confession of our human weakness takes place in quite another context for the one who utters it stands within the Jewish people and inherits its tradition. Its ethos still powerfully transmits even as it has transmuted its long tradition of commandment and aspiration. Among Jews, to be human is to strive to do one's duty and in that effort to attain one's dignity. And one knows that other Jews, though knowing you "are only human," will judge you by that standard. In this context, where a community strongly reinforces obligation, to say one is only human cannot function as a release from responsibility, as in our society we often hope it will, but only as a mitigation of our failing in what remain our legitimate responsibilities.

In sum, then, with the Emancipation, a new universalism, realism and scepticism came into the Jewish human ideal, but it cannot be said to have displaced it so much as to have reshaped its reach to others and its understanding of self. Thus, one may hope that as long as Jews remain faithful to their heritage, their new-found humanism will not lead on to the relativism and aimlessness that so sadly characterize much of American life but to a newly refreshed *mentshlekhkayt*. For a *mentsh*, it would seem, is only a post-Emancipation *tzaddik*,[41] a person more certain of human capacity and stupidity than of God's rules, one more concerned about everyday decency and compassion than about social conventions or institutional niceties, one as much a part of the global human race as of one's own wonderful people. The social and theological context has changed and with it the outer shape of the Jewish human ideal. But existentially, the underlying vision of what we are and ought to be remains remarkably the same.

Notes

1. Scholem, Gershom, "Three Types of Jewish Piety," *Ariel*, No. 32 (1973), p. 5. All citations from Scholem are taken from this printing. The essay first appeared in the *Eranos Yearbook*, 1969.

2. P. 7.

3. P. 9.

4. Briefly, at the bottom of pp. 8 and 9

5. E.g., Y. Bekh end and Y. Taan 2.2.

6. E.g., Sifre Dt. 1.13, Er. 36b, Ber. 35a and 63b. The term *hakham* is most commonly used in connection with the giving of rulings.

7. P. 10.

8. P. 11.

9. Kid. 40a–b.

10. P. 11.

11. P. 12. A somewhat similar figure is found in Hellenistic Judaism. David Winston describes one class in Philo's description of people as "those who are making gradual progress in virtue but are unable fully to attain it. . . . Since this class undoubtedly comprises the bulk of humanity, it is somewhat disconcerting to find no explicit statement by Philo regarding their final disposition." *Logos and Mystical Theology in Philo of Alexandria* (New York, HUC Press, 1985), p. 41.

12. P. 12.

13. *Mesillat Yesharim*, Moses Hayyim Luzzatto, translated by Mordecai Kaplan (Philadelphia: Jewish Publication Society of America, 1936) (hereafter: MY) p. 17. Note the duplication of *shehadikduk sheyidakdek* which makes the rendering "should be scrupulous" almost an understatement. While Kaplan's translation is somewhat loose by contemporary standards it not only renders the text with reasonable accuracy but with a certain English fluency that commends it for continuing use.

14. MY p. 53. I have rendered the term *yezer* in the Kaplan translation as "urge."

15. MY p. 57. This statement begins with a reference to one "who is an ardent worshipper" (*asher tilahet nafsho*), thus, perhaps, seeming to refer to someone seeking a goal higher than that of a mere *tzaddik*. I shall return to that matter below. Here I only wish to indicate that for Luzzatto, a person only on the 2nd level of his 10 step ladder to holiness must be concerned about generating considerable personal intensity. My point is that Scholem's account of the *tzaddik* does not sufficiently bring this out.

16. In rabbinic literature we have continual reference not only to the *tzaddik* but to the *tzaddik gamur*, "the complete *tzaddik*." One can thus find implicit in the talmudic notion degrees of the state, an ordinary and an extraordinary, the one satisfied with a plurality of righteousness, the other driving toward perfection. An exchange between Bar He He and Hillel is instructive. The latter, for all his proverbial mildness, did not hesitate to apply the distinction made in Mal. 3:18 "between the righteous and the wicked, between one that serves God and one who does not," to the difference between someone who had repeated his new learning 101 times as against 100. Though both might be called a *tzaddik gamur*, the difference between them was as real as the difference in rates mule drivers charge for having to go 11 as against 10 parasangs. Hag. 9b.

17. Pp. 18–19.

18. P. 21.

19. P. 10. R. Judah said that one who wishes to be a *hasid* should fulfill the laws of the tractates collected in the order Damages. Rava said the injunctions in the tractate of "The Fathers" (a figure of speech for the rabbinic masters). Others said those matters dealt with in the tractate Blessings. Kid. 30a.

20. MY p. 3. Luzzatto's book is not a manual for the would be *tzaddik* but rather for one who wished to become a *hasid* and perhaps go beyond it some steps to holiness. Following an old rabbinic teaching, there are 10 steps in Luzzatto's cur-

riculum. As Scholem indicates, one needs to be a *tzaddik* in order to become a *hasid*. Thus in discussing Luzzatto's notion of the *tzaddik* as against that of Scholem, I cited only his early chapters, those dealing with stages 1 and 2 of the training, whereas he reserves saintliness for stage 6. Much of late medieval Jewry seems to agree that *hasidut* can be cultivated by anyone for Luzzatto's work became perhaps the most widely studied of all the medieval Jewish moral manuals.

21. MY p. 147.

22. P. 23

23. Two factors confirm me in this method. The one is Jewish. The Covenant is made with the Jewish people, not with a given Jewish individual *per se*. Hence authentic if liberal Jewish thinking needs to proceed in terms of where the Covenant *people*, not merely the *individual* Jewish thinker, is to be found. I consider it a fundamental error of much liberal Jewish thought that it adopts, unthinkingly, the individualistic bias of philosophy or most Christian theology. It then never finds an easy way of understanding the appropriate claims of the Jewish people on the sovereign, individual Jew. The second arises from a recognition that modernity has taught us some truths which Judaism ought to accept (not infrequently after Jewish criticism and refinement). One of these, in the religious realm, is that personal experience (itself tested by reason but not screened by it) offers our best access to ultimate reality. As a contemporary Jewish thinker I therefore work from this two-fold, integrated stance.

24. My efforts to see if there was an equivalent term among American Sephardi Jews produced few results. Rabbi Marc D. Angel, Rabbi of The Congregational Shearith Israel, The Spanish and Portugese Synagogue, wrote in response to my query, "In Judeo-Spanish, the equivalent to 'mentsh' is 'benadam' (Hebrew for 'human being'), often pronounced 'benatham.' Obviously, it comes from the Hebrew. The word 'benadamlik' is used to refer to courtesy or consideration. I can't think of other terms that might be useful for your study. I have asked a friend here who knows Judeo-Spanish and I have also consulted a little Ladino-English dictionary. There may be other phrases but I am not familiar with them. Also, I do not know anything about Judeo-Arabic or other languages Sephardim have spoken." Letter of June 14, 1985.

25. In an unpublished manuscript on "Jewish Language," p. 7. I am again indebted to my schoolmate and friend of over 40 years, this time for sharing this extensive paper with me. Our relationship has flourished over the years precisely because we care enough about each other to criticize the other's thinking where it appears to be faulty.

26. I am grateful to Philip Miller, Librarian of the Hebrew Union College-Jewish Institute of Religion, New York, and Dina Abramowicz, Librarian of YIVO for their generous, gracious help, which pointed me toward such sources as existed and to others which we all hoped might turn out to be of greater value than actually was the case. Ignaz Bernstein and B. W. Segel, *Juedische Sprichwoerter und Redensarten* (Warsaw, 1908). Hanan Ayalti, ed., *Yiddish Proverbs* (New York: Schocken, 1949). Nahum Stuchkoff, *Der Oytzer fun der Yiddisher Shprakh* (YIVO, 1950). Shin. Esterson, *500 Gegramte Sprikhverter un Redensarten* (Jerusalem, 1963). James A. Matisoff, *Blessings, Curses, Hopes and Fears; Psycho-Ostensive Expressions in Yiddish* (Philadelphia: ISHI, 1979).

27. Op. cit., nos. 7, 9, 30 and 42, plus the examples cited below; additional sardonic ones are nos. 2, 16, 17, 22, 35 and 37, plus others fully cited. Pp. 164–167.

28. Ibid., no. 4. I bear the responsibility for the transliterations and translations.

29. Ibid., no. 23.

30. Ibid., no. 28.

31. Ibid., no. 36.

32. Ibid., no. 12.

33. Ayalti, no. 14, his transliteration and translation. Schwarzschild will find in this maxim additional basis for his suggestion, Ms. p. 7, that the Yiddish *mentsh* derives from the Hebrew *ish* based on Av. 2.6, "In a place where there is no man, strive to be [he prefers, to maintain proper Marburgian dynamism, "become"] a man." I see no basis for this supposition in the traditional understanding of the text. The classic Mishnah commentators ignore this phrase and the ones given in the printings of the Talmud understand it as a restatement of one's common duty to be Jewishly observant; thus, *ish* means one who fulfills one's obligations stated in Torah, not merely one's ethical responsibilities. Maimonides, of course, gives this statement his usual metaphysical twist. See Av. 7a, where it is enumerated 2.5.

34. Of the 49 not otherwise cited Bernstein/Segel proverbs, I see the following as sardonic observations on human nature: nos. 11, 14, 18, 19, 21, 31 (which says there is no justice), 32 (which together with 34 and 47 contradict 9), 33, 38, 39 and 40 (which say there is little ethics), and 48. Much of the Stuchkoff maxim collection repeats statements from Bernstein/Segel. Where it presents fresh usages, they are more likely to be descriptive than ethically exhortive. Op. cit., pp. 163 col. b and 164 col. a.

35. No. 16. See also no. 3.

36. Ayalti, no. 276.

37. Ibid., no. 316. I would also include in this category Esterson no. 224.

38. Bernstein/Segel, no. 20.

39. Matisow, no. 129.

40. Bernstein/Segel, no. 24.

41. I think we can say about when this change in attitude reached conscious expression among Yiddishists. Ruth Wisse ("The Politics of Yiddish," *Commentary*, Vol. 80, No. 1, July 1985) comments that *Yiddishkayt* "from the beginning of this century, and particularly in the period between the wars . . . began to assume a modern, ideological connotation," becoming a cultural process that "engenders *mentshlekhkayt*, humaneness," with the two eventually becoming identical terms, p. 29, col. a. I think she is speaking of an elitist development and that is one reason we find so little evidence of the ideological sense of *mentsh* in the sample of folk wisdom we examined. As she makes clear in her article, the generation descended from the immigrant Yiddish speakers largely abandoned the language. Insofar as they accepted the high-cultural notion of *yiddishkayt/mentshlekhkayt* they never had a chance to work it into the language they had grown up with but no longer used. Their continuing utilization of the Yiddish term *mentsh* seems then to express with particular power their desire to link the new vision with their old idealism.

18

Being a *Mentsh*, the
Psychological Aspect

In the preceding paper I discussed Gershom Scholem's three ideal Jewish personality types, the *talmid hakham*, the *hasid*, and the *tzaddik*, the sage, the pietist and the righteous one, suggesting that in modern times folk usage had added a fourth such figure, the *mentsh*. I should now like to speculate about a contemporary development of that term arising from our community's intense involvement with psychotherapy. I know of no literature treating this notion so to do so I shall draw on experience and intuition—and perhaps not a little Jewish optimism.

Most Jews, I think, now take it for granted that what Freud and his diverse followers have taught us is true, that we human beings are very much more creatures of our passions than our tradition or our common sense had previously indicated. Thus, to be a *mentsh* in the fullest sense of the term, one would need to pay very much more attention to the emotional side of existence than our forebears did. At this level, then, all we are speaking about is a further appreciation of the human fallibility which the onrush of modernity made so conspicuous a part of our folk ideal. The bridge between the older Jewish notion of a *mentsh* and that of today is well seen in their common high appreciation of having a sense of humor. A *mentsh* was always expected not to be so serious as to be unable to laugh at a good joke. Even more important today is being able to laugh at him or herself.

Abridged from "Mentshood," *Present Tense*, vol. 15, no. 6 (September–October 1988).

This new sense of *mentsh*-hood surfaces clearly in our current community attitudes toward play. Like all robust, long-lasting social enterprises, historic Jewish life had its currents of playfulness and foolery—and, occasionally, even a touch of the Dionysiac; our tradition certainly knows and encourages joy, happiness and celebration. But a gulf separates Sabbath rest or the delight of the commandments from the modern notion of "having fun." Thus, though it did not proscribe playing games, our sages did not consider that a worthy pursuit for mature adults. Surely much of this negativity arose from the economic constraints and social insecurity which characterized Jewish life in recent centuries. Yet the evidence of Biblical times indicates that it was also substantially a matter of cultural ethos. Few material differences distinguish the life of the Greeks from that of the Jews in late Biblical times, yet the one people made games central to their way of life and the other people did not. They simply had different values, the Greeks idealizing the human body where the Jews sought to imitate a bodiless, good God.

Today, American affluence and suburbanization have made play, particularly sports, a critical ingredient of "the good life." So for Jews, being a *mentsh* means not being one-sided, whether one is dedicated to intellect, business, or any other endeavor. Rather, a *mentsh* is well-rounded, one who knows how to take time off and relax, one who knows the importance of having a good time—and that generally means being able to play. Early on in modern times that appeared as the widespread Jewish interest in playing cards, a previously deprecated activity that became particularly attractive because if its accompanying sociability, Judaized as kibbitzing. Today, golf and tennis are the preferred recreations in up-scale circles. And the gymnasium, now repackaged as the health club, once abominated by Jews because of its association with Hellenic idolatry and homosexuality, has become a well-accepted part of rounded Jewish living.

A similar new Jewish openness characterizes the Jewish attitude toward the play we call sexuality. We are now quite proud that our tradition has always had a positive attitude toward sexual activity, seeing marriage and procreation as major means of serving God. Yet, pre-modern Judaism, reflecting its extended medieval history with its exaggerated dichotomy between body and soul, had a comparatively repressive attitude toward human sexuality. It was not a matter to be discussed openly and confronted directly as part of one's growing up. It was rather strongly equated with what the rabbinic tradition called the *yetzer hara*, "the urge to evil," and, being dangerous, had to be channeled within very carefully defined limits.

Most modern Jews accept the Freudian notion that sexuality is in and of itself neutral, if powerful, and that its coercive repression can be a major source of personality malformation and thus of human suffering. More important, they are convinced that the Freudian guide to greater healthfulness is correct, that, if I may take some license with the terms, expression ought to take the place of repression. We now commonly believe that a positive attitude toward and a proper exercise of one's sexuality is a major component of a fulfilled existence.

In hindsight, we can say that, even without benefit of Freud, as Jews modernized they began practicing a new, more pleasure-oriented sexuality. Already by the turn of the century, Jews who entered the social mainstream used contraceptives freely despite the admonitions of their religious leaders; most members of Orthodox synagogues seem to follow that practice today. In recent years, the freer attitude toward sexuality has made itself felt in the greater Jewish acceptance of quite diverse sexual arrangements. We are hardly surprised now that Jewish women are as concerned and open about sexual pleasure as are men, that husbands and wives feel it important to their relationship to work at their mutual sexual delight, or that young and sometimes not so young people live together without marriage. In striking contrast to our recent past, all that can be part of being a *mentsh* today. Indeed, we shall not consider someone who cannot love freely and joyously much of a *mentsh*.

Our *mentsh*, then, is the first Jew whose life is significantly attuned to the pleasure principle, one who makes care of the self and concern for the self, a major part of existence. In this transformation we can hear the cry of Philip Roth's Portnoy, cleverly caricaturing us, "We need to put the id back into the Yid." He is not far wrong; for much of our community the triumph of the therapeutic has meant learning to live more instinctually. But it is just this domestication of the id that creates a dialectical Jewish problem. As Hillel put it two thousand years ago, "If I am only for myself, what then am I?"—to which the modern answer would be, not much of a *mentsh*.

Concentration on the self produces a narrow, barren narcissism. But one might also attain a healthy narcissism, that love of self which is the basis of loving one's neighbor, the kind which breeds no illusions about our worth because it knows that, with all our faults, God loves us. One cannot be our kind of *mentsh* without being some kind of narcissist, but it is precisely the struggle to transcend simple self-gratification and become a healthy narcissist which would characterize our psychologized *mentsh*. How to become such a person therefore becomes the critical personal issue for this generation of Jews.

In the heady years of their first revelatory successes, psychotherapists often dreamed that treatment would replace religion, that giving up the discipline of the commandments for the regimen of therapy would more effectively ennoble our lives and transform society. It was, in other words, an attractive, alternative messianism.

Something like this is the ethno-religious basis for the disproportionate number of Jews who have regularly been involved in the "helping professions." The phenomenon, I would further suggest, also derives from the psychotherapist's role, one which nicely enfolds characteristics of the old, classic ideal Jewish types. Therapists are modern sages, possessing an exquisitely subtle, demandingly esoteric knowledge of human psychodynamics and a gift for the arcane casuistry of applying it in infinitely variable therapeutic situations. They are also secular pietists, often called upon to give inordinately of themselves by moving into emotional areas that threaten to overwhelm their own frail psyches as well as their capacity to understand and to heal. But above all, they increase righteousness in the world by helping people attain greater responsibility for what they do. They thus fulfill anew the treasured Talmudic dictum, "One who saves a single life is accounted as one who has saved the whole world." The helping professions therefore appeal to Jews because, on some existential level, they allow one to work toward their people's primal messianic goal.

Something of the power of this post-Freudian revolution is now also being felt on the lay level. So many of us have been or are in treatment that we now can see therapeutic concern as an integral part of our ideal way of life. What sort of *mentsh* is it who has no deep concern for others' feelings, one who continually creates emotionally oppressive situations which keep others from being true to themselves? Without some such enlarged sense of compassion even an otherwise admirable ethical activist can hardly now claim our full admiration. Our new *mentsh* will rather evidence a certain therapeutic sensitivity, responding to what others feel as well as to what they say and do, helping them grow emotionally as well as intellectually and ethically, creating, wherever possible, such psychic security with others that they can mutually improve their psychic well-being.

But is that all? Can we allow psychotherapy to dominate our contemporary vision of a *mentsh*? Is our healthy narcissism essentially being ready to enter and stay with therapy ourselves and to help others toward a similar psychic healthfulness?

Sweeping claims for treatment, I am convinced, now find little resonance among us. Our experience this century with psychotherapy, Marxism, science and so much else has shown them to be false messiahs. Thus, putting ego where id had been can effectively lessen suffering, a wonderful reason for pursuing that goal. But, though it mitigates our pain and increases our freedom, it cannot radically resolve the problems of being human. As the old Freud wrote, our discontents go deeper than analysis can reach. Surely one reason M. Scott Peck's *The Road Less Traveled* has such wide appeal is that it does not overstate what psychotherapy can accomplish or underestimate the dedication and sacrifice it requires.

In the Jewish community, our realism about therapy also comes from what the Holocaust taught us about human nature. Education, culture and traditional religion were inadequate bulwarks against the depravity of Nazism. Almost as chilling, the practice of democracy did not eradicate the latent though genteel anti-semitism that kept the allies from mitigating the effects of the Holocaust. Human motivation recedes ultimately and treatment can go on interminably. Meanwhile evil triumphs. Therapy may help—our common euphemism for it, "help," is literally true—but it does not "save" and that is why someone who completes treatment may not yet manifest the positive values that characterize a *mentsh*.

That returns us to what my intuition suggested about the Jewish embrace of psychotherapy, that it had a messianic root. As I understand it, therapy appeals to Jews not as an end in itself but as a means of increasing responsibility. To be sure, treatment cannot be judgmental and succeed—but where it retains its deep Jewish affinities, it also cannot be altogether divorced from a normative goal. Jewish health, *mentsh*-hood, is attained primarily not in rich feeling but in righteous doing. Even in modernity the repressed classic Jewish ethos returns: our psychologically oriented *mentsh* still needs to be a *tzaddik*, albeit a modern one.

This sort of *mentsh* fosters psychic well-being to ease the burden of creating a righteousness which must always mediate between what, in fact, one is, and what, by covenant, one ought to be. And that old goal of increasing justice and compassion requires that we enlarge our self-regard with other-love. Our Jewish task remains, then, as ever, as much social as it is personal, a truth as grounded in our historic past and oriented toward the messianic future as to the demanding present, a task as much set by values transcendentally laid upon us as autonomously worked out through our unique individuality. Jewish humanhood still means so to sanctify the everyday that those about us have more reason to hope the Days of the Messiah will come speedily.

Many Jews are content to leave it on that human level, speaking of what they most truly believe only out of what they most surely know, their experience and that of others like them. I think that is why the term *mentsh* remains so richly undefinable. It speaks of being human but it carries the weight of that which we know transcends our humanity and sets its proper standards. My experience and our tradition are less solipsistic than that. Humankind cannot explain its more than human depth or, more important, mandate its proper aspirations. If, to use Peter Berger's term, we find signals of transcendence in our humanity, then, showing the same courage we employed to face our emotionality, we should learn to face the Transcendent directly. That surely was what the classic Jewish tradition was all about.

I think I understand why many Jews are reluctant to speak of God. At best, that hesitation stems from our ancient respect for the One who grounds all reality and constitutes its standard and goal. Our awe is also associated with God's unfathomable transcendence, an experience we quickly identify with the Bible's symbols of sovereignty and sway. To link ourselves with that old God seems to mean allowing an all-dominating ruler into our lives. Such a God threatens to destroy what we have so dearly and importantly gained in modern times, the right to think and decide for ourselves, thus attaining true personal dignity. If we allow God to be our God, will it still be possible to be a *mentsh* with all the self-determination that term now involves?

Yet newly understanding our humanity also can give us fresh insight into the One in whose image we are created and with whom we stand in covenant as co-creators. Knowing it to be commandingly important that

242

we be a *mentsh*, we can see that our God is one who "makes space" for our self-determining humanhood. That does not make God any less the unique sovereign of the universe; only a god whose stature could be seriously threatened, only one who was insecure, would find such partnership intolerable. Rather this mature God gives our humanhood its unalienable dignity by calling us to intimate partnership despite our frailties and by refusing to give up on us despite our abuse of the freedom granted us. Being so loved, a *mentsh* will faithfully strive to love God and neighbors, working to create each day's small redemptions and, for the rest, waiting steadfastly for that time when all our hopes—and God's—will be realized.

19

When Is It Moral
to Have Intercourse?

A Personal Summary

I begin with a sense of outrage at the sexual tone of our civilization. For all the positive activities today between the sexes, there is all about us an unnatural, sick concentration on sex that is surely contagious. I suppose no age has ever been without serious sexual temptations. The rabbis speak of the prevalence of prostitutes, and Jewish medieval literature regularly ponders the difficulties occasioned by adultery and incest. Still it is difficult to find a comparable age when sex was prompted not just by physiology and neighborhood but by the continual pressure of the combined forces of the civilization. Today almost everything is suffused with sex, and the mass media, serving an exploitative economic apparatus, keep sex continually before us. Then, in a pious mood, society says, "Wait until marriage." The titillation is constant, but the ideals remain supposedly quite pure; this is the real obscenity of our time.

Moreover, we are continually being told that the modern, the advanced people of our time are already utilizing a newer, a freer sexual ethic. They are rebelling against the old repressiveness and are expressing themselves more fully, because more naturally. At its extreme, a whole way of live is involved. To live means to have fun. To be youthful means to gather new and exotic experiences. Everything should be tried, and sex is no different from travel or restaurants. And this is no esoteric theory, but the mood that prevails on many a campus, as in many a bar or resort. This is the sophisticated attitude of our time. To ask serious questions about it,

Originally published as "Speaking Personally," in *Choosing a Sex Ethic, a Jewish Inquiry* (New York: Schocken, 1969).

much less to want to think these values through is to mark oneself as odd or square or both. Even if someone asks you what you seriously believe about sex, the chances are that is a come-on for analysis and refutation to show how advanced they are and how old-fashioned you are. The name of the game is freer-than-thou. In such a milieu, who can talk about ethics, much less about God? If you believe anything, you learn to keep it well hidden. Most of us are really Marranos.

In such a social context I feel a great sense of compassion and admiration for those who, despite the prodding, the hypocrisy, the lechery, the confusion about them, are determined to be as thoughtful about their sex lives as they can be. No matter which of the standards they accept for themselves, I honor them for refusing to surrender as a self-determining person to our vulgarizing society. I hope this book has strengthened them in that resolve. This, more than any rule I could suggest about sexual behavior, is what will count in the long run.

I wish it were possible for me to ease the burdens by pointing out the single, unambiguous ethical truth. However, and this must be added to all the other difficulties of being a person of integrity today, our ethical situation itself is confused and complicated. People of another age faced their temptations with greater certainty than we can. When conscience appeared among humankind and the Bible was widely considered sacred, adultery, prostitution, and nonmarital relationships were forbidden. People knew this was right, and they were not troubled in that faith. They occasionally transgressed and felt guilty, but the standards, at least, were clear. No Job ever arose to argue the standards of sexual morality or any other ethical command with God.

We have a more disturbing form of guilt today: we feel we ought to know what is right, but we cannot be sure we do. No single standard regulating sex or most other serious human problems is without question. Inevitably several views compete for our assent, each backed by strong arguments, with even the most appealing not free from serious criticism. And since they are always partially contradictory, there is no way of accepting them all or combining the best of this with the best of that to avoid the problems of both. So we moderns, even when we feel as certain as we can, always leave a little room for doubt, for questions, for new knowledge, for a new approach. We can only make a choice for the time being, or insofar as we know. We may have to stake our lives on these commitments—in many issues, like marriage, not to take the whole risk is to give an answer worth nothing—but we abhor fanaticism and are leery of martyrdom. Basically we cannot be that certain. So our decisions are not absolute but the best we have been able to come up with. Our convictions are not without question, but this, as far as we can tell, is where we stand and who we are.

Such open certainty is not limited to modern secularists or liberal religionists. Being fundamental to the modern temper it affects religious orthodoxies as well. The Roman Catholic church may still claim to give infallible dogmatic guidance and have a God-given power to instruct the faithful in matters of faith and morality. Yet today it is greatly agitated over priestly celibacy, which is only a human, if ecclesiastic, rule, and birth control, in which conscience directs many against the official teaching. An Orthodox Jew will accept the rulings of the great legal masters of our day as the contemporary equivalent of the Torah God gave Moses on Sinai. Yet he can ask why in the face of radically changed conditions the contemporary practice should not follow the previously cited liberal suggestions of recent sages like Jacob Emden, Jacob Toledano, and Zeev Falk and permit the *pilegesh* relationship [literally, "a concubine," the medieval Jewish legal equivalent of the contemporary "living together"]. When orthodoxies include a doctrine of inner development, they are far more open, despite their certainty, than were their predecessors a century ago. At present this is, of course, the chief characteristic of religious liberals who believe God's will is always understood through the fallible and finite perceptions of humankind.

Thus, even one who does decide to approach sexual matters ethically can only hope to reach a limited certainty. This is not much—yet the concern for even this sort of standard is enough to cut us off from the lazy and indulgent and make us stand against our society's sick sexuality. This is not an easy time in which to try to be truly human. . . .

Depending on what you believe about human sexuality, about being a person, about marriage, each of the sexual ethics suggested today is somewhat convincing and ought to be accepted. Yet that is logically impossible. We cannot at the same time have the freedom of the mutual-consent ethics with the restrictions of the love standard or the greater restriction demanded by the marriage standard. What we require, therefore, is something far more pluralistic, a ranking rather than a comprehensive rule, a hierarchy rather than a single, synthesizing principle. I am thinking of something like the rabbis' multileveled judgment of what constituted sexual misbehavior. Some acts, like intercourse with one's betrothed, are forbidden, but once committed, the couple marries without penalty or official stigma. Some acts, like adultery, are within human jurisdiction to punish, but others, like incest, are left to God's own justice. Other acts, like rape or seduction, are matters of community concern, while still others, such as intercourse between consenting unmarried adults, are left to the domain of conscience. The Rabbis, though they sought to serve God in their legal and moral teaching, accepted a multiplicity of values in the variety of human behavior they knew people faced. This commends itself to me as a model for working out an approach to premarital intercourse that is not overly simplistic.

To begin with, I argued above that the healthy-orgasm criterion [that intercourse was justified by my sexual needs alone] was ethically defective because it made possible the subordination of one person's rights to that of the other. I believe—and it is no less important to me because I know that it is a matter of faith and not rationally demonstrable—that all persons are of equal moral worth and must be treated as such. That tenet of Judaism, which I affirm, makes it impossible for me to accept the egoistic, healthy-orgasm ethic. Any standard that might be used to invalidate the moral dignity of another person, I cannot consider ethical.

This rejection indicates why I must give some ethical status to the mutual-consent criterion. Here there is concern for both partners, as each is required to bring free, responsible assent to the act. This is an obvious ethical advance over permitting any form of coercion or exploitation in the name of self.

Yet more must be said. The very commitment to persons which made this position more ethical than that of healthy orgasm now makes it unsatisfactory as well. This standard is interested in only two aspects of the person, will and sexuality. Sex being good, a person is asked only to be a proper moral agent in undertaking it. In an almost Kantian sense, if the intention is right, if the act would be right for others in a similar situation and one treats one's partner with dignity, the deed is validated. But this means our moral function has somehow been isolated from all the rest of us. Who we are in our fullness, what the other means to us as a person and not just as free decision-maker, is not central to the judgment. Surely in sexual matters, where feelings and emotions are most intimately part of the central act—generally the immediate reasons for it—to limit the judgment only to the moral decision of parties is not to ask enough of them. Here emphatically a person is more than glands and will. A good deal of what we are as human beings is how we relate in fullness to other people.

In this insistence on fullness my Jewish concern for the moral dignity of persons has been extended by Martin Buber's teaching on what it means to be a whole person. Buber made a by now famous distinction between I–it and I–thou situations. An "it" is not truly a person; a "thou," someone addressed in the singular, as an individual, in terms of his or her full individuality, is a real person. For the most part, we are treated by others as "its." They are interested only in part of us—our clothes, our personality, our money, our status. They care for us largely in terms of what we can do for them or how they can use us. They do not relate to us as a whole person, as what we come to know we can be when someone does reach out to us from the depths and meets us in our own depths, as in friendship or love. That is how we know what it means to be a real person and why it is wrong to settle for anything less. The old Kantian concerns for the moral will may be a start toward full personal relationship, but in the I–thou alone can we see it consummated. To put it somewhat crudely, the only human contact demanded under the consent criterion is first of wills and then of genitals. This makes too little of human beings and allows sexual relations to be another activity where we are seen in terms of our parts rather than summoned to full human interrelationship. Here, of all acts, where man and woman are to be physically and emotionally in the closest unity, it would seem reasonable that they should be expected to be in the most genuine personal contact as well. If they are not concerned with each other as persons but only as sex partners, they are treating each other as "its" and thus, despite their free consent to the intercourse, are being unethical to each other as full human beings. How much truer the act would be if their sexual activity arose from what they meant to one another, if sex were not the reason for their intercourse but rather the natural outgrowth of all that they shared with one another. There is a radical difference between loving someone because he is sexy and having sex with someone because of your love.

I am far more concerned with the personal meaning of intercourse than with its physiological or psychological virtues because I believe one's body should, wherever it is reasonable, serve the whole self rather than the self be a servant to the body, though the two are obviously indivisible. Thus Jewish tradition made it a duty for a person to be concerned about health. You must eat regularly, fast only in moderation, see a doctor when sick, and bathe to keep clean. Yet narcissism or devotion to the physical for its own sake is not strong in the Jewish ethos. The same is true with sex. Judaism made marriage, regular intercourse, and having children primary religious commandments reinforced by intense community concern. But, it would have made no sense to believing Jews to suggest that accumulating orgasms was admirable, or that mastering every position for intercourse was a virtuosity worth pursuing. The closest one comes to such attitudes in Judaism is the man blessed in the number of his sons or the woman admired for her many children. A direct concern with sexual fulfillment is fundamentally physiological and egoistic, and probably quite impersonal, even though it may care about giving as well as getting sensation. The linkage of intercourse with marriage, however, concentrates on the human value of the sex, its significance for the family, the Jewish people, and therefore, human history.

We human beings are much more than our sexuality. That is what Judaism knew and Martin Buber helps us understand more deeply. Anyone who shares this high estimate of what it means to be a full person can hardly be satisfied with sexual relations based merely on consent.

Two standards which speak of the partners acting as whole persons have previously come before us. The one made friendship, the other, love, the necessary condition for the consent. The friendship criterion calls for what may be termed the "minimum personal relationship," because it wants to maximize the possibilities of ethical intercourse. The love criterion puts the emphasis on the personal relationship, and by demanding that much of the partners, limits substantially the possibility of ethical intercourse. The choice between them seems almost entirely to depend on how one balances one's need for intercourse against the need to be a full person.

I think highly of friendship, but sexual intercourse seems to me a rather extravagant way in which to express it. One should think so much of self and what this most intimate physical giving of self means, that one should not do so without the most worthwhile reason. Or, to put it more positively, I value intercourse too highly as an interhuman experience for me to find it an appropriate act with a person who is only a friend.

Socially, the problem in being fully human today is less a lack of sexual outlets than the insistence that we price ourselves cheaply as persons. To invest friendship with all the physical intimacies of love is to give fully in an essentially limited situation. Society continually asks us to make that bargain, to spend ourselves extravagantly but not make too many personal demands in return. We are early taught that love and compassion, individual attention and personal concern are too much to expect in our busy society, so acceptingly we learn to live without them. This is where the social revolution must begin. If we are persons, we must fight to be persons—and not just for ourselves alone but to make our entire society more humane. In sex I believe this means that intercourse should at least be reserved for those whom we love and not extended to one with whom we simply share friendship.

I think this high sense of the meaning persons ought to have for one another was implicit in the one nonmarital sexual relationship Judaism tolerated, the *pilegesh*. This was no temporary affair of two friends spending occasional nights or weekends together. In the small, medieval world they lived together in the man's home, in a community where everyone might be expected to know what was going on. They were legally man and "demi-wife." Our sources do not speak of their love, yet when we remember that in those pre-pill days children would most likely result from this arrangement, it is difficult to see so much structure and stability as a kind of friendship rather than of love. While the legal authorities ultimately did away with the *pilegesh*, apparently for ethical reasons, it did not so outrage their moral sensibilities that it was immediately intolerable. Some of the rabbis accepted it, and not merely, I feel, because the biblical precedents were so strong. Matters more fundamental to Jewish law have been reversed by rabbinic edict when the authorities felt it essential to do so. It seems more reasonable to assume that the lenient thinkers sensed some element of human decency in it, perhaps as against other possible nonmarital sexual activities, and this allowed them to tolerate it. This experience says something to me about the love as against the friendship criterion. Above I argued that the friendship standard is more ethical than the mere consent criterion because it is truer to what it means to be a person. Now I must take that a step further. The love criterion is more fully ethical still because it is more fully personal. That is its great appeal.

Need much be said about the value of love in a day when it has become practically the only unquestioned virtue, for many the only real faith? Love opens to us a sense of personal depth and quality we rarely find elsewhere in our civilization. It calls us to a life of richer meaning and value than anything our culture regularly sets before us. To share true love is to make life worthwhile, to make existence a privilege. In a society which specializes in exploitation and manipulation, in an era where despair and anxiety are characteristic, love is the most precious of accomplishments.

I do not see how I can deny the ethical quality of sexual acts that arise from and bespeak a genuine love—and it is much too late in the discussion to raise tedious cavils about self-deception and the need to make certain. Love more than any other experience commonly known to people exalts us from bestiality to humanity, from being used, to being ourselves. For people who truly love, to express that love in sexual relations cannot be called unethical. Particularly when contrasted to the human reality of most of what we do with other people whom we say we love, any lovemaking which is true to the love between us, even if we are unmarried, is right.

Yet I want to carry my pluralism a step further. Though I esteem love greatly, I believe we can reach an even more significant level of personal existence. Ordinary love is wonderful for the present, perhaps for the past as well. It does not work too well for the future, for it tends to go as it came. That is what, for all its preciousness, makes it ordinary love. But a person must live one's life not only in the present, if one would be a self, but into and through the future as well. People are more than moments of meaning. We are that integrity of self which carries on from birth to death. Because we know or fear time will make love end, we want to extract ourselves from the continuing flow of time, and withdraw from life as continuity. To do that is to lose true identity. If human beings only knew love-for-now, then they might have to deny time and content themselves with such oasis moments in the wilderness of existence. They know better, because they have more enduring loves. Indeed, every ordinary love takes on great joy at its inception because of the hope that it will be what we have always known we wanted, a lifelong love, one that will fill our lives not merely in the present but in all the future. Consequently, when such loves occur, they seem bigger than life, or as the Song of Songs puts it, "Love is stronger than death (8:6)." This is less a romantic exaggeration than the acknowledgment of the most meaningful possible human situation.

To affirm and uplift a person for a time is no small thing in our world, but to love for life and be loved in return is to make both persons, finally, fully what they might be. Great daring is required to bind one's future to another's.

I hasten to add that it makes no difference if this love later does not turn out to be rich enough to endure. Without taking risks there can be no authentic existence. In taking them we sometimes fail. The most important measure of success is responding honestly to the situation confronting us, not in always being right. Jewish experience shows that cherishing marriage and accepting the occasional necessity for divorce are not incompatible, at least in the sort of community the Jews created.

I find this sense of the distinction between love and love for all one's life missing from most of the contemporary discussions of love, sex, and marriage. This absence is particularly notable among the advocates of the new morality who talk so much about the personal. I think the uniform value attached to every variety of love derives from the feeling that our times are poor in love, even in its more modest manifestation, friendship. In such an underprivileged culture ordinary love is as much a source of value as most people can aspire to. Yet I see this failure to make distinctions reflecting something else, and I know that this particular insight of mine comes from my sharing Judaism's intense concern with history. Being satisfied with love-for-now rather than reaching for lifelong love seems a highly significant example of one of the great moral tragedies of our time: the devaluation of the future in the name of the present. We focus so sharply on ourselves in the here and now, that we have less and less concern for our continuity into what will yet be. We withdraw from the forward flow of historic time to try to pack the present as full of experience as we can. To be alive has come to mean the intensification of now. The moment that passes without high sensation or immediate self-validation is the equivalent of death. This style seems appropriate to our paradoxical historical situation. Life seems our chief good, and we have made great progress in extending and enriching it. Yet we all know that the military means exist, now, and by human will, to destroy us all. In a world where the plague is conquered and the West knows no famine, the bomb remains agonizingly real. Though we bury it deep lest we think of it, the concept of annihilation pervades the unconscious of modern civilization. Since we cannot be certain of a future, we want to live in the present. I think that explains much of the live-for-now mood of our time, in sex as in other things.

Affluence is another factor. Most of us are not yet so financially secure that we can abandon the future and spend now. Still, jobs and money will probably be available in the future, so to borrow from it to live in the present is a logical idea. And that is what we do when we move the criterion for intercourse forward from love-for-life to love-for-now, much less to momentary sensation.

If our culture has particular reasons for thinking of sexual relations in terms of the present, the single most conducive social context for adopting that point of view is to be found at the university. Students are old enough to act as adults, but we do not yet expect them to undertake full adult obligations, though many students do make a serious effort to expand their responsibilities. Students normally know their futures are mortgaged to this institution for four years at least; hence, they will not worry very much about the life to come until they are about to graduate. In the interim they have the heavy responsibility of staying in school and doing well there. What time they have for themselves is understandably devoted to enjoying the present. Besides, everyone else in this campus world is a peer, and they too are trying to take advantage of this breathing space. The older students become missionaries of the joys of immediacy, urging the neophytes to use the quickly passing pre-squaredom years to explore and experiment. The faculty, too, almost always focuses more sharply on what is wrong with accepted values than on what is reasonably certain to remain true for the rest of one's life. So one is almost irresistibly taken with the belief that youth is the best time of life, the model for what adulthood ought to be. There is a powerful temptation to believe that only what gives satisfaction in the here and now is worthy of pursuit. Thus love may authorize, but it should not bind or project the lovers' responsibilities into the future. Since most people rarely choose a sex ethic but adopt one from the group they want to be associated with, the move from home to school often involves a sexual crisis, though every campus has more conscientious objectors than libertines.

The university, because it provides a sheltered environment to a select community in the in-between years from adolescence to adult responsibility, is the social center of the love ethic for sexual intercourse.

This analysis has been deliberately overstated in the hope of making a point that is often strongly resisted. I believe—again my Jewish faith asserts itself—that a person can only be fully human through time and in responsibility. Becoming a whole person must include not just what one is and can enjoy but equally the enduring relationships and continuing commitments through which alone one can mature. The friendships which increase in understanding as in demand, the love that deepens to obligate as to quicken us over the years, these are what make us fully human. Integrity of self is not merely the work of moments or periods but the hard-won result of pursuing a continuity in our lives. Momentary genuineness is splendid, but we have not become true persons unless we can extend occasional authenticity to a lifetime of trying to be true. Experiment has its place, and joy must not be underrated. Still it is in what we do with our lives in the long run that we show how human we are. Marriage and a family are not an eventual necessity—an attitude that invites disaster before the vows are spoken!—but the preferred path of personal fulfillment. Without their intense commitment, demanding trust, unrelenting involvement, it is difficult to become fully human. They are worth working and waiting for, and this includes cultivating the values and attitudes that can make it possible for them to succeed.

Let me illustrate the difference between these two attitudes toward life by proposing a choice between two possible situations. Neither is really satisfactory, yet they represent what life offers to many people. In one case we will find love, rich and moving, but never great enough to result in marriage. Thus, while such affairs last months or even years, each inevitably ends, and the lovers go their separate ways. The other possibility is of a life spent in a marriage but one not initiated because of love. The couple has very genuine regard for one another, but it cannot be said to rise to that level of empathy and passion we call love. Yet knowing themselves to be unlikely to have a much richer emotional experience or to have a better partner with whom to spend their lives, they marry. Would you prefer a life of love that never comes to marriage over a life of marriage that knows regard but not love? The choice is, of course, odious, and one should not be forced into such an undesirable situation. Yet many people are. I like that choice no better than anyone else because I feel that life is best fulfilled in love-for-life and, therefore, marriage. Yet, seen from the perspective of time and of a whole life, if there must be a choice, then being married, even only in deep friendship, seems to me far more personally significant than being in love from time to time. If forced to choose, I confess I am not ultimately a romantic who thinks high moments are more important than continual personal growth. I value ecstasy, but I believe in almost every case becoming a person is more truly bound up with perseverance.

Thus, the most ethical form of human relationship I know is love-for-life. Its appropriate social and religious structure is the monogamous marriage. This being so, marriage is, if I may use the strange formulation of ethical pluralism, the most right context, that is, the best criterion for the validity of sexual intercourse. And I think every human being should try to reach the highest possible level of ethical behavior.

It is one of the besetting evils of our time that many people are satisfied to be "somewhat" ethical. "Doing the best I can" becomes an excuse for retaining self-indulgent bad habits. "I have to give in to myself every once in a while" or "I'm only human" is generally a rationalization for moral sloth or ethical unconcern. How easily the phrases become a philosophy, and what was an excuse becomes a way of life. I believe, as Judaism has taught, that to be a full human being means to strive continually for moral excellence and to make moral excellence not only the ideal framework but the increasing reality of one's existence. I am not saying that if you are not a saint you are not human—though I do not understand why people should consider it somehow more human not to be a saint (in Judaism, a righteous man). I am not saying people ought to spend their time morbidly worrying about whether they have been excellent in their behavior toward others—though I think the central importance of moral concern is often overlooked. I am saying that to settle for anything less than the highest possible ethical standards for our lives is already to compromise our humanity. There is plenty of time, after the act, to speak of our humanity and acknowledge our limitations. If we mean it sincerely, if that confession gives us the courage to resume our high standards as we face the next decision, Judaism then insists God will forgive and encourage us.

All of us who know our lives are tied to those of all other people should want to live by the highest ethical standards. Most of us, I am afraid, will be quite content to live by a modest morality or by none at all. Idealists must never forget how resistive to righteousness human nature is under all the fancy clothes and friendly etiquette. If the masses of people are not apt to act very ethically, then it is all the more important for the sensitive few to do as much as they can, to do the best deed for its own sake as well as for its example and benefit for all men.

I know what I am suggesting is not easy in our society, and I am pained with that thought. In any case, those who think as I do have an obligation to encourage people to marry young and to help them financially and emotionally to do so. One of our deepest sins is that we keep our youth so immature that, when they are biologically ripe for sex, they are hardly ready as persons for marriage. (Are they much readier for personalized intercourse without marriage?) Our new morality ought to begin by teaching us to see marriage, not love, as the place of human fulfillment. Then it ought to move on to demand that parents and, if necessary, the state, create the conditions—emotional and financial—which would make it practical. This would take a good deal of change in attitudes. I know no new morality which would not. It would not cure everything. But I know nothing that would, except, if I may say so, the coming of the Messiah. The best way of making that possible is for people who care about themselves and about humanity to do all they can to live by the highest ethical standards.

That surely has been the millennial concern of the Jewish people. It has stood for moral excellence not only on a personal level but in its community social style as well. Not every Jew has lived up to that high ideal, and many a Jewish community has been full of arrogance and contention. Yet over the centuries this people has remained surprisingly true to that ancient biblical vision of humankind ennobled. It has managed in the most diverse cultures, climates, economies, and social structures to convert its ancient dedication to moral excellence, to the more than moral excellence called holiness, into ways, habits, and disciplines that made prophetic values a community's way of life. Through this structuring of individual existence it helped people fulfill themselves and their people's destiny. As part of the Jew's stubborn continuity, they kept high standards of intellectuality, personal fidelity, and social concern before the world. And throughout the duration of the Jewish people they knew that this personal participation in the task of bringing humankind to its full human destiny would in the end of days be achieved.

I am saying that while every person should take the standards of moral excellence upon themselves, the believing Jew has special reason to do so. That is the tradition of this people. Moreover, if one practices Judaism as a member of its caring community, one will find in them as in it continuing support and stimulus for the effort to settle for nothing less than the accomplishment of the highest moral good.

This statement will indicate to some that I have ended precisely where I began, affirming the Jewish tradition. I do not think that is what has happened. I have, for the most part, not spoken in terms of Judaism, so to others it will seem a matter for criticism that a student of Judaism neglected it in order to talk instead about being or becoming a whole person.

What I have tried to do in this analysis is to comprehend the problem in its contemporary setting and speak to those it concerns in their own language. Many of the most thoughtful things college students themselves say about sex ethics are put in terms of what it means to be a person. I imagine they think of that as a purely secular value. For me it is a matter of religious belief. I see it as a part of American secularism only because Christianity once dominated western culture and infused it with a concern for persons, though that idea was radically extended in the spread of Enlightenment rationalism and now in existenialist concerns. I do not see how secularism alone might validate such a fundamental faith in persons—all persons—today. What shows us that persons are so important that they should be the criterion of all ethical behavior? Science cannot prove "persons" exist distinct from bodies, much less that they have an intrinsic worth. Philosophy is badly split over whether persons are undemonstrable, and therefore an illogical assertion, or are a self-evident fact, which is therefore more a creed or dogma than an idea. Modern politics is interested in power; business, in profits; the social order, in privilege; most people, in personal benefit. Where will a faith in persons strong enough to power lives and transform society come from and how will it be sustained? Had I not believed in what Judaism has taught me about what it means to be a person, I could not have written as I have. I spoke to a universal problem in universal terms in order to be understood. But all that universalism is based on a quite particularly Jewish faith. One might perhaps have such a faith if one were not a Jew. But if one were not somehow in the Jewish family of religions or under their influence, I am no longer sure, in this radically skeptical world, how one would come by it. Thus, knowing how my particular Jewish faith authorizes every universal affirmation made about persons here, I would see this discussion as deeply Jewish and deeply human at the same time, precisely the mixture I think the faith of Judaism requires.

Yet, as this personalist-Jewish analysis proceeded, a double transformation took place. The old Jewish attitudes toward sexual relations could not be validated in as rigid and single-leveled a form as they had become in recent centuries. The pluralistic stance I have taken is more liberal because more personalistic than that known by traditional Judaism. At the same time, the personalist emphasis on the individual and the present seems intolerably narrow when seen from the Jewish concern with time and structure. In turn, this makes me far more restrictive than existentialists or new-morality protagonists would be.

Perhaps it will help—certainly it will help me—if now, even briefly, I use something more like my natural language, that of internal Jewish religious discourse, to say what I believe and what it implies for sexual conduct.

God, as best we understand God, is not neutral but holy. We human beings knowing God, should try to bring that character of holiness into our lives. We are, when we are mature, free to do so, but we do not. This is the central problem of human history. By God's grace the Jews came as a people to know God and understand itself as bound to God and God's service in history. This extraordinary but continual community experience of relationship, now dramatic, as at the mountains—Sinai, Carmel, and Zion—now everyday, as in the long centuries of biblical struggle to integrate this consciousness, changed this people's character. The Jews pledged themselves as a people, its individuals and its community alike, to live by God's demands on them. Further, it took upon itself obligations that went beyond what all people are required to do so that it would reflect the highest standards of human behavior and endure as a particular people dedicated to God's service in history. It vowed to live that way until all humankind should come to know that God so well that they too would transform their lives in terms of God's reality. Generation after generation, the Jews renewed that promise, and now they and that service are inseparably intertwined. Though often, individually and as a community, they have failed to live up to that pact, God, they knew, never rejected them and their activity on God's behalf. Rather, in the mysterious way in which God managed to give continuing order to the universe, God sustained the people of Israel and would not let it, as a whole, disappear from history until its task had been completed. This relationship of mutual love and obligation between God and the people of Israel, Jews call the Covenant.

The Covenant is carried out by the Jews when it is made the basis of their existence and thus applied to every aspect of life. (Any religious-secular dichotomy has, therefore, little meaning in Judaism.) Yet the Jewish community has found no more central and significant form for the individual Jew to live in that Covenant than the personal covenant marriage. In its exclusiveness and fidelity it has been the chief analogy to the oneness of the relationship with God as the source of personal worth and development. In marriage's intermixture of love and obligation the Jew has seen the model of faith in God permeating the heart and thence all one's actions. Through children, Jews have found the greatest personal joy while carrying out the ancient Jewish pledge to endure through history for God's sake. Though Judaism knows sex can be one of the easiest ways to degradation, through the marriage covenant, it has made sexuality a chief means of serving God and becoming righteous. So Judaism has always deplored sexual immorality as a sin against God and human dignity alike.

Today Jews find themselves in a new social situation that presents them with a strange mixture of freedom and danger. They are marvelously at home in the non-Jewish world in a way they have never known. In their eagerness to become a part of it, motivated by their appreciation of its many virtues and eager to put far behind them any unnecessary and restrictive differences, many Jews have gone so far as to give up much of their old Jewish faith. At home now in a secular world such Jews are not sure how much they believe in God and therefore they are less certain of God's Covenant with the Household of Israel. So their interest in Jewish religious practice is small, and their substitute for it is to be, simply, a decent person. Many Jews think society should be made much better and their surrogate for corporate Jewish religiosity is to support, in high statistical disproportion, almost every activity which seeks to do that.

In recent years Jews have been quite concerned about the change in sexual attitudes. They still abhor adultery, for they know it destroys the possibility of marriage as it ought to be, and they want that and a loving family for themselves and their children. The latter they know will go on to a higher education and thus marry late. They are proud of the old Jewish sexual morality, but they sometimes wonder whether there is not something ethical about a young couple, really in love, having intercourse with one another, provided that they use contraceptives.

I think in this question as in many others they will have to consider whether the Jewish people, from whom they have gained and continue to gain so much, can long continue if it is satisfied only to try to be decent rather than struggle for moral excellence as a regular way of life. Jews who secularize the traditional terms of Jewish existence are ending its capacity to produce large numbers of people of value and are terminating its contribution to society. Those are secular goals. From the Jewish view they are breaking down Israel's Covenant with God. Ethical persons, in sexual as in other matters, are to be praised highly. But that is simply not good enough if human history as a whole is to be transformed and fulfilled. What we need today, as Judaism has always insisted in the past, is devotees of excellence in righteousness, that is, Jews, real Jews, devoted Jews, who will live the Covenant by sanctifying every aspect of their existence and most certainly their sexual behavior. Perhaps they will be a minority in the Jewish community today, as they occasionally were in the past. Yet I believe that there are such people in the American Jewish community today and that this faithful minority may once again be the most important part of this unusual people as it stubbornly continues on its messianic way. I do not know precisely what the details of such a sanctifying Covenant existence for every area of life would be like in this shifting modern world, nor do I think it easy in this civilization to stay for long on that level. Nonetheless, I believe much of the old Jewish life style is transferrable or adaptable to our situation, as I hope this discussion of sexual relations has manifested. I believe Jews who share this faith ought to have the courage to trust that, as we go forward in loyalty to that ancient Covenant, we shall, haltingly, find an authentic way to fulfill God's purposes in history with God's help.

257

20

Reading the Jewish Tradition
on Marital Sexuality

I have been asked to study what our heritage, particularly the Halacha, tells us about the proper sexual values in modern Jewish marriage. The request itself indicates a change in the concerns of many Reform Jews. Once we searched for texts which would show how "the sources of Judaism" supported "the best of modern culture"; today—with authoritative sexual guidance (and observable sexual practices) so varied, contradictory, and often seeming unethical—we want to know if classic Judaism can help us decide what to accept and what to reject in our society's sexual possibilities.

For the sake of this study, let us quickly by-pass the always nettlesome problem of an adequate data-base by working from the code literature. In Maimonides' *Mishneh Torah, Hilchot Nashim* (particularly chs. 14, 15, 24 and 25) and *Hilchot Kodashim* (particularly chs 1, 4, 8, 21 and 22) are relevant; in the *Shulḥan Aruch,* see *Even Ha-ezer,* chs. 21–25 (abridged in the *Kitsur S. A.* in chs. 150–155). But that only brings us to our central problem: It is difficult to determine what texts mean in anything other than the most literal sense. We cannot have the assurance of a Kaufmann Kohler, a Solomon Schechter, or an Israel Abrahams, that any modern mind reading these documents will arrive at pretty much the same sense of what they once meant, and what they *demand of us today.* What we think the texts meant to their authors will be determined by us as much by *our theory of how history moves* as by the words in the texts. Historians

From the *Journal of Reform Judaism,* vol. 29, no. 3 (Summer 1982).

then are only as useful to us in reading a text as their philosophy of history is persuasive.

Another problem then immediately asserts itself. Jewish scholars writing in English find it difficult to deal with classic Jewish legal texts applicable to a contemporary problem without becoming apologetic. Their Jewish readers are generally non-observant and critical. Besides, non-Jews may consult such works. The authors therefore tend to censor the more unpalatable requirements of Jewish law and practice, and translate its central regulations into as contemporary an idiom as possible.

Thus, Maurice Lamm, when discussing the purposes of marriage in his book, *The Jewish Way in Love and Marriage*, puts companionship first and deals with procreation only in that context. That tempts one to misunderstand the traditional Jewish teaching. Even a quick perusal of the relevant legal texts indicates that though the Halacha recognizes the importance and provides for the maintenance of marital companionship, its overwhelming priority in marriage is procreation. Lamm, as a good apologist, wisely stresses that aspect of Jewish tradition which commends companionship, but his presentation no longer yields a properly balanced sense of traditional Jewish law.

Jewish authorities, in their views of marriage (as in many other cases), commend many varied, complex, and partially conflicting values. They subtly balance them with and against each other. One cannot, then, give unqualified descriptions of the Jewish heritage on this topic. As I read the data, it is equally false to say that Judaism teaches that the purpose of marriage is merely procreation or companionship. The sages treat these values dialectically, trying to give a dynamic hierarchy to certain goods while avoiding a number of evils. Deducing "the Jewish view" is then further complicated by some renowned teachers who emphasize one aspect of the tradition, while other equally authoritative halachists emphasize its polar opposite. Citing only one authority or following only one stream of the legal process will not give us the whole view of classic Judaism.

Fortunately, a splendid English work exposes the full subtlety and dialectic of Jewish teaching on marital sexual responsibility. David Feldman's book, *Marital Relations, Birth Control and Abortion in Jewish Law*, lucidly sets the vast panorama of data before the serious reader. It sets the necessary basis for any responsible Jewish discussion of this topic.

How then shall we approach the classic texts of the Jewish tradition dealing with sexuality and marriage? As I read the variety of contemporary answers to that question, two separate hermeneutic issues tend to divide us. The first has to do with the *authority* we should grant to what we decipher as their meaning. In this regard, I can isolate five distinct positions among Jews. The second issue has to do with the contemporary theory we feel best renders the texts' *substantive* message. Here I find only two functioning major points of view. To some extent, the issues of authority and substance can operate independently of one another, which may explain why our community displays such hermeneutic diversity. And if eclecticism is added to our consideration, the reason we often appear to be anarchic should be clear.

As to authority, for some Jews the traditionalist reading of the law remains fully compelling. That is the Orthodox position, and one which some Conservative Jews share. I do not see how one maintaining such a position could long be comfortable participating in liberal Judaism, so I shall not consider it further.

I find contemporary liberal Jews exhibiting four additional easily identifiable responses to Jewish tradition's behests. One declares the law to be *authoritative*, except for very substantial reason. What constitutes sufficient grounds for change is part of the substantive aspect of hermeneutics. A second view grants Jewish law and tradition *as much* influence upon our decisions as it gives to the insights of modern culture, if not more. A third position considers the Jewish heritage a *valuable guide* to our decisions when its texts are read with the eyes of modern culture (the classic liberal hermeneutic). The fourth attitude holds that Judaism *can often* supply useful resources to motivate Jews to live by the values they have freely selected for themselves.

In sum, we differ as to the suasive power we assign to Jewish tradition and to contemporary culture.

We are also divided as to the *mode of description* we employ in speaking of values. I see only two fairly consistent modes of identifying the enduringly compelling substance of the Jewish tradition. The one describes it in terms of what is ethical; the other speaks from what constitutes a proper inter-personal relationship for Jews, i.e. the Covenant.

The ethical interpretation of Judaism is most widely known among us in its neo-Kantian form, as in the work of Hermann Cohen or Leo Baeck. With them, one reads Jewish texts with a Kantian eye for every aspect of freedom, creativity, and universality as employed in the Jewish understandings of law and duty. One might also do this out of another ethical system—a humanistic concern for persons, for example—and get a somewhat different but nontheless directly ethical appreciation of the Jewish heritage's continuing validity.

The relational position, which I espouse, differs in two important respects. It posits a personalistic rather than a rationalistic mode of interpretation. It also qualifies its universalism in terms of Jewish particularism; that is, it speaks of the *Jewish* relationship, not merely the one in which *all people* relate to one another or to God.

To explain further, I must declare my hermeneutic. I begin with my view of the authority of the Jewish tradition. I have broken with the older liberal practice of subordinating Jewish teaching to general culture, whether that is done rigorously, as by our Reform "Unitarians," or only in

considerable measure, as by most American Jews. I have less trust in contemporary wisdom and more in Judaism's independent validity than they
do. I am also too critical of the Jewish tradition to accept it as Halacha,
that is, as heteronomous discipline. Despite this reservation, I understand
Judaism to be, at the minimum, as good a guide to living as is our civilization. It therefore is as much a legitimate critic as a beneficiary of today's
understanding of the generally human. For me, Jewish teaching regularly,
but not always, functions more significantly in my decision-making than
does western culture, at least as far as values and grounding are concerned. These I interpret in a fundamentally personalistic way. That is, I
share Judaism's historic meta-Halacha, the Covenant relationship between
God and the people of Israel, out of which Torah arises.

Applying this value stance to specific questions, I mediate between
the demands of living in Covenant and the socio-historical, personal situation in which I find myself. My decisions and practice are, therefore,
characterized by a dialectical flow. They are relatively steady and consistent insofar as my faith and personal integrity remain stable. They are also
relatively free and changing insofar as I, at a given moment, detect a need
to serve God as part of the people of Israel's historic Covenant in ways
previously not utilized by me or the Jewish people. Covenantal personalism makes me more "liberal" than the halachists and less universalistic
and anarchic than the pure autonomists. From this stance comes my high
commitment to community pluralism and my respect for all interpretations of Jewish living and belief founded on serious concern for the claims
of Judaism "however differently perceived" (as the Central Conference of
American Rabbis' *Centenary Perspective* puts it).

This treatment of my liberal Jewish hermeneutic should explain how I
have gone about preparing my response to the question put to me: What
do you see making up the liberal Jewish ethics of sexuality in marriage
today? I have pondered the classic Jewish texts on the subject from my
personalistic, Covenantal perspective, and on the basis of a concern with
contemporary theories of sexuality going back over a decade to the writing
of my book on sex ethics.

I have been able to summarize my thoughts in the form of nine Jewish
positions and their dialectical, personalistic counter-concerns. So as to
cover many of the questions being raised in this field, I will present these
now in truncated fashion. I shall then point to two areas of my continuing
perplexity. I will conclude by returning to the systematic task by briefly
characterizing the general strengths and weaknesses of the Jewish tradition
and of modern culture as they emerge when subjected to this sort of confrontational analysis.

We begin, first, with the fundamental premise of the discussion. For
Judaism, marriage is an overwhelmingly important human duty and spou-
sal sexual intercourse is intimately bound up with its fulfillment. Though
the Halacha occasionally provides for celibate marriages (as contrasted to

261

non-procreative ones), as in the case of continual menstrual bleeding, it diametrically opposes those tendencies in Christianity, Hinduism, and elsewhere which seek to spiritualize marriage by eliminating intercourse. Our sages so oppose such a practice of celibacy that their occurrence qualifies women as well as men to demand that the Jewish court effectuate their divorce.

Yet, as the personalist perspective makes plain, the rabbis, for all their concern about sexual intercourse, give us relatively little instruction as to how we might best engage in it so as to reach its Jewish goals. They do provide us with voluminous, detailed instructions about various sexual prohibitions, most particularly when the wife is halachically a menstruant. By contrast, their positive inter-personal guidance is minimal and marginal. They seem rather inhibited about direct sex-education, fearing *nibul peh* (filthy speech) and immodesty so much that they prefer to err on the side of saying little. And when they do speak, their meaning is somewhat clouded by their addiction to euphemism. Modernity has taught us that we have a better chance of accomplishing our Jewish goals by being less covert about what is so important in our lives. To be better Jews we need to learn directly about human sexuality and to discuss it openly with our spouse so that we can recognize and respond to our individual and mutual needs. We also will benefit by learning how to educate each other about our sexuality as we face the personal and biological changes that continually reshape our marital relationships over the years.

Second, our tradition connects the act of marital intercourse with the highest expressions of holiness of which people are capable. That follows from our having a Covenant with the Most High, and has nothing to do with soil or blood or national destiny. But I do not see much of this tone of sacred sexuality in our early Jewish books. The Halacha, precisely as law, is concerned with the legal entailments of betrothal and marriage. *Kidushin*, despite all our homiletics, is essentially the setting apart of this woman for this man exclusively, just as a sanctuary is set aside from all other places and must not be defiled. Without doubt, elements of spiritual sanctification do enter the relationship, as the blessings under the *chupa* indicate. However, when the mystics employed a near-pagan symbolism for God to suggest a mythology of Divine fragmentation and reintegration through human religious behavior—only then did sexual intercourse become directly endowed with sacred overtones. If further evidence is required of the congeniality of this attitude to rabbinic Judaism, we need not seek far. The Talmudic halacha makes a wife utterly subject to her husband's sexual whims, but by the Middle Ages, the rabbis insist that he has no right to have intercourse with her without her free consent.

Yet, dialectically, by modern standards, the specific rules by which the rabbis safeguard the sacredness of human sexuality often seem no longer appropriate. The sages seem frightened of our having fleeting

262

thoughts or images of sexual pleasure (*hirhurim*). They warn us against these dangerous mental intrusions and suggest strategies by which to avoid them. These not succeeding, we should discipline ourselves to repress our sexual imagination. As a result, what might be one of our greatest human fulfillments is associated with what is dirty and defiling. Thus, they instruct us to have intercourse only in the dark and regardless of our window shades, never during the daytime. By contrast, the modern notion of sexuality as being natural to people seems far more likely to sanctify this drive. Our sexual fantasies usually testify to nothing more than our continuing vitality. How we allow our imaginations to influence our acts, not our day-dreams, is the truer indication of our character. Being creatures of whim and fancy, if we turn to one another in love by day, or enjoy seeing one another as we reach out by night, then surely these acts will only enhance the personal and, potentially, the sacred aspects of our sexual union.

Third, for all its insistence upon sexuality, rabbinic tradition felt it had only a limited place in marriage. The Covenant is for all of life, not merely to express our sexuality. In Judaism, the marital relationship encompasses far more than sexual satisfaction, because the sex act symbolizes the unique bond between the spouses. So much has been said about rabbinic Judaism being a worldly religion and having a positive attitude toward sex that we forget its countervailing tendency to sexual self-denial. The laws concerning marital separation during menstruation, most notably the insistence of seven clean days beyond the 4–plus days of actual flow, and the heavy condemnation of adultery, radically subordinate the sexual drive to a greater purpose. Moreover, males are often cautioned to limit their sexual activity to rather modest rates of intercourse. The modern world, by contrast, seems obsessed with sexuality and compulsive about better and more frequent sexual performance. It tends to subordinate the personal to the biological and the relationship turns into an idolatry of sensuality and orgasm. Restoring a Covenantal context to our sex lives would give us a more human sense of its virtues and limits.

Yet it must also be acknowledged that the contemporary preoccupation with sex arose in reaction to the heavy repression which all the religious traditions directed toward it. Thus, modern Hebrew writers of the turn of the century (such as Tchernichovski and Berdichevsky) welcomed the modern understanding of life for they felt their people had long been deprived of adequate love and sexuality. We may well attribute the morbidity with which much of ghetto Judaism invested sex to the stark dualism of body and spirit which medieval Jewish thought brought into our tradition. Nonetheless, we cannot deny that a similar negative note appears early on in Judaism. The Bible declares a man ritually impure until evening after he has had an ejaculation, and the rabbis regularly use repressive terms like *kof et yitsreinu*, subdue our (evil/sexual) urge, and *kovesh et yitsro*, conquer our (evil/sexual) urge, to describe how we should deal with our sexuality urges. The rabbis' rules and attitudes seem unduly restrictive when we view sexuality as central to human personality. Less fear of our libido and more ease with the free flowing nature of the personal life need to be infused into our contemporary Jewish sexual style.

Fourth, the Jewish writings consider the goals of intercourse to be far broader than sensual satisfaction. The Covenant between the partners is not founded on their facility in giving each other pleasure but in living together in sanctity. By contrast, Americans have come to value highly their technical know-how in producing and varying sexual pleasure. Often, then, what was once touted as an act of love becomes another test of our capacity to produce results. Not only does the relationship wither in the objectification, but the sex itself finally cannot live up to the anticipated ideal. The hedonistic paradox reasserts itself—directly pursuing happiness only makes it more elusive.

Although they occasionally acknowledged the human playfulness we so easily associate with personal sexual activity, the rabbis did not give it very much scope or recognition. Some silliness and foolishness is often a most delightful accompaniment to our sexuality. To deny it in the name of human dignity is to miss much of the positive reality of what it is to be a person.

Fifth, our tradition proclaims procreation to be the primary, though not the exclusive goal of marriage. The Covenant is made not only between the present partners but with the generations that were and with the generations yet to come. Infertility is thus a terrible calamity to a loving Jewish couple. We gladly summon every resource of medical science to make it possible for the spouses to have a child. And our community rejoices with happiness when we hear of a new pregnancy or the birth of a new child. Surely some special wisdom was attached to propagation since it was the first commandment recorded in the Torah, and it is one in whose fulfillment Jews have regularly known the *simcha shel mitsva*, the joy of the commandments.

Yet here too Jewish tradition interpreted a worthy value to the extent that the personal welfare of the partners was subordinated to the law and its communal-historical ends. Should the mother's life be threatened, contraception might or must be used. But severe economic hardship or human deterioration as a result of bearing many children were not halachically acceptable reasons for thwarting conception. Rabbinic literature has many discussions of the evils of wasting male seed and strategies to avoid this abominable occurrence. The modern mind is far more concerned with the human waste produced in the lives of the parents, the infant, and the siblings by insisting that mothers bear children even when the parents responsibly determine it is not to their or their family's best interest to do so. For us, companionship is a far more significant goal than procreation—though one wondrous aim of a true Jewish marital friendship is the genetic blending of persons to produce a totally new individual.

Sixth, from its earliest days, Judaism taught that marriage was the only acceptable social setting for the sexual relationship. It required some advancement beyond the common conventions of the ancient Middle East to reach the monogamous marriage. The logic of the Covenant, as exemplified in this most intimate of human relationships, led Judaism to insist that it involve but two partners. In marriage, the spouses undertook ultimate responsibility for one another, and for the possibility of producing a new life together and nurturing it to maturity. In the Divine model, God occasionally threatens the wayward Covenant partner, Israel, with a divorce, but their relationship was established for all time. Human beings, in all their fallibility, ought to strive for permanence as the ideal of Covenant life. Should they not be able to manage it, our tradition accepts the necessity of divorce, though it considers the dissolution of a marriage a tragedy.

But the stability of the Jewish marriage was procured at the cost of subordinating a woman's life to that of her husband. The idea of a wife as a full personality in her own right, entitled to pursue her individual goals as her husband pursues his, is a recent possibility indeed. Yet can we call the Covenant life between husband and wife humanly complete unless two equal partners bring it into being and maintain it? And that must hold true for the wife's sexual drives and aspirations as well as for her husband's. The flow of initiation, action, and reaction needs to be as open to the wife as to the husband, allowing her to act in ways previously considered unseemly for a Jew. What the ideal of equality will eventually do to transform the Jewish covenant of marriage, I do not think anyone can now know.

Seventh, sexual faithfulness is a cardinal sign of a good Jewish marriage and adultery is a most heinous sin. The Covenant bespeaks a unique relationship. Performing its unique marital privilege with other partners seriously damages the ties that once existed between the spouses when the intimacy they shared was unique to one another. On the Divine level, the prophets frequently denounce the people of Israel for its marital unfaithfulness. So too, though sexual loyalty requires abstention from other exciting sexual relationships and is a species of Jewish asceticism, nothing can take its place in a Jewish marriage. Our pledge to one another carries special weight when you and I know only each other as sexual partners. Should one of us break that vow of exclusivity, particularly if we do so willfully and self-consciously, we will damage our relationship most seriously. Indeed, even if we find a way to restore it, what we mean to one another cannot ever be quite the same. Some Jews today, fearing this disappointment, agree in advance to allow for occasional acts of adultery. In so deciding they practically invite the Evil *Yetser*, urge, to live with them and never can savor the hope and fulfillment of true Covenant. Their "open marriage" testifies to the diminished standards of human integrity common in our time.

Yet it is also true that the rabbinic laws of adultery are notoriously one-sided. Classic Halacha does not apply them in the same way to men as to women. Moreover, in the so-called "laws of jealousy" it gives husbands preemptive rights over their wives' acts so that mere suspicion of misbehavior becomes grounds for divorce. And shall we agree to the law that after adultery a husband may never take his wife back, ignoring every human consideration as to what brought the act about? Here the law speaks with implacable, impersonal rigor. In the name of community standards of sanctity it calls for depriving the people in the relationship of the right to a positive decision as to what might now best become of it. I do not see that it is a fatal mitigation of the seriousness of adultery to suggest that our modern understanding of persons requires us to introduce more compassion in dealing with a transgressor in this area than the Halacha did.

Eighth, incest is a major violation of Jewish marriage. The generations each have their place in the historical progression from creation to the Messiah. We do not mix our obligations to our generation with those that apply to the generations that came before us or the ones that follow us in turn. And the betrayal of exclusiveness found in adultery takes on special pain when we confuse those who are close enough to be loved uniquely with the one we love so dearly that ours is a bond of unique sexual sharing. The infidelity of incest not only breaches our special tie with them but does not allow our family relationships to function in that unparalleled Covenantal mix of high intimacy without genitality.

Here too, by personalist standards, the Halacha's impersonal specification of forbidden partners seems unduly extended. It specifies in great detail those whom we may not marry and does so without regard for age, needs, or other personal considerations. Incest may require a definition in largely impersonal terms so as to place an objective limit to our polymorphous sexual cravings. Nonetheless, the rabbinic extensions of the prohibited list of marriage partners (and perhaps even the far reaches of the biblical list) might, depending on the personal circumstances, warrant suspension in our ethics of marital sexuality.

Ninth, Judaism insists upon the communal context of our private sexual activity. What we do does not merely affect us alone but is an important part of the way the Covenant people seeks to live out its responsibilities to God. Being concerned with modesty, the sages directed that intercourse be quite a private matter. They not only barred the presence of all other adults and insisted on the seclusion of the spouses, they were also concerned about the possible presence of their children. At the same time, they did not consider Jews isolates who, when away from others, may conduct themselves in whatever fashion they might agree to. Being Jews, they should share in the high human standards and messianic aspirations of their people's Covenant wherever they are and whatever they do. Without its members living up to Israel's historic hopes, how can our people ever fulfill its responsibilities for bringing the Messiah? And the Evil *Yetser* being so strong and human will being so frail, are we long likely to remember the sanctity of our sexuality without keeping in mind the communal dimension of our private sexual life?

This social aspect of our sexuality can be conceded by the personalist without thereby vitiating the bite of the counterbalancing criticism, i.e., though the Jewish tradition richly informs us about our common human and Covenantal Jewish sexual goals, it offers us little help in learning how to express sexually just what two people mean to one another.

Consider a problem which has grown with our new knowledge and openness toward sex. How shall we continually transform the exclusivity of the Jewish marital pact in relation to the differing rates and paths of the partners' personal sexual development over the many years of an enduring marriage? Our sages have had little to say about keeping our sexual life fresh over the years. They either did not know about this problem or did not consider it worthy of their attention. Caring more directly about persons, we have a greater range of spiritual needs. Therefore, alongside static communal standards we need a sense of what enriches a modern Jewish marriage as the spouses age.

I realize that in this presentation of nine Jewish theses and their personalist counterpoises I have sacrificed depth analysis to comprehensive sweep. I am also conscious of not having touched on many other vital matters and of possibly suggesting that I have formed a focused judgment on all other issues. Permit me to remedy at least the latter failing by testifying to my—and perhaps our—continuing confusion in this area by saying a word abut two perplexing matters, one raised by the Halacha, the other by personalism.

I doubt that any category of Jewish law more seriously affects marital sexual life than the regulations concerning menstruation and separation. If we take our tradition seriously, we must acknowledge that these meticulously elaborated rules and their high emotional overtones cannot be censored out of the rabbis' understanding of how to consecrate a Jewish marriage. But what shall we liberal Jews make of them? Perhaps we can all agree on one step: the sexually proscribed seven clean days after the cessation of menstruation and the high fastidiousness of the sages about any later show of blood seem obsessive and ought summarily to be abandoned for a more humanistic, inter-personal evaluation of when sexual activity is fitting. But we are still left with endless, detailed regulations about the onset of the period, taboos during the flow, and what constitutes its proper conclusion. Does all this say anything to us? Here we most certainly need the help of our female colleagues and of Jewish women generally. They need to take the leadership in helping us rethink our old, often archaic feelings about blood and menstruation. Perhaps then we can find an appropriately personalized way for modern Jews to sanctify this significant aspect of female sexuality and thus of Jewish marriage.

The other problem arises from our contemporary culture. We liberal Jews have welcomed women's liberation and have taken some few but important steps toward making it a reality. But how will the presence of a fully self-determining, demanding as well as acquiescent wife, change the old tacit arrangements of Jewish marriage under which most Jews still operate? Consider, as one aspect of the problem, what the modern world has done to damage the male libido by harnessing it to economic or career-oriented ends. Our home lives have suffered and the market place has become foul with our displaced sexuality. If women should now similarly channel much of their sexual drive into the pursuit of success and power, what will become of the sexual primacy of the marital bed? How, we must now wonder, can liberal Judaism today combat the destructive power of a society bent on exploiting the new sexual freedom for women?

In sum, the Jewish teaching on sexuality continues to express with compelling power the mandates of existence under the Covenant. It provides us with a ground of value, standards of practice, and ideals to which to aspire. It directs us to structure our existence so that our lives are not a random sequence of events or experiences. It puts us in a historic context so that the present moment takes its place not only within our personal history but that of our family, our people, and thus of humankind slowly moving toward God's kingdom. It invests our sexual lives with sanctity, raising our animality beyond the human to where something of the divine image may be seen in us.

Despite this incomparable service, Judaism's sexual teaching shows three major areas in need of reform. First, its historical-communal institutional objectivity causes it to be relatively impersonalistic. We need to balance Judaism's preoccupation with abstract standards by a strong commitment to the individuality we consider basic to our mature existence. Second, its fearful understanding of the relationship between God and our genital activity easily can enshroud sexual activity with a heavy cloak of shame. We now recognize that exacerbating sexual fears and anxieties can cripple our humanity. Connecting our sex life with the transcendent needs to be done without making our sexual guidance damagingly repressive rather than therapeutically liberating. Third, and most obvious these days, classic Jewish texts are almost entirely concerned with male sexuality and male religious responsibility. A complete reworking of all these materials in terms of women's equality must now be undertaken. That cannot be done by males alone. The equal partner must have an equal voice. Indeed, considering the continuing prejudices of most of us men, leadership in this as in many other areas should be in the hands of women.

A similar dialectical evaluation of contemporary culture's view of sexuality is in order. Its weaknesses and strengths are largely the obverse of what I have just said about traditional Judaism. Too often our civilization is amoral about sex and not infrequently teaches shamelessness and the abolition of all guilt. It considers immediate pleasure the highest goal and has little sense of personal integrity through a lifetime and almost no concern for the individual as the channel for historic human destiny. By glorifying genitality and exploiting our repressions, contemporary society has largely stripped sexuality of its mysterious power to expose us to transcendence. Much of secular sexual attitudes so revulses people with a biblical sense of human dignity that it has sent them back to their Covenantal roots. We draw from them now to provide us with an elemental appreciation of the good so that we can discern and appropriate it when we discover it in modern sexuality.

For there is much that we have learned from our culture. The intimate relationship between sexuality and personality, the devious ways in which excessive repression ultimately expresses itself in pathology, the spiritual possibilities of a liberated but not libertine sex life, the technical and emotional therapies which revitalize our sexual functioning—all must be precious to liberal Jews. But above all, modernity has taught us what it means to be a person, living in full individuality and self-determination, yet paradoxically finding oneself most fully in a projected lifelong covenant of the highest intimacy and responsibility with one specific human being. An unmodernized Judaism may seem authentic, but that is only an appearance; the faithful Jewish continuity we seek is not captured in mere recapitulation but equally in a fresh, if daring, Covenant response to "the words which I, *Adonai*, command you this day."

21

On Homosexuality and the
Rabbinate, a
Covenantal Response*

Criteria for Liberal-Jewish Decision Making

In recent years, issues of what liberal Jews ought to do in a specific instance almost always devolve into debates over the proper criteria to be employed by us in making a decision. Let me then first briefly call attention to my paper, "The Autonomous Jewish Self" (reprinted here as Chapter 14) in which I detail my standards for determining Jewish obligation. In particular, I sought there to confront the tension that may arise between our ethical and other Jewish demands, a matter critical to the discussion of all questions of Jewish sexual ethics. As against the older style of Reform Jewish thinking, I do not begin with a universalistic, neo-Kantian rationalistic ethics on the basis of which I then seek confirmation from congenial Jewish texts. Rather, I understand Judaism as personal existence in Covenant. I therefore understand the "Jewish self," in full autonomy, inextricably linked to God as part of the Jewish people's historic Covenant relationship with God. Because of this shared relationship, the contemporary Jewish community and its past classic texts make a serious claim on me, as does our continuing need to live directed to our Messianic future. My selfhood remains critical to any decision, but it does not, as I under-

---

*Due to information I discovered after this paper was sent to the members of the Central Conference of American Rabbis, I realized my paper had come to a conclusion opposite to the one I now hold. This reversal is formally recorded and explained at the conclusion of the paper, which is given here in its circulated form as an instructive example of the moral interplay between the "is" and the "ought."

stand the "Jewish self," stand in isolation from God, the Jewish people, its past, present, and future. All must be part of my decision making for me to be true to my beliefs, that is, to be my kind of genuine Jew—though we may differ on how these interlocking factors come to bear on any given question.

This general theory of Jewish responsibility seems to me fully applicable to questions of Jewish sexual ethics. I could not have stated them explicitly in 1969 when I wrote on the question of the ethics of heterosexual intercourse, *Choosing a Sex Ethic*. Though it has taken me most of the intervening two decades to clarify my approach to liberal Jewish decision making, in retrospect, I find my current views implicit in my thinking then. More importantly, writing that book forced me to confront the conflict between what some contemporary ethical theories said about the rightness of intercourse and what I found that the classic teachers of Judaism, most notably in the halakhic tradition, understood Jewish duty to be, though with some dialectical variation. As a religious believer, my Jewish insight into the truth demanded at least an equal say in delineating what "Jewish" ethics were to be even if what made them "Jewish" was not simple acceptance of their premodern formulation. Thus, I discovered that I would now have to learn how properly to mediate between the occasionally clashing demands of classic Jewish obligation and the plurality of views that composed contemporary ethics. As I gained greater understanding of this task, I showed how this mediation operated, though in a somewhat sweeping way, in a paper for the Central Conference of American Rabbis Task Force on Sexuality, "Reading the Jewish Tradition on Marital Sexuality" (reprinted here as chapter 20). There I explored the clash between the Jewish side; that is, as requested, I began my inquiry with a reasonably objective reading of the central halakhic texts and then juxtaposed to their demands a personalistic view of marital sexual responsibility (that being the contemporary ethical view I find most cogent). In preparing this paper for the CCAR Committee on Homosexuality and the Rabbinate, I came to the conclusion that the issue of homosexuality (a term I use to include gay men and lesbians) did not require me to significantly alter or modify the standards or the process of decision making that I had previously worked out.

Let me also here add that though God's guidance is absolutely central to my conception of Jewish obligation, I make no explicit reference to it in what follows. That silence should not be misunderstood. My-our relationship with God is the constant background of the discussion; so to speak, I do this thinking in God's presence, conscious that I seek to determine what God wants of me, acknowledging my responsibility to God for all that I say and decide. For me God is no mere theological assumption or religious backdrop but a personal reality with whom I stand in living relationship, the "commanding" Other whose will for me as one of the Covenant people I earnestly seek to discern as I face this deeply troublesome, because intensely human, issue.

271

But I do not hear God directly "speaking" any specific command to me concerning this matter. To reason/intuit a decision here I must therefore proceed out of the ongoing context of my relationship with God and in terms of all that I know God requires of me. In other such cases I have found that sometimes I am later able to relate my decisions more directly to what I know God is asking of me, sometimes not. Nonetheless, direct or indirect, explicit or implicit, I seek nothing less than God's command for me/us, as best I can understand it. Since, as I have often indicated elsewhere, I think this subjective/personal element is necessarily built into the liberal decision-making process, I am committed to pluralism with regard to all conscientious efforts to delineate Jewish duty.

Universal Ethical Considerations

Since I believe Jews to be obligated to do more than what is universally ethical, I think it important to specify that by the term "ethics" I mean the good that any person, gentile or Jew, ought to do. This usage should enable us to be clear about any move we make beyond it to the obligations that arise from our particular Jewish relationship with God, the Covenant.

Philosophers today have no consensus as to how to find or define the good. Indeed, considerable influential opinion holds that, as rationality is generally understood today, substantive (that is, normative) ethics lies beyond the competence of philosophy. (So the much discussed recent books by Alasdair MacIntyre, *After Virtue* and *Whose Justice? Which Rationality?* [sic] and Bernard Williams, *The Ethical Limits of Philosophy* [sic].) That is the intellectual root of our current social ethical malaise. Our society goes far beyond the philosophers' pluralism in accepting divergent standards for determining the good, resulting in an astonishing diversity of what previously would have been called a-ethical or unethical behavior.

In the midst of this moral Babel, I can identify, with considerable over-simplification, four broad streams of substantive thinking about the ethics of homosexuality. They may be called social consequentialist, natural law, neo-Kantian, and personalist ethics. Let us consider them in turn.

(1) I have listed "social consequentialist" ethics with the other positions though it does not have the academic elaboration they do. Its philosophic equivalent would be a form of utilitarian ethics, but I have not come across an academic argument on homosexuality utilizing this position. However, many thoughtful people have argued that it would be bad for our society if homosexuals received equal rights. Specifically, they feel that any endorsement of homosexuality as an acceptable sexual alternative would weaken the family, an already threatened institution in our society. Directly, it would encourage people of uncertain sexuality and those whose psyches or traumas make acting out attractive to abandon the heterosexual family. Indirectly, it weakens the sacredness and status of the institution most fundamental to a sound society and further erodes what

272

strength traditional moral values still have in our society. All the intelligence and rhetoric of conservative social thought generally can be brought to bear on this topic with great ease. Since this perspective appeals to many conscientious people in our society these days, this position must be given serious consideration by those who believe that the people en masse are often as wise, if not wiser than, many of their intellectuals.

I have not seen a social consequentialist argument that advocates full equality for homosexuals.

I would agree that there is some measure of risk to our society in recognizing homosexuality as a sexual option fully equivalent to heterosexuality, but I do not see how anyone can confidently evaluate that risk. Indeed, this is one reason consequentialist theories of ethics have often been rejected: that one usually cannot reliably predict social consequences and moral outcomes. There also remains the difficult ethical calculus of weighing the problems generated by granting equal rights to homosexuals against the ethical good achieved by freeing homosexuals of discrimination as indicated below.

Moreover, our particular experience as Jews has some bearing on this universal issue. The reason consequentialism has never found a significant place in modern Jewish ethics is that it could easily validate a Christian or Moslem society refusing to grant equality to Jews or other dissenting minorities. We often heard that our emancipation would damage the society's ethos. Those dire consequences did not develop; to the contrary, once freed from major discrimination, Jews became a spectacularly beneficent social force. Based on this experience, Jewish philosophers have regularly espoused ethical theories that demanded rights even for minorities. Homosexuals are such an analogous minority in our society.

For all my primary rejection of consequentialism, I would agree that some prudential thinking must be part of any practical application of ethics. Yet I do not see that what is cogent in the consequentialist case about granting effective equality to homosexuals outweighs, as I shall develop below, arguments in favor of doing so.

(2) A strong case against the acceptance of homosexuality can be made (and often is) on the basis of natural law ethics, that is, that we learn what we ought to do by reading nature. Homosexuality is thereby adjudged unnatural. In religious natural law ethics, it is therefore clear why it is a sin against God.

Natural law ethics has been particularly strong among Roman Catholic thinkers, and with the contemporary difficulties of most utilitarian and deontological theories of ethics, it has recently found new secular as well as religious proponents. On the whole, however, most philosophers, particularly among non-Roman Catholics, have rejected it because of the critical difficulty of determining just how one knows what in nature is or is not ethically compelling. Homosexuality, of course, is not the sexual pattern of the overwhelming majority of creatures in most highly developed species. On the other hand, homosexuality does occur among animals and

273

seems to exist in a similar proportion of human beings in various cultures over the centuries. Arguing from nature that homosexuality is not the normal case would not logically vitiate the counter-argument that, for a given minority of people, homosexuality is natural and thus, religiously, God's will. The rejection of this contention forces us to face the problem that, in this sort of ethical thinking, one is not merely "reading" nature, presumably with simple objectivity, but, as in the judgment about the minority pattern, evaluating it. So to give some other examples, nature closely unites aggression and love, competition and cooperation, survival and altruism. By itself it does not give us an ethical mandate as to which of these impulses should guide its fellow. We must, then, utilize human discernment to distinguish what in nature is ethically directive from what is also in nature but is not suasive. Hence, I agree with those thinkers who find that natural law ethics either reduces to some other theory of ethics or, unpersuasively, reduces to a private intuition or a particular religious insight.

I have seen only one modern Jewish argument based on something like natural law. It contended that homosexuality was unnatural and gave as evidence the fact that human languages have only two sexual genders. I know of no philosophically competent thinker who has accepted this argument.

(3) Neo-Kantian ethics, the great exemplar of the deontological approach, employs certain essential benchmarks to determine what is rationally good, for example, prescribing as a duty only such acts as we would will to make a universal law of conduct and not treating any moral agent as a means only but also always as an end.

Just such considerations seem to have led people today to a new ethical perception of homosexuality. As they have come to know self-accepting, responsible homosexuals, they have asked why homosexuals should not be treated with the equality we extend to all other moral agents, rather than being discriminated against. And, putting themselves in the place of the newly familiar other, they have little problem ethically—emotions are another matter—asserting as a universal maxim that people should be entitled to their sexual preferences as long as they honor the free will and moral responsibility of their sexual partners. Together with many other people in our society, I find this argument ethically compelling.

(4) Personalist ethics considers good whatever contributes to making someone a genuine person (in Buber's language, a "thou").

If homosexuality is fixed in one's nature early in life, as much current opinion holds, it is depersonalizing—evil in this theory—to demand that homosexuals deny their fundamental nature/identity. Other than sexual orientation, there seems little if anything intrinsically different between homosexuals and other people. In the personalist understanding, therefore, it now becomes a significant ethical duty to help homosexuals accept themselves as worthy persons and unethical to continue to stigmatize and demean them as less than whole, fully human beings. Much of the concern of our colleagues, particularly the younger ones who have often had friends who were avowed homosexuals, stems from their strong ethical sense that we are depriving these human beings of their personhood. And the increasing evidence that many homosexuals, when freed of society's image of them as imperfect and flawed, are able to establish loving, stable, long-term relationships with others has increased their determination to fight discrimination against homosexuals. I also find this argument ethically compelling.

In sum, as I see the general ethical issue of homosexuality, aside from prudential considerations of uncertain significance, two major lines of ethical reasoning mandate a new, more accepting status for homosexuals in our society. That being the case, some of our colleagues wish to rectify the situation not only in our society but in the Jewish community and specifically in the Reform movement. Having long proclaimed Reform Judaism a "religion of reason," having identified universal ethics as a Reform Jew's overriding duty, how can we now not act upon this universal ethical demand?

If the human questions can momentarily be set to the side, what makes this issue so theoretically troubling, then, is that it forces us to clarify the relationship between our particular Jewish obligations and our universal ethical ones. And that, in turn, forces us to confront what, in actuality, we believe are the proper criteria for liberal Jewish decision making. If we still believe that universal ethics overrides all other considerations of Jewish duty, then homosexuality ought to be given full equality among us. Other than pragmatic considerations, the same ethical reasoning prompts many of our colleagues to perform intermarriages: a movement dedicated to universal ethics should not deny its blessings to two ethically well-matched persons. (Such colleagues may have great concern for the Jewish people, but when faced by an intermarriage, find the ethical priorities compelling.) So colleagues who do not intermarry in such a case reflect the view that, for all their concern for universal ethics, particular Jewish duty must be given priority.

I shall not add here to what I have written elsewhere arguing against equating liberal Jewish duty (as against possibility) with universal ethics or even giving it preemptive superiority over any other claimants to Jewish obligation. I stand with that large number of rabbis who would place a stringent interpretation on the Central Conference of American Rabbis' Centenary Perspective's statement: "The past century has taught us that the claims made upon us [by God as known through our people's relation with God] may begin with our ethical obligations but they extend to many other aspects of Jewish living. . . . " While ethics rightfully deserves a certain priority in our sense of Jewish obligation, that certain-ness derives from our knowing that our duty is multilayered, often as particular as it is universal. Much of one's response to the issue of homosexuality (as to many others) depends on the weight we attach to the claims that lead us equally to have major duties in the "other aspects of Jewish living" and how we negotiate these many, often mixed demands upon us. Surely we do not find it as easy as did a previous generation to take decisive stands on many issues, because we acknowledge we have more than one set of imperatives that impinge upon us.

This much having been clarified, I now turn to the particular Jewish questions that are equally integral to my deciding what I, a Jew, now need to do to serve God properly.

What Has Our Tradition Said?

How have the religious leaders of the people of Israel, in whose Covenant I stand, understood our obligations to God with regard to homosexuality? That is primarily, in classic Jewish terms, a halakhic issue and only secondarily one of biblical or agadic statement. Finding the rulings of the *halakhah*, in all their dialectical elaboration, is an academic matter, one independent of the scholar's sexual preferences or, for that matter, religion. All competent scholars should come to reasonably similar conclusions about them, and the differences between them could be judged by the usual academic criteria. Liberal Jews are particularly free to exercise critical detachment in such studies since they are not bound to follow or apologize for the content of their findings, though they may play some role in their autonomous decision making—in my case, a considerable but not decisive one.

I am not an expert in Jewish law, though I have for some years been concerned about the interface between the *halakhah* and Jewish theology and Jewish ethics. As far as I can tell, Jewish law prohibited homosexual acts and did so with none of the dialectic of opinion that it characteristically exhibits on most topics. So much is academic data. The slight difference of seriousness the *halakhah* attached to lesbian relationships seems to me simply an expression of the general sexism of the *halakhah*, a system that does not take women and their activities as seriously as it does men and their acts—but that is interpretation, not what the texts themselves say.

This introduces us to the next level of the problem, that the rigid separation of data and interpretation cannot rigorously be insisted upon. Texts do not simply speak to modern Jews. What they "mean" is already an act of interpretation and, all the more so, their "significance" or "implications." We move from words to meaning all the time, but just how to do so without reading ourselves into the texts is a highly disputed topic. As it applies to Jewish duty, it involves decisions about (1) what to take from modern culture; (2) what, independently of that, to affirm in one's Judaism and, were that not enough; (3) how best *(sic)* to combine the two sources of understanding. Let me contrast some responses to interpreting our data with my own.

Utilizing one or another form of a historical approach, some writers have taken the *prima facie* negativity of the evidence as a reflection more of its social setting than its religious intuition. They then generally distance themselves from the biblical and rabbinic authors since we have a radically different social context, one which, at least on this issue, gives us a superior understanding of the question. This enables or requires them to reject the position of classic Jewish law.

Two specific forms of this argument occur in discussions about a Jewish ethics of homosexuality. The one comes from thinkers who know, if only as a regulative idea for constructing a rational Jewish ethics, that the *halakhah* ideally moves toward neo-Kantian, universal ethical determinations. Thus, they can negate the content of the *halakhah* because we can be more fully universalistic than could our forebears. The second position is taken by thinkers who reason from the motives they understand to be behind the old proscriptions. Again, since we have a better understanding of the genesis and operation of homosexuality, we can assert a different sense of Jewish duty.

I do not share with these thinkers so clear a sense of my distance from the biblical and rabbinic authors; I cannot easily say that, for all the distance of time and difference of learning between us, that my sense of Jewish duty is wiser than theirs. Experientially, I understand us to stand in the same religious relationship, the Covenant. I therefore always seek to inquire, even where what they said seems strange to me (for example, the sacrificial system), what Covenantal significance they may have found in this pattern of duty. I may then find that what they knew they owed God, I do too, or now do not, or simply don't know, or do not yet know. I also seriously undertake this uncertain task, among other reasons, because I am sensitive to the Jewish difficulties raised by my insistence on individual autonomy as the ultimate though not exclusive or untrammeled authority in fixing liberal Jewish duty. I therefore seek to read the data in terms of its meta-halakhic, experiential/theological ground; that is, how does their/my affirmation of the Covenant issue in this/these rulings?

My question is speculative; the halakhists do not often articulate their meta-halakhic concerns. Since one's understanding of the fundamental nature of Judaism is at stake here, there will be a scholarly difference of opinion as to the result, another reason liberal Jews must be pluralistic. But one criterion of a reasonable inference is its coherence with what else we know of the halakhic way of life and its theological underpinnings. My inferences about the meta-halakhic basis for the classic Jewish proscription of homosexual acts arise from what I see as two major concerns of the sages, one negative and one positive, both of which cohere well with what we know about their socio-religious situation. Negatively, their sexual stringencies rejected many culturally acceptable sexual practices they saw around them because they found them incompatible with Covenant holiness. Positively, they saw in generative, heterosexual marriage a major, if not the major, human embodiment of the Covenant between God and Israel. It reflects their uncommon religious sensibility that historic time is central to serving God, that the people of Israel must have as many Covenant-faithful generations as are required to bring the Messiah. Israel being a small, endangered people, its sages vigorously sought to protect and foster their unique God-given mandate from what they considered gentile sinfulness. (The rabbis, it should be pointed out, ruled that homosexual acts were forbidden to Noachides as well as Jews).

I find this interpretation of the halakhic data persuasive, but that is a "historical" judgment, not a normative determination of my Jewish duty since I insist that only a decision of the self, not a finding about past precedent, can "command" me. But as a Jewish self, my understanding of the religious reality behind the *halakhah* will have a serious, significant impact upon my decision about my obligation as a Jew to God.

The Attitudes of the Jewish Community

I am, under the Covenant, as much a member of the contemporary Jewish community as I am a child of its past. I therefore seek to know what other Jews today understand their Covenant obligations to be. I know of no reasonably objective way to ascertain this. The issue is further complicated for me because in my Jewish decision making I do not give equal weight to every "Jewish" opinion. I am particularly concerned with those Jews who seek to live under the Covenant, that is, those Jews who attempt, in various ways, to build their lives on what God demands of them today as members of the Covenant people. They are, by my standards, the significant community of Israel in our time. I acknowledge that that is an ideal construct rather than an empiric reality, and some will sense it here and others there—another reason we must welcome pluralism in our movement. For myself, though I claim no special expertise in assessing where my ideal Jewish community stands on this issue, I feel reasonably satisfied with my understanding of it, based as it is on my decades of broad exposure to our people.

To begin with, I have been deeply impressed by many young idealistic colleagues and by Jews in our homosexual congregations who have made a case for the equality of the homosexual sexual preference under the Covenant. They are surely in my ideal community. Their ethical passion, their Jewish concern, and their human integrity have moved me greatly. They have an important job to do in instructing all of us with regard to this issue. They have already had an important impact upon the Jewish community, and I believe they will continue to change attitudes and open minds as to the differing ways liberal Jews may live in holiness under the Covenant.

Considerable inroads have been made in the community's prior, relatively unanimous, negative attitude toward homosexuality. But I see little openness to accepting it as a fully Covenantal equivalent to heterosexuality expressed in marriage. The traditionalists, whether halakhically firm or more pliant and dynamic, remain opposed to homosexuality as a Jewish option. While they may seek to extend whatever openness they can to homosexuals as persons and Jews, they do not see that the best homosexual relationships qualify as faithful Covenant living. They are reinforced in this attitude by a sense that Jewish life, particularly Jewish family life, has been substantially corrupted by accepting values from the general society. They believe it is important that we find ways to resist further deleterious encroachments by an increasingly pagan culture, of which they take homosexuality to be a significant manifestation. It is a matter which, as one turns from this group's modernized, humane representatives to others more inner-directed, is often addressed with vehement objection.

I find most liberal Jews sharing similar attitudes, though with two major differences. They do not, of course, identify the Covenant closely with substantial acceptance of *halakhah,* and a substantial minority among them feel strongly that we have an ethical responsibility to revise our Jewish attitudes to and treatment of homosexuals. As a result, advocates of homosexual rights have found a receptive audience when they have asked the Union of American Hebrew Congregations and the Central Conference of American Rabbis to endorse formally our society's granting homosexuals greater acceptance. But as the negotiations for the admission of homosexual congregations to the Union indicated, they have had less success in convincing the majority that homosexuality ought to be granted fully equivalent status with heterosexuality in the Jewish community.

As with the *halakhah,* I understand this liberal Jewish reticence in terms of our community's implicit sense of Covenant responsibility. Positively, I hear us asserting that the special imperatives that devolve upon Jews because of the Covenant necessitate our special devotion to the heterosexual, that is, the procreative family. Negatively, the imperiled situation of the Jewish community as a minority makes family unity a particularly important instrument of our survival. And here the general consequentialist arguments that the heterosexual family will be weakened become doubly significant for Jews.

As to the positive concern, the goal of the Covenant is the Messianic Time. Hence procreation is a major Jewish duty; if there is no new Jewish generation, and another and another, all the holiness of prior generations has lost its ultimate goal. Of course, one can be a good Jew without fulfilling this duty, but procreation remains a Covenantal mandate. Homosexual families can model the Covenant insofar as it involves interpersonal faithfulness in a lifetime. But when it comes to procreation, they divorce loving faithfulness and the generation of Jewish children. The love comes down along one line, so to speak, the generativity along another. To be sure, Jews who cannot have children are encouraged to adopt them; a pattern of such split relationships is known among us and has been transcended, but it is not our preferred state.

We must now turn to some prudential considerations. One of the new concerns in adoption is the attempts of adopted children to link up with their biological parents, occasionally causing some problems in their relationships with their adoptive parents. The same consideration needs to be taken into account with regard to the surrogate spouse in homosexual procreation.

The special Covenantal concern with having as integrated a family unit as possible has been reinforced over the ages, it seems to me, because of the perilous minority status of the Jewish people. Today, if anything, we face aggravated perils. From without, individualism and hedonism combine to erode family closeness and continuity—and they are substantial factors in leading Jews to intermarry. Within, we have agreed, somewhat grudgingly to be sure, that women are entitled to full equality in our families and that children should have increasing rights. These ethical imperatives have resulted in a restructuring of the family that is still under way, a restructuring that has subjected the Jewish family to great strain. While we have great hope that the ultimate results will be a major ethical-Jewish gain, the changes we have initiated have already put our families under such stress that liberal Jews, as I read them, are loath to do anything that might weaken it further.

In sum, I find our community continues to reflect a Covenantal concern, theological and prudential, in denying the equivalence of the faithful homosexual Jewish family to its heterosexual counterpart. I hasten to add that this is my present understanding of the case. Our community has shown its capacity to change its standards with regard to sexual standards, as the general acceptance of certain kinds of nonmarital sexual intercourse indicates. Perhaps it will do the same with regard to homosexuality and the homosexual family. But I do not now see any such significant shift of attitude under way with regard to homosexuality.

Again, as a liberal Jew I do not feel bound by what the Jewish community is saying on this issue, as best I understand it. But as one who shares the community's Covenant, I give its attitude very serious consideration.

An Instructive Special Case

By turning to a tangential issue, I believe I can show what leads me to resolve the conflict I feel between the claims of universal ethics and the Covenant with regard to this question. All of us are somewhat bisexual. Some people are more evenly balanced in this regard than others; an additional number are influenced by the circumstances of their life to move from one side of their sexuality to the other, and perhaps back again. In such people homosexuality is not a matter deeply integrated into the personality at an early age; it is a relatively free alternative of the kind most people know in relation to their sexuality. That is, when we are powerfully moved by our sexual urges of the most varied sorts, we are reasonably able to choose what we will do in response to them. Does our Judaism have a preference as to the decision a fully bisexual person makes with regard to his or her sexual options?

To me, the answer is quite clear. Given a choice, the Covenant requires Jews to elect the heterosexual option because in that mode they can, at least in principle, directly fulfill their duty to create the Jewish biological future. For my Judaism, then, heterosexual, procreative family existence is the preferred Jewish state, and everyone who is free to undertake it ought to do so to the extent they can. (Our community's responsibility to "singles" and our society's subjecting them to special peril are important topics that cannot be discussed here.)

But what of that significant number of persons who could only be asked to undertake this duty by doing violence to a central, ingrained element of their personality? Here the insights of modern psychology and our ethical concern for each person as a self radically modify for me our tradition's negative attitude toward homosexual activity. All of us need to serve God as much out of who we personally are as by what our community understands the Covenant to require of us generally. Furthermore, while every Jew has always been precious to our people, after the Holocaust a special responsibility rests upon us to include in our midst every Jew we can. Therefore, while maintaining its preference for heterosexuality, our community needs to do all it can to make it possible for homosexual Jews to share in our community life. That is not an unproblematic line of action to suggest. None of us likes to hear, "Yes, but . . . " when we ask for acceptance. Yet often, in the unprecedented situations modernity has confronted us with, the unconditional "Yes" does as much violence to our conscience as the unconditional "No" does to the person so summarily rejected. Then, as in the case of intermarried couples, "Yes, but . . . " may trouble those to whom it is said, but it at least indicates our desire to be as accepting as our own integrity allows. I know of no response to Jewish homosexuals that would not cause me greater anguish. Perhaps with loving goodwill we shall, together, find ways to lessen the difficulties it engenders.

Homosexual Rabbis

Two further premises guide me in extrapolating from the situation of Jews generally to that of rabbis: (1) to be a rabbi is not a Jewish right but a title bestowed as a special Jewish honor; (2) rabbis, in fulfillment of their special community status, ought to set an example of Jewish ideals. I think the former premise requires no further comment. As to the latter, the gap between our common human reality and our Jewish ideals prompts a further word. We rabbis know we are sinners as are all Jews. We also are determined to lessen the undesirable distance between rabbis and laity, and we therefore seek to make plain our sense of our common humanity.

Nonetheless, by dint of learning and life's dedication, rabbis ought, more than all other Jews, to be exemplars of living by the Covenant. And it is generally agreed that it is as model more than anything else that the rabbi teaches Judaism. Many congregations will settle for far less, most notably for a rabbi who is quintessentially a mentsh. In our troublesome social order, that is not an achievement to be denigrated. Nonetheless, for a rabbi only to be an exemplar of the b'ne noach at their best, that is, to be as good as a righteous gentile, is too little to ask even in our spiritually impoverished generation.

If we are dedicated to the Covenant with its special standards, then we should require of our rabbis, insofar as we are able, that they exemplify them. I am, therefore, against the ordination of homosexuals as rabbis.

Should the Central Conference of American Rabbis Act?

But the question of taking a stand on this matter is not addressed to me as an individual but to the rabbinic association of Reform rabbis, and that involves additional considerations.

I would agree that the CCAR should set a model of moral leadership for the Jewish community. It should often take a stand on ethical issues in advance of much of the Jewish community and even of the Reform laity. I derive this simply from our explicit, major commitment to the ethical dimension of what we understand God wants of us, our special sensitivity to this as caring rabbis, and our pragmatic recognition that much of the rest of the Jewish community prefers to wait on controversial issues, not the least because it prefers that we take the risks and receive the abuse that come with unpopular stands.

I can take that argument a step further. In a significant sense I think the leadership of the CCAR ought to be somewhat in advance of our membership with regard to such issues; real leaders ought to be moral pacesetters. And I believe that the members of the Conference, in their own independent way, desire guidance from their leaders, not hesitating, in turn, to let them know quite quickly when they find them moving too far too fast. Thus, despite the conclusion I personally reached above, I think it possible to argue that the leadership of the Conference should now take a courageous leadership and ask the membership to go on record as favoring a more open, positive stand toward homosexual rabbis by all our Reform institutions, national and local. Even if it produced few immediate practical results, it could be symbolically important in this moral struggle.

I am against asking the CCAR to exercise such moral leadership on this issue at this time for three interrelated reasons. First, the Reform movement is already in advance of almost all the rest of the organized Jewish religious community in its positive, public acceptance of Jewish homosexuals because of its formal acceptance into the Union of American Hebrew Congregations of synagogues that have a special concern for homosexuals. While that may not give proponents of full equality for homosexual Jews all that they wish, it has been a step that remains significantly in advance of the rest of the community, and more than just a verbal or symbolic step at that.

Second, all leadership must reckon on how many issues they can go beyond a clear mandate from their groups, and when they do take such a stand, how much in advance of them to go. Prophets, to be sure, do not reckon this way; thus, they have their special fate. We are not prophets, though we seek to emulate their insight and courage; we are rabbis working with communities. In the very highest sense of the term, we have political responsibilities to help our communities rise to greater holiness while keeping them in their American freedom a functioning community. Reform Judaism, in this case specifically the CCAR, has already moved so far out in front of the American Jewish religious community by its courageous experiment with patrilineality that it has threatened the unity of American Jewry. Action now, taking a further step toward the full acceptance of homosexuality, would in my judgment dangerously weaken the already fragile ties that keep most of American Jewry working together in matters of religion.

Third, there exist realistic alternatives for homosexual Jews other than the formal recognition by the Hebrew Union College-Jewish Institute of Religion and the Central Conference. The Reconstructionist Rabbinical College officially accepts all students without regard for sexual preference. (Though, it must be noted, this act of their faculty has prompted a call by some Reconstructionist congregations for reconsideration.) There also apparently exists some possibility that the Leo Baeck College in London may officially, or by some less indecorous British device, accept avowed homosexuals as candidates for the rabbinate. A far less desirable but nonetheless workable additional alternative is for homosexuals to come to the college, as a number have done over the years, staying "in the closet" until ordination. This will increase the number of homosexual rabbis in the Conference, perhaps enabling them to become a critical mass politically. (This depersonalizing situation will be somewhat mitigated these days by the significant number of students who will give such colleagues their full personal support during their studies.)

Utilizing the present alternatives may not immediately accomplish the goals of the proponents of CCAR action on this issue, but the Conference's not taking any action will also not permanently defeat their cause. By allowing the presence of Reform congregations specially concerned with homosexuals to have its familiarizing effect by working to help the gay liberation movement to change further the American acceptance of homosexuality, our Jewish communal receptivity may also change, thus making action on this matter less problematic, at least in some of its communal aspects.

Suggesting to people pursuing justice that they wait can easily be a form of the highest immorality. In this instance, I have such significantly substantive and practical doubt about our taking action that I believe taking none is what, as Jews, we ought to do.

A Correction

While this book was nearing production I chanced on information indicating I had made a major error in stating my conclusions. When I wrote this paper, I assumed that the Hebrew Union College-Jewish Institute of Religion still followed its old practice of actively (if imperfectly) screening homosexuals from admission and denying them ordination. Inadvertently and to my great surprise, I discovered in early May 1989—my paper reached the members of the CCAR committee in the last week of November 1987—that this is not the case. As interpreted to me, the College's present policy has been—the time of its inception is unclear—to maintain neutrality to the sexual orientation of applicants for admission and of enrolled students. Had I known this, I would not, of course, have concluded my paper by calling for no action by the Conference. My view of our Jewish religious obligations in this area requires me to dissent from the College's present policy, one I would characterize as passive permissiveness. I would instead now urge the Conference to use its good offices with the College to get it to return to its earlier practice as I and others understood and experienced it. In the meantime, I also believe that the Conference has an obligation to Reform congregations, our partners in the Placement Service. It should indicate to them that they can no longer assume that rabbis ordained by the College are usually heterosexual. Should a congregation wish for Jewish religious reasons (such as mine) to be led by a rabbi religiously committed to heterosexual existence, it would do well to ask candidates for its pulpit about their Jewish religious attitudes and commitments in this area. (May 22, 1989)

The Jew in Community:
Social Ethics

PART
FOUR

The Jew in Community:
Social Ethics

Since its modern beginnings, Jewish ethics has motivated generations of Jews to judge their Jewish authenticity largely by the quality of their participation in general human affairs. Perhaps the most telling evidence of the widespread adoption of this standard has been the boast of those who rejected the Jewish religion but argued for their superior Jewishness by pointing to their superior moral activity.

Recently the identification of Jewish duty with general social concern has found passionate critics. Staying close to the horizon of classic Jewish legal texts, they contend that an authentic Jew's overriding concern must be the affairs of this imperiled people. And this Jewish argument has been strengthened by the political conservative argument pointing to the difficulties of realistically carrying through programs for social betterment. The result has been a considerable dampening of the once famed American Jewish dedication to political moral action.

I do not deny the enormous complexity of the problems our society faces or how little direct guidance the Jewish tradition offers for alleviating them. Perhaps Judaism and other religions can be of the greatest help to society by providing the metaethical foundations that direct our evaluation of proposed solutions as acceptably humane. But though Jewish belief may not immediately guide us in drafting legislation or bureaucratic plans, it does give us practical counsel. The two main examples addressed here are the goals of business and the character of leadership. Many other writers have analyzed the social implications of various bioethical issues. Surely it requires no gift of prophecy to see that similar social questions will continue to puzzle a concerned citizenry. The Jewish community would greatly benefit from the development of a cadre of thinkers who were expert in the technical details of given social problems and likewise at home in the relevant halakhic literature. I am convinced that they would have much of considerable value to say to our community and to thoughtful others. Moreover, a body of such literature would be a major American contribution to the great chain of Jewish tradition.

22

Freedom

The Metamorphoses of a Jewish Value

The unique contours of the contemporary discussion about freedom appear most clearly against the background of classic Jewish views.

The Bible contains little direct reference to freedom. The fewer than two dozen direct references in it mainly concern the release of a slave or otherwise legally encumbered person. National freedom receives scant mention. By contrast, much of the Bible's legislation and literary allusion speak of slavery, personal and ethnic. While no sure inferences can be drawn from the writers' essentially negative attitude toward nonfreedom, the pervasiveness and significance of this attitude shape the later development of the issue.

This concern with freedom coheres well with the root reality of Hebraic religious experience, that the one and only God brought the people of Israel out of Egyptian slavery and gave them concrete instruction. Torah, the foundation of all other biblical values, placed its greatest emphasis on law and commandment. Remember and do, it continually exhorts; do not go after your own heart and eyes. In such a worldview, Torah delineates appropriate freedom, giving it proper scope and worth.

Both the economic and political aspects of freedom receive considerable adumbration in rabbinic literature. While accepting the institutions of slavery and temporary bondage, the rabbis increased responsibilities for owners and benefits for those in bondage. A number of teachers explicitly derogate a social status that inhibits the initiative they believe Jews ought

From *Contemporary Jewish Religious Thought,* ed. Arthur A. Cohen and Paul Mendes-Flohr (New York: Scribners, 1986).

ideally to bring to the observance of God's Torah. The same reasoning applies to the people of Israel as a whole. "Subjugation to the nations," a widely used rabbinic theological term, impedes the service the people of Israel owe God. For the rabbis, this punishment that has come upon their people is the equivalent of their ancestors' slavery in Egypt, and they fervently look forward to their own exodus and redemption. Personally and nationally, the continuity of the rabbis with the biblical writers stands out. Freedom remains an instrumental value, cherished as a condition for fulfilling Torah.

This fundamental notion takes another form in the Middle Ages. While the rabbis' concerns manifest themselves in the succeeding centuries—with the issue of personal status declining in interest—the focus of medieval Jewish thinkers becomes ontological. Since God knows everything, thus determining what is, how can one have free will with which to respond to the Torah's behests?

The question agitated medieval Jewish philosophers because it brings into contradiction two fundamental beliefs of Judaism (as of the religions derived from it): God's sovereignty and human responsibility. The former now required that God know everything, hence the future as well as the past. The Torah calls Jews to obedience to God's instruction, regularly exhorting them about the major consequences of their response. But if what they do is not a matter of their volition, the entire scheme seems irrational, particularly the retribution that so strongly characterizes it.

Almost all the major medieval Jewish thinkers refused to compromise on the reality of human initiative. Some argued that the problem lies beyond human capacity, whereas others preferred to conceptualize causation so as to allow for the free exercise of will. Only an occasional thinker found himself required to affirm some variety of determinism. The Jewish mystics, however, who often utilized philosophic notions, had little difficulty with this issue. They regularly reconciled paradoxes through the employment of an elaborate symbol system that could be manipulated in endless ways on multiple levels.

With the modern period, a revolutionary change occurred in Jewish status, both personal and ethnic. The term used to describe this shift, *emancipation*, literally means the formal process of freeing a slave. With the birth of democratic states and their new notion of citizenship, the term could be applied metaphorically to the granting of civil rights to those previously disenfranchised. On the human level, the results, though slow in coming and marred by a new anti-Semitism, were monumentally beneficial to the Jews. This extraordinary social progress permeated the modern Jewish consciousness and fundamentally shaped the contemporary Jewish discussion of freedom.

Theoretically, the modern democratic state derives from the idea of the dignity of each individual, a concept that emerged gradually after the late Middle Ages. Several major points in that development shape the modern Jewish version of the problem of freedom: Descartes's insistence on the individual's right to doubt all ideas until he could make them clear and convincing to himself; Rousseau's argument that this human capacity to think could be reconciled with government only if people were self-governing; and, above all, Kant's extension of this idea to the moral realm, that only an autonomous ethics is worthy of a rational person.

Though this Kantian notion of the modern person as self-legislating has dominated the agenda of modern Jewish thought, the fate of the problem of freedom of the will deserves some mention. When scientific determinism exercised considerable hold on thinkers, the problem did receive some general attention. But, as in the Middle Ages, life (if not intellect) seemed to refute the denial of freedom. Though research continues to unveil ever-further determinants of human nature, the general discounting of science's omniscience and the record of unpredictable human responses to the extraordinary (and sometimes ordinary) circumstances of this century have kept determinism at the outer periphery of intellectual concern.

Autonomy, however, strikes at the very heart of classic Jewish faith: God, not the self, gives law. If, then, modernity instructs the Jew to contravene what the sages of our day declare to be Torah, then the observant Jew will reject the blandishments of the philosophy of autonomy. For a minority of Jews, freedom within Torah remains the only way one can continue to be faithful to the covenant. The overwhelming majority of Jews, convinced by the spiritual benefits of emancipation, have sought some way of accommodating to it and thus to its emphasis on freedom.

The problem assumed its classic form when, for the sake of stemming conversion to Christianity, laymen started breaching accepted Jewish law so as to modernize the synagogue service and Jewish life. When thinkers began validating this process, they utilized the newly developed critical notion of history as continual change. To this they later added the scientific metaphor of evolution. For much of modern Jewry, historical development became the ideological validation for breaking with Jewish law or radically catalyzing its development. This ideology continues to function well wherever people can still believe that the onward march of events itself can, in some fashion, indicate where Jewish tradition needs to be maintained or modified.

Jewish thinkers who desired to give this notion philosophical respectability had Hegel and the Christian Hegelians available for their theorizing, but despite some efforts in this direction, no full-scale Jewish Hegelianism ever received much attention. Not the least reason for this was, by contrast to Kant, the highly limited place of ethics and thus human initiative in unreconstructed Hegelianism.

The first great modern Jewish philosophy, that of Hermann Cohen, makes ethics, and therefore human freedom, primary to the entire system. To Cohen as to Kant, human nature is identified with rationality, which, in turn, defined in terms of ethics, science, and aesthetics, is so self-evident as to require no justification. One cannot then deny human freedom without rejecting what makes us persons, not beasts. To be modern and rational, then, meant for Cohen to be autonomous and to legislate for oneself such laws of conduct as reason, so carefully defined by him, might dictate.

Cohen's notion of freedom goes one extraordinary step further, for he closely identifies reason with creativity. For him, the mind does not exist as such and then begin to think when energized by thinkers; rather, at our rational best, we create the apparatus by which the work of thinking proceeds—or somewhat less fundamentally, we originate an idea by which we will then rationally construct reality (in interaction with what we encounter, to be sure, but meeting that, of course, which our foundational idea allows to enter our experience). Creativity out of nothing, so to speak, is the apex of Cohen's rationalism. Thus for him freedom has as good as infinite worth.

In a Kantian, regulative sense, Cohen believed that his comprehensive, ethical worldview lay at the heart of Judaism, with the prophets providing its clearest articulation. With considerable polemic vigor, he argued that Judaism, of all historic religions, came closest to exemplifying his concept of a religion of reason. He realized that this theory only validated universal ethics as Jewish duty; proud Jew that he was, Cohen sought to provide a broader mandate to enable Judaism to survive. He did this by delineating the particular role remaining for religion once philosophy had done its work, and became more particular only when he occasionally argued that by its origination of the idea of ethical monotheism (in his sense) Judaism retained unique insight into it.

From Cohen's time on, a major focus of modern Jewish thought has been the proper limits of self-legislation. Two developments have raised this issue to critical importance. On the human level, explorations of ethical freedom have revealed not only new dimensions of personhood but also ethical proposals that radically contradict much prior ethical teaching. In the realm of Jewish experience, the strong rational validation of universal ethics makes the rest of Jewish practice seem optional in a time when Jewish ties badly need strengthening. No subsequent liberal solution to these problems has succeeded in winning a substantial number of adherents. How rationally to mandate an ethical system and how to justify group authority against individual autonomy remain utterly troublesome philosophic issues. Until this general problem of human authority is philosophically resolved, rationalistic theories of Jewish freedom are unlikely to return to liberal Jewish popularity.

As with regard to other traditions in America at large, liberalism's loss of its prior self-evident correctness and its continuing inability to transcend its weakened cultural props have made possible a revival of Jewish orthodoxy. Human freedom having shown itself unreliable if not destructive, God's gracious gift of Torah once again manifests its virtue as the only proper way for Jews. In modern Orthodoxy, much space can be made for the exercise of individual freedom and participation in contemporary culture.

Thus far, no systematic discussion of the proper role of personal freedom in Orthodoxy has yet appeared. In his essay *Halakhic Man*, Rabbi Joseph B. Soloveitchik demonstrated how rationality functions in the life utterly grounded in the law. That paper clearly lays out the Orthodox Jewish analogue of Hermann Cohen's rationality. But neither there nor elsewhere in his published works has Rabbi Soloveitchik given us an extensive analysis of the individual Jew's legitimate exercise of self-determination. He has, on occasion, made reference to possible tensions that might arise between the individual will and God's dictates. These he treats as the existential equivalent of sacrifices, with faithful Jews offering up their freedom at God's behest.

For all the fresh appeal of Orthodoxy, most modernized Jews have not been willing to accept it; they prefer the notion of tradition to that of Torah as discipline. At its best, this response acknowledges that, for all their failings, modernity and its central notion of autonomy must find a place in Judaism. The immediate issues that have forced this question upon the community have been women's rights in Judaism and the place of democracy. On both counts, there seems a fundamental clash between what much of the community believes to be ultimately right and what the overwhelming majority of sages declare to be halakhically binding.

National freedom has similarly been thoroughly recast in modern times. The human initiative asserted on the personal level gave rise to the notion of ethnic self-determination, most notably manifest in nineteenth-century nationalism. Among Jews this produced Zionism, despite the accepted understanding of the Torah that God alone, through the Messiah, should reestablish Jewish political sovereignty—a difficulty still manifest in the continuing ambivalence toward Zionism of the most observant sector of the Jewish community.

The establishment and positive accomplishments of the State of Israel have won it the support and admiration of almost all of world Jewry. But the continuing confrontation with perilous circumstances has aborted the occasional efforts to turn Zionist thought from ideology to systematic analysis. In particular, the problem of what limits there should be to the exercise of Jewish national freedom has received little theoretical discussion. In part this has been due to the intense community opposition to any public discussion of Diaspora Jewish concern with particular policies of given Israeli administrations. In equal part, at least, the problem also arises from the difficulty of establishing standards, certainly from a secular point of view, by which to make such judgments.

I have sought to approach these issues by adumbrating a theory of Judaism in terms of the particular relationship in which the autonomous Jewish self stands. In my personalist understanding of the covenant, Kant's secular autonomy has been radically transformed. Rather than reason guiding the self, the individual stands in intimate relationship to God, and from that—or from the tradition or the teachers who authentically articulate the consequences of this relationship—the individual discovers what must be done.

That is true universally; all humankind shares in the Noachide covenant. The Jewish self, however, does not stand in isolated relationship with God but shares in the people of Israel's historic covenant. Jewish duty derives from this and is, therefore, as ineluctably particular as it is universal, social as it is personal. Yet it must ultimately be individually appropriated and projected. For all that the Jewish self comes before God as one of the Jewish people, the Jew remains a self with the personal right to determine what God now demands of the people of Israel and of any particular member of it.

Often this personalist approach to Jewish duty will lead to acknowledging the lasting value of classic Jewish teaching and thus to simple obedience. But it may also require modification or abandonment of an old practice or the creation of a new form adequate to the continuing reality of an ancient relationship. Discipline has thus been internalized, but the consequent subjectivity has been contained by defining the self in terms of its relationship with God and the Jewish people. Were there enough Diaspora "Jewish selves" who lived by this standard, communal norms of Jewish duty might once again arise, though in forms different from those created when Jewish discipline was essentially objectified.

This convenantal understanding applies equally to the State of Israel as to individual Jews. Here, too, freedom becomes responsible only in the service of God in continuation of the Jewish people's millennial relationship with God.

23

Social Justice, the Liberal Jewish Case

Though esteeming highly the spiritual worth of the individual, the Bible authors give priority to the corporate human relationship with God. I would speculate that they do so largely because they view humankind as essentially social. Looking at Adam, they have *Adonai* say, "It is not good for man to be alone: I will make a fitting helpmate for him."[1] And the tower of Babel story comes to explain why the history of humankind is essentially a record of the conflict of peoples and nations.[2] Even the account of the Israelite patriarchs serves to introduce the emergence of the Hebrew nation and explain its possession of Canaan.[3] The historical books then tell what happened to the covenanted people, and the prophetic books criticize, threaten, remotivate, and redirect its efforts to create a communal life holy to God. Social ethics is obviously fundamental to the religion of the Bible.

We shall have little difficulty specifying the content of biblical social ethics as long as we see it as a body of abstract ideals. Can there be much doubt that the Bible, in all its diversity of authors, attitudes, voices, and concerns, unambiguously aspires to a time when people live together in plenty and not in poverty, in justice and not in oppression, in love and not in hatred, in peace and not in war?

Our difficulties in accepting and applying biblical social ethics arise as we move from the Bible's idealism to its profound human realism. Its

Originally published as "The Critical Issue in The Quest for Social Justice: A Jewish View," in *Contemporary Ethical Issues in Jewish and Christian Traditions*, ed. Frederick E. Greenspan (Hoboken: Ktav, 1986).

writers accept as axiomatic the premise that human beings are no longer in the Garden of Eden because we are creatures who regularly will to sin. They see our stubborn, perverse rejection of God's will as the motive power of human history and the problem that God's loving, saving power must overcome. The biblical lawgivers, envisioning people this way, created statutes by which they might effectuate their God-inspired social ideal in their immediate, concrete social situation. The prophets, by divine revelation, clarified what God was doing in the particular local and international affairs of Jewish history.

In due course, direct revelation ceased in Israel, and altered social circumstances demanded a more appropriate statement of what God now wanted of the people of the Covenant. The rabbis in their unique way then continued the Bible's practical social concern in the exquisite details of talmudic law and the inspirational lessons of midrashic lore. That tradition of vision and application, of text and interpretation, of precedent and application, of enlargement and augmentation, of creative development and new enactment, goes on to the present day. A substantial body of classic Jewish writings treats of ethical issues, and a not inconsiderable and growing contemporary literature seeks to apply them to our time.[4]

From this point on, the characterization of contemporary Jewish social ethics confronts two difficulties. The first of these it shares indistinguishably with the field of Christian ethics. The move from ethical ideal to specific injunction increases the pluralism of opinion among learned, thoughtful, faithful students of these matters. The classic differences over how idealistic we ought to try to be at this moment or how little we should settle for, human nature being so refractory, are exponentially multiplied today by the irremediable ambiguities created by the technical complexity of many social issues. How does one discover which economic theory provides the most reliable foundation for a program to lessen poverty, or which perception of military realities explains what hardware we require, or worse, how to combine the two of them in a time of stagflation?

More troubling than specifying content, I believe, is the challenge arising from those people who loyally come to the synagogue or church and consider social ethics in its broad sense peripheral if not irrelevant to their central spiritual concerns. This problem takes on special form today in the Jewish community but one which reflects the present situation of all biblical religions in America. I think I can best be of help in clarifying the central issue of biblical social ethics as well as in making plain the unique contours of contemporary Jewish religious thought by dealing with the metaethical rather than the material level of our question. I propose to expound and respond to the arguments of those who question why pious Jews in our time ought to have a major commitment to transforming society.

Like all our other visible, voluble pietistic movements, the American Jewish social quietists gain their strength largely in reaction to the liberal, activist interpretation of the Jewish social ethic which dominated our community for the first twenty years following World War II. One must keep in mind that our secularization had started earlier and proceeded more effectively than that of American Christians due to our heavy urbanization, our commitment to higher education, and our identification of the secular as the realm where we would meet less prejudice.[5] Liberalism had become the essence of Judaism for much of our community in a movement far more intense than the parallel Christian activity. Indeed, by the late 1960s, when this identification of Jewish social ethics with activist, liberal politics peaked, there had been over a century of unprecedented Jewish involvement in every cause for human betterment in which Jews had been permitted to participate. Surely this must be ranked among the proudest achievements of Jewish history. Not only did Jews devote themselves to the general welfare in strikingly large numbers, disproportionately so, and give creative leadership in almost every field they entered, they did so without long-established models to emulate but in spontaneous, enthusiastic response to their emancipation from centuries of a degraded social status.[6]

The rejection of Jewish social ethics as equivalent to liberal political activity has been gathering power for over a decade. It substantially derives from the universal American shift to the right.[7] With the American economy stagnating or in decline, the rising expectations of many once-quiescent groups in our society can no longer be met. Fierce competition for limited means has become common, and self-interest has increasingly replaced the common welfare as an immediate political concern. In this atmosphere, ethnics have turned to their roots rather than to the American future to find a sense of security, and old social coalitions have broken down as the groups seek greater gains for themselves. They have also lost their program of change. Increasingly people feel that liberalism did not and cannot resolve our social problems. Rather it created a host of new ones in the name of social improvement. To some extent this mood draws on the historic prejudices of Americans against various minority groups, for they are vulnerable and subject to attack in ways that were unthinkable a decade or so ago. Less debatably, the concern with the self and its satisfactions has for a growing number of people been understood in more isolated and less social a fashion than previously, the notorious narcissism of our times.

The American Jewish community reflects all these currents but does so in forms refracted by Jewish ethnic experience and values. Consider the issue of social class. Political liberalism had appealed to a community of acculturating immigrants who were poor in means, experience, and even opportunity but rich in hope. The overwhelming portion of the native-born, unretired American Jewish community is now solidly middle-class, and perhaps more of it is upper-class than any other religio-ethnic group. It may have had to make its way through a relatively unfair and discriminatory system, but its present status and privileges depend on the continuing functioning of that system. Today, by sharp contrast to fifty years ago,

American Jewry has a stake in not greatly altering this country's socio-economic structure.[8]

Moreover, a small but significant community role is now played by a relatively recent group of Jewish immigrants, those who arrived as refugees during the Hitler period or, more importantly, since then. A large proportion of this group had not previously come to the United States for religious reasons. The country was synonymous with assimilation and nonobservance. In many cases, too, their form of Orthodoxy required limited participation in general society. Having survived the Holocaust and determined to continue their Jewish lives, they have little desire to learn from or accommodate to gentile ways. Their attacks on English-speaking, beardless, university-attending, American-oriented Orthodox Jews has mitigated much of the social concern visible among what, in the 1960s, came to be called "modern Orthodoxy."[9] Their presence and Jewish militance have posed a special challenge to what remains of the old, outer-directed American Jewish communal leadership. It had already been discredited by the heavy burden of guilt which historical reconsideration had fixed upon it for failing European Jewry during the Hitler years. American Jews had been so concerned to be part of the American war effort that they would not break ranks and press the special claims of the Jews the Nazis were murdering en masse. Worse, research disclosed that the liberal leaders the Jews had adulated had not cared enough for the Jewish victims to give such help as might have been possible, for example, bombing the death camps.

These special Jewish factors intensified the effect of the new general American ethnic assertiveness. As a result, many voices in the Jewish community began to oppose the dogmatic liberal identification of Jewish interests with those of all other American minorities.[10] The liberal political agenda, they charged, takes no account of the special needs of the Jews as a religio-ethnic group and ignores the unparalleled heritage of Western anti-semitism that still functions against this people. To hope governmental social and economic programs will create a society of such widespread contentment as to vitiate the old Jew-hatred is as naive as was the Jewish Communist dream that the proletarian state would eliminate anti-semitism. To the contrary, liberal-sponsored programs like busing, affirmative action, and opposition to government aid to Jewish all-day schools directly lessen the chances of American Jews building a strong Jewish community life in the future.

The emerging Jewish right, as it has gained the economic strength and political sophistication to express its will—again paralleling Christian phenomena—has pressed a strong polemic against the Jewish authenticity of the Jewish liberals. By identifying Judaism with general ethics, they legitimated assimilation. Those who wanted to escape their Jewish identity could claim that by helping humankind they were, in fact, being good Jews. Generally they could be counted on to fight for the rights of every people except their own. Thus on the university campus, they impeded or fought the introduction of courses in Jewish studies. Consistent with their devotion to humanity, the liberals' Jewish religious practice tended to be minimal and their knowledge of Judaism superficial. Even the articles written by those who sought to show the harmony of Judaism and universal ethics are little more than a few biblical verses or rabbinic apothegms, often snatched from their context, utilized to Judaize a Western intellectual position. A Judaism which has no discipline and demands no sacrifice is unworthy of being called a religion. How then could such people speak authentically in Judaism's name and hope to apply its values to the problems of society as a whole?

Rather than pretentiously assert a Jewish mission to all humankind, Jewry should devote itself to what its millennial history best suits it for, sanctifying the lives of individuals and families. If Jews were properly observant, they would also be decent citizens. Devoting themselves mainly to the preservation and enhancement of their community, they could not help also being a positive force in society and making a major contribution to its welfare. Besides, in this time of social peril, Jews need to base their lives on the primary lesson of the Holocaust: in a crisis, no one else can be counted on to help Jews but other Jews. We are historically mandated and ethically entitled to make concern with our people's welfare the sovereign content of our social ethic.

This account of the ideology of the new Jewish right has thus far omitted one major factor which, in quite complicated ways, makes its appeal quite compelling, that is, the deep American Jewish concern for the State of Israel. No other Jewish cause remotely comes close to motivating American Jewry as does the survival of the Israeli state. It represents our people's primal, life-affirming response to the Holocaust and, in the face of excruciatingly difficult political pressures, exemplifies in its democratic, social-welfare orientation the age-old social values of Judaism. As the State of Israel perceives its needs, or better, as American Jewish leaders, eager not to repeat the failures of the Holocaust, understand their need to lobby for Israeli causes, the agenda of American political liberalism—domestic welfare—is soft and unrealistic. The major problems of our day are, rather, international. Hence America needs to become staunchly anti-Soviet and thus militarily unimpeachable.[11]

The reeducation of American Jewish leadership in this regard may well be dated to 1967. Lyndon Johnson informed a group summoned to the White House that if the State of Israel was to get the jet planes it desired, American Jews would have to stop backing the protests against the Vietnam War. Similarly, the lesson of the critical dependence of the Israeli army on the American arsenal for resupply in the decisive early days of the 1973 war was not lost on many American Jews. If the State of Israel is to survive, America must be militarily strong—and it would help if the Pentagon saw the American Jewish community as its backers.

From those days to the present, the rhetoric and formal organizational stands of most American Jewish organizations have shifted rightward; that is, general human concerns have essentially been displaced by ethnic and Israeli ones. This move has been justified by the ideology that Jewish concerns are the proper, authentic focus of a Jewish social ethic. It must be noted, however, that all this has not yet produced a clear-cut, major statistical reorientation in Jewish voting patterns, if the presidential elections of 1980 and 1984 have been rightly assessed.[12] The old liberal ethics of most American Jews has, in any case, surely lost its old elan and weakened to the point where it may well soon become empty. Historically, it is far too early to say what is likely to happen or when, and events in this century have been so unpredictable that speculation is most unwise.

Intellectually, the issue before Jews as individuals and as a community may be put this way: should the social ethic of contemporary Judaism as it concerns general society be achieved indirectly, as a side effect of particular Jewish observance, or should it be another major, direct, active concern of faithful Jews, comparable in some measure to their devotion to the Jewish community in its service of God?

I respond to this question speaking officially for myself alone, but articulating a position which I suggest many American Jews roughly share socially, though not perhaps theologically.

We too are deeply concerned about Jewish authenticity and therefore have no wish to gloss over the failings of doctrinaire Jewish liberalism. Any Jewish ethic worthy of that name cannot be purely universalistic, so concerned with humanity it has no interest in the Jewish people. Jews loyal to the Covenant with God must necessarily accept the responsibilities it places upon them to build their specific community and through it bring humankind to its messianic goal.

With all that, a word is in order in defense of a previous generation of Jewish universalists. They may have allowed their enthusiasm at the emancipation of the Jews to carry them too far in jettisoning Judaism's protective particularity. They should also have had a more realistic view of human nature and social change. For all that, their radicalism accomplished much for their less adventuresome fellow-Jews. They articulated the ethic by which Jews still participate in general society, developed a style for Jewish involvement in general causes, accomplished much to improve human welfare, and served as living proof that one can be a proud Jew and thoroughly involved in the great social issues of our time. The challenge of their stance still cannot be ignored: will we long remain a vital community if in our democratic situation we try to reinstitute a ghetto orientation to Judaism?

By this brief digression I wish most emphatically to deny that the faults of Jewish liberalism totally invalidate its substance. The choice before us is not the either/or of a tarnished liberalism versus a refurbished, modernized traditionalism. Modern Orthodoxy and right-wing Conservatism, both strongly linked with the move to right-of-center or rightist political stands, would not exist had they not adopted much of the pioneering liberals' ideology. Right-wing Orthodoxy, as indicated by its fanatic, antipluralistic acts in the United States and the State of Israel, is too self-centered for most of us to accept it as an authentic Judaism for modern Jews. An excessive universalism need not be replaced by a particularism so overwhelming it has little direct interest in the pressing concerns of humankind. There are many Jews who counsel that we withdraw from the social arena except where Jewish interests are at stake or our allies in achieving them require our help. The older liberals have convinced many of us that Jews, having been welcomed as equals in society, should now understand that our faith demands of us that we share in seeking to meet the problems all human beings now confront even as we give special attention to the specific needs of our own people.

Our ethical choice hinges largely on our interpretation of our recent history. What does our experience of Emancipation from the ghetto mean to us? Ought it to bring us to introduce a major change in the traditional Jewish social ethic, making it more universally oriented and activist in seeking to attain its newly inclusive goals, or, in limited response to our new freedom, ought it to cause us only to extend when necessary our classic inner-oriented social ethic? On theological as well as practical grounds, I believe the Emancipation should influence our understanding of Judaism as profoundly as it now seems to us the destruction of the Second Temple did when it ushered in the era of rabbinic Judaism. Further, as I shall explain in due course, I do not consider the Holocaust to have invalidated the universal imperative of the Emancipation but, if anything, further to have reinforced it.

Let me begin my response on the practical level. The Jewish people, through its major centers in the State of Israel, the United States, and other free countries, has indissolubly linked its destiny with the other free peoples. Should there be a major energy crisis, an economic collapse, radical atmospheric pollution, a global failure of democracy, an atomic war, the Jews will not escape unscathed. I cannot respond to such threats as easily as Jews of the ghetto era would have done by saying, as some Jews still do today, "What has all that to do with us? The people of Israel is eternal. God will guard us." Most of us live too intimately as part of Western society not to be deeply affected by its failures and successes, and all but the most self-isolated of our Hasidim would suffer significant spiritual dislocation if they could no longer live as free, emancipated Jews.

If so, we have a simple ethical responsibility to help those among whom we live shape our mutual destiny. Jews of other centuries were not allowed to share in the determination of their society's policies. We, having both the situation and the incentive, have become socially involved in ways unknown to other Jewries, and rightly so. Any retreat from this activist stance ought to be fought as inappropriate to our radically altered sociopolitical situation.

That argument can legitimately be extended. Having gained exceptionally from our freedom, as the result of great industry and application, to be sure, Jews have a special responsibility to give of their gains to society. To make a contribution only to the extent others do would seem too little on several counts. Most people do not give very much of themselves for the sake of society, one reason conditions are as bad as they are today. Many others, having benefited modestly from our social order, have neither the means, the energy, nor the know-how to do very much for anyone but themselves. It seems only morally right that those who have had greater success should give a greater proportion of their strength and their means to help those less fortunate. Then the Jews, who have fared spectacularly well in the United States, have a simple ethical responsibility to work for the common good in special devotion. And the long heritage of Jewish social concern should spur Jews on to bolster a society which makes it an important part of its life to promote the welfare of its indigent, handicapped, and otherwise deprived citizens.

On a more spiritual level, I want to argue that two of the great experiences of Diaspora Jewry in our time mandate a strong commitment to a universal ethic. In the first case, the Holocaust, I partially agree with the Jewish right. Jews ought to continue their exemplary response to the death of the 6,000,000 and the threat to all of us by vigorously upbuilding and furthering Jewish life today. I differ with those Jews who argue that the cruelty of the Nazis, the indifference of the "good Germans," and the callousness of the Allies' leaders demonstrate that Jews have no genuine share in Western society. We have been the classic outsider for millennia, they say, and despite surface changes we remain the great available victim.

I readily concede that Jews ought not to underestimate the continuing virulence of anti-semitism or overestimate the changes wrought by some decades of democracy, goodwill, and ecumenism. But if we deny that a common standard of goodness applies between all human beings, strongly enough to command them to override their group concerns so as to respect the humanity of those their folk considers aliens, how can we fault the Germans for their bestial ethnocentrism? If there is no universal ethics which one should follow even under extraordinary social pressure, how can we condemn the Nazis and those who quietly went along with them? And if out of the bitterness of our suffering we insist upon the paramount importance of such interhuman responsibility, then how can we not exemplify it in our own lives? Instead of responding to the utter negativity of the Holocaust by confining our social concern largely to ourselves, thereby validating group moralities, we ought to demonstrate its evil by our own active concern for people far removed from our immediate situation.

I cannot leave the argument there. I do not see that we can insist today that the promise of the Emancipation finally be fulfilled by the Western world if we do not ourselves resolutely affirm and live by universal ethical standards. We may claim rights among humankind because all people are part of one human family and ought to live in equal status, though that requires them to overcome millennial prejudices in which, as individuals and as classes, they have many vested interests. And, again, if we demand that others ought to effectuate that ideal, so should we who proclaim it, presumably because it is true and not merely because it now benefits us.

To me the Emancipation, for all its equivocation and unrealized promises, is a religious experience reminiscent in its own lesser way of the great revelatory exodus of our people from Egypt. Recent generations of Jews also passed from a long, painful "slavery" to a new freedom, and that passage should become a new motive for Jewish social behavior even as the ancient redemption motivated our people's social legislation—"you know the heart of the stranger, for you were strangers in the land of Egypt." Particularly as we begin to move personally away from that transition, we need to memorialize the experience of our release from the ghetto, *shtetl*, and *mellah* so that it can shape our social consciousness. Few people in our society know intimately what it means to suffer for centuries as pariahs and then come to positions of power and influence. Our own family histories teach us that a society is judged best by the way it treats its most powerless people, those the Bible once identified as the widow, the stranger, and the orphan. Today, Jews are in a unique position to identify with and help do something for such sufferers. We ought to accept that as our modern Jewish duty in order to be true to what we ourselves have endured and what we know we share with all other human beings.

In responding to the Holocaust and our Emancipation by dedication to action for the redemption of all humanity, I believe we can set a proper model of human behavior before all creatures. That is a far cry from the old liberal notion of the mission of Israel to all humankind, but in our contemporary confused and troubled human situation, it is hardly less an exaltation of the people of Israel's potential historic role. And its high estimation of the Jewish people comes from no assertion of Jewish spiritual superiority or expectations of what we shall actually accomplish, but only of what may result when we respond in Covenant faithfulness to what has happened to us.

Two pragmatic considerations seem to me to prompt the Jewish community to take an activist stance in social-ethical matters. The first is a reiteration of the classic modernist perception of the best long-range strategy for securing Jewish security, that Jews will fare better in a society more adequately meeting the needs of its citizens. If so, for their own sake, Jews ought to be involved in trying to overcome the major problems of the society. In doing so, they should be particularly concerned about the rights of underprivileged groups, for their treatment mirrors what may next happen to the Jews.

None of the recent traumas of Jewish history has changed the truth of these assertions. True, there are no guarantees of Jewish security; and Jews cannot do very much to change society or decisively alter its established patterns of inequity; and these social tasks do not nearly conduce to Jewish survival as much as will direct involvement in traditional Jewish responsibilities. Differently put, an outer-oriented Jewish social ethics ought not to take on the messianic dimensions for us that it did for a previous generation. Our hard-learned realism may temper our immediate expectations. It constitutes no reason to deny what our ideals and our enlightened self-interest motivate us to do with our lives.

I should like to suggest a second practical reason for not confining our energies largely to our own community. When we need political allies to help us fight for our cause should some Jewish interest be at stake, we shall be unlikely to find them or to find them receptive if we have not been available when they were carrying on their own struggle for greater social justice. Being a tiny minority in America—perhaps 5,800,000 in a population of over 220,000,000—we must depend on the goodwill of others in order to sway the democratic process. Our potential allies need to be able to count on us for regular aid. Better yet, we may best expect to gain the support we seek when the people we desire it from already stand in our debt for our having long been at their side in their fights.

We cannot, however, any longer assert unequivocally that the liberal rather than the conservative political program is necessarily the better or the more ethical way of achieving Judaism's vision of the good society. The old, dogmatic equation of Jewish ethics with political liberalism no longer is convincing. The transfer of religious ideals to concrete social plans always involves highly complex and contingent considerations. No point of view may reasonably claim that it invariably has the whole truth on such matters. Liberalism can assert a special affinity to biblical ethics because of its concern with benefiting the masses directly and its insistence on taking immediate social action to do so. Nonetheless, its recent record of ambiguous results has vitiated much of its theoretical promise and made it necessary to ask whether in any given instance the conservative option may not better effectuate our ethical goals. As with so much of our life, a revitalized Jewish social ethic must make room for a vigorous pluralism, in this case of political judgment, and out of a thoughtful dialectic over appropriate means, speak to the inquiring Jew.

In one fundamental respect, however, the liberal position seems to me to have special validity to anyone who takes the modern Jewish experience seriously. The Emancipation of the Jews did not come about by benignly waiting for internal developments, market forces, the private sector, or personal growth to grant Jews rights. It came by government initiative. Only in countries where governments acted and formally granted Jews equality and then demanded, if slowly, that their often unwilling citizenries live up to that grant, did Jews truly enter society. Unless Jews are prepared to deny the experience of their own families and ethnic group, they must emphatically reject the notion that government has no proper role in the moral improvement of the social order. Without resolute government leadership in furthering the goals of democracy—in America so closely linked to those of the Bible—the ethical dimensions of our social life may be counted on to contract. Human nature and social interaction being what they are, exploitation, injustice, and what the rabbis poignantly call "free hatred" will slowly but certainly strengthen their hold on our lives. Conservatives, who claim to be realists about human beings, ought to see that as clearly as they see the corruption of good government by those who must operate it. Whenever we are sensitive to the distance we still remain from our social ideals, we must ask what we can all do together, through government, the one "community" through which we all can act as one, to achieve them. And that is not to say that governmental action is always indicated because we consider it the only, the infallible, or the ultimate source of social transformation.

But for me and some other Jews, the most compelling reason for an activist Jewish social ethic is theological. The Emancipation has simply changed our view of what God wants of Jews in relation to all humankind. Or more precisely put, the changed horizon of effective Jewish social ethics exposed by the new scope given Jews for their lives has helped us realize that until recently Jews were only partially able to envisage and effectuate their duty to God. Having gained a broader vision of humankind, Jews like me can no longer delimit what we intuit God wants of us as overwhelmingly, if not exclusively, consisting of acts oriented to our own community.

The classic biblical and rabbinic chasm between Jews and gentiles does not yawn as deeply between us and our neighbors, and many bridges connect us with one another. We all stand before the same God. To be sure, we still find continuing merit, some would say cosmic significance, in sustaining our side of our people's distinctive Covenant with God. At the same time, we have come in ever more intimate ways to recognize our common humanity with gentiles. In very many ways, particularly in many moral and spiritual aspirations and not merely in our joint human needs, we are very much like one another. Working with one another, studying together, cooperating in various community projects, we cannot easily ignore how precious all humankind is to our God and therefore needs to be to us. And our personal postghetto perspective, so radically extended by our education outside of classic Jewish texts and now regularly stretched by the wonders of electronic communication and jet travel, keeps expanding. We can envisage a day when we consider the entire globe our neighborhood and everyone in it the neighbor we are called upon to love even as we love ourselves.

For us, proclaiming God is One must freshly mean appreciating and living out God's active care and concern for all human beings. Acting on that faith, we must devote ourselves in considerable measure to working with all people and not just with other Jews to make the sovereignty of God real on earth.

To this extent the Emancipation has been revelatory; it has given us a more extensive intuition of what God expects of us by having set us in these radically changed social circumstances. For all our disappointments and suffering in these near two centuries of freedom, Jews such as me still believe in the promise of the new, inclusive social order into which we have come and now comprise so integral a part. Authentically living by our people's Covenant with God in this time and place necessarily yields a conception of Jewish duty expanded from that which evolved in the previous fifteen hundred years of isolation, segregation, and persecution. And that has led some Jews to an activist Jewish social ethic which we believe our community as a whole will ignore or forget only at the cost of its great spiritual peril.

Notes

1. Gen. 2:18.

2. Gen. 11:1–9.

3. Note the command as well as the promise in Gen. 12:1–3, the first mention of the Covenant relation and its entailments.

4. See the most helpful article by Sid Z. Leiman, "Jewish Ethics 1970–75: Retrospect and Prospect," *Religious Studies Review*, 2, no. 2 (April, 1976):16–22. It not only provides a listing of all the relevant writings for those years, but includes translations and other materials dealing with the history of Jewish ethics. I know of nothing comparable for the years since. Leiman's qualifications notwithstanding, I suggest that Sh'ma: A Journal of Jewish Responsibility remains the best way of remaining in touch with the scope and variety of contemporary Jewish ethical concerns, though I am not a disinterested observer.

5. So already my "The Postsecular Situation of Jewish Theology," *Theological Studies*, 31, no. 3 (September, 1970):460–475.

6. Dawidowicz and Goldstein, "The American Jewish Liberal Tradition," in *The American Jewish Community*, ed. Marshall Sklare (New York: Behrman, 1974), and see the bibliography there on "The Politics of American Jewry," pp. 372 f. Also Eugene B. Borowitz, *The Mask Jews Wear* (New York: Simon & Schuster, 1973), chaps. 2–4.

7. Much of what follows is speculative, but it is not uninformed or essentially ideological pleading. In general, minorities reflect majority trends; Jews, still quite eager to belong and not be thought too different, reflect majority currents faithfully if in idiosyncratic ways. Indeed, they are so sensitive to certain winds of social change that they often serve as a good indicator of the new directions most Americans will one day take, e.g., the almost universal adoption of contraception among modernized Jews in the 1920s.

8. Milton Himmelfarb, an astute observer of the American Jewish community and an early, trenchant critic of its unreflective liberalism (*The Jews of Modernity* [New York: Basic Books, 1973]), denies that a class shift is responsible for any Jewish voting change. Jews in poor, not well-to-do precincts are more likely to vote Republican. See his "Are Jews Becoming Republican," *Commentary* 72, no. 2 (August, 1981): 27–31 and Lucy Dawidowicz, "Politics, the Jews, and the '84 Election," *Commentary* 79, no. 2 (February, 1985):25–30.

9. Because this sector of the community is inner-directed, where it publishes, it tends to do so in a Jewish language, Yiddish (sic), but not modern Hebrew. Being wary of the gentile world, it confines the full strength of its views to oral communication. Some sense of these subterranean attitudes may be gained from perusing the issues of the weekly English newspaper, the *Jewish Press*. A more accommodationist but still militantly rightist stance is taken by the *Jewish Observer*, the slick monthly publication of Agudath Israel, the somewhat non-Zionist Orthodox international religious organization.

10. For an early statement of a thoughtful revisionism, see Charles S. Liebman, *The Ambivalent American Jew* (Philadelphia: Jewish Publication Society, 1973), chaps. 7 and 8. In reading Jakob Petuchowski's "The Limits of Self-Sacrifice" (in *Modern Jewish Ethics* [Columbus: Ohio State University Press, 1975]), one should bear in mind that "self-sacrifice" means the liberal suggestion that Jews put devotion to the general welfare ahead of certain specific Jewish interests.

11. For a more detailed statement of the argument concerning the State of Israel plus a deeper analysis of those points on which I argue that the old liberalism needs to be modified, see my "Rethinking the Reform Jewish Attitude to Social Action," *Journal of Reform Judaism* 27, no. 4 (Fall 1980):1–19.

12. See the data and attitudes of the articles cited in note 8.

24

Hillul Hashem

A Universal Rubric in the Halakhah

The need to rethink the theory of modern Jewish ethics arises from the loss of the meaning the liberals assigned to the words "Jewish" and "ethics." For Hermann Cohen and the many who utilized his ideas, the neo-Kantian definition of ethics determined the meaning of the word "Jewish." Today, the several competing versions of philosophic ethics all operate under a cloud of uncertainty, as Alasdair MacIntyre's widely discussed *After Virtue* (Notre Dame: University of Notre Dame Press, 1981) makes plain. Thus, one mode of reestablishing a compelling theory of Jewish ethics involves studying contemporary options in ethics and applying the most appealing of these to Judaism.

An alternate path explores the independent meaning the term *Jewish* should have in such a theory. Self-respect demands that it be given at least equal weight with Hellenic or Germanic philosophy, specifically, that they not be allowed to dictate what Judaism properly understands to be "the good and the right." From this perspective, mediation between Judaism and ethics begins from the Jewish side and does so in terms of authoritative Jewish teaching, namely, with concern for the *halakhah*.

Orthodox and postliberal Jews can easily share this approach to Jewish ethics though they are likely, in due course, to come to different conclusions about contemporary Jewish responsibility.[1] In doing so they must face the continuing difficulty generated by this procedure: how to recon-

Originally published as "*Hillul Hashem*: A Universalistic Rubric in Halakhic Ethics" in *The Life of Covenant*, ed. Joseph Edelheit (Chicago: Spertus College, 1986).

cile a particular people's legal system with the sense of goodness available to all human beings.

This study arises as a continuation of my interest in this approach evidenced recently by a response to Aharon Lichtenstein's much-discussed paper, "Does Jewish Tradition Recognize an Ethic Independent of *Halakha?*"[2] There I pointed to the ambiguous and subordinate status of the "ethical moment" in *halakhah*, thus impugning the commanding power of Jewish ethics. Here I propose to study a specific halakhic provision which illumines Jewish law's relation to universal human moral judgment, namely the category *hillul hashem*, insofar as it shapes Jewish duty in terms of gentile opinion.

An inner theological dialectic lies behind the legal tension to be explored. God has given the Torah to one particular people, the Jews, and its rules distinguish between those who do and those who do not participate in the system. The same Torah indicates that God stands in a similar relationship, if a legally less demanding one, with all humankind, the children of Noah. Hence they may be said to have a legitimate basis for judging Jewish conduct.[3] The potential tension between what the Torah permits to Jews and a harsh evaluation gentiles might make of it creates the subset of the laws of *hillul hashem* to be studied. (On its meaning, see below.)

While the term *hillul hashem* does not occur in the Bible, its equivalents are found in several biblical books, with heavy concentrations in Leviticus and Ezekiel. The *peshat*, simple meaning, of these texts may be classified as moving from concrete acts of profanation, to those which directly or indirectly cast aspersions on God, and finally to an abstract sense of *hillul hashem*.

Since the book of Leviticus pays considerable attention to cultic acts which sanctify God—to the extent that various items can be called God's "holy things"—so, by extension, mishandling them profanes God. (Thus Lev. 21:6, 22:2, 32; Mal. 1:12; and perhaps Ez. 20:39.) Idolatry—specifically, sacrificing one's child to Moloch—is a desecration (Lev. 18:21, 20:13). Ezekiel accuses certain women prophets of equivalent sacrilege (Ez. 13:19). The theme also encompasses noncultic violations, of which swearing falsely by God's name is a similarly direct profanation (Lev. 19:12). And it includes unethical acts like a father and son having sexual relations with the same girl (Am. 2:7) and the Jerusalemites reneging on their solemn pact to free their Jewish slaves (Jer. 34:16). Ezekiel envisages this notion abstractly and four times, in consecutive verses, proclaims God's determination to sanctify the Divine name which the people of Israel has profaned through its sinfulness (Ez. 36:20–23).

The social dimension of several of these acts of profanation deserves particular attention. The heinousness of the sacrilege derives as much from what the act says about God to others, a public, as from its intrinsic profanity. The biblical authors consider God's social, corporate acknowledgment even more important than the equally indispensable private faith of individuals. The political term, king, so often used to refer to God, testifies to this social understanding of God's reality. Hence acts which imply that there is no God or which as good as do the same by testifying falsely to God's nature or commands, profane God's "name," that is, our understanding of God or, equally, God's reputation. Much of rabbinic teaching in this area derives from this social context.

A direct line runs from the Bible to the Talmud's teachings about *hillul hashem*.[4] Thus, since Jews are enjoined to sanctify God's name by martyrdom rather than commit murder, idolatry, or sexual offenses, failing to give up one's life then profanes God's name. So does rebelliously transgressing commands of the Torah. This identification of God with God's commands results in a significant rabbinic expansion of this theme, namely, that "important people," scholars being the chief case, must live by a higher standard than ordinary folk. People take rabbis and other such dignitaries as models for proper behavior. They therefore ought to avoid acts which the Torah otherwise permits but which, done by them, might lead to a lowering of communal standards and, in turn, to lesser sanctity in God's people, thus profaning its God.

A motif of particular importance for this investigation emerges from this preliminary survey. The concept of *hillul hashem* has extraordinary power.[5] When properly invoked, it can, so to speak, change the contours of Jewish duty. It does so by overriding a previous permission granted by the Torah and negating it, thus determining duty anew.

The *halakhah* contains such a possibility because its piety emphasizes the corporate dimension. Here the individual's "prior" options are limited to enhance the community's religious life and to safeguard it from sin. (With the Bible, the rabbis consider leading others to sin a qualitatively worse level of iniquity than is private transgression.) While the rabbis occasionally refer to the possibility of *hillul hashem* in private (*betzinah* or *beseter*)—of which the most notorious example is the advice to one overcome by lust to satisfy himself where he is not known—their overwhelming attention is given to acts in public (*befarhesiya* or *berabim*).[6]

Recognizing the cosmic importance the rabbis attached to the Jewish community and its practice of the Torah, the imperative, internal, social quality of *hillul hashem* seems quite logical. But considering the general corporate (as against individual) denigration of the gentiles, the *umot haolam* or *goyim*—who are usually identified as "wicked," and thus deserving of God's judgment—it comes as something of a surprise to discover that the same process operates in relation to them. The rabbis prohibit certain acts to Jews, not because the Torah proscribes them, but because of what doing them might lead gentiles to think or say.[7] In such cases, potential gentile opinion leads to a change in the "prior" contours of Jewish duty: hyperbolically, in some cases the gentiles "make" Torah.

In itself, this concern for the religious judgment of idolators is worthy of note. It testifies to the universalism implicit in *halakhah*. Of even greater interest, these prohibitions take precedence over Jewish economic loss, which the rabbis normally avoid in keeping with their principle, *hatorah hasah al memonam shel yisrael,* "the Torah has compassion on the funds of Jews." This unusual aspect of *halakhah,* with its intriguing parallels to recent ethical thinking about the universalizability of ethical judgment, deserves investigation.

Before proceeding, an important disclaimer must be made. In each instance to be studied, the majority of sages say Jewish law directly prohibits the act involved. They then rule that it carries a double opprobrium because it also constitutes *hillul hashem.* Here we are interested in the well attested if minority usage of *hillul hashem* which some sages invoke to prohibit Jewish acts toward gentiles which they otherwise consider permissible. (It would also be of great interest if historians of the *halakhah* could elucidate the socio-temporal circumstances to which the rabbis may have been responding in these rulings.)

We may group the sixteen specific applications of *hillul hashem* we are studying into three categories: (1) the prohibition of acts directly disparaging God's honor or doing so by dishonoring the Jewish people; (2) the prohibition of possible stealing from gentiles whether direct or indirect; and (3) the prohibition of acts, national or individual, that might be perceived as deception.

Three acts fall into the first category. Only one is explicitly described as a direct affront to God: taking law cases to a gentile court.[8] This might be seen as testimony to the superiority of the gentiles' god or, with homiletic license, as indicating the denial of the God of Israel.[9] The other two cases dishonor the Jewish community: publicly taking charity from gentiles[10] and permitting gentile contractors to work for Jews on the Sabbath when it is clear that they are working for Jews and gentiles do not permit work on their own Sabbath.[11]

The remaining cases, the overwhelming majority, concern thievery and deception. For *halakhah,* then, gentiles become a decisive factor in shaping the law mainly in ethical matters. The editors of the *Talmudic Encyclopedia* consider the most embracing category of this theme *gezel hagoy,* "the robbery of gentiles." They not only treat it as the leading instance of the invocation of *hillul hashem* relative to gentiles[12] but they devote a substantial independent article to the topic.[13]

The problem is most easily confronted via a Tanaitic tradition cited in Y. B. K. 4.3. Two Romans, sent to learn all about Judaism, commented after having studied it that they admired Jewish law save for the provision that Jews are permitted to rob gentiles (perhaps, more narrowly, that Jews may keep what has been stolen from gentiles).[14.] Thereupon Rabban Gamaliel prohibited the robbery of gentiles because it involved *hillul hashem.* Here not only do we have gentile opinion shaping Jewish duty (to the economic loss of Jews) but an indication that the permission once operated and the prohibition was instituted later. In any event, Jewish law proscribes the robbery of gentiles, whether because intrinsically forbidden by the Torah and doubly abominable as *hillul hashem*, or, according to some authorities, forbidden only under the latter rubric.

That would seem to settle the matter. Yet the robbery of gentiles arises in other specific matters which, for the sake of greater specificity, I consider below under the rubric of potential deception. A further set of problems arises probably because human cupidity is strong and Jews have been steadily persecuted. Thus, some authorities acknowledge that acts considered the robbery of gentiles might not become known, thus removing them from the prohibition of *hillul hashem*. But this means permitting such acts according to those sages who do not consider them intrinsically prohibited.[15]

Two prohibitions may be said to have been instituted to avoid even a gentile perception of Jewish theft. In the first instance, though Jews in the home of a Jewish owner may eat of that with which they are working, that practice is forbidden when the owner is gentile. He might conclude that Jewish laborers steal from their bosses.[16] In the second instance, a synagogue menorah which is the gift of a gentile may not be exchanged for anything else, even to perform a commandment, though that is possible for one donated by a Jew. And the sages explicitly note that invocation of *hillul hashem* is to prevent the gentile complaining about Jews appropriating his gift.[17]

Five cases, most of which traditionally are connected to the notion of *gezel hagoy*, seem to me better considered as forms of interpersonal deception. Thus, one may not lie to a gentile[18] or mislead him in negotiating to buy his slave.[19] A particularly intricate case involves *hafkaat halvaato*, the abrogation of a gentile's loan. In the original case, the loan was made by one gentile to another who then became the lender's slave until the loan was paid off. A Jew who purchases that slave should normally pay off the loan, but some authorities say Jews are not obligated to repay loans to gentiles.[20] Thus, Rashi, commenting on the talmudic text, says that this is not really *gezel hagoy*, only the refusal to give him back his money.[21] Sages following this legal line allow for keeping gentile money but consider this form of doing so less troubling a matter than outright *gezel hagoy*.

Hafkaat halvaato also arises analogously to other cases, described below (and, as we shall see, remains a living consideration for contemporary halakhic practice). The editors of the *Talmudic Encyclopedia* seem sensitive to the ethical problems involved in this issue. They therefore conspicuously feature an opinion that restricts this option, namely that of the Meiri, perhaps the leading traditional liberalizer of Jewish law regarding gentiles. In sum, once again the sages divide between those who hold *hafkaat halvaato* intrinsically forbidden and also a *hillul hashem*, and those who proscribe it only when it leads to a profanation of God's name.[22]

Two other forms of interpersonal deception are forbidden because of possible detrimental gentile opinion. One involves making a private condition when swearing an oath to a gentile under coercion, thus rendering it invalid.[23] The other concerns taking advantage of an error made by a gentile in the course of a negotiation.[24]

The five remaining cases seem more social in focus and if not prohibited might lead gentiles to consider Jews untrustworthy. A Jew may not oppress a gentile,[25] or keep something he has lost,[26] or deny him the testimony he seeks, even if this involves a loss to another Jew,[27] whenever such an act might lead to a profanation of God's name.

Perhaps the most troublesome of these issues is the avoidance of taxes imposed by a gentile government. While it is clear that "the law of the [gentile] country has the force of [Torah] law," a body of opinion clearly holds that in certain cases avoidance is permitted—but not if it might involve *hillul hashem*.[28] Finally, as the case of the Gibeonites made clear to the rabbis, the Jewish people may not break a treaty it has made with another people, even if false pretenses are involved, should that act result in the disparagement of the Jews and thus the profanation of God's name.[29]

One can therefore say about these sixteen instances that the evidence abundantly demonstrates that in certain cases, mainly ethical ones, gentile opinion can be a decisive, overriding factor in determining, even altering, *halakhah*. It would be of the greatest interest to know what constitutes the necessary warrants for invoking *hillul hashem* in a given case and what limits there are to its uncommon power. Nothing in the literature studied touches directly on the theory of the utilization of *hillul hashem*. Indeed, we do not find it characteristic of any given sage and it seems, on the surface, to be used with as much randomness as consistency.

So much is classic *halakhah*. To see how this motif might be of help to us in clarifying the nature of Jewish ethics today, it will help to take a brief look at its contemporary employment. A search made by the Institute for Computers in Jewish Life through the responsa program of the Bar-Ilan Center for Computers and Jewish Studies provided the necessary data. It generated a list of sources in which the term *hillul hashem* appeared in close association with either *goy* or *akum* (literally, "idolator"; legally, "non-Jew"—though hardly a happy association). In the works of three eminent respondents of our time, Yechiel Weinberg *(Seridei Esh)*, Moshe Feinstein *(Igrot Moshe)*, and Eliezer Waldenberg *(Tzitz Eliezer)*, seventeen possible *teshuvot* dealing with our topic occurred.[30] Of these, only eight were relevant to this study, the others either could not be found, had no reference to this topic, or related only to *hillul shabbat*.

Yechiel Weinberg is best represented in this sample, as five of his *teshuvot* deal with *hillul hashem* in relation to gentiles. He uses the term *hillul hashem* in these texts only in the citation or summary of the traditional dicta. The case topics are: (1) martyrdom *(Seridei Esh*, vol. 2, no. 79); (2) teaching gentiles Torah, where he adduces the case of the Romans *(Seridei Esh*, vol. 2, no. 90); (3) selling a synagogue seat to satisfy a debt, where the sale of synagogue property is discussed *(Seridei Esh*, vol. 3, no. 63); and (4) the robbery of gentiles *(Seridei Esh*, nos. 74–75—in the latter, beware of the misprint at the top of page 254 which indicates that this is responsum no. 57 rather than no. 75).

Only two responsa of Moshe Feinstein are relevant to this study. Both involve the issue of *gezel hagoy* with one merely mentioning the classic opinions (*Igrot Moshe, Yoreh Deah*, vol. 1, no. 103). The other is somewhat more interesting since it seems to be the only instance of this concept being used in a fresh application as against the citation of classic precedent (*Igrot Moshe, Hoshen Mishpat*, vol. 1, no. 82). He suggests that the sages did not absolutely require the return of a gentile's lost article because while voluntarily doing so can lead to sanctifying God's name among gentiles, having to do so might, on occasion, lead to *hillul hashem*. It should be noted, however, that this unique example of a contemporary creative use of the concept of *hillul hashem* occurs in a theoretical discussion of the law of the rabbis living among idolators.

The one relevant *teshuvah* of Eliezer Waldenberg has special interest since the questioner proposes a new application of *hillul hashem*. Quite conscious of the concept's special power, he suggests that wearing his *tzitziyot* so that they are visible, rather than obscured by being under his other clothes, may lead gentiles to set inordinately high standards for his behavior (since most Jews are not this pious). This might lead to what he ingeniously calls *avak hillul hashem*, "a hint [literally, "the dust"] of a profanation of God's name" (*Tzitz [sic] Eliezer*, vol. 8 no. 3). Hence he inquires whether, since this does not involve either giving up the practice or altering it to avoid gentile mockery, he may wear his *tzitziyot* obscured. To which the answer is a firm negative, with the possibility of *avak hillul hashem* apparently of so little substance that Waldenberg never discusses it.

From this sample, limited in authorities and to the questions they have chosen to answer and publish, some tentative conclusions may be drawn. Apparently the major *poskim* of our time use the concept of *hillul hashem* only in the cases and contexts in which it came down to them. They do not seem to apply it to any new situations or in terms of any different perception of gentile opinion. Insofar as they are indicative of the broad sweep of contemporary *halakhah*, we may say that Jewish law internally recognizes that in certain instances, largely ethical, it should be governed authoritatively by gentile reactions to Jewish behavior or their perceptions thereof, if the sages, by standards and methods remaining obscure, deem such fresh legal determinations warranted.

At this point, liberal (and postliberal) Jews demur. For these authorities the Emancipation has changed nothing, and gentile opinions are still thought of as if there were no Jewish political equality amid functioning democracies. By the very grant of full civic status to Jews and the continuing effort to overcome the powerful vestiges of fifteen hundred years of legally established anti-semitism, gentiles and their ethical opinions are worthy of very much more consideration than they were in pre-Emancipation times. The appeal to Jews of the Kantian insistence on the universalization of ethics rests on this intellectual-social basis. Rabbinic Judaism understood that "a decent respect to the opinions of mankind" can mandate Torah law. The changed behavior of gentiles toward Jews, and the continuing realities of Jewish equality, demand greater concern with and respect for the ethical judgments of those who are not Jewish.

The liberal concern with ethics stems from this religious perception. The search by postliberal thinkers for a new understanding of Jewish ethics may involve rejecting the liberals' insistence that Jewish obligation be universalizable. However, the new particularism does not invalidate the essential truth that Jews today must sanctify God's name in significant part by attending to universal, that is to gentile as well as Jewish, moral opinion.

Recent Jewish suffering at gentile hands bolsters rather than refutes this affirmation about the significance of gentile understandings of ethics. True, the Holocaust ended Jewish liberals' messianic enthusiasm at gentile goodwill. And the continuing manifestations of anti-semitism must keep Jews wary, not only of our enemies but of our own wishful thinking. Such bitterly won realism does not constitute reason to deny that the Emancipation radically changed relations between Jews and gentiles. It raised universalism from a largely neglected human theoretical notion to an ideal which continues to exert powerful political pressure on much of humankind. If particularistic standards of ethical behavior are to be restored to supremacy, it will be difficult to argue that the German people had no right to do what it did; or, of equal significance today, that all humankind should have stood up to protest the barbaric German violation of fundamental human rights. More, if democracy cannot be trusted, not only is most of world Jewry unsafe but so is the State of Israel, whose survival depends on the continued health of free nations.

Let me illustrate the divergence of these two Jewish views of attention to gentile ethical judgments by showing how they affect or might affect one aspect of contemporary Jewish ethical responsibility, namely, a Jew's religious obligation to pay taxes to a non-Jewish government.

Herschel Schachter, professor of Talmud at Yeshiva University, devotes half of a recent study to this issue.[31] One might assume that the well-known talmudic principle *dina demalkhuta dina*, "the law of the country is [Torah] law," applies to taxation, a civil matter. The question is not that simple, and Schachter clarifies the background and substance of a significant difference of opinion on a gentile government's right to levy taxes. He writes, "This dispute . . . is not just a hair-splitting technicality. Upon the resolution hinges the major question of whether a Jew living under a non-Jewish government has to consider the laws of the land as legitimately binding [in Jewish law] upon him or not. . . . It is not necessary at this point to follow through to the end of the technical dispute; suffice it to record that practical halakhah generally accepts that the ruler does have certain legitimate powers over the individuals under his control, and that to some extent, as part of keeping the Torah, Jews must accept these restrictions or guidelines." (Note the qualification, "generally accepts," which allows a loophole that will grow at the next level of the discussion.)

Schachter then continues with a discussion of the sages' differing opinions as to the extent of the government's right to levy taxes.[32] Since the matter remains unresolved, he can only continue the discussion, "Assuming that the government has the legal right to levy taxes, and that the citizens are obligated to pay these taxes, *like any other debt that any individual owes to someone else*"[33] (emphasis added, as it returns us to the rabbinic notion of the Jew's right not to pay back a gentile loan). He then goes on to ask, "What would be the status [in Jewish law] of one who does not pay his taxes; or does not pay the full amount that he should legally be paying?"[34]

The difficulties now deepen. "If however it is a non-Jewish government to which one owes taxes. . . . The Talmud clearly forbids 'gezel akum' stealing from a nochri [sic], but 'hafka'as halva'oso' is allowed. That is to say that although theft from a nochri is forbidden, *not paying back* a debt which one owes to a nochri is not considered an act of gezel (theft). If this be the case, then the non-Jewish government has all the legal right to levy just and fair taxes; still, what is to forbid the individual from failure to pay his taxes on the grounds that 'hafka'as halva'oso' (non-payment of a debt) of a nochri is allowed?"[35]

Schachter apparently cannot bring himself to translate the term *nochri*, which means "gentile" (literally, "stranger"). Reading the paragraph without the euphemism of the Hebrew term changes its ethical impact, precisely the question of gentile opinion (and perhaps that of poorly informed Jews as well who assume that Torah law is generally ethical and not discriminatory).[36]

He further notes that with the proliferation of small businesses the issue is a real one, but the sages do not definitively settle it. He continues, "To the question of whether it is permissible to operate a store and not collect or not pay sales tax, we find a mixed response."[37] He then explicates different views on this topic. He indicates, in one sentence, that the Vilna Gaon and "other Poskim" (though only *Kesef Mishneh* is cited in his note) permit nonpayment. Since there is no further citation, it is he who adds that "if one might possibly create a situation of 'chilul hashem' by not paying taxes, there is no doubt that the 'heter' [permission] of 'hafka'as halva'ah' [not repaying a gentile loan] of akum [here not 'nochri' but the old legal term for gentile, 'idolator'] does not apply. In the *rare instance* where (a) there is no question of signing a false statement, and (b) there is no possibility of causing a chilul hashem, this group of poskim does not consider it forbidden."[38] He then continues with a discussion of the opinion of those who insist on payment and, tellingly, raises the further issue of patronizing such an establishment, recording a statement of Rabbi J. B. Soloveitchik that is forbidden.

To the postliberal Jewish ethical sensibility appropriate reverence for the teaching of prior generations has here been carried too far. Almost every authority cited in Schachter's discussion lived under conditions of political inequality and discrimination, as well as in an economy of scarcity. Like the three contemporary respondents cited above, nothing in his discussion takes cognizance of the Emancipation and of the radically changed relations of Jews and gentiles.

Suppose, following the story of the Talmud of the Land of Israel, that gentiles, long told they cannot truly understand Judaism unless they understand *halakhah,* come to study it. And they learn that devout Jews in America are still guided by their sages to consider whether the American government does or does not have religious validity, does or does not have the right to tax them, and whether they, in turn, do or do not have an obligation to pay taxes, or indeed, to pay back gentile loans (if, of course, in the exercise of *halakhic* creativity they can be reasonably certain of not being detected and avoid *hillul hashem*)? Should not some contemporary Rabban Gamliel, indeed the *halakhic* community as a whole, rise up and decree that the very discussion of these matters in these terms, much less acting upon them, constitutes a *hillul hashem*?

But why wait for such a discovery and thus allow a grave sin to occur? Why not admit that in our changed situation, we ought to broaden our appreciation of human ethical opinion and, giving it greater scope than it once had in the life of Torah, allow it to override such elements of civil discrimination and inequality as have come down to us? The task of mediating between *halakhah* and ethics remains a difficult one for postliberals. But the fresh will to be guided by classic Jewish teaching must not be allowed to wipe out the truths of universal ethics on which, in fact, we build our Jewish existence day by day.

Notes

1. I use the term "postliberal" to distinguish those non-Orthodox thinkers who consciously distance themselves from the earlier liberal equation of Jewish ethics with universal ethics (generally formulated in a neo-Kantian structure) and who thus gave inadequate weight to the *halakhah's* independent striving for the good. The postliberals seek to remedy this by treating the classic Jewish legal sources with at least equal dignity.

2. Lichtenstein's paper is found in Marvin Fox, *Modern Jewish Ethics* (Columbus: Ohio State University Press, 1975). My response, "The Authority of the Ethical Impulse in Halakhah," appeared in *Studies in Jewish Philosophy,* vol. 2, and in somewhat different form in Jonathan V. Plaut, ed., *Through the Sound of Many Voices* (Toronto: Lester and Orpen Dennys, 1982). For the view that ethical considerations per se play no part in halakhic decisions, see David Weiss Halivni, "Can a Religious Law be Immoral?" in *Perspectives on Jews and Judaism,* ed. Arthur Chiel (New York: Rabbinical Assembly, 1978).

3. See the admirable study by David Novak, *The Image of the Non-Jew in Judaism* (New York: Edward Mellen, 1983). I am not fully persuaded that the sources bear out the philosophical underpinnings that Novak finds in the origin and development of the category of Noachide law, but he has made a most impressive case for a considerable if implicit rationality in these laws.

4. This study of the *halakhic* sources on *hillul hashem* is based on the relevant articles in *Entziklopediyah Talmudit*, 17 vols. (Jerusalem: Talmudic Encyclopedia Institute, 1955–), henceforth ET, namely, *"goy"* (vol. 6), *"gezel hagoy"* (vol.6), and, particularly, *"hillul hashem"* (vol. 15). My independent check of a number of the sources cited indicated that, other than what a historical-critical hermeneutic might add, the articles faithfully and intelligently represented the texts cited. For ease of reference, I shall therefore cite the rabbinic materials underlying my analyses by reference to the apposite encyclopedia column or footnote, all from the article *"hillul hashem"* unless otherwise specified.

5. ET, col. 347ff., the subsection on the "important person."

6. In keeping with the methodology of this study, I forebear from citing the many *agadic* passages which testify, with the usual hyperbole, to the seriousness with which the rabbis deplored the sin of *hillul hashem*. See the collection in ET, col. 356ff.

7. ET, col. 344.

8. Many sages are quite explicit about this and make such statements as, "lest the gentiles say, 'The Jews have no Torah,' " (n. 160), "or they might say, 'Why did God choose thieves and deceivers to be His portion?' " (n. 161), or it might lead them to cast aspersions on the Jewish religion (n. 163).

9. ET, col. 347.

10. ET, n. 91.

11. ET, col. 356; cf. *"goy,"* vol. 6, col. 310.

12. ET, col. 355. The only *teshuvah* of David Hoffmann dealing with *hillul hashem* involved this sort of case (*Melamed Lehoil*, pt. 1, *Orah Hayyim* 35). We shall encounter another one below in our consideration of contemporary *teshuvot*.

13. ET, col. 351.

14. ET, vol. 6, col. 487ff. The article has nine columns of text with 134 notes in the usual condensed style of ET.

15. There are several variations of this story with the Romans making somewhat different complaints in them, e.g., *Sifre Deuteronomy*, ed. Louis Finkelstein, p. 401. The issue of the robbery of gentiles occurs only in the Talmud of the Land of Israel. Corroborative material, however, may be found in the discussions cited in B.M. 111b.

16. The issue of the robbery of a gentile becoming known is raised repeatedly by the sources cited in the article on *gezel hagoy*.

17. ET, col. 353, nn. 174–75.

18. ET, col. 355, nn. 209–15.

19. ET, nn. 160–61.

20. ET, nn. 167–68.

21. ET, n. 169, but see the extended treatment in the article *"gezel hagoy,"* col. 493.

22. Ibid., nn. 97–98.

23. Ibid., nn. 102–3.

24. ET, *"hillul hashem,"* col. 353.

25. ET, n. 169, and see the long discussion in the article *"gezel hagoy,"* col. 494f., and see particularly n. 127 which is the case we are discussing.

26. ET, n. 170, and the discussion in the article *"gezel hagoy,"* nn. 108–11. The usual understanding of this is failure to pay one's debts. It may thus only be another way of putting the issue of *hafkaat halvaato*, but I have adduced it here for the sake of completeness.

27. ET, n. 169, and the discussion in the article *"goy,"* col. 359, nn. 153–57.

28. ET, nn. 216–17.

29. ET, article *"dina demalkhuta dina,"* vol. 7, col. 301.

30. ET, cols. 353ff.

31. I do not know what to make of the following statistical anomaly: though more *poskim* spoke of *hillul hashem* in relation to *goy* than to *akum* (six pages of printout to four), the bulk of the classic respondents used the former, less derogatory term while a much higher proportion of modern *poskim* (arbitrarily, those later than the Maharsham—Shalom Mordecai Shvadron, 1835–1911) used the latter term. In our sample, sixteen of the seventeen responsa were listed in the *akum teshuvot*, and the one indicated with the usage *goy* (though it did not appear in the cited sentence) could not be located due to a difficulty with the printout at that point (*Igrot Moshe*, possibly *Hoshen Mishpat*, vol. 3, no. 3).

32. "Dina De'malchusa Dina," *Journal of Halacha and Contemporary Society* 1, no. 1 (Spring 1981, Pesach 5741): 103ff.

33. Ibid., 107–11.

34. Ibid., 111.

35. Ibid.

36. Ibid., 112–13.

37. Ibid., 113.

38. Ibid., 113f.

25

Tzimtzum:

A Mystic Model for Contemporary Leadership

If sex was another generation's "dirty little secret," as D. H. Lawrence termed it, surely ours is power. Now that we can admit we bear this primal lust, we see it operating everywhere, often more decisively than money, class, conditioning, genetics or the other usual determinants of behavior. The "purest" relationships reveal a political structure. In sex and not only between parents and children, in education and not only in political dealing, in religion, art, literature and culture and not only in business strategy, most decisions are made on the basis of power. So our hope of accomplishment in most fields rests largely on how power is organized there or what can be done to change that arrangement.

Perhaps we should not have been shocked to discover the extent to which power determines most human affairs. It is more than a century since Nietzsche proclaimed our will to power to be our dominant characteristic. Yet what has moved many in our generation to despair is neither the ubiquity nor the decisiveness of power but rather the recognition that almost everywhere we see power in action we see it abused. Ethically we may be far more relativistic and contextual than previous generations were. But even if we have given up ethical absolutes and moral rules many of us still cling to the notion that each of us is a person, not merely an animal, and that, a la Buber, we ought to be treated by others as persons and not as things. Hence we retain a strong ethical sense, though it often pits us against the forms which once claimed to make the dignity of persons explicit but today only operate to demean it, e.g. children should be

From *Religious Education*, vol. 69, no. 6 (November-December 1974).

seen and not heard. In an imperfect world, we could probably tolerate the fact that most relationships are inevitably hierarchical, particularly when more than a few people are involved for more than a few months. So we would not mind some people having power if they used it much of the time to enable us and others to be persons, that is, to be true to the self we know we ought to be. But they don't. Again and again, people—parents, lovers, teachers, politicians, chairmen, bosses, nurses, bureaucrats, counselors, friends, therapists, children, hosts, and hostesses—force us to be something other than what we know we are. We despair because the abuse of power seems endemic.

Our constant experience is that we have not been consulted, or have not been listened to, or have not really had a voice in matters which deeply affect our lives. In short, we exist in the continuing consciousness of being the object of someone else's power rather than being a person in our own right though we are involved with people of greater status than ours.

Modern times brought democracy into human relationships. This change may properly be called a revolution for, despite the varying forms in which it was effectuated, it gave those of little power some significant power. By contrast, the best previous generations had been able to do to humanize people's will to power was to appeal to our better nature, to beg the mighty to act with mercy. Thus, in the Bible's classic formulation, the test of the Covenant Community's faithfulness to its gracious Partner-God is its treatment of the widow, the orphan and the stranger, the figures who epitomize social powerlessness. Much remains to be said for inculcating compassion in the possessors of power, that is, all of us. Yet the sad truth is that despite their occasional acts of charity, truly benevolent tyrants are rare. Rather than rely on sovereign's goodwill we prefer to share in power. So today almost every social arrangement we know is under pressure to transform itself in the direction of more effective democracy.

I

The problems involved in moralizing the use of power are so great that any contribution to their mitigation should be welcome. While I believe that our best hope in this direction lies in giving ever greater power to the people, it also seems clear to me that we are nowhere near the stage where we can have leaderless associations. I therefore want to make a suggestion which might help ethicize the leader's role and which does so by going a step further on the road which turned the benevolent tyrant into the responsive chairperson executive. I believe we can find a fresh model for contemporary leadership in the mystic speculations about God of Isaac Luria (1534–1572) of Safed in the Holy Land. The reasons for utilizing Luria's extraordinary teaching will, I trust, become clear below. Here a word is needed about the methodological validity of transposing images of

321

transcendent being into a purely human dimension. I here follow Ludwig Feuerbach's insight that statements about God are, In fact, projections of our sense of what it is to be a person. Hence to Feuerbach, concepts of God are essentially concepts of humankind and theses about the way God relates to the creatures are implicitly theses about the way people ought to relate to each other. Feuerbach, of course, thought that theological assertions were assertions only about humankind. I think that aspect of Feuerbach's thinking is wrong, but surely it is not the only case in intellectual history of a useful idea being turned into an all-embracing absolute by its enraptured creator. Hence I propose to bracket the question of what God-talk says about God while still utilizing a Feuerbachian analysis to determine what Luria's visions of God say about us.

Luria's doctrine centers about two themes rarely treated so directly in traditional Jewish literature yet of intense concern to us today: God as creator and people as co-creator. Though creation grandly opens the book of Genesis, it and all the later texts are extraordinarily reticent, for ancient documents, of what was involved in God's creating. This anti-mythological bent became law, for the Mishnah (compiled about 200 of the Common Era) decrees that one may not publicly teach *Maaseh Bereshit*, The Work Of Creation. So we can find only hints of this esoteric doctrine until, centuries later, mystic writings begin to record some of the possibilities, reaching a spectacular climax in Luria's rather detailed description of the process.

What appeals to our generation in the focus on God as creator is that God's power is used to bring others into being. By contrast, the normal Biblical/liturgical terms, Lord and King, speak of God's status and power. This sense of God's power is modified by images which envision God as using it lovingly, e.g. God as Father, Husband or Lover. Yet remembering the realities of Near Eastern life and the continuing tradition of male dominance in Jewish life, even these symbols speak strongly of sovereignty and obedience.

Luria's teaching about God is appealing because it makes us, quite literally, God's co-creator. His teaching involves so complete a shift to human activism that scholars can even speak of God becoming passive in the process.

The Lurianic doctrine is most conveniently discussed around three major terms: *tzimtzum, shevirah, tikkun*. Since these are three stages in the Work of Creation it will be best to explain the theory as a whole first and then draw its implications for leadership. (In the description which follows I work largely from the analyses of Gershom Scholem, the pioneering master of the modern study of Jewish mysticism.)

Creation is commonly thought of in spatial terms and is envisioned as a movement of externalization: what was God's will now is turned, by an application of power, into a reality "outside" God. Think for a moment of Michelangelo's Sistine Chapel depiction of the creation of man. The mighty God stretches forth the full length of an arm to one fingertip and thus brings man into being. For us humans, creation is normally an act in extension of ourselves, of producing something "there" that was previously only within us.

Something of this picture is to be seen in the Biblical texts despite their apparent efforts to avoid the gross anthropomorphism of Near Eastern creation stories. Thus, in the first version, Genesis 1, God utters words in order to let the light be and, if some modern translators are correct ("When God began to create the heaven and the earth—the earth being unformed and void . . ."), there already was material external to God to shape. The story in Genesis 2 simply begins with the dry ground and then, with explicit externality, has God mold man out of the dust of the earth before putting the breath of life into him. Creation as externalization is fully explicit in the neo-Platonic teaching (from the first century of the Common Era on) and thus in the Jewish mystic tradition which often borrowed from it (from the early Middle Ages on). Here creation is generally spoken of as emanation, the gentle but efficacious spilling over of the plenteous being of God. The usual image is of a fountain which, out of its fullness, pours water over its basin, thus creating new pools. God has such plenitude of reality that some of it emerges in a lesser form, which, in turn makes possible an emergence in even lesser form, and so on, down a series of variously interpreted gradations, until our world exists. The neo-Platonists and mystics thought in this way to ease the problem of the infinite God creating finite beings. To us it seems reasonably clear that the very first movement from infinity to finitude—no matter how extensive the finite is thought to be—is as difficult to understand as the Universal God creating ants or pebbles. In any case, the doctrine of emanation, though it links all creatures to God by an unbroken progression of being, is a clear expression of our usual sense that creation is a species of externalization.

II

Luria felt otherwise. I cannot say to what extent his radical shift of creation images was due to the memories and continuing effects of the mass expulsion of the Jewish community of Spain in 1492. The fact is, Isaac Luria alone created a radically new mystic theory of creation. It will be simplest then to limit ourselves to his intellectual trail, and we may best prepare ourselves for his ideas by confronting a logical issue with regard to creation. If God is everywhere, how can there be any other place outside, in which the creation can arise? Michelangelo, for example, had to limit God to one majestic sized human figure if he was to leave room to paint an Adam. But God is not a man and we are taught that God fills all space. If that way of speaking about God is unsatisfactory because spatiality is a poor metaphor for God, consider the question in ontological form; if God is fundamental being, fully realized, how can there be secondary being, that is, being only partly realized? Or, if God is all-in-all, how can the partial or the transitory, which must depend upon God for their being, ever come to exist?

One response might be to deny the reality of creation as much Hindu thought has done (and as, from the Divine perspective, the later Jewish mystic, Shneour Zalman of Lyady, 1747–1813, would do). Luria is too much under the influence of classic Jewish creation theory for that. Instead he boldly suggests that creation begins with an act of contraction, *tzimtzum*. God does not initiate the existence of other things by extending himself. There would be no place for them then to be, no area of non-being or partial being in which they might exist. Hence to create, God must first withdraw into himself. God must, so to speak, become less so that other things could come into being. So great, says Luria, is God's will to create; so great is God's love for creation.

It is not without interest that Luria has utterly reversed the older meaning of the term *tzimtzum*. In the rabbinic usage from which he almost certainly took the term, the verb form means "to concentrate" but in an externalizing way. The reference there is to God being especially present between the cherubim atop the Ark of the Covenant in the Holy of Holies. And the comment is made that the God of all universes "concentrates" particularly at that point in space. For Luria, *tzimtzum* is the exact opposite. God concentrates not out there, at a point in the world, but within. God draws deeper into God and by this withdrawal leaves a void in which the creatures can come into being.

Tzimtzum, then, is not itself creation but the necessary prelude to it. Now the externalizing act can occur, but with certain ultimately troublesome consequences derived from its taking place in a realm from which God has withdrawn. Of course, God could not be totally absent, for without some aspect of the divine reality being present nothing at all could exist. Luria says God leaves behind, in the creation-space, a residue of the divine reality, something like the oil or wine, he nicely notes, that is always still there after we think we have emptied the jug.

The positive externalizing movement of creation begins with God sending forth a beam of light into the void. From this light, in various extraordinary stages, the creation we know eventually took form. For Luria, then, creating is a two-fold process, a contraction which leads to an expansion. More, it is a continuing double movement, for God continues the work of Creation each day, continuously, and hence all existence as we know it pulsates to the divine regression and egression. Here Luria's sense of time and the opportune moves in a mystic realm no fine-tuned atomic instrument can ever hope to clock.

Perhaps we should already be prepared by the doctrine of *tzimtzum* for the next major stage in creation but most people find it not only dramatic but somewhat disturbing. Luria teaches that the creative act speedily results in a cosmic catastrophe, that creation begins with a calamity. Luria describes it in metaphors which today could easily be taken from our experiments to harness thermo-nuclear energy, specifically to find "containers" for the enormous heat of the plasma gases involved in the fusion process. As the divine beam of created light comes into the void, it goes through various transformations. Ultimately it produces certain "vessels" which are to come to full existence when they are filled with the creating light. But now, as God's great power fills some of the lesser vessels, it proves too mighty for them and they are shattered, the *shevirah* mentioned above. The result is an imperfect creation, one in which things are not as they ought to be or were intended by God to be, a cosmos which from almost its very beginning is alienated from itself, a created order where evil abounds instead of good.

Luria, however, is not a pessimist. Once again his sense of the dialectic implicit in all things reasserts itself and he turns the doctrine of a flawed creation into the basis of humankind's having cosmic significance. To begin with, the *shevirah* does not mean that the creation collapses into nothingness. It cannot, for God's energy was poured into it. True, what we see around us today is largely the "shells" or "husks" of what should have been, without their proper kernels of God's energizing light. But by their very existence we know that something of God's power is in them. Thus Luria speaks of the divine sparks which are to be found everywhere in creation. If all these sparks were lifted up from the husks and restored to their proper place in God's spiritual order for creation, then all things would become what they were intended to be. Creation can be restored and *tikkun* means restoration, the reintegration of the organic wholeness of creation, the reestablishment of the world in the full graciousness of God's primal intent.

What astonishes us here is Luria's bold insistence that *tikkun* is primarily humanity's work, not God's. In everything one faces, in every situation one finds oneself in, one should realize that there is a fallen spark of God's light waiting to be returned to its designated spiritual place. Hence, as people do the good moment by moment and give their acts of goodness a proper, inner, mystic intention—more specifically, as the Jew practices Jewish law and manifests Jewish virtues with full concentration of the soul on the task of uplifting the divine sparks—the shattered creation is brought into repair. The ailing cosmos is heated. The Messiah is brought near. People do that, each person by each act. And if enough people did that enough of the time, Luria teaches, God would send the Messiah. Or, to put it with more appropriate divine passivity, if people, by their acts, restored the creation to what god had hoped it would be, then all the benefits of God's gracious goodness would be available to them. Such a messianic estimate of human initiative is unique—so much so that some scholars have argued that Luria's ideas, transmitted by Christian Cabbalists and transformed by late Renaissance and early rationalist humanism, were influential in producing the heady confidence in humankind of the 18th century enlightenment. But I do not think we need carry Luria's ideas any further.

III

The excitement of the Lurianic teaching arises from its radical shift in the application and hence the structure of cosmic power. Traditional creation theories focus on God and the effectuation of the divine will. God is understood in a transitive mode. In such an approach, the creatures are, so to speak, only the objects of God's activity. So, by Feuerbachian inversion, leadership comes to mean using power to achieve one's ends. The greatest leaders, then, are the people who mobilized massive energies to accomplish vast projects. And since, until recently, social power has been political-military, most of the great figures of world history were warriors of warrior-kings. Though today we might add executives or administrators to the list of those eligible for adulation, our ideal leader remains the achiever, the person who imposes designs upon reality.

The Lurianic God moves in radically other ways. Now God is understood in a reflexive mode. From the very beginning, thinking of God involves consideration of God's creatures; how can their independent existence be assured? where will they find sufficient emptiness of being to make their limited reality significant? With this in mind, the exercise of God's power is drastically re-directed. It must first be applied to itself, to the extent of constricting its all-encompassing quality. Only when God withdraws can God create—if God's creatures are to have full dignity.

This readily translates into contemporary human terms. We seek a leadership construed not primarily in terms of the accomplishment of plans but equally in terms of its humanizing effect on the people being led. Our ethics demand a leader who uses power to enable people to be persons while they work together. Such a leader, as against the stereotype of the cruel general or ruthless executive is not essentially goal oriented, but recognizes that people are always as important if not more important than the current undertaking.

The extension and the withdrawal visions of creation retain something in common. Even tyrants know that people can be pushed only so far and the biblical God, who by having unlimited power could have been the greatest of tyrants, nonetheless creates people independent enough to resist God. On the other hand, in the Lurianic theory, though the creatures are given initial consideration, the creation is not oriented to their satisfaction but by the divine will. Yet though these creation visions overlap, they assign quite different status to those of lesser power and so must be considered alternative models for exercising leadership. Think of the sort of leadership we all have known in groups of small to moderate size, the family, the classroom, the church or synagogue. (One could easily expand the list.) These institutions have goals to accomplish. Yet in being part of them, it has made all the difference in the world to us whether we felt our parents or teachers or clergy were using us to accomplish their purposes or helping us grow as we labored for our common ends. I suggest that the

326

ability to practice *tzimtzum* can sharply distinguish accomplishment-directed from person-fostering leadership.

Leaders, by their power, have a greater field of presence than most people do. When they move into a room they seem to fill the space around them. We say they radiate power. Hence the greater the people we meet the more reduced we feel—though as in fascist or fantasy adulation we may hope that by utterly identifying ourselves with our hero, we can gain the fullest sort of existence. So in the presence of the mighty we are silent and respectful, we await their directions and are fearful of their judgments. Who we are is defined by what they think of us. Like God the preeminent have true existence and we, their creatures, exist only in part. In such a system the activists strive for the day when they will be god and others will have to serve them. Professors, who suffered through the indignities of the old Ph.D. apprenticeship system and have finally made it to full rank and tenure, today face students who increasingly demand to be treated as persons, that is, as partners whose independent reality is respected in the relationship. But the professors, having finally become Number One in the academic hierarchy, want to realize the benefits of that status, not the least as a compensation for the pain of achieving it. They want to rule as they were ruled—and that is only one of the many varieties of refusing to make room for others so neatly summarized in the term "ego-trip."

The Lurianic model of leadership has, as its first step, contraction. The leader withholds presence and power so that the followers may have some place in which to be. Take the case of a parent who has the power to insist upon a given decision and a good deal of experience upon which to base that judgment. In such an instance, the urge to compel is almost irresistible. Yet if it is a matter the parent feels the child can handle—better, if making this decision and taking responsibility for it will help the child grow as a person—then the mature parent withdraws and makes it possible for the child to choose and thus come more fully into being. *Tzimtzum* here means not only telling the child what to do but not manipulating the decision by hinting or "sharing" experience or "only" giving some advice. Leaving room for the other means just that, including allowing the child sometimes to make a foolish choice. Not ever to be permitted to choose the wrong thing means not truly to be free. Parents, like all other leaders, should seek to emulate God's maturity. God gives God's children their freedom even though they may use it against God because God knows the divine dignity cannot be satisfied in the long run with anything less than a relationship in which in which we come to God freely rather than in servility.

Tzimtzum operates in a similar way in the leadership of teachers and clergy. Normally both are so busy doing things for us that they leave us little opportunity to do things on our own and thus find some personal independence. Both talk too much—so much so, that when they stop talking for a moment and ask for questions or honest comments, we don't believe them. We know if we stay quiet for a moment they will start talking again. We realize that their professional roles have been built around creation by extension of the self, so they will have to prove to us by a rigorous practice of *tzimtzum* that they really want us to be persons in our own right.

One common misinterpretation of this approach is to think it calls for a swing from dominance to abandonment, a sort of petulant declaration that if one's lessers do not want one's guidance then they should get no help at all and suffer the consequences of being on their own. There are many parents who vacillate between enforcing a harsh law and granting complete license. In school or church situations, withdrawal to give others freedom easily becomes a rationalization for indolence, the refusal to plan, or provide resources, or make proper demands upon the community. Luria's God does not indulge in *tzimtzum* to sulk. His God bears no resemblance to Aristotle's self-centered god who was not only pure thought, thinking, but thought only about the purest of things, God. *Tzimtzum* is rather the first of a two-part rhythm, for it is always followed by sending the creative beam of light into the just-vacated void. The withdrawal is for the sake of later using one's power properly. Contraction without a following expansion, regression without subsequent egression does not produce creation. But once room has been made for another, even simple applications of power can prove effective. How often it has been the seemingly casual word, the side comment, the quizzical look we got which, coming from someone we knew respected us, powerfully affected us. So in the classroom, though the teacher's summary of the data or interpretation of the material is regularly needed, it is also the good question, the challenge of stimulating options, the pause which is receptive that is the most effective means of educating. Indeed, perhaps the greatest effect one can have on someone seeking to become a person is to provide a model. Here the exercise of power is, directly speaking, all on oneself and only indirectly on the other. Yet in creating persons, the effectiveness of a good example, particularly as contrasted to laying down rules or verbalizing ideals, is immeasurable.

Leadership in the Lurianic style is particularly difficult, then, because it requires a continuing alternation of the application of our power. Now we hold back; now we act. To do either in the right way, is difficult enough. To develop a sense when to stop one and do the other and then reverse that in due turn is to involve one in endless inner conflict. An example will make this clearer. In a seminar, though the teacher may have spent a lifetime on a topic, the teacher elects to sit silently so as to give the student an opportunity to speak. If the teacher does not keep still, allowing, say, slight errors of fact or misinterpretations to pass by uncontested, but regularly interrupts, the student's presentation, and self, are as good as destroyed. At the same time, incompetence can be tolerated only so far. If the student is well on the way to ruining an important topic for the class or making such major misstatements that all which follows will be false, the teacher must interrupt. Danger lurks equally in action and inaction. Premature or too frequent intervention is as fateful as missing danger signs or giving insufficient aid. And with all this, we cannot help but realize that our judgement to intervene may only be a power-grab while our decision to stay silent may really mean we are unwilling to take the responsibility for interrupting.

The seminar situation illustrates well the complexities of functioning as a Lurianic leader. No wonder then that the call for a modern style of leadership throws many people into great anxiety. Their masters did not use their power this way and no one now can give them a rule as to when and how they ought to step back or step in. So failures in trying to exert the new leadership abound and examples of successful leadership are rare even in face to face associations, much less the giant organizations of which our society is so largely composed.

IV

Some implications for leadership of the ideas of *shevirah* and *tikkun* also deserve mention, though they are perhaps at greater distance from Luria's teaching than the ones mentioned above. Those who lead by *tzimtzum* must quickly reconcile themselves to the fact that leaving room for others to act is likely to mean their own purposes will be accomplished only in blemished form. The student will, in terms of the content presented or material covered, not lead the seminar as well as the teacher could. The children who write their own college application biographies or seek out summer jobs themselves are not likely to do as expert a job as the parent. The congregants who read or create a service will probably not reach the level of expression nor educe the religious traditions in a way the clergy might have. *Shevirah*, imperfect creation, is the logical consequence of leadership by *tzimtzum*. Hence, if our eyes are only on what has been accomplished in our plans and we cannot see what has happened in the creation of persons, we are likely to be deeply disturbed. The next step is to take over ourselves. It is, indeed, often easier to get things done by doing them oneself rather than allowing others to do so, particularly in their way. But to seize power from others is to deprive them of the possibility of significant action and thus of dignity. We must learn to trust them if they are to be given a chance to be persons and that means learning to "put up" with their bumbling ways. God, we say, "bears" with us. Without forgiveness for our sins, we would not be able to continue as real shapers of history. The graciousness implicit in *tzimtzum* is not only the grant of space in which we might have being but the will to forgive the faults we may commit once we have that independent being. Anyone who would lead by *tzimtzum*, then, must know that *shevirah* is likely if not inevitable. Thus Lurianic leadership depends not only on an exquisite sense of inter-personal rhythm but a capacity to forgive and go on working with those whose need for independence is a major cause of the frustration of our plans.

The strength to persist in so frustrating a role can come from recognizing that the leader's *tzimtzum* and the resulting *shevirah* are the occasion for the followers' work of *tikkun*, restoration and completion. The group's objectives may not have been accomplished now but the leader may be confident that the effort will go on. Its continuation no longer depends upon the presence of the present leader. By the act of *tzimtzum*, confirmed in bearing with the *shevirah*, the leader has taught the disciples to work out of their own initiative and not by coercion from above. The painful process has created a new generation to carry on the work. And it, in turn, following the leader's model, will create another generation of workers, *ad infinitum*, until the goal has been accomplished. This is as much messianism as we are entitled to in human endeavors. So the parents who see their children able to make their own decisions maturely, though they choose a peculiar life style; so the teachers who see their students become competent scholars, though they reach conclusions at variance from what they were taught; so the clergy who develop a laity committed to living religiously, come what may, though they transform the traditions they received; such leaders by *tzimtzum* know they have done as much as people can do to save a troublesome and treacherous world. Their hope, then, arises from seeing the present and the future as two parts of a whole. They are patient during the *shevirah* and endure the self-denial of their *tzimtzum* to create an indomitable commitment to *tikkun*. Leadership with so long a view is not muscular enough for Michelangelo's God, or his heroes, Moses and David. The great Florentine was a Renaissance man and believed power meant lordship, not person-making. We can still learn much from Michelangelo's sense of grandeur but we must move beyond it to implement our new sense of humanity.

Did Isaac Luria himself see, far before Feuerbach, that his vision of a withdrawing creator could be a model for personal leadership? We cannot quite tell. In some respects he seems to have been unassertive beyond the customary humility of the pious. Thus, we are told that he usually allowed one of his disciples to walk ahead of him—an act firmly prohibited in the etiquette of respect for a master—because the student considered it a special honor. He is also reported never to have bargained over the price asked for any object he needed for religious purposes nor questioned his wife's requests with regard to household or personal expenses. So too, he emphasized to his followers that they were all parts of one organism and therefore needed to care and pray for each other. And he was quite uncommunicative about his deepest mystical doctrines, not only refusing to write anything down but apparently instructing his most trusted adepts only by hints and allusions.

But we dare not press this interpretation further. In most respects Luria seems to have exercised authority in the typical kingly fashion of one who is recognized as wearing the crown of the Torah. He organized his disciples into a group called The Lion's Whelps (a pun made on the initials of his title, Rabbi Isaac, gave him the title The Lion) and he set high admission standards which were stringently enforced. He then divided them into two categories, apparently according to how much mystic knowledge he felt he could share with them. The extent of his dominance of the group may perhaps be gauged from the fact that he refused Joseph Karo, the greatest authority on Jewish law of that time, permission to be part of the inner circle. Another intriguing fact gives us some indication that Luria's leadership had limited effectiveness. He arranged to have all his followers live together in a sort of commune, but within a few months there was considerable difficulty among them. The texts say, typically enough, that the wives began to quarrel among themselves and this caused the disturbances among the adepts. Yet, if this seems to compromise Luria's stature somewhat, we should also keep in mind that his career as a mystic teacher in Safed comprised just three years, after which he died. In that short time he changed the course of Jewish mysticism and did so, apparently, by imbuing his disciples with so deep a commitment to his doctrine that they, and their followers in turn, spread it throughout the Jewish world. More, they brought it into the thought and life style of much of Jewry, the first time that mysticism, which had always been an elitist interest, became part of mass Jewish living. So if we cannot know whether Luria led by *tzimtzum*, we can nonetheless say that his leadership had an extraordinary effect in his day and his teaching retains a powerful message for our time.

26

The Rabbi's Special Ethical Responsibilities

All Jews are commanded not to profane God's name (Lev. 22:32). This is the negative side of the positive imperative to sanctify God's name, even, if necessary, by martyrdom. *Hillul hashem*, the profanation of God's name, is a most serious sin, as may be gauged by the difficulty the *halakhah* ascribes to gaining atonement for it: R. Elazar b. Azariah said (after enumerating various sins and their forgiveness), "But if one has been guilty of *hillul hashem*, then *teshuvah*, repentance, has no power to suspend [punishment], nor Yom Kippur to procure atonement, nor suffering to [finally] wipe out [the sin], but all of them together suspend [the punishment] and death wipes it out." (Yoma 86a, one of two classic talmudic passages on this theme. What follows this dictum specifies what various rabbis said constituted such a profanation, and these form the substance of many later halakhic citations on this topic.)

Anyone considered by a community an *adam hashuv*, an "important person," perhaps "a significant public figure," falls within a special category of Jewish law, both for privilege and restriction. Thus, he (so the historical Jewish usage) may read by a *shabat* light or use a gentile physician to treat a wound, acts forbidden to ordinary Jews (Shab. 12b and 28a). In this special freedom, one can hear the echo of the less legitimate license those in power often arrogate to themselves. However, in keeping with the *halakhah*'s special concern for the community, such a person's role also imposes extra responsibilities upon him. Thus, he should not do anything that would bring shame on himself and make his community despise him (Rashi to Taan. 14b). Interestingly enough, there is a somewhat similar, though more limited, category of laws for an *ishah hashuvah*, "an important woman," generally understood as the daughter of a prominent family. As the halakhah evolved, the tone of strictness predominated, and the effective rule became that "in our generations" all the stringencies remain in effect, but "importance never bestows [special] ease of obligation." Those who differ with this ruling agree that being a leader does not convey special privileges but insist that the community retains the right to extend special leniency to him (Taz to O. H. 72.100 alef and Omer Hashkahah 61).

As a result, an adam hashuv carries an especially heavy level of obligation with regard to hillul hashem, though here the category begins to overlap with the special obligations of the talmid hakham, the student sage, or the tzaddik, one recognized as a righteous man. The principle involved here is that of role model. Again and again the sources contain comments such as, people "learn from him and if he is not careful with his deeds then lesser folk will disparage the Torah . . . for such a one has acted profanely" (Rashi to Shab. 33a). This prohibition means that he may not do acts otherwise permitted by the Torah; how much more heinous is his deed should he violate a commandment since "others will learn from him to do the same," thus making him, as it were, guilty of the specially grave offense of causing many to sin (Rashi to Kid. 40a). So "an important person needs to be especially stringent with himself" (Shab. 51a, a theme often echoed by Maimonides).

Perhaps as good a general statement of what constitutes an act of hillul hashem by a talmid hakham is that of Isaac of the School of R. Yannai, "Anyone about whose acts his colleagues are ashamed to hear" (Yoma 86a). Later writers pick up this theme and say it is someone who begins to have a bad reputation or who is suspected of being a sinner (Rashi and Meiri ad loc.). R. Nahman is cited in the same talmudic passage as saying that one who has committed hillul hashem causes his colleagues to pray God will forgive his deeds. The scope of what might be considered hillul hashem for a talmid hakham, it must be emphasized, extends far beyond what the halakhah requires of ordinary Jews. Thus, one early posttalmudic source comments that a scholar should be careful even about matters that people might consider to be sins even though he does not consider them such; he should be as sensitive to people's judgments as he is about that of God (SMK 85).

Here is a sample of some specific acts that, if done by a talmid hakham, constitute a hillul hashem: not paying one's butcher promptly (where the butcher does not come around to collect payment); not being honest in business or cordial with people; feasting frequently; joking around or eating and drinking with vulgarians, ame haaretz; or, worse, getting drunk in their presence. A rabbi can even say, though this is agadic hyperbole, that a scholar who has a grease spot on his garment deserves death (for causing people to despise God, so close is the association of learning with God's presence) (Yoma 86a; MT Yesod. Hatorah 5.11 and Hil. De. 5.3; Shab. 114a). Yet it is not at all a hillul hashem if a talmid hakham works at a generally despised craft in order to get his livelihood (Rashbam to B.B. 110a). A second *agadah* may serve as a useful summary. "Don't wear *talit* and *tefilin* and go commit sins for this is, literally, taking God's name in [to the] vain" (Pes. Rab. 22).

As to the punishment of an *adam hashuv*, the community should, when his deeds become known, publicize the sinfulness of the hypocrite—that is, the wicked one who seeks to appear righteous—for he is profaning God's name (Yoma 86b and the Tosefta to chap. 4). No special leniency is shown such a sinner even though he be a *talmid hakham*. If there are evil reports of him, we are required to put him under a ban. Some say that if we do not do so, then we too are guilty of a *hillul hashem*. The classic story in this regard (MK 17a) concerns R. Judah, and it is worth citing fully:

> Of a certain scholar of whom there were evil reports [of sexual misconduct, as the text implies below], R. Judah asked, "What shall we do? Ban him? But the rabbis have need of him. [Rashi: he was their *rav*; Steinsaltz: he is great in Torah.] Not ban him? God's name will be profaned." He asked Rabbah bar bar Hanah, "Have you ever heard a teaching concerning such a case?" He replied, "Thus taught R. Yohanan, 'What is the meaning of the text, for the priest's lips should guard knowledge and they should seek Torah from his mouth, for he is a messenger of *Adonai Tzevaot?*' When a *rav* is like a messenger of God, they should seek Torah from his mouth. But if he is not, they should not seek Torah from him." So R. Judah pronounced a ban on him.
>
> In time, R. Judah became [seriously] ill and the rabbis came to inquire of him [whether he would lift the ban], and that man was also along with them. When R. Judah saw him, he laughed. The man said, "Isn't it bad enough for 'that man' that he is banned and now he is [you are] laughing at him!" R. Judah said, "I was not laughing at you but, since I am going to another world, I was happy to think that I showed no partiality even toward a man like yourself [Steinsaltz: but followed the law]."

Even after R. Judah's death, the effect of the ban continued, as the story goes, until that scholar's own death, as the result of being stung on the penis by a wasp. Though he was then initially turned down for burial among "the Pious," he was finally given a place among "the Judges." When the question is asked why he was even admitted there, the answer is given that he had acted according to R. Ilai's notorious dictum: "When one sees that his *yetzer* is overcoming him, let him go where he is not known, put on black clothes and a black wrap and do the deed his heart desires rather than profane God's name publicly" [Cf. Kid. 40a]. Thus, according to this interpretation, there might have been a halakhic basis for his sexual misconduct. Nonetheless, being a *talmid hakham* he should not have acted on R. Ilai's "permission," and that is why R. Judah placed and kept him under a ban.

R. Judah's fearless action defines the later *halakhah*. The *talmid hakham* who commits a *hillul hashem* is the twenty-third of the twenty-four persons specified in the list of the *Shulhan Arukh* itemizing the transgres-

334

sors who should be placed under a ban (Y. D. 334.43). Indeed, the code specifies (Y. D. 334.42) what is involved in punishing a *talmid hakham*. (For further data and a fuller exposition of the laws, see the *Talmudic Encyclopedia*, the articles *"adam hashuv,"* and *"hillul hashem."*)

A Theological Comment

Our Reform rabbis' association met to discuss what might be done about our colleagues of whom there have been "evil reports," or, equally important, how to help our colleagues from getting into such situations. At the meeting, Debbie Zecher reminded us that the psychologist Rabbi Jack Bloom had found many rabbis deeply troubled emotionally because they were expected to be, in his term, "symbolic exemplars." I do not know how Jack understands that term, but it means a good deal to me. Rabbis easily become overwhelmed by the very special demands people make of them. Identifying the rabbi with God/parents, people have expectations that are impossibly varied and grandiose, expectations that extend far beyond the special standards the rabbi expects of him or herself and has tried to teach people ought to be expected of a good Jew.

The notion of "symbolic exemplar" runs contrary to the effort we have made in recent decades to transform our role as rabbis. We have tried to humanize it, to lessen the distance between rabbi and laity, to be more a person and less a special Jewish and human case. So when everyone expects us to be a *tzaddik* we would gladly settle for being, like everyone else, a simple *mentsh*; the tension can become more than we can tolerate. From that agony, the *yetzer hara*, the Urge-to-do-evil, draws power.

I wish to speak to one dimension of this problem, of the role in it of proper Jewish faith. My Judaism recognizes no split between "ordinary" people and "symbolic exemplars." All human beings are "symbolic exemplars." They are, all of them, created in God's image; they thus have an ineradicable dignity and responsibility no other animal has. Any lesser view of human beings, of some people as just "ordinary," is a creation of the secular mind, specifically of much of social science, and the beginning of the self-denigration of humankind.

Among human beings, all Jews are a special class of "symbolic exemplars" for they are a people who by destiny and choice are intimately identified with God. Even in our secular age, we know that how Jews behave, particularly in the public eye, affects the way humanity thinks of us and thus of our God. We still properly expect more of Jews, for all our humanity, than we do of other people.

And rabbis are the Jews' "Jews." Because of our learning and life's dedication, because of what we do and believe, paltry as it may seem to us, because of our venerable title, Jews—people—expect everything of us. We cannot do or be everything they want us to do and be; even worse, we cannot do and be even what we would like to be. But in failure as in accomplishment, these are the right standards; this is our true vocation.

I think it would greatly help colleagues face the special trials of our lives if we could bring ourselves to recognize and reject the secular view of what a person is or ought to be and, thus, of what a rabbi today might hope to be. When rabbis yearn to be as secular as other people seem to be, the *hillul hashem* has already begun; only the occurrence remains to be specified. Jewish faith, continually sought and renewed, needs to ground our psychic, our human struggle. If we can win through to a Jewish meta-psychology, if we can find ways to hold fast to it through the years—*emunah*—we shall know why our people and God lay very special obligations upon us, and we can hope that, with all our faults, we may live up to them.

27

Jewish Meta-ethics and
Business Ethics

In our contemporary debates over business ethics, too little attention has been given to the role of our beliefs as the cause of our differences of opinion. To validate this judgment, let us consider two highly regarded theories of correct business behavior and contrast them with a modern Jewish viewpoint.

The obvious place to start is Milton Friedman's book, *Capitalism and Freedom.* There he writes, "There is one and only one social responsibility of business, to use its resources and engage in activities designed to increase its profits so long as it stays within the rules of the game, which is to say, engages in open and free competition without deception or fraud." He therefore condemns as "a fundamentally subversive doctrine" in our free society the suggestion that corporations use their profits for charitable purposes or otherwise be concerned with their supposed social responsibility.

Professor Albert Z. Carr argues that business can best be understood in terms of contemporary game theory. Like all games, it has certain expectations and rules by which you are expected to abide. Business ethics, then, means staying within the rules of the game. One's goal in this activity as in other such pursuits is quite clear: it is to win. Friedman and Carr—and others who think similarly—are therefore quite insistent that the proper conduct of business is independent of the imperatives of personal morality. These should be left to the individual heart and will, or, where coercion is necessary, to democratic decisions via government.

From Sh'ma, a Journal of Jewish Responsibility, 18/350 (March 18, 1988).

In rejecting the adequacy of these views let me not be misunderstood as also denying the truths they know but wrongly absolutize. First, a business needs to make a profit. In our society you cannot long stay in business without making money—though some people are remarkably successful at doing so. Second, business is highly competitive. If you are not meeting the needs of your customers, someone else will soon likely do so and take them away from you.

Choosing to Whom One Is Moral

From a modern Jewish perspective, concentrating one's entire philosophy on these realities yields an unduly restrictive sense of responsibility. They limit one's ethical horizon to one's shareholders or owners—and to them alone. That is a kind of economic ethno-centrism—the sort of unacceptable parochial ethics which mean those who are not part of my tribe may expect to receive less than full human concern from me. In its ghetto configuration, Jewish ethics, in tone even more than in precept, made a number of sharp distinctions between Jews and gentiles—a pattern derived from its alienation from the ethics of idolaters and its later experience of persecution at the hands of its daughter religions. Since we had suffered badly because of others' limited ethical vision, when we gained equality modernizing Jews utilized the implicit universal commitments of Judaism to create an explicit Jewish obligation of embracing scope. Having attained this moral maturity, how can we now regress to distinguishing in business between the favored "us" as against the non-person "them"?

The restricted moral focus of the ethics of Friedman and Carr leads on to a more serious ethical deficiency. It introduces a radical split into our lives, a wall of separation between what we are supposed to do in business and what more broadly we ought to do as an ethical human being—precisely what is meant by the dehumanizing effect of our contemporary society. When we cannot apply in our economic activities a reasonably full range of our ethical sensibilities—our empathy, our compassion, our sense of justice—we are being forced to deny that part of us which Judaism teaches makes us most truly human.

Even on this theoretical level, these ethical views are highly problematic. But as they have filtered into our society they have become ever more pernicious. Tell people that profit is the essential business good and the evil urge quickly leads them to indulge their greed and selfishness. Tell them that business is only a game which one plays to win and they easily apply to it Vince Lombardi's theory of competition: winning isn't the most important thing—it's the *only* thing! If so, one will do *anything* to win—and then immorality becomes a reasonable if secretive way of doing business. For a deleterious minority, what might have been merely a dehumanizing ethics has become a rationalization for violating the oldest rule of business ethics: don't keep two kinds of measures, one for yourself and one for everyone else.

The Principles Over Which We Disagree

The wide divergence between the modern Jewish and the Friedman-Carr ethics turns us inevitably to the meta-ethical level of the discussion whence it arises. To begin with, why am I so certain that the philosophies of Professors Friedman and Carr are profoundly unsatisfactory, indeed wrong? It cannot be because their theories of ethics are not rational in the contemporary usage of that term. Both thinkers argue with high technical competence, presenting acute analyses, relevant evidence and compelling argument. They move without logical hitch from their assumptions to their conclusions. They are fine exemplars of what our century has come to look for in "rational ethics," tight reasoning rather than the character of the moral good being elaborated.

The Jewish community, by contrast, still tends to use the term "rational ethics" less as a comment about the rigor of one's argument than as a sign of its qualitative sense of duty. Carrying on the early modern Jewish universalization of our ethics, we assume that "ethics" still means something like Immanuel Kant's moral theory as liberals applied it to our tradition. They made "moral law" the essence of Judaism and provided a rational basis for insisting that the practice of justice and compassion is fundamental to modern human existence. But the Kantian notion of reason as necessarily including an independent ethics has been subjected to devastating philosophic challenge in our time. Instead, philosophers today generally empty the term "rationality" of any ethical substance. For them a rational ethics is characterized by its technically skilled reasoning about a question of what one ought to do. They often then seek to compensate for its lack of primary ethical assumptions by adding in various human considerations. By such standards, Friedman, Carr and other careful reasoners are fully entitled to call their views "ethics," indeed "rational ethics"—by these standards more rigorously rational than ours! So we can hardly claim to disagree with them as a matter of simple rationality.

Are Humans by Nature Moral?

Shall we then say that we deny the ethics of Friedman and Carr because our socially concerned view of human responsibility is truer to human nature than is theirs? Surely at this late date in our traumatic century the evidence hardly confirms a belief that people are naturally good. Human nature seems far more competitive than altruistic. When people face a crisis, they regularly show themselves to be highly self-centered. And our culture demonstrates that even luxury can bring out the ego in us. Despite our relative affluence, narcissism, not concern for others, characterizes us. We shall not move decisively toward greater human solidarity if we insist on basing our business lives on the ethics intrinsic to the human animal.

Then why do Jewish teachers assert that number-or victory-oriented business ethics are utterly inadequate, indeed noxious in their popularized

339

forms? We do so because of what we know ethically as a matter of faith; that is, we do so because of our Jewish beliefs about humankind, its duties and its destiny. We know, with an utterly deep and ultimate knowing, that people are not created as isolates but as ineluctably social creatures who are called to build a human community suffused with justice and compassion. Hence people always have qualitative obligations not only to themselves alone but also simultaneously to others. As Hillel said, "[Yes,] if I am not for myself, who will be for me? But [being a social creature] if I am only for myself, what am I?"

As a result, the Bible gives far more attention to our social than to our personal responsibilities. Its legislation brands gossip a sin, but it is far more detailed in specifying our need to have just weights and measures. It unambiguously charges us not to lie, but exhorts us with far greater rhetorical intensity not to abuse our social power.

And these are not mere suggestions to us, sage counsel we would be wise to consider. They are commandments whose violation makes us radically unworthy but whose fulfillment honors all that we are and ought to be. Our lawgivers, prophets and sages knew that every aspect of our lives had to reflect a sense of good, one that derived from something other than themselves, one they knew was utterly primary to the universe. And we, as much the beneficiaries of the way of life they shaped as of their teachings, are committed to our modernized versions of their ethics because we "know" they were right—though, by contemporary standards, it is a more than rational "knowing."

The Religious Foundations of Our Ethics

In short, and to stop indulging our obsolete agnosticism, our Jewish standards of ethics derive from our experience of God (in whichever modern Jewish sense we use that term). In our own fashion, we, like Jews of the past, affirm that the One God of the universe lays a necessary standard of conduct upon us, one we might not have created for ourselves but which we know calls us to our highest human capacity, being God-like.

Yes, we are free to transgress that Divine standard, and our puny resolve and worthy habits must constantly struggle with the ever changing forms of temptation. With what extraordinary power does the Evil Urge within us fashion new lures for us which promise to fulfill one of our true passions. And because we always lust for very much more than we can ever admit to ourselves, it often overcomes us. Our hope of resisting it, then, rests in no small measure on what we ultimately believe and how deeply we care about those beliefs. And in that depth struggle of the self, Judaism asserts, rests the ethical hope, the messianic future of our world.

Please do not misunderstand me. I know there are people who fervently believe in God who are scoundrels. But, often, they are untrue to their religious tradition which itself would denounce their acts as sinful.

Moreover, some believers fail to meet our modern moral standards because they have not allowed their beliefs to be affected by the ethical truth found in democratic social existence. I know, too, that there are people whose lives I would judge to be highly ethical who say they are atheists or complete agnostics. I gladly acknowledge the joy I have found working with them in a social struggle. But they face a long term problem. What once seemed the sure, purely human grounds of enlightened ethics have now radically eroded. Such humanists are, as I see it, living off capital, to be specific, the moral capital invested in this society by a people nurtured in the Judeo-Christian tradition, the many generations who made the Bible's human and social goals an integral part of our democratic American ethos. Unless something like a modernized reading of the Bible again undergirds our civilization, it will not long evidence the ethical devotion which has been one of its chief glories.

Transcending Our Own Old Assumptions

This unanticipated cultural turn radically reverses what has been American Jewry's basic self-understanding since mid-century. Most modernized American Jews once were happy in their agnosticism because they took it for granted that peoples' religious beliefs were irrelevant as long as they were ethical. Only now we discover that having a substantive as against a formal ethics—in this instance, even in our business ethics—depends quite directly upon what we believe. Ultimately, the choice between a business ethics based solely on profit or winning or, worst of all, winning above all else, as against the Jewish demand that we try to realize justice and compassion in every aspect of our lives, is what you fundamentally believe—about people, about society, about duty, about self, and thus, about God, the reality upon which all these values rest.

I derive from this the synagogue's role in resisting the contemporary devaluation of substantive business ethics. That is not, primarily, to preach about the sin we see around us, an activity to be undertaken more to avoid mistaken inferences from its silence than to hope to change things by even realistic moralizing. Rather the synagogue mainly needs to help us reclaim—or assert with new dedication—the Jewish meta-ethical basis of our business lives and, if it needs saying, of our lives as a whole. We need to face with unblinking honesty our joint responsibility to live dedicated both to what God demands of us and the profit we must make to survive in our competitive business world. But having a glimpse of the supremely real and worthy, knowing that it mandates high humanity from us, acknowledging that its realization cannot remain private and quietistic but must be effected in every public and private realm, we are emboldened, against a venal minority, to find the honored Jewish way between a realism that is idolatry and the premature messianism which defaults from history.

341

I can provide some simple guidance as to how to find that middle way. It is, like most other sensible advice today, more dialectical than linear. Let us, first, ground our business ethics in the meliorative idealism of the rabbis. The Talmud and the rest of Jewish law are most easily read as a continual effort to find ways to work within given economic structures while seeking to transcend them. The rabbis want Israel to survive, but they also want Jews to sanctify their lives.

Thus, our sages did not categorically forbid Jewish slave owning. Halakhically observant Jews today could, technically speaking, resinstitute slavery. Of course, these new owners of Jews who sold themselves into slavery would have to conform to the rules the rabbis instituted for them. Abbaye, we are told (Kid. 20a), made this response to the challenge why, when the verses on slavery could be interpreted stringently, he read them liberally. "It is written (Dt. 15:16), 'Because he [the slave] is happy with you.' He must be 'with' [equal to] you in food and in drink so that you should not eat white bread while he has black, you drink old wine while he has new, you sleep in a feather bed and he sleeps on straw. That's why people say, 'Whoever buys a Jewish slave is liking buying a master for himself.' " This may be more sermon than operative law, but it clearly conveys the spirit of the laws of Jewish slave owning as Maimonides later codified them.

"But if not now," Hillel said, "When?"

The danger of a melioristic ethics is that the powerful are forever saying "not now," and so the downtrodden become accustomed to thinking that they must always be patient with injustice. The prophets of Israel knew better. Against the entrenched privilege of the monarchy, the nobles, the wealthy, they said, "God hates evil. We can and must rid ourselves of it right now." They remind us how much sin can hide behind a paternalistic "Look at how much progress we've already made. You can't ask us to do more." But God wants us to exercise justice and compassion now, not merely some day. Consider the problem of women's compensation. Despite all the progress in giving women who wish to do so an equal opportunity to work, the statistics unambiguously show that women still earn very substantially less than men holding the same job. Against the rabbinic meliorism that can become passivity, the prophetic conscience asserts its dialectic ethical demand that this discrimination stop now.

How, practically, can those who must make a profit in a competitive world, balance these divergent Jewish mandates? Talmudically, we need to be part of that minority in our business or profession which is at the forefront of applying its ethical standards. Prophetically, we need to be alert to those times when radical changes in our practices can be made, and we need to be part of those pressing for them.

These injunctions are somewhat contradictory and no one can provide us with a rule by which we can safely, ethically, mediate between them in a given case. So, like our Talmudic forebears, we shall have different opinions about what concretely constitutes proper Jewish ethics in a specific business situation. Writ large, this means the Jewish majority must acknowledge that one can be an ethically sensitive Jew and a Republican or a neo-conservative. Of course, as with one's being a Democrat, the final ethical judgment depends on what one proposes to do about tolerating or ameliorating America's social malpractice. Learning to live ethically with conflicts over whether a patient rabbinic or an urgent prophetic attitude on a given issue is Jewishly wise will be a major test of our developing American Judaism.

How fortunate we are then to have largely internalized the lessons of secular democracy and made them a part of our modernized Judaism. For, in ways our tradition could not envision, it has taught us how to tolerate exasperating contrary opinion and, from the clash of views, better to find our own conscientious way. To us, that generally means seeking reasons that will convince us. Often, however, we remain in a troubled, indecisive "gray" area. Then, the common wisdom holds, we should reach down into "our gut" to intuit what, being who we are, we finally must do. I believe that is the secular equivalent of saying that when reason, knowledge, good counsel and common sense seem inadequate to a decision, we should reach for what we most deeply believe and see what action it entails.

It is just here that who or what our God is will be critical for how we live—and on this point, modern Judaism, for all its various understandings of God, agrees with our tradition in full unanimity. For the God we can allow ourselves to believe in is the God in whose image we must seek to shape ourselves. Believing in false gods, we become untrue to the person we might have been. It is no easy task distinguishing God from the many gods who today claim our allegiance. Nonetheless and despite all its own confusion and doubt, there is no better community than the synagogue in which to pursue that search. And with the gray areas of ethical existence steadily expanding, there is no more critical task in rebuilding our business and general ethics than solidly reestablishing their meta-ethical foundations.

28

Temptation in a
Capitalist Context

A generation or two ago, when I graduated from the university, a wicked prayer made the rounds testifying to our aspirations: "Oh Lord, should temptation come my way, give me the courage to give in to it." Agitated by rising expectations of freedom, we thought ourselves unbearably restricted. We wanted release from our crippling constraints—financial, sexual, social, familial—and thought thereby to achieve full maturity, perhaps even redemption.

Today, even in jest, I cannot commend the virtue of temptation to you. All around us, freedom moves through permissiveness to license. Violation is an esteemed form of creativity and sinfulness a highly marketable commodity. By contrast, we now regularly suspect that the seeming virtuous are really moral double agents. Consider, during the years of your studies you have come to know Michael Deaver, the President's erstwhile confidant who awaits jail, and Larry Speakes, the President's one-time official spokesman who lied about what the President had said; and, to give Democratic iniquity equal time, there was Gary Hart who fornicated with so little concern to cover his marital deceit, we knew he could not be a good President, and his fellow candidate, Joe Biden, who plagiarized speeches his staff was not smart enough to write. The Governor of Arizona has been impeached and found guilty, perhaps soon to join those former members of Congress and the Federal judiciary who are serving time. E. F. Hutton has paid fines for laundering cash and kiting checks while Ivan

Baccalaureate sermon, Colgate University, May 29, 1988.

Boesky and his Wall Street ilk have taught us new by-ways in fiduciary responsibility. Stay tuned, Drexel Lambert and the many others under investigation are certain to enlighten us non-insiders as to the new financial meanings of innocence, guilt, or merely being very shady. The list, as you well know, could easily be expanded.

Surrendering to temptation is so common it now carries little aura of convention-defying heroism but rather quickly justifies itself by its banality, as epitomized in the cynical ethics of "Everyone does it." Indeed, one widely trumpeted indictment of university education today is its failure to throw this moral cancer into remission, as if knowing where the various Platonists and Aristotelians of each generation have differed would endow us with upright character and active social conscience. For all my awe of and pleasure from the cerebral cortex, I feel quite certain that our problems lie far deeper in the self, in those fundamental dispositions of our individuality we, in true poesy, call our soul. So I rise to remind you of it and of all those who taught you over the years about your soul's reality, those people, now anonymous or remembered, whose words still instruct you, whose example still inspires you, whose lasting influence still compellingly appeals to you not to cohabit with sin.

No, I do not propose to define my terms. I remain sufficiently confident of most people's basic decency and in the power of the Judeo-Christian idealism our forebears invested in this country, to let you define them for yourselves. Besides, I am not only a committed religious liberal, I am here to preach, not indulge my analytic proclivities as a professor of theology.

If venality has properly lost some of its stench in our time, we may largely ascribe it to our ethical desire to surrender our illusions about human motivation. Marx taught us money moves the world, Nietzsche made it power, and Freud said libido ruled over all. They were all partly right. So when the villain of Hollywood's *Wall Street*, Gordon Gekko, lectures us on the virtues of greed, we are moved by his half of the truth, not the least because we cannot deny our momentary covetousness when we hear about some real people's almost unreal incomes. Why shouldn't we be "players" in whatever game we fancy and wallow in the kind of money whose regular accompaniments are power, sex, and adulation. In theory, socialism's goal of the common good would organize us more ethically. Realistically, we know that self-aggrandizement gets people to produce far more. So we Americans remain committed to using selfishness to power our social engine.

Quickly we discover that to make the system work we must often morally compromise. Long before we get to the university we learn that some lying and much silence are required to get along and get ahead. How odd of God to exile us from the Garden of Eden and not yet permit us to see the Days of the Messiah—but as long as we live in this in-between age, perfection will be denied us and sainthood will be far beyond the common reach. Such virtue as we may hope to attain will have to arise out of a strange mix of faith kept and betrayed. In the Jewish tradition, obsessed for millennia now with holding survival and righteousness in sacred tension, some socially lubricative lies are commended, the classic being, understandably enough, every bride is beautiful.

Acknowledging that we are this maculate has placed us on the ethician's fearsome "slippery slope." Once we agree to live by compromise, where do we draw the line? We all claim to have our limits, but the demands made upon us regularly outrun our capacity to say "No" and mean it. Besides, who can be certain of what is evil in a time when the good, as in the case of women's rights, keeps being defined differently than it was a few years ago? The gray area expands inexorably, and when we recognize that the white can hardly be discerned we insist, "We can handle it." Len Bias, the prize of last year's collegiate basketball draft, who, like you, looked forward to graduation, surely thought so. So too did those of your friends you've seen ruined by drugs. The epidemic of crack is, in a way, all over our society, everywhere that addiction to money, power, sex, stroking, alcohol, even security, eats away the moral will. The Talmud says, "The urge to do evil is first as flimsy as a spider's web but soon becomes as unbreakable as cart ropes."

Knowing this human predicament, the Buddha taught that, to overcome evil and avoid suffering, we should rid ourselves of all wanting, all grasping, all holding on. It is not this or that for which we yearn that engenders and perpetuates evil but the very act of desiring itself. Only when we renounce all craving, when, indeed, we surrender the very notion of a substantive self that wants and longs and needs, will we be truly free. And to those for whom the path to full enlightenment was too arduous, he commended accepting life's conventional demands serenely, transformed by the moral insight that all its wanting is folly.

We Americans, the product-hungry result of history's greatest hucksterdom, are so steeped in discontent that the Buddha's message of renunciation, or its various separatist analogues, seems a desirable if risky cure for our near-terminal case of living by our lusts. Against all our common American expectations, then, a minority among us have opted to withdraw from the system insofar as they can, convinced that only a stringent self-segregation can save them from being defiled by it.

The rest of us, despite our sense of moral peril, know that we cannot be fully human if we give up the Judeo-Christian project of seeking in everyday life to sanctify the selfishness that so effectively drives it. So we look to our benevolence to others, particularly the powerless and underprivileged, to the faithfulness of our relationships and the caring communities we create, to see if we have indeed lost our faith. A great Jewish teacher was once asked how, in the last judgment, the righteous could be identified. He said that they would be those who had given bread to the hungry and drink to the thirsty, who had offered hospitality to the stranger and clothing to the naked, who had visited the sick on their beds and the prisoners in their cells. And he did not hesitate to add, "I tell you, insofar as you did this to even the least of my brothers, you did it unto me."

This audacious Judeo-Christian insistence on channeling our randy selves to God's service as we stand in the marketplace and the public forum means continual exposure to powerful temptations. Ours is no century in which to hope that some momentary moral triumph has decisively weakened the Devil. Nor is it one in which to proclaim that religion will save us from sin, not while Jim and Tammy Bakker await likely indictment and trial, not with Jimmy Swaggart speedily back in the pulpit to resolve his cash flow problems, not with rabbis in jail for tax scams and priests guilty of molesting their charges. Our religions give us no guarantees, no leaders without clay feet, no one in whom we can fully believe, no one, that is, but God, the One who merits our trust but whom, too often, we find we cannot understand.

What a risky enterprise, then, is this, the soul's venture capitalism. We daringly propose to deny the self free exercise of its appetite for power and pleasure, even while assuming the moral jeopardy of living by its unprecedented effectiveness in feeding the hungry, satisfying the thirsty, welcoming the alien, clothing the naked, caring for the sick and seeking humanity for the felon. We hazard the dangers of this strategy in loyalty to all those who, over the years, awakened our power to do the good: the parents who have tried to love us better than they may have been loved; the friends who saw something in us more valuable than a mere means to their gratification; the teachers who unleashed our capacity to learn and thereby taught us a critical means of self-transcendence; the people, known or anonymous, whose simple goodness or high moral valor endowed us with models of what we ought to be; and everyone who has truly loved us and thereby shown us the self we must yet be. They all accompany us in our wearying but incomparably ennobling effort to be human.

As does God. Only a dogmatic secularism could suggest that it is truly our gut we must reach for when all our moral preparation seems inadequate to a particularly seductive temptation. The raw self will give us only raw guidance—but there is that in us which transcends our ingenious animality and models our Creator. When all else fails us in the hour of temptation, that is our final human resource. These days, the university does not directly teach us very much about this critical art of spiritual search and decision. But it pays tribute to it by retaining this unsecular exercise called a Baccalaureate service. I should like to believe this is its way of reminding us that there is more to education than courses, more to character than grades, more to human destiny than what passes for success. Then let us, in joy and thanksgiving, acknowledge all we have received from God who, in the words of the Jewish blessing for such occasions, "has kept us alive, and sustained us, and brought us to this joyous day," and who we pray will deliver us from temptation and empower us for good, for as long as we may live.

Amen.

29

The Role of Shame
in Business Ethics

Business ethics may profitably focus on the decisions individual workers must make, or on the accepted standards of a given area of activity, or even on the overall sense of right and wrong which guides a civilization's economic activity. My remarks will treat the global rather than the individual issues, largely because I find most people's business ethics derive from what they believe others, in their trade or in the marketplace as a whole, consider to be proper.

I suggest that one useful strategy for judging the adequacy of business ethics is to compare any such system with another which has worked reasonably well for a considerable length of time. Specifically, I propose to delineate some of the characteristics of the ethics of Judaism which have made it, as such things go, rather successful. I am not asserting that Jewish ethics has found a way to keep Jews from becoming scoundrels or that it has turned me and my co-religionists into marketplace saints. The Talmud, with its usual hard-headedness about human nature, records the comment, "The greater the man, the greater his will to do evil." Only the coming of the Messiah will end human sin. But, among human institutions, the Jewish tradition, modernized in response to the Jewish emancipation from the ghetto, has had an unusual record of producing successful business people who retained high regard for the human and social consequences of their profit making. What, then, made Judaism a more than merely adequate inculcator of ethics?

Untitled in *Ethics and Corporate Responsibility* (New York: Hebrew Union College-Jewish Institute of Religion, n.d.).

Let us first consider what we may call some of the formal characteristics of the Jewish approach to ethics. To begin with, Jewish morality is not simply left to the conscience or good will of the individual, though these have their place in Jewish piety. The great Jewish teachers, from Moses on, made a sustained effort to set down in plain words what is expected of people. Biblical religion includes commands like paying a day worker's wages at the conclusion of the work and not some time later. This, in turn, is the subject of Talmudic and later rabbinic discussion as various new forms of social and economic labor relations arose.

Judaism also created a system of education to communicate these rules and dicta to those coming into, that is growing up in, the community. Jewish study, even for children, has largely been the study of texts, and advanced Jewish study has always meant the study of Jewish law. And no one could ever be considered a good Jew without life-long study.

The verbalization of Jewish wisdom did not become static. Often within a given period of Jewish history, we can trace the development of new legal-ethical patterns as times changed. However, Jewish history was not confined to one social structure alone. The laws of the Torah were largely completed under the conditions of Jewish self-rule during a millennium-and-a-half before the Common Era. They were expanded into the Mishnah code of 200 C.E. under Roman domination, whose official interpretation is the Talmud completed in Babylonia, Iraq, about the year 500 under Parthian rule. Its later applications received codification about 1070 by a Spanish Jew who had migrated to Egypt, Moses Maimonides. Then, about 1550, a Turkish Jew, Joseph Karo, gave the ensuing developments classic form in a code, the Shulḥan Aruch, which European Jews accepted only when a Polish rabbi, Moses Isserles, adapted it to their circumstances. And Jewish ethics today, whether in Orthodox continuity or liberal adaptation, continues that chain of tradition.

This legal literature, and the explicit ethical teaching which was its twin in the Oral Law, was not essentially the result of theory or speculation. The writers of the Talmud were apparently officers of the state, authorized to regulate the markets and adjudicate the disputes that arose in them. For two millennia the rabbis' rulings arose out of the confrontation of ethical ideals and traditional norms with the reality of business conducted under conditions of economic scarcity and threats to Jewish survival.

The resulting literature is full of what we call the conflict of values and the need to assert priorities. As a religion of history, Judaism had to be realistic while holding on to and effectuating high spiritual goals. It did so by evolving a subtle interplay between legal requirement and moral ideal. The law generally set forth the ethical minimum which, in a given time and place, one was expected to do. But no spiritually significant tradition could be satisfied with establishing only a moral floor upon which a community could practically move about. So Jewish law is inseparable from a teaching of ethical goals and aspirations which, though not legally enforceable, were expected to be part of a good Jew's life.

This sophisticated system required the creation, maintenance and honoring of a class of legal-ethical experts, the rabbis. They were the masters of this tradition and, though we have been through radical disruption and remain puzzled as to how to apply the old teachings in our radically complex modern situation, we contemporary rabbis remain the continuators and amplifiers of their work.

These formal considerations—articulation, education, development, testing in experience, confronting internal value conflict, realism abut the gap between what can be expected and what ought to be done, and the institutionalization of expertise—all received their power and effectiveness because there was a community which took them seriously. Individual Jews regularly sin, we are taught, and some in every age are called wicked, but the people as a whole believed in its law and lore and sought to live by it. Mothers and fathers taught Jewish rules and values to their children and in significant part judged their actions by them. Jewish heroes were great of spirit; the Jewish sanctuary focuses on a book of guidance and law, the Torah; and Jewish worship addressed the God who gave the commandments and their accompanying ethical instruction.

Participants in the Jewish community shared a common sense of desired quality. Put humanistically, it was a notion of what a decent person ought to be and therefore do—what the Yiddish so untranslatably calls a *mensch*. At its depths, Jewish ethics was a response to the God whose holiness is not essentially found in sacred rite or mystic contemplation but in the proper treatment of human beings. Isaiah exemplifies Judaism's highest intuition of God's proper service when he says, in God's name (1.14-17): "Your new moons and seasonal feasts fill Me with loathing; they are become a burden unto Me, I cannot endure them. When you lift up your hands, I will turn My eyes away from you; though you pray at length I will not listen. Your hands are stained with crime. Wash yourselves clean. Put your evil doings away from My sight. Cease to do evil. Learn to do good. Devote yourselves to justice. Aid the wronged. Uphold the rights of the orphan. Defend the cause of the widow."

Despite the pressures which often forced the Jewish community to restrict its vision and its human expectation, the prophetic sense of Jewish priorities never disappeared from this people. Of all the religious acts Judaism demands of Jews none is more important than acting ethically. Some people thought the tragedy of the nursing home scandal of New York some years ago was our public disgrace in that the leader of one of our international religious organizations was convicted of cheating the government and, in effect, stealing from his elderly patients. What far more deeply revolted most Jews was the notion that he or anyone might think that meticulous observance of religious rites might in any way take the place of a Jew's moral responsibility.

An effective system of ethics must have sanctions. If ethical violations do not have repercussions in the real world, our talk about ethics is only that contemptuous activity, moralizing. At one time in the Jewish community, the sanctions were enforced by the community's court and God's judgment. People were fined or beaten or excommunicated for their violations—and God, too, gave recompense. Today, the Jewish God like the Jewish courts, is largely impotent. Such few sanctions as remain in the Jewish community—a matter of the greatest concern in this time of ethical degeneration—are largely personal and social. Those who continue to care about what it means to be a Jew still largely judge themselves by their ethical performance. And those who remain sensitive to Jewish community opinion know that their character will be gossiped about with weightier judgment than their looks, their goods, their contacts, or their power. As sanctions go, these are not much—but that is precisely an indication of our current moral decline. Nobody cares much about ethics. There is even something exciting about associating with the notorious or even being so.

I would be untrue to my vocation as a theologian if I suggested we need not pay much attention to the formal signs of an adequate business ethic. But I would be false to my Jewish faith and the experience of my people if I did not say that a good system means nothing without a community of people who are deeply committed to it, who share its sense of quality, who give its behests high priority and who exercise sanctions against those who offend against it.

Perhaps my message can best be summed up this way: we will again have no significantly effective business ethics until we once again learn to feel shame for our business immoralities. We moderns, for all the unflappability we seek to project, are not beyond being ashamed. If we were to miss or badly bungle a major, obvious business opportunity, we would privately berate ourselves and would become highly sensitive to what our associates and competitors were saying about our stupidity. We would feel shame for being so bad at business.

But we are not likely to feel anything nearly as intense about making an unethical business decision or going along with one. To feel shame, one needs to care about what one is doing and how others will feel about it. Most of us care a lot about success, money, power, acceptance or other common business and professional values. On the whole, we are not that invested in Judeo-Christian ethics. Indeed brazenness, rather than moral sensitivity is often trumpeted as the sign of a competent executive. No matter how heinous the behavior these days, people come before the cameras to proclaim their innocence. They expect their lawyers to get them off and their public relations people to make everyone forget about it as speedily as possible. Even when we are found guilty, we do not consider it unseemly to be publicly contrite.

The rabbis of the Talmud termed this attitude *azut panim*, literally, strength of face. One musters the inner strength to face down every twinge of conscience in oneself and every glimmer of human reproach that might arise in the eyes of others. The rabbis said that *azut panim* was the sin which caused the destruction of the holy city of Jerusalem and its Temple.

I fear that those who accept the rise of such brazenness as a business ideal may be inviting the impending decline of our civilization. If we would halt that slide, we need to create, wherever we can, the sort of business communities which by their concerns as well as by their formal ethics restore a healthy sense of moral shame to those who do business.

Relating to Groups,
Mine and Others

FIVE

Relating to Groups,
Mine and Others

Few blasphemies in religous history have been more egregious than the license groups have given themselves to treat "sinners" in ways they denounced as grossly perverse when others practiced them. Not the least example of religious groups' inability to abide by the Golden Rule has been their customary defensiveness in the face of criticism; the biblical prophets received little acclaim. Rather, one's sincere challenge to the adequacy of a given faith or one of its doctrines quickly becomes no less than an affront to the one and only God.

I sometimes ruminate as to why few writers have reflected on the ethical problems involved in our relations with our own community, with other groups within one's faith, and particularly with other faiths. On the latter topic, I believe I have given the most detailed Jewish analysis I know of the ethical standards for interfaith theological discussion.

I think it important to reemphasize that the very possibility of exchange as equals—the only way it could be ethically conceived—has resulted from the growth of the democratic ideal. I also see in many Christian participants in dialogue (as in other aspects of theology) a recognition I had not noticed in a prior generation that most moderns will largely evaluate the merit of a given faith by how it treats religious strangers and aliens.

As one of the few avowed Jewish theologians, I have often been called upon to participate in interfaith dialogue. Occasionally I have responded to the invitation not only by studying substantive matters of mutual concern but by reflecting on what we ought to be doing with one another. I am particularly pleased that I have recently been able to extend this experience at theological dialogue with Christians to an exchange with an eminent representative of Buddhism. That has allowed me to make some observations that go beyond Jewish-Christian discussions to a broader religious horizon—here complicated by the fact that the theologians present their faiths as creative reinterpreters, not primarily as faithful transmitters of a tradition.

In these papers I do not often speak directly about the ethical issues involved in interfaith exchange. I do not have to, my partners understanding them largely as I do. But the sensitive reader, even if skeptical about the possibility and value of such conversations, should have little difficulty in extricating the values here being put into practice.

30

Rethinking the Reform Jewish
Theory of Social Action

You have asked me, as a friendly outsider, to utilize an academic point of view to help us figure out how, in the present complex historical situation, we might best conceptualize the Reform Jewish commitment to social ethical responsibility. I am very pleased to have received your invitation since I have always had a great sense of the importance of the Commission on Social Action and considered it a body which has lent dignity and weight to the Reform movement.

1. The Premises of Our Classical Social Action Stance

What once made social action a matter of the highest priority for Reform Judaism? I shall try to answer that question in terms of our theoretical position, our pragmatic concerns and the general social spirit of the time.

Theoretically, there were two fundamental theological commitments which gave power to the Reform Jewish interest in social action, it being taken for granted that Judaism is an activist religion. The first thesis was that the essence of Judaism was its universal ethics. Specifically, we argued that the prophetic tradition was central to Judaism and that prophecy emphasized ethics over ritual. The second thesis was that the universal social ethics of prophetic Judaism was best expressed in, or was the equivalent of, liberal politics. As a result many Jews believed that

From the *Journal of Reform Judaism*, vol. 27, no. 3, (Fall 1980).

liberal politics was Jewish ethics in action and, hence, if you were so involved you were, in fact, fulfilling your central Jewish responsibility.

Implicit in these two commitments was the assumption that people were essentially good. We talked about the perfectibility of humankind, believing that if we could change the situation in which people functioned—the educational, the occupational, the nutritional—what was inside them would respond by creating goodness. If their social circumstances were altered, people would activate themselves to build a better world. The great symbol of this activist perfectibility was the Messianic Age. We were confident that all newly caring people, not just one extraordinary agent of God, the Messiah, would bring that age about. And liberal politics was our chief agent for achieving it. That yielded the equation: Judaism equals ethics equals liberal politics equals the coming of the Messianic Age. Consequently we dedicated ourselves to social action with a messianic fervor.

Pragmatically, as well, a devotion to liberal activism seemed the most practical course of action for Jews to take. I do not consider that a false Jewish standard. A truth which does not function in history hardly seems Jewish. Since Bible times truth has been validated for us by being carried out in the real affairs of people, their politics and their history. Therefore, that what is theoretically true also turned out to have a pragmatic justification fit in nicely with our basic Jewish attitude.

The pragmatic justification could be short-range; namely, if we won rights for all people, specifically for the underprivileged, we would secure our rights as Jews. It was to our interest, then, to work actively for the rights of others. In the longer view, making society more fully equitable, having democracy work for more and more people, would also reduce the possibility that there would be outbursts of anti-semitism. We were so sure democracy could be made to work on this long-range basis that we were willing to accept certain short-range disabilities for the sake of our long-range goal. Thus, the commitment of Jews in the United States to the public school system made life incredibly difficult for Jewish education. We accepted that because we saw public education creating a pluralistic society as well as giving us the sort of training we needed to get ahead in this community.

Besides, the times seemed to favor the liberal attitude. The *Zeitgeist*, the spirit of the age, was liberal in the circles in which Jews moved, that is, among the urban and well-educated. We had come from either the lower class or the bottom of the middle class and were making our way up the social ladder. Having long been outsiders, we were determined to be insiders and culturally sophisticated. We avidly shared the notion that a liberal spirit was on the move that would change, even save, the world. As time passed, we could point to specific social victories which we and our allies had won, and thus our sense of being in the vanguard of a coming change reinforced our theoretical and pragmatic interest in liberalism.

One helpful feature of that time was being able to identify the enemy. It was the privileged class. Entrenched in power, they were preventing the underprivileged, indeed the masses as a whole, from exercising their rights. That the Jews themselves had ever been emancipated was a tremendous, symbolic victory for liberalism. Basic to the consciousness of the sensitive Jew in that period was a personal sense that a radical change had taken place in society which reversed 1500 years of steadily worsening discrimination against Jews. Many people in the Jewish community had parents or grandparents who could remember not being free. Therefore the liberals, who worked for oppressed minorities, such as we were at the end of the eighteenth century and, in some cases, remain, were our saviours. Liberalism overwhelmingly commended itself to us on a personal level and this historical perception lies behind much of what I shall be saying.

All this fit in well with the major social drive of the Jewish community. Because the Emancipation had only become practical for most of us in the period after World War II, we had a burning desire to move out into the world, to become involved in its problems, to add to our ethnic horizon of significance the universal cares of humankind. The times were liberal and we were eager to join the rest of humanity. These combined drives made liberalism irresistible.

2. The Loss of the Old Foundations

Now I must be negative and discuss what has made social action today much less significant to the whole Jewish community and particularly to Reform Jews. Let me be clear. Our situation is not that no one cares or does anything. The mail from the Union of American Hebrew Congregations indicates that our national movement and some congregational committees are doing extraordinary things. Many people should be admired for their ethical stamina. And I admit that, to a surprising extent, Jews are still largely voting liberal. Yet the preponderant weight of evidence of all sorts—spirit, elan, emphasis, priorities—indicates that something has radically changed. The intellectual basis for that transformation is clear. All the previous reasons I gave for our being involved in social action now seem substantially wrong or inaccurate. We have lost our old rationale and no longer have a secure ground on which to base our political activism. And, lacking assurance, we have lost passion.

Let us review our premises in reverse order, starting with the spirit of the times, going on to the pragmatic arguments, and finally ending with a consideration of religious theory. The mood of our age is substantially anti-liberal—and not just among Jews. In the varied circles in which I move, the enemy is not just the privileged class but often the liberals themselves. Many people actively distrust them as problem solvers. They seem to create new problems, sometimes worse ones, than those they had answered. At the moment, they do not seem to have any new ideas. Mostly they still call for more government action or some professor's theory on how, say, to settle the economic or energy trade-offs. Their ideas sound like dressed-up versions of the same ones we have heard for years and which have not proved satisfactory. The liberals' basic notion, that institutions are the primary means of increasing social righteousness, is highly unappealing. Most institutions seem substantially corrupt; almost all of them have failed us badly. We tend not to trust them. To look to them to change society radically makes little sense.

Besides, we now feel that social problems are too complex for easy solution. Once things were easier. When we had a social difficulty, we read our liberal magazines and got the answer. Today, with a greater information flow, we are quickly convinced that the experts hopelessly disagree and no answer is unproblematic. The old liberal way of finding remedies and going out to fight for them against the children of darkness therefore seems somewhat immature.

Perhaps that mood is intensified because we oversold liberalism. We believed social action would bring the Messianic Age—and all we got was the 1970s. If we hadn't expected so much, we wouldn't feel so bad. But having been deeply disappointed, people have little confidence in the liberal approach to social betterment.

Permit me an editorial comment. One sign of the low state of liberal ethics is the current poverty of its rhetoric. When liberals write articles today, they sound badly tired, using phrases that no longer ring and reasoning that hardly carries conviction. The sharp, interesting writing is by conservatives. They seem to have new things to say, and though much of it is criticism, by contrast to the liberals' writing, it seems quite wise.

This general American mood has its repercussons in the Jewish community. Among self-respecting Jews, the *Zeitgeist* is not universalistic but particularistic. We are concerned with our survival and fearful for our people. We delve into our roots and identify ethnicity with authentic Jewishness. As the CCAR *Centenary Perspective* (statement on our spiritual situation) puts it, the Holocaust, the current spiritual emptiness of western civilization, and the accomplishments of the State of Israel have made our people, not our world, our highest priority. Social action is therefore of marginal Jewish interest.

Were liberal activism still pragmatically valuable we might fight this cultural shift. Clearly that is not the way many Jews view things. They feel that liberal politics now does not promote but runs counter to our Jewish interests. Our social situation has changed. We are not among the underprivileged groups in this society. We are either one of the most, or the most, successful religio-ethnic community on the North American continent. This high status has been obtained in the present social structure. Any proposed change in an order which has given us our gains would

immediately affect our status and privileges. The obvious example is busing, and I am sure you could give many more.

Furthermore, the notion that we should take short-term losses to
achieve long-range general democracy seems naive and utopian. We cannot honestly believe that social-political action, particularly to the point of
ethnic sacrifice, will create so good a society that people will stop being
anti-semitic. The Jewish role in general political decisions is not very
great. In the meantime, we would be taking Jewish losses for a dubious
political goal. So people ask, "Why should this small and troubled community handicap itself in a conservative time for a long-range goal whose
attainment is questionable?"

Internationally, "what's good for the Jews" is almost undebatable. For
many American Jews, universal social action regularly conficts with
American Jewish responsibility to the State of Israel. Members of this Commission had to battle the issue of the Vietnam War and spilled their blood
on the floor of the Union of American Hebrew Congregations biennial convention to fight for what was, in my opinion, the mandate of Jewish ethics.
They can testify that there are pressures generated by our commitment to
the State of Israel which demand we not get involved in universal ethical
issues. Thus in the current United States budget, the State of Israel needs
guns but social action calls for more butter for the poor. "If you are for
Jews, why aren't you for guns? And why are you involved with butter?" So
goes the common refrain.

Our basic political situation is not complicated. The State of Israel
needs American Jews as its lobby, not as an independent ethical community. The political rules are clear. Political leaders want support, not dissent or the diversion of energy. Martin Luther King was no longer invited
to the White House once he got his nose into the Vietnam War. The Israelis
need American Jews to support the United States defense budget and an
anti-Soviet American foreign policy, not directly to devote their political
clout, such as it is, to improving American democracy. I call that essentially a right-wing political stance. I think it fair to say that what the State
of Israel has meant within the American Jewish community is a drastic
reorientation of Jewish political concern. If "what is good for the Jews" is
identified—as very many people in our community do—with what is
good for the State of Israel, then supporting Israeli objectives means damp-
ing one's liberalism.

This is a most troublesome issue. Fortunately, on many levels it simply dissolves because we know that nothing so well exemplifies the Jewish will to live and do so with quality as does the State of Israel. Compare
its accomplishments, despite its crushing burdens, with those of other new
countries founded since World War II. The Israeli effort—to be democratic,
to take in refugees, to build a welfare state, etc.—may not be perfect.
Nevertheless, it is also, on a simple human level, awesome. In large part,
we may take great ethical encouragement from what even Jewish secularity
retains of a Jewish sense of the desired quality of human existence. None-

theless, something has substantially changed. At one time it looked as if the politics connected with the State of Israel would be positive, ethical, humanistic and universal. That is no longer the case.

Moreover, as long as it was a question of Israeli survival, our leaders could say "no" to any attempt whatsoever to criticize or disassociate oneself from the State of Israel. Think what that does to conscience. It denies that it is possible to love, identify with, be involved with, care for, struggle for a cause on almost every occasion but at certain special moments legitimately to say, "It's enough. There are limits. There are some things we not only can't do, but we shouldn't be asked to do."

I believe (with Abba Eban and others) that the treaty with Egypt has changed the Israeli problem from that of survival to only, *nebbich*, that of security. If so, that should allow for open, critical discussion among American Jews about Israeli affairs and some revival of universal concerns. But that is too subtle for most Jews. And it certainly does not serve the political needs either of the State of Israel or of the Jewish fund-raising apparatus in the United States. Both prefer the solidarity that crisis engenders. I admit that choosing which issues you are going to fight about is a major sign of maturity and character. Whether there is an issue with regard to the State of Israel worth publicly fighting about has to be approached with the most serious deliberation. Any such criticism on the part of this Commission or of the Reform movement as a whole would be an extraordinarily difficult act and might even prove radically counter-productive institutionally. I can well understand official bodies of the Reform movement evading such issues for organizational reasons. But I deny that all individual Reform Jews ought to keep silent about them.

Because the Israelis' present political needs are generally antithetical to the usual universal social ethical concerns, we see a radical diminution of the latter. The strategy of incorporating political action for the Israelis into our social action programs will, therefore, not allow us to revive the classic liberal concerns. We no longer get synergy, but a large measure of conflict.

Thus, locally and internationally, social action is pragmatically contra-indicated rather than mandated. The older theological basis for social action has similarly been shaken. Were it not, ideological certainty might enable us to overcome the shift of the *Zeitgeist* and the practical arguments against universal social devotion. Any strengthening of the Reform commitment to social action will, therefore, have to be preceded by a rethinking of its theological foundations.

A practical consideration must be introduced at this point. During the last generation the participants in these theological discussions have increased both in number and in points of view represented. At one time, Jewish ethics was largely the province of Reform rabbis. Today we not only expect Conservative and other liberal Jews to treat ethical issues but, as the most recent entrants to the arena, Orthodox Jews as well. Of particular interest is the participation not only of the so-called "modern Orthodox," but of rabbis and laity who stand even further to the religious and cultural right. All these thinkers bring an expanded range of Jewish learning, intellectual concern and personal sensitivity to the debates. This has radically altered the way the ethics of Judaism must be discussed by sophisticated people. The critique of the older theological foundations of social action, which follows, is not limited to the Jewish political right, regardless of their religious affiliation. It summarizes my sense of where Jewish intellectuals generally stand, though much of the criticism which has brought them there has originated on the right. (Obviously, too, the frequent identification of the religious right with the political right is applicable here, most closely with regard to the previously discussed conflict between the imperative deriving from our commitments to the State of Israel and to universal ethics.)

To begin with, the assertion that the essence of Judaism has been universal ethics now seems historically unwarranted. Academically, how could one know or demonstrate what the spiritual essence of any centuries-old people is? Our liberal forebears confidently answered this question out of the assumptions of German critical-idealistic philosophy. We no longer give it that credence. Worse, as we look at the classic Jewish texts which the liberal thinkers cited to prove their case, we almost always find them reading into them their own, modernistic liberal ideas, most frequently by taking the passages out of context. The contemporary academic approach to the texts finds little direct universalism in them and results in a far more particularistic view of Jewish responsibility than was given by the early liberals.

If students of Judaism see anything as central to the Jewish experience, it is Jewish legal obligation. That is not the same as ethics. Thus the Bible has many words for God's regulations, but none for abstract ethics. Neither the prophets nor the rabbis of the Talmud saw ethics as a category distinct from Torah, The Law. While that term has acquired unfortunate overtones as a result of Christian polemics against it, taken in a Jewish sense, that is, incorporating *agadah* (love) as well as *halakhah* (the law), the Psalms as well as Deuteronomy, it is a useful term to characterize the encompassing Jewish sense of loyalty and response to God. As one reads the books in which the Jewish sense of religious obligation has been elaborated, the genuinely *universal* ethical must be described as few and marginal. They are there and they are not unimportant. To overlook them would be to distort traditional Judaism. But they are not the major concern or the principal religious consideration of Jewish duty as our liberal teachers would have had us believe. There were historical reasons, I am convinced, for the special horizon of these pre-Emancipation texts, and it was the genius of the early Reformers to see that a new social context demanded a new balance in the priorities of Jewish obligation. Nonetheless, if anything can be called central to rabbinic literature in which Jewish duty was explicated over the centuries, it is the survival of the Jewish people for its service to God. If that is true, then any contemporary effort to call an ethical position authentically Jewish will have to validate itself in terms of its roots in Jewish law and its relation to the survival of the Jewish people as well as its service to God.

This attack on the older liberalism has special poignancy because it is occasionally coupled with a telling analysis of the motives which led many to utilize this position as an ideology. Not a few liberal Jews wanted ethics to be the essence of Jewish responsibility for that freed them from having to do acts which might openly identify them as Jews. Judaism as essentially social action is thus often an apparently noble rationale for Jewish assimilation. One sees it in the extreme case: the more fanatic the Marxist the less Jewish religious duties one maintained and, for a long time, the less ethnic responsibilities as well. Today, by contrast, serious-minded Jews will substantially judge the Jewish authenticity of protagonists of a universal cause in terms of what specific Jewish disciplines their beliefs also lead them to undertake.

Even assuming that universal ethics has a major role in Jewish duty, its old corollary thesis, that ethical values means liberal politics, is now denied. Surely on many specific issues, Jewish survival seems to mandate conservative positions, for example, government help to religious day schools and limited freedom for abortions. It will not do to argue that such stands will destroy democracy, for there are other functioning democratic nations which do not have our American arrangements on these matters. The least one can say today is that the political application of the ethics of Judaism is an open matter. Perhaps it might be best to describe Jewish ethics as often having plural political outcomes. That is, our faith can often only give us a general sense of the good, but when it comes to specific political decisions or social structures in which they are to be realized, different interpretations are possible. That there is something Talmudic about the need to tolerate both liberal and conservative political positions in Judaism only makes it seem more genuinely Jewish than the older identification of Judaism with liberalism.

It should come as no surprise, then, to assert that the view of humankind which underlay the old liberal theology has undergone serious revision. I will not repeat here what the CCAR *Centenary Perspective* says about the effect of the Holocaust upon us in this regard, or what I and others have written about this matter. Having finally faced up to the Holocaust and, somehow with it, to the mess we have made of western civilization and American democracy, we cannot any longer easily be optimistic about human nature. It seems ridiculous to speak of people as perfectible, to believe that they are so basically good that if we only provide them with the proper social circumstances they will create a messianic time. That does not mean that we Jews now propose to take on the classic Christian view of human nature as fallen or, as some put it, perverse. Rather, the modern liberals' estimate of the human potential for good seems less realistic than the Talmudic notion of the human will-to-do-good being fought by a powerful, wily, relentless inner will-to-do-evil. None of us is so good as to become perfect on our own, not even Moses, and none of us is so wise or pious that we cannot, at any time, be seduced by the evil urge. That seems to explain people as we know them, if we are honest. It certainly explains why we regularly subvert even the best of our human institutions, of which marriage, the family and our schools are obvious contemporary instances.

Thus it seems laughable now to think of politics in messianic terms. Even Marxists seem to know better these days. The rest of us are not being merely cynical when we cannot get aroused by a certain candidate or a given bit of legislation. We know they will not change human nature. For all the good that people can and should do, we are spiritually problematic creatures. We do not trust ourselves as much as we used to, certainly not as in the days when we had such confidence in human power that we had no reason to be concerned about God. I think it is not an exaggeration to say that, as we have become more realistic about our finitude, we have become more open to God's reality and place in our own lives. Our quiet minority resurgence of Jewish spirituality in the past few years is the result of a reverse *tzimtzum* (mystic self-contraction): as people have withdrawn from omni-competence, they have made room for God in their world.

I apologize for what may seem undue negativity, but I do not see how we can move forward without honestly facing up to the fact that we have lost much of the old theological, pragmatic and social justifications for our Reform Jewish theory of social action.

3. A Dialectical Commitment to Social Action

Can the present situation be changed? I do not know. There is too much which affects us which cannot be anticipated. What, for example, will be the general human situation in western civilization in the next generation? Setting aside all the problems of simple human survival, what will be our spiritual condition? Will we move into a moral decline or remain at our present level of dejection? Will we find a renewed sense of our human capacity to effectuate righteousness? Who can answer such questions with any assurance? Yet I think there is a special Reform Jewish commitment to thinking through and putting into effect the universal aspect of our Jewish responsibility. Practically put, if we do not undertake that task today, no one else in the Jewish community is likely to do it. Historically, and for good reason, in my opinion, universal ethics has been a major concern of our movement and its daring willingness to face up to the implications of the Emancipation of the Jews. Any move to reform our pursuit of social justice should be based on the commitments we share with our Reform forebears, though it will necessarily apply them in a fashion appropriate to our present situation.

That is emphatically true in one critical respect: Reform rejects the notion that our legitimate choices are limited to either/or, either ghetto Judaism or modern Christianity, Jewish Orthodoxy or social assimilation, classic liberalism or contemporary conservatism, perhaps allied with religious orthodoxy. The failures of liberalism should not drive us back to a pre-liberal attitude toward Jewish duty, but on to a post-liberal, socially realistic recommitment to our universal ethical responsibility.

The first step in that new stance is to recognize what remains valid in the older liberal teaching concerning Jewish ethics today. Four themes may be quickly identified.

The first of these is the primacy of ethics in Jewish duty. This is not the same as saying that ethics is the essence of Judaism, though it is surely related to that assertion. Instead we declare that nothing is a more significant test of the "good Jew" than ethical behaviour. That may not be all a good Jew has to do, but it is the least one expects. No amount of other Jewish observance will, in our eyes, substitute for a refusal to "Cease to do evil; learn to do good. Devote yourself to justice; aid the wronged," in whatever modern form these injunctions of Isaiah 1:15f appear. That this is not simply an odd Reform Jewish attitude is attested by the almost universal revulsion in the Jewish community at the conduct of Bernard Bergman in the New York nursing home scandal.

The second such theme is the notion that the universal aspect of our Judaism must be a significant aspect of our present Jewish practice. Had many people in western civilization not come to think universally about human responsibility, we Jews would still be in the ghetto or worse. Intellectually, the notion of universal ethical duties is the foundation of the Emancipation of the Jews and the basis of our right to participate as equals in general society. Unless we affirm such an ethic, we deny the grounds of our unimpeded participation in western civilization and the basis upon which we assert that our Emancipation still needs to be completed.

I do not see that this classic liberal assertion has been invalidated by the Holocaust. Though it may teach us a new and bitter realism about human nature, the Nazi brutality is the antithesis of our liberal conviction that no group is exempt from being treated with justice and mercy. Thus, our moral outrage at the Nazis is premised upon our insistence that they knew what acts human beings ought never to do. They were guilty, despite all social pressure, only because there is a universal morality all people can know and should follow. Shall the Jews, who have suffered so much from the particularism of other peoples, now fail to give appropriate devotion to their duties to all of humankind?

Practically, too, it ill behooves a people so worried about its security effectively to deny its responsibilities to its society. What moral judgment must be made of a group which has benefited extraordinarily from participating in the general community—as a result of its hard work, to be sure—now refusing to give back to that community a significant measure of its interest and energy? Most Jews who advocate the least practical amount of involvement in general social affairs refuse to speak of it

368

openly, for they know it would be self-incriminating. The effects of this closet ethnocentrism are very widely felt in the Jewish community.

Again, I wish to assert that this commitment to universalism is felt far beyond the boundaries of Reform Judaism. Permit me to give a somewhat debatable but, in my view, exciting example. I refer to the increasing pressure for giving women full rights in the Jewish religion, since universalism contradicts sexual discrimination. Despite the difficulties that the ideologues are having with it, I detect a slow but steady movement in all sections of the Jewish community to give women full rights. Even among Orthodox Jews, where women may be willing to maintain their subordinate status to men as "separate but equal," new models of work and marital relationships, as well as a new sense of what is permissible within the law, have appeared. I suggest that is because a universal sense of personhood is now being applied to the special class called women.

Third, we continue to affirm the thesis that political activism is, in our time and place, a valuable way to create righteousness. Traditional Jewish law does not call for civic involvement; however, for emancipated Jews to utilize their franchise to bring greater social justice into being seems to us an obviously legitimate form of Jewish duty. Its clear-cut example is Zionism. Everyone talks about Reform Jews being anti-Zionist, but the State of Israel does not exist because of traditional Jewish law. People rarely discuss the Orthodox who fought Zionism as a heretical assumption of the Messiah's prerogative and an interference with God's providence. The notion that people ought to be politically active is a modernist ideal we Jews learned from western democracy, not from the Torah. As a result of it, not only were we emancipated in Europe but we finally learned to emancipate ourselves. I do not see how modern Jews can turn their backs on political activism as a significant means of living as a Jew.

The fourth modern affirmation which the Jewish tradition, in a comparable manner, did not hold is that all human knowledge is seriously limited and, therefore, pluralism is a social necessity. For liberals, no one possesses the absolute truth which all others must accept. All have equal rights and may engage in the continual search for a more adequate view of the truth. Modern history has taught us that to identify any human being or institution with the absolute is to invite tyranny and run the risk of fanaticism. We recapture the virtue of liberal democracy every time the reactionaries come to power. The Ayatollah Khomeini in Iran has done more to rehabilitate liberalism by his negative example than most of us have been able to do by our positive accomplishments. What might result if the Orthodox right should ever come to power in the State of Israel is not totally dissimilar from what we see in Iran. We cannot simply assume that all Orthodoxy is modern and democratic, as much of it tends to be in the United States. The notion of a unique revelation by God does not easily come to terms with democracy and pluralism. Many orthodoxies have found a way to do so, but it should be clear that on these values there is a conflict between us and our unreformed tradition.

369

What I have just said suggests a reversal of the old justification of liberalism. It arose from our sense of the goodness of humankind. Ironically, it is now required because of our deep-seated evil urge and the consequent abuse of power by people and their institutions, most notably government. No one is good enough not to have a check on him or her. All of us need to share power so that we may help keep others from doing us evil.

I believe these four continuing liberal theses validate a significant and substantial social action commitment. I think we can make a good case for them, but they are not messianic in their claim or aspiration, and that marks their major divergence from the older view.

Our realistic view of human nature mandates another departure from classic theories of Jewish social action. We can no longer be content to be the passive recipients of the truths of western civilization's liberal political thinkers. These need to be balanced by some criticisms we make of them on the basis of our Jewish faith and experience. Though I now do so in the language of our culture, I think the substance of these four assertions stems out of the Jewish tradition.

First, our Judaism insists that not every exercise of freedom is ethical and not every exercise of freedom, even if ethical, is necessarily "good for the Jews." One of our contemporary problems is that freedom as such has been raised to so high a value that whatever one does authentically, whatever one feels one must do to be true to oneself, is recognized as good— regardless of what is done or what its effects are. Self-indulgence has become a moral creed. Even ordinary people succumb. The world is too big and too complicated; people know it can't be changed and they don't want to get involved too much. So they pamper themselves. Living the "good life" is now often not an ethical, but an aesthetic value. Against all such radical individualism, our Judaism denies that one can be properly human without a significant social conscience.

It would further insist that even the ethical use of freedom is not a sufficiently high standard of action for a "good Jew." The classic example is intermarriage. Two people may be free and authentic with one another, but if they are not both Jews, their marriage is not "good for the Jews." So Jewish tradition argues, and a substantial number of Reform rabbis agree.

One may put this in another fashion. Ethics may be our highest priority, but the ethical is not all one needs to do as a Jew. Today, if one asks, "Rabbi, if I do the right thing but don't come to the synagogue, I'm a good Jew, isn't that so?" my answer must be, "No." Ethics are indispensable to Jews, but they do not nearly exhaust Jewish duty. Rather our ethics need to be one part of our whole sense of Jewish responsibility.

Second, the universal ideal—that individuals should work for all humankind—did not arise easily in human history. The obvious empirical evidence is that people are quite varied. They have different abilities and can accomplish different things. On any practical basis one would never arrive at the idea that all individuals are equal. Certainly when one looks at cultural differences, it is a mystery where the idea of universalism arose. Only when we see the unity beyond the multiplicity and acknowledge its commanding power can universalism have sway. People can take humankind seriously only from a particular base in monotheism or its spiritual equivalent. We are universalists because we are Jews. Christians and Moslems can be universalistic because they derive that idea from the Jewish Bible. But not every "bible" and not every religion or philosophic point of view will bring one to universalism. Therefore, if we are committed to humanity as a whole, it is because we start from a Jewish faith-base. That being the case, our Jewish universalism had better not be overemphasized and thus destroy our Jewish particularity, or we will cut the very ground out from under our ethical stance.

Third, the secular realm is not necessarily ethically or Jewishly desirable. By secular, I mean those social areas where we Americans have decided that religion will not make any difference. In a post-Puritan age we must ask if secularity still contains an ethical content, specifically a sense of social responsibility, a commitment to sharing with others. At one time, we could trust that any intelligent person would know one had to be ethical in this corporate sense. Then, in the days before a proselytizing libertarianism, one could assume that any educated, cultured, sophisticated person would be socially responsible. That assumption has very substantially passed. Today it is difficult to know what are the secular reasons for being obligated to others than oneself. That it is often convenient or useful to do so, that it is part of the tradition of our country, that we need it to get along with one another, that our mothers and fathers taught us so—these are practical and useful reasons but hardly compelling ones. They do not yield an imperative. They do not tell us why one *must* care about the good, why one *must* devote oneself to the good, why against the dehumanizing forces of society one *must* resist. With our high confidence in human rationality and goodness eroded, it is not clear on what secular, non-religious basis one would assert a persistent, commanding social ethic.

Moreover, it may be useful to agree that in our American society we will allow for a large secular space in order for everyone to be able to get along, but that is not the Jewish ideal. Judaism calls for all people to acknowledge God's "rule" and live by God's laws. If, in fact, the secular is empty of the ethical, can Jews be happy with so much neutral, aethical room in our lives? Must we not ask whence the qualitative input is now to come in our culture? Our secular society seems to swing between two moods, exhilaration and dejection, and both conduce to nihilism. We say, "I can do anything, *anything*; I can't do anything right." On the one hand, we have a freedom which destroys values: I am able to change any rules, make myself whatever I wish and explore anything I desire. On the other hand, in the midst of extraordinary affluence and opportunity, people are chronically depressed and unable to energize their moral capacities. Judaism cannot be satisfied to adapt to such a secularity but must seek to transform it.

This leads to my fourth balancing Jewish thesis, which is that our social ethics now must have a spiritual quality. Jews are classicly committed to social ethics for religious reasons and would criticize any efforts to try to create them on a purely secular basis, although tactically it might be wise to join with secularists in various affairs. Our tradition declares that there is something other than ourselves in the universe, something that charges us with the responsibility to be better than we are and gives us humans a power to create the good which will not come into being unless we create it. This otherness will not let us rest at yesterday's or this morning's moral achievement but urges us on to messianic goals. It will not let us be satisfied with our doing this individually but requires us to do it with all other people.

Because this command transcends us, ethical action has a primary, persistent place in our lives. Because of it, we know all human beings must live with moral quality and Jews ought to be a people of special ethical excellence. Because this command stems from what is most real and lasting, we Jews do not give up. We fail, our projects go wrong and our politics turn out not to be redemptive, but the worth of our ideals and their ultimate triumph are assured because they are based on God. So I know that I personally am worthwhile, despite all my failures, because God does not forsake me or my people. What is not accomplished in my lifetime or in this generation will yet surely be accomplished. The Jewish people is not defeated, for God does not die and the Covenant remains in effect. From this realistic point of view, our social action commitment arises more because of our faith in God than out of our trust in humankind and its capacity to do the good.

Our new theory of social action must, therefore, be dialectical, one in which we balance what democratic society has taught us by what Judaism now teaches us needs to be done to rehabilitate liberalism. In typical Reform fashion, we want a mixture of what our new view of human nature tells us is the best of our old ethical theory and the continuing truths of our tradition. Such a new theory can partially be worked out in abstraction by our theoreticians. The greater part, I think, needs to be created in terms of specific cases, figuring out in the face of hard reality how one balances the Jewish and the modern affirmations against each other. Even more important than the conclusions reached, I believe, will be the style and manner in which the new social action decision-making process will be carried out. Permit me to make six suggestions as to how the procedures of social action might now be appropriately fashioned.

4. Reshaping the Work of Social Action

One, to claim Jewish adequacy, that is, to claim one is speaking from a social ethic that is authentically Jewish, one must ground one's discussion in Jewish law, the core of traditional Jewish teaching. That does not mean we have to agree with *halachah* in all of its decisions. Since its classic documents were formulated in non-democratic societies amid economies of scarcity, I suggest that we cannot do so much of the time. But as Jews we must begin with an honest engagement of the full range of sources, liberal or reactionary though their substance appear. Then we need to be quite open and honest about where we agree or disagree with them and, in the latter case, explain why we think that disagreement is legitimate. It seems to me that one of the major tasks before us is to create a body of specialists in Jewish law who can help us study the various kinds of issues we must face.

Second, a major consideration in any position that purports to be a Jewish decision is its Jewish consequences. Our version of an environmental impact statement is a Jewish welfare impact statement. How will taking this stand affect the present needs and interests of the Jewish community? That does not mean we have to do what many other people think is in the short range interests of the Jewish community. But it must be clear, if we are committed Jews, that we are concerned with the Jewish people and its needs and that we have made that concern a major factor in evaluating the risks our decision may engender.

Third, any position that we want to consider must be elaborated in terms of plural alternatives and ought to explain our evaluation of them. It is no longer obvious that every question has one answer—and that a liberal one. How seriously do we consider the various available options? Why do we finally choose one over the others? More, can we help other people learn how to choose among alternatives? Our major ethical goal today, in my opinion, is the responsible use of our freedom. In our pluralistic time, that means facing many options and learning how to choose between them.

Fourth, our new realism requires us to be systematically suspicious of any easy solutions to significant human problems, particularly those which rely on government. I do not envy anyone who has the responsibility of trying to give the Jewish community guidance on SALT II, inflation and the energy crisis. Is it really true that we know how to deliberate over and come to a Jewish answer on such issues? When one considers who may be sitting in any congregation in terms of academic, intellectual, business and human expertise, it is very hard to believe that anything less than the most searching deliberations will receive much respect from our thoughtful members.

In the old days it was possible to judge our social action effectiveness by the number of opinions we turned out. We had answers then because we had the relatively simple identification of Judaism with ethics and political liberalism. If those easy identifications are broken today and the problems are far more complex than we once thought, then the process will be as important to us as the result. I even venture to say that how we think issues through, struggle with them and try to come to a responsible Jewish response to them is almost more important than the results themselves. In my opinion, unless we have Jewishly grounded, realistically confronted, alternatively elaborated decisions, intelligent people will not find our opinions worth much.

Finally, I do not see that we can make any immediate messianic claims for what we are doing. We may be inching toward the Messianic Age but we are on a long, long road. People just cannot do as much of an ultimate nature as we once thought they could. I think we can work out of passion as well as duty, for we are able to increase justice and peace. But we must leave something for God to do. And, fortunately, because of God, we know all our defeats are temporary.

Does that effectively take the action out of social action? We seem to have wound up with a study group. In part, that is what I am advocating. That is appalling by the older liberal style of social action, which gloried in putting us on record as supporting every good cause. I am against resolutions being our central concern—but I equally oppose only studying. It seems perfectly clear to me that there are legitimate exigencies in decision making. Sometimes they are forced upon us by the society as a whole, sometimes by inner need. There are times in the political process when one cannot wait any longer to come to a decision. There are some issues which one does not have time to study and work up deliberately.

In the present situation, if we have to err, I think it ought to be on the side of proper process. Exigency can easily become an excuse for going back to grinding out our answers and taking quick stands. I do not believe we can speak responsibly to very many issues. Indeed, I think trying to figure out which ones we ought to face up to is the skill we most immediately need to learn. Then, perhaps, when we have accepted our limits, we may be able to learn how responsible, post-liberal Jewish decision making ought to be carried out. And the more experience we have in working on long-range topics, the easier it will be for us to live up to our new standards when we come to a situation of emergency and must reach a decision speedily.

With all the limits of this appraoch, it seems to me a proper reflection of our contemporary notion of human maturity. A mature person today is not doctrinaire, but often uncertain and conflicted, perhaps confused a great deal of the time. Nevertheless, such a person knows that in the midst of all the difficulty one needs to fight for one's integrity. When I meet people who remain persistently ethical despite being battered by social complexities and personal vacillations, I admire them. I would like to see our movement become like that, neither orthodox nor optimistic, neither self-confident in its wisdom nor willing to be passive in the face of injustice. I would prefer it to become more deliberative than vocal, more studious than opinionated, speaking only when it counts and, by the manner of its speech, counting.

374

31

The Prospects for Jewish
Denominationalism

I would propose a thesis and a question to serve as the focus of discussing the virtue of having diverse organized religious movements in American Judaism. The thesis is that in the context of contemporary Jewish life, the differences among American Jewish religious movements are relatively but not entirely insignificant. That observation, in turn, raises the question, How shall we live with one another? More specifically, how shall we deal with our differences from one another?

My assertion of the relative insignificance of the differences between us begins from simple sociological feel. Regardless of the label attached to the synagogue with which they affiliate, there is little to distinguish the day to day behavior of American Jews of different denominations from one another. In their masses they are not observant or informed or devout. The overwhelming majority may still like lighting candles or having a Seder but they are not fundamentally concerned with or respectful of Jewish law. They believe, like good American consumers, in picking out what in Jewish practice gives them personal satisfaction. Intellectually put, they dissolve corporate *halakhah* into personal autonomy. Thus our precious minority of searchers seeks guidance from *The Jewish Catalog*, the *Shulḥan Arukh* laid out for a generation accustomed to the appeal of Sears-Roebuck or Neiman-Marcus. Before long the remnant of our pre-World War II European-born or immigrant-oriented oldsters will die out and the post-World War II immigrants will have completed their integra-

From *Conservative Judaism*, vol. 30, no. 4 (Summer 1976).

tion into the American culture. Then the overwhelming majority of American Jews will, in their general apathy, be relieved only by flashes of Jewish sentiment and piety, and will be even more undistinguishable than they are today a block away from the synagogue building.

I think most American Jews know that, and so they increasingly hear our assertions of denominational superiority as simple ideology. Marx defined it bluntly: ideology is a system of ideas invented to cover the fact that one is acting out of economic self-interest. Freud expanded the notion by defining rationalizations as the ideas used to justify what our psyche needs. Listening to most rabbis talk about Torah-true Judaism, or changing *halakhah* by halakhic methods, or the importance of personal autonomy, most lay-people hear only "members." They probably mean what they say, but what they really are after is customers, not just good Jews. Or, as you and I have often thought, listening to lay people or colleagues putting down other Jews or extolling their own movement, they say more about themselves than about their group. Mostly what comes through is some unconscious trauma they live with, perhaps the pain which often accompanies strict observance in a permissive culture, or the guilt which comes from having broken with full-scale allegiance to *halakhah*, or the worry that one is somehow not as accepted as one would like to be.

These two negative and perhaps vulgar aspects of indifference to denominationalism should be put in a more positive context. As Mordecai Kaplan taught us, living in a democratic society inevitably suggests pluralism as the appropriate standard of Jewish communal behavior. Democracy, of course, tolerates political difference but by that attitude implicitly indicates that no position has the whole truth. I cannot see any *logical* reason why American Orthodoxy should accept the pluralistic demands of American Jews. Thus, some minority of Orthodoxy, mostly the European-oriented, though not exclusively them, refuses to participate in our democratic, "umbrella" religious activities. It is strong testimony, then, to the power of our social context that most Orthodoxy, despite doubts about the Jewish equality of our denominations, accepts pluralism as part of the American Jewish way of life.

The necessary effect of such democratization of the community is that *klal yisrael*, the whole of our people, rather than any of its divisions, is seen as decisively important. In my opinion, this has not gone as far as Kaplan hoped, that is that the people of Israel becomes the dominating, God- and Torah-generating basis of Jewish life. Nonetheless, insofar as anything is central to most American Jews, it is the Jewish people rather than some version of being Jewish.

Perhaps history has been more decisive in this respect than the democratic experience. Having lost 6,000,000 Jews under Hitler, who has the temerity now to add to our losses and say, "These Jews are not Jews"? We also have seen the State of Israel unify the most radically diverse Jews in its midst and in the diaspora for its support. So few Jews are prepared to

376

say, against the slogan of the UJA, "we are not one." And in the face of the common dangers to the Jewish people—the growing pressure on the State of Israel, the terror in Syria and Iraq, the reduction of immigration from Russia, the threats to Jewish life in South America, and the possibility that anti-Semitism may yet revive in the United States—our denominational differences seem of small account. What separates one group of religious Jews from another is simply not worth much of the severely limited and greatly overburdened energies of caring Jews.

There are parallel considerations among our thoughtful elite. They largely know that building a rich Jewish life in this society is an overwhelming task and none of us has a sure way to do it. Assimilation saps our vitality. Secularism destroys the validity of our faith. By vitiating the God who authorized and was the focus of Jewish observance it turns *halakhah* into a mere option, at best a recreational activity, at worst another alternative for personal enrichment (and we have so many alternatives that we neglect almost all of them). In the face of such peril, every ally in making Jews more Jewish, in increasing the quality of Jewish life, in making the Jewish religion come alive, is to be welcomed. Different people respond to different Jewish approaches. Who, then, will be so bold as to say that only *their* way leads to the Jewish future?

Moreover, when the experts in our movements seek Jewish responses to modern problems they do so in reasonably the same way. All work with the university model of the proper application of rationality to an issue. All want to know what sociology or psychology or economics or history can tell us about what we are going through and what might work in our situation. And all, believing that the Jewish tradition is relevant to Jewish life, if not, in fact, the best single guide we have to who we are and what we ought to be doing, will study our classic texts to see what they direct us to do. Regardless of how bound we feel by the results of such a search, we will proceed similarly, using scientific editions, being critical of sources, working chronologically, applying philological expertise, studying the relevant secondary literature. In the subsequent debate over which option seems best for the Jews, we shall normally argue according to the canons of modern academic debate. In brief, even as you read the discussions in *Sh'ma* magazine, with all their limitations, to be sure, you cannot generally tell the denomination of the author until you get to the conclusions—and sometimes not then. And since I have spoken *pro domo*, permit me a further personal observation. In recent years it has often been remarked upon, occasionally with a certain glee bordering on self-congratulation, that Reform Jews are becoming more traditional. I think there is truth in that observation and that this openness of Reform Jews to the Jewish heritage is part of the growing sense of Jewish unity I am describing. But what is also true and what is rarely if ever remarked upon is that most American Jews have now adopted as their own many of the principles for which Reform Judaism came into being and for which it had to carry the fight for most of the past 175 years or so: that Judaism can adapt to modern culture and yet remain authentic; that we should study our tradition scientifically; that our tradition has changed and must continue to change; that we need to carry on our Jewish debates in terms of those standards of the intellectual world which are congenial to our tradition. These and other ideas pioneered by Reform are the now common premises of much of American Jewish life. I suggest, therefore, that another reason for our sense that we have so much in common is that, on this level, we are now all Reform Jews.

Comrades of the Spirit

Though it impinges on the area of our differences, this analysis can be carried forward another step. For many of us, what unites us religiously is far greater than what separates us. In our concepts of our relationships to God, or understandings of the people of Israel, we do not substantially differ. God is variously spoken of as idea, process, Eternal Thou, mystery or He who searches for us, in any of our groupings; that the Jews are not a church but an ethnic group with all the trappings of peoplehood is the accepted self-understanding of almost all American Jews. We may differ as to whether, fundamentally, God chose Israel, or Israel discovered and pledged loyalty to God, or the two found each other and entered into a covenant relationship, but these options are personal intellectual choices, not denominational characteristics. We all acknowledge that we are part of a relationship between God and the Jewish people, begun most dramatically at Sinai and continuing down to our own day. Even if we go on to differ over what inaugurates or results from that relationship, Torah, specifically the Law, it is clear that we still hold a great deal in common religiously.

In another time, when almost all Jews apparently were believing and observant, merely to have shared in the Jew's relationship with God but not to have lived it in the one, generally accepted way, would have been the Jewish equivalent of heresy. Some small number of Jews still insists that this remains the only standard of Jewish authenticity. Yet that criterion today effectively rules out of Judaism all but the tiniest handful of Jews. If only for the purpose of bringing the Jewish people back to Torah-true Judaism some new approach is required. This often results in a new Orthodox attitude to the non-observant. In a pragmatic effort to come to terms with widespread non-observance, American Orthodoxy (and much of the rest of our community) now operates with a new criterion of a person's Jewishness: Do they take being Jewish seriously? Is Judaism only an activity they engage in, a profession they practice, a field they show expertise in, a set of routines they handle skillfully, or is it, while perhaps any or all of these, something which goes to the core of their being? Is their being Jewish the foundation on which they live? This new criterion is personal and existential. It allows us to see a greater Jewish authenticity in a deeply caring Jew whose practice still largely consists of Rosenzweig's fa-

378

mous "not yet" rather than in a mechanical *mitzvah*-doer whose life is given to exploiting others while aggrandizing the self. This new sense of existential Jewishness enables us to find comrades of the spirit in places where, with other perspectives, we might not have thought to search for Jews. It is the most radical challenge to the old adjectival Judaism, for labels do not guarantee seriousness. In this mood we hear God saying, "Would that they forsook Me, My *Shulḥan Arukh*, and their denominations, and grounded their lives, in full existential depth, on their Jewishness, for the ultimacy with which they then faced personal and social existence would bring them back to Me and My service"—and if that turned out, in fact, not to be the old *halakhah*, then it would be a modern Jew's equivalent of it.

What Divides Us

For all these reasons I believe that the diffferences between our movements are relatively insignificant. Nonetheless, what divides us is not unimportant. Three decades ago Milton Steinberg distinguished traditionalist from modernist Jews. They gave different answers to the questions: May we introduce changes in Judaism only through the traditional institutions of change? May we change the institutions of change themselves? On this issue the Orthodox and the Non-Orthodox split; but, as usual, the matter is largely though not entirely clear-cut. To the best of my knowledge, no major Orthodox authority publicly accepts the halakhic rulings of anyone other than another Orthodox rabbi, and almost all Reform rabbis and very many Conservative rabbis recognize that their rulings on matters of Jewish practice divide them from the Orthodox. Yet there remain Conservative colleagues who hope that since *halakhah* as changed by the Conservative movement is done by recognized halakhic authorities within the norms of the halakhic process, as in the case of the revised *ketubah*, marriage contract, Conservative *halakhah* could and perhaps will be accepted by Orthodoxy. This seems also to have motivated Conservative leaders in refusing to join with Reform Jews in the State of Israel for a common fight to legitimate the non-Orthodox rabbinate there. Perhaps my view of these matters is somewhat skewed, but I do not see the Israeli rabbinical establishment or American Orthodoxy ready to accept a pluralistic attitude toward *halakhah*. Perhaps the Orthodox can accept a convert who in agreeing to observe the Law understands that to mean, a la Conservative *halakhah*, that, for certain purposes, electricity may be used on the Sabbath. I find it difficult to believe, however, that they would not look askance at weddings which, while carried out in full observance of Jewish law, accepted as kosher witnesses people who rode on the Sabbath, to shul of course, in keeping with Conservative *halakhah*. But then again, I may not understand the flexibility of the contemporary Orthodox establishment or the full traditional validity of all the decisions of the Committee on Jewish Law and Standards.

In any case, assuming now the distance I see between traditionalists and modernists, the problems of living together can become quite difficult indeed. I see no need from the liberal side to challenge the right of any Jew to be Orthodox. Were there, however, Orthodox denials that Jews can legitimately take up the modernist option, it would be essential to assert the Jewish legitimacy of generational and even personal autonomy. Moreover, if change is the accepted pattern of all previous Jewish history, then the liberal approach, which seeks the changes necessary to make Judaism live today, would in fact seem to be the more authentic one.

Differences between Modernists

But with most of the Orthodox rabbinate not present, we cannot usefully discuss how modernists can best live with traditionalists. Instead, let me address myself to the differences between the modernists and what we should do about them. I leave out of consideration that minority of Conservative rabbis who feel they are, in truth, fully Orthodox and that minority of Reform rabbis who insist Jewish tradition has no claim on them. Where the rest of us stand in relation to one another seems to me very much more a matter of temperament than of principle.

Take, for example, one of the few efforts in recent years to elucidate some of the principles by which Conservative Jews approach *halakhah*, namely that of Seymour Siegel. Siegel affirms that fundamentally *agadah*, lore, determines *halakhah*, that, in effect, what Jewish tradition teaches us God wants of us as persons and as a community must be the criterion of our sense of Jewish duty today. I know of few Reform Jews who would argue with that principle. To be sure, by temperament Siegel would start with the full panoply of Jewish observance and invoke a transcendent agadic purpose only as he felt *halakhah* clashed with it. The result would be a much more traditional pattern of observance than that derived from the same principle by my average Reform colleague. The latter would likely reject the *halakhah* as an *a priori* and, starting from common decency and some Jewish sentiment, proceed to construct a Jewish life from those aspects of the Jewish tradition which seem to lead to Judaism's agadic goals. Though Siegel's pattern seems more Jewish, it cannot be defined merely in the name of tradition, for it breaks sharply with the halakhic system in asserting the primacy of the *agadah*. Once that is done, how can one argue that radically to employ the agadic criterion is somehow less Jewish? Instead, I suggest, it is the existential criterion which should be decisive. As long as *agadah* is taken seriously, as long as it generates a real and compelling sense of Jewish duty to God, as long as it is considered part of the Jewish people out of some sense of continuity with the Jewish past and in commitment to the Jewish hope of bringing or awaiting the Messiah, I do not see that, in theory, it is less consistently Jewish than Siegel's position. Rather I can understand that from mutual commitment to the same princi-

380

ple the two groups will have much in common, as is evident in the growing overlap of the Jewish life-styles of Conservative and Reform rabbis.

Some Conservative rabbis feel it critical that changes not be made merely by individuals but under the guidance of some communal body. This seems quite a difference from the Reform procedure. The only corporate halakhic body in the Central Conference of American Rabbis, our Responsa Committee, is, contrary to the rules for all other committees, forbidden to have its decisions discussed at a Conference meeting; its decisions carry only the authority of the individual who signed them. Yet I wonder if, practically, there is very much more than a difference of tone between us. When the Committee on Jewish Law and Standards is unanimous in its decisions, the rulings are theoretically binding upon Conservative Jews. Yet I do not know of any cases where the Rabbinical Assembly has taken action against a colleague for violating its religious rulings. That may not have been necessary since in many cases where the vote has been unanimous, the matter has long since been accepted by most Conservative Jews or is no longer of much interest to them. In matters about which there is controversy, the Committee will almost certainly have a divided vote. In that case, the individual rabbi will be the arbiter for his community, a somewhat optimistic notion which seems, practically, to Reform Jews, to be what they are also doing.

An even less significant difference between us is the notion that halakhic changes ought to be made on the basis of knowledge of and somehow in conformity with the *halakhah's* own procedure of change, even if these need to be applied creatively in our own day. Any Jew who cares for our tradition will rejoice in the possibility of having a growing body of literature in English in which classic Jewish texts are studied with reference to modern questions. I am quite certain that the readership for such materials is growing in Reform and general American Jewish circles. (One of the standard complaints with *Sh'ma* is that we are long on opinion and short on the citation of sources.) Indeed, in the Reform movement we have had an ongoing effort to apply halakhic learning and reasoning to changes in the law. I refer to the many volumes of responsa by Solomon Freehof. If his work is disparaged by some Conservative colleagues it is not because he does not know the law or that his sinuous way in reaching his decision is without precedent among *poskim*, Jewish legal decisors. The trouble with Freehof is that he is a compulsive *meikil*, almost always giving a highly lenient decision. He uses his knowledge and the vagaries of halakhic reasoning to find ways to be permissive. It is this combination of legal acumen put at the service of relaxed observance which many Conservative and not a few Reform rabbis find uncomfortable.

The Rate of Change

But perhaps I take the significance of the halakhic style of reasoning too lightly; I await the response of the Conservative colleagues here assembled. I do know that for most Reform rabbis, while it can be valuable, it is not fundamentally decisive—and I wonder if that is not the case for many Conservative rabbis as well. Let us take, for example, our respective decisions with regard to contraception. The major contribution of a Conservative response to this question a few years back was the citing of a halakhic parallel in which, on the basis of her subjective judgment, a woman was allowed to set aside what was otherwise the law. It is difficult for most Reform Jews to see in this nicety of erudition an advance over what Jacob Lauterbach said to the Central Conference of American Rabbis on the same subject in the 1920's when the subject was much more controversial. Lauterbach concluded his search of the *halakhah* with a straightforward appeal to conscience unbuttressed by talmudic citation or precedent. It seemed then and seems now to most Reform Jews a quite appropriate Jewish approach. If such reasoning cannot really be accepted by Conservative Jews, then the gap between us is wider than I think.

What I have termed a matter of temperament comes out most clearly when we must face the issue of the rate of change. Comparatively speaking, Reform Jews seem quite uninhibited when it comes to abandoning the past and trying something new. From mixed seating to major services on Sunday, from vernacular prayers to organ-accompanied hymn singing, from late Friday services to substituting cornets for the shofar, Reform Jews have reveled in innovation. They apparently consider it their equivalent of a Sinaitic mandate to feel for what Jews ought to be doing now, and then to do it. I recall Salo Baron once commenting that it was this impetuousness of Reform Judaism which practically made it necessary for a Conservative movement to come into being and, by waiting around for the Reform Jews to make fools of themselves, to then serve the many Jews who had been offended in the process. (Of course, Professor Baron put it very much more kindly.)

Temperament and Jewishness

I do not see that it will help us much with this theme to talk of the past. The record of past decades is too overlaid with the controversies of German and East European Jewish immigrants to be very clear on matters of theory or temperament. I suggest we consider this question of the rate of change in terms of a contemporary issue, the rights of women in Judaism, specifically the right of a woman to be a rabbi. Here the Reform Jewish stand is clear and to most Reform Jews (and apparently to not a few Conservative Jews) quit convincing. Simple conscience demands that women be allowed the same access as men to roles for which they are equally qualified. The Jews, Judaism and the rabbinate can use more gifted, able, devoted people. There are Jewish women fully capable of acquiring rabbinic learning and giving rabbinic leadership. There is a growing number of institutions and communities which will accept them. There are many good reasons for having women rabbis. That this has not been done before and somehow contravenes the sexist ethos of a traditional Jewish community, many of whose emotions on this matter trace back to medieval notions of female inferiority, hardly seems worthy of serious consideration. The Reform Jews have moved forthrightly in this area—not, to be sure, without some grumbles from people who have been annoyed to discover how sexist they are. I almost hesitate to raise this issue here for fear that we may lose the occasional students who now come to the Hebrew Union College-Jewish Institute of Religion because the Jewish Theological Seminary will not accept women in the rabbinical school.

Reform Jews see little virtue in this Conservative reticence. If the issue is halakhic precedent, it is difficult to believe that with all the halakhic learning and subtlety present in Conservative Judaism something could not be found which, as in the case of the contraception responsum, could not be made to serve as a precedent for setting the old law aside. Or if, as some claim with regard to the question of women being counted in a *minyan*, the problem is built into the very system itself, then surely all the talk that we have heard about the flexibility of *halakhah* and its inherent ability to meet new situations must now either be shown to operate, or the ideologists of an adaptive *halakhah* should forever hold their peace. Yet I think we all know that if there were an egalitarian will we would find a halakhic way. The problem is indeed temperament. Official Conservative Judaism prefers to wait a few years, a decade perhaps, or more, to see how things turn out. That is, I suppose, prudence—perhaps even responsibility. But from a Reform Jewish perspective it borders on indecent calculation. As we see it, the rest of the community holds back in holier-than-thou self-satisfaction and allows the Reform Jews to take the risks of experimenting for American Jewry. Then, when the results are reasonably clear, the community co-opts the successful patterns as its own while deriding the Reform Jews for those that failed. So at least it seems to us.

There are, I admit, grave problems with this Reform Jewish willingness to take risks. They emerge most clearly in our current tension over the problem of performing intermarriages. Again, eliminating the fringe groups in this controversy, the struggle among the rest of us is how best to preserve the Jewish people. Not performing an intermarriage is the classic sign that one has reached a limit beyond which Reform Jews will not go in their accommodation to society. Here one hopes that couples facing such a refusal will realize how serious a breach of Jewish life they are contemplating and thus be moved to break off their relationshp or seek conversion. The contrary position, for all that I disagree with it, is regularly based on the conviction, backed by some statistics, that conducting an intermarriage will lead to the children of this couple being raised as Jews. My colleagues hope thus to gain additions to the Jewish people. I think such rabbis do less good and, in the aggregate, cause more harm than they realize. Their stand does more than disturb me; it profoundly hurts me for it impinges on my deepest sense of what constitutes Jewish loyalty and dignity. Yet for all my pain I respect their Jewish right to experiment and be wrong. For all the damage I think they may be causing, I support them in their conscientious daring to risk the past for the sake of the future of Judaism. And it is this, ultimately, which makes me a Reform and not a Conservative Jew. I prefer to take the risks of training women now to be rabbis even if that means having to identify myself with intermarrying colleagues. I do not have the temperament to stand around and wait for someone else to find the new, needed patterns of emerging Judaism. I want to be part of the group that faces the perils, endures the trials and occasionally has the satisfaction of creating what everyone knew was needed but could not bring themselves to search for or try to create. I do not think I underestimate the importance of a difference or temperament. It is surely enough to justify our staying two separate movements.

Besides, what would a merger accomplish anyway? It would make us all the more anonymous than we now feel in our gigantic asociations, all the more subject to bureaucracies which despite their efforts to treat us personally cannot help but think that their bigger is always a Jewish better. Our differences can be useful to God and the Jewish people if they help us keep each other honest about our ideology. If, indeed, there is no Judaism without *halakhah* and Conservative Judaism is the best instrumentality for contemporary halakhic development, then Reform Jews will be useful when they ask: Just where are these halakhic Conservative Jews and on just what issues does Conservative Judaism give leadership to American Jewry? If, indeed, Reform Judaism is committed to experiment for the sake of a better American Judaism, then Conservative Jews will do us a service by regularly asking: Just what experiments are you now undertaking and how can their results be related to the Jewish people and the Jewish heritage?

Yet if what I have said above is correct, our differences from one another, while of some importance, are relatively insignificant. Mostly we must not take our adjectival distance from one another too seriously. We fight the same enemies, we share the same goals, we serve the same God as part of the same people in loyalty to the same tradition, awaiting the same reign of God on earth. We may differ in temperament but that is a small matter in the face of the Jewishness which binds us radically one soul to the other.

384

32

Co-existing with
Orthodox Jews

Orthodox spokesmen have often proposed a simple solution to the problem of Jewish unity. They suggest that, since we Progressive Jews adapt to
so much else in the modern world, we agree for the sake of Jewish unity to
accept classic Jewish law in all matters related to Jewish identity. The
analogy to *kashrut* serves as a paradigm for this argument. "You can eat in
my house but I cannot eat in yours. Why do you not then agree to follow
our practice?"

In my experience, thoughtful traditionalists—the extremists, intellectual and moral, of both camps being omitted from this discussion—often
cannot see the element of religious principle in Progressive Judaism. From
their perspective, there doesn't appear to be any. The classic Jewish
sources focus on faith in terms of practice rather than belief, but many
observances central to traditional Judaism—Shabbat, *kashrut*, Jewish marriage, Hebrew *davening* (praying)—seem to have little meaning to many
Progressive Jews, some even feeling free to discard them altogether. Thus it
appears puzzling that the vaunted flexibility of Progressive Jews cannot,
for the sake of the Jewish people, embrace at least some few disciplines of
classic Jewish law.

Our first task, then, is explanatory: to indicate that what others perceive as our rejection of Judaism, arises from what we see as an even
deeper level of Jewish belief and devotion. It is not enough merely to point
to the changes that Jews instituted in response to shifting historic circumstances. That once controversial notion of ours has largely become the

From the *Journal of Reform Judaism*, vol. 33, no. 2 (Summer 1987).

common property of all modernized Jews. The critical issue then becomes not whether Jews ever ought to change, or even the rate of that change, but the criteria and, in turn, the structures for reshaping Jewish duty. In sum, the issues between us are not descriptive but normative, not how the *halakha* functioned but how our meta-halakhic commitments indicate it now ought to function.

Elucidating the Contradictory Views of Commandment

In all our theological variety, we Progressive Jews mostly agree that the primal ethical thrust of classic Judaism now demands greater weight than it once had in determining our Jewish obligations. And its immediate consequence is a greatly increased regard for the dignity of the individual Jew, that is, for the Jewish "conscience." As a result, wherever human welfare is involved, we hear an ultimate command being laid upon us which demands priority in our Jewish living. We do not thereby deny the indispensability of symbolizing all the other dimensions of our historic faith. We only know that sanctifying human relations is our primary Jewish responsibility and thus a major criterion of the life of prayer, ritual, and study which inspires and guides us in our messianic service. We also are convinced that this heightened concern for persons must begin with each individual Jew's unique capacity for religious experience and understanding.

Many Progressive Jews abuse the freedom we esteem. But we do not consider the continuing ubiquity of sin a refutation of our ideal. Surely no useful lesson in comparative Judaism will result from comparing the most admirably sincere Orthodox Jews with the most vulgarly non-observant in our midst. I have no fear of the result of our comparing the pious elites of our movements with one another, or, for that matter, seeing what we would learn by similarly studying those among both groups who claim our name but refuse our respective disciplines.

If we are to argue our theories in terms of what best contributes to the survival of the Jews, I am convinced that we Progressive Jews have taken the right risks. In a time when people are overwhelmingly educated and socialized to think for themselves, only a Judaism that demonstrates ultimate respect for the conscientious decisions of individuals can long hope to survive and flourish. To me, that is not merely a pragmatic consideration but a faith I find expressed in the Torah when it says we are "created in the image of God." To be a person has come to mean exercising self-determination. Thus all human beings, including Jews, need to be given adequate scope for the exercise of personal autonomy and the grounding which will enable them to do so with mature responsibility.

Two emphases would help make plain to others that these commitments obligate us even as *halakha* does other Jews. First, of course, is our actions. We would make our case to the Jewish world more convincingly if our pious elite were larger and its activity more visible. Obviously, that goal commends itself intrinsically, but in the context of this discussion it will also help to keep its political significance in mind. Second, other Jews would better understand the depth of our religiosity if, instead of talking about human feelings or needs, we would speak of what God wants. Note the circumlocutions I resorted to above in stating our religious case, "primal, highest, essential, intuition, ultimate." I utilized such humanistic terminology so that as many people as possible would feel comfortable with my survey of our common belief. Historically, such language was a new midrashic style we created to make Judaism believable again in a day when God and Torah had so overwhelmed Jewish consciousness that human initiative had stultified.

But ours is no time in which to idealize human capabilities in such a way that we remain embarrassed to speak directly of God. We modernists may envisage God differently. Nonetheless, we all assert that the imperative power of the ethical and the inalienable dignity of the individual are not merely our human idea or hope but a result of who God is and what God has done. Formally, we do not speak of God and duty differently than do other Jews. We, too, assert that our obligations derive from what we believe God wants us to do. And our Progressive Jewish versions of Jewish responsibility derive from our several perceptions of how God wants us to live the Covenant today. Put in those terms, the common language of our tradition and the true language of our faith, few people would ask us to deny our sense of God and Torah for the sake of a less disputatious Jewish community.

That having been established, we must face a harsh reality: if conscience is to be respected, we cannot ask Orthodoxy to violate its own faith and accept Progessive Judaism, de jure, as a fully equivalent, if alternative, interpretation of Judaism.

Setting aside all considerations of power, as we did when considering our own case, let us continue to focus on the question of belief. Theologically, Orthodoxy cannot recognize the teaching of Progressive Judaism as valid. The basic, authoritative Jewish texts of Jewish law clearly classify our modernist reinterpretation of Judaism as our tradition's equivalent of heresy, apikorsut. Ideally, it can never be condoned.

On both sides, then, the protagonists stand on principle—and the stands are irreconcilable. Were that not the case, our problem might already be moving toward resolution as a result of a little goodwill or dialogue.

Finding a Jewish Way Nevertheless

Yet for all their intractability, I do not believe our difficulties are beyond substantial amelioration. Both sides have a deep, though subsidiary, faith that might now help us overcome the present impasse: their commitment to *Ahavat Yisrael,* the love of the Jewish people and of individual Jews. The higher politics, that is, political action as a climax of our social ethics, might, with God's help, find a way to move us from this common ideal to a pattern of mutually acceptable existence.

As a matter of *halakha,* Leviticus' commandment to love your "neighbor"—literally, your "fellow-Jew"—as yourself, is conditional upon that Jew's observance of the commandments. Two contemporary realities tend to mitigate this restrictive reading of the law. First, we all remain deeply wounded by the Holocaust. Enough Jews have already been lost in this generation, making almost all of us desirous of finding ways to keep us from losing more. Second, most modernized Jews prize the benefits pluralism has brought to social relationships. Even groups that cannot easily validate granting rights to those espousing error appreciate the human security and social opportunity tolerance has brought to minority group existence. So, too, in our community, experience with democracy has taught us the virtues of finding ways to live with Jews with whose beliefs and life style we may radically disagree.

Somewhat hesitantly, I wish to suggest that a third factor may also give us some measure of hope, namely that while neither group is without substantial power, neither is strong enough to force the other to its will. While there are great regional variations and each group draws on different strengths, we have a rough balance of power among us. Orthodoxy demands respect for its unbroken tradition, its venerable institutions, its sages' impressive learning, its adherents' dedication and self-sacrifice and the not unambiguous value of its many fanatics. With all that, if we inquire about the faith people actually live, Orthodoxy appeals to but a small minority of Jews.

Progressive Judaism may lack centuries of experience to authenticate its modernized Torah. Nonetheless, it bespeaks the unarticulated faith of most contemporary Jews, regardless of their institutional affiliation. They want to be Jews but they also want their Judaism to manifest what they have found precious in modernity: democracy, pluralism, the dignity of each person, and the virtue of not insisting that one generation's social arrangements cannot be changed by those that follow it. On all these counts, they know Progressive Judaism is right even when they cannot publicly admit it. Their tacit assent is our greatest political asset.

With neither group able to enforce its view on the other, realism may lead them to permit their love of Jews to guide them to some mutually acceptable accommodation.

It will not do, however, to suggest that this process can be hastened by asking Orthodox and Progressive Jews to subordinate their special interests to the needs of *Kelal Yisrael,* Jewry as a whole. That appeal seriously misconstrues the present impasse. Neither group believes Jewish unity is the overriding Jewish value. Had *Kelal Yisrael* been our most significant concern, we would never have brought Progressive Judaism into being, for its creation seriously divided the Jewish community by defying the accepted community leadership and the established traditions of our people. The same is true of Zionism, our movement's secular counterpart. If further proof is needed, should Meir Kahane ever become Prime Minister of the State of Israel, no fervent appeals to *Kelal Yisrael* will keep the overwhelming majority of modernized Jews from dissociating themselves from his administration.

The concept of *Kelal Yisrael* has even less weight in traditional Judaism. Neither the Bible nor Rabbinic literature significantly employs the term. Rather, its recent currency derives from secular Jews who, having abandoned God and Torah, love the Jewish folk enough to make it their supreme value. Believing Jews—and here Progressive and Orthodox Jews stand as one—will seek the good of the Jewish people not in some low though common denominator but in terms of what they believe God wants of this people.

A critical concern of classic Jewish social theory—accommodation to reality—may also give us some hope in this quest. The Torah reflects a transcendent idealism. But it is meant to be lived by real people in real history. Hence, though it demands holiness, it also seeks ways to make its ideals practical and livable.

Over the centuries the *halakha*, the Jewish legal tradition, demonstrated an extraordinary capacity for finding the fine line between God's lofty demands and the Jewish community's actual capabilities. Indeed, Progressive Judaism became a necessity only as that genius faltered before the unparalleled challenges of the Emancipation. In any case, Rabbinic Judaism commends the piety of a certain species of compromise. It must not make Jews cynics by its easy sacrifice of our ideals, as the Hellenists once did. Yet it also may not aim for such purity that it becomes unrealistic, like that self-destructive sect that left Jerusalem for a holiness attainable only in Dead Sea isolation.

The move to compromise fuels extremist indignation at the betrayal of principle. In this dispute we may confidently expect the prophetic voices in Progressive Judaism and the super-pious among the Orthodox will righteously spurn any proposed middle way. At their best, they will remind us of the ideals that any arrangement will, in part, have sacrificed. But human and Jewish history assure us that such radical efforts to implement God's fullest demands now cannot build a community or keep it alive in history. Jews may be inspired by their prophets and *Chasidim* but Judaism is the creation of rabbis. We work at the higher politics by way of their measured idealism. So we do not ask our leaders to devise practices even our fringe groups will find acceptable but only ones the bulk of our community feels it can support with full Jewish integrity.

In pursuit of this goal our leaders must give special consideration to one group among us, Jewish women. Equal Jewish rights having so long been denied them, they are properly sensitive about their status, particularly in matters relating to Jewish identity, and they are rightly touchy about who presumes to speak and rule on them. There still being few women in positions of genuine power among us, we must ask our leaders to make certain that feminist Jewish concerns receive due consideration as we move toward Jewish unity. Lest males once again create the structures of female existence, we must, in turn, ask feminists for some specific guidance. Even though their major energies must still be given to confronting a community slow to change, we shall need to know which aspects of traditional Jewish practice they might, for the sake of unity, abide.

I do not see that the substance of any possible arrangements with the Orthodox can be worked out in public. If anything, the media, with their preference for controversy and their practice of provocation, are a hindrance to the resolution of contentious issues. Even in private it should be clear that neither side will negotiate matters of principle. But since doctrines always co-exist with administrative variation, it may be possible to find or create some significant areas of mutual activity. At the very least, people who respect one another's piety and power will want to learn from one another something of the other group's concerns and openness. That might make it possible for each group, independently, to adopt a course of action that the other could live with. Perhaps the most useful thing we can do in public is to indicate our sincere, if principled, devotion to seeking a reasonable accommodation with one another. I can, I think, best contribute to that process by considering an example or two of the specific sort of issues that might arise and how we might usefully approach them.

Facing Some Realities of Compromise

The late, great *posek* (decisor), Harav Moshe Feinstein, *zichrono livrakha* (may his memory be for blessing), issued a daring halakhic ruling that weddings conducted by Progessive rabbis do not create what the *halakha* considers a marriage. Superficially, that seems an egregious insult to our rabbinate and the many Jewish families its rites have consecrated. Yet the Jewish legal effect of Reb Moshe's ruling has quite another tone. It as good as ends the halakhic problems created by our wedding ceremonies. Couples married by us would not need a traditional *get* (divorce document) should they divorce. More importantly, their children by a subsequent marriage are not *mamzerim*, the Jewish bastardy which bars marriage to a kosher Jew. Other authorities disagreed with Reb Moshe's conclusions and insist that Jewish law must consider our wedding ceremonies legally binding, thus leaving the evil consequences intact.

In my case, Reb Moshe's juridic analysis and conclusion corresponds, in fact, with my subjective intent and resulting practice. I do not seek to perform "halakhically valid" wedding ceremonies (in the technical sense of that phrase; its only proper sense, I believe).

I imagine some people will disparage the integrity of any rabbi who says he has no interest in performing a "proper Jewish" wedding ceremony. Their attack utterly misconstrues my meaning and misperceives my purpose. I take Reb Moshe's legal language literally, which is generally what legal writers wish their readers to do. At a wedding I do not seek to act as an agent of the traditional Jewish legal system conducting a juridically valid ceremony that thereby renders the couple subject to its provisions covering marriage and descent. Were that my intention I should do many things I, in fact, do not do. Thus, I should carefully investigate whether the witnesses to the *ketuba* (the marriage contract) are halakhically fit to execute this document and I should insist upon an act of *kinyan* (acquisition) by the groom to formalize his serious legal intent in this transaction. I not only dispense with these and other serious legal matters; I do not make a great effort to become expert in this aspect of Jewish law. I would gladly agree to the understanding that no Jews married by me should ever have to issue or receive a traditional *get* or have a child who might be given the status *mamzer*.

All of this, to my way of thinking about Judaism, has little to do with the *Jewish* legitimacy I seek to convey by a wedding ceremony. To me, Jewish authenticity arises from a Jew's continuing personal appropriation of the people of Israel's Covenant with God, not in following specific juridic procedures by which Jews in prior ages and today have sought to express it. I hope by the marital rites I conduct to help two Jews sanctify their personal relationship as the most basic level of their people's historic, ongoing Covenant with God. To accomplish that personalist-ethnic-spiritual task, I study what Jews once did and now do in such rites, utilizing whatever I and other rabbinic colleagues have found useful in our tradition and creating new forms where present needs remain unfulfilled.

From my Progressive theological perspective, I deny that there is anything Jewishly *inauthentic* about my practice for all that it is technically unhalakhic. But if it will help to reduce barriers between Orthodox and Progessive Jews, I will gladly indicate on whatever *ketuba*-like document I sign that the rites to which it attests were not meant to create a halakhically valid marriage. (Were a formula to that effect added to the Hebrew text, it could have legal effect without generally confusing most of our laity about our religious goals.) To me, such a practice would represent so slight a compromise of principle and so great a gain in Jewish unity that I would not hesitate to commend it to my colleagues.

Of course, wherever possible, I prefer, as a continuer of our people's Covenant with God, to utilize its classic, halakhic forms to do so. They often express today, as they have for ages, the living reality of our ongoing relationship with God. But in the cases where they do not, loyalty to God takes precedence over faithfulness to legal procedure.

I do not assume that if we made a few adjustments to Jewish law, like adjusting our practice to Reb Moshe's ruling, and if there were some independent halakhic flexibility by the Orthodox, we could easily overcome our present difficulties. Much of what stands between us is emotional, not

391

rational, and our passions are intensified by our various investments of power and ego. Consider another possible compromise we might be called upon to make.

We have long taught that ritual practices should not be invested with the high significance we bring to ethical concerns. If, then, a difference in ritual tended to separate us from most of the household of Israel, we should not find changing it very troublesome. Yet apply that reasoning to the custom of some elements in Progressive Judaism to pray bareheaded. That practice is not only different from that of almost all other Jews but also distasteful to many of them—a fact we know and adapt to without much difficulty, for example, when we are at Progressive services in the State of Israel. Praying bareheaded once symbolized our desire to be fully integrated into Western civilization. But that social goal having largely been achieved, most of us today give higher priority to affirming our place as Jews among the Jewish people as a whole. I think it clear that our contemporary Jewish goals would best be met and Jewish unity considerably advanced if all Progessive Jews prayed with covered heads. So much for the logic of the case.

But were we to advance such a suggestion—it could be no more than that in Progressive Judaism—it would arouse passionate objections: "We weren't brought up that way"; "We aren't used to wearing skull-caps"; "It feels uncomfortable, even embarrassing"; "The old usage defined us and now we're becoming Orthodox"; "Why must we do all the changing?"; "Why can't we simply let things alone?" I think there are good, rational responses to each of those comments. I doubt that they will have much effect until the emotional backlash created by the proposal has been overcome—if ever. So this small step toward greater Jewish unity would likely engender considerable dissension among us. We must not underestimate the power of emotion in religious affairs.

If that is true of Jews who believe in the value of Jewish change, how much the more may we expect that various Orthodox Jews will greet their sages' possible halakhic creativity with hurt and outrage. As I understand their mood, they bring to these issues a deep-seated resentment against non-observant Jewry. It abandoned *halakha* for the benefits of Western civilization, now shown to be largely spiritually bankrupt, and in the name of its new, superior way of life isolated the Orthodox and as good as discriminated against Orthodoxy. For the first time in the more than a millennium since Rabbinic Judaism became widely accepted, the pious have had to defend Jewish law against the practice of Jews—and now these one-time uncaring others ask those who have faithfully preserved the tradition to suggest modifications of it. Such suggestions are likely to raise deep emotional responses. And where Orthodoxy enjoys privilege and an established community position, the passion to maintain them will greatly intensify the feelings.

I have concentrated so on the fearsome challenges we face because I think easy optimism and subsequent disappointment may lead us to despair of making any progress. But I do not consider these dauntingly diffi-cult issues of practical social ethics insoluble. Rather, I believe that realistic people of goodwill and fertile imagination may yet find ways to resolve them. In this century, with its often dismal human record, two people from religions other than ours, Mahatma Gandhi and Martin Luther King, *hasidei umot ha-olam*, righteous gentiles indeed, have shown us that higher politics remains possible despite the harsh realities of power and the ugly strength of prejudice. What Jews now need is leaders who show their moral courage and political sagacity, creating out of what can be done a faithful reflection of what ought to be done.

No one can give our leaders a rule by which to distinguish an unwor-thy compromise or an overly idealistic demand from what, as best we can figure it out, God wants of us in our particular here-and-now. That is where their leadership as well as their character and faith will be tested.

May I also suggest that, in a way, the heavy burdens our leaders carry differ only in scope from those each of us shoulders in his or her own life? God calls us all to be holy not in some general, abstract spiritual way but in the humdrum particularities of making money and spending it, of work-ing with some people and against the designs of others, of loving and hat-ing and being indifferent, of the situations we are stuck with and those we can create to our will. Our Judaism seeks to make us realists who are not cynical, idealists who are not fools. But we, facing the hundred compro-mises each day requires, must ultimately proceed on our own, mediating between God's demand for holiness and the particularity of the creation in which God bids us work it out. We, too, each in our own spheres, must practice the higher politics, the high art of living Torah.

33

On Theological Dialogue
with Christians

The critical issue concerning Jewish-Christian dialogue is not whether it shall be but only what kind it shall be. The world has anticipated any theoretical discussion of the issue. It is busily at work forcing people in a dozen different ways to confront their neighbors of many climates and states as well as faiths. If Jewish thinkers choose not to engage in dialogue and show how it ought most appropriately be conducted, neither Jews nor Christians will remain blissfully ignorant of its possibilities. Our society in its mindless mixture of exploitation and chance will teach them what an informed leadership might have hoped to guide to responsible goals.

Religious leaders of both faiths should have a special interest in this new world-become-a-neighborhood. Morally we must confess that a good deal of the prejudice which separates neighbor from neighbor, nation from nation, race from race, has been empowered by religion even where it has not arisen in its midst. For that prophetic judgment we must be grateful to those secular critics who, judging us by our own standards, have called us hypocrites. Such prejudice cannot be ended merely by giving people facts, for its roots lie beyond the rational. Yet the word "Jew" will sound differently when Christians know the countless lives of sanctity created by post-Biblical Judaism, and the term "goy" will lose its repulsiveness when Jews know what the mass and the cross and the creeds represent. The very fact that one faith deems other faiths worthy of serious concern will itself help to make dialogue more than superficially effective.

From *Judaism and the Interfaith Movement* (New York: Synagogue Council of America, n.d., probably 1969).

Yet the most positive reason for inter-faith conversation is that the search for new neighbors should always be a primary task of those who wait for the coming of God's Kingdom. We do not stand and serve alone. God knows all people as the covenant with Noah and his children makes clear. As our individual religious communions sustain the individual, so the knowledge that other religious communities stand alongside ours in the night of history should give us all added hope as we seek to survive in faithfulness.

These truths, and others, can hardly be gainsaid. That is why they may be stated with such brevity. What keeps Jews and Christians both from applying them in their institutions is not the falsity of the ideas but our fear. We are afraid that if we affirm that which we mutually believe we shall lose our individual faith. That dread is particularly great within the Jewish community. In the century and a half that Jews have been coming out of the ghetto they have seen how social integration leads to religious defection. If the rate of conversions to Christianity has not been high in recent years it is only because religion is out of style and ethical secularism a far more attractive because less identifiable option. With society so seductive, shall a minority faith concern itself about dialogue with other faiths? It hardly has the energy to transmit to its own people an introductory understanding of its view of humankind and God and history. And after centuries of Christian persecution climaxed by the Nazi horrors (which Christianity may not have caused but for which it provided the background and against which it did not vigorously protest), how can one say it is important for Jews to learn about Christian belief?

These special Jewish fears are widespread among believing, caring Jews. They must not be repressed among Jews or in discussion with non-Jews. They must be stated. What makes Jewish-Christian discussion possible today is that such candor and honesty in speaking of one's fears is welcomed and appreciated. So the very negative statement itself, predicated as it is on some people's willingness to listen to other people speak their heart's pain, is not the end of dialogue but its beginning. To know one is welcome, to acknowledge one's apprehension to people who genuinely care, is already to initiate the process and transform the broken past in a slight but significant way.

These diverse tensions explain the strange paradox of Jewish attitudes toward discussions with Christians. There is virtual unanimity in the Jewish community that in matters of social welfare Jews should welcome opportunities to work together with Christian groups. Wherever education, race relations, poverty, health, the aged, the handicapped, world peace and other such issues are at stake, Jews should not hesitate, but rather make a positive effort to join inter-faith programs which will call attention to the evils and seek to remedy them. Moreover, this is a Jewish religious obligation and therefore it will not do to have the Jews represented by secular agencies but only by the religious organizations—congregational, educational, or rabbinic.

There is little question too as to how such inter-faith activity should be carried out. A generation ago Jews were so eager to speak to Christians that they snatched at every chance to be seen together. Today the emphasis is on mature self-respect. Jews may be willing to engage in dialogue, even to initiate some programs for it. They are, however, no longer willing to be the perpetual initiators of such talks nor the major financiers of projects to encourage them. Once inter-faith activity was often the only Jewish concern of the Jewish participants. Now it is clear that Judaism can only be properly represented by those who believe it, know it and practice it. Jewish faith must be the foundation of any significant contact with Christianity. That being so, it is clear that though such extra-communal concerns are not primary to Jewish existence, they have a legitimate if secondary claim upon the believing Jew. Thus, the insecurity which leads either to total withdrawal or to fawning and obsequiousness is no longer acceptable. A mature democracy makes it possible for a self-respecting Judaism to co-operate with an interested Christianity in a way which can only serve to benefit them and their society.

That positive attitude toward dialogue does not, however, carry over into the realm of theology. There a substantial difference of opinion divides thoughtful people in the Jewish community, and these differences, while largely following Orthodox versus non-Orthodox lines, do to some extent cut across the denominations. Yet even here some areas of almost universal agreement remain. What is not debated is the need to study and understand contemporary Christian theology. That activity, it is conceded, may teach Jews much today, whether by disagreement or concurrence, even as it did in the classic periods of Jewish philosophy. Here too the security of contemporary Jewish belief as over against the blandishments of contemporary intellectual movements asserts itself. There is no longer a great fear of such ideas or systems sweeping Jews from their faith by the power of their modernity. Thoughtful Jews have seen these intellectual fashions come and go so frequently in recent generations and have learned enough about the lasting truth of Judaism, even in its modern dress, not to fear confronting the best that modern Christianity has to offer, or to refuse to learn what it might have to teach.

What is being argued in the Jewish community is whether Jews ought to participate in face-to-face discussions of theology with Christians. Four major reasons have been advanced against such exchanges. Since Christianity is now past its historic peak and is no longer the controlling spiritual power of our civilization, Jews need not concern themselves with it on a practical level. Psychologically, Christianity is too intimately involved in Jewish minds with the guilt of the Holocaust for Jews to be able to speak or listen freely to it, and the silence of organized Christianity during the Six Day Arab-Israeli War has only increased those emotional barriers. Humanly, it is not reasonable to be expected to participate in conversations with those whose only interest is in converting you to their faith. And theoretically, religious faith is so private a matter that it cannot meaningfully be discussed between faiths.

All these contentions contain some measure of truth to them, yet I do not find them persuasive either individually or collectively. Rather, it seems to be that together with the insights that they offer there is a good deal in them that is at best shortsighted and at worst immoral.

To call this a post-Christian age does not mean that Christianity has lost all influence on our civilization. It remains the single most important non-governmental institution known to Western civilization. It shapes much of the thinking and the lives of the tens of millions of its adherents, and by its very presence in the culture exerts a powerful effect on the admittedly substantial minority of those who are not its members. To say that Western culture is becoming increasingly secular is not thereby to say that Christianity is dead. Much of the good inherent in contemporary secularity derives from the Christian civilization which gave rise to it. Without it, where will modern secularity find the basis for a strong ethical or culturally humanistic drive?

At the fall 1966 Harvard Divinity School Jewish-Christian Colloquium, many Jewish speakers in the discussion group on Torah and Dogma seemed to find it some indication of the truth of Judaism that ours had become a post-Christian era. In my remarks then I termed this attitude "Jewish triumphalism" and events since then have confirmed the accuracy of that term. After centuries of hearing Christianity laud itself over Judaism because of its numbers and power, Jewish resentment has finally found a decisive response. In preferring secularity to Christianity the world seems now to have learned what loyal Jews always knew, that Christianity is not true enough. The next implication would seem to be that Judaism, having said so for two thousand years, is thereby justified and validated. Such notions say more about the psychology of their proponents than about cultural or theological realities.

Should Judaism, as a matter of deliberate policy, prefer people to be secular rather than Christian? That might be the case if with typical nineteenth-century optimism it might be assumed that educated, enlightened people will be ethical, perhaps even religious in a general sort of way. Surely it is difficult for a descendent of the prophets to have such trust in contemporary secularity. It is one thing to appreciate an anti-Puritanism which leads to a more natural acceptance of pleasure. It is quite another to see that become the new life principle that self-gratification is the primary goal of existence and fun the measure of how alive one is. The old Protestant ethos may have known too much of restraint, but to turn Christian freedom into modern anarchy, to create an ethical mood whose only barrier to action is "why not?" is to set loose a new possibility of immorality that can only appall those who love the Bible.

Jean-Paul Sartre points the way. Freedom is the only good and to choose freely the only virtue, regardless of the content. What atheist existentialism expounds, affluence empowers in a post-Christian era. Can anyone concerned for Jewish authenticity welcome the new immoralism which this has begun to bring into the Jewish community? Is a post-Christian culture which teaches Jews the secular virtues of sensual indulgence and living for oneself in the present a social context Judaism should welcome? It is naive to think that secularism without the Bible will somehow be Christianity without Christ or the Church, that it will be, so to speak, closer to Judaism than Christianity is. The more realistic view would seem to be that a secularism unguided by Christianity and paying no attention to its handful of believing Jews would become a new paganism, one far more dangerous than anything the prophets and rabbis ever fought against. With its idols internalized and pandering to every creature need of people to keep them productive, that new paganism, in its sophistication and immediate appeal, will make Judaism appear to be irrational self-denial, a masochism swathed in illusion.

Already its power makes itself felt. Jews no longer convert to Christianity. Why take on even its burdens? Rather they drift into the new secularism and, except for the tiniest minority, they are not even distinguished by a strong ethical impulse as was the old socialist or liberal substitute-faith. When they make a commitment to the good life, they are speaking in terms of personal pleasure, not moral service.

If that is the drift of a post-Christian era then Judaism and Christianity are at least united in having a common enemy. Judaism has far more in common with Christianity than with a secularism going pagan. That is not meant as a denial of the real and disturbing differences between the two faiths. Much critical remains to be said about the concept of a Judeo-Christian tradition (though Jewish triumphalism often asserts itself in such discussions). Yet with all such qualifications one cannot assert that it makes as much sense to speak of a Judeo-Greek or a Judeo-Roman tradition as a Judeo-Christian one. There are unquestioned fundamental similarities in these two faiths. They may not be so evident when they are compared to one another, but they emerge quite clearly when the contrast is to an unbelieving, unethical cultural style. Judaism needs Christianity as its ally against the paganization of our civilization unless it prefers to withdraw to a self-imposed ghetto or quixotically try to do the job alone. Realistically, then, theological dialogue is necessary to determine to what extent Judaism and Christianity can be partners in this critical social enterprise.

That is a relatively pure motive for talking to Christians about theology, yet there is a parallel matter whose overtones are less noble. It has to do with the strange discontinuity in discussion as one moves from matters of social welfare to theology. In the former case Jews are eager to speak and work together with Christians. In the latter they fall silent and withdraw. Is that a reasonable condition to put upon such a relationship? Can we really expect people to work intimately with us in areas of vital human concern and yet refuse to speak to them, politely to be sure, when they inquire about our values or commitments? The anomaly is made all the more pointed because Jewish participation in inter-group activities, it has been demanded, ought to take place only under religious auspices. How then can one close off in advance inquiries about what faith grounds Jewish concerns in an area of social action or what beliefs guide them in taking a given stand on a certain issue?

The suspicion cannot be repressed that Jews advocating such a schizoid relationship to Christians are less concerned to work together as human beings than to use Christians for Jewish social ends. Where the issues immediately affect the Jewish community, as in fair employment practices or ending university restrictions, the Jewish gain is clear. But even in such apparently disinterested matters as race and poverty it is obvious that any right secured for minorities below the Jews in the American status scale makes the position of Jews that more secure. But Jews have nothing to gain, they believe, from theological dialogue, so they will not talk. If Jews come to issues of social ethics only as another power bloc interested in alliances with those who share their power aims, then they should say so. To mask such motives with the ideology of inter-religious cooperation is intolerable. If the basis for joining together in the activity is religious, then it should be discussable.

To say that one simply cannot talk to Christians on the level of faith because of the anti-semitism necessarily inherent in Christianity, or more specifically because of its inevitable association with the Holocaust, does not mitigate the charge of exploiting inter-faith social activities. If all Christians are potentially Nazis or have the shadow of a Nazi about them, how can one in all integrity join them in social ethical projects? To do so, if that is one's experience or belief, would be the height of hypocrisy. That is not only a reason to break off theological discussion face to face but to withdraw from contacts of every kind with Christians. Surely for those who have been indelibly scarred by the Hitler fury that would be understandable. Yet that has not been the decision of the majority of those who came through the Holocaust and for the overwhelming majority of Jews brought up in America. The word "goy" has lost much of its ancient bitterness. A phobia toward Christians and Christianity seems more pathological than the virulent hatred it sees behind every gentile face.

The silence of the Christian organizations during the June 1967 Arab-Israeli war seemed to many to provide some support for the previous argument. When there was a Jewish crisis of the first magnitude, when American Jews needed the support and help of the churches and church bodies it was not forthcoming. The silence was damning, and official statements after the war calling for the Israelis to surrender Old Jerusalem or the West Bank have only made matters worse. American Jewish sentiments run high on this issue. That is precisely why it is desirable to apply as much rational analysis to it as possible.

Perhaps the first thing to do is to put what happened in perspective. Individual Christians were not silent during the first few days of the war. It was quite clear that the sympathy of most American non-Jews was with the Israelis, and they did not hesitate to say so to almost any Jew whom they recognized. Many highly placed Christian clergymen were heard from, often without being asked, and in the weeks after the closing of the Straits of Tiran and before the war, certain Christian bodies did call for justice for the State of Israel. One cannot then equate being Christian with being against the State of Israel.

More important, specifying that it was the institutional church, not all individual clergy or most church members who were most grievously absent, should refute the more critical assertion: anti-Israelism is only the new form of traditional Christian anti-semitism. That is simply not true, as individual Christian attitudes demonstrated. The position taken by the official bodies is less likely the result of some residue of ancient Christian anti-Jewish phobia than of the special concerns of institutional Christianity as contrasted to individual Christians.

That would seem logical unless one assumes that any person who takes a stand against the State of Israel in a critical matter is *ipso facto* an anti-semite. Some Jews feel that way and it makes no diference to them whether the critics are Jewish or Christian. They are Jew-haters. But no believing Jew can place a political entity, even a Jewish one, beyond all judgment. One wonders what such nationalists would have said to the prophets. To the Jewish heart there may have been little ambiguity in the recent Arab-Israeli war. Only to a jingo could there have been none. Yet if some twinge of doubt about the war could agitate even those who love the State of Israel surely it is possible for those whose loyalties are not primarily concerned with the Jewish people to confront the same ambiguous proposition and decide against the State of Israel. For myself, I believe that almost any person of reason and morality could have seen the necessity of Israel's fight against the Arabs and should have championed her cause. Yet I can understand how some people of reason and morals might disagree. There are surely anti-semites who have condemned the Israelis for winning and refusing to give back what they have won until a cease-fire becomes a formal peace. Their voices are heard in respectable journals and in respected institutions. But not every one who argues against the State of Israel is sick on the subject of Jews.

The institutional church has a hierarchy of value different from that of most American Jews or most individual Christians on this matter. Where the one gives the highest priority to Jewish survival and the other high value to Israeli forbearance and democratic accomplishment, church bodies have their responsibilities to Christian Arabs and their hope of converting the remaining Arabs. United States support for the State of Israel identifies Christianity with Israeli interests in Arab eyes and makes the possibilities of conversion that much more difficult. The churches may be concerned about Jews and anxious to right ancient wrongs. They are more concerned with their Christian Arab brothers and their missisn to convert the world to Christianity. That is not hatred for the Jews, even indirectly. It

400

is a scale of value which, when applied to an ambiguous situation, might well make possible a decision which would prefer silence to pro-Israeli declarations. I think that decision was wrong, by my standards even immoral, but I do not think it was pathological. It disturbs the free flow of conversation as any great difference of opinion will. It does not prove that it is impossible or undesirable.

How odd it is to hear Jews charge that if Christian groups do not support Jewish interests in critical matters, Jews should not engage in theological dialogue with them. It comes with incredibly poor grace from the lips of those who have righteously insisted that dialogue is impossible with Christians since they are only interested in converting Jews. Now the truth appears. These Jews are only interested in dialogue if they convert Christians to positions valued by the Jewish community! Surely any discussion entered with only one possible outcome is necessarily ugly and objectionable. That is not to say participants in dialogue should not want to change the other's point of view. There is little sense talking unless you believe what you are saying and want others to see the truth of your view. What is unseemly is to insist that if they do not agree it was not worth talking, or to listen to what they say only as a pretext for pressing one's own view. Obviously Christianity desires the conversion of the Jews in a way that Judaism does not reciprocate to it. Yet insofar as many modern Christian theologians and some churches influenced by them have seen such conversion of the Jews as an eschatological rather than a contemporary matter, a task more for the Second Coming than for the church today, there is a new openness possible from the Christian side in such discussions. From the Jewish point of view, the very failure of organized Christianity to understand how peoplehood is a theological category to Jews and how the State of Israel becomes a concern of Jewish faith, is precisely a reason to intensify theologial discussion not end it. And that does not mean Christians will always thereafter agree with Jews but only that in their new moments of decision they may understand the Jews and Judaism as they understand themselves.

Can such conversations be at all significant if religious faith is at its heart so private and personal a matter as we moderns have come to know it to be? How can there be a meaningful exchange when what is at stake is simply unutterable? Surely people cannot tell others the fullness of the truth their hearts have come to know. That is not a Jewish truth but a modern existentialist dictum. It is as well known to Christians as to Jews, if not better. Hence there can be no illusion on either side that any such discussion can present all that either faith holds dear. Rather, each tradition knows that in its own midst there are areas where communication ceases and privacy must rule. How much the more will that be true between different religions. That is agreed.

Now, however, the real question can be raised. Since not everything can be said, is there nothing at all worth saying? That hardly seems the case. In the first place, it is clear that saying faith is ultimately too personal for utterance is already to communicate something about it. Faith is not beyond all meaningful statement. That is not a philosophic quibble for there are practical consequences to the ability to say something about one's faith. One studies one's own traditions about it because one knows they can help one in a way one often cannot help oneself. One speaks with others of one's community to understand what is common and what is individual in one's affirmations and is thereby enriched. One can learn from the books of other faiths something about one's own. And in the case of converts one can know enough of what they have come to learn and believe of Jewish faith that they can responsibly accept it. Only because it is reasonably clear that they affirm it in their private way with sufficient authenticity, may they be accepted in the Congregation of Israel. These things are all possible and real in the realm of what can be said about faith. They explain why theological dialogue may hope to accomplish much in an exchange between faiths even though they must stay within the bonds of finitude.

We can be enriched by the non-verbal as well. How true it is that one understands a faith better by knowing its believers rather than reading its theoreticians. The faithful convey something beyond words of its style, its feel, its effective nuance. This is as critical to understanding its validity as its ideas if not more so. Hence we must stand in polemic over-againstness not just to the minds of men of other faith but to their faith-full lives as well.

This is where the real issue of conversion arises. We confront the adherents of another faith in the full human dimension of the truth on which they stake their existence. If they do any less, if they do not really believe, if their faith is only an intellectual game, their practice and stance an unmeant routine, they are not worth speaking to on these matters. If they are fully present in their faith, their authenticity makes its demands upon us. Simply being there they challenge us to accept their saving truth for ourselves. We cannot deny them that right without asking them to sacrifice themselves in all their personhood. To engage in this sort of polemic, then, must mean to hold oneself open to the demand made by the other's very person, that we accept their truth. The risk of dialogue, even polemical dialogue, is conversion. But it applies to them as well as to us. They must be as open to us and our truth as we are required to be to them. They must be as willing to risk what may happen when we talk as we are, and neither of us must in all good conscience exert any influence upon the other to make a decision other than what logic permits between minds and respect between persons.

The risk of conversion is worth taking for those who seek the truth passionately and are reasonably secure in the road that they have thus far come, for the customary alternate to such conversion is a new and fundamental self-affirmation. To know in the depths of one's being that the other's truth is not one's own generally means to be sent back to one's own truth with some new insight into its nature. That may, at best, be an existential variety of negative theology, yet it is also true that negation is one of the classic means of definition. In knowing who we are not, in having some intellectual and personal sense of why we are not sharers in other faiths, we become more fundamentally rooted in our own. That is not an easy or a troubleless path, but compared to the slander and hatred of other faiths into which religious groups have regularly allowed themselves to be drawn, it is one far more worthy of our God.

What an extraordinary contribution religion could make to the contemporary world if it could show people how to understand one another in their difference! What vulgar sinfulness infects every level of our social relations when we must deride and defame those who differ from us in order to affirm our own world. It is but one step from this hatred of the different to its destruction. Does not the Bible itself remind us that the first religious polemic, one over the nature of sacrifices, ended in Cain's murder of Abel? The time is ripe, as it always has been, to learn that lesson. We are all of us children of Adam, though some of us still till the fields while others tend the flocks. Whose sacrifice the Lord will in due course accept God alone can fully know. Until then we shall serve God best in being ourselves, not trying to become our brothers, in accepting them for what they are even where they are not like us, and thereby accepting ourselves as well in all our distinctiveness.

34

Finding a Way to Peace among Religions, a Response to Hans Kung

There is so much that I agree with in Professor Hans Kung's paper, "No Peace in the World Without Peace Among Religions," that I could easily devote a good portion of my own to showing how my Jewish belief leads me to join him in many of his affirmations. Perhaps I can summarize my agreement in this way: as a believing Jew, I find Professor Kung's politics of high humanism a noble statement of the hopes of my faith and the experience of my people. And in his soaring spirit, with its ethical passion and rich human concern, I find a soul-brother to whom I know myself bound, despite our different contexts of faith. These firm convictions form the foundation of everything I now wish to contribute to this symposium.

Let me begin, as Professor Kung did, with a personal experience. I was surprised and continue to remain instructed by the great wave of negative Jewish reaction to the meetings between representatives of our religious community and the Pope not quite two years ago. Nonetheless, nothing in my recent experience has given me a better understanding of the continuing imperative of inter-faith dialogue and the substantial barriers standing in its way. I speak about these matters as one who deeply appreciates the continuing growth over the past two decades or so of healthy religious discussion between Jews and Christians in the United States. To give one

A paper contributed on behalf of Judaism to the UNESCO-sponsored symposium on "World Religious and Human Rights" on the occasion of the two-hundredth anniversary of the Declaration of Human Rights, February 1989. Portions of this paper were adapted from an address to the Tenth Annual National Workshop on Jewish-Christian Relations, November 1987.

example, but an exceptional one, each year for a decade now, our two American religious communities have held an annual National Workshop on Jewish-Christian relations, at a number of which I have been privileged to speak. These shift from one major city to another, requiring local initiative and enterprise to organize and carry through the program. Despite this they have steadily grown in the number of those attending, both locally and from all over our country, until now the attendance is measured in the thousands rather than the hundreds. At these workshops, the range of topics under consideration, the breadth of experience and learning of those leading the sessions, the palpable goodwill all about, the open recognition of all our past hurts and present problems, and our growing ability to speak of our deepest faith so as to enlighten but not to impose are a splendid human accomplishment.

But more important than these transformations of the old suspicions and antipathies has been the progress we have made in being able to disagree with one another. Twenty years ago, when the ecumenical movement began to reach out to the realm of inter-faith activities, I dared to suggest to a meeting of the Religious Education Association that, for all its importance, we should not settle merely for attaining civility between us. The true sign of friendship is the ability to confront the friends' serious differences of opinion. That suggested to me that we should not be talking to one another properly until we had learned how to have loving disagreements, what I termed an I-thou polemic. I still believe that. To love our neighbors as long as they agree with us hardly requires a commandment. Learning how, appreciatively, to differ on matters of great significance to us is a spiritual attainment everyone of goodwill should admire. So, for all my appreciation of our positive interchange, nothing impresses me more as a sign of our maturing relationship than our increasing ability to speak candidly, but with undiminished regard, of what the other is doing or saying that troubles us.

Some people do not understand that inter-religious discussion can involve a frank exchange of differences of opinion; indeed, that for old antagonists it is a major achievement. Thus to me, the meetings of the Jewish representatives with the Pope, for all the genteel clash of opinion, seemed a healthy outcome of a growing understanding between Jews and Catholics. Of course, I would have preferred that the gap between the divergent views had radically lessened. Nonetheless, compared to what has until recent years been a most sorry history, a face to face exchange of mutual concerns and disparate perspectives was a major step forward.

I shall return to that instructive experience later. I have introduced it this early in my paper to indicate in what sense I shall devote most of it to disagreement with Professor Kung. Perhaps "disagreement" is too strong a term. His paper is so finely nuanced, so delicately balanced in its dialectic—an approach I find thoroughly appropriate to this topic and congenial to my soul—that it may only be that I have missed something of the tension of positions he so delicately set before us. Or it may be that I wish to change the balance somewhat. In any case, these talmudic responses to the instruction I have gained from him are meant to further our exchange and thus what we will still learn from him.

Professor Kung spoke of an instructive experience he had in Lebanon, and his reflections on it stimulate me to my first comment. He is convinced that had there been serious dialogue between Christians and Muslims twenty years ago, which their communities supported, "Lebanon would not have slipped into a catastrophe of this magnitude." This could be interpreted as meaning that the conflict in Lebanon is essentially a religious one and that if the religious issues could be settled then other questions, difficult though they might be, would be settled in turn. On the most idealistic and theoretical level, I would agree with him. Christianity and Islam, as best I have come to understand them, seem to me to care centrally about peace. Were people fully imbued with their spirit to sit down together to solve critical problems facing them, I believe their goodwill would be an important factor in helping them find ways to do so.

But on a realistic level, that is, the level of analysis which in the Jewish tradition must be conducted on the basis of the Evil Urge operating in all people, I see religion as a secondary if not lesser cause operating in most supposed religious conflicts. Consider whatever examples you wish in whatever part of the globe—if one could disentangle the economic factors which cause them, the political, national, and tribal interests they further, and the heavy burden of historical enmity they camouflage, how significant a role does religion truly play in them? And how important a role might harmony between religions have in mitigating struggles founded on such strong social energies? Surely you will not misunderstand my meaning to think that I am suggesting, as I certainly am not, that religion abandon the role of peacemaker in whatever capacity it might carry it out—one most important being the case in which the hatreds are most implacable. I am only saying that in this sinful world we should beware of overestimating the immediate *political* effects of goodwill between religions. I surely agree that there will be no world peace without peace between religions. But, for all our hopes, it is not realistic to suggest that peace between religions will bring world peace.

I am not optimistic about our immediate prospects because of the long historic propensity of religious institutions to ally themselves with those in power and find religious justifications for the aims of the powerful. There are, in every faith, I add, thank God, those saints and prophets who speak truth to power. But mostly religious leaders wisely calculate that without the support of rulers and the rich, their institutions will be diminished; and should the mighty be antagonized, they will be badly limited or even destroyed. The record of religious institutions standing up to those who would make war and foment hatred is not good. Professor Kung knows all this and talks about it. It leaves me very much more skeptical than he is about what we, for all our idealism, might accomplish.

406

Let me extend this line of thought a bit. It seems to me that, as I view the scene, many religious groups would make their most valuable contribution to peace by first creating it in their own midst. As long as those who share a world of belief and practice live in strife and conflict, their global political or inter-faith efforts for peace will be compromised. Peace needs to begin at home where the real problems of human difference can more immediately be felt and responded to in a common universe of belief. Facing and overcoming such realities provides unsurpassable credentials for speaking to people of other faiths about inter-religious peace. But on this score, Professor Kung can surely instruct us all.

I turn now to the theoretical problem which forms the heart of Professor Kung's paper: how can we integrate an unswerving devotion to the truth of our own particular faith with an equally compelling dedication to the universal occurrence of other faiths which are also true? His own answer, which has great practical resonance for those of us who have lived as part of persecuted minorities, is to be found in the universal ethical standards which, as a consequence of the European Enlightenment, were then "realized with greater consistency" than had heretofore prevailed in his faith and, I would imagine, in many others. If, to put it too concisely, all the world religions could find their own reasons for accepting the understanding of proper personhood that he symbolizes in the term *Humanum*, then it could prompt us to work for peace among us and thus in the world without vitiating our individual conviction that our religion is true.

I must now attempt a most intricate, because highly consequential, theoretical maneuver. I cannot deny the validity of some universal truths without opening the possibilities that Jews will once again be relegated to the ghetto, *shtetl*, and *mellah*, and all the precious equality we have gained in the past two hundred years will be wiped away. After fifteen hundred years of discrimination and persecution in the Western world, Jews received equality wherever the notion of universal rights or its like was accepted; where that was not the case, Jews never became equals, and that is so until this day. Politically, I wish to affirm universal rights and thus the validity of certain universal values and judgments. But as a Western academic intellectual, I do not see how Professor Kung or anyone else I have been reading any longer knows how to establish rationally the philosophic necessity of such universal ethics.

It will help in my analysis if I take a helpful word of Professor Kung's out of context. It occurs in his critique of three strategies of inter-religious relationships that he finds faulty. After rejecting the "fortress" tactic of saying only one's own faith is true and the "religious stew" of saying all religions are equally true, he turns to that of "embracing" other religions as a subsidiary level of one's own. He rejects this view because of its deleterious consequence of elevating one's religion into what he nicely calls a "supersystem."

The logical point is quite clear. In order to embrace many particulars, one claims to be on a higher level and, by transcending them without vitiating their truth, understands better how they properly relate to one another. That notion, I think, concretizes our problem and his solution. How can we transcend the truth of the individual faiths—which he knows is basic to all else we do—yet provide ourselves with a "supersystem" which not only requires them to create peace with one another but will be the criterion by which anyone can know which faiths are true and which are not. I think it only reasonable to call a system which provides for such judgment a "supersystem." My interest in this usage is not to score a verbal point in this discussion by charging Professor Kung with calling for the same intellectual step he found faulty in others. It is rather to show how important in his presentation the universal ethical realm is. And, that being the case, the grounds that establish its truth, a truth which is sufficient to judge all religions as true or false, must be most closely scrutinized.

I reiterate, I am in heartfelt agreement with Professor Kung's political goals but that sympathy does not persuade me that he has given us a convincing *intellectual* reason for accepting his "supersystem." This is not the time to refer to all the academic problems standing in the way of trying to establish the truth of an ethical universal, all those difficulties so concisely summed up in the title of Alasdair MacIntyre's most recent book on ethics, *Whose Justice? Which Rationality?* Merely consider how logically "super" a supersystem would have to be to claim the right to judge the truth of all religions; or consider how often what was confidently asserted as universal has been unmasked as another self-serving invention of Western, white, male, middle-class professors.

Professor Kung surely knows all this, but great-heartedly chooses to by-pass it, giving us practical and human, perhaps even pragmatic reasons for accepting his proposed supersystem. Thus he observes, "It cannot be overlooked that religion has always proved to be the most convincing where . . . it effectively lifted up the Humanum"; "*progress toward humaneness* within all the various religions . . . is unmistakable since their entrance into the modern world"; "many conversations . . . have convinced me that in the future we will see a vigorous growing consciousness in all the great religions in reference to the preservation of human rights"; "the hope . . . is not unfounded that in the question of *human rights* and universal *ethical criteria* . . . an elementary basic consensus on the basic premises of human life and community could take shape."

I do not think that Professor Kung will find many who are attending this symposium who will disagree with his observations or his project. That is what has brought them here. I, for one, find much that he is saying congenial to my faith and to Jewish experience over the centuries. As to the former, Judaism's God is universal and that God has an intimate relationship with all humankind, the covenant made with Noah and his descendants. Jewish tradition gave that doctrine its fullest measure of authority when it made it integral to the *halakhah*, the law, and ruled that any gentile living up to the commandments of that covenant would have a share in "the life of the world to come." And after their long, painful experience with persecution, modern Jews have made universal ethics a central tenet of their faith. Thus these Jews, like me, would gladly agree with Professor Kung's ethical goals, though, considering what we have seen in this century and what we now know people fully capable of, I find his judgments about history and ethical progress unduly optimistic.

But recognizing how congenial to the attendees at this symposium this practical line of argument will be has led me to wonder about those who are not here. That is, what of those Jews and those adherents of other faiths who are not only not present at the symposium but would refuse, as a matter of principle, to attend. While I have no hesitation in this matter as in many others to go my own religious way without them, I cannot ignore them in this discussion. And I know that while I may speak for my understanding of Judaism and for what I hope are the not inconsiderable number of Jews who will agree with me, I also know that there are many others I certainly do not speak for. That was at least one thing I learned from the passionate negative reaction to the Jewish meetings with the Pope.

Professor Kung's proposal is addressed, I take it, not just to that small elite of modernized, democratized religious believers who are eager to see a more global perspective brought into their faiths but to the religious bodies proper to which they belong. I and many like-minded Jews, I believe, could find ways of joining in Professor Kung's practical project. But would the bulk of our community be behind us? And even if some numerical majority would do so, would it include those who have been most intense about their faith, those most devoted in their observance, those most dedicated to its continuity? Until we consider them, the believers from every religion who would resist this proposal, we shall not have a realistic grasp of what is involved in trying to have peace between religions.

Let me formulate my inquiry this way: Why, despite all the good accomplished through inter-faith activity and the manifest evil of inter-faith controversy do many people in each of our groups remain resolutely opposed to inter-religious dialogue? Why do they not only eschew inter-faith exchange but often consider it a spiritual danger one should avoid?

I shall, shortly, carry on a small thought experiment about Judaism, inquiring what some Jews find in it that makes them feel that it mandates such separatism. I am convinced by what I have studied over the years that every religion has resources for self-isolation and self-exaltation even as it also has ones, generally much better known and publicized these days, for appreciating our common humanity. I want to probe some of the resources for inner-directedness in the Jewish tradition, ones I believe to be fairly typical of what one can find in most other world religions, though mostly we find ways to repress these aspects of our traditions, particularly when speaking to those outside it. I suggest that while I am doing this, my audience consider what an equivalent search in their tradition would yield that would have a similar import. I hope this somewhat risky enterprise will enable us to gain greater insight into the varied dimensions of our faiths and more realistically enable us to think what we might do to universalize the attitudes of those who prefer talking only to fellow believers, and then, preferably, ones of their own kind.

To indicate something of the mood of this portion of my community, let me first present a sample of the objections Jews raised to the meetings with the Pope: "The Jewish community gained no major concession from these exchanges. The Pope said nothing new about the Papacy's actions during the Holocaust, said nothing new about the meeting with Yasir Arafat and Kurt Waldheim, and did nothing about the Holy See's refusal to grant full, formal recognition to the State of Israel." Some went even further, asserting, "It is demeaning for Jews to meet under such conditions with the Pope, coming to him as if we were petitioners appealing for something which he, as a matter of simple morality, ought to do on his own."

I think such people speak only for a minority in our community, but it is a sizable one. For many of them, inter-faith activity makes sense only in political terms. They have no interest in understanding others as a human act valuable in itself which, if nothing else, turns the threatening stranger into an acquaintance. They see no point in discussions which are simply open-ended, and they approach talks with others with a strict cost-benefit standard, asking, "So what did you get?"

I would not deny that I hope inter-faith discussions will have practical outcomes, that our getting to know one another better will result in valuable human and religious gains. But I carry no list of immediate social desiderata into most inter-religious discussions so I do not measure their value by what specific concessions I gain as a result of them. True, I should probably not long go on meeting with people who do nothing as a result of our discussions—beginning, of course, with myself—but with one God meaning one humanity, I am more intrinsically than consequentially concerned with inter-faith activity. By contrast, some in my community are almost exclusively concerned with results and little else counts for them. These Jews, for whom dialogue is a front for political gain, seem to me our Jewish equivalent of those Christians who speak of dialogue with Jews but mean converts to Christianity. All thinking Jews spurn dialogue-partners whose true purpose is proselytization not exchange. Following Hillel's Golden Rule, however, they should understand that those of other faiths will similarly withdraw from people who say dialogue but mean negotiation.

More substantially, behind these attitudes, and indeed behind the openness of much of the rest of our community, is our sensitivity to what we have suffered. Our people have been so battered by recent history that on many a supposed universal ethical issue a disinterested moral stance is impossible for many Jews and impractical for many others. To give the most telling case, I feel certain that to this group I need not rehearse the long, unhappy history of Christianity's attitude toward and treatment of the Jewish people. And what some decades ago might have been merely an aching memory has in our time been given bitter reality by the various levels of Christian implication in the Holocaust. No discussion of Jewish self-isolation should omit the emotional, moral wounds Jews have suffered in recent decades.

This most particularly must include the immediate reality of our fear for our survival. We were, already before Hitler, the smallest of the world's great historic religions. Having lost a third of our number in the Holocaust we are now smaller still. More important, we know that our fears for our continued existence are real, not paranoid. People of education, culture, and rich civilization did their methodical best to kill us all—and the liberal nations of the world stood by and did not do what they might realistically have done to mitigate if not to end the murder. This Humanum, too, is a reality.

As a result caring Jews are deeply dedicated to the survival of the Jewish people. And we are inordinately sensitive to any suggestion that Jewish continuity is not a primary value, a given that requires no justification in terms of something else. Or that there is a level of human existence of such universal validity that, though one may well wish to exemplify it Jewishly, Jewish existence itself is only a secondary value to what is universal. After the Holocaust, though we esteem the universalism which makes possible our participation in the world as equals, most of us will resist it if it comes in a form which, even by implication, suggests the secondary value of the significant, independent survival of the Jewish people.

Let me be more specific, Professor Kung strives heroically to show that his universal ethical standard for world religions is compatible with his deep respect for their individual integrity. He is careful to point out that they must each judge on the basis of their own internal criteria the extent to which they can affirm his vision of the Humanum, but he is confident that they will all be able to find ways to do so. Judaism, as I have indicated, clearly has a classic religious basis for affirming a universal ethical reality. To that extent we agree. But his formulation does not stop there, at the confluence of the agreement of the religions on various aspects of being human. He sees the ethical as a realm independent of them, sufficiently so that it can *judge* them. It becomes, willy-nilly, a "supersystem" in the sense that it determines which religions are true and which are not. Thus, if what it says "allows human life to succeed and be happy . . . [and] makes possible an optimal human development," if what it knows to be "humane, truly human, and enhances human existence," if what it sees as "a meaningful and fruitful existence" should clash with the behests of Judaism, then Judaism is to that extent untrue.

I have two objections to this formulation, substantive and formal. I know what the word human means mostly because of my religious faith, though I have nuanced it substantially as a result of my modern democratic existence. But it is clear to me that of these two affirmations, my Judaism is the primary one. This brings me to my second difficulty, that Professor Kung's proposal implies that I know a truth more ultimate than

411

my faith, that there is a system "super-ior" to the one on which I have based my life until now. I cannot say that this is impossible—but after my many cycles of doubt and rewon faith, I find that most unlikely. In any case, such a greater truth would surely have to commend itself with extraordinary power to win my primary allegiance in place of Judaism. It is just because universal humanism has so little basis in contemporary rationality and recent historic experience that particular religions, new and old, have flourished so in recent decades.

The point is a sensitive one in the Jewish community because of our experience with universalism. Embracing it avidly as we did when we were permitted into the modern world, we discovered that it could easily be a new path to the end of the Jews. In its bourgeois form in western Europe, it took the form of radical assimilation which found in humanism the noble fulfillment of everything to which the old traditions of Judaism had in their limited way aspired. In its communist form, in eastern Europe, it took the form of a radical rejection of the Jewish religion and of Zionist nationalism that was the equivalent of cultural genocide. Today, believing Jews will consider it a major criterion of all theories of humanity and religion to see whether they understand that Jewish existence is primary and not derivative of anything but God's will and our answering determination.

In sum, since I know no truth superior to my Judaism, it is, in Professor Kung's terms, my "supersystem." I have not found, in more than twenty years of inter-faith theological discussion, that this has impeded my being able to speak to others, a further worry Professor Kung had about the "embracing" strategy. I should like to think that, if anything, it has made it more interesting to speak to me. And I believe that there are limited but effective ways that those of us who see no other way to speak to others but from within our circle of faith might nonetheless proceed to clarify what we share in common. I shall return to that later. But first, as one who speaks from an "embracing," traditional perspective, let me turn to my examination of particularistic themes within Judaism and our means of overcoming them.

I detect three religious motifs in Judaism which often serve as the basis for rejecting inter-faith dialogue. The first of these is the converse of xenophobia, the general theological presumption that gentiles, immemorially, hate Jews. Hebrew Scripture prefigures this antagonism in the conflict between the two brothers, Jacob, he who is Israel, and Esau, whom the rabbis take to be the prototype of the gentile nations. Two Israeli professors of political science, Charles Liebman and Eliezer Don-Yehiyah, in their book, *Civil Religion in Israel*, described this motif as part of their effort to analyze Israeli religious groups and their effect on political life. They write, "The traditional Jewish view of Jewish-gentile relations is symbolically expressed in the phrase, 'Esau hates Jacob' (Gen. 33:4). As Rabbi Simeon the son of Yohai said, 'Is it not well known that Esau hates Jacob? But at that moment when he ran and saw Jacob, his pity was really

412

aroused and he kissed him with his whole heart.' " [They are citing Rashi, the standard Jewish commentator to the Torah, *ad. loc.*] The authors continue, "The sages found it necessary to explain Esau's sign of affection. This is consistent with the main line of the Jewish tradition which found anti-semitism to be the norm, the natural response of the non-Jew, whereas the absence of anti-semitism required explanation. 'Esau hates Jacob' symbolized the world the Jews experienced. It is deeply embedded in the Jewish folk tradition" (p. 138).

That is one reason some Jews will not engage in inter-religious activity. They do not believe Christians, Muslims, and non-Jews generally are capable of genuinely overcoming the long Western tradition of anti-semitism. I take it that one could find in a number of other faiths somewhat similar strains which anticipate difficulties with certain people or which set up considerable barriers between those within and those without the circle of faith.

Moreover, there are specific religious distinctions in the Jewish religious tradition (specifically, in normative Jewish law, *halakhah*), between acceptable and unacceptable gentiles. In classic Jewish faith, the world is divided into three groups: Jews, good gentiles—those who observe the stipulations of the Noachide covenant—and wicked gentiles, characteristically, idolaters. Muslims having so stringent a monotheism, almost all Jewish legal authorities consider them outside the category of idolaters. (The few who do have questions about the status of Muslims raise them because they are unclear whether Muslims, as Jewish law says they should, accept their status because it was so established in the Torah.) However, a minority of our sages rules that Christians come under the category of idolaters. The critical issue for Jewish law in this regard is what one may licitly associate with the one God. Specifically, does Christian Trinitarianism—particularly as understood in the Middle Ages when these judgments were made—involve what Jewish law considers an unacceptable association with God, thus rendering Christians technical idolaters?

The great majority of Jewish legal authorities ruled that Christianity is not idolatry under Jewish law. Nonetheless, the greatest single legal decisor of the Jewish Middle Ages, Moses Maimonides, followed by some other sages, if a minority, ruled that Christianity must legally be considered an idolatry. As a result, there will always be some Jews who say that they follow Maimonides in this regard and, considering Christianity an illicit religion, will refuse to be involved with it in any religious way. Again, my sense is that there are honored teachers and texts in most world religions which similarly deny the fundamental truth of other faiths.

The final theme in this gallery of exclusiveness relates to the provisions of Jewish law which, regardless of the issue of idolatry, make important distinctions between Jews and gentiles. Let us take as an example a matter which recently became of some significance in Israeli life. According to the Jewish religious calendar, the year 5747, 1986–87, was a Sabbatical year. As a result, observant Jews in the Land of Israel, following the

413

commandments which call for Jews to let their soil lie fallow then, would not eat any produce grown on land owned by Jews. Some decades ago, the then Chief Rabbi of Israel, Abraham Kook, ruled that it was permissible to sell the Jewish land to a gentile for the Sabbatical year, thus making its produce edible by observant Jews. But, a minority of sages hold that a Jew may never sell a parcel of the Land of Israel to a gentile, even for a brief period of time. As a result, some pious Jews in Israel called upon the government to use some of its hard currency reserves to import food grown abroad during the Sabbatical year.

There are a number of other such provisions in Jewish law which distinguish between Jewish responsibility to Jews and to gentiles. One who is sensitive to the mood of such directed praxis can easily understand the law to be directing Jews to stay as far away from gentiles as possible, something most sages and observant Jews do not see mandated by Jewish law or belief. Once more, I direct your attention to those aspects of your own faith which call for significant distinctions in how one acts toward those who share it and those who do not.

Let me now restate my concern. I cannot participate in this symposium as a representative of Judaism as if almost everyone in my community agreed with my views. A sizable minority does not. We all need to know this. But if I, as I do, find very much in Professor Kung's proposal and the theme of this conference that is humanly commendable and Jewishly worthy then either I misunderstand the implications of Jewish faith or most believing Jews ought to agree with me. Since the latter is not the case I have tried to understand the resources for exclusiveness in my faith so that I can properly respond to them. How might I—that is, all of us—seek to do so?

I find three customary strategies for circumventing the barriers to openness in religious traditions. The easiest way is to point out that they are minority positions. Customarily, in Judaism, we follow the majority when it comes to religious practice. Instead of citing and following the Maimonidean texts which rule that Christianity is idolatry, should we not, then, basing ourselves upon the differing opinion of most other sages, cite those Maimonidean texts in which he praises Christianity and Islam for paving the way for the coming of God's Kingdom? This, in fact, seems to be what the majority of Jewish thinkers have done and, knowing it, many Jews have followed their lead.

Following the tolerant majority leads to a temptation which must be avoided. Anxious to advance the cause of openness, we decide to quote only those texts which reflect Jewish religious tolerance and universalism. I, for example, regularly prefer the texts which I cite in religious discussions, intra- or inter-faith, to those cited by other people. But the troublesome texts cannot be ignored. Limiting one's tradition to its canon of tolerance enables opponents of dialogue to challenge the integrity of your position since you have not represented your tradition fairly. And those who naively thought their tradition spoke only in terms of love and com-

passion can be devastated by having to hear, for the first time, of the resources for intolerance in their tradition.

We might, then, seek to apply a historic hermeneutic to the exclusiv-
istic texts. This allows us to say that not only is their language ancient but
it conveys the values and social situation of their pre-democratic time.
Perhaps in those historic circumstances our predecessors may have understood this to be God's guidance for their relationships with believers in
other faiths. But we live in quite another social structure. We associate and
work harmoniously with an astonishingly diverse group of people and
year by year gain increasing proximity to an ever less foreign world community. The exclusivist views that may have been religiously appropriate
to a world of smaller horizons seem far too constricted for our day.

This mode of reinterpretation comes with some traditional precedent
behind it since each of our faiths has, on occasion, applied it to some of
the writings we consider inspired. In classic Jewish legal literature, a most
apt example is provided by the Meiri (Menahem ben Solomon of Perpig-
nan), a great thirteenth-century French Jewish legal authority and the piv-
otal exponent of Jewish religious tolerance. He ruled that a new openness
to Christians and others was called for because "the nations" had, over the
centuries, become reasonably moral due to their religious transformation. I
am sure many examples quickly come to mind from the history of other
faiths.

However, this approach, generally so effective because it is so much a
part of our modern way of thinking, carries little authority with many religious traditionalists. To begin with, it is never clear when history may be
factored into our reinterpretation of an old text. As with the selection of
texts to be relied upon, I am quite happy with my good judgment in doing
so but often quite suspicious when others introduce it. For once one begins
using historic change to relativize old pronouncements, nothing is safe
from revision. As a result, many pietists view the modern understanding
of history with profound suspicion. Its devotion to unending evolution, to
change as the sign of life, allows for no lasting truths or eternal values to
be beyond its transforming power. And when this position is reinforced by
a profound unhappiness about the demoralization of our society, deep
emotions can easily refute what good sense or conscience might otherwise
commend to us. Surely the widespread turn to religious conservatism, so
notable a religious phenomenon of our time, is testimony to the widespread appeal of such logic.

The third and perhaps easiest way of neutralizing the religious resources for intolerance is to identify them with our human contribution to
religious forms, textual and ritual alike. Being finite, people necessarily
have a limited capacity to understand and express the fullness of God's
own truth. Thus, not infrequently, we may be responsible for obscuring it.
Two important implications for openness follow from this. First, that all
the texts and acts I love are, for all their supreme, decisive value, somewhat limited. I may hope to gain additional if subsidiary insight into what

God wishes by paying some attention to what other people know to be God's truth. Second, the great teachers of my tradition, while instructing me in what I know to be God's word, also convey to me some personal understandings of their own. Unwittingly, they may thus authorize a prejudice and hostility which runs contrary to their central teaching concerning God's over-arching unity and the consequent oneness of all humankind. This personalizing hermeneutic is well attested even in traditional Jewish legal thinking where it is common to speak of a given sage's "system" of interpretation or to acknowledge that some authorities are characteristically lenient or stringent in their rulings.

The human factor is so widely accepted as a reality among us that many people will not deny that exclusivist utterances may more often be personal predilection or conditioning than divine inspiration. But to those believers who know God's own hand lies behind every critical text and its proper interpretation, the argument from human finitude will have quite limited appeal.

Reluctantly, but necessarily, I conclude that there is no easy theological way of reconciling the more universal and the more particular emphases in a given religion. We must therefore expect to have continual tension in all our communities between those who believe that serving God requires considerable openness to others and those who know that it mandates a careful exclusiveness.

To my mind, such realism makes inter-faith work all the more important. By its very existence and spiritual vitality, by creating a model of openness to others yet faithfulness to one's tradition, it constitutes an appropriate spiritual challenge to those who will not join us. Pragmatically, it may create a critical mass to influence those in our communities who are less the foes of dialogue than simply unaccustomed to it. And it may also help our world cement its commitment to unity in diversity so that it will not easily be swept away should a tempest of old prejudices sweep by.

Yet if theory provides no clear way of reconciling these two approaches to God's service, a social factor may yet give us its practical equivalent. I refer to the modern experience of democracy.

I shall speak now out of my American experience though I believe that in my national particularity I am reflecting a sense of spiritual truth felt far more universally. What makes it possible for us Americans of several faiths, indeed what impels us toward outreach to one another is our nation's commitment to and experience of creating unity out of pluralism. The recent celebration of the bicentennial of the Constitution of the United States forcibly reminded us how a great founding ideal of our country, religious freedom for everyone, is embedded in the legal foundation of our national life. I am awe-struck that this utterly secular text has taught us all a compelling religious truth, one our individual traditions may have sensed but whose social form it alone clearly mandated. By its formulation that there be impartial religious pluralism among us, the Constitution required us to live peaceably with people with whom we may

416

profoundly disagree. And that, in turn, led us to learn how to find, often after great argument, mutually acceptable means of advancing the common welfare. Against all that our histories led us to anticipate, two centuries of seeking to live up to this standard have taught us that by practicing pluralism we are much the better human beings *as our own religions define that*. And, we have also surprisingly discovered that we are truer to our own particular faith when we make democratic pluralism an integral part of its religious morality. For America has not only taught us the spiritual benefits of living in peace with people of other faiths but of creating a similar sense of communal *shalom*, peace, in our own disputatious faith communities.

It is on this pragmatic level that I can begin to join Professor Kung in his hopes for the future. Wherever democracy is vital, there is greater human well-being in our religious midst than there was in the societies of our ancestors of which we have much data. *E pluribus unum*, out of those who remain many, it is possible to create a unity and thus come closer to our spiritual ideals. That truth, made manifest in daily living, will, I hope, exercise a compelling spiritual influence on all of us everywhere.

I think it is possible to add one further line of development, one suggested by Professor Kung's reference to the relationship between the legal codification of human rights and the modern humane consciousness which underlies it. I cannot tell whether I detect more of a difference than Professor Kung does between these two levels of activity. Nonetheless, I see a rather clear distinction between being able to agree on specific courses of action, even standards of behavior, and necessarily agreeing on the universal principles which lead one to them. I am quite willing, as a result of much experience, to find ways that I can join with others in improving the common welfare without our having to agree on the ethics, metaphysics, or faith which leads us to them. I suggest that it is this pragmatic approach which those of us who follow the "embracing" strategy can best take to work toward peace between religions. It is one that sounds often in Professor Kung's paper though I see him as far more concerned with universal truth claims than I am. For all my philosophic interests, I, as my kind of believer, have a certain tolerance for those occasions when life seems responsibly to have moved ahead of our ability to conceptualize what is taking place. As I see it, then, peace among religions must come from a partial, practical outreach to one another as our faiths allow and our experience suggests. While I would prefer messianic wholeness to come now and while I agonize over all the sin our indolence allows to continue, I will be content if we move in little, though steady, ways toward it. I hear Professor Kung calling us to just such an openness to the spiritual possibilities of this time, and I am happy to be associated with him in that high cause.

35

Judaism and Christianity on
Recent Historic Events

Several discussions about my book on contemporary Christologies[1] suggested to me that I occupy an uncommon situation in the field of contemporary Jewish thought. Most of my professional colleagues are philosophers, specializing in the medieval Jewish or modern general areas. I am one of a tiny number identifying themselves as Jewish theologians and, rarer still, one with postrabbinic training in Christian theology. Standing between these two disciplines, then, I propose to undertake a comparative theological inquiry here, hoping thereby to gain insight into the distinctive faith of each tradition. Somewhat recklessly, I should like to work holistically and try to characterize the current situation in each faith by focusing on one broad theme. I can, perhaps, reduce the risk of so grandiose an enterprise by starting from a description of the Jewish situation, which I know better, and then move on to what appears to me to be its closest Christian parallel. I hope the heuristic gains of this effort compensate for its substantive shortcoming.[2]

Jewish Interpretations

For about two decades now, Jewish religious thinkers have centered most of their attention on the theological[3] implications of recent historic events. Five distinct interests can be delineated. The first two, the "death

Originally published as "Recent Historic Events: Jewish and Christian Interpretations," in *Theological Studies*, vol. 44, no. 2 (June 1983).

of God" and the State of Israel, aroused far more participation than the three other topics I shall explicate.

The early novels of Elie Wiesel and the first group of Richard Rubenstein's theologically revisionist articles appeared in the late 1950's. Yet it was not until the mid-1960's that large-scale Jewish discussion of the meaning of the Holocaust began.[4] I remain convinced[5] that an important factor in finally legitimating this topic was the emergence of the Christian death-of-God movement then. In any case, the debate continued vigorously for about ten years and still sporadically resumes, though in rather ritualized fashion.

What moved the Jewish theoreticians was less the classic issue of theodicy than responding to the actual, awesome events under Hitler. Rubenstein's argument and title made Auschwitz the symbol for the new form of an old problem.[6] He, Wiesel, and Emil Fackenheim asserted that the Holocaust was unique in the history of human evil. It therefore demanded totally new responses from Jews. It was, for all its negativity, our Mt. Sinai. Wiesel insisted that its singularity took it far beyond our ability even to frame proper questions about it, much less to provide answers. Rubenstein demanded a radical rejection of the received God of Judaism, in whose place he now saw the Holy Nothing. Fackenheim, after years insisting that God's revelation (understood in Buber's contentless I-thou terms) must be the basis of modern Judaism, could no longer speak of God's presence in history. Instead, he built his Jewish commitment on the unconditional command to nurture Jewish life which came to the Jewish people from Auschwitz though no commander was discernible.[7] The responses to these views were based on new ways of restating the old defenses: it is good that people are free and responsible, even to be Nazis; God is finite; having some reason to have faith, we can trust in God even though we do not fully understand God.

The second major discussion arose out of the Holocaust controversy as a result of the 1967 Israeli Six Day War. In the weeks prior to and during the news blackout of its first two days, the possibility of another "holocaust" loomed before world Jewry. This mood was intensified by our first experience of war by television. Those experiences were sufficient to arouse Jewish ethnic concern to levels previously unprecedented. They were then heightened by the details of an incredible victory—deliverance—and, even more miraculously, by seeing Jews enter Old Jerusalem and, for the first time since the State of Israel had been established, being permitted to pray before the Temple Mount Western Wall.

The effect of those weeks on American Jewry was profound, lasting, and utterly unanticipated. Our new affluence and success in an expanding American economy had made us lukewarm to our ethnic identity and rather indifferent to the State of Israel. The frightful threat and wondrous triumph of the Six Day War made us realize how deeply Jewish we were and wanted to be, and how organically we were bound to the State of Israel. Once again, we were not alone in changing our social self-perception.

The growing urban strife in America and the consequent burgeoning of ethnic consciousness in all groups undoubtedly influenced us.[8] And the ensuing years of international isolation for the Israelis and the rise of a new international anti-semitism strengthened a post-Holocaust community's determination to make Jewish survival primary.

Theologically, the issue became what spiritual weight one should attach to the State of Israel. To Irving Greenberg it was, with the Holocaust, the second irresistible imperative transforming Jewish modernity into a new pluralistic traditionalism.[9] Fackenheim went further. He proclaimed the State of Israel the contemporary absolute of Jewish life. This followed logically on his evaluation of the Holocaust. The Commanding Voice of Auschwitz had laid an unconditional obligation upon the Jewish people to deny Hitler a posthumous victory. The State of Israel was Jewry's collective, life-affirming fulfillment of that commandment. Hence keeping it alive and flourishing was the unimpeachable, overriding Jewish responsibility.[10]

Opposition to this Israelocentrism faced the difficulty of communicating the difference between the extraordinarily important and the essential or indispensable. Specifically, the protagonists of the opposing view sought to establish that, on the biblical model, Jewish statehood must be subordinate to other beliefs, certainly in God, but also in the Jewish people itself.[11] Two political tangents of this discussion deserve mention. The one had to do with the right and criterion of criticizing the Israeli government. The other considered the long-term viability of Diaspora Jewry should the State of Israel disappear.

A third recent theme, notable mainly because our Orthodox writers rarely debate theology, centered about the possible eschatological implications of Old Jerusalem coming under Jewish sovereignty for the first time in nearly two thousand years. Some thinkers, taking seriously their daily prayers for God's return to Jerusalem, saw the spectacular events of 1967 as possibly the first glimmers of the messianic redemption. Other thinkers, chastened by the long, bitter Jewish experience of premature messianism, cautioned against this view, despite its special appeal in explaining our recent experience of terrible travail as "the birth pangs of the Messiah."[12]

Fourth, a broader segment of our community has seen the Vietnam War, Watergate, and other socially disillusioning events requiring them to rethink the old alliance between Judaism and modernity. This has a social as well as an intellectual aspect. American Jews have long considered themselves fully at home here. Some thinkers now suggest that we must revive the category of Exile. To a considerable extent, they argue, Jews are aliens in this society. They propose utilizing the term Exile not merely in its existentialist, universal connotation of alienation but in a particular Jewish fashion, in the Bible's nationalistic usage, without thereby yielding to the Zionist secular definition, which is purely political.[13]

A rather more compelling question addresses the balance between the authority of American culture and Jewish tradition. If, in our new realism, our culture is less worthy of religious devotion, then our tradition newly commends itself to us. Not only does it suggest itself as the antidote for our society's ills but as an independent source of human value we have long ignored. We therefore need to be "more Jewish" in belief and practice than we have been.[14] The two most exciting spiritual phenomena in our community during the past decade have been the new traditionalism of liberal Jews and the ground-swell founding of *havurot*, small communities for Jewish celebration and experience.[15] Unexpectedly, too, Orthodoxy has emerged as an option for modern Jews desirous of living an authentic Jewish existence. Both movements have parallels in the general American turn to the right. The specific Jewish contours of our developments arise from considering the failures of America and the re-emergence of anti-semitism against our memories of the Holocaust.

Fifth, our most recent issue has come out of our everyday experience in these years. Not long ago many writers were saying that our entire Jewish way of life must now be rebuilt around the Holocaust. With most of us day by day finding normality the basic condition of our lives, that older view seems faulty. Frightful disasters occur and dreadful horrors are still regularly perpetrated. We must never be blind to the hells about us or to the potential of their occurrence. But our lives are very far from a recapitulation of Auschwitz or even greatly illuminated by its uniqueness. Even God, who in Rubenstein's formulation was absent to us—"we live in a time of the Death of God"—has reappeared in the living search of at least a minority of the Jewish community.[16]

This transition can most readily be seen in the thought of Irving Greenberg, who has devoted himself wholeheartedly to the intellectual and communal tasks imposed by the Holocaust. In his earliest writing it was not clear whether he seriously dissented from Wiesel, Rubenstein, and Fackenheim that Auschwitz had taken the place of Sinai for us. Before long he not only gave it equal rank but began speaking of moment-faiths and the continuing place of God in our lives.[17] Most recently he has given further prominence to Jewish continuity, though with the radical revisions required by living in a post-Holocaust age.[18]

It seems to me that abstract, academic themes dominate contemporary Christian theology, save for liberation theology (of which more later). By contrast, Jewish thinking overwhelmingly centers on living social questions prompted by recent historical events. In theological language, my Jewish colleagues are asking, "What is God saying in what has happened to us?" To be sure, we do not hear that question articulated in those words. Jews retain a certain traditional reticence about speaking directly of God. Surely, too, some of our thinkers remain so sensitive to the agnostic Jewish environment in which they grew up and continue to move that they habitually bracket out the God-question, preferring instead to speak about the Jewish people or Jewish duty. Nonetheless, our debates involve more than ethnic interests or social concerns. They inevitably reach down to our ultimate convictions about Jewish responsibility. In the typical selectivity of a secular generation, we tune out the most important frequencies of our "signals of transcendence."

Before asking how Christian theologians approach recent events, I think it important to test and thereby try to strengthen the comprehensive hypothesis I have sought to establish. Let us inquire to what extent historic events are a long-term or only a recent Jewish religious interest. The evidence from biblical-talmudic Judaism is unambiguous. One might even argue that this religious concern with history is as unique to Hebrew tradition as is monotheism. The prophets and rabbis regularly sought God's hand in the major historic occurrences of their time. While the theophany at Mt. Sinai may ground and limit Jewish life, the Bible spends comparatively little time on what transpired there and devotes itself in great detail to what happened in later centuries when Jews sought to live by the Torah. Though the rabbis restrict where revelation may be found,[19] they quite organically react to the destruction of the Temple or to rulers such as Hadrian by indicating what God is teaching the Jewish people through these calamities.

This pattern of interpreting the triumphs and trials of Jewish history as the operation of God's justice continued until Jewish modernity. Characteristically, it now surfaces among us only in the speeches of one or another of our European-oriented *yeshivah* heads, that is, the leaders of that part of our community which has resolutely refused to modernize. For the rest of us, as early as the nineteenth century, modernization meant secularization, substituting a scientific world view for a religious one. Those modernized Jews who maintained some effective belief in God quickly gave up the old mechanistic, Deuteronomic reading of history. The modern concepts of God made history almost entirely the domain of social forces and human moral decision, not God's direct action.[20]

This modern demythologization of history is of some importance for our theme. Consider, for example, the response of Jewry to the "Holocaust" of its time, the 1903 Kishinev massacre. Jews world-wide could not imagine such an act occurring among civilized people, and the conscience of much of Western civilization motivated almost universal protest. Despite the pain, the modernists did not try to explain this tragedy in terms of theological verities they had long given up. Rather, the outrage was blamed, variously, on a failure of conscience and reason, a cynical governmental diversion of the masses, a capitalist plot against the proletariat, or a result of the Jews not being expected to stand up in self-defense. Rubenstein's charge, half a century later, that the Holocaust made it impossible to believe in the old God of history may have applied to the Jewish traditionalists who still affirmed Deuteronomic justice in history. (Factually, some recent data disputes this charge.[21]) However, this interpretation of the death of God simply did not apply to the mass of modernized Jews. They had secularized long before the Holocaust and were largely atheistic or agnostic. Those who had liberal concepts of God knew nothing of a God who was "the ultimate omnipotent actor in history."[22]

If so, did secularization mean the end of the classic Jewish perception of history as a continuing scene of God's self-manifestation? A surface examination of liberal Jewish theologies in the early decades of this century bears out that surmise. Hermann Cohen, whose neo-Kantian, philosophic reinterpretation of Judaism set the standard and problematic of most of the succeeding thinkers, described Judaism in terms of its central, that is, its regulative "idea," ethical monotheism. His younger German compatriot Leo Baeck yoked religious consciousness to the master's rationalism and spoke of "the essence" of Judaism. Both notions derived from German idealism, in which the empirical is radically subordinated to the rational—as good as dissolving history into concept.

I wish to argue that, on a deeper level, this seeming ahistoricalism is itself their response to what God was doing in their history. Their idealistic Judaism arose, though they do not remind us of it, as a means of coping theologically with Jewish Emancipation. The political and social enfranchisement of the Jews in the general society was not one event but, by their time, a century-long process. While most Jews enthusiastically accepted their new human equality, many doubted they could adopt a way of life determined by their society and yet remain authentically Jewish. The decades of experiment in worship, observance, and rationalization finally reached maturity in the thought of Hermann Cohen. If the University of Marburg philosopher did not discuss his system as a response to Emancipation, it was only because he took that move for granted even as he exemplified its benefits. Note that his philosophy of Judaism elevates Judaism's eternal idea against the books tradition says were given at Sinai. He thus validates the authority of contemporary reason in Judaism, making rational relevance the criterion of Jewish authenticity. Baeck employed a similar strategy to reach similar goals. He only expanded the dimensions of the immediate experience which Jews would now make sovereign.[23]

As the twentieth century moved on, the succeeding philosophers became more historically self-conscious. Our other great rationalistic system-builder, Mordecai Kaplan, is a good case in point. Kaplan justifies his radicalism by pointing to the reinterpretations brought on by the prior major turning points in Jewish history, the Exile and the destruction of the Second Temple. He argues that the Emancipation is another of these, requiring us to rethink and reshape Judaism stringently to our democratic social situation. Since our cultural ethos is scientific, Kaplan reconstructs Jewish institutional life, practices, values, and ideas in naturalistic terms. In this system, American naturalism replaces German philosophic idealism but the function of reason remains the same: to establish the emancipated Jew as the master of the Jewish past, though also its beneficiary. This, once again, is a philosophy of the "revelation" given by historic events.[24]

A decade earlier in Germany, Martin Buber had reached his unique insight about the reality and authority of genuine interpersonal encounter. In this nonrationalist "system," history has renewed importance. The homogenized chronology of rationalism now is accompanied by the person-alistic experience that some moments are far richer in meaning than others. By this theory Buber reached the same goal as the rationalists: he had acknowledged the revelatory authority of the Emancipation and met it by giving the present encounter hegemony over tradition.

At the same time, Buber had provided modernized Jews with a non-Orthodox understanding of how God might be speaking in contemporary events. Israel, the people, can today, as in the past, encounter God, this time in the wilderness of contemporary history. Buber responded to events in his lifetime from this perspective. Zionism was to be the modern coun-terpart of the ancient Hebrews' corporate relationship with God; the *kib-butz* was the noble Jewish effort to live community in full dimension; the need of the Israelis to reach out and make common cause with the Arabs was the test of Zionism's Jewishness; though Eichmann was guilty of the most heinous crimes against the Jewish people, Buber argued that it did not befit our character to take his life. The Holocaust so troubled him that he rethought his theory of evil, acknowledging now the terrifying biblical truth that, on occasion, God withdraws from us, "hiding His face."[25]

The other two distinctive system-makers of this century, Franz Rosen-zweig and Abraham Heschel, would seem the exceptions to my hypothe-sis. Since I believe I can somewhat mitigate the refutation by way of Heschel, I shall speak first about him, though Rosenzweig wrote nearly half a century earlier.

Heschel interpreted Judaism as a religion centered on time rather than space.[26] But he did not initiate the contemporary Jewish theological inter-est in historic events. Before 1967, the opposite was actually the case. In his system, which was fully elaborated prior to that fateful year, contem-porary history has no role, except perhaps as secularizing villain. I read Heschel's work as a religionist's protest against the desanctification of the world and, in particular, against the liberal secularization of Jewish faith. In quite classic fashion, therefore, Heschel made the recovery of revelation the goal of his apologetics. He thereby returned Sinai and the prophets to their authoritative place and made the rabbis their legitimate interpreters. In his Judaism contemporary history was only another arena for the appli-cation of these eternal truths. At that stage his attitude to recent history merely involved him in reversing the liberal Jewish manner of accommo-dating to modernity, though he retained its ethical thrust.

The return of Old Jerusalem to Jewish sovereignty changed that. He-schel's book *Israel, An Echo of Eternity* movingly describes what this place, Jerusalem, means to him as a Jew, and therefore what this event of return means to Judaism.[27] Intriguingly for so traditionalistic a thinker, he makes no messianic argument. Rather, he limits himself to the theological significance of geography. He provides a phenomenology of standing on the sites which constitute some of the people of Israel's most sacred sym-bols. Thus, though Heschel's thought was based on the classic tenet that ancient revelation determined contemporary Judaism, he too was religiously overcome by a modern event.

We cannot say the same for Rosenzweig, though it must quickly be noted that he died in 1929 after a meteoric intellectual career, in the last few years of which he was incapacitated by an almost total paralysis.[28] Like Heschel, he saw revelation as the heart of Judaism, though Rosenzweig posited a nonverbal, "contentless" (by classic Jewish standards) encounter with God.[29] As a result, Rosenzweig too had no significant doctrine of the Jewish people and, alone of all twentieth-century Jewish thinkers, turned his back on contemporary events (though accepting the Emancipation).[30] He made history a Christian domain, with authentic Jews already participating in eternity by living the Torah. They thus had no religious interest in what passes for history.

Rosenzweig's thought clearly counts against my argument concerning the centrality of history to modern as to ancient Jewish theology. If he is correct, the concerns of my generation are an accident of our situation but not Jewishly essential. I think it fair to rejoin that this aspect of Rosenzweig's thought has been an embarrassment to those who would follow him. On the issue of eternity, not the moment, he has been almost totally rejected by the Jewish community on the basis of its lived experience. Any theory that would render the Holocaust and the State of Israel peripheral to being a Jew cannot be right. I suggest that Rosenzweig came to his extreme stand because of his heavy polemic agenda against the opposing views of Judaism, the Orthodox, the liberal, and the Zionist. This caused him to emphasize God and contentless revelation to the detriment of the folk and human aspects of Judaism. Consequently, the philosophical idealism which Rosenzweig was seeking to escape managed to reassert itself and frustrate the protoexistentialism he had creatively initiated to take its place.

Let me sum up my Jewish case by adducing one further piece of evidence. With the exception of Buber, the great system-builders give almost no attention to the Mt. Sinai experience. The rationalists as good as dissolve it into mind and conscience. Heschel assimilates it to his general theory of revelation as sym-pathos, despite his commitment to Sinai's uniqueness. Rosenzweig, describing revelation as love, speaks of Sinai only symbolically. Buber, applying the I-thou relationship to the national level, searches the Exodus account with intriguing personalistic openness.[31] But having devoted one chapter of one work to the topic, he does not return to it. Thus the Jewish concern for history in these thinkers is not attention to a unique occurrence in the past but to the events of their time.

It may well be countered that this is so because the thinkers I have analyzed, except Heschel, are liberal Jews. If only Orthodoxy can be Judaism, my argument again fails. But I see no useful way of debating the issue of what constitutes authentic Judaism. I would only point out how Orthodoxy itself has changed as a result of events. Particularly notable is its about-face toward Zionism. What was almost a complete rejection of this irreligiosity when modern secular Zionism arose, has now become almost total support, mainly enthusiastic but partially grudging. This transformation was not the result of a changed philosophy of history but of a realistic response to what happened. Moreover, I cannot here treat any Orthodox Jewish philosopher because there are no twentieth-century systematic expositions of traditional Jewish faith comparable to those of the liberals. The least that can be said of my hypothesis, then, is that it characterizes such Jewish theology as we have. I gladly acknowledge that I am speaking about liberal Judaism. I must add that the systems I have described raise to the level of academic reflection the beliefs of the overwhelming majority of concerned American Jews.

Christian Interpretations

In turning now to contemporary Christian theology, let me identify a methodological problem. The differing Christian attitude toward recent events I perceive is not totally distinct from that of the Jewish theoreticians. Polemicists prefer to draw battlelines sharply. They force a decisive choice—and then the advocate is tempted to delineate the two stands so as to make the decision well-nigh irresistible. I think no false sense of ecumenism secretly makes me see only indistinct lines of dissimilarity between us. Even in disagreement the positions partially overlap. Living in the same culture, brought ever more closely into contact by democracy, media, and travel, utilizing the same repertoire of civilization symbol-structures, we are bound to be alike. That does not rule out genuine, fundamental opposition, but it explains why seeking to discern where our disagreements begin and leave off is a most subtle and often frustrating task.

To some extent, the greatest similarity in dealing with recent events may be seen in the attitudes of some evangelical Christians and Orthodox Jewish thinkers. Both can discern in the happenings around them signs that the *eschaton*, the end time, is breaking in. I do not know how much weight to attach to the different historical valences they consider meaningful. The Christian thinkers work with the negative aspects of events and resonate with vibrations of the power of the Antichrist. Because of Jerusalem, the Jews are overwhelmed by a positive indication the Messiah may be nigh.

Even in this convergence I detect somewhat contrary evaluations of the pre-Messianic history in which we stand. The evangelicals seem to me to esteem the Second Coming and its salvation so highly that present events are, by comparison, of small significance. Accepting the Christ and remaining steadfast in one's faith, while devotedly awaiting, even anticipating, his speedy return are the religiously desirable virtues. Obviously, these will affect one's everyday life. But the time frame radically distinguishes between the value of this era and that which was when Jesus walked this earth and that which will be when he returns.

Jews, for all their commitment to the coming of the Messiah, are less eschatologically oriented. God's Torah directs them to the here-and-now, not to the life of the world-to-come, though it awaits them. Their sense of the Messiah remains so human that figures as ordinary as Bar Kochba and Sabbetai Zevi could be taken for the Shoot of Jesse. Though the great eschatological drama of resurrection, judgment, and eternal life ensues in due course, the advent of the Messiah will occur in profane, not transformed, history. I suggest, then, that even on the right we can distinguish between the faiths on this theme. With some hesitation, I find here what I see more clearly elsewhere: the Jewish thinkers can be deeply moved by *specific* happenings, while the Christian theologians seek to read the signs of the times *in general*.

The contours of difference emerge more readily when I read less orthodox thinkers. The most dramatic confrontation with contemporary history would seem to occur in the European praxis theologians like Moltmann and Metz, and the South American liberationists. In the late 1960's I would have described the European movement as a response to the student revolution and the prospect of great social change. But for more than a decade now, no particular occurrence—the Polish worker's revolt, for example—has had anywhere near similar impact. And Hispanic liberation theology likewise seems far more socially than historically oriented.

Something also must be said now about the power of events to reshape theology. For the Jews, the Emancipation, the Holocaust, the State of Israel, the gaining of Old Jerusalem, and, potentially, other happenings can cause fundamental revisions in our thought. These events changed the thinkers' teaching concerning God and Torah and, most markedly, their doctrines of the people of Israel. I do not see historical incidents impinging as strongly on Christian thinkers. Recent experiences may transform Christian witness and the tone of Christian existence, as in recent years, but I do not see events causing so fundamental a rethinking of faith among Christians as among Jews. Somewhat less hesitantly now, I would identify the Christian concern as responding to the culture generally, while the Jews have reacted more directly to specific historic occurrences.

Perhaps I can go a step further. The socially oriented Christian theologians seem to me to be answering the Marxists' legitimate criticism of the society and the church. The leftists co-opted and perverted the church's social ethics. Now that the ethical duplicity of the secular critics is plain, the church can reclaim its social values, challenge the Marxists for their institutional failure, and, by co-opting the Marxist social analysis, renew its mandate of stewardship. My ethical admiration for that stance does not change my judgment about our diversity in theologically confronting our time.

427

Somewhat similar attitudes emerge in two lesser themes of Christian writing. One is the continuing effort to create a theology of culture. While this activity seems less lively to me in recent years than it did in the exciting days of H. Richard Niebuhr and Paul Tillich, little similar work surfaces among Jews. Far less predictable is the outcome of contemporary Christian thinkers' engagement with Asian religions, now freshly seen as dialogue partners rather than as objects of missionary zeal. I read this as a broadening of contemporary Christian theology's cultural horizon from barely beyond the West to include the whole globe. Accompanying it has been an enlarged sense of the equality of humankind and the universality of genuine spirituality. This poses a new challenge to Christian as to other faiths' particularity. But these activities fit in well with my earlier speculations about the central orientation of Christian thought.

Even clearer insight is yielded by a retrospective look at the Protestant death-of-God agitation of the mid-1960's. The four theoreticians who formulated the issues under discussion then, Paul Van Buren, Thomas J. J. Altizer, Gabriel Vahanian, and William Hamilton, based their positions, different as they were, on cultural considerations. Altizer's cyclical view of opposing spiritual epochs, based vaguely on Mircea Eliade's view of religion, yielded a negative judgment about Western civilization and contemporary religion. Van Buren called for demythologizing the Son to conform to the philosophic temper of the times. Vahanian and Hamilton examined immediate religious experience and found it empty. In our culture, they proclaimed, God was dead. Not until Richard Rubenstein's writing came to their attention did it occur to them to argue that an event in their lifetime, the Holocaust, was an immediate refutation of the existence of a good and omnipotent God. And the Nazi experience never did play much of a role in their subsequent discussion.

In the near twenty years since those days, some Christian thinkers have acknowledged that, at the least, this event requires some reconsideration of theologies formulated before evil like the Holocaust could be imagined. Roy Eckardt, Franklin Littell, John Pawlikowski, and others have tried to rethink their Christianity in terms of this human and Jewish horror. Paul Van Buren has gone even further and now has begun to study what it might mean to think rigorously of Christianity as an offshoot of Jewish religious experience. Such Christian theologians are doing very much what Jews have done, but I shall not further consider their work. I cannot tell to what extent they are responding to what happened or to the challenge of Jewish colleagues for whom attention to this matter is a condition of dialogue. How such an event might find a proper place in Christian thought remains unclear to me. My doubts arise from the fact that the overwhelming majority of Christian theologians do not yet consider the Holocaust a sufficiently significant event to merit much attention in their thinking.

I have come across only two Christian thinkers who have responded to historic events somewhat as Jews have. Karl Rahner has pondered the theological implications of the declining world influence of Christianity and its potential fall to a minority impulse in Western civilization. To Jews, long accustomed to Christian apologists arguing that the success of Christianity demonstrates its truth, the change in Christian power over the past two decades has been striking. Rahner resolutely rejects all such temporal criteria of worth as contrary to the kenotic traditions of the church. To the contrary, Christianity most authentically fulfills its mission as a servant church. It may now well be required by God to become a church in diaspora, serving in the humility befitting a relatively powerless, scattered institution. But that will only confirm, not contradict, its central truth.

Rahner's effort here is comparable to the reconsideration forced on Jewish thinkers by the Emancipation drastically changing their social status. But where their experience could compel them to rethink radically the nature of their Jewishness, Rahner's reaction to this apparently substantial historical shift barely impinges upon his central understanding of Christianity. The notion of a church in diaspora is only hinted at in his comprehensive volume *Foundations of Christian Faith*.[32]

A far more direct investigation of the meaning of historical events in Christianity may be found in Wolfhart Pannenberg's *Human Nature, Election and History*.[33] Pannenberg's interest in history is well known, since he contended in *Jesus—God and Man* that an academic historical approach to the evidence available validates the factual occurrence of Jesus' resurrection. In the last three of these lectures he probes the meaning of historic events since the Christ. He deplores those tendencies in Christianity, from Augustine through Luther and beyond, to separate the true domain of Christian existence from the commonplace realm of sociopolitical affairs. This led, after the collapse of the medieval effort to establish a proper Christendom, to the secular modern state, where religion is reduced to a private activity. Pannenberg calls for a proper recognition of the social dimension of Christianity. He emphasizes the importance of the "people of God" motif in the New Testament and Christian belief, holding it to be more important even than the notion of church, but, in any case, equally significant a doctrine as that of individual salvation.[34]

I was particularly curious to see what he made of this as he applied it to our time. Permit me to explain my special interest. In my paper on contemporary Christologies, I had excoriated Pannenberg for his religious anti-semitism. He had continued the old Christian-Protestant-Lutheran charge that with the crucifixion the religion of the Jews died. I was outraged that he, a post-Holocaust theologian, in Germany of all countries, seemed to have no consciousness of the social consequences of centuries of such teaching. The anti-semitism of Christian theology had made it possible for secularists to transform "Judaism is dead" into "Jews should be killed." While reworking this material into book form, I learned that in a work of the early 1970's Pannenberg had modified his earlier view. He then described his prior statement as "the resupposition of a view widespread in German Protestantism, that the religion of the Law and the Jewish religion

are identical."[35] But when Richard John Neuhaus kindly brought us together to discuss this matter, Pannenberg could not understand why I
should assess his thought in terms of the previous German generation's
actions, which, plainly enough, he considered totally reprehensible. I
therefore was particularly interested in what he might say about recent
historic events.

In his final lecture Pannenberg devotes one long paragraph to the
meaning of the two World Wars, which he discusses in terms of modern
nationalism. Because it has been secularized, nationalism has been affected for evil as well as for good, as has the other chief organizing principle secularism utilized, liberalism. (Both nationalism and liberalism
have Judeo-Christian origins, he argues.) The evil effects on nationalism
have been most pronounced, leading to World War I's orgy of European
self-destruction and an end to Europe's world domination. Worse, "It
meant that the divine vocation that was perceived earlier in experiences of
national chosenness, had been forfeited by nationalistic self-glorification."
He then continues:

> That judgment became definitive with World War II. Among the hardest
> hit was the German nation. The single most serious reason for that in theo-
> logical as well as in historical terms may have been the persecution and
> attempted annihilation of the Jewish people. This attempt disclosed to the
> world the radical nature of that nationalism. The German case demon-
> strated in a particularly decisive way the dangerous potential of national-
> ism, but it is uncertain whether the general significance of that experience
> has yet been properly understood in the contemporary world.[36]

The ethical import of this passage is admirable. But it leaves a Jewish
reader troubled. Events can apparently teach a Christian theologian something about nationalism, in this case particularly about German nationalism, though here that instance is sublimated to the world's problem with
it. Events do not, in this instance, cause the theologian to take a hard look
at his own religious tradition. Surely, that such an evil made itself manifest in the birthplace of Protestant Christianity and still one of its most
important intellectual centers, is not a trivial matter. How could a nation
with such a vigorous church life, Catholic as well as Protestant, have become so demonic? Should there not be a thorough critique and rethinking
of the intellectual factors in the church which made this possible?

If we follow the Talmudic dictum of judging others by looking only at
the scale of merit,[37] we may say that Pannenberg's lectures, for all that
they do not say so explicitly, are a judgment on and a reconstruction of
Christian theology. While Pannenberg does not discuss Christian theological anti-semitism here, he does isolate and correct the basic error he sees
in prior interpretations of Christianity: it was too individualistically oriented and now needs to take more direct responsibility for the nation in
which it functions. If that is the proper understanding, Pannenberg is one
of the few Christian thinkers I have encountered who have allowed their
basic faith to be modified by recent events.

Can we now provide some reasons for the dissimilar interests of contemporary Jewish and Christian theologians?

Let us say the simplest yet most important thing first: we do not know when or where or why God acts. All religions know moments highly charged with meaning and long stretches when memory must take the place of revelation. Who is to say that perhaps in recent years God chose to act toward the Jews with a directness and significance God did not in the same period manifest to Christians? In other centuries one might have made the same observation the other way around. Let us therefore proceed with great humility. We may be seeking to fathom matters which radically exceed our depth of penetration. But let that not keep us from seeking to explore that which mind and soul make available to us.

In this spirit of tentativeness, two sociological caveats ought to be introduced. To begin with, the distinctive Jewish theological concerns may reflect the situation of those who do it rather than Judaism's essential faith. Most Jews writing in this area are not professional theologians. Their agenda is not set by a well-established guild and they are not centrally concerned with the academic challenges one's seminary or university colleagues may raise. Even those of our writers who are academics work in disciplines other than Jewish theology. As a result, we are far more likely to attend to the realities faced by our community than to the abstract issues made significant by generations of learned, abstract, academic debate.

Second, our community is small, conscious of being a tiny minority everywhere but in the State of Israel and sensitive to the perils to its survival. We magnify every trauma, and having recently undergone previously unimaginable pain—even in terms of the long, anguished history of Jewish suffering—we have been humanly and spiritually changed. But we have also been overwhelmed by several unbelievable triumphs in our time. We can, therefore, often find ourselves quite confused as to how such extremes as we have known can testify to one ultimate reality.

By these familial Jewish standards we find it almost incomprehensible, for example, that when the Christian Lebanese were under severe assault by their Moslem Lebanese brothers and their Syrian allies, there was no Western Christian outcry. Perhaps the vastness of Christianity simply gives a different scale to any individual event. Thus, for all Rahner's genuine humility, he can know that even a diminished church will contain some hundreds of millions of remaining believers. That should surely keep it alive until the Spirit manifests itself again in the church's social status. We do not have this numeric assurance. Nonetheless, Jews may well ask what God is saying to them in keeping them so few and so imperiled. However, with this question about the theology of Jewish sociology, we have moved on to the more important level of our analysis.

I wish to suggest that the differing responses of Jewish and Christian theologians to recent historic events is largely due to their different paradigms of religious reality. For Jews, that is the Covenant with the people of Israel begun at Mt. Sinai; for Christians, it is the New Covenant made

431

through the life and death of Jesus the Christ and carried on through the church. If we contrast these two religions to Asian faiths, the many similarities between Judaism and Christianity quickly stand out. The structure and content of the relationships with God clearly show a "family resemblance."

Yet there remain major differences between them. For our purposes, let me point to the rather diverse balance each faith gives to God's role and to that of God's human partner in the covenants. I believe we will find this theological divergence determinative of the phenomenon to which I have been calling attention.

In Judaism God initially fulfills the Covenant promises to the patriarchs by expanding Jacob's family to a populous nation, by taking them out of Egypt, giving them the Torah, and setting them as a people on their own Land. The act of receiving the Law-and-Teaching climaxes the early relationship and sets the conditions of all that is to follow. But it includes a commitment to the everyday history which will come after Sinai, in which God's care will regularly make itself felt. Then, too, the people of Israel, though utterly subordinate to their King/Lord/Creator/Only-God-of-the-universe, are active agents in the Covenant-making process. More, by assenting to being yoked to this God, they agree to bear the personal and corporate responsibility of living out God's Torah in history. By rabbinic times and the emergence of the doctrine of the Oral as well as the Written Law-and-Teaching, the rabbis become the effective shapers of the continuing meaning of Torah. They then richly endow the ordinary Jew with duties to sanctify life as perhaps only priests had thought of doing in prior times.

With secularization, modern Jewish thinkers transformed the ancient notion of the Covenant. Under the impact of science, God's providence was reinterpreted as less active, while the formerly limited role of human agency in the Covenant was extended almost to the point of dominance. As I analyze it, this transition did not negate the old covenantal faith that God was continually involved in the people of Israel's efforts to live by Torah. Thus, despite modernization, Jews could remain open to the possibility that contemporary history might be revelatory. To put this in the less tortured language of a simpler age, they could still ask what God was saying to them in their history.

It seems to me that Christianity's New Covenant does not as easily provide for such a modernized religious interest in recent events. What is involved, I am suggesting, is a sense of time which, for all its similarity to Judaism, here exposes its difference.

At the heart of the New Covenant lies God's utterly gracious and incomparable generosity in sending the Son and thereby assuming personal responsibility for atoning for human sinfulness. God's act-of-love in the Christ is so extraordinary that God's action cannot have the same sort of continuity in Christian lives that God's partnership has after God's gift of

432

the Torah at Mt. Sinai. To be sure, when the Parousia comes, all that was promised and foreshadowed in the life of the Christ will be gloriously ful-filled in ways beyond our imagining. In the interim God does not, of course, forsake the newly-called-forth people of God. The Holy Spirit is with them, acting in their lives, their institutions, and their history. But I am suggesting that the interim work of the Spirit, though real and power-ful, is of a different order than that of the God who gives a Teaching rather than a person of the triune Godhead. For the God of the Sinaitic Covenant remains personally involved with those who, alone in all the world, seek to live by God's Torah.

To better understand the differentiating thrust which will influence contemporary Christian theologians who seek to modernize the classic doctrine of the Holy Spirit, we must first seek what the traditional notion of the New Covenant makes of the role of the human partner. To Jewish eyes, Christianity's overwhelming sense of God's graciousness renders hu-man beings in the New Covenant more thoroughly subordinated and pas-sive in relation to God than are the Hebrews of the Covenant of Sinai. To be sure, there are major differences here between Catholic and Protestant teaching. Yet, in terms of the Jewish religious self-perception, Christianity as a whole seems to create a rather different balance between God and humankind. Christianity does call on us to open our hearts to faith and be ready to receive God's truth. In various interpretations it stresses the im-portance of the church and the life of sacraments as crucial to salvation. Yet, as Jews view it, in classic Christianity the balance is radically weighted toward God's side by the utterly unparallelable act-of-love God once did. Moreover, it should be noted that Christian salvation is primarily directed to the individual by God, though in varying interpretations the group, that is, the church, plays a role in it. Hence what happens to indi-vidual Christians is likely to have more significance to them than what happens to their community. Thus, Rahner appears to be predominantly occupied with the individual human being and God, and only secondarily with the church. By contrast, when Pannenberg needs models for his newly socialized Christianity, he draws them almost entirely from Hebrew Scripture.

The modernization of the New Covenant pioneered the radical activa-tion of the human role and the de-emphasis on God's providence which is typical of liberal religion. What happens to the Holy Spirit in this, and where it is now seen to operate, I am speculating, keeps contemporary theologians from envisioning recent events as "revelatory." This is not to argue that events can never play such a role in Christianity. In a previous time, when Providence was strongly activist, the Holy Spirit might be seen in happenings as varied as the Crusades or the Reformation. Today, with our scientific view of existence making the Holy Spirit less likely to be seen as objectively active, historic events retreat in importance for Chris-tians. Rather, with salvation understood in primarily personal terms and religion now conceived of largely in experiential terms, the Holy Spirit is more likely to be seen acting in the inner life of individuals than in the occurrences which befall the church as a whole or some significant part of it. But I have now strained my thesis to its limit. In extenuation, I ask you to remember my intention: I have been trying to clarify why what seems so obviously critical to one faith, Judaism, has not been so to another faith, Christianity, though both lived through the same history.

At least we can say that this investigation illustrates again the notion that we are apt to perceive about us that which our perspective on reality permits us to see. Perhaps in the clash of all the other factors which affect our perception, understanding our theological lenses does not explain very much. But if it helps enable once contentious religions to understand and live better with one another despite their differences, that will be accomplishment enough.

Notes

1. *Contemporary Christologies: A Jewish Response* (New York: Paulist, 1980).

2. In many ways I see this paper as an extension of the method utilized in *Christologies* (cf. #1–9).

3. When Jews can bring themselves to use this term, they do so in a sense far looser than that of Christians. Not having dogma or creed as Christians do, working instead out of the rabbinic openness to ideas and images which is structured by required action rather than by confessions of faith, Jews tend to be wary of theology lest it mean required statements or specifications of belief. Yet we have always had thinking people who, while living by this believing way, have tried to determine what it meant to them abstractly. In our time of high intellectual activity and social challenge, there has been a great deal of such thought. This matter recurs in this paper. Note, e.g., the discussion below of the people who work at what I would call Jewish theology.

4. The Eichmann trial and Hannah Arendt's provocative thesis on the effect of Jewish cooperation with the Nazis gave the discussion initial impetus. That was under way by 1963, but it was not until 1966 that the first major Jewish gathering dealt with the issue, the then annual symposium sponsored by *Judaism*. Fackenheim, Popkin, Steiner, and Wiesel participated, and their remarks were published in *Judaism* 16 (1967) 269–84, under the telling title "Jewish Values in the Post-Holocaust Future."

5. This theme has concerned me in a number of my articles and books where I have dealt with the change which has come over Jewish thought in the past two decades. With Jews anxious to protect the status they had gained as one of America's three major religions, they could never admit the widespread agnosticism of secularized Jews. Hence the Protestant death-of-God movement seemed for a time a positive liberation from the long-repressed hypocrisy of Jewish religiosity. And it is the collapse of that self-perception (of not needing religion) which has brought about the new Jewish interest in personal spirituality.

6. Note the title of his book, which became the focus of this discussion: *After Auschwitz* (Indianapolis: Bobbs-Merrill, 1966).

7. For a summary discussion of this material, see chapter 9, "Confronting the

Holocaust," in my book *Choices in Modern Jewish Thought* (New York: Behrman House, 1983). Most of the distinctive positions in the debate are discussed there. Note particularly the contribution of Michael Wyschogrod, who has given the most careful analysis of Fackenheim's argument, originally in "Faith and the Holocaust," *Judaism* 20 (1971) 286–94. My own argument concerning the uniqueness of the Holocaust is given at the end of the chapter noted above.

8. My treatment of this material may be seen in *The Mask Jews Wear* (New York: Simon and Schuster, 1973) 58 ff., and see the context.

9. The most easily available statement is in *Auschwitz: Beginning of a New Era?* ed. Eva Fleischner (New York: Ktav, 1974), in his statement "Cloud of Smoke, Pillar of Fire" (31 ff.).

10. See e.g., his paper "The Holocaust and the State of Israel: Their Relation," in Fleischner, *Auschwitz* 205 ff., and passim in his papers collected under the title *The Jewish Return into History* (New York: Schocken, 1978).

11. My rejection of this position may be found in two articles, originally one long paper, published as "Liberal Judaism's Effort to Invalidate Relativism without Mandating Orthodoxy," *Go and Study*, ed. Samuel Fishman and Raphael Jospe (New York: Ktav, 1980), and "The Liberal Jews in Search of an 'Absolute,' " *Cross Currents* 29 (1979) 9–14.

12. See the symposium "The Religious Meaning of the Six Day War," *Tradition* 10, no. 2 (Summer 1968) 5–20. A further exchange between Shubert Spero and Norman Lamm in the wake of the Egyptian-Israeli Yom Kippur War of 1973 is instructive: *Sh'ma* 4/73 (May 3, 1974) 98 ff. Also Shubert Spero, "The Religious Meaning of the State of Israel," *Forum*, 1976, no. 1, 69–82. A related discussion is found in Lawrence Kaplan's "Divine Promises—Conditional and Absolute," *Tradition* 18, no. 2 (Summer 1979) 35–43.

13. The literature on this topic is too diffuse for easy citation. A good example of diverse opinions is found in *Dimensions* 5, no. 3 (Spring 1971) 5–21. One of the earliest statements of the existentialist interpretation is found in Arthur A. Cohen, *The Natural and the Supernatural Jew* (New York: Pantheon, 1962) 179 ff.

14. On the new traditionalism, see chapter 10, "A Theology of Modern Orthodoxy," in my *Choices* (n. 7 above).

15. Eugene B. Borowitz, "The Changing Forms of Jewish Spirituality," *America* 140 (1979) 346–50.

16. Ibid.

17. Notice the section on "Moment Faiths" in the paper cited in n. 9 above.

18. So in a number of presently unpublished papers, including one delivered at a meeting in June 1981, "The Transformation of the Covenant."

19. Note how limited and how ambivalent their relation is to the *bat kol*, their closest counterpart to the biblical spirit of God: article "Bat Kol," *Encyclopedia Judaica* 4, 324.

20. *Ideas of Jewish History*, ed. Michael A. Meyer (New York: Behrman, 1974) xii, and note the tone of all the historians mentioned from Heinrich Graetz on.

21. Reeve Robert Brenner, *The Faith and Doubt of Holocaust Survivors* (New York: Free Press, 1980) 222 ff.

22. Eugene B. Borowitz, "God and Man in Judaism Today," *Judaism* 13 (1974) 298–308.

23. For a fuller discussion, see chaps. 2 and 3 in *Choices* (n. 7 above).

24. He is treated in chap. 4 of *Choices*.

25. The best analysis of this material remains Maurice Friedman, *Martin Bu-*

ber, *The Life of Dialogue* (New York: Harper, 1960). For the early and late stages of Buber's thought on evil, see chaps. 15 and 16.

26. *The Sabbath* (New York: Abelard Schuman, 1952).

27. *Israel: An Echo of Eternity* (New York: Farrar, Straus and Giroux, 1969).

28. Nahum N. Glatzer, *Franz Rosenzweig: His Life and Thought* (New York: Schocken, 1953) 108 ff.

29. Ibid. 285, where the theory is succinctly put. Its critical consequences are spelled out in the correspondence with Buber, reproduced in Franz Rosenzweig, *On Jewish Learning* (New York: Schocken, 1955) 109 ff.

30. See my discussion on "The Problem of the Form of a Jewish Theology," *Hebrew Union College Annual* (Cinn.) 40–41 (1969–70) 391–408, where I discuss the similarity of structural form in Heschel and Rosenzweig.

31. For Rosenzweig, the material in n. 29 above is apt. For Buber, see his *Moses* (Oxford: East and West Library, 1946) 110 ff.

32. New York: Seabury, 1978.

33. Philadelphia: Westminster, 1977.

34. Ibid.,e.g., 100–101, 106–7.

35. See the Foreword to his *The Apostle's Creed in the Light of Today's Questions* (Philadelphia: Westminster, 1972).

36. *Human Nature* 104–5.

37. Pirke Avot 1.6.

Jewish Critiques of Christian Ethics

A Dissent

The Jewish reader of James Gustafson's work, *Christ and the Moral Life*, is likely to emerge from it with two complementary impressions. First, because of differing responses to the Christ, there is a surprising variety of Christian ethical thinking. Gustafson deliberately eschews discussing the thinkers in terms of typologies and thus cannot be accused of exaggerating their differences by the form of his presentation (p. 5). Much of the diversity one finds in the work of these theologians arises from their disagreement as to where to place the primary emphases in Christian ethics, particularly because the Christ and his work may be interpreted in many ways. Gustafson thus inadvertently makes it clear that anyone wishing to compare Christian ethics with other views of morality requires substantial orientation to the varied topography of Christian ethical positions. What outside critics might assume Christianity lacks may turn out to be an authentic interpretation of Christian responsibility but one that is not popularly known as such.

The second impression derives from the first. There is an extraordinary disparity between Gustafson's presentation of Christian ethics and the perceptions Jews have had of them in the past century and a half. Jewish spokesmen have almost always identified the ethics of Christianity with the principle of love presented in the two love commandments and the Sermon on the Mount. From the single-mindedness with which Jewish writers have contrasted the inadequacy of love as a basis for human exis-

From *Contemporary Christologies, a Jewish Response* (New York: Paulist, 1980).

tence with that of justice, one would have thought the former quality was the sole normative content of Christian morality. Gustafson's work shows any such view is simplistic, perhaps even ignorant. Since, from the Jewish side, the debate over ethics has been a critical matter in comparing the value of the two religions, this theme is worthy of detailed examination.

Beginning early in the nineteenth century a denigration of Christian ethics (Protestant ethics is almost always meant) has been central to the defense of Judaism against the appeal of the modernist, majority religion, Christianity. Already in the writings of Joseph Salvador (1796–1873) and Elijah Benamozegh (1823–1900), the first notable modern Jewish polemicists, the standard lines of this attack appear. Christianity is individualistic and other-worldly in its primary orientation. Unlike Judaism, which is social and this-worldly, Christianity has no proper ethical orientation (Jacob, 1974).[1] These polemical attitudes first rise to the level of serious academic significance in the work of Hermann Cohen (1847–1918), the founder of the Marburg school of neo-Kantianism. Cohen saw Kant, as he reinterpreted him, providing a rationally valid understanding of humanity's place in the universe. This secular philosophy, which Cohen worked out in the final quarter of the nineteenth century, had religious implications since the idea of God played a central role in it. First in occasional writings and then after his retirement in 1913 in a sustained major treatment, Cohen applied his philosophy to Judaism. He found it, of all historic religions, to be the one that most clearly embodied the neo-Kantian notion of "religion of reason." Cohen saw the special relation between Kant and Judaism centering on Kant's double emphasis, that ethics is a major, distinctive characteristic of human beings and that properly rational ethics takes the form of law. (For one, explicit statement see "Affinities Between the Philosophy of Kant and Judaism" in 1971.)

Both themes were important in Cohen's defense of Judaism against Christian claims to final truth. In the Kantian frame of reference, rational beings would seek ethics, not faith. They would build their lives on a morality of law, not one of love. Cohen, who argued that ethics is the essence of Jewish law, had thus demonstrated the rational superiority of Judaism. It is as useless as it is irresistible to speculate whether Cohen's decision to undertake the academic effort of rehabilitating Kant was not in some significant way due to the usefulness Cohen intuited it might have for a modern Jewish apologetic. Cohen's neo-Kantianism has always been described as straightforward philosophical creativity; yet I cannot read the Jewish essays he based on his philosophy without the sense that their polemic against Christianity, implied or expressed, is highly important to him. To be sure, Cohen has a number of other major intellectual enemies, specifically mythology and pantheism, Spinoza being connected with the latter. But it tells us a good deal about Cohen's attitude that he often links Christianity with mythology and pantheism to expose it as insufficiently rational.

From the late nineteenth century on, the Jewish argument against

Christianity was shaped by the Cohenian critique: rational people could not accept Christianity. By contrast Judaism could be seen as the finest exemplar of "religion of reason" chiefly because, in an age of acculturation and secularization, the essence of Torah could be equated with Kantian morality. This construction of reality was so useful to Jews living as a minority in a Christian world that it became the common ideology of modernizing Jews. Though support for neo-Kantian rationality has long since eroded in academic circles, most Jews today still go back to the language of rational religion when they seek to justify Judaism against the attractiveness of Christianity.

Cohen's philosophy was not directly known to most of the Jewish community. Its influence was mediated to the masses by the many Jewish scholars whose attitudes were shaped by study in Germany or by the reading of German-Jewish intellectual works, most of which were strongly influenced by Cohen's ideas. Though the extent of Cohen's influence upon them is debatable, two of the most influential Jewish teachers of the early twentieth century indicate clearly the way neo-Kantian approaches to rationality and ethics shape the common Jewish perception of Christian moral theology. Taking them chronologically let us consider the perceptions of Christian ethics of Ahad Ha-am and Kaufmann Kohler.

Ahad Ha-am was the pseudonym of Asher Ginsberg (1856–1927), one of the classic figures of the East-European Hebrew enlightenment, the *Haskalah* movement. In a series of essays written in the two decades before the First World War he crystallized the ideology that came to be called "cultural Zionism." In opposition to Theodor Herzl's emphasis on political legitimization for the creation of a Jewish state, Ahad Ha-am thought nothing more important than strengthening the quality of Jewish national existence. In the spirit of the folk-psychology of the period, he believed each nation had an individual "soul" that gave its culture a distinctive cast. The Jews were especially gifted, he contended, in spiritual creativity. Being agnostic, he meant this in a secular sense, that the Jews had a talent for ethics and culture. He insisted that Judaism contained a distinctive, naturalistic morality.

While he often referred to this view, his most explicit expression of it came when he contrasted the ethics of Judaism with those of Christianity. It appeared in 1910 in response to the publication by a British liberal Jew, Claude G. Montefiore, of a two-volume commentary called *The Synoptic Gospels*. Montefiore's attitude may be gauged from this unusual statement, "If Judaism does not, as it were, come to terms with the Gospels, it must always be, I am inclined to think, a creed in a corner, of little influence and with no expansive power" (Simon, 1946, p. 127). Ahad Ha-am's essay on this matter was entitled, notably, "Between Two Opinions" (the phrase is taken from Elijah's challenge on Mt. Carmel to the Israelites to accept either God or Baal, 1 K. 18.21). Ahad Ha-am's concluding paragraphs indicate how radically he took this matter of distinctive national will and identity.

"But every true Jew, be he orthodox or liberal, feels in the depths of his being that there is something in the spirit of his people—though we do not know what it is—which has prevented us from following the rest of the world along the beaten path, has led to our producing this Judaism of ours, and has kept us and our Judaism 'in a corner' to this day, because we cannot abandon the distinctive outlook on which Judaism is based. Let those who still have this feeling remain within the fold; let those who have lost it go elsewhere. There is no room for compromise" (pp. 127–128).

His central contention is that "the Jewish people, in contrast to the rest of the world, has a preference for the abstract ideal in religion and morality" (p. 129). Ahad Ha-am shows how, in contrast to other faiths, this operates in relation to God and, in contrast to Christianity, in the Jewish conception of the Messiah. He contends that the "preference of the Jewish mind [is] for the impersonal" and this is the basis of the distinctive Jewish moral and religious goal. "Judaism conceives its aim not as the salvation of the individual, but as the well-being and perfection of a group, of the Jewish people, and ultimately of the human race" (p. 130). He will not argue that this is a higher value than individual salvation, only that it is distinctively Jewish and is part of "the essential character" of the Jewish people (p. 131). This leads on to a discussion of the differing senses of morality in Judaism and Christianity and a defense of Hillel's negative version of the golden rule. "The moral law of the Gospels asks the 'natural man' to reverse his natural attitude towards himself and others, and to put the 'other' in place of the 'self'—that is, to replace straight-forward egoism by inverted egoism. For the altruism of the Gospels is neither more nor less than inverted egoism. Altruism and egoism alike deny the individual as such all objective moral value, and make him merely a means to a subjective end; but whereas egoism makes the 'other' a means to the advantage of the 'self,' altruism does just the reverse. Judaism, however, gets rid of this subjective attitude entirely. Its morality is based on something abstract and objective on *absolute justice*, which attaches moral value to the individual as such without any distinction between the 'self' and the 'other.' On this theory a man's sense of justice is the supreme judge both of his own actions and those of other men. This sense of justice must be made independent of individual relations, as though it were a separate entity; and before it all men, including the self, must be equal. All men, including the self, are under obligation to develop their lives and their faculties to assist his neighbor's self-development, so far as he can. But just as I have no right to ruin another man's life for the sake of my own, so I have no right to ruin my own life for the sake of another's. Both of us are men, and both our lives have the same value before the throne of justice" (p. 132). Ahad Ha-am then cites two sections of the Talmud in which, in varying ways, the question is raised whether one is obligated to give one's life for one's fellow. (Though one case is clearly undecided in the Talmud, he argues that the rabbis prove his point.) It is a tribute to Ahad Ha-am's influence that the two cases, where one man has a jug of water sufficient

440

to take him but not his comrade through a desert (Bava Metzia 62a), and the question whether one may commit murder to escape a threat to one's own life (Pesahim 25b) became commonplace in later discussions of the ethics of Judaism.

Two other items in Ahad-Ha-am's analysis are worth noting. First, he pictures the Days of the Messiah in terms of absolute, impartial justice. " . . . Judaism . . . looks forward to the development of morality to a point at which Justice will become an instinct with good men, so that in any given situation they will be able to apply the standard of absolute justice without any long process of reflection. . . . Personal and social considerations will not affect them in the slightest degree; their instinct will judge every action with absolute impartiality, ignoring all human relations, and making no difference between X and Y, between the self and the other, between rich and poor" (p. 135). Second, he argues that while the Jewish morality of justice can easily be carried over into the sphere of international relations "the altruism of the Gospels provides no sort of basis for . . . [it]. A nation can never believe that its moral duty lies in self-abasement or in the renunciation of its rights for the benefit of other nations. . . . Hence Christian nations have not been able to regulate their relations with one another on the basis of their religions; national egoism has inevitably remained the sole determining force in international affairs . . . " (p. 137).

Not only decades but unanticipated historic and cultural changes separate the contemporary reader from Ahad Ha-am. To many modern scholars he ignored the Jewish concern for persons and Judaism's teaching of compassion and love, reworked Jewish teaching in terms of a Kant-like rational ethics, denied such an option to Christianity, and ignored all Christian ethical teaching other than Jesus' statement of the golden rule understood as self-sacrificing neighbor-love. Perhaps one may explain his limited purview in this essay by recalling that he was responding to a work on the Gospels and, in general, that the popular polemics regularly directed against the Jews contrasted Christian love and Jewish legalism. As he puts it, "That Jewish morality is based on justice, and the morality of the Gospels on love, has become a platitude . . . " (p. 131). When one sees him as polemicist and not as the objective dispenser of abstract justice he calls true Jews to be, we can understand better his limited perception of Christian ethics. It is also somewhat surprising that he does not inquire whether the Christian choice of grounds to distinguish between Judaism and Christianity is correct. In his widely read essay "Slavery Amidst Freedom" he had criticized Western Jews for giving up their independent sense of Jewish values to adopt Christian standards. Here he accepts the Christian interpretation uncritically and seeks to show the superiority of an ethic of justice, though he does not make an explicit statement of judgment. Obviously, if Kantianism is the criterion and Judaism is identified with it, the case for Judaism is not difficult to make.

Ahad Ha-am's ideas were influential not only in organized Zionist circles but, more significantly, among the many East-European intellectuals, particularly the educators, who made ethnic loyalty and cultural creativity, particularly in regard to the Hebrew language, central to their Jewish existence. In America the Reform rabbinate and, some decades later, the Conservative rabbinate disseminated a related sense of Christian and Jewish ethics. Kaufmann Kohler, the author of *Jewish Theology* (original U.S. edition 1917), popularized this position. He had an exceptional influence on American Jewry because his book was the first full-scale English interpretation of modern Judaism, and for nearly two decades Kohler was President of the Hebrew Union College, the seminary for Reform rabbis.

The concluding chapter of Kohler's *Jewish Theology* is entitled "The Ethics of Judaism and the Kingdom of God." It is obviously meant as the climax to all that has been stated before. By contrast, the volume has no section on law, though some aspects of Jewish observance and obligation are mentioned in the last half of the book. This may stem from Kohler's understanding of theology as dealing only with matters of belief or from his Reform Jewish sense that the older understanding of Jewish law was now outmoded. In any case, his general inattention to conduct makes his explicit attention to ethics all the more significant.

Kohler declares, "The soul of the Jewish religion is its ethics. Its God is the Fountainhead and Ideal of Morality.... Accordinly, the kingdom of God ... does not rest in a world beyond the grave, but ... in a complete moral order on earth, the reign of truth, righteousness and holiness among all men and nations" (1917, p. 477). Kohler is convinced that the ethics of Judaism are unique and that this is due, in substantial measure, to the unique capacities of the Jewish people for the life of the spirit. Thus he can say that "the election of Israel presupposes an inner calling, a special capacity of the soul and tendency of intellect which fit it for the divine task ... [the people] must have within itself enough of the heavenly spark of truth and of the impetus of the religious genius as to be able and eager, whenever and wherever the opportunity is favorable, to direct the spiritual flight of humanity toward the highest and the holiest" (pp. 326–327).

Kohler's treatment of ethics is, from the beginning, comparative and polemical, downgrading in turn, though with various degrees of appreciation, nonreligious, Asian, Buddhist and Hellenic ethics. Though he also utilizes folk-psychology, Kohler rejects Ahad Ha-am's understanding of Jewish ethics. Reflecting his religious, anti-Zionist sense of Judaism, Kohler contends that "In contrast to purely altruistic or socialistic ethics, Jewish morality accentuated the value of the individual even apart from the social organism" (p. 482). From this emphasis on the worth of each individual he develops a polemic against an ethic of love. As in Ahad Ha-am, the argument is carried out in relation to the negative version of the golden rule and the proper interpretation of neighbor love. "Taken in the positive form, the command cannot be literally carried out. We cannot love the stranger as we love ourselves or our kin; still less can we love our enemy, as is demanded by the Sermon on the Mount. According to the Hebrew Scriptures we can and should treat our enemy magnanimously and forgive him, but we cannot truly love him, unless he turns from an enemy to a friend. . . . Love of all fellow-men is, in fact, taught by both Hillel and Philo" (p. 485). It is also implied in Deuteronomy and explicit in Rabbinic teachings. "However, love as a principle of action is not sufficiently firm to fashion human conduct or rule society. It is too much swayed by impulse and emotion and is often too partial. Love without justice leads to abuse and wrong, as we see in the history of the Church, which began with the principle of love, but often failed to heed the admonitions of justice. Therefore justice is the all inclusive principle of human conduct in the eyes of Judaism. . . . The Jewish conception of justice is broader than mere abstention from hurting our fellow-men. Justice is also a positive conception . . . the very principle of ethics of the Mosaic law, the principle for which the great prophets fought with all vigor and vehemence of the divine spirit [is] social justice" (pp. 485–497). "Judaism cannot accept the New Testament spirit of other worldliness, which prompted the teaching: 'Take no thought for your life, what ye shall drink, nor yet for your body what ye shall put on' or 'Resist not evil.' Such a view disregards the values and duties of domestic, civic, and industrial life, and creates an inseparable gulf between sacred and profane, between religion and culture. In contrast to this, Jewish ethics sets the highest value upon all things that make man more of a human being and increase his power of doing good" (p. 489). Kohler continues in this vein, contrasting the Jewish esteem for marriage and wealth derived from labor with the Christian values of celibacy and poverty. "As has been well said, Judaism teaches a 'robust morality.' . . . Jewish ethics excels all other ethical systems, especially in its insistence upon purity and holiness" (pp. 489–490).

The popular polemics against Judaism that formed the background for the early twentieth-century Jewish writings on ethics have been mentioned above. Kohler also has in mind the attacks on Judaism by contemporary Christian scholars. Internationally known figures, such as Bossuet, Delitzsch, Harnack, Weber and Wellhausen, in their investigations of the origins of Christianity, sought to justify their faith against its Jewish background. They regularly contrasted the New Testament doctrine of love with the aridity of Pharisaism, the Jewish legalism. Kohler considered it a major responsibility of Jewish scholarship to refute their misunderstanding of Judaism. Since Kohler-like attitudes toward Christianity persist in the contemporary Jewish community, it is important to point out that Kohler was not concerned with theological ethics. Though he wrote a book he called *Jewish Theology*, his interests were primarily historical and literary. He did not consider, therefore, the teachings of Thomas, Calvin, Wesley or Maurice, to mention some of the thinkers Gustafson treats. Their ideas would have made Kohler's Jewish ethics seem less distinctive than he took them to be.

This stream of ideas surfaces most visibly in the contemporary Jewish community in Leo Baeck's essay, "Romantic Religion" (in Baeck, 1958). Since its publication in English, it has been the major document on Christianity before American Jewish intellectuals and it therefore merits our detailed attention.

Baeck declares that there are "two forms above all" in piety and religion and that they are "exemplified especially by . . . Judaism and Christianity. In essential respects they confront each other as the classical and the romantic religion" (p. 189). The latter is characterized as follows: "Tense feelings supply its content, and it seeks its goals in the now mythical, now mystical visions of the imagination. Its world is the realm in which all rules are suspended; it is the world of the irregular, the extraordinary and the miraculous, that world which lies beyond all reality, the remote which transcends all things" (pp. 189–190). Romantic religion is distinctively "feminine . . . passive . . . touchingly helpless and weary; it wants to be seized and inspired from above, embraced by a flood of grace which should descend upon it and possess it—a will-less instrument of the wondrous ways of God. When Schleiermacher defined religion as 'the feeling of absolute dependence,' he condensed this attitude into a formula." As a result, "Romanticism, therefore, lacks any strong ethical impulse, and will to conquer life ethically. . . . All law, all that legislates, all morality with its commandments is repugnant to it; it would rather stay outside the sphere of good and evil; the highest ideal may be anything at all, except the distinct demands of ethical action" (p. 192). In a telling aside, oblivious to the fact that Immanuel Kant was not a rabbi, Baeck says, "Therefore the romantic 'personality' is also something totally different from, say, the Kantian personality who confronts us as the bearer of the moral law and who finds himself, and thus his freedom, in being faithful to the commandment" (p. 193). Though Baeck admits that no historic religion is without a mixture of the two types he is contrasting (p. 195), he goes on to identify Christianity as the romantic religion *par excellence*, attributing this to Paul (pp. 196ff). "Later on, the Catholicism of the Middle Ages softened this conception and granted a certain amount of human participation. But Luther then returned to the purer romanticism of Paul with its motto, *sola fide*, through faith alone . . . " (p. 205).

Classical religion is activist and ethical as even the history of Christianity shows. "It is, therefore, no accident that peoples with a live sense of independence have turned, consciously and unconsciously, towards the paths of classical religion. . . . The history of Calvinistic, Baptist piety with its affinity to the Old Testament, its 'legalistic' orientation, and its ethical stress on proving oneself, shows this clearly. And it was the same story wherever the social conscience stirred; it, too, had to effect this reversion, for it, too, runs counter to romantic religion. The social conscience finds romantic religion repugnant because it is at bottom a religious egoism. . . . [I]n it the individual knows only himself and what God or life is to bring him, but not the commandment, not the mutual demands of men" (p. 211). Thus Christianity has had "calamitous" problems with the theory of work.

Both Catholic ethics, because of its dualism of heavenly and earthly vocations, and Luther, essentially opposing lazy monks, demonstrate this difficulty. Calvinism is an exception and Baeck says it was "in this respect, too, returning closer to Judaism" (p. 213). A similar point is scored against the Lutheran division between Church and state. "Much as was demanded of the state ecclesiastically, little was asked from it morally." Baeck admits that episodes of Jewish romanticism also show Judaism making peace with tyrants. Nonetheless, romantic religion by its fundamental concerns fosters social conservatism and thus "The problem of culture cannot be solved under a romantic religion" (p. 214). The exceptions grow in Old Testament soil. "From there, too, came the Protestant social movement. The genuinely romantic Pauline faith . . . can confront a culture only as an outsider without any real access to it. . . . This faith cannot as a matter of principle do justice to the tasks which the social conscience imposes on man . . . " (p. 215). The concept of Christian culture does not refute this for it is essentially a result of syncretism, a product of "the desire to fuse everything [which] is characteristic of romanticism" (p. 215). The modern notion of an independent culture is essentially un-Christian. "It was able to prevail only by fighting the Church, the Protestant Church just as much as the Catholic" (p. 217).

After a substantial discussion of the evil effects of romanticism as shown in miracle, sacrament, dogma, priesthood and ecclesiatic authority, Baeck takes up the classic Jewish polemic stance, the defense of justice. In romantic religion justice "is preserved . . . only as an old-fashioned word: the content is completely different. Veracity and justice as active virtues no longer have any place in romanticism. For the believer there is no command to do anything. . . . Paul merely gave this notion its most exaggerated formulation . . . . Justice is for him exclusively something that happens to man: man therefore need not exercise it; he only must believe in it. Thus it presupposes as its very condition that the will to be just . . . is negated. . . . The whole theology of Paul revolves around this negation" (pp. 240–241). Though in the face of human need this position was changed, as in James and in the later teaching of the Catholic Church, Luther restores Paul's transformation of justice (p. 243). "The Pauline faith deprives ethics itself of its basis. . . . Ethics was from now on reduced to a subordinate, if not altogether superfluous, position. . . . Religion now becomes the opposite, the contradiction of ethics; each excludes the other in principle. Either faith or ethics! That is the innermost meaning of the fight which Paul and Luther waged against the 'Law' " (pp. 248–249).

Baeck, who maintains the stance of the impartial, descriptive analyst throughout the work, now seeks to show his openness by a brief discussion of the psychological validity of the romantic approach (pp. 294f). His intentions are made clear, however, by his opposition to any efforts to ethicize Christianity. "Where the Pauline doctrine is ethicized, as happens at times today as a concession to what is felt to be modern, the doctrine is deprived of its very essence, loses its own character, and ceases to have its own path.... Ethical religion is in this context a contradiction in terms...." Baeck is so determined to fit Christianity to his ideal types that he can neatly gerrymander the New Testament record. "Paul himself was still too deeply rooted in Judaism and hence made moral demands time and again. These demands are genuine insofar as they proceeded from his honest and deeply ethical personality and from his living past from which he could never disentangle himself entirely. But they are not genuine insofar as they did not proceed from his romantic religion which he proclaimed as that which was most truly his own.... They proceed from his personality but not from his faith, and they constitute the contradiction of his character" (p. 250). So the Church could never make ethical duties more than "a mere appendix of religion," and Protestantism did little better, often giving the civil magistrate the effective concern for the moral realm (p. 251). A polemic on Luther's passivity then reaches it climax, characteristically, in the comment "It becomes quite evident ... how impossible it is to derive Kant from Luther, as a certain construction of history suggests from time to time. For Kant the liberating and redeeming power comes from the Law.... Kant's ethics, almost still more than his critique of knowledge, represents the most extreme antithesis of that which was Luther's certainty.... Kant's philosophy of the Law is the very antithesis of all romanticism" (pp. 254–255).

In the concluding section of the essay Baeck mounts another attack on the possibility of Christian ethics. "In the Church, ethics has basically always caused embarrassment. It was there ... but the faith lacked any organic relation to it.... It was considered antiquated and outmoded, a truth no longer valid, something to which only a relapse to a lower stage could lead back. In spite of all this, the religious desire for ethics has, of course, not vanished in the Church.... But ... this quest was vain, and the lot of ethics ... got lost in mere enthusiasm ... pious prayer in some ... in others ... hollow sentimental pathos; or this path led to the collecting and classifying activity of the casuists." This is his judgment of the Catholics, many Lutherans and most specifically, Schleiermacher (pp. 256–257).

One can detect in the Gospels a genuine ethical and prophetic thrust (p. 261), but Baeck insists this has been a problem to the Church. The Catholics solved it by giving responsibility to the elite. "Protestantism, on the other hand, became utterly helpless at this point" (p. 262). The commands of Christ are then interpreted away. This is carried a step forward in modern New Testament scholarship where the virtues taught by Jesus are expounded at great length with the understanding that in life as opposed to faith the very opposite of poverty, not swearing and not resisting evil are validated (p. 263). This is the sentimental side of Christian ethics; it makes "ethics ... an experience" (p. 265). Baeck then tries to connect romanticism and ethical casuistry, claiming that it is "erroneous to associate it exclusively with Catholicism, as if it did not also have its place in Protestantism" (p. 268).[2] Once again the section concludes with a reference to Kant's conception of morality as the proper criterion for measuring religious ethics. The essay then turns to questions of last things and concludes with a final claim for classical religion. In it "longing strives ever again for the goal which is to unify all men and impels them to follow the commandment of God: after all, these two things really mean one and the same thing. For all future is here the future of the commandment, the future in which it is realized and fulfilled. Perhaps it is this [as against the subjectivity and self-centeredness of romantic religion] that we find the most clear-cut difference between romantic and classical religion" (p. 292).

This exposition of Baeck's essay, which summarizes much of the common Jewish attitude to Christian ethics, should clarify why the Jewish reader is likely to be shocked by Gustafson's rich presentation of ethics founded on the Christ. To take one case, there is a world of difference between Baeck's understanding of Luther's sense of justice and Gustafson's treatment of the ethical implications Luther sees in Christ as humanity's justifier. Baeck's performance here can be excused only if one assumes that his reader knows this is polemical literature which one reads in anticipation of seeing the opponent humiliated. That sort of debate had supposedly gone out with the Middle Ages and, in the modern style, Baeck presents himself here as an impartial scholar. Baeck undoubtedly thought that he was being objective because he followed an accepted modern methodology, namely typology. Yet the method he adopted enabled him to ignore all contrary data. He could dismiss contrary appearances as momentary aberrations from the true types of faith he had in mind. Moreover, because the types inhere in the essence of a religion, the historical cannot truly change. Christianity cannot become fully ethical; Judaism, despite its nonethical law and its mysticism, has been and always will be an essentially ethical faith. The discussion seems learned and reasonable; in fact it is fundamentally dogmatic and arbitrary. We are never told how one discovers the two types, why there are no more, or why they have these rather than other possible qualities. Baeck knows and does not explain. He relies on the sweep of his argument and the richness of his reference to carry the reader along with him. It is an odd sort of rationality indeed since no counterargument is ever possible in such a context. For Baeck to have operated in this manner seems particularly ironic. He claimed a superior sense of ethics. Yet he judges with unequal measures, a positive one for his religion, a negative one for his neighbor's.

One can easily imagine the Jewish community's reaction were the situation reversed. Suppose a Christian thinker discussed the merits of Judaism and Christianity in terms of a typology of religions that were either neurotic, because they emphasized law and judgment, or autonomous, because they centered about love and persons. To be sure, one could say some positive things about the neurotic personality. Its need for structure and institution produces stability, its drive to accumulate merit produces good works and all of us, in one way or another, are neurotic. One would, however, have to deny it any genuine association with ethical autonomy, the sort of true freedom which the Christ, as justifier, brings us to release us from our inevitable, incapacitating guilt. The neurotic, as such, is never truly free and cannot therefore reach authentic personhood. That would simply be untrue to its type.

I do not consider this appeal to the absurdity of the procedure far-fetched. Baeck identified the Torah and *halakhah* with Kant's sense of law and insisted Jewish obligation was essentially what was required by the categorical imperative. That is not what traditional Judaism in the past or observant Jews today understand Jewish obligation to be. Why should my typological polemicist not be as free to describe Judaism as neurotic dependence on law as Baeck is to make Christianity romantic and hence a-ethical?[3]

Baeck's performance makes it necessary to restate the fundamental premise of proper comparative religious study. One cannot discuss other people's religion until one has come to understand it in a way that they would find recognizable. "What is hateful to you, do not do unto your neighbor." A reading of Gustafson's treatment of Christian ethics requires the judgment that much of what Jews have written on this topic does not meet this standard.

Notes

1. This work is useful as a speedy survey of these two authors as well as many other Jewish thinkers who have given some attention to Christianity, but its approach is uncritical and defensive.

2. Baeck's exposition of this casuistry is among the least clear and convincing parts of the entire essay.

3. On the problems raised by identifying Judaism with Kantian ethics, see Fox (1975) and particularly the essay by Aharon Lichtenstein, "Does Jewish Tradition Recognize an Ethic Independent of Halakha?" Particular attention should be given the resolution of the topic in the penultimate paragraph, 83, where the imperative attached to ethics is declared to be as authoritative as that of the *halachah* but with the critically significant yet unexplained qualification, "in its own way."

Bibliography

Baeck, Leo	1958	*Judaism and Christianity.* Philadelphia: Jewish Publication Society, 1958.
Cohen, Hermann	1971	*Reason and Hope.* Eva Jospe, ed. New York: Norton, 1971.
Fox, Marvin	1975	*Modern Jewish Ethics.* Columbus, Ohio: Ohio State University Press, 1975.
Gustafson, James	1968	*Christ and the Moral Life.* New York: Harper and Row, 1968.

Jacob, Walter	1974	*Christianity through Jewish Eyes.* Cincinnati: Hebrew Union College Press, 1974.
Kohler, Kaufmann	1917	*Jewish Theology.* Repr. Cincinnati: Riverdale, 1943.
Simon, Leon	1946	*Ahad Ha-am, Essays, Letters, Memoirs.* Oxford: East and West, 1946.

37

Jesus the Jew in the Light of the Jewish-Christian Dialogue

I turned to the subject of "Jesus the Jew in the Light of the Jewish-Christian Dialogue" with the same expectations I had when I wrote a book on contemporary Christology. I knew that as I investigated that subject I would run into a variety of theological descriptions. It was perfectly plain to me that the currents that run through theology in one religion in the western world would also be present in others. That turned out to be the case. But I thought I would have a somewhat easier time preparing to talk about Jesus the Jew. It seemed a relatively accessible theme, one which it would be easy to get one's hands on—until I began to explore it seriously. Jesus the Jew turns out to be, as far as I can tell, a quite illusive figure.

That is the case because, to begin with, the facts about Jesus are extraordinarily difficult to find. If I ask, for example, about the historical Jesus, we run into all the problems that historians of the New Testament period have raised with regard to the sources. What shall we do about the differing pictures of Jesus we get within a given gospel, much less between the four gospels of the New Testament? The sources we use to construct a picture of the historical Jesus turn out to be rather ambiguous. The result is that, one after another, historians come along with a somewhat different history or method of research, examine the sources and emerge with a somewhat different figure. What we have then is less a picture of Jesus the man in that historical period than an account of how a modern theory of structuring history produces its historical Jesus.

From *Proceedings of the Center for Jewish-Christian Learning*, College of St. Thomas, vol. 2 (Spring 1987).

If that were not difficult enough, trying to talk about one's Jewishness in the first century compounds our difficulties. The truth of the matter is that almost all the sources that we have with regard to the practice of Judaism in this general period come from a time after Jesus. They become more plentiful and more reliable as we turn from the first to the second century of the Common Era. We can then read back from the Jewishness of the second century into the descriptions of Jesus given us in the gospels, but we are, in fact, reading back into history and it is not quite clear whether or not there had been a development in the practice and theory of Judaism from the time of Jesus to the second century.

Moreover, the accounts given in the New Testament, specifically in the gospels, are the best documents available to us for the practice of Judaism during Jesus' lifetime. There are no other substantial contemporaneous sources for Jewishness in that period. Only these records come to us from people who are speaking out of Christian faith, not out of a desire to record data as impartially or sympathetically as possible.

Thus, trying to get a clear historical picture of the Jewishness of Jesus turns out to be extraordinarily difficult. I decided to give up that quest, leaving it to the historians in the hope that they will, in due course, enlighten us on this score.

I then decided I would instead look at how our contemporaries see Jesus and then deduce what I considered to be the Jewishness of that Jesus. Quite quickly, it once again turned out that the Jesus I sought was quite illusive. Thus, as I turned on my television set one Sunday morning, I encountered Robert Schuller speaking from the Crystal Cathedral assuring me with the most beneficent smile that Jesus meant only compassion, happiness and peace. But when I picked up my Sunday *New York Times* and read Eugene Kennedy's article about David Tracy, I discovered that his Jesus is not only loving but "absolutely terrifying." The clear picture of Jesus I sought again disappeared from view.

I therefore decided I would take the subject of this session quite literally. That is to say I understand my invitation to speak to you about "Jesus the Jew in the Light of Jewish-Christian Dialogue" to mean "Who is the Jesus mediated to me, a Jewish theologian, by a Christian dialogue partner?" I now seek to encounter not the Jesus of history or of any popular theology, but the Jesus of the person who comes to meet and speak with me out of his or her Christian faith; the one who, standing beside me in all openness, yet believing in his or her own faith, reaches out to me from an intuition that somehow for all our differences—which may be quite radical—we yet share something; this person whose belief in Jesus encourages encounter with me a Jew, who sees in me as a Jew something of Jesus' faith. Who is the Jesus mediated to me and communicated to me by this dialogue partner? I can hope to recognize the Jewishness of this because, in fact, I am being asked to recognize something about myself which the other has seen in me and the faith I bear and identified with the Jesus of his or her Christian faith.

451

This Jesus, to begin at the most fundamental level, is a Jesus who obviously loves God. And I have no difficulty recognizing who his God is. It is the God of Israel, of Abraham and Sarah, of Isaac and Rebecca, of Jacob and Leah and Rachel. And this Jesus not only seeks to serve that God but does so in ways which I find quite familiar for they are ways commanded to the people of Israel of which I am a part. That is, this Jesus understands serving God primarily as loving people and reaching out to them. Thus Jesus is continually involved with people; sometimes they are individuals, sometimes small groups, sometimes large groups, but he is always involved with people recognizing that the service of God is to be carried out among human beings.

Jesus carries on this service in a wonderful old Jewish style. He is mostly a teacher, one involved in instruction. He has a quite familiar pedagogic style. Sometimes he cites familiar texts from the Torah like, "Thou shalt love the Lord thy God with all thy heart, with all thy soul and with all thy might," a citation from the book of Deuteronomy (6:5). I know it well, for we recite it regularly. So too, he cites a passage from the book of Leviticus (19:18), "Thou shalt love thy neighbor as thy self." He also cites the prophets, my prophets. Though probably people spoke Aramaic in his day, rather than utilize the Aramaic translation of the Bible he almost certainly cited them in the original Hebrew which, to this day, we still read in the synagogue on Saturday mornings or on holidays.

He is, however, a somewhat unusual teacher because he often speaks in parables. That's not an unfamiliar method. In the Midrash, the exegetical Jewish literature dealing with the biblical text, the rabbis very often used what they call a Mashal. They often teach by telling stories about a king, or about a father who had a son, or about a mother who had a child, or about an animal. It is an old Jewish way of teaching but one that he utilizes with extraordinary creativity, insight, and compassion. Jesus has a quite admirable genius for telling a quick little story which touches the hearer's heart and soul.

He's also a somewhat unusual teacher because he is often quite concerned with people on the fringe. That is, he is not satisfied merely to reach out to the usual run of Jews one might instruct in the Land of Israel, but he gives himself to people who are by and large social outcasts. Of course, that doesn't sound entirely strange to me. In his outreach I hear echoes of that old biblical refrain that we must have special regard for the widow, the stranger, and the orphan. We are commanded by the biblical prophets to be concerned about the powerless people, the outsiders, the ones who may not be able to negotiate the normal activities of society. Therefore, when I come across a Jewish teacher who is interested in sinners, publicans, in others, I recognize a person of some special yet nonetheless not uncommon Jewish concern.

But he doesn't always speak to those people. He really also wants to speak to the usual run of people. This teacher likes to go to synagogues, not just synagogues for outcasts, synagogues for ordinary Jews. Occasionally he even speaks to large groups who gather to hear him. He seems to be something of a popular preacher, speaker, religious type, and one of his primary themes is that they should repent. That's quite a familiar message; it is one of the key doctrines of Judaism. You cannot give people commandments and tell them what to do, recognize that they are human and not also tell them what to do when they don't live up to the commandments. Indeed, one of the high spots of the Jewish ritual year is the Day of Atonement, when the community gathers in an annual rite of confession, repentance and atonement. Indeed we do not even take a survey of how Jews have been behaving in any given year to decide whether we need that holiday. It's scheduled. But it is only the climax of something which is done every day. The daily prayers of the Jews include prayers for not only insight and understanding but prayers for forgiveness and for God's help in carrying through our work of repentance. So when I hear this Jewish preacher exhorting his fellow Jews to repent, I hear him echoing a Jewish tradition sounding strongly in the law and climaxed in the prophets in Ezekiel's marvelous sermon (chapter 18) on individual responsibility.

What is more, I hear a quite recognizable lesson when Jesus says that the immediate purpose of this repentance is to be ready for the imminent coming of God's rule on earth. The dialectic is typically Jewish. What at first seems like such a pessimistic message, "you're a sinner; repent," is also incredibly optimistic. God will rule! The power of evil will be overthrown! History can be utterly transformed! It might happen now—get ready by repenting your sins. This theme is not as fully and immediately developed in the prophets who say it in their own way and for their own times. But it is only unfamiliar in urgency, not in substantive content.

What I find particularly attractive about this Jewish teacher—particularly compared to some religious leaders today—is his activism. He seeks to serve God by doing things with people amid general society. He is not satisfied to go off to the Judean desert to isolate himself and his followers in a community near the Dead Sea. He's in the world. Indeed he is willing, despite the risks, to go up to Jerusalem, the center of his society and its power. I like that kind of religion; it reminds me of Nathan's and Amos' faith, one which connects the service of God with the reality of human life and social existence, one that confronts and seeks to change real people facing real situations.

This Jesus is a Jewish type I can easily place. He's a Galilean pietist, an itinerant preacher and teacher who wants Jews to be more Jewish, who wants them to take their religion more seriously, to express its inner belief in their lives, to add sanctity to their day-by-day affairs as part of a people dedicated to God and pledged to see that God's rule ultimately triumphs in history. When I meet this Jesus, the Jesus I find in the eyes of someone who meets me in honest dialogue, I recognize I have come across something particularly precious.

I know that to be true because this is such a new Jesus for Jews to confront. It is only 20 years or so since serious dialogue has been taking place between Jews and Roman Catholics, and not much longer between Jews and Protestants. After 1,600 years, that is, ever since the Edict of Toleration made Judaism a permitted but a degraded religion in the Roman Empire, after 1,600 years of discrimination, oppression and outright hatred, to encounter a radically changed attitude and therefore to see the possibility of another Jesus, one I recognize, is quite an extraordinary experience.

But if I have spoken about the Jesus who can be seen in the light of Jewish-Christian dialogue, what must yet be said about the Jesus who stands in its shadow? We can only hope to appreciate what we have gained if we recognize what many people yet still lack. What about the people who will not participate in dialogue, Jews and Christians alike, or those who will talk to others but only with the deepest suspicion or barely contained anger or contempt? Or those who do become involved in dialogue but do so because it is the correct thing to do and therefore participate without real interest or openness? Or those who seek to be genuine yet strictly limit what they discuss, who quickly become evasive even on permitted topics, or who insist on focusing the exchange on their private agendas? Who is the Jesus seen when dialogue is not fully present?

Worse, should the old Jewish-Christian animosities somehow reassert themselves, then on the Jewish side Jesus once again appears as the symbol of centuries of persecution and untold suffering. This Jesus is the one who validated the hatred and oppression of his own people. He is the Jesus who stands for crusades, inquisitions, ritual murder charges and forced conversions. He is the Jesus who did not protest the Holocaust. That Jesus may not hate his kinfolk in his heart, but he has stood idly by while his kinfolk bled.

We remain fearful of that Jesus, the one who is the only way to the Father, the son who comes to supersede all prior covenants, the Lord whom everyone should and one day will come to serve. If you do not see the shadow, you won't appreciate the light.

Thus, when the Church, assembled in full ecumenical council, says formally that there must be genuine dialogue, an extraordinary step has been taken to reverse an old and painful relationship. And if the Church in any nation has been able to appreciate what this new openness might mean, it is the Church in America. This country has had unparalleled experience with pluralistic living and it has taught all its citizens how they might live harmoniously with one another despite radical differences of culture, class, race and religion. Are we, then, reading *Nostra Aetate* with our democratic, American eyes and not as the Church truly means it? I hope not. I hope we are only reading it as, in fact, it is written and as the Holy Spirit intends. I hope that our effort at genuine dialogue is not something peculiarly North American but a genuine response to the commanding voice each of us hears from our deepest faith.

Let Jesus have the last word. When the Son of Man comes to rule and separates the sheep from the goats, the sheep are surprised to discover that they are being honored for having recognized and honored their Lord and master, and they say, "Lord, when did we see you hungry and give you food, or thirsty and give you drink? When did we see you a stranger and invite you home, or naked and clothe you? When did we see you sick or in prison and visit you?" And the king will answer, "Truly, I say to you, as you did it to one of the least of these, my brethren, you did it unto me" (Mat. 25:37–40). I read these words literally. "What you do unto the least of my brethren, the Jews, will show me—and show them—the real Jesus."

38

The Challenge of Jesus the
Jew for the Church

There is something about intellectuals that requires them, the minute they begin to speak, to explain why they cannot address the topic as it was announced. Perhaps that is because the modern mind, when it looks at things, instantly begins to have doubts and raise questions. Some of the blame may be laid at the door of Descartes who introduced us to the notion that ideas ought to be made clear and distinct; otherwise, one should not believe them. With his morning's topic, my diffidence also stems from our contemporary reluctance to tell other people what they ought to do. Who am I to say what should challenge the church? I do have a perception of what the Jewishness of Jesus might mean; I spoke of it last night, and, by extension, I shall speak of it again this morning. I also have an understanding of the ways in which this reading of Jesus' life might pose certain questions for the church.

But I am not *of* the church. I do not have an insider's feel for the ways in which things that appear to me to pose potential problems for the church have already been resolved by it and, thus, within the circle of Christian faith, are not real difficulties at all. Thus, many of you know better what it is that I ought to speak about this morning than I do. True, my years of study of Christian theology and acquaintance with Christian theologians have given me a certain perception of what may be found in the church. I will speak from that perspective, but I take it that I am also to learn from you this morning where my understandings are unfounded

From *Proceedings of the Center for Jewish-Christian Learning,* College of St. Thomas, vol. 2 (Spring 1987).

or poorly founded, and how my faith, the faith of Jesus as I know him, functions or ought properly to function within the church.

I have said all this since the initial point I had prepared to make in this discussion may rest on a misconception of mine, or, at least, so it now appears to me after the address of Fr. John Pawlikowski last night.

John said, in distinguishing the features of Jesus' religiosity from that of Judaism, that he found a certain intimacy between Jesus and God which he thought might be different from that of the Judaism of Jesus' time. My notes for this morning's presentation call for me to open the discussion by suggesting that Jesus' characteristic intimacy with God is typically Jewish and appears to create something of a problem for the church. We obviously have different ways of reading the New Testament data concerning Jesus' religion. I am hopeful that one of the things we will do this morning is deal with this apparent conflict of perception, thus helping each of us understand better our own religion as it relates to that of the other person.

My first point, then, despite what I heard so persuasively advocated last evening, is that the challenges to the church raised by Jesus' Jewishness seem to me to begin with his peculiar Jewish intimacy with God. That is to say, Jesus turns to God directly and immediately. He has no difficulty in the field, in the synagogue, wherever he is, addressing God, knowing that God will at once be available to him. He does not feel that to speak to God he needs the help of any of the priests of the Temple or of the Temple rites. He is not even concerned with any particular ritual of address. He feels that he can, whenever he wishes to, address God immediately, that he can turn to God personally, in his own language and his own way, and establish communication. Or, to put it the other way around, the God of Jesus is directly accessible and is ever-present.

I see nothing whatsoever unusual about this for a first century Jew. In this respect, every human being—not even every Jew, but every human being—is God's child, a son or daughter of God. This direct access to God is fundamental to Judaism's teaching about humankind and derives from its teaching about the covenant of Noah (Gen. 8 and 9). Through the pact made with Noah and his seed, God has a significant, serious relationship with all the nations and tongues of the world into which the family of Noah was split after the Tower of Babel. It is only because humankind fails to live up to that relationship that God decides to call a people for himself. (Please excuse the masculine reference; I spent my formative religious years utilizing the accepted sexist way of speaking about God, and from time to time, despite my efforts to transcend it, I find I occasionally don't know how to escape the masculine pronouns of reference.) God chooses a People to serve God particularly. This new covenant with Abraham does not end the covenant with the nations. In Jewish law, as well as in Jewish lore, it is clear that God's relationship with Gentiles is still in effect.

The most direct evidence of this doctrine is the Book of Jonah. Jonah is sent to Nineveh, the capital of Assyria, the symbolic center of the enemies of God's own people, the people of Israel. God is planning to destroy

Nineveh for its wickedness. Jonah doesn't want to warn the Ninevites about God's intention, so he flees. Whatever Jonah's reasons, a topic marvelously interesting to contemplate, God gets Jonah to Nineveh anyway. Though some people care only about the fish story, it is only now that the important part of the book occurs.

When Jonah makes his proclamation, these Gentiles, these Assyrians, believe God, repent of their evil ways and God immediately forgives them. (This turnabout embarrasses Jonah terribly, engendering such an outburst of prophetic petulance one hardly knows whether to laugh or cry.)

What happens to the Ninevites, despite the prophet, should make plain God's direct accessibility in Judaism. Even hated enemies of the Jewish people, the Assyrians, can reach God and attain God's forgiveness on their own and without benefit of Jewish priest or sanctuary or rite or ritual. How much the more will a pious person know God intimately! I, therefore, see the Jewishness of Jesus as the basis of his sense that he can always turn to God and find God close.

I chose the story of Ninevites to make my point because it is precisely in this disputed area of the doctrine of God's forgiveness of sin that the Jewish understanding of the availability of God becomes tellingly manifest. Consider Jesus' preaching to the Jews of his time. He says to them, "Repent, for the Kingdom of God is at hand." He does not tell them, "Go to the temple and participate in the rites of the Day of Atonement." He does not advise them, "Have one of the priestly class lead you through the established rites of repentance." He doesn't say such things because he takes it for granted that the Galileans or Jerusalemites to whom he is speaking can, in fact, carry out teshuvah, repentance, entirely on their own. His preaching, in this respect, reflects, as I understand it, his ancestral Jewish faith.

Or consider the act of prayer. When Jesus himself wishes to pray, or when people ask him how they should pray, he does not insist, "You must first gather 10 people and then follow certain routines," which Jewish law came to require for a complete, community service, Jesus says to them, "pray this way," taking it for granted that, individually, nothing stands between them and God. (Our historians suggest that in this period even the communal Jewish liturgy still had a quite open form. Although a service probably had required themes, the prayers had no verbal fixity until many, many centuries later.)

Think of the liberties the Psalmists take in their relationship to God. To be sure, they are sometimes filled with trust, gratitude and adoration. But they also have no hesitation in complaining to God or calling God to account. They wonder where God is and why God's help is so slow coming. They unburden their hearts, itemizing their physical ailments and detailing their suffering. Their sense of God being at hand and open to their personal woes is astonishing in itself. But consider that these poems were made a part of Jewish sacred Scripture—and more, that they were then seen as so representative of proper Jewish spirituality that they were extensively utilized in the synagogue and the church.

I have taken considerable time with this topic because of my surprising discovery last night that John and I, who have read one another and occasionally talked to one another over the years, see Jesus' intimacy with God as intrinsic to our particular faith. Clarifying this matter should provide an interesting example of the way we still need to learn from one another. So, to sum up my view, I see Jesus' Jewish intimacy with God as a challenge to the church, which, as I understand it from the outside, manifests a somewhat different sense of God's availability.

Now, to some other themes, again with the proviso that I await your instruction. As a Jew, Jesus has a very special attachment to the Land of Israel. He is a figure of that country and life, is conformed to its villages, its fisherfolk, its great lake. He is connected to it in a manner that can be called an extension of the Incarnation. In the Jewish tradition, too, though it cannot be called incarnation, God has a unique relationship to this particular bit of geography, though God is clearly the creator and concerned "owner" of the entire world. It is not that God is literally *in* the Land of Israel. Yet, in the Judaism of Jesus' time, this is the place where God and the creation are in the most intimate contact. Then, as today, the Land of Israel had a special hold on all Jews, Jesus among them. Quite naturally, at a given point, he goes to Jerusalem, the center of the land, to bring his life's work to climax. To demythologize Jesus' immediate physical environment, to take the words "Galilee" or "Jerusalem" as if they were the equivalent of slides flashed by a modern director at the back of a stage to situate the actors, to not see the place names of the gospels as real places, to not understand that there are really hills and mountains and valleys in the Land of Israel, that its dust is real dust, its rocks are real rocks, is to neglect a significant element part of what I should think Christians mean by the Incarnation.

And that's why going to the Land of Israel and walking through it, being in the places where Jesus himself was, changes forever the way one reads the Bible. I say that out of my own experience with Hebrew Scripture. I thought myself a relatively realistic, modern person, one who knew from concerned study how to accept my Bible in the fullness of its humanity while remaining open to the voice of God speaking in its pages. Then I made my first trip to the Land of Israel and realized that walking around there was the most significant act of exegesis I should probably ever do. I assume there is something emotional, indeed sentimental, in this and who knows what else. But long after the lump had left my throat and the mist my eyes, the land still had its effect on me. I cannot read the Bible the same since being there. If, then, the land is so significant to Jesus' Jewishness, one challenge to the church is, "What is the place of the Land of Israel in a Christianity centered around Jesus the Jew?"

That inquiry extends, of course, also to Jesus' people. To American ears the term "people" often has an abstract, almost empty sense, as if it meant no more than human being, as in "They're nice people." But to capture the Jewish self-understanding, the term "people" needs to be given a much more specific, perhaps more European, certainly more Hebraic, content. Let me put the critical issue somewhat more bluntly than perhaps I should—the Jews are not a church. We are a folk, a people like the Hittites, the Hivites, the Jebusites, the Perrizites, the Girgashites and the Canaanites. We are the Hebrews. That's how Hebrew Scripture describes us. Like other ethnic groups, we have a language and a land and a history and heroes and other ethnic involvements as well. That is why our sacred Scripture is so full of political and social and economic matters, ones which hardly sound religious at all. Indeed, there isn't a metaphysical chapter in all of our Bible. But there is constant concern about this folk seeking to establish itself as an ongoing social reality in the Land of Israel.

To make certain you have this Jewish sense of folk or people, let me use a daring word, "nation." The Hebrew nation would be of as much genuine interest to us today as are the Perrizites if it was simply another people of the ancient Middle East. What makes the Jews unusual is that they are God's folk. Unlike all the other peoples, those who descend rather naturally from the children of Noah after the Tower of Babel, this ethnic community is called into being by God. God says to Abram, "I will make you a mighty nation." And this nation, for all its human frailty and obstinacy, finally agrees to bend its ethnicity to the service of the God who has chosen it. Our Bible is full of the "Now we love you, now we don't" of the Jewish people confronting God. In a way, that proves how real this history is. If the Bible said the Hebrews had immediately accepted God's rule over their lives and then dutifully carried it out, they would be unrecognizable to us. They would certainly not be like the Jews I know, who in respect of their vacillating yet ultimately enduring faithfulness are very much like their stiff-necked ancestors.

Over the centuries of experience and prophetic leadership, this folk sought through its community, its monarchy, its military life, its economic arrangements, to be true to God. What an extraordinary agenda this ethnic group set for itself! Page after page, the Bible tells us what happened as these Jews sought to bend to God's will the realities of power in society as in individual life.

Jesus is part of this daring folk. He seems primarily concerned with his fellow Jews. He spends his life with Jews and addresses himself to his ethnic kin. He could easily have traveled across the Mediterranean to talk to other people—but he didn't. And I don't need to remind you of those passages where Jesus seems to restrict his message to his own religio-ethnic community. Besides, he is as much a part of its culture as he is native to its land. He knows his people's literature; he speaks its language; he utilizes its distinctive style of instruction. To appropriate Jesus' Jewishness, that is, to accept him in his full Incarnation, one must accept Jesus' Jewish ethnicity. To me, that raises a question for the church, "How should Christians relate to the Jews as a folk and not another church?"

That brings us, as it must, to the great contemporary reflection of Jewish ethnicity, the revival of the corporate life of the People of Israel as an ethnic group on its own land, namely, the State of Israel.

Here is Jesus' Jewishness revitalized in a fully functioning, ongoing social form. That State is more secular than I would like, and in some respects more ecclesiastical than I would like. But like every other human institution, with all its faults, of which I take it you have seen some in other institutions, here is God's work being done in our time. What, then, is the church to make of the State of Israel, of the Jewish community of Jesus—now, may I borrow a word borrowed from us—of Jewish nationhood resurrected on its own land in full national form?

All this brings me to a most painful problem of Jesus' Jewishness, one which we partially share, but one which also takes us in somewhat different directions. That is the problem of the Holocaust. Had Jesus been under Hitler's sway, he would likely have died in the Holocaust. The Holy Family and all the disciples would have all been sent to the gas chambers because Hitler's understanding of Jews was racial. He believed the Jewish genetic material was malignant, like cancer, and needed to be excised from the human race. A new faith made no difference. Only Jewish biology counted—and Jesus of Nazareth had it. He was that—Jewish.

On one level, we share a problem here. We who are brought together by common faith in God now must ask, "How could our God have allowed such a terrible extermination to happen?" And by that I surely mean not just the terrible extermination of six million Jews—all the Nazis could process—but all the millions of other human beings who were so rationally, so industrially murdered.

However, we immediately part ways if Christians approach this problem with their classic response to the enigma of suffering. Christians have a powerful theological symbol for understanding tribulation, the cross. As a result, for them suffering is a way, or can be a way, of serving God. Such an interpretation of the Holocaust will meet with a stony if not hostile reception in the Jewish community.

Long before the Holocaust, out of centuries of painful experience going back to Sennacherib and Nebuchadnezzar, Jews learned that suffering has no special virtue for getting us close to God. Saints can take the sufferings of life and transform them into a path to intimacy with God. Most of us cannot. We find suffering a terrible challenge to God's justice and compassion. Suffering often destroys us; not infrequently it destroys our faith. We do not have a theology of the cross in Judaism. Most tryingly, we have heard others suggest that we should bear our pain nobly because they have a doctrine that suffering is a way to God. The often unspoken Jewish response to such ideas is that those who have a doctrine of suffering as a particularly efficacious way to God should apply it to themselves, not to others.

The Holocaust does, I think, create a special problem for the church but it is not one of the theology of the cross. That is a postulate of Christian faith, and religions, as I see it, need not validate their beliefs by nonbelievers' standards as long as they find their doctrines making good sense within their own tradition. The church's special Holocaust problems seem to me to arise from the way Christianity made possible the Holocaust, at least the Holocaust as it applied to Jews. To be sure, Nazism is not only un-Christian but profoundly anti-Christian. Moreover, the Nazi racialization of anti-semitism is a classic example of the secularization of religious teaching, in this case leading not only to its extension but to its demonization. Nonetheless, had there not been centuries of Christian teaching and, more significantly, Christian approval for the practice of anti-semitism, the Holocaust would not have been possible.

Alas, there are still some people who understand Christianity in some deep-seated way to allow them to hate Jews. This continued hatred is, if fortunately a minority reality, another problem raised by the Jewishness of Jesus, one which, happily, the church has moved in the last 20 years forthrightly to answer.

Finally, the Jewishness of Jesus raises the issue of Jesus' people continuing in unbroken Jewish form what we see as Jesus' piety. That Jewish religiosity and spirituality that I see in the Jesus of the gospels, the Jewishness I have tried last night and today to delineate to you, is still alive among us. The Jewish community continues to be moved by it. Yes, we have been strongly buffeted by the winds of secularization, perhaps more so than any other religious community. And our religiosity has been substantially shaken by that process. But if we are to speak comparatively, we ought to compare the best of each community to one another or the worst.

I wish, then, to speak of the best of our community. They live by their relationship with God as part of God's covenant with the People of Israel centered in the Land of Israel, devote themselves to sanctifying the life of this people and its members, and by this service testify to humankind that one day God's rule will be established on earth. It is an old covenant, but old only in the sense of ancient, surely not obsolete or outmoded. We know that because, at our best, we find, as Jews have found for millennia, that our spiritual lives remain fresh and flowing and challenging and, indeed, directive. We are, of course, a tiny people, some 11–12 million people worldwide, that's all. There are hundreds of millions of Christians, hundreds of millions of Moslems, hundreds of millions of Buddhists. There are perhaps 12 million Jews. How can so small and so vulnerable a people have survived these painful millennia and have done so faithful to their covenant and as a blessing to humankind? Surely it is because God, our living God, whom we have so often failed to serve, has never—despite all our suffering and trials—ultimately failed us. We remain a people in history because we remain in some obscure yet certain way, God's "treasured folk."

Accepting the Jewishness of Jesus means accepting the fact that the piety from which he arose continues in living faithfulness to this day. What does the church make of this presence of God among us? What does it say about our inspiring experience that our covenant keeps us and our children and our children's children, as it has kept our forebears for more than four millennia, lovingly in God's embrace?

I have asked many questions this morning and I shall be greatly rewarded if, as a consequence of our continuing discussion, I learn how, in the future, to ask them more appropriately.

39

Buddhist and Jewish Ethics,
a Response to Masao Abe

Having long puzzled about how to explain Judaism adequately in English terms—the language being so substantially shaped by Christianity—I greatly admire Masao Abe's accomplishment in conveying his Buddhist understanding of ultimate reality. The problems facing him are far more daunting than those confronting Jewish theologians since he does not share a common Scripture and God with Christians as Jews do. Decreasing the linguistic barriers to greater understanding, as Masao Abe has so well done in his lengthy paper "Kenotic God and Dynamic Sunyata," seems to me one of the most realistic and important aims of inter-faith dialogue.

He also shows commendable openness to his dialogue partners' thought, not only seeking to learn from them but then integrating these insights into his statement of his distinctive Zen philosophy. Moreover, while not repressing the issues Christianity and Judaism raise for his own thought and belief, he can firmly indicate his considerable questions concerning them. He thus admirably demonstrates the potentially transformative moral power of inter-faith dialogue.

Though his primary discussion is with Christianity, Abe also seeks to understand how Jewish thinkers have come to terms with the Holocaust, hoping in this way to initiate Buddhist-Jewish dialogue. It is, to the best of my knowledge, the first step in direct academic exchange between these faiths though Leo Baeck and Martin Buber had written about Buddhism

Entitled "Dynamic Sunyata and the God Whose Glory Fills the Universe," in an exchange of papers between Masao Abe and western thinkers to be published by Orbis Press in 1990.

464

many decades ago.[1] I feel privileged to have been invited to enter into dialogue with Professor Abe.

There are many matters on which I can find Jewish points of agreement with him: indidividual responsibility is substantially corporate; an exaggerated thirst for life and attachment to things is a major source of evil; people need insight into a reality which is beyond the everyday, and it is as much dependent upon "grace" (my discomfort with the Christian overtones of this term is so great that I had to signal it) as upon will and act; "salvation" might come at any moment, thus the present can be heavy with significance; thing-ification easily bars the way to true understanding; and much more. Yet, since holistic context radically shapes the distinctive significance of a specific theme in a given faith, all these points of agreement point us toward a more fundamental disagreement. Thus, if I may make a disinterested academic observation, Abe's reinterpretation of the Son's *kenosis*, his self-emptying to take incarnate form, seems to me quite utterly to transform it from what I have understood contemporary Christian theologians to be saying; I therefore look forward to seeing how they respond to him.

The heart of the Jewish-Buddhist discussion may most easily be approached by beginning with the second of the two questions Abe asks of Jewish thinkers at the conclusion of his discussion of the Holocaust. He inquires, "If the rupture caused by the holocaust is not a rupture of this or that way of philosophical or theological thinking, but of thought itself, how is *Tikkun*, that is a mending of the rupture, possible?" (p. 95) To Abe as a Buddhist, "mending," *Tikkun*, has to do with thought or understanding, in a Mahayana sense, to be sure. That follows logically from his insight into the human situation and its remedy. *Avidya*, ignorance, is the fundamental evil, and thus enlightenment, *vidya*, true understanding, is its "mending" (pp. 72–77). If, then, thought itself has been ruptured, the indispensable remedy is no longer available and all appears lost. How, then, can Jews still speak meaningfully of *Tikkun* after the Holocaust?

Abe's question is based on a citation from the writings of Emil Fackenheim and it will help to read it again. Fackenheim writes, "For the first time in this work [*To Mend the World*], we are faced with the possibility that the Holocaust may be a radical rupture in history—and that among things ruptured may be not just this or that way of philosophical or theological thinking, but thought itself" (p. 93). I understand Fackenheim to be saying that the Holocaust may be "a radical rupture in history," one so comprehensive that "among things ruptured" is thought—which is to say that the meaning of the Holocaust, *among other things*, exceeds the capacities of the intellectual activities the West calls philosophy or theology.

What, besides cognitive construction, does Fackenheim feel is now decisively challenged? More significantly than philosophizing, this qualitatively unique evil radically throws into doubt the Jewish people's very Covenant with God and the way of life it authorizes—and by extension it also threatens the covenant between God and all humankind, the Children of Noah. The ultimate issue is not how we can now think, though that is important to *homo sapiens*. Rather, it is how we might now mend our Covenant/covenant relationship with God so that the essential *Tikkun*, the mending of human history, can take place. In its Jewish context, *Tikkun* is attained by how one (everyone) lives, not primarily by what understanding one achieves. Thus, as Fackenheim has emphasized, Jews have "coped" (to use Abe's verb) with the radical rupture of the Holocaust by rededicating themselves to living in Covenant; not the least significant part of this *Tikkun* has been their insistence on not merely continuing their inherited religious way of life but by creating various new-old ways to live in Covenant. Thus, Fackenheim's own hope for *Tikkun* is not based on an elevation of insight but by our building our lives, as best we can, on the example of those Jews and gentiles whose deeds demonstrated that the death camps could not destroy their spirit.

It should be emphasized that neither philosophy nor theology is the basis for identifying the critical Jewish response to the Holocaust. Instead, the surprisingly positive activity of the Jewish community in the post-Holocaust period finally forced Jewish thinkers to reflect on its meaning. They did not lead or even significantly direct the Jewish people's response to the horror. In fact, it took them about two decades to confront directly the questions raised by the Holocaust. Only then, after the living responses were well established, did the thinkers' ideas begin to have a significant impact upon our community. It is still not clear to me whether the Christian death-of-God movement and, probably more importantly, its underlying cultural ferment were more responsible for bringing Holocaust theology into being than any indigenous demand by Jews for a fresh statement of their faith.[2] When Jewish thinkers did confront this challenge, then, at their best, they sought to understand, learn from and interpret what the Jewish community had been going through—and it is on this secondary level that they have had their influence in reshaping Jewish life. In these observations I am, of course, reflecting my own understanding of Judaism as the enduring Covenant between God and the Jewish people, hence a religion as much of the group as of, at least to liberals, individuals. Unlike the Descartean bent of western philosophy, I believe Jewish thinkers must constantly seek to think out of communal Jewish experience, seeking as best they can to understand its significance, though they must also do so out of their specific individuality.

Some comparative considerations may be helpful at this point. For Judaism the fundamental human concern is not redemption from sin. The God we stand in Covenant with "knows our frame and remembers that we are dust" and thus, as the prior verses say, directly has compassion upon us and forgives our sins (Ps. 103:8–14). This God can be heard by Ezekiel calling the people of Israel to repentance by saying climactically, "I have no pleasure in the death of him that dieth, says *Adonai*, God, therefore turn yourselves and live" (Ez. 18:32). Having no doctrine of original sin, Jews believe that the responsibility and the capacity to turn from evil are given not only to Jews but to all humankind, as the example of the Ninevites in the book of Jonah demonstrates. We further believe that people, Noachides or Israelites alike, are not fundamentally ignorant of how they ought to live because God has given us instruction (*Torah*) to that end and, in various ways, continues to do so. One requires no unusual intellectual or spiritual gift to know in the usual case how one ought to live. One learns it as much if not more from one's family and community as from one's formal religious training and from the great teachers of each generation. Thus, believing Jews are not surprised to discover genuine religion and morality, in quite diverse forms to be sure, among many peoples and faiths.

For Judaism, the primary human task is creating holiness through righteous living. The responsible deed, the one which simultaneously acknowledges God, others, time, place/nature and self in Covenantal fulfillment, not only mends the torn but fulfills the promise inherent in existence.

What is at stake here is precisely the level of seriousness with which one should take this ethical/spiritual human capacity. For Masao Abe it is a deeply felt and humanly quite significant matter, one whose importance may certainly not be trivialized. But it is only level "2" of the three dimensions of his thought (p. 79ff.). Thus, "all issues are properly and legitimately understood *ultimately* from the vantage point of the third dimension" which is that of "a transhuman fundamental dimension represented by religious faith or awakening," that is, dynamic Sunyata. In it, all such dualities as good and evil, holy and profane are overcome and transcended. By contrast, in the classic Jewish understanding, ultimate reality has indelible quality, God is holy—and that means, most closely, that God is good. There is nothing more ultimate. And because God is holy/good,[3] Jews are to be holy/good, which means to do holy/good deeds and create a holy/good human order which ultimately embraces nature in its fulfillment, with God's help.

Because the holy/good deed has such ultimacy, Jews have made it their primary concern and have now enhanced this traditional activism with the dynamism of modern self-assertion. This existential commitment has provided the motive power for the extraordinary Jewish contribution to modern civilization. Even Jews estranged from their religious tradition tend to measure their worth by what they do for humankind. As a consequence, the almost unanimous response of Jewish thinkers and laypeople to the Holocaust has been to try to act to frustrate its goals and prevent its replication. Negatively, that means opposing evil wherever one sees it; positively, it means fostering goodness to the extent that one can. And this form of *Tikkun* has been the most important Jewish response to the Holocaust.

Leo Baeck, the one Jewish theologian (liberal, to be sure) to have been in a concentration camp during the Holocaust and to have survived, wrote these lines as part of the conclusion to his post-Holocaust book of theology: "The great task of dark days, and the greater one of bright hours, was to keep faith with the expectation. Man waits for God, and God waits for man. The promise and the demand speak here, both in one: the grace of the commandment and the commandment of grace. Both are one in the One God. Around the One God there is concealment. He does not reveal Himself, but He reveals the commandment and the grace. . . . Every people can be chosen for a history, for a share in the history of humanity. Each is a question which God has asked, and each people must answer. But more history has been assigned to this people than to any other people. God's question speaks stronger here. . . . It is so easy to remain a slave, and it is so difficult to become a free man. But this people can only exist in the full seriousness of its task. It can only exist in this freedom which reaches beyond all other freedoms."[4]

With this worldview, the caring Jewish community will overwhelmingly reject the suggestion that, for all the trauma connected with the Holocaust, we ought to understand that it *ultimately* has no significance; or, to put it more directly, that *ultimately* there is no utterly fundamental distinction between the Nazi death camp operators and their victims. For most Jews, a response to the encompassing evils of our day—world hunger, political tyranny, religious intolerance and warfare, the threat of nuclear destruction—cannot properly be made with a consciousness that they are truly second-level concerns, that bringing people to a higher level of understanding is the most significant way to face them. And I cannot imagine them agreeing that the ultimate response to the Nazis would have been for Jews to raise their consciousness from a radically moral to a higher, post-moral level.

Does this then mean that, as Masao Abe inquires in his first question, "The holocaust is an isolated event entirely unrelated to other events in the world and history and thereby has a fixed, enduring absolute evil nature?" And if the latter is true, "How can (the) Jewish people come to terms with the holocaust and with God, who ultimately allowed the holocaust to occur?" (p. 95). In some sense the answer seems reasonably unequivocal. Even Fackenheim, the thinker who has made the strongest case for the qualitative uniqueness of the Holocaust, does not suggest that it was "an isolated event entirely unrelated to other events in the world and history." He and the rest of the Jewish community would not be so sensitive to the Christian background of Nazi anti-semitism if they thought the Holocaust so unhistorical, nor would they be so concerned that it retain a place in human consciousness to spur people to do the good.

Does it, then, have "a fixed, enduring, absolute evil nature"? Yes and no. It is, as far as we can tell, uniquely significant in telling us about human evil. Until some other, more horrific event occurs—Heaven forfend—and as long as memory recalls it, no small matter to Jews, it seems "fixed (and) enduring." But is it "absolute"? If Abe means does it carry the same ultimacy that, for him, Sunyata does and Jewish holiness does not, then I must say no. In my understanding of Judaism, only God is "absolute," though I would assert that only in a metaphorical, weak sense. (Were God a strong absolute, as Bradley indicated, there could be no creation and no independent human will.[5]) And insofar as the "absolute" God is holy/good, the Holocaust is enduringly evil.

In that event, to continue with the question, "How can (the) Jewish people come to terms with God, who ultimately allowed the holocaust to occur?" Here, I think, the phrase "come to terms," requires a more intellectual response than the one I gave in my previous discussion of how we "coped." I believe a brief discussion of Holocaust theology and the Jewish community's response to it will be most instructive for clarifying Judaism's distinctive affirmations as I understand them.

To the best of my knowledge only one Jew who has written extensively on the Holocaust, Richard L. Rubenstein, has followed the logic of the problem of evil to the conclusion that God cannot be good. He suggests that, after the Holocaust, God ought better to be understood as "the Holy Nothingness, known to mystics of all ages, out of which we have come and to which we shall ultimately return. . . . The limitations of finitude can be overcome only when we return to the Nothingness out of which we have been thrust. In the final analysis, omnipotent Nothingness is Lord of all creation."[6] While Rubenstein never developed this notion very fully, there is much in what he did write concerning it which might lead Masao Abe to fruitful dialogue with him.

The Jewish community agreed with Rubenstein that the Holocaust posed a radical challenge to its inherited or reappropriated tradition. But his conception of God found few echoes in what then developed into Holocaust theology. I think it is clear why: it did not provide a ground for qualitatively distinguishing between Nazis and Jews. It had explained logically why "God" could "ultimately allow the holocaust to occur" but had done so only by denying that there was any ultimate reason for being morally outraged to begin with; if ultimate reality is morally neutral—and perhaps negative since Rubenstein calls death the only Messiah[7]—one has as much right to be a Nazi as a Jew. That way of "coming to terms" with the Holocaust was, for all its logical rigor and grim courage, antithetical to the fundamental religious intuition of the Jewish community.

I cannot recall a Jewish thinker who has dealt with Holocaust theodicy who has not begun with a vigorous reassertion of the so-called "free-will defense." Consistent with what has been said above, most Jews see the Holocaust as an indictment of humankind, specifically of the Nazis for their demonic use of their freedom. For the Jews I know, theological speculation must not be allowed to shift the primary responsibility for the evil from the Nazis to God. Some human beings, often after considerable deliberation, decided to carry out the Holocaust—and many renewed that decision day after day for years. They were the worst. But in a similar but qualitatively different human failure, the western democracies and even Jewish community leadership did not do what they could to stop or protest the Holocaust; the human guilt is proportional to the human power.

While Jews may have been aghast that God would have allowed human freedom to proceed to such evil lengths, no one seriously suggested that a good God should have deprived people of their freedom or, almost the same thing, severely limited its effective scope. The holy/good deed can only come from a free person. That notion is so central to the Jewish intuition of ultimate reality that humankind's action and nature, not God's, must be the primary level of the discussion.

Those Jews who sought a rational understanding of how God could allow the Holocaust found their solution by denying God has encompassing power. They had no difficulty producing numerous citations from rabbinic literature in which God is depicted as limited. Moreover, the notion of a finite, perhaps growing God had considerable appeal because it heightened the moral responsibility of humankind. One could not now sink into passivity, throwing oneself utterly into God's saving hands and abandoning what one might have done to save oneself and the world. It is a concept that has brought much solace to Jews in a troubled time and, universalized and popularized in Harold Kushner's *When Bad Things Happen to Good People* (Schocken), it has been a healing balm to many troubled Americans.

Surprisingly, considering the alleged rationality of the contemporary Jewish community, the idea of a limited God has not become dominant. For all its helpfulness and logical clarity, it seems to many people to create as many new problems as it resolves old ones. On the human level, it leaves people with no cosmic recourse when they are sorely stricken and have exhausted their human power struggling against their ills. God may then be a co-sufferer but God is also as helpless as we are and thus cannot offer much solace. And it is not clear in a post-Holocaust age that we can count on humankind to perfect God's limitations, since we have so many of our own. How then will the Messiah come and history be redeemed from mere neutrality or worse? Moreover, on the ontological level, troublesome questions are raised by that power which is not in God's hands. Is there a force or being over against what we had understood to be the one God? And how shall we now transcend our rationality and have faith that despite God's limited power, God's goodness will ultimately prevail in our universe?

Such questions or their human equivalents have, paradoxically enough, engendered a significant return to the God of the Covenant who, we were told two decades ago, was dead, at least in our time. A minority among us, but an unabating one, is in the midst of a probing spiritual quest. As I have analyzed this movement over the years,[8] it has seemed to me generated by a search for a more adequate ground of value. Once, the high human quality that modern Jews have so prized seemed common to all rational, educated, cultured people; thus humanism could be a substitute for religious faith. In recent years, human frailty and perversity, institutional failure, cultural vacuity and philosophy's inability to mandate substantive ethics, have increasingly threatened to make our civilization amoral or worse. To be more in touch with what one ultimately believes, to find greater power to resist, as one knows one must, these corrosive social forces—perhaps even to harness them for human betterment—people have turned to traditional religious belief. Sophisticates who once would have found that unthinkable given the attractions of radically autonomous human reason and Nietzschean self-assertion, now find those alternatives largely discredited. They have few moral credentials to present to a generation concerned with value. If anything, they are more the problem to be overcome than a proper standard for its solution.

How do these almost-traditional Jewish believers "come to terms" with the Holocaust? Unable to sacrifice God's goodness, or power, or deny the reality of evil, they reluctantly sacrifice the certainty of logic in the face of what they know to be the ultimate commanding power of living in holy goodness. They believe, in their fashion, even though they do not understand in any ultimate way. Like classic Jewish pietists, they hope the goodness of God day by day will set the context for their confrontation with evil. Creating that day to day appreciation of God's continual giving goodness is more important to them than understanding the theological ground of the limit case of gross suffering.

Perhaps such a piety, even in its modern guises, sounds strange for a people so proud of its intellectuality. But there is a certain classic Jewish reticence to probe too deeply into God. Christian theologians like Jurgen Moltmann find it congruent with their trinitarian faith to speak of what transpires in God's interior. Masao Abe suggests that from his Buddhist perspective they ought to move on to "the still greater interior of the interior" (p. 37). On this score, the central tradition of the Jewish people has been resolutely agnostic. It does not know much about God's essence because, as a religion of revelation, God did not say much about it. In recent generations, as thinkers have reinterpreted revelation in terms of human religious experience, this aspect of Jewish awe has, if anything, been strengthened. Almost all Jewish thinkers readily acknowledge that they have little knowledge of Godself though they claim empowering understanding of how God wants us to live. The power of the holy/good deed remains that strong among us.

There is an important exception to this characterization of Judaism, namely, Jewish mysticism, and a brief consideration of its career is in order. Our earliest records of the Jewish mystical tradition—from the time of early rabbinic literature—and its first books focus on how God created the universe and exercises power through it, quite roughly, the classic concerns called *maaseh vereshit* and *maaseh merkavah*, "the work of creation" and "the work of (God's) chariot (as per Ezekiel 1)." We hear of heavenly palaces and angelic beings, even of the dimensions of God's "body" but not about God's inner life.

About a millennium later, theosophy had emerged as a major Jewish mystical concern with the appearance of the Zohar, the classic work of the Jewish mystical tradition, at the end of the 13th century c.e. Strongly influenced by medieval Jewish rationalism's emphasis on unity, the author of the Zohar knows God to be, in utter identity and unbroken unity, both *En Sof* and *Sefirot*. The former term translates easily as "Without End"— but thus, if the meaning is taken rigorously, God is the one about whom nothing at all can be said, not even, in a way, this, since saying inevitably suggests limits. Some mystics have even gone on to call God, in this understanding, "Nothing." But they and other Jewish theosophists also radically affirmed that the *En Sof* is also the *Sefirot*, the ten "spheres" of interactive divine energy whose configurations and interplay may be described by a range of metaphors so daring and so grossly material they sometimes leave moderns aghast.

In the 16th century Isaac Luria extended the notion of God's pervasive unity to the extent that creation could only be accomplished by God's "contraction" (a sort of "emptying"?) to make "room" for the universe. Two centuries later, the Maggid of Mezeritch, the second generation leader of the new Hasidic movement, mystically knew that God alone was truly real and thus in his teaching, a clear distinction between a "relative" human level of affairs and an "absolute" divine one holds sway. Much Hasidic doctrine still features this understanding though the extent to which it remains part of esoteric as against the folksy, exoteric instruction given by Hasidism is unclear. And, it should be noted, for all this doctrine of two levels of reality, Hasidim have been most faithful in their observance of even the minutiae of Jewish law and custom. Masao Abe should find much in this development in Jewish mysticism which is congenial to him though its sense of ultimate reality is that of pervasive fullness rather than that of dialectical emptying.

The bulk of the Jewish community, however, continues to reject such mysticism. Most Orthodox Jews find its teachings about God suspiciously unlike those of the Bible and the Talmud. These Jewish classics accept the reality of creation and the ultimate significance of the holy act. They find this inherited tradition not only self-commending but fully coherent with their experience. Jewish liberals generally find the enveloping mystical sense of God at variance with their own sporadic, tentative religious experience. More critically, knowing God so intimately, Jewish mysticism tends to bend human freedom utterly to God's will. But what if, as in the case of women's rights, people find they must trust their own sense of the holy/ good more than the regulations and customs, indeed more than the "revelation" they have inherited? Again, the primacy of the sense of proper human value reasserts itself and insists upon its central place in any affirmations that are to be made about God. I believe that religious sensitivity is at the root of the general community rejection of asserting God is All-in-All, thereby entailing, ultimately, that there is no real evil—not even the Holocaust. Modernized Jews may wish to make increasing room for God in their lives but, as I understand them, they do not propose thereby to wipe out but to empower what they know to be demanded of humankind: "Seek good and not evil, that ye may live; and so *Adonai*, the God of hosts, will be with you, as you say. Hate evil, love good, and establish justice in the gate" (Am. 5:14–15).

Notes

1. All references to pages in Masao Abe's paper are given in the body of the text and the notes are reserved for other matters. Baeck, in *The Essence of Judaism*, describes the Buddhism of apparently "static" Sunyata as the typological opposite of Judaism; Buber compares and contrasts Zen Buddhism and Hasidic Judaism in his essay, "The Place of Hasidism in the History of Religion," published both in *The Origin and Meaning of Hasidism* (Horizon) and *Hasidism* (Philosophical Press).

2. See my *Choices in Modern Jewish Thought*, chapter 9, "Confronting the Holocaust," particularly pp. 187–190.

3. I am not satisfied with either the term "holy" or "good" by itself to convey the quality of the mandated, desired Jewish act. "Holy" alone often carries the connotations of "churchy" or of a segregated spirituality. "Good" is too easily secularized into humanistic ethics. The fulfilled Jewish act is more life-involved than the one, more God-oriented than the other. This dilemma surfaces in another way in trying to translate the term *tzedakah*. We variously render it as "righteousness" or "justice," but it is as likely to mean "faithfulness, reliability" and it comes to mean what English terms "charity."

4. *This People Israel*, pp. 397 and 402 (Holt, Rinehart & Winston).

5. I discuss the equivocal applicability of the term "absolute" to the God of Judaism in my paper "Liberal Judaism's Effort to Invalidate Relativism Without Mandating Orthodoxy," *Go and Study, Essays in Honor of Alfred Jospe* (B'nai Brith Hillel).

6. *After Auschwitz*, p. 154 (Bobbs-Merrill).

7. Ibid, pp. 184, 198.

8. While this topic is found in many of my articles over the past two decades, it was the fundamental theme of my analysis of the situation of American Jewry in *The Mask Jews Wear* (Simon and Schuster) published in 1973 when Jewish discussions of the death of God were at their height. (See, particularly, the Afterword, and compare the chapter on the 1980s in the second edition published by Sh'ma, Inc.) Cf. the later statements at the end of chapters 2 and 3, Part Two of my *Liberal Judaism* (Union of American Hebrew Congregations).

40

When Theologians Engage in
Inter-faith Dialogue

Paul van Buren devotes the third volume of his systematic Christian theology to his christology, entitling it, most significantly, *Christ in Context*. While he directs it primarily to Christian readers, I am certain he hopes, as do all of us who write for publication, that others will learn from it. As a Jewish theologian, I am particularly interested in his work because of his rigorous effort to rethink Christian faith in terms of its Jewish origins. And now he has sought to discern Jesus as the Christ not merely within the context of his Jewish social environment but specifically within the circle of its faith. His thinking on this topic so intrigued me that it prompted this reflection on the special contours of inter-faith dialogue between academic theologians. I discern some unexpected features in such exchanges as contrasted to those between local clergy or lay groups, or, most certainly, to those of officials of our groups in formal session—the closest approximation we have to dialogue between "Judaism" and "Christianity."

To give my observations some hope of broader validity, I propose to expand my consideration to include the thought of a Buddhist thinker, Masao Abe. He has been extensively involved in Buddhist-Christian dialogue and in a recent paper directed to Christian theologians he raised some questions to which he thought Jewish thinkers might fruitfully re-

Adapted from an address marking the opening of the Center for Jewish-Christian Learning and Relations, General Theological Seminary, New York City, May 1988. Delivered in this form at the inauguration of the Franklin Moosnick Lectures in Judaic Studies, Lexington Theological Seminary, Lexington, Ky., March 1989.

spond. Let me, then, begin my analysis with the thought of this eminent contemporary Buddhist thinker.

Masao Abe's philosophy arises from the fundamental religious insight of Zen Buddhism that ultimately there is only dynamic Nothingness. We westerners may perhaps most easily understand this view as the direct antithesis of Heidegger's famous query, "Why is there anything at all?" Zen, so to speak, rather inquires, "Why is there nothing at all?" With change and ephemerality the most common human experiences, the Zen masters lead us on rigorously to the startling insight that there is, simply, nothing at all. Abe, in turn, inquires why, with so much historical and human evidence of the nihil around us, with so many western thinkers, like Nietzsche, concerned with nothingness, Christian theologians do not take the doctrine of *kenosis* to its logical conclusion. At the heart of the Christian conception of the Triune God lies the Son's extraordinary act of emptying out the exclusivity of his role in the Godhead so that he might also take on human form, thereby to suffer and die to redeem humanity. This Christian religious intuition, Abe urges, should be given more comprehensive scope. God should be understood to be fully kenotic, a Godhead so fully emptied out that God can finally emerge as the primordial Nothing Zen also acknowledges as ultimate reality. Abe takes a similar line with Jewish theologians, this time extrapolating from their discussions of the Holocaust. Does not the utter absence encountered in the Holocaust testify that at the heart of human affairs, as in nature itself, only a dynamic nothingess can be seen?

Abe's thought would, thus far, be quite recognizable as a thoughtful restatement of Zen. But he then surprises his reader with a call for Buddhist ethical activism in the western sense of the terms. With great intellectual creativity, he argues that *Sunyata*, the elemental dynamic negativity, should not be conceived in terms of a linear emptying out but a reflexive one. If negation is all, it must also negate negation itself, thus originating a certain positivity. He then connects this notion of reflexive *Sunyata* with the loving practice of the *bodhisattvas*. These noble souls attain enlightenment but, out of their deep compassion for suffering humanity, turn back to the world to redeem humankind from the bad *karma* in which it has been immemorially immersed. In the vow, *pranidhana*, all enlightened Buddhists should take to save others, not him- or herself alone, he sees a generative ethical impulse. Combining this with the Buddhist concern for right action, he sets before us a world-oriented, ethically active, Zen Buddhism. As he puts it, "*Sunyata* endlessly, ceaselessly turns itself into vow and into act and thus dynamically centers itself in a focal point of this dynamism."

This Buddhism of Abe's is quite different from any statement of this faith I have ever previously encountered. It radically reverses the common western image of Buddhism as, in our perspective, a world-denying religion. What, then, are we to make of an eminent academic representative of his or her faith who presents it to you in a form that, in terms of all your prior efforts to understand it, goes contrary to what you have thought it taught?

I also found Paul van Buren's christology unlike, perhaps antithetical to, any doctrine of the Christ I had ever before encountered. Thus, van Buren invokes neither revelation nor faith to explain how he knows Jesus was authorized by God; for him it is, rather, a simple deduction from his extraordinary effectiveness. He takes Nicea and Chalcedon's doctrine of two natures in Jesus to be logically incoherent, a blunder resulting from the church becoming anti-Judaic and then forcibly tearing Jesus out of his religious context. For him, the resurrection is not a factual, historic occurrence—an approach to it he considers mythological. Rather it is a way of pointing to the continued functioning of the Christ after his death to bring people, most notably gentiles, to God.

All this climaxes in van Buren's radical assertion that Jesus communicated no new religious truth; there is nothing religiously novel about his role or his message. To be sure, he was (and is) uniquely powerful in communicating God's claim on us human beings, and he did (does) this with incomparable effectiveness because of his matchless personhood. But he not only was a Jew who lived as a Jew and taught as a Jew might teach; what he taught, then and now, is only the truth of Judaism. In short, van Buren takes the title to his book with utter literality. He rethinks the Christ-hood of Jesus " . . . in Context," that is, with radical concreteness and specificity, rigidly insisting that Jesus's faith and role be delineated only in terms of the Judaism of his day. Any other kind of christology radically rips him out of his theological context, a theological blunder initiated by some anti-Judaic early Christians who, to van Buren's great sorrow, have set the church's dominant tone down to our own day.

Not only Jews but most Christians, I suggest, will find van Buren's Christ unlike any previously known to them. Perhaps I can put it best this way: in the past, Christian theologies have regularly been supercessionist, dissolving the Israel of the flesh into the true Israel, that of the spirit, the church. Paul van Buren's Christianity is not merely anti-supercessionist; it is uncompromisingly *successionist*. For him, the church knows no substantive truth not already to be found in classic Judaism, though as the community of gentiles called to Israel's God its way of celebrating its faith will necessarily be its own.

My first reaction to this unknown Christ was to criticize van Buren for so transforming his received faith. But I quickly realized I was being as unreasonable as I had thought some of my Jewish colleagues were some years ago for their criticism of my book on christologies. There I had analyzed what a committee of Christian theologians recommended to me as a representative sample of contemporary doctrines of the Christ. My Jewish colleagues were unhappy with my work because they did not find in it the Christ they were accustomed to reject. All they wanted to know was, "Where is the traditional doctrine of the incarnation?" If contemporary Christian theologians did not impute to the incarnation the meanings they associated with it—largely from Jewish polemical arguments, I thought—they denied that these new theologies could rightly be called Christianity. Naturally, it seemed to me that Christian theologians, particularly ones considered to be representative, had a greater right to say what constituted Christianity than did a group of Jews. And now I found myself reacting to Paul van Buren's christology with exactly the same argument I had rejected in my critics!

The least one can say, then, about academic theological inter-faith dialogue is that it may allow one to discover that other religions are different from what you thought they were. Nonetheless, the question remains cogent: Can theologians who drastically transform the substance of their inherited traditions properly be considered representative of them?

But again, that same question could be asked about my own theology. Classically, Judaism has based itself on an objectified, verbal doctrine of God's revelation, understanding it, in particular, to center on the law(s) God gave the people of Israel as well as the procedures for their continual amplification. I envision God's revelation and commandment as essentially personalistic, that is inner but relational realities. Instead of vesting authority in the sages of the Talmud and their successors, I place it in the hands of each learned, conscientious Jew. I therefore condone changes in Jewish practice and doctrine as well as a pluralism of Jewish obligation that, by the standards of Jewish tradition, render me the Jewish equivalent of a heretic.

Why, then, do I feel entitled, even commanded, so radically to transform Judaism and now feel the urge to protest Abe and Van Buren doing the same? The issue is particularly pressing with regard to Paul van Buren's theology since we utilize the same model—personal relationship—to communicate religious truth. It therefore ill behooves me in carrying on a dialogue with my two academic colleagues to deny them an intellectual right I consider essential as I seek to explicate my community's faith authentically. Therefore, instead of confronting the Buddhism and Christianity I think they ought to have, I must, if we are to meet as equals, confront their particular Buddhism and Christianity even as I will expect that they attend to my interpretation of Judaism.

Surely many Jewish traditionalists object to inter-faith theological dialogue just for this reason. For there can be little doubt why these three thinkers have taken their unexpected stands. Having been involved with thinkers of other faiths, or academic students of religion, they have heard various critiques of their faiths. In reaction to them, they have then rethought their understanding of their beliefs. This aspect of inter-faith dialogue, certainly among academics, is often quite covert, most certainly at the early stages of acquaintance when people are overjoyed merely to be talking civilly rather than carrying on polemics. At some point in a growing relationship it becomes important to explain why you are not the other. Doing so necessarily involves a critique of the other's faith, even if only set forth in terms of the religious truths particularly dear to you. That communicates the understanding that your partner does not appreciate this or that facet of spirituality as he or she ought.

Our sample of thinkers shows the effect of such interchange. Abe specifically indicates that he has been influenced by the western charge that Buddhism is too ethically passive and unworldly, in the western sense of those terms. As a result, one can see that he restudied his tradition and drew from it those motifs which correspond to westerners' ethics. So, too, van Buren has been deeply affected by the criticisms of Christianity as fundamentally, even doctrinally, anti-semitic. As a result, he has radically reinterpreted Christianity in a fashion that radically purges it of any reminder and possibility of that ancient sin.

My own thought also involves a response to external challenges, less, I think, those raised in dialogue with Christian theologians than by reading secular thinkers analyzing the human condition (to whom many Christian theologians have also responded). Thus, by contemporary personalist standards, traditional Judaism appears too little concerned with the individual and too much centered on the community, its legal procedures and institutional necessities. Acknowledging some religious legitimacy to these values, though less to the judgments, I conceptualize the Covenant in relational and personalistic terms rather than the more familiar contractual, ethnic or (neo-Kantian) ethical ones. So I place a heavy emphasis on the human role in the Covenant without thereby, I devoutly hope, demeaning the active involvement of an independent, other God, the senior partner in our intimate association.

Clearly, just this process disturbs the traditionalist Jewish critics of theological inter-faith dialogue. They worry lest the dynamic of such exchange lead Jews to vitiate the classic content of our spirituality. By contrast the much publicized present strength of orthodoxies arises from their confident, detailed knowledge concerning the truth of our relationship with God. I am a religious liberal because I do not have their assurance or agree that theirs is warranted. Moreover, for all its compelling quality, I know how limited is my understanding of God's will. Having confidence that their truth is God's truth, they see no reason to speak of it in equal exchange with skeptics or unbelievers. One might then, out of simple courtesy, be called upon to respond to the dialogue partner's non-acceptance of it and the need, responding in the other's terms, to reformulate one's faith in such a way as to betray it.

In my experience, something quite different occurs. Theologians worthy of their calling know their primary responsibility is to God and that they and their ideas are continually subject to God's judgment. As people of integrity they can respond to others only as their faith allows them to do. When someone suggests that Judaism has a lack, I do not, out of my insecurity rush to satisfy my dialogue partner. I also do not bristle at the possibility that someone else may know a spiritual truth my community has not thought of or has given too little emphasis. Rather, I evaluate whether there is Jewish merit in the suggestion. My standard will be the truth on which I stand as a member of my religious community and on which I stake my life. As I see it, then, the effect of my heritage remains dominant, assimilating to it the influences arising from dialogue.

Each of the three theologians under examination manifests just this limited reponsiveness. In each, the classic emphases of their faiths re-emerge as critical to their creative reinterpretations of them. Not the least indication is the subtle way that this summons up Judaism's old dissent from them. Thus, though Masao Abe has presented what westerners will recognize as an ethically activist Buddhism, he explicitly indicates that this moral thrust has only proximate but not ultimate religious significance. Rather, the ethics he commends can only properly hope to be spiritually significant if it is carried out as an outgrowth of the fundamental insight that dynamic nothingness is at the heart of reality. His Buddhist "categorical imperative" is not to do the good, but to gain enlightenment, *satori*. To my Jewish soul, that must radically denature the quality and tone of Abe's ethics. In this shift of ultimate concern from right action to right understanding he reinstates the fundamental spiritual divergence of Judaism and Buddhism.

In Paul van Buren's case, the religious innovation of Christianity lies in enabling the gentile nations to come into a true relationship with God. He very carefully specifies that he makes no triumphalist claims for the church; the Christ is not the only way to come to God. There may be other modes of doing so but for gentiles who become Christians, the Jew Jesus is the means by which they arrive at proper intimacy with God.

Yet, despite his universalism, intimately linked as it is to the elimination of all Christian anti-Judaism, his Christianity contains the basis of a conflict with Judaism that I believe he must eventually face. It arises from the stubborn fact that Jesus seems not to have recognized the fact that his real role, as van Buren depicts it, is to bring gentiles into the Jewish covenant with God. For as van Buren notes, Jesus came to his own people and preached only to them. Some of the witnesses to his ministry picture it as exclusively directed to Jews. Van Buren responds that he only came looking for "the lost sheep of the house of Israel," what in a telling phrase he describes as "lapsed, assimilated, alienated, or unrighteous Jews." Surely, then, a church which has reclaimed the Jewish Jesus would be entitled to reclaim the Jewish task of Jesus, now no longer a mission to evangelize the Jews and make them Christians but one to make better Jews of all those Jews whom we rabbis and professors continually criticize as apathetic and uncaring. And that returns us to our ancient Jewish-Christian dispute over how Jews ought now best fulfill their Covenant.

My own theological work discloses a similar development. In recent years, I have been giving increased attention to the actional implications of my thought. That may only be because I have satisfied my methodological perplexities about doing Jewish theology. But it is equally likely the result of my view of the Covenant, which for all my personalism, stresses that a Jew's relationship with God is fulfilled mainly by action in community as part of the people of Israel. Thus, I now often reflect on what ethical and other deeds one ought to do day by day to carry out the Covenant. I know that until I have clarified the entailments of Covenant responsibility in significant part, I cannot be greatly confident that my restatement of Jewish faith is valid. Or, more traditionally put, I have a Jewish responsibility to indicate my personalist equivalent to what has been, since talmudic times, Jewish obligation as rabbinic law. Once more, the characteristic religious concerns remain central.

There seems little doubt, then, that when creative theologians engage in dialogue, they speak for themselves alone, not an "ism" like Buddh-ism or Juda-ism, or an "ity" like Christian-ity. One therefore will understand them and their faith better if they are situated on the spectrum of religious positions held in their community. Thus, the man and the tradition are illuminated if we realize that Masao Abe is a Mahayana Buddhist, a Zen Mahayana Buddist, a Japanese Zen Buddhist of the Kyoto School with its special interest in western philosophy and its admirable effort to speak to westerners in their own terms of the message of Zen. Paul van Buren is an Episcopal priest, one who is part of that glorious tradition of Episcopalian Protestantism which encourages some of its theologians to adopt positions so radical that they provoke not only much of the church but contemporary society as well—a tradition much honored also among modern Jews. And I am found on the theological right of the left wing of the believing Jewish community. Or, to unpack that metaphor, my theology is much too liberal for traditionally observant Jews while also unacceptably pious and demanding for many of the liberal Jews with whom I am properly identified.

To be sure, ours is not the only way to do theology. Many eminent thinkers eschew the blandishments of novelty. They seek only to convey the received truth of their faith community, though articulating it in a contemporary guise they hope moderns will find appealing. They work by close attention to historic precedent and by the copious citation of texts that validate their reading of their tradition. Another group of interpreters seeks to communicate where the bulk of believers now find themselves spiritually. Theirs is more a sociological approach, seeking through various techniques to find out where "the people of God" believe themselves to be.

Innovative theologians, such as the three we have been analyzing here, should not be understood as speaking for "the" sangha, "the" church or "the" Jewish people. I doubt that they are even primarily concerned with speaking to their communities as they are. They address them as they know they ought some day to be. They seek to present, as it were, the faith of the future. At any given moment, one cannot know what their communities make out of what they are saying. Some of their cobelievers will repudiate them; most will ignore or forget them; a few will learn from them; and some, they hope, will accept their theologies as the best presently available way of articulating their tradition's millennial sense of the

480

ineffable. If, then, you want to learn about Buddhism or Christianity or Judaism as such from its creative thinkers, you must wait a century or two to see what "the" Buddhists, or "the" Christians, or "the" Jews think of these versions of their faith.

Innovative theology requires considerable venturesomeness. Yet for all its risks, one critical element of it in our time is inter-faith dialogue. We engage in it because we believe that our religions will be less true to their fundamental affirmations, less vital in their spirituality and less likely to continue in their service of God without it. For openness to other people's understandings of the Ultimate helps us better appreciate our own distinctive truth, not the least by making us ask whether we are seeing its full implications. Besides, our religions, in their own visions, look forward to that day when all of humankind is united. We seem far from it today, but by learning to speak in utter depth to people of views different from our own, in placing our radical disagreements with one another in the respectful, loving context of that eschatological vision, we seek, here and now, to do what we can do—and often have not done—to bring nearer that devoutly desired consummation.

A Concluding Reflection

41

The Resulting Task

I believe the ethical enterprise pursued in these papers to have validated itself on an initial basis, not the least by its reasonable coherence, if more in method and self-involvement than as theory or conclusions. It also provides a plausible understanding of what, from a Covenantal perspective, constitutes an independent Jewish perspective of our duties to one another. Equally important to me, it demonstrates that one can deny final trust to both tradition and philosophic ethics, though giving metaethical priority to Judaism, be guided by them both, and learning from the choices one must make within and between them, emerge with ethical direction.

I have learned a good deal from this effort that clarifies the method I believe one should employ in carrying it forward. Let us begin with the general ethical side. For all the clash of ethical theories today, in fact, through them something quite useful can be learned. Nonetheless, until very much more philosophical consensus exists, or one view clearly demonstrates that it best comports to our Jewish metaethical vision, contemporary ethical discussions will mostly be of value to us as applied to individual questions. These are vigorously discussed today from many different perspectives, ranging, for example, in economic matters from anarchism and libertarianism at the one pole to various forms of Marxist collectivism at the other. Most other fields show similar diversity. One ought not, then, if one truly wishes to learn from contemporary ethics, simply to select the one that seems most moral to one and argue that it is "the" accepted ethical view today—a characteristic of much recent non-Orthodox Jewish ethical writing. We can learn much by directly confronting the choices forced on us by this ethical pluralism. At the least, our ethical horizons are expanded by the possibility that the good may be found elsewhere than in the thinkers we have come to rely upon. More significantly, reflecting on why one must reject a given proposal often gives one insight into the silent affirmation that compels it. This greater understanding of one's ethical commitments, very often of a metaethical kind, can be most helpful in clarifying the relationship between one's ethics and one's Judaism. Since the practical work of ethics largely consists of applying these primal values, the gain can be most significant.

Something similar can be said about the Jewish side of the process. Ethical writers, of every Jewish affiliation, often give one only the Jewish sources they believe will bolster their case even when they give evidence from the *halakhah* proper priority in supporting their decisions. While the dialectic of opinion in the *halakhah* comes nowhere near approaching the broad pluralism we see in general ethical discussions, it often exists and ought to be considered when speaking of "the" *halakhah*. Generally, the variety of opinion is of a formal variety, where a law is to be classified or how it is to be derived. But these technical considerations not infrequently lead on to a fresh substantive conclusion. Perhaps the decisor came to his conclusion simply out of formal logical considerations, but he did not hesitate, then, to declare his ruling *halakhah*. Had it been substantively unpalatable to his Jewish sensibility, he would not have done so. Hence, one concerned more with the metaethical than the halakhic-formal grounds for a decision can still often learn much from the dialectic of views in a given halakhic area. And other, more substantive considerations can lead to a divergent opinion. For a concerned Jew, the substantial citation of the dialectic of halakhic opinion on a given topic must therefore be a major criterion for the Jewish adequacy of a Jewish ethical discussion.

This daunting conclusion would seem to preclude any but halakhic experts from participating in this field, one reason that so much ethical-halakhic writing in recent years has come from Orthodox thinkers. Fortunately the growth of interest in Jewish law and the continuing application to its sources of the major Western academic modes of doing research have eased the task for the many who, like myself, are not scholars of *halakhah*. Tools like the *Talmudic Encyclopedia* and the Bar Ilan University computerization of the major Jewish respondents have greatly eased the task of gaining a good data base from which to carry on one's Jewish investigations. And there is every reason to believe that the growing number of such resources will increase with time.

The major methodological difficulty in working with these materials from an ethical perspective is finding a way to let them speak to us with proper independence. Only in that way can the Jewish tradition make its proper contribution to our quest for guidance. But we are often overcome by what we *want* the Jewish sources to be saying to us, occasionally by what we know they ought to say, and so we censor out part of what is there and simply read the rest in terms of our needs. Eisegesis, reading in, replaces exegesis, reading out. The difficulty is that one cannot make a sharp distinction between "what the data says" and its interpretation by us. What constitutes the relevant data and, more important, how it is to be read to be "understood," already constitutes a contemporary reconstruction of the past; there is no objectivity in the confident sense of some decades ago. And I would argue that even many of those who claim to read the old sources as part of the unbroken continuity of their classic study style, often do so subtly influenced by their changed historical-cultural situation.

I suggest meeting this difficulty in the following ways. One begins by trying to acquire as substantial a base as possible of relevant halakhic material. One sign of this is that one considers the major opinions that later halakhic writers refer back to. As against most of the traditional sources for the data, we moderns find it helpful to have the material in careful chronological perspective; for example, we do not take it for granted that the classic commentary to the Talmud, that written by Rashi (1040–1105) in France, necessarily correctly interprets the talmudic text of some five centuries earlier in Babylon. Reading each text as reflective of some authoritative Jewish opinion of its period and place enables us better to see what variation took place in formulation of the argument and, more important, in defining Jewish duty.

Some limited observations about the material are helpful at this stage. Can the variations be simply characterized, for example, as more stringent or more lenient? Have reasons for the view, particularly if there is a shift, been offered that move beyond formal halakhic considerations, for example, Meiri's new openness to Christianity based on "the nations'" increased morality? But to suggest that this or that historic circumstance or social condition was the basis for such a variation in halakhic position seems to me more speculative than a close attention to the data can allow.

A warning sign that one has moved on to interpretation or mediation should be seen when one sees, as history, a discussion of the halakhic texts in terms of the contemporary ethical discussion, for example, when one suggests that medieval decisor's respect for individual autonomy brought them to rule that a husband's talmudically specified right to do sexually whatever he wishes with his wife is qualified by her need to consent. When values are seen in an old text that were not commonly part of its worldview as disclosed by the range of texts of that period, we probably are no longer getting the text's independent input but reading it our way. There is a time for that step in the investigation, but not until the two prior tasks have been completed, knowing the variety of modern opinion on the topic and the way the halakhic process treated the topic over time.

It is precisely here that the difference between the older liberal pattern of doing Jewish ethics and the postmodern one I am advocating becomes most pronounced. At this point the classic liberals would proceed to *interpretation* while I call for *mediation*. With some exaggeration, we may say that the liberals read the sources of Judaism in terms of their modern ethics; what was now "Jewish" was what was (universally) ethical, together with a certain historic and ethnic tone to this statement of duty. Contemporary Orthodoxy largely proceeds in the other direction, learning from *halakhah* which of the many contemporary calls to action are proper Jewish obligations. Having ultimate confidence in neither, though more in Judaism than in our culture, I propose letting each help us evaluate the other critically, confronting us with what we, faced with their agreements and dissents, ought to do. On some occasions, as in the controversy over feminism, I find myself largely agreeing with one vision of the general culture. On others, as in the Jewish refusal to separate business from the totality of the human self as recommended by Milton Friedman, I side largely with our tradition. And sometimes I find myself, as on most sexual questions, largely more traditional than most general ethics, but also far more permissive than is classic Jewish law.

Thus far, I see no rational or classic Jewish consistency to my Jewish ethical stands. However, I find them a coherent way for my Jewish self to carry out its obligations to God under the Covenant. It does not yet greatly trouble me that others using relatively the same method come to different definitions of duty. I see such pluralism as a necessary adjunct of our modern Jewish affirmation of the religious importance of the self, and there is substantial evidence that, at least in some periods, selfhood in Covenant allowed for substantial individual diversity.

But the Covenant was not given to me as an individual but to the people of Israel as a whole. A postmodern Jewish ethics may begin with individual selves seeking an authentic way to be Jewish, but if it is to take proper Jewish form, what begins with the self will lead on to community. From individuals who care and think and live this way, the nucleus of such a contemporary Covenantally loyal community might develop. Around it, others less dedicated might gather. From their personal decisions, ones which also included concern for the others, common patterns might then develop, in time exerting their own influence on individual decision making. That is as close as we are likely to come to postmodern Jewish "law." It is a lot to aspire to—but hope, I take it, is a major virtue in Jewish ethics.

Index

Religion (*cont.*)
goodness, 67–68; forgiveness in, 65–66; freedom of, 121–22; God as goal of, 45, 47; and God's covenant, 62–63, 65, 66; and human worth, 46, 62; institutional, 55–56, 219–21; liberal *vs* traditionalist perspectives on, 115–18, 121; moral crisis in, 49–57, 85–88; and psychotherapy, 41–48, 240–41; resurgence of, 53–54, 86, 87, 88, 109–10, 147; and role of denunciation, 55; secular critique of, 58–59; and selfhood, 63, 64–65; separation of state and, 114, 118–20; teaching about, 120, 123–24, 132, 133–39; Tillichian concept of, 49–50; traditional, fear of, 87; traditional, universal claims of, 89; value-filled, 45–46, 50. *See also* Christian ethics; Interfaith dialogue; Jewish ethics; Jewish ethics, individual
Resurrection, 20
Ritschl, Albrecht, 50
Road Less Travelled, The (Peck), 241
Robinson, Theodore, 140 n. 5
Roman Catholic Church, 187, 245–46, 273, 433, 444, 445, 446
Roman Empire, 95
Rosenzweig, Franz, 181, 184, 214, 378–79, 424, 425
Roth, Philip, 240
Rousseau, Jean Jacques, 205, 291
Rubenstein, Richard, 419, 421, 422, 428, 469

Sachar, Howard M., 143 n. 25
Salvador, Joseph, 438
Samuel, 126
Samuel (Amoraic master), 127, 128
Sartre, Jean Paul, 82, 180, 209–11, 397–98
Schachter, Herschel, 315–16, 317
Schleiermacher, 444
Schlipp, R., 224 n. 57
Scholem, Gershom, 226–30, 231
Schools: prayer in, 140 n. 2; and religious education, 120, 123–24, 132, 133–39

Schuler, Robert, 451
Schwarzschild, Steven S., 143 n. 30, 196, 197, 198, 210–11, 232, 237 n. 33
Scott, R. B. Y., 140 n. 7
Secularism: achievements of, 59–61, 65; ahistoricalism of, 423; in American Judaism, 146–47; in covenant with religion, 68–69; critique of religion, 58–59, 115–16, 146; and Emancipation, 145; and ethical content, 371; guilt and depression in, 65–66; and hope, 153–54, 155, 160; and immorality, 39, 50–53, 54–55, 61–62, 397–98; loss of faith in, 39, 66–67, 109, 115; and modernity, 22, 146; oriented to present, 154–55; religious denunciation of, 55, 115; and selfhood, 63–67
Sefer Hachinuch, 127
Segal, B. W., 233, 236 n. 26, 237 n. 34
Self, autonomous: of Buber, 212–15; and community authority, 215–21; and conscience, 185–87; and democracy, 185; and Enlightenment view, 177–78; ethical responsibility of, 64, 178–79; freedom and constraint in, 182–83; of Habermas, 211–12; and healthy narcissim, 240; and Jewish law, 176–77, 183–84, 188–92; of Kant, 205–6; of Marx, 207; and nationalism, 207–9; problem of authority and, 204; relationship to God, 64–65, 179–81, 182, 215, 270–71; of Rousseau, 205; of Sartre, 209–11; self-centered, 63–64; *vs* tradition, 165–75, 291; unfulfilled, 63
Sephardic Jews, 236 n. 24
Sexual ethics, 244–84; absence of, 244–45; contradictory, 245–46; and friendship criterion, 248–49; and healthy-orgasm criterion, 246–47; highest standards of, 253–54; in Jewish law, 189–91, 258–60, 262–68; and Jewish tradition, 254–57, 260–61; live-for-now viewpoint in, 251–52; and

Eugene B. Borowitz is the Sigmund L. Falk Distinguished Professor of Education and Jewish Religious Thought at the Hebrew Union College-Jewish Institute of Religion, New York. He is also a rabbi. He received the D.H.L. degree from Hebrew Union College-Jewish Institute of Religion and the Ed.D. from Teachers College, Columbia University. His publications include *A Layman's Introduction to Religious Existentialism*, *Choosing a Sex Ethic*, *Understanding Judaism* (a children's textbook), *Choices in Modern Jewish Thought*, and *Liberal Judaism*.

The manuscript was prepared for publication by Jana Currie Scott. The book was designed by Joanne E. Kinney. The display and text typeface is Melior. The book is printed on 50-lb. Glatfelter paper. The hardcover edition is bound in Holliston Mills Roxite A-Grade cloth and the paperback cover is 10 pt C1S.

Manufactured in the United States of America.